THE NICOLAI CASE

Fig. 1. Georg Friedrich Nicolai at forty-four, a photograph
made in Copenhagen for the second edition of
The Biology of War.

THE NICOLAI CASE

A BIOGRAPHY

WOLF ZUELZER

WAYNE STATE UNIVERSITY PRESS, DETROIT 1982

Library of Congress Cataloging in Publication Data

Zuelzer, Wolf W., 1909–
  The Nicolai Case.

  "Chronology of G.F. Nicolai, life and selected writings": p.
  Bibliography: p.
  Includes index.
  1. Nicolai, Georg Friedrich, 1874–1964.
2. Scientists—Germany—Biography. 3. Pacifism—History. I. Title.
Q143.N5Z83   327.1'72'0924 [B]   82–1990
ISBN 0–8143–1701–4   AACR2

Contents

Illustrations

The Discovery—In Lieu of a Preface

Few men have occupied a more conspicuous place in the battles of their time, and few have been relegated to oblivion more unjustly, than Georg Friedrich Nicolai, pacifist and humanitarian, scientist and dissident. He was born in Berlin in 1874 and died in exile in Chile, a legendary figure, ninety years later. Between 1914, when he provoked the wrath of Imperial Germany by denouncing the Great Patriotic War as the senseless destruction of European civilization, and 1922, when nationalist fanatics drove him from the Weimar Republic as a traitor, there was never a time when there was not a "Nicolai Case" of some kind pending before a military, parliamentary, academic, or legal tribunal and being debated by press and public.

Even in Argentina, to which he fled, it was the same: his arrival gave rise to stormy controversies between the revolutionary students at the universities and their liberal and socialist sympathizers, on the one hand, and the defenders of the old order, on the other. His forced departure from the country nine years after his arrival itself caused an outcry that echoed throughout the entire nation. In Republican Spain he was first welcomed as the prophet of a new age, then sent away as a liability to the embattled government. Chile finally gave him a lasting asylum, but not until he had survived furious attacks from both the extreme Right and the extreme Left.

Nicolai's admirers compared him to Martin Luther, Galileo, and Giordano Bruno as a harbinger of mankind's liberation from the shackles of an oppressive past. His enemies called him a renegade and betrayer of man's most sacred ideals. His attempt to provide a scientific proof for the argument that war—which he called an atavistic remnant of a primitive stage in human evolution—was obsolete and unavailing in the era of modern technology was a milestone of pacifist thought. His book *The Biology of War*, written in defiance of the Prussian military and at the risk of his life and liberty, was the most powerful anti-war document of the First World War and was translated into nine languages. His later writings on social, philosophical, and scientific subjects teemed with novel ideas and had a profound impact on two generations of Latin American students. Citizen of a world without national barriers in an age of virulent nationalism, radical pacifist in an age of violence, rational thinker in an age of irrationality, brilliant, aggressive, and unafraid to stand up for the truth as he saw it, he was always in the thick of battle, whether as the focal point of fanatical hatred or the object of intense loyalty.

Before 1914, Nicolai had enjoyed an international reputation as a physician and a physiologist. During the war he appeared like an erratic comet in the darkened European sky, soon to vanish from the sight of both admirers and detractors to complete his orbit in the remote South American space. At the beginning of the war his manifesto, "Appeal to the Europeans," was signed by no less a figure than Albert Einstein, and Romain Rolland, the French novelist revered as the spiritual heir of Tolstoy, bestowed the sobriquet "Le Grand Européen" on him. After the war Rolland enlisted Nicolai's support for a manifesto of his own calling for the reconciliation of Europe's intellectuals, a document signed by such luminaries as Benedetto Croce, Hermann Hesse, Heinrich Mann, Bertrand Russell, Franz Werfel, and Stefan Zweig.

Nicolai's writings appeared in virtually every leading liberal and socialist magazine and newspaper of the young Weimar Republic. He was chosen to lead the German delegation to the international conference that met in Bern in 1919 to discuss the formation of the League of Nations. Like Albert Einstein, Harry Kessler, E. J. Gumbel, and Carl von Ossietzky, he belonged to the Bund Neues Vaterland, that select group of men and women working for peace, democracy, and social justice in postwar Germany. In 1922, only weeks before he left for South America, the Bund sent him to Paris as head of a three-man delegation charged with preparing the way for a Franco-German rapprochement. On the eve of his departure for Argentina his supporters staged a demonstration in his honor that served at the same time as a public forum for denunciation of his persecutors. In Argentina he was revered as a symbol of cultural and spiritual renewal. In Chile—and, in the end, in all of Latin America—his pronouncements on Communism and Fascism, the Second World War, atomic energy, education, birth control, and virtually all other questions of public interest had the force of an oracle.

Why, then, was this man forgotten within a decade of his death by all but a handful of disciples? We shall see that in Germany Nicolai was not so much forgotten as deliberately buried. The forces to which he succumbed were the same forces which would soon raise Adolf Hitler to power. They saw to it that Nicolai was made a non-person, deprived of his reputation and his livelihood, threatened with extinction, and at last spat out of the national mouth like an indigestible morsel. He was slated for oblivion not only for opposing the war but for daring to attack the illusion of German moral and cultural superiority, an illusion which had sustained the Germans in their battle against the rest of the world. At the height of the war, he publicly challenged the myth of a peace-loving, blameless nation forced to defend itself against a host of enemies bent on its destruction. After the war he denounced the equally cherished "stab-in-the-back" legend fostered by the defeated military leadership and later vigorously exploited by Hitler, according to which the unbeaten German army was robbed of victory by traitors on the home front.

As an apostle of reason and champion of European unity, he was too radical for his nationalistic German contemporaries: his logic was too remorseless, his sense of reality too keen, his truth too painful. Nor could the memory of such a man survive in South America, least of all in such countries as Argentina and Chile, whose dictatorial regimes are by their nature anti-intellectual, anti-rationalist, and anti-libertarian. Nicolai's ideas found their audience among two generations of Latin idealists; they were lost in the bloody silence that later enveloped these countries.

Character is destiny. Nicolai was a brilliant thinker but an impatient and abrasive personality, conscious of his intellectual superiority and little inclined to spare the feelings of his fellows. He persuaded and dazzled or he offended and shocked them. Convinced of the scientific objectivity of his views, he was never willing to concede a point or compromise in matters of principle. As a pacifist and democrat in a militarist and monarchist society, such a man was bound to arouse violent enmities; as an independent thinker in the polarized society of Latin America, he aroused the ire of conservatives, Catholics, and Communists alike.

But the psychological explanation alone is not sufficient to account for the hostility which Nicolai faced throughout his lifetime. In his native country he represented a certain tradition which had its origin in the Enlightenment and reached its apogee in the writings of the great liberal emigrants of the period between the Napoleonic wars and the Revolution of 1848—Heinrich Heine, Georg Büchner, Ludwig Börne, and Georg Herwegh. It was the tradition of German Idealism, not as an abstract concept but as a practical program of political freedom and human dignity inspired by the French Revolution.

For a time the struggle for democracy and the resistance against the petty dynastic rulers of the Metternich era merged with the cause of national unification, but with the advent of Bismarck the dynastic principle became the foundation of the national state. In 1914, under the pressure of a war that threatened the very existence of the nation, the authoritarian state and the national idea were fused into a single patriotic notion, and he who opposed German militarism found himself opposing the Fatherland (even the Social Democrats, though pacifists in principle, refrained from doing so). Nowhere did the Bismarckian state find more whole-hearted acceptance than among the members of the educated middle class. A member of that class who condemned the war and saw England and France as indispensable members of the European community rather than mortal enemies must be a blind man at best and a traitor at worst, and no one believed that Nicolai was blind—on the contrary, like Cassandra, it was his uncanny perspicacity which aroused the hatred and the fear of his countrymen.

Nicolai not only played a sharply defined historical role but could and did speak for himself in a highly articulate manner. In addition to his numerous writings in German and in Spanish, he hoarded so many documents concerning both his public and his private life that one must conclude that he expected to be "rediscovered" after his death. He kept every piece of paper relating to his person: official documents, newspaper clippings, drafts of his speeches and lectures, business and legal papers, love letters, drawings, photographs, even an unpublished novel combining autobiography and science fiction and bearing the revealing title *Herr der Erde* (*Lord of the Earth*). He was not a hypocrite and made no attempt to conceal the shadows in his character. The documents he left behind testify to a bold intellect, profound erudition, personal courage and willingness to sacrifice for his principles and to fight for freedom and human rights, and at the same time a healthy appetite for life's pleasures. He was at once

3

martyr and epicurean, altruist and egotist, idealist and rake. But these traits existed in a kind of emotional vacuum. Those who knew him speak of his charm, his stimulating conversation, his wit, and his brilliant mind. But he loved humanity, not the human beings around him. As a person he was selfish, quarrelsome, indifferent to the feelings of others. Among his papers are unopened but carefully preserved love letters, evidence of a supreme indifference to others coupled with a sort of collector's compulsiveness. There are lists of the many women he seduced throughout his lifetime, prepared with scientific exactitude and recorded not only by name but by nationality, racial orign, and civil status—virgin, married, divorcée, widow—and the circumstances of the seduction, as if he were recording a series of biological experiments. Letters show him as a petty tyrant in his circle of family and friends, bills and receipts betray the cunning businessman, notes testify to his extreme egocentricity and vanity. But again and again such impressions vanish in the face of his life-long struggle for justice, truth, and reason. For these he risked his life, sacrificed his career and his birthright as a German and a European, and went to live in exile at an advanced age rather than bow to expediency.

My discovery of this figure was not unlike an archeological excavation that begins with the accidental discovery of a marble fragment in a heap of rubble and ends with the uncovering of a burial chamber. A quotation in an obscure book written by the Dadaist Hugo Ball in 1918, which had been gathering dust on the shelves of the Zentralbibliothek of Zurich ever since, set me on a trail that ended with the discovery of Nicolai's papers and the writing of this book. The quotation was from Nicolai's *Biology of War (Die Biologie des Krieges)*, published the previous year. The title was hardly less intriguing than the passage cited by Ball, which dealt with an actual conversation between the German chancellor, Theobald von Bethmann-Hollweg, and the British ambassador, Sir Edward Goschen, on the eve of the invasion of Belgium by German troops. Bethmann-Hollweg had implored England not to join the war on account of a mere "scrap of paper," meaning the international treaty which guaranteed Belgium's neutrality. Sir Edward rejected this plea on the grounds that the fear of consequences could not justify the breach of solemn obligations. Nicolai commented that here "every word spoken by the British ambassador was inspired by the ideal of duty, every word of the German by the notion of utility," yet Bethmann-Hollweg was raised in the Kantian tradition of the Categorical Imperative, while the Englishman owed his sense of duty to the despised Utilitarianism of the British school. "I think that in view of these facts," Nicolai went on, "our philosophy professors should cease to prostitute Kant and themselves, and say, with Bethmann-Hollweg: '*Pater peccavi*, under the pressure of events we have allowed selfish but understandable concerns for our own welfare to push us into a breach of sacred commitments, but we hope to make restitution at a later time.'"

Who had written these words, I wondered. What German—obviously a person with an academic background—had the courage to hurl such truths in the face of his compatriots? England was then the most hated enemy, a nation of hucksters that had plotted the war against innocent Germany in cold blood, jealous of a rival which threatened its dominant position in world trade—that is how England was portrayed in every newspaper, every speech, every article from the pens of German "philosophy professors." Clearly, the author of this passage was worth investigating.

The Zurich library possessed a copy of *Biologie des Krieges*, published in 1917, and there I found ideas of breath-taking boldness for the time and circumstances in which the book was written. It warned that the war was a threat to Western civilization and to the very existence of the states for whose sake it was being fought. It viewed the nations of Europe as interdependent cells of a single organism. Educated men had the duty to prevent this organism from suffering the fate of the Greek city-states, which had been destroyed for want of a collective structure. The current war would produce no victors, said the writer, only losers. The conditions of the peace must not become the source of future wars.

The book was a veritable gold mine of prophecies long since fulfilled and of ideas fifty years ahead of their time. But who was Nicolai, and what had become of him? The library had only one other sample of his writings, a slender volume of political essays published in 1921. Then the earth seemed to have swallowed him up. Had he died young? Or had this eloquent man nothing more to say after that?

At this point the story of Nicolai's rescue from oblivion must involve his chronicler's own history. The very fact that I chose this man as the object of a biography points to a certain affinity, but actually the task of exploring this life was imposed on *me* by a remarkable set of circumstances. Chance—or fate—threw so many clues my way that I felt obliged to write the book. Like Nicolai, I was born in Berlin, into an academic family. Like him I became a physician and a scientist. Like him I have certain extracurricular interests, among them history. I too left Germany—Hitler's Germany, in my case—to spend the greater part of my life in a freer world. At this point the parallels end, but they gave rise to a special empathy.

I had the opportunity to attempt to satisfy my historical curiosity during a sabbatical year in Europe. The question I hoped to answer was why the Weimar Republic, the society in which I had grown up, had failed. To what extent was the debacle attributable to the absence of the historical and spiritual requirements for a democratic commonwealth? The question necessarily led me to the period preceding the Revolution of 1918. Did the Germans at the end of the First World War understand the causes of the collapse and its inevitable consequences, or were they still caught up in the illusions with which they had entered the conflict? Was there in fact even a semblance of an informed public, the very essence of the democratic process, in which a genuine debate over the catastrophe could have taken place? There was war-weariness and a longing for peace, there was a dull, unfocused resistance to Ludendorff's military dictatorship, an unrest among the masses that led to hunger strikes, but was there a clearly informed and genuine opposition?

The Social Democrats had supported the war to the very end, its imperialist character notwithstanding, and had dutifully joined the last Imperial cabinet. A reading of the newspapers for October, 1918, a month before the collapse, showed that even the more radical Independent Socialists had remained passive, not daring to tell their followers that the abrupt decision to end the war had been Ludendorff's, not that of the pathetic civilian government to which he had assigned the role of scapegoat. After four years of military censorship, with Germany and her allies in control from the Channel coast to the Caucasus, with Russia beaten and the Western Front still seemingly intact, the German public was unprepared for defeat and unable to react to it rationally. The utterances of the political leaders of every shade in those last days of the monarchy have a ghostly, unreal air. Not only the bourgeois parties but the Socialists remained uncomprehending in the face of the disaster. There was no informed public opinion, no meaningful debate, no plan, no decision. The Weimar Republic was the child of ignorance.

In the midst of this depressing rubble of history I discovered Nicolai, a realist and virtually the only German to oppose the war from the beginning, refusing to be intimidated by the military and its partisans, calling for a negotiated peace while there was still time, appraising Germany's plight in an objective manner, and urging his countrymen to face the facts. It was an exciting discovery, but what I had found was barely enough material for an essay. Too bad, I thought, for not only was the notion of an anti-militaristic, democratic, cosmopolitan German professor of the period an intriguing one, but also I had the nagging feeling that as a child I had seen this man in my parents' home. Professor Nicolai—the name suddenly had a familiar ring. Had he been a friend of my father? The probability was great, for both men were internists and physiologists, both held teaching positions at the University of Berlin, were of the same generation and moved in the same social circles, lived in the same part of town, and must at least have met each other. If so, I had been too young to remember him.

The next clue came the following spring, when I visited my sister in Taormina during my sabbatical. It occurred to me that she, five years my senior, might remember so vivid a personality, but she had no recollection of him. I told her of my discovery, then we dropped the subject. The next day, however, she asked for the name once more. Nicolai? Yes, she knew a person by that name, though he could not possibly be the man I was looking for. His first name was Otto, he was in his fifties, and he was an inmate in an institution for the mentally retarded in southern Germany whose directors were her friends. She now recalled that Otto, afflicted with mongolism, good-natured like most of his kind and by no means completely dull, had often greeted her warmly as the daughter of a friend of his father. Could Otto the feeble-minded be the son of the author of *The*

Biology of War? I wrote to her friends at the institution and learned that Nicolai—my Nicolai!—was indeed Otto's father. He had emigrated to Argentina in 1922, leaving his two-year-old retarded son behind. His widow was still alive, but afflicted with loss of memory. However, a niece living in Baden-Baden, Dr. Ruth Katz, could surely give me information about her late uncle. It was as if I had suddenly found the door to that burial chamber under the heap of rubble.

But what would the tomb contain? What could the niece tell me about a man who had vanished fifty years ago, presumably forever, from the horizon of a young girl? Meanwhile, I had gone to Munich, for unrelated reasons, and this visit proved crucial. "There is no such thing as chance," Dr. Katz wrote in response to my inquiry about her uncle. Nicolai's papers—he had died only six years earlier—were in the custody of her daughter, Frau Marianne Katz, who lived in Munich. I was welcome to call on her and inspect the documents.

I had found the burial chamber. In the chain of circumstances beginning with the accidental discovery of a long-forgotten book, and the vague feeling that I had seen its author in my youth, to the equally accidental visit to my sister in Taormina and her acquaintance with the feeble-minded Otto and memory that our fathers had known each other, to my trip to Munich, where the literary estate of Nicolai had been shipped from Chile after his death, I recognized a pattern that allowed only one interpretation: I was destined to write this biography.

The undertaking turned out to be a formidable one. The collection of Nicolai's papers, gathered after his death in Santiago by Peter Feldmann and sent to Dr. Katz, filled nine packing crates and had never been catalogued. It contained personal, scientific, political, historical, and literary documents from the Bismarck era through Wilhelminian Germany, the First World War, the beginnings of the Weimar Republic, and forty eventful years in Argentina and Chile. His travels in the Orient, the Arctic, tsarist and Soviet Russia, Italy, France, Spain, the United States, and Mexico were documented. There were autographs from Albert Einstein, Romain Rolland, Georg Brandes, Jane Addams, Heinrich Mann, Theodor Heuss, Pablo Neruda. Most of the documents were in German or Spanish, but there were also letters and articles in French, English, Swedish, Danish, Russian, Romanian, and even Esperanto. The collection included a series of fraternity bulletins from the 1890s illuminating little-known aspects of German political history; theatrical reviews of Nicolai's, giving a glimpse of the German stage at the turn of the century; papers on medical and physiological subjects from an exciting period in the history of medicine; books by Nicolai on the electrocardiogram, the conditioned reflex, Relativity Theory, sociology, education, eugenics, the economy of South America, the Soviet Union, dialectical materialism, psychoanalysis, Goethe, and Cervantes; an unpublished autobiographical novel; and manuscripts and drafts of speeches whose themes ranged from travelogues to discourses on Pascal's triangle.

It was clear that Nicolai had been a true universal genius, and this literary treasure exceeded my fondest hopes. At the same time it became clear that so rich a find could not be digested in the remaining months of my sabbatical year. Here, too, fate smiled upon me. I was granted permission to take the material home for leisurely examination. As this manuscript went to press, the Nicolai heirs had donated the Nicolai archive to the Institut für Zeitgeschichte (Institute for Contemporary History) at Munich, where it is now deposited.

At this point many other sources came into view. The Humboldt University of East Berlin refused to grant me access to its Nicolai files, and the old German army archives in Naumburg in the German Democratic Republic were likewise inaccessible, but these deficiencies were outweighed by abundant information from other sources. Romain Rolland's diary of the war years proved to be a veritable treasure trove. The Romanian pacifist and writer Eugen Relgis visited Nicolai in Berlin in 1921 and recorded his impressions in a book, later expanded and reissued in Spanish. Many people who knew Nicolai were interviewed, among them Frau Friederike Nicolai, his widow; Dr. Dietrich Blos, a nephew, in Berlin; Mme. Marie Romain Rolland, in Paris; Albert Einstein's stepdaughter Margot Einstein and his secretary, Helen Dukas, in Princeton; Nicolai's translator and good friend Diego Abad de Santillán, in Buenos Aires; Augustin Souchy, a kindred spirit now living in Munich, who visited him in Rosario in 1929 and in Santiago in 1963; his associate of many years Dr. Carlos Lovazzano, in La Jolla; Kurt Grossmann, of Kew Gardens, N.Y., a former member of the Bund Neues Vaterland; the Feldmann family, who looked after his needs in his last years; and the friends who spoke at his funeral in 1964.

Among other colleagues and disciples interviewed in South America were Drs. Francisco Bendicente, Vladimir Mikieliecich, Richardo Orta Nadal, and David Ostrovsky, and Dr. and Sra. Alfredo Castellanos, all of Rosario; Dr. Jorge Orgaz, former rector of the Universidad Nacional de Córdoba, participant in the early days of the Reforma, and author of *Reforma universitaria y Rebelión estudiantil*; "ALONE," the literary critic of *El Mercurio*, Professor Alfonso Asenjo, Sr. Peter Feldmann, Sr. Cesar Godoy Urrutia, Professors Aljandro Lipschütz, Hector Orrego Puelma, and Agustin Tellez, and Sra. Aggie Woelfler-Feldmann, all of Santiago; Dr. Luis Alberto Sanchez, former rector of the Universidad Nacional Mayor de San Marcos; and Sr. Victor Raúl Haya de la Torre, leader of the movement for workers' universities and founder of the Peruvian political party APRA.

The archives of the Universidad Nacional de Córdoba, the Faculty of Economic Sciences of the Universidad del Litoral, and the Biblioteca Argentina in Rosario and the library of the University of Chile in Santiago provided additional information. I acknowledge the help of all these persons and institutions with deep appreciation.

My special thanks are due to Frau Marianne Katz of Munich, former custodian of the Nicolai archive, who first allowed me access to the material and who contributed many invaluable ideas over the years; and to Mrs. Jean Owen, who as editor provided guidance and advice.

The book begins with Nicolai's struggle against the militarism and nationalism of his compatriots, which he believed was the cause of the First World War. It was the conscious attempt of the scientist to combat the forces of unreason which were then threatening a seemingly rational order and which have since come to dominate a large part of the world, as he foresaw. This is a biography, not a historical study, though it is often difficult to draw the line between the two. Apart from the drama of Nicolai's career as a perpetual dissident, apart from the complexity of his character, apart from the originality of his mind and his ideas, in his life the ultimate issues of modern history find their expression: the struggle of freedom against coercion, reason against violence, science against ideology, global unity against nationalism, civilization against the dark, destructive urges of the human psyche. Nicolai's experiences as a student in Wilhelminian Germany, as a conscientious objector during the First World War, and finally as a pariah in the academic community in the early days of the Weimar Republic show the consequences of the "treason of the intellectuals," the lapse of a civilized nation into the depths of barbarism, with an immediacy no historical treatise can provide. Similarly, his experiences in Latin America as an independent thinker in a traditionalist society demonstrate, more vividly than any social or cultural history can, the dilemma of the free spirit in the modern world.

I. A VOICE
IN THE WILDERNESS

1. One Man's War against War

In the spring of 1917, the old Swiss firm of Orell Füssli added a chapter to the annals of publishing and a footnote to the history of the First World War by bringing out—ostensibly against the author's wishes—a book with the forbidding but timely title *The Biology of War*.[1] It came from the pen of one Georg Friedrich Nicolai, a lowly private in the German army then serving as an orderly at the base hospital of Fortress Danzig but in peacetime professor of physiology at the University of Berlin, sometime consultant physician to the Empress Augusta Viktoria, and more recently senior cardiologist for the Seventeenth Army Corps. Added to this strange mixture of antecedents was the fact that he was under strict surveillance by his military superiors for having expressed "antinational" views. Those who took the trouble to follow parliamentary debates in the midst of the war knew that the "Nicolai Case" had repeatedly come before the Reichstag.

The manner in which the manuscript of *The Biology of War*, a highly subversive book in the eyes of the German government, had come into the Swiss publisher's hands remained a closely guarded secret. The text was incomplete, occasionally distorted, and not always in the proper sequence. The author had never seen the proofs. In a letter written tongue-in-cheek in compliance with an order from his commanding officer, he had protested the publication of his own work and requested the return of the manuscript, a request which, to no one's surprise, had been ignored. For Orell Füssli the strange publishing venture was an act of faith, evidently tempered by businesslike caution, for the printing was held to two thousand modestly paper-bound copies. Prospects for reaping material rewards were indeed dim, for Nicolai was unknown outside the medical profession, the title of his book suggested a dry technical treatise, and the market for pacifist literature addressed to German readers had never been good and was at an all-time low just then.

In spite of such handicaps *The Biology of War* proved to be a spectacular success. It electrified the forlorn band of exiles who were nursing the prostrate cause of peace on the neutral soil of Switzerland and overnight catapulted its author into a position of moral and intellectual leadership among pacifists everywhere. In an unprecedented gesture of homage, the *Friedenswarte* in Bern, principal forum of pacifism in German-speaking countries since the turn of the century, devoted the lead article of its June issue to a review of Nicolai's book. To be precise, the review dealt only with the first three chapters, for at that point the reviewer—none other than the venerable pacifist and editor Alfred Fried himself, winner of the 1911 Nobel Prize for Peace—despaired of doing justice to the remaining twelve and contented himself with enumerating their titles. In what was surely one of the most potent compliments ever paid a writer, Fried advised the German government not to ban the work, because "to forgo such a prohibition is worth more than any victory on the battlefield."

The advice, needless to say, was not taken. The *Friedenswarte* itself was banned in the Reich, and the German High Command had no interest in moral victories. For Messrs. Hindenburg and Ludendorff, war was not an evil but a natural and by no means undesirable attribute of human existence, a glorious challenge to the greatness of the nation and—at worst—a technical problem to be dealt with by experts as disease is dealt with by physicians. For them the object of the war was not the chimera of a lasting peace but the acquisition of strong positions from which to fight the next war. In their professional view, which at the moment was the law in Germany, anything short of total military victory was tantamount to failure. The mere wish for peace (other than that to be imposed by a triumphant German army upon a beaten enemy) was *Flaumacherei*, defeatism if not downright treason. Fortunately, all printed matter was subject to military censorship, and the officers to whom that task was entrusted could be relied upon to protect the public against the poison of peacemongering. *The Biology of War* was duly banned, or rather an earlier preventive ban was reaffirmed, but even the vaunted efficiency of the German bureaucracy could not prevent a sizable number of copies from reaching booksellers in various parts of the country. The hardheaded Swiss could be quite imaginative when it came to outwitting German officialdom. The drab gray volumes, whose specially printed jackets bore the innocuous title *The Grain Economy of Switzerland*, passed customs with ease and were sold in brisk under-the-counter trading to a select clientele.

From Vevey on the shores of Lake Geneva, where he lived in voluntary exile during the war, the French novelist Romain Rolland wrote to his fellow pacifist Albert Einstein, then on a visit to Switzerland:

> I have read Professor Nicolai's book with passionate interest. I believe he is a friend of yours. Please let him know how much I liked his book. I have been virtually living with it these past few months. It is a wonderful thing in these terrible times to come upon such a great, free, and serene soul, an experience that is ample reward for the great folly of this second universal Deluge. But the Ark is afloat and will come ashore safely.[2]

The message, delivered by Einstein in due course, was the beginning of a long and cordial friendship between the two most outspoken opponents of the war. In his book *Les Précurseurs*, an homage to the prophets and martyrs of peace, the Frenchman devoted a chapter to the German pacifist, on whom he bestowed the title "Le Grand Européen."[3] Later he wrote the preface to the second edition of *The Biology of War*. Nicolai in turn translated Rolland's postwar manifesto calling for the reconciliation of Europe's intellectuals and undertook the difficult task of soliciting the support of Germany's embittered cultural elite. During the debate on the Treaty of Versailles another Frenchman, the Socialist leader Albert Thomas, told the Chambre des Députés that Nicolai and a handful of like-minded Germans had saved their country's moral integrity, and—for the sake of these few just men—urged France to grant the defeated enemy more lenient peace terms than those demanded by the implacable "Tiger" Clemenceau. This plea, too, fell on deaf ears.

To the publisher's delight, the two thousand copies of *The Biology of War* were quickly bought by those lucky enough to know the right booksellers in Germany and by the reading public of Switzerland and other neutral countries. Despite great difficulties, not the least of which was the fact that the author was more closely watched than ever, a second edition, revised, expanded, and carrying a handsome photograph of Nicolai, was readied with all possible speed. Danish, Swedish, and English editions followed, the latter appearing simultaneously in London and New York and in time the work was translated wholly or in part into Italian, Spanish, Russian, Romanian, Finnish, and even Japanese.

The only major nation whose public never had the opportunity to read the book in its own language was France, where censorship during the war was just as rigid as in Germany. It appeared immediately after the country had passed through the shattering experience of its army's mutiny in the wake of the disastrous spring offensive on the Aisne of General Nivelle ("le buveur de sang"), and the government, desperately struggling to revive the nation's will to fight, was in no mood for pacifist ideas, least of all those of a *boche*. Although the book was an attack on German militarism (*Le Temps* ridiculed it as the naive attempt of a modern Doctor Pangloss to restore the best of all possible worlds by wishful thinking), the French censor was taking no chances. Once the fighting had ended and it seemed that Germany could never again disturb the peace of Europe, few Frenchmen cared to know what a former enemy had written at the height of the conflict. The book did earn Nicolai an invitation to Paris (he was one of the first Germans to set foot on French soil after the war) for the purpose of establishing contact with French pacifists, but the mission was not a lasting success. In December 1921, the aged Anatole France, returning from Stockholm after receiving the Nobel Prize, stopped off in Berlin for the express purpose of meeting "two great Germans"; as he put it, Albert Einstein and Nicolai, but the accolade by one of their most famous compatriots failed to impress the French. Three years after the armistice their bitterness was still too intense, and a French edition of Nicolai's book remained a poor publishing risk. Even Einstein, invited to lecture at the Collège de France only a few months later, thought it wise to slip into Paris in the dark of night. He found himself faced with the threat of a walkout by thirty "Immortals" at the Académie Française. In 1923, Premier Raymond Poincaré dealt a heavy blow to the hopes of pacifists everywhere by sending French troops into the Ruhr. The last French echo of *The Biology of War* was the lament of *L'Ère nouvelle*, a Socialist newspaper, that Nicolai's wartime warnings were as timely as ever. To the chagrin of the francophile author, no French edition of his book ever appeared, Romain Rolland, Albert Thomas, and Anatole France notwithstanding.

Nicolai's volume was indeed a remarkable document. The most original and unquestionably the most potent antiwar book of its time, it combined a brilliant and impassioned critique of German militarism with a coldly factual inquiry into the biological effects of modern warfare on the species *homo sapiens*. But the most remarkable thing about it was the fact that it was written in the midst of the war by a German—and a German professor at that—living in Germany. It had been written, moreover, not in the grim year 1917, when the toll of the previous year's suicidal battles of Verdun and the Somme and the deprivations of the past "Turnip Winter" had begun to sober many minds, but in the summer of 1915, when the tide of war enthusiasm was still running high among the German public. The delay had not been of Nicolai's making, nor had he intended to publish his controversial offspring abroad. On the contrary, he felt that the impact of his dissent depended in large measure on its appearing in Germany as the legitimate publication of a German author, presented to the German public by a German publisher. He insisted that his was the truly patriotic view and refused indignantly to wear the label "subversive," which the flag-waving advocates of war-to-the-finish stood ready to pin on any "slacker." (The term "slacker," incidentally, was broad enough to include even the chancellor, Herr von Bethmann-Hollweg, who had admitted that the invasion of Belgium was a breach of international law and who opposed unrestricted submarine warfare.)

Nicolai, whose views were considerably more radical than those of the imperial chancellor, was determined to make himself heard. He had persuaded Curt Thesing, a personal friend and owner of a publishing firm in Leipzig, to undertake the printing of his book. The authorities could not possibly object to a purportedly scientific work. It was not until the police—alerted by his own staunchly patriotic father-in-law—impounded the type and confiscated the galley proofs that he abandoned his original plan. A diplomatic courier secretly in sympathy with his views took a copy of the manuscript across the Swiss border in his official pouch. Someone else eventually placed it with Orell Füssli in Zurich. Nicolai's military superiors got wind of the project and ordered him to stop the publication. He wrote to Zurich under duress, wording his letter in such a way that not only the recipient but the commanding officer in Danzig could read between the lines. The result was a court-martial for violation of the Prussian press law.

The author of *The Biology of War* was thus clearly a marked man, but he had not left the country. Unlike most of the dissidents who, if they were not locked up in jails or insane asylums, either sought refuge abroad or subsided into silence, Nicolai, for the time being, remained in Germany, enjoyed a liberty of sorts punctuated by brief arrests, and was not at all silent. On the contrary, he continued to be a gadfly to his superiors and a troublemaker to the German government. Drafted into the army, he refused to take the oath to the colors. Demoted to the rank of private and assigned menial duties as an orderly in the medical corps, he remained every inch the professor and generally had the best of it in his dealings with the undistinguished army doctors, who would have looked up to him as to an authority under normal circumstances but who now found themselves in the unhappy position of having to give orders to this difficult subordinate. He was involved in more than one court-martial and in numerous disciplinary proceedings. The War Ministry had a voluminous dossier on him. The Reichstag, no longer as impotent as it had been in peacetime, was the scene of repeated questions from the floor concerning the army's treatment of the problematical private, questions which the representative of the War Ministry answered evasively; at one point the Kaiser himself intervened on Nicolai's behalf.

Then in his early forties, a strikingly handsome man of military bearing (Fig. 1), Nicolai could have passed for one of the glamorous aviators or submarine commanders whose photographs decorated the display windows of stationery shops throughout wartime Germany. To make the illusion complete, he affected a monocle (which he was forced briefly to abandon during his career as a private) and displayed several conspicuous saber scars acquired on the dueling floor. As he would characterize himself later, he was thoroughly bourgeois in his outlook, "even a bit of a nationalist." Less than three months before the outbreak of the war, he had married the daughter of Geheimrat Carl Busley, who was, among other things, a senior official of a leading manufacturer of naval armaments, a founder of the Imperial Yacht Club, and an intimate of the Kaiser: in a word, a very pillar of the Establishment. The Nicolai wedding at the Hotel Adlon, smothered in roses and graced by beribboned and bemedaled Wilhelminian personages (see Fig. 15), was one of the noteworthy social events of that last golden season of peace. The groom, already a physiologist of international stature, a prominent physician, author of numerous scientific papers, and member of all the proper professional societies, was approaching the summit of a brilliant academic career. Yet, to judge from *The Biology of War*, he was as much at home in the worlds of Aristotle and Plato, Hobbes and Kant, Pascal and Montesquieu, Goethe, Dostoevski, and Nietzsche as in the laboratory, at the bedside, or for that matter in the drawing room.

The gentle Romain Rolland, ever generous with adjectives, had called him "great, free, and serene." He could not know how far he was from the truth, at least with respect to the last of these attributes. As for greatness,

> rightly to be great
> is not to stir without great argument
> but greatly to find quarrel in a straw
> when honour's at the stake

says Hamlet. Nicolai's "great argument" was the war, a challenge to his scientific and moral convictions to which he responded as if it were a personal matter, passionately and with all the resources at his command. By publishing his book in defiance of an all-powerful government, he put his career, his wealth, his freedom, and, for all he knew, his life in jeopardy and in due course became a wanderer on the face of the earth. Along the way there were plenty of other straws in which to find quarrel, and he plucked them as they came, but he was equally willing to quarrel when honor was not at stake and to stir without great argument. He had in him

17

a measure of greatness, compounded by a powerful mind and the unflinching courage to stand up for the truth which that mind illuminated for him. Far from being serene, however, he was a compulsive scrapper and a restless spirit. From the beginning his life had been a series of quarrels, indiscriminately involving his parents, teachers, classmates, fraternity brothers, colleagues and superiors, sister and brother-in-law, policemen, cabdrivers, passers-by in the street, and strangers in restaurants. In his book he called for the curbing of man's aggressive instincts as a condition for the survival of the human race. In his private life he was as aggressive as he was brilliant. This contrast between intellect and temperament, insight and action, was the tragic paradox that governed his destiny.

As he matured, he learned not to control his aggressive impulses but to channel them in worthier directions. In the irrational war his rational mind had at last found an issue large enough to satisfy his combative urge, and in the mighty Prussian war machine he had met an enemy he could respect. He was not so much a man of peace as a rebel whom logic and temperament drove to fight for the cause of pacifism at the very moment when it was most dangerous to do so. The fact that he stood virtually alone suited him to perfection, for to be a member of a group, even as its leader, was to accept restraint, share responsibility, divide the credit, and lessen the risk. In *The Biology of War*, written after he had been banished to the Prussian fortress town of Graudenz early in the war, he spoke of the crushing effects of his intellectual isolation, of "the dread hours of doubt that none are spared who walk alone," and he compared his plight to that of a little ant, "forced to fight without the help of a single fellow ant, a hundred paces from its colony." But such rhetoric was meant to dramatize his role as a martyr rather than to express his true feelings. Nicolai was not above striking a pose when it suited his purpose. He knew no doubts, and the simile of the ant was an odd choice for one of the most unbridled individualists who ever trod this earth.

His true feelings found expression in the words with which he introduced Rolland's "Declaration of the Independence of the Spirit" to the dejected postwar German intelligentsia.[4] There had been active resistance to the war in the ranks of the proletariat, he said, referring to the imprisonment of Karl Liebknecht, the leader of the radical wing of the German Social Democrats, and to the great strikes of 1917 and 1918, but not among the intellectuals. "To my knowledge I was the only one who openly refused to bear arms and who faced the consequences. In 1914, all those who by their nature should have opposed the war failed: the Christian Community of Saints, the Alliance Israélite, the Social Democrats, the scientists, the philosophers, and the pacifists. This total failure of all moral forces must not recur." He welcomed the support of those who had belatedly seen the light and embraced the cause of peace, but he denounced those

> who had spent their lives as after-dinner speakers preaching the unity of civilization and who then, equally drunk with patriotic fervor, blasphemed the Internationale of the spirit. For they simply did not

do their duty. Not for their own pleasure had they been elected chairmen and speakers at international meetings. Rather, they had been placed as sentries at the gate of the future so that they might hold fast some day and set an example to the masses. Nor could they plead surprise, for they had talked about international solidarity so often and so enthusiastically that one had to assume they had paid some attention.

Nicolai had a right to be critical. He himself had not been among the "sentries," having dedicated his life to medical science, a field to which he had made impressive contributions. In collaboration with his chief, Friedrich Kraus, he had written the first authoritative text on the electrocardiogram, a subject whose importance for the diagnosis of heart disease was only beginning to be grasped by clinicians. As an investigator, a teacher, and a physician, he had been a busy man. No doubt he had felt secure in the knowledge that despite the Kaiser's saber-rattling and the hue and cry of the chauvinists on both sides of the Rhine, a European war was too insane an undertaking to become reality. When it came nevertheless, he rushed into the breach—or rather threw himself against an intruder who had already entered the citadel. Perceiving far more acutely than most of his compatriots that the war, regardless of its outcome, posed a threat to European civilization, he felt that it was up to the bearers of that civilization, the scholars, scientists, artists, and writers, to defend it against the barbarians on both sides. It was as a citizen of the Republic of Letters that he stepped forward. He quickly learned that he was out of step with the other citizens of that republic, or, as he might have put it, that they were out of step with him.

Like most of his contemporaries, he had been caught unaware by the cataclysm. The assassination of Archduke Franz Ferdinand in a remote Balkan town by fanatical Serbian nationalists was unfortunate, to be sure, but hardly rated as a *casus belli*. People pitied the old emperor, Franz Joseph, who had suffered yet another violent loss in his family. (His brother Maximilian had been executed in Mexico, his wife Elisabeth had been assassinated in Switzerland, and his only son, Rudolph, had committed suicide.) But it was to all appearances a family matter, or at most an Austrian matter. No one knew that Vienna intended to exploit the incident as a pretext for a military adventure; no one knew of the "blank check" the Kaiser had secretly given to the Austrians; no one expected a general European war. The Kaiser himself quietly consulted his advisers and, on being assured that Germany was ready for any emergency, boarded his yacht for the annual summer voyage to northern waters, thereby allaying any fears the public might have. The public had none. Those who could afford it went to the seashore or the mountains. It was vacation time in Europe.

Nicolai, having taken his bride on a honeymoon to the Riviera in May, did not take a vacation that summer. He was busy preparing a paper for the forthcoming International Congress of Electrophysiology at Lyons, to which as an authority on the electrocardiogram he had received a special invitation. He would deliver his talk in French, which he spoke fluently, having spent a semester in Paris as a student. He had come away enchanted with the language, the food, the people, and above all the *mores* of France, had gone back several times, and was looking forward to the return visit. En route he would have an opportunity to see his sister and his brother-in-law in Karlsruhe, and perhaps take a quick side trip to the Dobel, his recently acquired mountain retreat in the Black Forest. Ignoring the now rapidly swelling chorus of war hysteria—what else could it be but hysteria?—he then departed happily for the last international congress to be held in Europe for a long time. His wife stayed behind in the vast, lovingly decorated apartment at Rankestrasse 34 in Berlin's prosperous "New West," where the couple had taken up residence only a few short months before.

He almost failed to return, for by the time the congress was over France had begun to mobilize. Jean Jaurès, the French Socialist leader and apostle of peace, had been assassinated, crowds were shouting "à Berlin," bands were playing the "Marseillaise," and a hysterical fear of German spies was sweeping the nation. Nicolai unhurriedly and politely took leave of his French hosts and boarded a train for the frontier. Coming fresh from an international gathering of scientists with its atmosphere of exquisite politeness and brotherhood, he was unable to take the patriotic fury of the mob quite seriously, though it interested him as a natural phenomenon, as a swarm of angry hornets would have interested him. At Belfort, a key fortress in the French defense system and just about the most sensitive spot he could have chosen, he left the train and nonchalantly strolled through the town, observing the behavior of the crowds and the assembling of military formations with the detachment of a Gulliver studying Brobdingnagian affairs. As he would say later, it was the opportunity of a lifetime to see a French mobilization, and he had no intention of missing it. With his monocle and his dueling scars, he was soon recognized as an enemy alien. He was seized and barely escaped being shot as a spy then and there, but he insisted on being taken before the commandant, to whom he presented his credentials and explained the purely scientific nature of his interest. The incredulous officer agreed to send a telegram to Lyons to verify the prisoner's claim that he had been the honored guest of a French professor. On receiving an affirmative reply, he dismissed Nicolai with a show of *politesse* worthy of a Cyrano de Bergerac. As a francophile, Nicolai was charmed: at least it would be a chivalrous war.

He was soon disillusioned. By the time he reached Berlin, German troops had invaded Belgium, Cossacks were reported to be looting and burning East Prussian towns, England had joined the fray, and to a man the German Social Democrats had abandoned the international solidarity of the working class and joined the bourgeois parties in the Reichstag to approve the war credits. It was rapidly becoming apparent that the war would be neither chivalrous nor short. What was not yet apparent was the fact that in this war dashing heroism and brilliant strategy would prove less important than industrial organization, economic resources, an efficient system of transportation, raw materials, and foodstuffs. The public—and for that matter the High Command—was thinking in terms of enemy troops killed or captured, of breakthroughs and encirclements, strong-points taken and territory gained. And as far as the public knew, the war was going extremely well for Germany.

The Belgian fortresses fell, not quite on schedule, but with impressive speed nevertheless. The public was not privy to the timetable of the General Staff and could not know that the fall of Liège was announced before the event to keep morale high. Nor, under a censorship that permitted only victories to be reported, was it told that the battle of the Marne had ended with a decisive setback. The capture of Antwerp, a mere consolation prize after that debacle, was presented as a triumph of German arms, notwithstanding the fact that the Belgian army had gotten away to fight another day. Above all, there was Tannenberg, the great victory in the East that annihilated a huge Russian force, relieved the threat to East Prussia, and gave rise to the fatal myth of the invincibility of the twin heroes Hindenburg and Ludendorff. Visibly the Lord was on the side of the Fatherland. Bells were tolling from every steeple and black-white-and-red flags were flying from every balcony.

Whatever his sources of information, Nicolai did not share the general optimism. For him the war, apart from its senselessness, was a problem of resources. Having lost the advantage of surprise, Germany could not hope to match the Entente in manpower, raw materials, or industrial capacity. In the midst of the victory celebrations he sat down and drew a simple graph, which he sent to the General Staff. It consisted of two curves representing the war potential of the opposing camps. In the manner of a biology professor explaining the energy metabolism of an amoeba to a beginners' class, he told the gentlemen with the red stripe on their trousers that one could predict the general shape of the two curves even if one did not have knowledge of the actual figures, which must surely be available to the war planners. The curve representing German strength would rise more rapidly than that of the Allies because Germany was better prepared for war, but would level off and eventually decline at the very moment when the curve representing the enemy could be expected to rise steeply. The outcome of the war rested upon the time it would take for the two curves to intersect. That would be the last possible moment for a negotiated peace.

We have no record of the reaction to this piece of unsolicited advice at General Headquarters. Nicolai later said that the number of Germans who understood the implications of his graph could have been counted on the fingers of one hand. While this was an overstatement—the prompt creation of a War Raw Materials Office at the suggestion of another civilian, the industrialist Walther Rathenau, shows that there were people who recognized the problem—the charge was not entirely without justice. The public, understandably proud of the feats of German arms and hypnotized by the huge territorial gains east and west, continued to expect victory to the very end of the war. Bethmann-Hollweg, who presided over the government during the first three war years, saw clearly enough that the timing of a negotiated peace was intimately connected with the shifting balance of resources, but in his strangely inconsistent way he clung to war

21

aims which, however modest they were in comparison with those of the superpatriots, could only have been achieved at the point of the sword. In any case, he lacked the power to challenge an omnipotent High Command that was utterly impervious to the kind of civilian logic embodied in Nicolai's graph. Indeed, in the spring of 1918, long after the two curves had intersected and the unlimited capacity of the Allies to produce tanks and airplanes had made German hopes of victory illusory, when a huge American expeditionary force was already assembled on French soil, Hindenburg and Ludendorff would still mount gigantic offensives on the western front, hoping somehow to avert the inevitable. If Nicolai's logic still eluded the generals at a time when defeat was staring them in the face, it must have impressed them as the ravings of a lunatic or a crank at the beginning of the war, when the smell of victory was in the air.

Having given the military experts the benefit of his advice, Nicolai offered his talents in a field where no one could call him a dilettante: he volunteered his services as a physician. In that capacity he remained a civilian. Unlike most German males, he did not hold a reserve officer's commission and was not liable to being called up. Antimilitaristic even in his youth, he had chosen to forgo the year-long stint that led to the coveted reserve officer's patent and absolved the volunteer from serving the three years demanded from those who lacked a high-school diploma. How he as an able-bodied male had escaped military service is a matter for speculation. In a society based on class privilege such as Imperial Germany, those with connections could obtain special treatment, and Nicolai had never been averse to making use of his connections. Except where his principles were at stake he was a thoroughly practical person. He had in any case never worn the "king's cloth," as the uniform was called in Prussia, and as a married man of forty he was exempt from military service when the war broke out. Theoretically he was liable to be drafted into the Landsturm, the home guard composed of older men, but this device was almost never used in the case of physicians. In time it would become a convenient and unobtrusive means of dealing with pacifist troublemakers against whom the authorities could find no other legal grounds to proceed. Being surrendered to the tender mercies of a Prussian drill sergeant was an effective damper on dissent, and no one could complain that he was being punished for holding perfectly lawful but insufficiently patriotic views because he was made to fulfill his obligation to his country.

Such possibilities, however, were still unimaginably remote for Professor Nicolai, a member of the Establishment in good standing who had not yet come in conflict with the military. On the contrary, he had just shown his willingness to do his part. As a physician he could serve without violating his pacifist convictions (or sacrificing the amenities of civilian life). A civil contract with the War Ministry made him chief of a large cardiac service at a military hospital in Tempelhof, on the outskirts of Berlin, permitting him to maintain his private practice in town and to teach at the university. He continued to live in his luxurious apartment, whose front rooms, in keeping with Continental custom, served as his consulting offices and contained an electrocardiograph, an X-ray machine, a well-equipped laboratory, and a splendid scientific library. At Tempelhof he had four assistants and a challenging position. It was an ideal arrangement for reconciling the conscience of a pacifist with the enjoyment of a useful and interesting career.

The event that stirred Nicolai's wrath and propelled him toward rebellion and martyrdom was the appearance of the "Manifesto to the Civilized World," later to become notorious as the "Manifesto of the Ninety-Three."[5] In this extraordinary document the flower of Germany's intelligentsia defended the rape of Belgium and in ringing tones proclaimed its solidarity with German militarism. The list of signers read like a *Who's Who* of German scholarship and art. It included Max Planck, Wilhelm Roentgen, Emil Fischer, Paul Ehrlich, Emil von Behring, and August von Wassermann, to name only a few of the lasting glories of German science. The fame of the artist-signers was to prove less durable—most of the seventeen in this category fell into oblivion in little more than a generation—but to their contemporaries they represented the epitome of the national genius. Among the poets were Richard Dehmel, a friend of Nicolai's mother, and Gerhart Hauptmann, acclaimed as the successor of Goethe and Ibsen. There were two composers, Richard Wagner's son Siegfried and Engelbert Humperdinck. There was the conductor Felix von Weingartner; the theatrical genius Max Reinhardt; Wilhelm von Bode, guiding spirit of Berlin's great art museums; Ulrich von Wilamowitz-Moellendorff, Germany's leading classicist; Rudolf Eucken, grand old man of German philosophy; and Friedrich Naumann, a leader of the Progressive party. Twelve ranking theologians, some considered liberal, seven jurists and political scientists, five art historians, four professors of philosophy, and four of literature and languages lent their names.

The heart of the manifesto was the matter of Belgium. The invasion of that small neutral country in the first hours of the war had horrified a world still clinging to the illusion of the sanctity of international treaties. The horror had grown when the harsh reprisals of German troops against the civilian population, the wholesale shootings of hostages, and the burning of Louvain became known. The rape of Belgium made it difficult to claim that Germany was the victim; German actions might be defended on grounds of military expediency, but not on the lofty plane of morality.

The Ninety-Three tried to do just that. The chancellor had at least been candid in calling the treaty guaranteeing Belgium's neutrality a "scrap of paper" that must not be allowed to stand in Germany's path in the hour of her need, and he had promised to make restitution at the earliest possible moment. The standard-bearers of German culture insisted that Germany had every right to occupy the little country. After a preamble attributing the "calumnies and lies" circulating abroad to their enemies' frustration over being unable to prove "ficticious German defeats" (a delicate reference to the setback on the Marne), they made six points, each prefaced by a ringing "It is not true."

It was not true that Germany had started the war: "Not until our people was attacked from three sides by superior forces long lying in wait at the frontier did it rise as one man." It was not true that Germany had criminally violated Belgian neutrality: proof was at hand that England and France had been about to violate it on their part if Germany had been foolish enough to wait. The life and property of not one single Belgian had been harmed except in self-defense. The ambushing of German troops by civilians was the act of despicable assassins; the burning of Louvain had resulted from the necessity of avenging "with a heavy heart" the treachery of a frenzied populace, and in any case the famous town hall had been saved by the heroic efforts of German soldiers. Germany was adhering to the international rules of warfare. Those who had chosen to ally themselves with Russia and Serbia—nations obviously regarded as barbaric by the signers—had no right to pose as defenders of European civilization, all the less because they had armed Mongolians and Negroes to help them fight white men! Lastly, it was not true that the fight against "our so-called militarism" was not a fight against our culture: "without German militarism German culture would be wiped off the face of the Earth." To a world that was at the mercy of the poison arrows of enemy propaganda the signers cried out: "Believe us! Believe us that we shall fight this battle to the very end as a *Kulturvolk*, a civilized nation, that holds the legacy of a Goethe, a Beethoven and a Kant no less sacred than its hearth and soil."

The ending alone was enough to infuriate Nicolai, who saw in Goethe the European, in Beethoven the composer of the "Ode to Joy," in Kant the author of the *Treatise on Eternal Peace*. War was bad business under the best of circumstances, but it was the business of the military. One could not hold it against soldiers if they followed their trade, nor was it to be expected that the uneducated masses would resist the tide of chauvinism. He had seen the French mobs at Belfort and knew that German mobs were no different. What was unforgivable was the blind nationalism of his peers, the scholars and artists, representatives of a German culture in whose mission he believed deeply but which he considered an integral part of a wider European civilization. The supposed upholders of a great tradition had failed in their most sacred duty. For Nicolai the manifesto amounted to intellectual treason. If no one else would stand up for the true, the universal Germany of Goethe, Beethoven, and Kant, he would.

He drafted a countermanifesto which he took to Albert Einstein and Wilhelm Förster, a distinguished astronomer, for their approval. Both agreed to sign the document as coauthors. The "Appeal to the Europeans," as it was called, deplored the war as a catastrophic disruption of cultural ties between kindred nations at the very moment in history when developments in technology and communications made the unity of civilization a necessity. "That such a state of things exists should not surprise us, but those who take even the slightest interest in this universal civilization have a twofold obligation to defend these principles. Yet those who might be expected to do so, scientists and artists above all, have thus far said nothing to counteract the impression that they care little for the resumption of the severed international ties." This attitude could not be excused by any degree of national passion. "It is unworthy of the ideal of culture as it has been understood hitherto by the whole world, and it would be disastrous if it were to be adopted by educated people in all countries."

The "Appeal" contained two remarkably accurate predictions. The calamity was a threat not only to civilization as a whole but to "the very thing in whose name all these barbarities are perpetrated"—to the "existence of the warring states as national entities." "Thanks to technical progress the world is smaller today, and the countries of the great European peninsula are as close to one another today as were the city-states of that smaller peninsula, Greece, in ancient times." Even bolder for a document written so early in the war (it was intended for release in October 1914 as a rebuttal of the Ninety-Three) was the second prediction that "this war in all probability will leave behind no victors, only victims." Looking ahead still farther, the signers added a third warning: "It is therefore not only desirable but a dire necessity that educated men of all nations make their influence felt, so that whatever the outcome of the war, the terms of the peace do not become the source of future wars." The physiologist, the physicist, and the astronomer showed more insight into human affairs than was later given to the statesmen who devised the treaties of Versailles and Brest Litovsk. With magnificent disdain for the realities of the moment, the "Appeal" declared Europe ripe for union so that she might save her soil, her inhabitants, and her civilization. It closed with a call for the signatures of kindred spirits, "determined like us to create the strongest possible echo of the will of Europe."

Exactly one kindred spirit was willing to sign, and he was a personal friend of Nicolai and very much under his influence: Dr. Otto Buek, private scholar, writer, critic, and dreamer. That Albert Einstein associated himself with the quixotic venture testifies to Nicolai's persuasiveness, for Einstein never again publicly opposed the war, having reached the conclusion that such gestures were futile. The "Appeal to the Europeans" remained unpublished until Nicolai resurrected it in the introduction to *The Biology of War*. Its prophecies had already in large measure come true by the time the book appeared.

Nicolai took comfort in the thought that Einstein, whom he even then considered to be the greatest scientist of the century, had put his name to a document which Nicolai had unsuccessfully submitted to the elite of Berlin's academic community. Even so, he was bitterly disappointed. The experience, he said in a postwar speech, caused him "to wonder for the first time whether the edifice of German science, so splendidly solid in its outward appearance, might not be inwardly rotten." The speech, significantly enough, was titled "The Moral Tasks of the Proletariat—An Indictment of Bourgeois Science."

If he singled out the scientists for special censure, it was because they had shattered his most cherished belief, the illusion that the intellectual integrity of the high priests of science was on a par with their technical achievements. For him science was not a mere method for determining facts of the physical world but a search for the truth that illuminated the whole of life and demanded from its professants a commitment to objectivity in every sphere of human endeavor. For a scientist there could be no double standard of truth, no compartmentalizing of values. It was a difficult and austere credo, but he lived by it and would in time accept degradation, exile, and poverty for its sake. "Everyone," he wrote in *The Biology of War*, "is entitled to consider as true anything of which he is morally convinced, as long as he does not pose as a 'representative of science.' For it is the chief characteristic of the scientist that he accepts nothing as true unless he has convinced himself by impartial observation that it is so."

The sixfold "it is not true" of the Ninety-Three was therefore unworthy of men accustomed to abide by the strictest rules of evidence. "Any scientist ought to have been appalled by the wording, even if he approved of the sentiment." No one could know, for example, whether the reprisals against Belgian civilians were carried out with brutality or "with a heavy heart," whether the German soldiers had committed crimes or acted under duress, whether militarism and civilization were indissolubly linked or irreconcilable opposites. No one could in good conscience assert that not a single Belgian had been harmed except under dire necessity. All this was hearsay. The most a scientist in his laboratory or a scholar in his study could have said was that it came from a usually reliable source, though Nicolai would not grant even that much, for the source was reputed to be the Reichstag deputy Matthias Erzberger, a clever politician in whose truthfulness he had little faith.[6] Some of the signers later claimed that they had not read the manifesto, allowing their names to be used in the belief that they were supporting a good cause, an excuse which Nicolai considered worse than the original act.

If the public remained unaware of the abortive countermanifesto, the authorities were not. Einstein was a Swiss citizen, and Förster—who incidentally had been among the Ninety-Three and had made amends to his pacifist conscience by signing the countermanifesto—was very old and presumably harmless, but Nicolai would bear watching. Indeed, it was not long before he again offended official sensibilities by giving lectures at the university on "War as a Biological Factor in Human Evolution." One could surmise the tenor of these lectures from this title, but the authorities were sensitive to the charge of interfering with academic freedom. Since no basis for legal action could be found—the Reich prided itself on being a *Rechtsstaat*, a state founded on law—it was best not to tip one's hand and to deal with the troublemaker in other, more subtle, ways. In the spring of 1915, the famous Professor Nicolai suddenly found himself transferred from his comfortable post at Tempelhof to the little garrison town of Graudenz, where he was assigned as a mere assistant to a unit for contagious diseases, a field in which he had little experience (Figs. 2–3).

The transfer was typical of the way the government dealt with influential people whom it regarded as dangerous to war morale. As yet Nicolai had given no offense that would have justified disciplinary action. He had merely revealed himself as the holder of undesirable views. Such men, if they came under military jurisdiction, were called up for service; if not, they risked disappearing in a mental institution, a perfectly logical fate for people whose insanity was only too obvious to the warlords, if not to the psychiatrists. Baron Hermann von Eckardstein, a former councillor at the German embassy in London whose revelations threatened to belie the myth of England's war guilt, was a case in point, though he was eventually released, thanks to the efforts of the Socialist leader Philipp Scheidemann. Prince Karl Max Lichnowsky, head of the same embassy, whose even

Fig. 2. Postcard from Albert and Ilse Einstein, 2 April 1915.

more damaging memoir was widely circulated, escaped being locked up but was expelled from the Prussian Herrenhaus and pronounced *non compos mentis*. It was even possible to be declared insane in absentia.

Things had not yet progressed that far in Nicolai's case. The man was a nuisance, but he was a professor and probably harmless, and in any case he had connections. Though a civilian, he was subject to army orders by virtue of his contract. It seemed best to remove him from the scene as quietly as possible via the administrative route. No official reason other than "a combination of certain regrettable circumstances" was given for the transfer of the noted heart specialist to a contagious disease hospital in the hinterland, where his talent would be wasted, and only a crusty old surgeon general of the Imperial Guard was frank enough to admit the truth. All the professor had to do, he told him bluntly, was to abandon his

Fig. 3. Postcard greeting from Albert, Elsa, and Ilse Einstein after Nicolai's banishment to Graudenz, one of several such parodying the prevailing patriotic fervor. The face shows the heads of the Central Powers, the Kaiser, the Sultan of Turkey, and the Emperor Franz Joseph. Einstein has written above the faces "Einigkeit macht stark!" ("Union Is Strength"). The printed motto reads "In Battle United."

lectures and he could stay in Berlin; otherwise he would have to go to Graudenz. Nicolai chose Graudenz.

Graudenz was an old Prussian fortress known chiefly as the place where Fritz Reuter, a popular humorist and novelist, had been imprisoned in the darkest days of the Reaction for singing patriotic songs considered seditious in the realm of the Hohenzollern kings. The Reuter room had since become a tourist attraction and a shrine for the few liberals left in Nicolai's day. Nicolai would make the most of this fortuitous circumstance, claiming that he had been inspired to write his book "by this room where a German patriot spent years as a prisoner," leaving it to the reader to draw the obvious parallel. "Those who today still decry Goethe's conception of the European as treasonable will subscribe to that conception within a few years, even as the commandant of this fortress, once Reuter's jailer, must now maintain his cell as a museum."[7]

Somehow the Reuter legend spawned a Nicolai legend, the first of many that grew up around him in his eventful career as a dissident and one that he never chose to disavow, for he found it useful. Since *The Biology of War* was written at Graudenz and since he spoke at length of Reuter's cell, the impression got about that he had been confined to that very cell. Nothing could have been farther from the truth. He was not a prisoner, nor—as his translators abroad would claim with pardonable exaggeration—had he been relieved of his academic position or his property confiscated. On the contrary, life in Graudenz had its pleasant side, and it is doubtful that he spent much time in the Reuter cell or indeed in any part of the fortress. The commandant proved to be a reasonable man, who realized that Nicolai's talents were going to waste and who arranged for his appointment as consulting cardiologist, not only for Graudenz but for the entire Seventeenth Army Corps district. It was a position of authority and permitted Nicolai to save many a soldier accused of malingering from being sent to the front by some overzealous army doctor.

He had by no means given up hope of returning to the capital, and he sent a continuous stream of protests and petitions to various authorities in Berlin. To Wilhelm von Waldeyer, the famous anatomist, then dean of the medical faculty and a signer of the "Manifesto of the Ninety-Three," he complained about the reassignment of his courses, which he fully expected to resume in the near future, to a colleague. To the minister for religious and cultural affairs he protested vigorously against the infringement on his academic freedom. The minister replied, in technically correct fashion, that the matter did not come under his jurisdiction, Nicolai having been transferred on orders of the War Ministry, not as a university professor but as a physician under contract to the army. So sure was Nicolai of returning that he prepared his forbidden lectures for the next semester. Not until it became apparent that the unseen powers in the War Ministry had no intention of relenting did he conceive the idea of expanding his notes into the book that became *The Biology of War*. Meanwhile he inquired about riding horses, ordered a hunting outfit (Fig. 4), purchased a rifle and ammunition, and joined the commandant in rabbit and fox hunts in the pleasant environs of Graudenz. The two men were getting along famously, their differences in viewpoint notwithstanding. As yet, to use a German expression, the tablecloth between Nicolai and official Germany had not been cut.

That event, however, was not long in coming and, fittingly enough, took place at a luncheon at the Königlicher Hof, Graudenz's best hotel, toward the end of August 1915. The war had entered its second year, the end was not in sight, and Nicolai's curves were moving inexorably toward the point of intersection. Italy had joined the enemy, showing how a former ally and perfect weather vane was judging the wind to blow. The sinking of the *Lusitania* had brought Germany to the brink of war with the

United States, a catastrophe which the chancellor temporarily averted by forcing the navy to abandon unrestricted submarine warfare. This act of intestinal fortitude had earned him the epithet "coward" in national circles. Though the Kaiser privately deplored the breach of chivalry that had doomed women and children, the country was elated. The United States was considered to be a contemptible foe. The *Lusitania*, purportedly

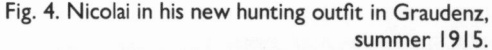

Fig. 4. Nicolai in his new hunting outfit in Graudenz, summer 1915.

armed and deceitfully flying the American flag, had richly deserved her fate. A medal was struck to commemorate the event, showing the sinking vessel with the bridge blown away, flames shooting to the sky, and waves washing over the stern, encircled by the legend "No Contraband!" The equally dramatic obverse pictured a top-hatted war profiteer and other unsavory characters thronging to the ticket window of the Cunard Line, where a grinning skeleton relieved them of their cash underneath a sign reading "Business Above Everything." One more enemy could not destroy the will to conquer. The western front was immobilized, but in the east Hindenburg and Ludendorff were winning spectacular victories, wresting all of Poland from the Russians and taking prisoners by the thousands.

The academic community was not exempt from the general euphoria: *l'appétit vient en mangeant*. The professors, no longer defensive about German *Kultur*, now clamored for the outright annexation of Belgium and other territories east and west. In June an Independent Committee for a German Peace was formed under the leadership of the ultrapatriotic historian Dietrich Schäfer to stiffen the timid chancellor's spine. In July the so-called Seeberg Petition, named after the equally rabid theologian Reinhold Seeberg, was submitted to Bethmann-Hollweg.[8] In it more than twelve hundred scientists, historians, churchmen, and other luminaries voiced their unshakable determination not to rest until the bastion that was Germany was made large and secure enough to guarantee the independence of generations to come. They (and the German people, they asserted) had only one fear—that once again, as at the Congress of Vienna, the pen of the diplomats would rob them of the spoils of the sword.

This might have sufficed, but the professors, being professors, wanted to prove that they were not oblivious of Germany's spiritual future. "The concern for the German spirit," they declared, "does not belong among the war aims or the peace terms." Forgetting that Beethoven and Goethe had lived when Germany's political fortunes were at their lowest ebb, they added: "Germany must be politically and economically secure before she can pursue her spiritual goals." Indulging in an unmistakable bit of blackmail directed at the chancellor, who was suspected of leaning toward a compromise peace, they warned that a statesman who returned from the (as yet imaginary) conference table without the title to Belgium, without other large territorial gains, without billions in reparations, and above all without having achieved "the most ruthless humiliation of England" would face not only the displeasure of the lower and middle classes but the wrath of the highest circles, threatening the very foundations of the monarchy. There was a counterpetition from the more moderate elements in academia, signed by Albert Einstein, Max Planck, and the philosopher Edmund Husserl, among others, but even this minority, clearly expecting a German victory, did not in principle rule out annexations of foreign territory.

It was in this climate that the fateful conversation in the dining room of the Königlicher Hof took place. It was the noon hour, and space was at a premium. A stranger, espying an empty chair at the table where Nicolai was sitting with a friend, bowed stiffly, mumbled his name, and asked permission to sit down. Permission granted, the waiter brought a menu for the new arrival, and the conversation continued where it had left off. As usual, the topic was the war, and as usual Nicolai was in the midst of a diatribe against the makers of Germany's war policy. Perhaps he had in the past been more cautious in his choice of words, or his colleagues, sensing the genius of the man, had shielded him against the consequences of his more seditious remarks. His dining companion, a Dr. Boenheim, was completely under his spell. Perhaps, frustrated in his attempts to return to Berlin, Nicolai was in an angry mood or possibly he felt ebullient and reckless because he had nearly completed his book. Perhaps—as occasionally happened—he simply did not like the stranger's face and decided to shock him with an outrageous remark. Be that as it may, he threw caution to the winds and gave it as his opinion that certain acts of war committed by Germany, to wit, the invasion of Belgium, the sinking of the *Lusitania*, and the use of poison gas, were not only criminal but stupid, for they invited retribution. This was strong stuff, and the ominous stranger, a military surgeon named Dr. Knoll, lost no time in reporting it to his superiors. Nicolai was now embarked on a martyr's career that was to shape the rest of his life.

Even then the action taken by the authorities was curiously restrained. Nicolai, who meanwhile had been taken ill with rheumatic fever, was questioned in his lodgings by the chief of the military hospital, a Dr. Knoch. By a strange coincidence, the names of almost all his antagonists during the ensuing troubles had a harsh Teutonic ring and a sinister or grotesque meaning: Knoll ("clod"), Knoch ("bone"), Böse ("evil"), Schwer ("heavy"), Klauer ("claw"), and Pusch. It was as if they had been chosen by a supernatural playwright to symbolize the gray evil that now descended upon him. The invalid's first remarks sufficed to convince his examiner that he indeed harbored the "antinational" views of which he stood accused. Official patience was at an end. Knoch's report went through channels, and on 13 September Nicolai received notice of another transfer, this time to the end of the world, a camp for Russian prisoners of war at Tuchel, on the edge of a moor called Tuchler Heide, where he would be assigned to the infirmary.

Although the transfer was clearly punitive, no charges were preferred against Nicolai. The matter was treated once again as an administrative problem. The order, signed by Dr. Böttcher, acting surgeon general of the Seventeenth Army Corps, was addressed in proper form to "Herr Professor Nicolai, Hochwohlgeboren," and read as follows:

> It has come to my attention that your Hochwohlgeboren has expressed toward third persons, although not hospital personnel under your supervision, views which I must consider antinational. In the interest of the service I deem it necessary that you should change the scene of your activities. Accordingly I have proposed to the Generalkommando XVII Army Corps that you be transferred to the prisoner-of-war camp Tuchel. Kindly await your orders to that effect. I cannot refrain from calling your attention to the fact that indications of treason are considered to exist when antinational views are expressed toward foreigners.[9]

Nicolai did not take this challenge lying down. He considered himself no less patriotic than the next man and a better or at least more farsighted German than most. "I assert," he wrote from the clinic of his friend Professor Brugsch in Berlin, where he had had himself transported in the meantime, "that I have never held or expressed antinational views." He crossed out the next sentence of the draft, which he had scribbled on the back of Böttcher's official missive. "On the contrary," it had been his first impulse to write, "it requires either the highest degree of stupidity or deliberate malice to construe my remarks in this fashion." In a calmer, though scarcely less telling, vein he continued: "To my mind, the views I have expressed are in the true interest of our country and, as I stand ready to prove if necessary, correspond to those held by the responsible authorities of our government."

With this allusion to the chancellor's position he was touching a raw nerve, for in army circles Bethmann-Hollweg was seen as the chief obstacle to the ruthless pursuit of victory at any cost, yet he was nonetheless the head of the legally constituted government and as such enjoyed the vacillating but—at critical moments—wholehearted support of the monarch. He had admitted at the very outset, albeit in language that was far more temperate than Nicolai's, that the invasion of Belgium was morally wrong. His rash promise to make restitution once the war was over had thrown a monkey wrench into the plans of the annexationists before they had time to develop. When they developed anyhow, he had tried, and was still trying in 1915, to keep them from being aired in public. More realistic than his critics, aware that after the fiasco on the Marne the prospects for a "German Peace" were dim, he could not afford to be driven into a corner by the strident cries of the Pan-German annexationists, which aroused the most sanguine expectations at home and furnished grist for the propaganda mills of the enemy. Persuasion being useless with people whose very menace lay in the fact that they knew themselves to be always right, he had taken the unheard-of step of applying wartime censorship measures, not against the Social Democrats and other doubtful elements but against German patriots, generals and admirals, bearers of proud titles and respected members of the middle class. It was unbelievable and, fortunately, ineffective. The patriots had money and mimeograph machines and saw to it that their views as to what constituted Germany's rightful war aims were given the widest, although clandestine, circulation. They also saw to it that the chancellor's cowardly attempts to suppress these views became known, for the man plainly lacked the will to win.

But Bethmann-Hollweg's greatest crime was his opposition to the ruthless submarine warfare ceaselessly clamored for by Grand Admiral Alfred von Tirpitz, the powerful Navy League, and all good patriots in and out of uniform. The U-boats, they insisted, were a sure-fire weapon without which Germany was like a man fighting for his life with one arm tied behind his back. It was absurd to forgo this weapon out of fear of the United States, an effete commercial nation infested with the spirit of democracy and unlikely to fight. Herr von Tirpitz unleashed a vast campaign amounting to a guarantee that England would be "forced to her knees" within six months. An impressive man in his grand admiral's uniform and his magnificent beard, Tirpitz had behind him one million members of the Navy League, a pressure group of his own creation, and the financial backing of industry, notably the producers of naval armaments (including the Schichau Yards, of which Nicolai's father-in-law happened to be the representative), as well as the vocal support of the nationalist press. But the chancellor stood his ground and was able to continue his policy of appeasing the United States. In the end Tirpitz resigned in disgust.

Nicolai was thus entirely correct in claiming that his remarks concerning Belgium and submarine warfare only reflected the views of His Majesty's government. He was, to be sure, a far more radical pacifist than the chancellor, and his language had been more colorful, but that was not the issue. "I therefore maintain," his protest continued, "that a transfer that might be construed as a punitive measure is unjust. On these grounds I ask Your Excellency to reverse the order, or else institute disciplinary proceedings against me, so that it can be proved unequivocally that the charges against me are without foundation."

The demand for disciplinary action against himself was to become a favorite (though always unsuccessful) stratagem in Nicolai's attempts to smoke out evasive opponents. Anxious to avoid becoming involved in a cause célèbre and fully aware that the legal case against the cagey professor was weak, Böttcher once more took refuge in administrative procedure. His reply was short and to the point: "The transfer to Tuchel is not a punitive measure," he wrote disingenuously, "but a step taken in the interest of the service. Please return this letter, as well as the communication of 13 September."

It had dawned on the acting surgeon general that he had walked into a trap when he based the transfer on the untenable charge of antinational views on the part of such a well-known and well-connected personality as Professor Nicolai, and he hoped to extricate himself by retrieving the original order before it could be exploited by a skillful opponent. But it was Nicolai's turn to be disingenuous. Recognizing the value of the compromising document as clearly as his superior, he blandly denied having it. Böttcher, now throughly alarmed, became insistent. "Your statement that you no longer have the letter in your possession is considered insufficient. Where is it?" Nicolai progressed from an untruth to a half-truth. He had used the back of the letter, he replied, to draft his answer—this was true—and subsequently discarded it along with other pieces of business. This was not true. Nicolai rarely discarded so much as a postcard of the most cursory interest, let alone a document of such vital importance, and Böttcher's letter remained in his files to his dying day.

As a stickler for the truth he could excuse his white lie on the grounds that he was engaged in a struggle with a powerful and deceitful adversary who threatened, by banishing him to the outer darkness, to wreck the effort he had come to regard as his mission in life. That adversary was not the insignificant Dr. Böttcher but the War Ministry, and behind it the hated spirit of Prussian militarism. In this struggle a slight prevarication was justified, as long as it did not involve a sacrifice of principle. He knew full well, moreover, that the other side had consistently lied to him in pretending that his transfers were routine administrative measures. Böttcher had slipped, and Nicolai was prepared to make the most of it, like David exploiting the sun in Goliath's eyes.

David had many more stones in his shepherd's bag, and though he failed to smite the Philistine with his brass helmet, his coat of mail, and his spear that weighed six hundred shekels, he used them with great skill to prolong the battle and inflict painful wounds on the enemy. With David, Nicolai might have said: "What have I now done? Is there not a cause?" The events of the past year had given a keener edge to his dissent. As a pacifist of long standing he abhorred the war as senseless butchery. As a European he deplored the destruction of a common civilization. As a scientist he considered what he contemptuously called "Katzbalgereien mit Kanonen" (the brawls of alley cats armed with cannons) as an obsolete and wasteful method of pursuing national goals. As he put it in *The Biology of War*, it was absurd to kill one another over energy resources that were large enough to satisfy the needs of all mankind. But now, amidst the clamor for the spoils of a war not yet won, he was reaching the new and still more daring conclusion that the main obstacle to an early and sane peace was the Germans' expectation of victory.

In the eyes of his countrymen this was indeed akin to treason. But Nicolai took a broader and in the end more realistic view. Inbued with the traditions of German Idealism as represented by Kant and Goethe, no less than with fierce pride in the scientific heritage of a Humboldt, a Helmholtz, or a Virchow, he feared the increasing brutalization of the national spirit and the total ascendancy of the military which a prolonged war was bound to bring with it. The prospect of territorial conquests which dazzled the generals, the professors, and the public at large was an irrelevant detail that could under no circumstances justify the colossal risk of destroying Germany as a civilized nation. A man whose house is on fire can ill afford to make off with his neighbor's heirlooms. To jeopardize what Nicolai believed to be the essence of the German heritage for the sake of spoils of at best dubious value was sheer madness. His might be a voice crying in the wilderness, but he was determined to make it heard.

The transfer to the godforsaken prison camp at Tuchel was therefore a deadly blow to him. He needed to find a publisher willing to risk his money and perhaps his freedom for the now-completed *Biology of War*. This was not something that could be done from a distance. Berlin was the center of action and his home ground, the place where the influential figures of the publishing world could be found, the place also where he could move about with comparative freedom and use personal contacts to exert his considerable powers of persuasion. Graudenz, though otherwise pleasant, had been unsatisfactory as a base of operations. Tuchel would be infinitely worse. He would be cut off from the world, deprived of his books, and dependent on slow and irregular censored mail. He would be treated more like a prisoner than a person of authority and, given his record, would be kept under close surveillance. He would also miss the amenities of life, which he by no means despised. If he could help it he would never go to Tuchel.

Knowing what obstacles his book would face, he had not waited to complete the manuscript before starting the wheels turning. As yet, publishers with a clean record did not have to submit publications to the censor in advance, though they faced suppression or confiscation if they stepped too far out of line. *The Biology of War*, despite its innocuous title and its scientific trappings, was at bottom a virulent attack on the very foundations of Prussian militarism, drawing on history and politics as much as on biology for its argument. Once it was available for inspection, no censor would pass it, censorship being vested in the commanders of the military districts into which Germany was divided. Curt Thesing, owner of the Verlag Naturwissenschaften, a friend and fellow pacifist in whom Nicolai had placed his hopes, was with the army in France.

The faithful Otto Buek in Berlin was exploring other possibilities, but he was clearly not the man for the job. Timid, diffident, and impractical, he often forgot to date his letters or give his return address and had difficulties in interpreting the necessarily cryptic messages Nicolai sent him from Graudenz. He admired his resourceful friend Georg, on whom he depended for moral support in these depressing times, but he was aware of his own limitations. "Dear friend," he wrote on one occasion, "I thank you for your consolatory letter. It raised my spirits temporarily but not for long. You just happen to be lucky in everything. In the most godforsaken place"—he meant Graudenz, not Tuchel—"you succeed in finding people with whom you can harmonize and whom you can influence, and moreover you have your happy confidence in the meaning of the run of the world and thus can always find strength and interest enough to work and be active." He himself was not in good health, he reported, afraid of losing his tutorial position and despairing of the future. When Nicolai upbraided him for his lack of progress in the matter of the book, he defended himself by describing once more the state of his mind: "What you interpret as lack of energy or inertia is not want of goodwill or of the proper spirit, but congenital disposition. To conquer this lethargy one needs faith, which unfortunately I do not possess. Pessimism and the fear engendered by the spectacle of unreason triumphant throughout the world, together with lack of confidence in my own strength and in humanity at large—these things are too deeply imprinted on my mind."

In spite of these drawbacks, Buek was invaluable as an errand boy, and it was he who, from the depth of his pessimism, emerged with the eminently practical suggestion of approaching a Swiss publisher. Nicolai would not as yet consider this solution. Instead he wrote to Maximilian Harden, editor of *Die Zukunft*, the most influential and least corruptible journalist of the Wilhelminian era. Harden, once a protégé of Bismarck, had been an ardent advocate of annexations early in the war, but had lately begun to see the light. Still, he was not ready to go as far as Nicolai. "I am very interested in the contents," he wrote on an open postcard, postcards being less likely to be read or intercepted by the censor, "but whether it is 'possible' seems very doubtful, to say the least." Already Nicolai's correspondence had assumed a conspiratorial cast.

His brightest hope was Franz Pfemfert, a kindred spirit, in his way as unorthodox and aggressive as Nicolai himself. A dynamo of a man, Pfemfert had single-handedly made his magazine *Die Aktion* the brilliantly illuminated stage for the writers and artists of Expressionism, a movement whose common denominator was the radical rejection of the social, cultural, and political pretensions of Wilhelminian Germany. In the pages of *Aktion* the arrogance of the military, the gray despair of the tenements, the hypocrisy of the middle classes, the injustice of the political caste system, and the picture-postcard perfection of Wilhelminian art had been castigated by writers whose talent often matched their courage. Though *Aktion* had renounced political topics during the war, Pfemfert violently opposed the course on which Germany had embarked. He therefore used his connections with publishers to find a berth for *The Biology of War*, and when every door was shut in his face he printed some of the less seditious chapters in his own magazine. He supplied Nicolai with reading material whose shipment entailed risks for sender and recipient alike, such as *Die Internationale*, a history of Marxist socialism by Franz Mehring and Rosa Luxemburg. Recognizing a critical talent when he saw one, he also sent Nicolai a copy of *Händler und Helden*, a violently anti-British concoction by the renowned economist Werner Sombart, asking him if he would "take care of this 'work' from the historical standpoint" in a lead article for *Aktion*. The project came to nothing, but Pfemfert remained a loyal friend and staunch ally.

Pfemfert's letters to Graudenz were lively and informative. He had gone to see the publisher Eugen Diederichs, editor of the magazine *Die Tat* and an influential figure in literary circles, whose vague idealism found expression in protests against the soulless industrial age. Pfemfert expected Diederichs to be sympathetic but had found him completely *verschweint*, an untranslatable coinage meaning roughly "turned into a pig." Like most German intellectuals, Pfemfert said, Diederichs had had a change of heart. "He regrets his former work, considers Tolstoy a nightmare and, as he confessed to me, has 'umgelernt' [revised his thinking]." There was no hope from that quarter. "Fischer [head of the great publishing firm S. Fischer] is still out of town. He remains my white hope. If not, I still have other ideas. If no one else, the *Aktion* will do the printing."

The hope did not materialize. Pfemfert was as impatient as Nicolai. Dismissing the latter's secret negotiations with a Leipzig publisher named Klemm as "nonsense," he announced that he would not wait much longer. "As soon as I have time—first I must sell a lovely old painting to a man I know—I shall give up this stupid waiting," he wrote before he had even seen the complete manuscript. "Perhaps I shall start immediately anyway. The prospect of having you in Berlin again is the only pleasure of the next few days. Please write—and return this letter." Pfemfert too had reasons for not wanting compromising letters to remain in Nicolai's file, though they differed from Böttcher's. But before he could make good his offer, Nicolai's book was formally outlawed, and thereafter no German publisher could risk its publication.

In the late summer of 1915, however, Nicolai's hopes were still undimmed. He was moving heaven and earth to avoid the transfer to Tuchel. From his sickbed in Brugsch's Berlin clinic he made the opening move. On 27 September, he sent a new appeal to the Commandatura in Graudenz. "No one will believe that the transfer is not a punitive measure," he wrote.

If the authorities feel that it is not in the interest of the service for the slanderer [he meant Dr. Knoll] and his victim to be in the same unit, let him be transferred who committed the wrong. This, as I happen to know from personal contacts, is also the feeling of at least the majority of my colleagues in Graudenz. One more thing: in the interest of the *Burgfrieden* proclaimed by the supreme commander I have thus far refrained from suing the author of these slanderous reports for libel. All the more do I have the right to expect the protection of my superiors, although it is also in their own interest to avoid the impression that they are lending official support to libelers. Hoping that nothing more than this hint is needed to redress the grave—albeit, I am sure, unintentional—injustice, I respectfully ask you to revoke the transfer, or else open disciplinary hearings. But, should it against all expectations be considered desirable to remove me from Graudenz, then, given the interest of the army in my special field of competence, I respectfully request a transfer to Berlin.

The letter was vintage Nicolai, at once aggressive and crafty, self-righteous and highly practical. He was turning the tables on his accusers. He suggested a superficially plausible reason for the transfer order, namely, the undesirable effect of having two colleagues who had become enemies on the same post, a reason which the authorities clearly had not in mind but which he offered them as a face-saving device should they wish to reverse themselves. He found a way to claim the moral support of his fellow officers; he made it appear that the *Burgfrieden*, a notion pertaining to national politics, was applicable to his private cause; and he ended with the suggestion that the penalty of a transfer to Tuchel be converted into the reward of an assignment to Berlin, where he had wanted to be all along.

The maneuver failed, not unexpectedly, but Nicolai had gained precious time. The Commandatura of Graudenz informed him that it did not consider itself competent with respect to a disciplinary hearing. "Your dossier," the carefully worded answer read, "may show whether the denunciation was made by a colleague, but it has been forwarded to the inspector of prison camps [at Tuchel]. The original transcript of your deposition is at the War Ministry." The mills of the military bureaucracy had begun to grind.

Nicolai's next protest was addressed to General Von Schack, commander of the Seventeenth Army Corps in Danzig. Exploiting the opening Böttcher had given him when he based the transfer order on the charge of antinational views, he argued that the measure was clearly punitive rather than administrative, and therefore improper. The general's answer, dated 31 December 1915, found him still in Berlin. "It is stipulated that the utterances with which you are charged were made only in private conversation, albeit in a public place, and prior to the release of the proclamation of the Seventeenth Army Corps of 15 August," it stated, referring to a new set of strict regulations, issued perhaps in response to Nicolai's own breach of the code for army personnel. "Therefore you are not liable to punishment." But Von Schack would not disavow his acting surgeon general: "I too consider the statements reported under oath by Dr. Knoll as evidence of antinational and anti-German views and must therefore reject your complaint against Dr. Böttcher concerning the expression he used in his letter of 13 September. Your transfer is not to be regarded as punitive, but it is in the interest of the service, for your statements are widely known and have been discussed by your subordinates."

The general was undoubtedly right: Nicolai's assistants and orderlies had been questioned and talked freely. He himself had probably told them—not without a grim pride—of the incident at the Königlicher Hof. At this juncture he appealed to the emperor as the court of last resort. He was not favored with a reply, but he had sources of information and learned that His Majesty had written a benign marginal gloss on his dossier: "The man is a well-meaning idealist, let him be."[10] Perhaps the Kaiser, at heart a decent man, felt kindly toward the physician who had attended the empress. Still, as supreme warlord he did not wish to overrule the decision of a high officer. "His Majesty is willing to believe that your thoughts are guided solely by your concern for the welfare of the Fatherland," General Von Schack informed Nicolai on 16 March 1916. "Nevertheless, the All-Highest could not disagree with my interpretation of your conduct. In view of the seriousness of the times every German must do his share to make sure that the will to win is not turned into timid doubt. The utterances of an influential person such as a physician, made in a circle of doubtful discretion, show lack of a full sense of responsibility."

Perhaps the All-Highest had learned that Nicolai had once again defied the War Ministry by resuming his objectionable lectures at the university during his extended sick leave in Berlin. The only way to deal with such a brazen provocation was to remove him from the scene. His orders were activated, and at last he departed for Tuchel, having managed to draw out his stay in the capital for six precious months. But no sooner had he arrived there than he received orders to report to the headquarters of the Seventeenth Army Corps in Danzig. The record does not show whether the Kaiser's lenient remark had inspired second thoughts in some bureaucrat at the War Ministry, whether General Von Schack on mature reflection had decided that it was best to keep such a slippery character as Nicolai in sight, or whether the army was afraid of repercussions in the Reichstag, where the dissenter had friends among the Progressives and Social Democrats, a useful fact that he was not likely to conceal. He had in fact taken advantage of his stay in the capital to strengthen these connections. The Reichstag, to be sure, was a contemptible "chatterbox," as Bismarck had called the national parliament, but one of the few rights the Bismarckian constitution allowed the chatterers was that of approving or disapproving the war budget. In these perilous times it was better not to offend parliamentarians and best to oblige them with small favors. The army was confident that it could handle Nicolai, wherever he might be stationed.

The sudden change of orders had a ludicrous sequel which gives us a glimpse into the great pacifist's private morals. Not the least of his many gifts was the irresistible attraction he exerted on women. He considered them fair game and never allowed conventions or circumstances to interfere with his pleasure. To console himself for the hardships of Tuchel he had arranged for his latest conquest, Hannah Boenheim, wife of the colleague with whom he had lunched on the fatal day at the Königlicher Hof, to visit him at his new post. Hannah came as soon as she could find a pretext, but discovered him already gone. She spent the night staring at the dreary walls of the village inn. Perhaps Nicolai, who was rarely considerate in his dealings with women, had not bothered to let her know that he had received new orders, or perhaps there had not been time. He was in any case en route to Danzig.

Danzig was not Berlin, but it was a large and lively town and a vast improvement over Tuchel or even Graudenz. As a comparatively recent acquisition of Prussia, to which it was awarded at the second partition of Poland in 1797, the ancient city had preserved an independent if not downright anti-Prussian spirit that was bound to appeal to the rebel in Nicolai. But it would be some time before he could enjoy its amenities, such as they were in wartime. He was now face to face with Dr. Böttcher, who had not forgotten the trouble Nicolai had given him and who lost no time in letting him know that he was under a cloud. Upon reporting for duty—still as a civilian under contract to the War Ministry—he was peremptorily ordered to refrain from all political utterances. Coming from an officer who was responsible for the morale and discipline of his men, and given Nicolai's record, this was not an unreasonable demand, but it was met with open defiance. As a civilian Nicolai claimed to be exempt from military discipline. Böttcher promptly closed the loophole. Within a few days the civilian found himself confronted with the demand that he take the oath to the colors, which would place him under the same discipline as regular army officers. Again he refused, citing three reasons. First, there was no legal precedent for the request. Thus far no civilian physician had been asked to take the oath. Second, he objected to taking the oath as a matter of principle, for it implied a willingness to support the war. And third, the suddenness of the demand proved that it was a mere piece of chicanery, aimed at his person because of his refusal to knuckle under to the military.

Reichstag or no, the army had enough. By the standards of a Prussian institution accustomed to unquestioning obedience, Nicolai's superiors had been more than lenient until now. Plainly the man was asking for trouble and had to be brought under control. He was suspended and ordered to restrict his movements to the city limits of Danzig. On 1 April 1916 his contract with the War Ministry was annulled. He was then drafted into the Landsturm as a private, assigned to Fortress Danzig as *Militärkrankenwärter*, a medical orderly, and ordered to report forthwith to his new superior, a Dr. Schwer. As far as the army was concerned, that was that. The thought that a private under orders could give trouble to his superiors did not occur to men brought up in the Prussian tradition. They did not know Nicolai. For him the fight had just begun.

NOTES

1. *Die Biologie des Krieges, Betrachtungen eines deutschen Naturforschers* (Zurich: Orell Füssli, 1917); copy in Nicolai archive. Hereafter cited as *The Biology of War*.

2. Rolland to Einstein, 21 August 1917, quoted from *Einstein on Peace*, ed. Otto Nathan and Heinz Norden (New York: Schocken Books, 1968). Romain Rolland, the French writer and pacifist, winner of the Nobel Prize for Literature in 1916, was considered by his admirers to be a latter-day Tolstoy. In exile in Switzerland during the war, he served as a rallying point for pacifists in the belligerent countries.

3. Rolland's essay on Nicolai originally appeared in 1917 in two parts in the pacifist magazine *Demain*, published in Geneva, under the title "Un Grand Européen: G.-F. Nicolai" (*Demain* 2, nos. 18–19 [October–November 1917]:337–57, 13–30). It was later reprinted in Rolland's *Les Précurseurs* (Paris: Albin Michel, 1923).

4. "Déclaration de l'indépendence de l'esprit," Rolland's postwar appeal for the reconciliation of Europe's intellectuals, is quoted in full in his wartime diary, *Journal des années de guerre 1914–1919: Notes et documents pour servir à l'histoire morale de l'Europe de ce temps* (ed. Marie Romain Rolland (Paris: Albin Michel, 1952). He read it to Nicolai for his approval at their first face-to-face meeting in March 1919. Nicolai's commentary appeared in the Preface to his translation, *Romain Rollands Manifest und die deutschen Antworten, mit einem Anhang über den Fall Nicolai* (Charlottenburg: Mundus Verlagsanstalt, 1919), p. 15.

5. "Aufruf an die Kulturwelt," quoted in full by Nicolai in *The Biology of War*, pp. 4–6.

6. As if to confirm Nicolai's skepticism, Erzberger was soon placed in charge of German propaganda abroad, perhaps on the strength of this achievement. He was a leader of the Center Party and a rabid annexationist early in the war. Later, however, he became the architect of the Reichstag Peace Resolution of 1917, signer of the Armistice in 1918, and finance minister in the early days of the Weimar Republic. He was assassinated in 1921 by right-wing fanatics.

7. Introduction to *The Biology of War*, pp. 12–13.

8. For details, see H. P. Bleuel, *Deutschlands Bekenner, Professoren zwischen Kaiserreich und Diktatur* (Bern: Scherz Verlag, 1968).

9. Original is in the Nicolai archive.

10. According to Nicolai, the Kaiser's marginal note was reported to him by "a reliable officer." He incorporated it verbatim in the pamphlet *Warum ich aus Deutschland ging* (*Why I Left Germany*). It is quoted here from Nicolai's *Aufruf an die Europäer, gesammelte Aufsätze zum Wiederaufbau Europas*, edited by Hans Wehberg (Leipzig: Verlag der Wiener graphischen Werkstätte, 1921).

2. The Last Encyclopedist

"Some books are to be tasted," wrote Francis Bacon, "others to be swallowed, and some to be chewed and digested." *The Biology of War*, while eminently readable, belonged to Bacon's third category. It made, in fact, considerable demands on the reader's intellect, if only because of the bulk and variety of the observations with which it confronted him. Though written in a lucid and refreshingly unprofessorial style, it was not, nor was meant to be, a popular book. Nicolai, for whom mass culture was still a contradiction in terms, was addressing the educated public from whose awakening he envisioned the salvation of Europe. He fully expected his readers to be familiar with the traditions of western civilization, to understand literary and historical allusions, and to follow the rigors of scientific reasoning.

On the other hand, *The Biology of War* was not a work to be read only by experts. Nicolai no doubt chose the intriguing title both to startle the public by the juxtaposition of two hitherto unrelated notions and to keep the censor from looking too closely at what promised to be a dry technical treatise. It was anything but that, of course, and despite its unglamorous title it became the bible of pacifism in the closing years of the war and for some time thereafter. It was the message of a scientist in possession of vital knowledge that he felt compelled to impart to intelligent but poorly informed laymen in terms they could understand. As Nicolai saw it, the future of mankind was bound up with its biological fate, and the experts— much like the atomic physicists of a later age—had the duty to enlighten the world about the dangers of modern warfare to the well-being of the species. A war in which millions of human beings, chiefly the young and able-bodied, were killed or maimed and other millions were threatened with famine and disease was a biological event of the first magnitude. Misconceptions about the "wholesomeness" and the "invigorating effects" of war had been current in Germany in peacetime and were rampant in the flush of the victories of 1914 and 1915. Men of the caliber of Ernst Haeckel, the doyen of the natural sciences, were hailing the conflict as a Darwinian struggle for life and equating the survival of the fittest with Germany's victory over England. Nicolai, who considered these ideas as pernicious as they were unscientific, felt that it behooved him as a scientist to challenge them.

But it was not only as a scientist that he raised his voice. He was speaking as a German against German militarism, as a European against a fratricidal war, as a civilized human being against the suicide of a civilization. On balance, *The Biology of War* was more political than scientific, more polemical than objective. Strictly speaking, only five of its fifteen chapters were devoted to the biological aspects of war, and even there the facts from the realm of natural science were liberally interlaced with ideas from other spheres. It was not for nothing that Nicolai had spent years collecting materials for his lectures on the topic of cultural-biological interactions in human evolution. War was merely a special—though now, in the summer of 1915, a desperately urgent—case of such interaction. He wished to examine it from every angle, as a natural phenomenon and evolutionary cul-de-sac and as a moral and political problem, as an example of misdirected technology and faulty utilization of energy and other resources and as a social disease, as both cause and result of aberrations in national and individual behavior. It was an ambitious undertaking, well beyond the capabilities of the ordinary biologist or, for that matter, the ordinary man. But Nicolai was no ordinary biologist. His background and his phenomenal memory enabled him to draw freely upon resources in virtually every field of human endeavor; perhaps no man since Aristotle and Saint Thomas Aquinas had achieved greater mastery of the sum of knowledge available in his time. The reviewers who tried to summarize the contents of his book were torn between admiration and despair.

Nicolai's magnum opus was no mere display of erudition, however. He saw himself above all as the lone defender of Germany's intellectual honor. In the "Manifesto of the Ninety-Three" the nation's intelligentsia had condoned the rape of Belgium in the name of Kant and Goethe, linking the survival of German culture to the triumph of Prussian militarism. This betrayal of German Idealism, as he called it in the Introduction, could not be allowed to go unanswered. Not without malice, he quoted the manifesto in its entirety, complete with the names of the signers, some of whom no doubt had had second thoughts by then. Following a devastating critique, he then reproduced the counter-manifesto which he, Einstein, and Förster had drawn up in the fall of 1914 and which had not yet reached the public. A more powerful opening would be difficult to imagine, for by the time the book finally appeared Nicolai's warnings had taken on the force of prophecies fulfilled.

As a scientist Nicolai was aware of his obligation to be objective, and he took care to define the limits of his objectivity at the outset. Natural phenomena such as earthquakes or floods could be viewed with detachment, he said, even though they might destroy human lives, for they were not subject to control by humans. War, on the other hand, was not a natural catastrophe or an act of God but a human act, and as such open to judgment. To refrain from taking positions for the sake of scientific objectivity was to obscure the very nature of the problem. "I have therefore gathered the material in as objective a manner as possible in order to use it under the aspect of one guiding idea: the idea of humanity."

The material he had thus gathered was impressive. The index alone occupied fifteen pages, with more than 660 entries, beginning with Abélard and ending with the contemporary zoologist Otto Zur Strassen. Among those quoted or referred to in the text or in the footnotes were the church fathers from Origen to Saint Augustine; medieval figures such as Peter of Amiens, Saint Francis, Saint Thomas Aquinas, and Dante; the humanists of the Renaissance; Cervantes and his contemporary, the Spanish Jesuit Francisco Suárez; poets from Homer, Virgil, Calderón, Goethe, and Walt Whitman to Ernst Lissauer, author of the odious "Hymn of Hate" against England; philosophers from Spinoza to Comte and moralists from Pascal to Tolstoy; satirists from Rabelais to Swift and from Voltaire to Anatole France; and political theorists from Machiavelli to Grotius and from Montesquieu to John Stuart Mill. There were references to military authorities from the inevitable Clausewitz to Admiral Mahan and from the elder Moltke to General Friedrich von Bernhardi, the notorious prophet of the current war; and social critics of every shade, including Jeremy Bentham, Fourier, Marx, Lassalle, and Kropotkin, as well as Charles Kingsley and Ibsen. Scientists, needless to say, occupied a prominent place among Nicolai's sources. The list included physicists from Galileo and Newton to Faraday, Planck, Einstein, and Marconi; mathematicians from Pythagoras to Henri Poincaré; naturalists from Humboldt and Darwin to Helmholtz and Pasteur; Pavlov, the discoverer of the conditioned reflex; and Fritz Haber, the inventor of the first poison gas used to kill human beings. And, inevitably, there was the whole array of Greek and Roman authors and German classics without which a book from the pen of a German professor was unthinkable.

But Nicolai was not trying to dazzle the reader with mere scholarship. He aimed at nothing less than a new religion of humanity, a moral code based on the common biological and cultural denominators of mankind. He conceived the species as an organism held together by its biological heritage and its history, evolving in a direction fixed by the evolution that had manifestly taken place in the past and must inevitably continue in the future. "To be human means nothing less than to have understood the evolutionary history of mankind, to know whence we have come, to sense whither we are headed, and to try to adapt ourselves accordingly to the general process of nature which, for us, unfolds in the development of the human race." To trace this process was to invoke the voices of those who had advanced the common cause, the poets who had beheld man's destiny in their visions, the thinkers whose wisdom had pointed the way, the scientists who had given mankind the understanding of the laws of nature, and the discoverers and inventors who had freed it from its physical limitations. War had no place in this scheme of things, for it no longer served the purposes of the species. Physical aggression was an example of an instinct that had lost its usefulness in the course of human evolution. War might be defended by the supernatural religions—for example, by a watered-down Christianity—as the will of God. As the will of man it could never be reconciled with the religion of humanity, a creed born of knowledge and reason instead of revealed truth. "To feel the reality of the human community is to have one's roots in the world, to have religion, to love one's neighbor."

Although Nicolai, strangely enough, did not expressly acknowledge his indebtedness to Auguste Comte, his conception was in fact an updated version of the French philosopher's *Religion de l'Humanité*. Like Comte he rejected the metaphysical notions of God and eternal life, finding the inspiration for his creed in the workings of the human mind. To know the knowable, nature and man, was enough. To go beyond, to leave the plane of reality, was both futile and dangerous. The guiding principle of human conduct must be sought in the understanding of human nature itself. Intuitive knowledge had given way in modern times to science as a means by which man could understand his environment and himself. Comte's dictum "savoir pour prévoir, prévoir pour prévenir" ("to know in order to look ahead, to look ahead in order to prevent") would have been the perfect motto for *The Biology of War*. The supernatural religions, though they embodied many profound truths, had failed man because they rested on something other than reality. Those who did not know that God does not exist, Nicolai said, could derive their morality from Him, but "he who knows that God does not exist, and yet concocts for himself some fantastic notion of a power that he defines as God, is acting foolishly, and in this sense the most naive idol worshiper is much saner than many a learned philosopher."

Like Comte, who had proposed the idea of humanity, "Le Grand Être," as the religion of the future, Nicolai saw the concept of the brotherhood of mankind as the only possible substitute for the absolutes of revealed religion. What was new in his approach was the emphasis on the biological basis of man's destiny. Comte, creator of the science of sociology and, indeed, of the very word "sociology," had seen the human race as a socially perfectible but biologically fixed species. Though he considered biology to be one of the fundamental sciences, he had not lived to read *Origin of Species* and *The Descent of Man*. Nicolai conceived humanity as a way station on the path of evolution. He insisted that morality, that is, the social code of man, must henceforth be compatible with the biological goal of a new and better breed. Man must rid himself of the old destructive rivalries, for as an intelligent being he is capable of recognizing them as obstacles to his proper biological progression. Having taken his future into his own hands and being able to anticipate his own evolution, he must consciously change his behavior.

Nicolai laid the groundwork for these conclusions with typical German thoroughness. He surveyed the history of ideas concerning war from Confucius and Heraclitus (whose unfortunate dictum "war is the father of all things" he balanced by the same author's view that the sense of the world was "harmony and peace") to Woodrow Wilson. He traced the development of weapons from stone axes and arrowheads to dum-dum bullets and poison gas grenades. He quoted chapter and verse, both well-known authorities and remote sources whose existence a cursory search for usable quotations would not have disclosed. He was thoroughly at home in the fine print of the footnotes that so often prove more interesting than the text to which they are appended. He knew the out-of-the-way corners of history, and in passing dropped such pearls of information as the number of witches and heretics estimated to have been burned before 1700; the drop in the value of British consols in the wake of the Boer War; the fact that the Second Lateran Council in 1139 had banned the use of the crossbow against fellow-Christians (though not against heathens and Saracens); General Wolfe's deathbed exclamation that he would rather have been the author of Gray's *Elegy* than the conqueror of Quebec; the names of the German poets who had glorified the "War of Liberation" against Napoleon without ever seeing battle; and the effect of the Franco-Prussian War on the number of side-wheelers built by the Saxon-Bohemian Steamship Company.

His knowledge of military history was not limited to the exploits of famous conquerors such as Hannibal, Alexander, Caesar, Tamerlane, Cortez, Charles XII, Napoleon, and Moltke. He referred with equal familiarity to less well-known figures such as the Macedonian commander Polyperchon, the Mongol warlord Batu Khan, the Hussite general Jan Žižka, and the Russian rebel chieftain Pugachev. His acquaintance with English writers was no less extensive. He cited not only the great poets and philosophers but authors little known in Germany as David Hartley, William Paley, and Richard Price. He was equally at home in the writings of the French encyclopedists and physiocrats. He quoted from the works of lesser Russian novelists like Andreyev and Lermontov. It goes without saying that he was thoroughly familiar with the history of the major European nations, but he had not neglected the smaller peoples. Few Germans of his generation would have been able to name any Czech historical figures other than Jan Hus and perhaps the ill-fated King Ottokar, who lost his crown to the first Habsburg emperor. Nicolai mentioned George of Podiebrad, a Czech prince of the fifteenth century, as the first statesman to propose a federation of European rulers; Žižka as the leader of a people's army that had inflicted the most humiliating defeats on the noble knights of the German emperor Sigismund; Peter Chelcicky, founder of one of the earliest communes of conscientious objectors and author of *Sít Víry*, the "Net of Faith," in which he had branded the knightly warriors of his time as criminals and murderers; and Johann Amos Comenius, the great Moravian educator, who had held similar views, though he was better known as the founder of modern pedagogy than as a pacifist.

Nor was this all. Nicolai offered his readers the solid fare of statistics and facts, making liberal use of charts, graphs, and tables, as well as diagrams and drawings from his own hand. He quoted birth rates, comparisons of war casualties with accidental deaths, production figures for German industry, the share of various European powers in world trade, the relative speed of the various means of transportation and communication, the number of steam engines built in the nineteenth century, the energy consumption of bacteria, animals, and man, and the tax load imposed on the average German citizen by the war. He examined with equal anthropological detachment the instinctual roots of tribal loyalties and those of modern nationalism. He even discussed the sacred subject of motherhood in the cold light of its biological function. He met the claim of the patriots that war was morally elevating by citing an increase of 50 percent in juvenile crime in the city of Berlin during the first year of the war. And he offered ethnological, etymological, and historical arguments to demolish the theory of the Germanic master race, so avidly proclaimed by the apostate Englishman Houston Stewart Chamberlain and so eagerly believed by German university professors and janitors alike.

So much erudition was unusual, especially in a man who could be called anything but a bookworm and who, moreover, was a renowned physician and physiologist. Nicolai was also a skillful writer. *The Biology of War*, however scholarly, is anything but dull. Nicolai's sentences are short, concise, and often pungent. He presents the reader with a unique blend of scholarliness and polemic, objectivity and sarcasm, facts and anecdotes, science and pathos. To illustrate the persistence of useless instincts he used two examples. The first was the case of the city dog who vainly scratches the asphalt pavement because his wolflike ancestors had buried their excrement in order to keep their enemies off the scent. The second and more pointed example was the behavior of the angry man who bares his teeth and clenches his fist in a reflex that his progenitors in the trees had developed to frighten would-be aggressors, hardly a becoming gesture for civilized Europeans. Modern war, the reader was told, was "a kind of life insurance" for the physically and morally unfit who stayed behind. War was above all an atavism, on a par with cannibalism and slavery.

As for the notion of national honor, had the Germans lost theirs once and for all because Napoleon had been the better strategist? Was it honorable to fall upon a small neighbor like Belgium? The greatest crime of the war-happy German intellectuals was their earnestness, "the same damned earnestness with which once upon a time white-robed inquisitors fertilized the 'heavenly palm' with human blood," the earnestness with which they attempted to "reconcile the destruction of human lives with the dignity of man." Nicolai was willing to concede that no one could be expected to curb his enthusiasm for the war just because Kant, Germany's greatest thinker, had been an avowed pacifist, but when Professor Max Scheler tried to prove from disconnected passages that the sage of Königsberg had been at heart a war-lover, one might ask a little more respect for the truth, especially from a professor of philosophy.

Biologically speaking, mongrels were superior to purebred dogs, just as the ethnic mixtures that populated Europe were preferable to pure stocks, unless one were willing to admit that "the Jews are the flower of creation." And the purists who wished to purge the German language of "foreign elements" should remember that the German words for "ink," "writing," "letter," "church," and "pastor" were of Latin or Greek origin. From whom, then, had the Germans learned to read and write? Were they willing to abandon the use of the telegraph, together with the word for it, because its inventor had been an American?

The thrust of Nicolai's scientific argument was against the spurious Darwinism that served his compatriots as a quasi-biological justification for the war. On the contrary, he contended, from the biologist's point of view war was no longer useful or necessary. It was in any case a political institution, not a biological attribute of man. Darwin's great conception had been misinterpreted and perverted. The struggle for life was a struggle between different species, not war between members of the same race, let alone the same civilization. Competition within the species was desirable and indeed unavoidable, but it did not require mass killings. In any case, war had ceased to favor the selection of the fittest. As a means of improving the physical condition of young males it was inferior to a reasonably designed program of sports and physical education. Individual valor and resourcefulness counted for little in the face of an artillery barrage or a gas attack. If there was any martial virtue left in the industrial age, it was not courage but the talent for organization, for having troops, guns, ammunition, and food supplies in the right place at the right time, for running an efficient railroad system, talents which the Germans possessed in the highest degree, but which were virtues only when used for creative purposes. Meanwhile the unfit, the cripples, the malformed, the mentally defective, and the criminals remained at home and could reproduce their undesirable traits, while healthy young men died by the millions.

Man's future in any event depended less and less on bodily strength and agility and more and more on the brain as the means of controlling the environment and creating new tools with which to extend and amplify his limited physical powers. The strongest athlete could not stop an onrushing train, any more than the gatekeeper's little dog who ran yapping alongside, but anybody who knew how to loosen a single bolt on the track could derail the most powerful locomotive. Fitness was all well and good but—and here spoke Professor Nicolai, founder of the first sports laboratory in Germany and a passionate sportsman himself—it was not their physical prowess that had made men like Werner von Siemens, Alfred Krupp, or Albert Ballin leading figures in modern Germany. The men who had done the most for the nation's material strength had not made their reputations as prizefighters.

Man owed his dominant position on this planet to the evolution of his brain. Having surpassed his competitors in the animal kingdom by virtue of his superior intelligence, he should now turn that weapon toward the conquest of nature's energy resources, rather than toward killing and enslaving his fellow men. These resources were large enough for all mankind and needed only to be tapped efficiently to ensure prosperity and peace. War was nothing but a primitive struggle for energy in its various forms: food energy obtained directly from grain and cattle or indirectly from the land; ore and gold that the winner took from the loser; and labor that could be coerced from prisoners and slaves. The purpose of war therefore was theft and the exploitation of someone else's labor—in a word, slavery. This method could be justified only as long as it was considered proper for the victor to demand slave labor from the vanquished, and practical only as long as it was possible to coerce human beings into slavery. But slavery had been superseded by more efficient methods of production. In the machine age war was an obsolete means of improving the human condition.

It was true that aggressive instincts were part of man's biological heritage, but this did not mean that they had to be accepted passively. Rousseau had started the cult of the instinct, and ever since there had been those who placed instinct above reason. But it was reason that had made man master of the earth and allowed him to analyze his instincts and subordinate them to rational purposes. The infallibility of instincts was a fallacy that had been deduced from the apparent perfection of instinctual behavior in animals, for example, the nest-building of birds or the economical construction of the honeycomb by bees, who build their hexagonal units without knowledge of the theory of statics. But instincts were neither infallible nor truly purposeful. They were simply adaptations that had favored survival of the species, whereas unfavorable responses had led to extinction. Useful instincts, however, could become useless or even harmful if the environment to which they were adapted happened to change. In that case a species might become extinct, for evolution was an irreversible process, and instincts were highly specialized functions that tended to persist, like rudimentary organs, long after their original purpose was lost. Only man could escape the consequences of this biological specialization, for in his brain he possessed a universal organ that allowed him to modify his environment, create limitless numbers of artificial organs, and deliberately change his behavior.

This ability to influence and transform his own species imposed on man the obligation to master and reject those instincts which he recognized as harmful. Admittedly this was no easy task. Even the most sincere pacifist, for example, had a deep-rooted urge to fight. But he need not yield to this urge, for he had a choice. The warlike instinct only proved that at one time fighting had been a necessity; it did not prove that it was still necessary. People, Nicolai added, "who in this day and age still abandon themselves to their warlike desires bring to my mind's eye—I can't help myself—the image of the dog scratching the asphalt."

But man did not have to rely exclusively on his reasoning powers to counteract this innate aggressiveness. From the time when the ancestors of *homo sapiens* descended from the trees and formed primitive societies, whose success depended on cooperation, humans had been endowed with strong social instincts. The question was not how a predatory animal became peace-loving man, but rather how a social animal developed warlike behavior. Man's anatomy alone—his lack of horns, tusks, claws, hooves, and armor—proved that he had been a peaceable creature who succeeded in establishing himself on the ground only because he lived in hordes whose members divided the various tasks necessary for survival according to a common need. The horde was the oldest human institution, antedating the family and indeed the species. It was true that the higher apes lived in small families, but the lower primates from which human evolution had branched off at some early stage lived in hordes and possessed strongly developed social instincts. Their imitativeness and their chattering and grimacing were reminiscent of human behavior and could have arisen only in connection with a communal form of life. Primitive human tribes, whether Eskimos, Tierra del Fuegans, Andamans, or Bushmen, still showed similar patterns of social cohesion and behavior. But the surest proof of man's descent from social animals was human speech, for this form of communication presupposed the existence of complex social relationships within a group of individuals.

Social instincts, then, were deeply rooted in human heredity. They were as essential for a global society in the age of communications as they had been for the isolated Stone Age tribe, if not more so. They must be cultivated in every way, for man's destiny again depended on his ability to cooperate. (This line of reasoning is almost identical with the warnings uttered almost fifty years later by the geneticist J. H. Muller at the Third International Congress of Human Genetics.) War was not only a destroyer of lives and property but an obstacle to the further evolution of the human race.

Much had been made, Nicolai wrote, of the alleged benefits of war as an instrument of natural selection. A German clergyman had gone so far as to call the war "God's great winnowing machine by which He separates the chaff from the wheat." But selection meant survival of those members of the species who were best adapted to the conditions under which they lived. The gazelle most likely to escape the lion was the one with the sharpest sight, the keenest hearing, and the fastest legs. These qualities meant nothing to the tortoise, whose survival depended on the thickness of its shell. Both species were ideally equipped to cope with the specific threats to their lives as a result of natural selection. Similarly, if war should become the principal business of mankind, natural selection would ultimately produce a race that was ideally endowed for life in the trenches. Nicolai then painted a grim Orwellian picture of this new rabbitlike human race. It would not desire the finer things in life, for these were not to be had in the trenches anyway. It would have a poorly developed sense of smell, if only to be able to stand the stench of rotting corpses, but good eyes and ears and quick reflexes, so as to dive with lightning speed into the foxholes. The sharp eyes would also be needed for aiming guns, "though experience teaches that in perpetual battle the joy of killing wanes and interest in finding cover grows." The new breed would have low intelligence, for its tasks would be simple. It would despise the works of peace, "for it is a basic trait of human nature to consider only one's own occupation as important." Its emotions would be centered on food and drink. Its only redeeming trait would be a certain esprit de corps, but its chief characteristic would be hatred and fear of the enemy. Such would be the selective advantages of perpetual trench warfare.

If this was satire, aimed at the earnest believers in war as nature's or God's remedy for national decay, Nicolai was serious in conceding that there might be one case in which war could be defended on logical grounds. That case, paradoxically, was the complete extermination of the enemy. Since obviously that was not the purpose of the present war, because the Germans and French expected each other to survive as a nation and to find some day a modus vivendi, they might as well stop slaughtering each other immediately. At bottom the war was a quarrel between relatives who might hate each other and begrudge each other their possessions, but who still recognized each other as members of the same family. It would be altogether different if one side no longer regarded the other as part of the human family. A race that looked upon its enemies as subhumans or nonhumans (*Untermenschen* or *Unmenschen*) might feel justified in exterminating them to make room for the better breed. In that case, however, the rules and conventions of so-called humane warfare to which modern states were paying lip service should be dispensed with altogether.

If genocide (the word itself had not yet come into use) was the objective, then children in the womb, babes in their mothers' arms, the aged, and the crippled logically must be slain without mercy.

Even Nicolai, whose insights were often prophetic, could not have foreseen that within his own lifetime the legitimate government of his beloved Germany would carry this reasoning to its ultimate conclusion. Hitler's genocidal madness was the corollary to the myth of the Germanic master race, a myth Nicolai did his best to combat. The mass murder of the Jews stemmed from the notion that they were biologically, intellectually, and morally inferior to the Germans. Even if allowance is made for the sadistic mentality of the executioners—the overseers of the death camps who separated husbands and wives, parents and children, in front of the gas chambers, the SS men who dashed the skulls of Jewish infants against the pavement before their mothers' eyes, the engineers whose locomotives hauled the victims to their final destination—none of these minions of the Third Reich could have carried out their gruesome tasks if they had not felt that they were squashing loathsome creatures rather than human beings.

Genocide might be the ultimate horror, Nicolai wrote, but it made sense in a case in which one culture felt itself threatened by another, totally alien culture. Europeans had no business killing one another, but he could understand the feelings of those who considered the "Mongolian" race—a term that included the Chinese and Japanese—as the natural enemy of the white man. Conceivably a situation might arise in which "we or the Mongolians might say: 'Only one of our races can rule the world, and we wish it to be ours.'"

Three pages of *The Biology of War* were devoted to a curious dissertation on the possibility of such a confrontation. While the European war overshadowed all other issues, Nicolai was looking beyond, for he perceived clearly that it was the beginning of the end of European hegemony over the colonial peoples. The notion of an armed conflict between West and East was by no means farfetched. The Boxer Rebellion had been a severe jolt to the smugness of the white man, and the Japanese victory over Russia in 1905 had been the first successful challenge to European supremacy. If a small nation after only a few decades of exposure to Western technology could beat a huge empire that was part of the West, what would happen when China with its huge population entered the modern age? Deep-rooted historical memories had risen to the surface, for the great invasions of the Huns, Tartars, and Turks had never been erased from the consciousness of Europe. Once upon a time irresistible Mongol hordes had conquered Russia, destroyed Poland, overrun Hungary, crushed a German-Polish army at Liegnitz, and then mysteriously vanished to the east, but seven centuries had not extinguished the horror. To the average European the distinction between Mongols and Chinese was vague. He was afraid of a race that was hardy, clever, dangerous, and totally alien.

It is against this background that Nicolai's concern with the "Mongolian threat" must be seen. One of his reasons for opposing the European war was his conviction that it must inevitably weaken the West. What would happen when China introduced conscription and began to manufacture modern weapons, as the Japanese were already doing? As yet the Yellow Peril could be stopped by brute force; in another twenty years it might be too late. Instead of indulging in a "silly struggle for mere power," the Europeans should weigh the dangers of a confrontation with Asia. Nicolai was convinced of the cultural superiority of the West, but he conceded that the yellow race might possess the greater stamina. He did not advocate a war of extermination, which in his opinion was neither morally justified nor practically feasible; Europe would do better to concentrate on surpassing its rivals by using its scientific, technical, and economic assets to develop a stronger, more resilient breed.

The waning of European hegemony in world affairs was a cause for regret for the "good European" Nicolai, not because he approved of exploiting backward countries but because he believed that Western man was farther advanced on the road that all mankind must travel. It was the combination of universal curiosity and active energy characteristic of Western civilization that had made man the master of his environment and that in due course would free the whole of humanity from indolence and superstition. Other civilizations might have produced spiritual, social, and artistic forms of equal value, but the unique blend of Greek inquisitiveness and love of freedom, Roman discipline and law, Judaeo-Christian spirituality and modern science had moved the world forward. If, as a later age might put it, human evolution was entering the cultural channel, it was doing so under Western leadership. A setback for Europe was a setback for humanity.

The strange digression on the Yellow Peril nevertheless reveals a crack in the armor of Nicolai's idealism. "His heart trembles only at the sufferings of the white race, and his humanity stops at the frontiers of the yellow peoples," the shrewd Romain Rolland confided to his diary when Nicolai visited him at Villeneuve after the war. Rolland, who was troubled himself at the prospect of a conflict with Asia, found his visitor strangely unsympathetic toward Asiatics. "He manifests a sort of instinctive aversion for Asia," Rolland wrote, even before he learned that Nicolai's attitude was shaped by his personal experiences in the Far East. When he decided to probe more deeply, Nicolai "at first tried to put me off with biological arguments which did not seem at all sound to me, and which in fact are pure unreasoned prejudices. A yellow person seems to him a different animal from a white, a stranger, whereas any European of whatever nationality is not a stranger to him." Nicolai told Rolland how shocked he had been when, aboard some ship, he had seen a Chinese put his legs against the railing next to those of an American. "How dare he put his legs next to those of a white man?" he had thought. In such a progressive thinker this bespoke a rather archaic subconscious, Rolland commented, adding that Nicolai had good-naturedly conceded the point. "He believes in a *genus humanum*, but he cannot yet make his heart accept it."[1] Rolland had hit the nail on the head. Nicolai had formed his opinions of the Chinese in the course of an extended stay in the Orient at the turn of the century. He described to Rolland the inhumane conditions under which they had worked, but he was able to find extenuating circumstances. He spoke of the need to impose Eurpean civilization—here the horrified Rolland put a sarcastic exclamation mark—on a barely humanized population. "All in all," Rolland concluded his comment on these candid revelations, "it is clear that Nicolai views these infamous practices . . . with the fatalism of the thinker who sees humanity as it is, namely, in the last stages of barbarism, and who does not attempt to change it or shorten the course."

As a mature scientist Nicolai saw the human race as a single species, if not a single organism, but it is doubtful that his emotional response to its nonwhite members ever changed. As a biologist, however, he saw the unity of the species as an inescapable fact. Writing at a time when the mechanisms of heredity were not yet fully understood, he based this concept on the continuity of the germ plasm as demonstrated at the turn of the century by August Weismann's studies on *Hydromedusa*. The germ plasm (a later generation would define it as DNA) was for him the tree of life through which all individuals and all races were connected; it was the imperishable substance, carried in individual mortal vessels but unitary in nature. Sexual reproduction, "amphimixis," was the means by which the separate parts of the whole communicated with one another and maintained the unity of the species.

But biological unity was not enough. "As yet the time for universal brotherhood is not at hand, nor should it be. As yet the gulf between whites, yellows, and blacks is too deep." This was a descriptive statement rather than an endorsement of racism, and Nicolai hastened to make his meaning clear. He opposed any purely biological definition of "race," not only ridiculing the notion of separate races within Europe (and in particular the myth of the Germanic master race) but refusing to admit the validity of a biological distinction between a "European race" and Asiatics, Africans, or North American Indians. Physical characteristics, common descent, or linguistic relationships did not suffice to establish meaningful divisions between groups of human beings, he asserted. Those who wished to use such criteria would have to exclude the Finns, the Hungarians, the Basques, and even the Prussians from the European community to which they so obviously belonged. The concept of a people, of a nation, of a grouping of peoples, "and even of a race" made sense only if it rested on the multiple criteria of common history, culture, language, and physical characteristics that were "halfway distinguishable from those of other races." Well ahead of his time, Nicolai had recognized the mutual feedback between biological and cultural influences. In advance of Spengler and Toynbee, he had reached the conclusion that the units of history were neither racial nor political groupings but civilizations. It was in this sense that he took pride in being a European and spoke of *Kulturpatriotismus* as the only acceptable form of patriotism.

At a time when the war was fanning the flames of chauvinism everywhere in Europe, this was a remarkably broad conception. Though Dr. Johnson's saying, "patriotism is the last refuge of a scoundrel," had somehow escaped Nicolai's notice, he shared the sentiment. At bottom patriotism was inseparable from, or rather identical with, chauvinism, he declared. But why did otherwise sensible men become chauvinists? First, because they were unable to resist mass suggestion, and second, because they lacked the inner sense of belonging to a civilization that allowed free minds to look beyond national borders and freely choose their values where they found them. What could be better suited for the support of the weak-minded than the feeling of belonging to a mass movement? "It is an uplifting sensation for every idiot to be part of a majority of several millions of the likes of himself, and thus in time the need for [emotional] support becomes an irresistible force." That was the positive element in chauvinism. The negative side was chiefly its hatred and envy of all things foreign. War was "the trigger and at the same time the sounding board" of chauvinism.

Nicolai cited examples of what he called the bankruptcy of the German intellect under the impact of war-engendered chauvinism. People were greeting each other with "Gott strafe England" ("may God punish England") or with "Hiddekk," an acronym derived from words signifying the hope that England would be taught a lesson. The tasteless cartoons of *Simplicissimus* were beneath notice, as were the coarse insults heaped by the daily press on the Japanese, Belgians, and Serbs. The claims for German superiority—the philosopher Adolf Lasson said "never has there been anything so perfect as Germany," Gerhart Hauptmann called Germany "the soul of Europe," and truthfulness, love of nature, scientific spirit, conscientiousness and loyalty were all proclaimed exclusively German virtues—were not to be wondered at, for "the blowing of our own horn and the bluster are the heritage of our primitive animal ancestors." Still, the attacks of presumably intelligent and educated people on the enemy were beyond belief and beyond excuse. The Lutheran theologian Adolf Harnack called England a traitor against civilization, Professor of Germanic Languages Gustav Roethe considered her "the great cold hypocrite," Rudolf Eucken, the dean of German philosophers, attributed England's actions to "repulsive frivolity," the dramatist Carl Hauptmann to "hucksterish envy." The poet Richard Dehmel said that Shakespeare and Byron on close examination turned out to be cynics and that Englishmen in general were "ravening beasts." German newspapers demanded that prisoners of war should be fed in pigsties, together with the swine. A report that the British Navy had rescued some shipwrecked German sailors gave rise to the editorial comment that it would have been better to die than owe one's life to such riff-raff. One of Nicolai's colleagues confided to him that he was considering ways of secretly entering Russia in order to infect the population with some sort of virulent germs, for in dealing with this rabble anything was permissible. (In 1915 bacteriological warfare was still a shocking notion, at least to Nicolai.) And the poet Ernst Lissauer, "the comical gentleman" whose hatred of England was as irrational as it was vicious, stated "very appropriately" that the verses of his "Hymn of Hate" should be hissed rather than spoken. "Bravo for the self-criticism," Nicolai commented wryly.

This kind of patriotism was no longer a moral commandment to defend the sacred goods of hearth and soil, but rather the frenzied swarming of hornets or ants defending the hive or the anthill. So potent was this impulse that even the new republican regime of Russia, composed of men who hated tsarism worse than any external enemy, had agreed to continue hostilities—a statement, incidentally, that shows that as late as the spring of 1917 Nicolai still had ways of communicating with his publisher in Switzerland. Exclusionary patriotism had nothing to do with spontaneous love of home and country. It was, Nicolai noted, a modern disease, not more than a hundred or a hundred and fifty years old. Geared to the petty national states of contemporary Europe, it must be overcome by a larger, more spacious European patriotism, just as the parochial loyalties of Prussians, Hessians, and Bavarians had been dwarfed by their common love of a united Germany. America was setting the example, for there the old dynastic allegiances of the European settlers had been transformed into a free and responsible *Kulturpatriotismus*. For the time being this cultural patriotism was still inseparable from the ascendancy of the white race: "When the Americans say 'America for the Americans,' they really mean 'America for the free descendants of the white Europeans,' for despite all the enthusiasm for the emancipation of the slaves, the feeling for racial differences from non-Europeans is nowhere stronger than in the United States, where—especially in the South—it often assumes ridiculous and grotesque forms." (In the 1950s the aged Nicolai remarked that already in the span of two generations the American Negro had achieved cultural equality.) Europe, however, must take care lest it lose its cultural leadership permanently to the New World. This too was an original idea in 1915.

From the vantage point of a later generation, many of Nicolai's ideas may seem commonplace, but one may take this as a token of their soundness and effectiveness. In the time and place in which they were written, in the Prussian fortress town of Graudenz in the summer of 1915, they were novel, daring, revolutionary. Amidst the hysteria that had seized virtually every German from Thomas Mann to Max Planck, from the Conservatives to the Social Democrats, from barons to day laborers, from Gentiles to Jews, Nicolai raised the voice of sanity.

His objections to the war were aimed not so much at the loss of human lives as at its backwardness, its uselessness, and its brutalizing effects on the national psyche. Although the horror of Hiroshima was still unimaginable, the technology of the First World War was gruesome enough. There were the so-called wolf pits in which soldiers speared on concealed stakes were left to die a lingering death, barbed-wire abatis in which men became entangled and which were "cleaned out" when the concentration of "material" made it worthwhile (Nicolai used the quotation marks to express his outrage at the very jargon that described the destruction of lives in terms of sewage disposal), electrically charged fences on which human beings hung like dead flies, concealed land mines, flamethrowers, gas grenades, and aerial bombs. There was no such thing as humane warfare in the technical age, he concluded. The prospect that men would become inured to such horrors was as frightening as the horrors themselves.

Nicolai's revulsion reflects the shock rational people felt at the enormity of a war that swept away the illusions of a civilization long accustomed to peace and international collaboration. Mankind had seemed on the verge of solving its problems through technological progress, enlightenment, and goodwill. War was something one read about in history books or in newspaper accounts of Balkan brawls. War between civilized nations was as unthinkable as an outbreak of cholera. Nicolai was not a sentimentalist. His reaction to the new barbarianism did not cloud his objective assessment of the extent of the losses caused by the war. Writing in 1915, when the great battles of attrition of Verdun and the Somme had not yet been fought, he coldly calculated that the killings thus far had not significantly affected the mortality of the world's population as a whole. Instead of sixty people per minute, about sixty-four were now dying, he wrote. In peacetime thirty-five thousand people died yearly from accidents in Germany alone. In Europe only about half a billion man-years had been lost in the preceeding hundred years as the result of battle casualties, an insignificant number as compared to the thirty-six billion man-years wasted because lack of medical care and poverty deprived so many workers of a large part of their natural life span.

Nicolai's assumption that the death of large numbers of vigorous young males and the sparing of the unfit under wartime conditions could lead to unfavorable selection has been overtaken by "progress" in the art of aerial bombing, which has deprived civilian populations of their former advantage over actual combatants. Some modern anthropologists have questioned the thesis that war has any genetic consequences (unless nuclear weapons are employed) on the grounds that the periods of time are too short and the number of fighting men too small to affect the existing equilibrium through the slow process of natural selection. Whether this holds true for small countries upon which overwhelming concentrations of modern weapons are brought to bear for long periods of time remains to be seen. Nicolai, who was horrified by the use of poison gas and the prospect of bacteriological warfare, did not envision defoliating agents, let along MIRVs with atomic warheads. He might have pointed to the Thirty Years' and the Seven Years' wars as examples of profound disturbances of a natural equilibrium. He undoubtedly would have refused to consider the problem solely in biological terms and would have been intensely concerned with the effects of cultural disruption on the living organism of a nation as a whole. He was in any case the first to investigate the biological aspects of modern war in a comprehensive manner, and despite both the limitations imposed on him by the state of knowledge of his time and the emotional bias with which he approached the subject, he produced a body of generally sound conclusions. In an era when his compatriots and colleagues believed in all seriousness that war—"the bath of steel"—was God-given, necessary, invigorating, noble, and desirable, his attempt to take the scientific view was a large step forward. His thinking has remained relevant in an age in which death, disability, and disease have been inflicted on a colossal scale on countries like Vietnam and Cambodia by people whose notions of national honor and of the state's claims upon its citizens are perhaps not so different from those of the German policymakers of 1914 to 1918.

Nicolai knew that war is not a mere matter of aggressive instincts. He recognized its dependence on the organization of mankind into sovereign national states, and he knew that its preparation and execution involve complex symbolic processes as well as a highly integrated social and economic system. If he nevertheless emphasized the role of instincts, it was because he wanted to refute the assumptions then prevailing in Germany, both in scientific circles and among the public at large, regarding the biological and moral soundness of war. In the context of the Social Darwinism that was being preached to his countrymen, the proof that aggressive instincts had lost their evolutionary raison d'être was a powerful argument. The complementary idea, derived largely from the writings of the Russians Peter Kropotkin and Nicolai Novikoff, that social and altruistic instincts are an equally important basic part of man's inheritance led him to conclude that the well-being and indeed the survival of the human race would require fostering the social instincts and channeling aggressive instincts into productive rather than destructive activities. Like the geneticist Herman Muller, he saw man's present condition as a stepping stone in a process of evolution that man himself could and must control, a process that depended on cooperation and intelligence. Above all, Nicolai had the courage of his convictions and felt obliged to express them. He would not have approved of the restraint shown by the majority of the members of the American Anthropological Association in 1967, when they defeated a motion calling on the United States government to end the war in Vietnam on the grounds that such a motion would jeopardize the purely scientific character of the organization. Right or wrong, he believed that the scientist must take a stand on the moral and political issues of his time.

NOTES

1. *Journal des années de guerre 1914–1919: Notes et documents pour servir à l'histoire morale de l'Europe de ce temps*, ed. Marie Romain Rolland (Paris: Albin Michel, 1952), pp. 1758, 1760.

3. The Soil and the Seed

It would hardly be an exaggeration to say that the intellectual distance separating the author of *The Biology of War* from the vast majority of his countrymen could only be measured in light-years. For him the war was a foolish game with dangerous toys in the hands of destructive children; for them it was a holy crusade. He foresaw the decline of the west, win or lose, while they dreamed of the rise of a victorious fatherland. The scholar who had breathed the morning air of international congresses where colleagues from many countries joined in a common search for the universal truths of science deplored the end of a golden age. The patriots welcomed a pretext for cutting unwanted ties with treacherous foreigners. Nicolai regarded German militarism as the residue of a barbaric past; they saw it as both the shield and the touchstone of Germany's greatness. His outlook remained that of a rational observer; theirs had become that of participants in an emotional orgy.

What Nicolai called "the bankruptcy of the German intellect" was a form of collective insanity which neither facts nor logic could dispel. Paradoxically, the most seriously afflicted group was the academic community, his own colleagues. Learned societies expelled enemy nationals; German scholars resigned from foreign academies and returned their medals and diplomas. The eminent sociologist and economist Werner Sombart welcomed the war as a reason for discontinuing German participation in international congresses and for reducing international trade as well as cultural exchanges. Germany's contribution to science was so superior that it would be no loss if every international journal ceased publication and the exchange of scientists stopped altogether for a few decades, he declared: "When all is said and done, we Germans have no need of anyone in the cultural-intellectual field. No nation on earth can give us in the fields of science, technology, art, and literature anything worth mentioning that it would be painful for us to do without."[1] This was written in the summer of 1915, at the same time as *The Biology of War*. For Nicolai, who had worked with Pavlov in St. Petersburg and with Willem Einthoven, the founder of electrocardiography, in Leyden, the jingoism of his academic brethren amounted to intellectual treason. Such men were deserters from the cause of civilization, comparable to soldiers who leave their post under fire, he wrote.

The jingoists, on the other hand, saw themselves as the upholders of the heroic *Weltanschauung* or, in Sombart's words, "the last bulwark against the slimy waters of commercialism that have engulfed or are about to engulf all other nations."[2] Similar views were expounded by thousands of editorialists in the press, shouted from the pulpit by thousands of clergymen, and offered as the fruit of profound learning by thousands of professors. The special object of their rage was England, for the British declaration of war had caught the German public unaware. England had played a waiting game in order to stab a trusting Germany in the back. She was in fact the sole culprit and real instigator of the war. She had betrayed her Germanic heritage by allying herself with Slavs and Gauls against her kinsmen. A war fought by industrial nations with all the devices of modern technology was seen as a matter of tribal loyalties, the struggle between the powers of darkness and light from which a radiant Siegfried would emerge victorious while the traitor Hagen went to his amply deserved doom. Britain's foreign secretary, Sir Edward Grey, was the embodiment of evil, responsible for the devastation wrought by the war, the streams of blood, the tears of orphans and widows. The historian Hermann Oncken, in an article entitled "England's Solvent Morality," accused the British of being cold-blooded hypocrites who let others do the fighting for them, who hired not only "murderous Cossacks" and "treacherous Japanese" but Senegalese and Herreros and cannibals from the South Seas. "A nation of Pecksniffs!" he cried.[3] Ernst Lissauer, the poet of Jewish extraction, called on Germans to swear an oath of everlasting hatred for England. "Some day peace may return, but our hatred for you shall endure," he wrote in his "Hymn of Hatred."

Nicolai, as noted earlier, referred to the author of this piece as "a comical gentleman," but so much venom was hardly a laughing matter. It was almost worse, however, when the venom *was*—or was intended to be—a laughing matter, namely, in the cartoons of the humor magazines. The crudest, most brutal insults passed for patriotic wit. The English were portrayed as utterly devoid of human feeling, insensitive to suffering, ready to sacrifice their own children for the sake of profit. A series of cartoons in *Simplicissimus* entitled "Rogues' Gallery" showed front and side views, in mug-shot fashion, of Sir Edward Grey ("Arsonist"), Herbert Asquith ("Document Forger"), and Winston Churchill ("Pirate"), alongside the killer of Sarajevo, Gavrilo Princip ("Assassin").

The Germans had no monopoly on bad taste or tunnel vision, however. Caricaturists of every belligerent country showed the enemy as dangerous yet contemptible, cruel and evil yet cowardly and weak. Nicolai rightly saw this mentality as a threat to the reconciliation of Europe. But the fact that the affliction was universal did not relieve educated Germans of the obligation to resist it in their own country. Each nation, he said, was responsible for its own sins. On the first page of *The Biology of War* he acknowledged the risk of being accused of anti-German bias. His answer was that he knew German chauvinism better than its counterparts abroad. Let Frenchmen criticize France, Englishmen England. His mission was to hold a mirror to the Germans at the risk of giving comfort to the enemy, to preach to his countrymen as the prophets of old had preached to the Israelites. Like the prophets of old, Nicolai failed. The crudities of *Simplicissimus* reflected the mood of the country. In an unsolicited testimonial, Thomas Mann wrote: "Where else in the world is there another satirical and patriotic polemical magazine of this quality, a magazine that manages to be at once so artistic, so literate, and so close to the people?" And on a still lower plane, literally and figuratively, an imaginative toilet manufacturer made a killing with the sale of commodes at whose bottom there shone in full color the glazed likenesses of Sir Edward Grey, Winston Churchill, and Raymond Poincaré.

Lapses of taste apart, the Germans were sincere in their belief that the war had been forced on them. The declarations of war against France and Russia and the rape of Belgium were seen as acts of elementary self-defense. The skillful manipulation of public opinion during the July crisis had rallied even the Social Democrats behind the flag. Had not the Kaiser said "we seek no conquests?" Had not their own leader August Bebel once said that war against tsarism as the oppressor of the toiling masses might some day be justified? Now the sinister autocracy in the East was on the march; France had only waited for the moment when she could avenge the defeat of 1870 and regain Alsace-Lorraine; and England, like Shylock rubbing his hands in anticipation of a handsome profit, was behind the whole thing. The fear of encirclement which had preyed on the minds of two generations had become a reality. The chauvinists who had clamored for a preventive war had been right all along.

The Germans, moreover, considered themselves a very special people, destined somehow to bring salvation to the rest of the world, if necessary by force. War was not only a practical necessity but a moral duty, at once a trial laid on a peace-loving people and a glorious challenge to a nation of heroes. Not that they were bent on aggrandizement, for, to quote Sombart once more, they had more important things to do. "Rest easy, dear neighbors," the professor said grandly, "we shall not gobble you up. What would be the good of an indigestible lump in our stomach? Nor do we have any desire to subjugate half-civilized or primitive peoples in order to pour German culture into them." If, however, it should be desirable to enlarge the *Lebensraum* of a great nation, "we shall take as much land as we may deem necessary," and if strategic considerations should require more drastic action, Germany would seize whatever strong points were needed to assure her position as a world power, say, Dover, Malta, and Suez. In the face of such wildly contradictory statements Nicolai might well speak of intellectual bankruptcy. The last vestiges of political realism were crumbling.

Each of the warring powers suffered from its own brand of paranoia; each feared its neighbors and believed in the righteousness of its cause; each had become convinced of the inevitability of a general war. A diplomacy geared to the subtleties of the Congress of Vienna could deal neither with the pent-up energies of modern nationalism nor with the realities of the new technology. The self-defeating system of opposing power blocks had created a tension which the slightest atmospheric disturbance could trigger.

Nicolai understood this, and, writing for a German public, he took pains to avoid the question of war guilt. Between the lines, however, he left little doubt that in his opinion the beam in the German eye was considerably larger than the mote in that of the Entente. After the war he was more explicit. In judging the question of war guilt, he wrote in 1919, the technicalities mattered little. "It is of no account whether some telegram was delayed, whether an order for mobilization was issued an hour earlier or later. The verdict of history will ask solely whose national policy was so oriented that war became inevitable in the end, which state was so organized that its continued existence was most dependent on power politics."[4]

But in August 1914 technicalities mattered greatly, and they continued to matter until the Reich was at last destroyed, for they shaped German attitudes toward the Peace of Versailles and ensured popular support for Hitler. Nicolai was right on the mark when he wrote in *The Biology of War*, "The harm consists in the fact that a nation which denies its share in the responsibility for the war will do nothing to avert [war] in the future." The myth of Germany's innocence lived on and, reinforced by the companion myth of the "stab in the back," which blamed its defeat on traitors at home rather than on Allied superiority, played a major role in the genesis of the Second World War. Nicolai's courageous plea for a national soul-searching fell on deaf ears.

To be fair, in 1914 war was not yet looked upon as the absolute evil that later generations have come to see it. All governments considered it a legitimate, albeit regrettable, means of achieving national goals, and few people had any inkling of its destructiveness. War still seemed to be what Clausewitz had called it: the continuation of politics by "other means." But in Germany it was more than that. There, militarism was a way of life, a *Weltanschauung*, as Nicolai called it, rendered dangerous by German efficiency and doubly dangerous by the belief that war was desirable in and of itself. Military discipline was the perfect model for human relationships in a society that saw in the pyramid of command and obey the reflection of a God-given order. At the head of that pyramid stood the warrior caste, as secure in the industrial age as it had been in feudal times. War was still looked upon as a chivalrous calling and a developer of character and loyalty; peace was enervating, leading to softness, intellectual inertia, and moral decay.

Helmuth von Moltke, the victor of the Franco-Prussian War, had said: "Eternal peace is a dream, and not even a beautiful dream, and war is a link in God's order of the world. Here the noblest aspirations of man unfold themselves: courage and renunciation, devotion and willingness to make sacrifices and risk one's life. Without war the world would bog down in a quagmire of materialism." Nicolai quoted this passage as proof of an outworn morality, but the Moltkean view of war was still prevalent. "Peace," a certain Herr Schmidt-Gibichenfels had said in a book called *War as a Cultural Factor, Creator and Preserver of States*, "carries the danger of *Superkultur* and supercivilization, which can only be averted by a timely war." He would not deny the blessings of peace, but peace "only in healthy alternation with war, for therein lies the germ of everything that is great, beautiful, and noble, in nature as in any true *Kultur*."[5] In an article with the intriguing title "Psychiatry and Politics," a physician named Dr. Fuchs asked why the rulers of Germany were reluctant to follow the example of Frederick the Great and start a war that was long overdue. Who were the nation's heroes? Not Goethe, Schiller, Richard Wagner, or Karl Marx, but Barbarossa, Frederick the Great, Marshall Blücher, Moltke, and Bismarck, "the tough men of blood who sacrificed thousands of human lives. It is to them that the folk soul pours out its tenderest feelings, a flow of truly worshipful gratitude."[6] And when the war finally did break out, Heinrich Class, president of the powerful Pan-German League and a notorious chauvinist and anti-Semite, wrote with unconcealed elation, "We have longed for this day." The murky idealism that inspired these ravings found its poetic expression in a sonnet by Georg Heym, "A Longing To Escape Our Time," which ended with these lines:

> In luxuries of peace we feel a deadly fear.
> We know not "must" nor "shall" nor "can,"
> We feel a longing, we cry out for war.

The war, then, had come as an emotional release for many Germans. For the professional soldier it was the long-awaited break in the peacetime routine. For the middle class it was an outlet for frustrated aggressions. For the working class it was a sense of belonging, a reconciliation with a nation that had rejected it as its internal enemy. The certainty of the righteousness of the German cause sanctified anger and hate and gave them a target. The urge to kill and rape is infinitely enhanced by a clear conscience. Inhibitions and taboos fall away, and the spiritual awakening is intoxicating. The man who goes out to fight and perhaps to die in battle sheds his workaday responsibilities. He is already a hero; he is free.

People rarely clamor for a fight unless they expect to win. The German army's invincibility was an article of faith, and the question was not whether but when the enemy would be beaten. "Wir Deutsche fürchten Gott, aber sonst nichts in der Welt" ("We Germans fear God, but nothing else in the world"), Bismarck said. His addendum, "and the fear of God alone suffices to make us love and honor peace," was somehow forgotten.

Militarism, Nicolai's bête noire, was the sine qua non of Germany. As the Manifesto of the Ninety-Three had said, "without German militarism German culture would be wiped off the face of the earth" and "the German Army and the German people are as one." On this point Nicolai and his adversaries agreed. Militarism was not merely a protective shield but an all-pervading fact of life. The soldier, or, to be exact, the officer, was the symbol of the nation's glory. The Kaiser saw himself first and foremost as a soldier and supreme warlord. Bismarck's three wars had made Germany into a nation. The soldier's was a noble calling, infinitely superior to that of a mere civilian, a "stupid civilian," as the Kaiser liked to call people who did not have to conform to the beautiful simplicities of military discipline. In a state founded on the semi-feudal traditions of the Prussian squirearchy and dedicated to the proposition that the Prussian officer was the crowning glory of God's creation, it was bad enough to be a civilian, let along a pacifist, a democrat, and an individualist. Nicolai, who was all of these things, was bound to hate militarism with a passion, quite apart from its ultimate purpose as a machinery for making war.

Spit and polish was a fetish whose magic extended far beyond the parade grounds. The much-caricatured ramrod stiffness of the Prussian officer was widely equated with manliness. A smart military bearing was essential for the man who wanted to get ahead, and the uniform was the indispensable symbol of authority. For some, the civilian was simply a person who lacked an essential attribute of manhood. He was often portrayed as flabby, flat-chested and flat-footed, near-sighted, and suffering from hernias, bunions, and other complaints conducive to ridicule. Indeed, compared to the dashing officer in dress uniform, complete with helmet, monocle, saber, and spurs, he cut a sorry figure, standing uneasily at public ceremonies in his cutaway and striped trousers, the corners of his starched collar cutting into his double chin, his feet aching, rivulets of sweat forming between top hat and scalp. Such at least was the caricaturists' view, and since German males were seldom civilians by choice but usually because of some physical defect, it was not wholly inaccurate. For an athletic man in superb condition like Nicolai to avoid military service was most unusual. An ardent devotée of many sports, he at least was one civilian who need not be ashamed of his physique, and if he donated his time to lecture other civilians on the benefits of exercise, as he had done before the war, it was because he wanted to prove that soldiering was not the only road to physical fitness.

Fit or not, the civilian was a nuisance. A man who did not have to follow orders might have a mind of his own. He might be a Liberal and a believer in parliamentary government, if not a Socialist. Such men sat in the Reichstag, a body elected by universal suffrage and sheltering Progressives, Social Democrats, and Jews. Herr Von Oldenburg-Januschau, a crusty old Junker from East Prussia, had spoken the mind of his fellow-Conservatives in 1913, when he said that he would hate to see the day when a lieutenant with ten men could not close the Reichstag. Just such a thing had in fact happened in 1848, when General Wrangel politely but firmly closed the revolutionary Prussian Assembly.

Militarism, then, was a two-edged sword, a weapon against both internal and external enemies, and Nicolai saw it as such. For him it was the embodiment of blind obedience within the state and the instrument of aggression without. Who benefited? For a man reared in the liberal tradition, the answer was obvious: the dynasty and the privileged Junker class, the same powers which had crushed democracy in the aftermath of 1848. "Gegen Demokraten helfen nur Soldaten" ("soldiers are the only remedy against democrats") was a piece of doggerel from that era which accurately expressed official Prussian attitudes down to Nicolai's day. In his eyes the army as the tool of a self-serving, socially irresponsible officer caste was both the enemy of civic progress and a perpetual threat to peace.

Nicolai devoted a whole chapter of *The Biology of War* to the Prussian army, from its beginnings as a mercenary force to the contemporary system of universal military service, showing how it had been turned into a tool of the dynasty. Even the people's militia, designed ostensibly as a home guard, had been placed under the command of professional officers and sent abroad as early as 1814. In 1848 it had been used to subdue the revolutionaries. The present German army, still controlled by the Prussian War Ministry, was the opposite of a democratic institution. The draft system merely served to magnify the state's capacity for war. Whereas earlier wars had been waged with small mercenary forces that could do little damage, the modern state was a huge machine geared for total war. As a mere cog in this machine, the individual was in effect a slave. Moreover, the arming of a country for total war inevitably forced its neighbors to follow suit; even England was about to adopt the draft under the stress of the present war.

A dilemma arose from the fact that republican France also employed the draft and in fact had only recently extended compulsory military service from two to three years. The potential for aggression was therefore not tied to any particular form of government. The crux of the matter was neither the size nor the composition of an army "but solely the use one intends to make of it." The cat was out of the bag: it was not militarism as such that was evil but militarism in the service of an immoral state—dynastic militarism, German militarism. The remedy was not a balance of power between sovereign states, each armed to the teeth and looking upon war as the continuation of power politics, "but one and only one thing: international democracy." This was the faith of classical nineteenth-century liberalism, the belief that once the kings were chased from their thrones the peoples of all nations would lie down together like the lion and the lamb. Nicolai lived to see this illusion shattered and to seek the deeper causes of human failure. In 1914, however, the illusion was pardonable, for the universe that came crashing down in the bloodiest war in history had been seemingly too perfect and too full of yet greater promises to fall of its own accord. There had to be a villain, and the swaggering militarism of Germany's rulers seemed to fill the bill.

Nicolai was too good a historian not to know that militarism was not necessarily identical with aggressive nationalism. The latter was a post-unification disease afflicting the growing organism of Bismarck's young Reich, whereas militarism was a centuries-old Prussian institution designed to protect the scattered territories of the Hohenzollern against predators. It was therefore basically rational, disciplined, and generally cautious, in contrast to the new German nationalism, which was none of these things. It is, of course, a dangerous business to have a loaded gun in the house, and if such a gun is placed in the hands of an irrational, over-wrought person, the odds are that it will go off some day, as indeed it did. This was the gist of Nicolai's argument. Inherently, however, the Prussian brand of militarism was not especially aggressive. Rather, it was a way of life, a straitjacket to be sure, but one in which the wearer felt on the whole quite comfortable—so much so that he would have resented any attempt to remove it.

Prior to the First World War, Prussia had generally behaved with restraint. Before 1864 most of her territories had been acquired by inheritance or treaty rather than by conquest. Bismarck's wars against Denmark, Austria, and France, however Machiavellian in design, were carefully calculated means of unifying Germany under the royal house of Prussia after the revolutionary solution of 1848 had failed, and they did not lack a certain logic. Clausewitz's definition of war was the perfect expression of the Prussian spirit. After the war with France, the ever-pragmatic Bismarck had opposed extensive annexations, refrained from further military adventures, and declared Germany to be "saturated" with respect to territorial needs. Even the swashbuckling Wilhelm II had repeatedly backed away from war, being more a lover of parades, maneuvers, naval inspections, and twenty-one-gun salutes than the ruthless conqueror his enemies made him out to be.

In recent times, however, the cautious Prussian spirit had been overwhelmed by the dual current of German nationalism and the curious blend of *Kulturpessimismus*, Social Darwinism, and the archaic code of honor which Sombart called "heroic *Weltanschauung*." The new nationalism was not simply the pride of a people at last unified in a powerful state. It manifested itself in a noisy, intolerant, and aggressive super-patriotism. "No line can be drawn between patriotism and chauvinism," was the heading of a paragraph in *The Biology of War*, and Nicolai argued that both had their roots in self-love and fear. Perhaps it was as good an explanation as any. Unlike the nationalism of the preceding generation, whose vision of a united Germany had encompassed the ideals of liberty and human dignity, the new movement was antiliberal, antiintellectual, and authoritarian. The old nationalism had been part of a broad European current directed against the reactionary regimes of the Metternich era and therefore was democratic if not revolutionary, especially in Germany, where the many petty dynasties stood in the path of unification. The sense of being part of a common European cause had created a genuinely fraternal feeling toward other nations, including Frenchmen and Poles.

The transformation of this spirit into its opposite had occurred almost overnight in the new Reich Bismarck created. Why? Nicolai's generation grew up in a powerful and prosperous state. France had ceased to be a threat, the tsars and the Hohenzollerns were traditional friends, and England was neutral as long as the Continent was at peace. The German army was the strongest in the world, and Bismarck was the arbiter of Europe. The economy was flourishing and generally stable. The Industrial Revolution posed no worse problems in Germany than elsewhere, and in fact Bismarck's advanced social legislation had taken the wind out of the Socialist sails and kept the workers reasonably contented. The cultural life of the nation was gratifyingly active. High standards of scholarship prevailed in the numerous universities, attracting students and professors from all over the world.

The serpent in this Garden of Eden was not the Social Democratic party, although that role had been assigned to it by Bismarck, who outlawed its assemblies, by the Kaiser, who called it the enemy of the state, and by conservative circles generally. The "Sozis" were a tame enough lot, more revisionist than revolutionary, and in any case without any political influence. They controlled no state or national offices and were shunned like lepers by the men in power, notwithstanding the fact that they were the largest party in the Reichstag. The German worker was the best-educated in Europe, but insofar as he was a Socialist he stood outside the mainstream of public life. Nor did the petit bourgeois, who later would help Hitler into the saddle, trouble the peace of Wilhelm II's realm. He knew who his betters were, had reasonable security, and accepted life pretty much as he found it.

The malcontents came from the ranks of the educated middle class, the sons of the Liberals of 1848. Unlike their fathers, these men did not oppose the regime. Staunchly monarchist, they considered the government as, if anything, too liberal. Their quarrel was not with the state or the social order but with the world in general. The unification of Germany had left them without concrete goals, and the ruthless moves with which Bismarck had created the Second Reich had denied them even the pride of authorship.

What bothered them? They were disappointed that the millennium had not come. Ill-equipped by their classical education to understand the forces of capitalism and industrialization, they were repelled by the crass materialism of the age. They saw no improvement in their own situation, even while observing the rapid rise of the newly assimilated Jews. Though secure in their positions and suffering no real hardships, they felt sorry for themselves and hostile toward those whom they did not recognize as their own kind, Jews, Socialists, and foreigners.

From these frustrations, real or imaginary, had arisen that arrogant super-patriotism whose chief elements were glorification of the German past, the claim of innate superiority of the Germanic "race," intolerance for divergent opinions, and noisy anti-Semitism and chauvinism. The high priest of this cult was the historian Heinrich von Treitschke, a renegade Liberal who extolled what were purported to be the specifically Germanic virtues of courage, loyalty, love of freedom, and devotion to duty and who reduced German history to an unbroken series of martial feats. He was also the author of the dictum "the Jews are our misfortune." His influence on the academic youth of Nicolai's generation was enormous. One observer, the poet Hermann Bahr, described the effect of his lectures as "Old Testament with *furor teutonicus* added."

The modern *furor teutonicus* found its targets in two ready-made enemies, Jews and Frenchmen. Anti-Semitism had not yet succeeded in shaping events as an overt political force, though the attempt had been made by the notorious Court Chaplain Adolf Stöcker, a demagogue who combined ostensibly religious sentiments with eminently practical proposals for the protection of honest Germans against the people who killed Christ. Stöcker lost his following because he was not radical enough. From then on it was not religion but "race" that made the Jew objectionable. The government discouraged anti-Semitism as a challenge to law and order, but, like an occult virus, the movement remained latent in the consciousness of the nation, ready to flare up in times of stress.

German superiority and Jewish inferiority—or rather Jewish greed and lust for power—were notions that could easily be combined with the ideal of a pure race rooted in the German soil and possessing the sturdy virtues of the plowman, fused somehow with the warrior spirit of yore. The word *Volk* ("the people") acquired a mystical quality. The Volk was uncorrupted, spontaneous, and creative. Here was the eternal German soul, resistant to pernicious modern influences. For, though the Reich was restored, it somehow seemed to lack a soul. To the old antagonisms between north and south, Protestants and Catholics, new ones had been added: labor against capital, industry against agriculture. What was needed was a return to the simple tribal loyalties of olden times. Not until then would the Kyffhäuser Mountain open and Emperor Barbarossa sally forth once again to lead a united nation to everlasting glory.

In this vision, nourished by men who spent their lives in badly ventilated offices and classrooms, the yearning for fresh air and the joys of rustic life was an important element. The peasant who tilled the fields under God's open sky was somehow more valuable than the "uprooted" city dweller. Traders, intellectuals, and politicians were at best a necessary evil and at worst exploiters of honest, simple folk. Blood and soil, these were the ultimate values of the Volk movement. It was the slogan under which the fight against the complexities of modern life was fought, the incantation with which to banish reality.

Not that the break with reality was complete. When it came to financial support and propaganda, the dreamers had their feet firmly planted on the ground. Their political home was the Pan-German League, whose founder, Heinrich Class, never ceased to berate the government for its reluctance to go to war. Any pretext, or for that matter no pretext at all, would have done. The connections between the Pan-Germans and heavy industry were of the best. No less helpful were the connections with high-ranking army and navy officers, with Conservatives and National Liberals in the Reichstag, and with the Wehrverein and the Flottenverein, pressure groups on behalf of the armed forces which in turn were linked with industry and government. An influential press was always at the disposal of the Pan-Germans, as were the pens of sympathetic university professors.

The Pan-German brand of patriotism amounted to a chauvinism unparalleled in the history of a prosperous nation at peace. Until Britain's treachery was revealed in 1914, the target of this cult of hate was France, "the hereditary enemy." She was portrayed as a menace, smarting from defeat in the war of 1870–71 and plotting revenge, yet decadent and corrupt. "No nation is so irreconcilable, so unmovable, so tough as the French in their thirst for revenge," the noted historian Friedrich Meinecke warned his readers. "No other halfway civilized European people is so low, so vice-ridden, so inferior," said the *Post*. The traveller should avoid France "as one avoids sewers when crossing the street," another newspaper advised. There was a perpetual clamor for preventive war with France, although, according to one editorialist, fighting so inferior an enemy would be a dubious pleasure for German warriors.[7]

As for the Slavs, with whom Germany had no substantive quarrel whatsoever, their turn would come, once the battle between the "Romanic" and "Germanic" races was settled. Then the world would witness an epic struggle between the Germanic and Slavic races. England—before the war—was treated with a mixture of grudging respect and ill-concealed envy as a nation of shopkeepers which stood in the path of German expansion. Sooner or later it would have to cede some of its colonies to provide *Lebensraum* for German settlers, but it would never interfere with the continental conquests that were uppermost in Pan-German minds. Still, one could not be too careful, as the *Allgemeiner Beobachter* said in 1912 on the occasion of the visit of the noted British economist Sir Norman Angell, representing the English Peace Society. He was "a paid agent trying to snare German simpletons with a peace propaganda based on pseudoscientific economic arguments, but thank God he has been firmly rebuffed in the universities and even in Berlin."

In this overheated atmosphere pacifists were virtual outcasts. Along with socialism, anarchism, women's rights, and temperance, pacifism ranked as a menace to the established order. An avowed opponent of war was at best a crank—this was the view the Kaiser would take of Nicolai—and at worst a weakling and a traitor. Still, the Pan-German view had not gone unchallenged. The chancellor himself had said that it was not necessary "always to carry one's sword in one's mouth." The great metropolitan newspapers of liberal hue had warned of the dangers of unbridled chauvinism, supporting the government in its efforts to curb the hysterics of the war party. But it was a losing battle. The voices of reason were drowned out by the chorus of hate. "Why all this hellish noise?" the writer Ludwig Thoma asked in 1913: "The chauvinist press has seen to it that all threads are broken, every word and every gesture is misunderstood, humanity and love of peace are jeered at by every screaming stay-at-home. . . . Public opinion has been poisoned drop by drop. Empty slogans and lies have become unshakable truths. This press has carried the day, let us admit it."[8]

The chief bulwark against the chauvinist tide had been the Social Democratic party. According to Marxist dogma, the proletariat had no interest in the power struggles of capitalist states. The only meaningful war was the class war, and even on this front the party had abandoned all thought of violence. Only days before the outbreak of hostilities it sent emissaries abroad to discuss a position of solidarity with the French Socialists. But leaders and rank and file—in Germany as in France—had proved better patriots than Socialists. On 4 August 1914 the Social Democratic delegation in the Reichstag to a man approved the war credits. The comrades justified their abrupt turnabout on the grounds that the war was purely defensive and directed against reactionary Russia, but their leaders could hardly fail to see through the notion of a "defensive war" which could only help to sustain the capitalist system they were sworn to destroy. Some had cast their vote in the interest of party discipline, among them even Karl Liebknecht. But the elected representatives knew that the masses would not follow a leadership that appeared to desert the Fatherland in its hour of need. They knew that they were betraying their most sacred principles, and many of them suffered greatly, but the majority succumbed to the patriotic tide, happy to be received at last into the fellowship of good Germans from which they had been excluded for so long. As Konrad Haenisch (who later as minister of education would play a benevolent but ineffectual role as Nicolai's protector against vengeful nationalists) confessed, it had been hard to resist the mood that "surged and raged all around us, a mood which—if one looked deeply into one's heart—had already taken possession of one's soul." He spoke of the moment when "suddenly the terrible tension dissolved, when one dared to be one's true self, until—in defiance of all the petrified and wooden principles—one could for the first time (the first time in nearly a quarter of a century!) join with an overflowing heart and a clear conscience, without the dread of being a traitor, in the roaring battle cry 'Deutschland, Deutschland über Alles.' "[9]

Haenisch's "true self" and that of many of his comrades had been not that of the class-conscious Socialist but that of the frustrated bourgeois, the good monarchist and patriot at heart who had suffered from the slights inflicted by a callous society. Time would prove that they were believers in law and order, republicans *malgré soi*, and respecters of authority, especially military authority. In their postwar republic, industrial tycoons, Imperial generals, unreconstructed monarchists, East Elbian squires, Bavarian separatists, and fanatical Hitlerites could comfortably coexist with a well-behaved proletariat.

German Social Democracy, Nicolai wrote in *The Biology of War*, was "the most faithful mirror of the German people: a mixture of doctrinaire idealism and practical militarism." The dumping of those "petrified and wooden principles" enabled the party to condone the invasion of Belgium and, later, unrestricted submarine warfare and, tacitly, the predatory Peace of Brest-Litovsk. The only party which included pacifism in its basic creed allowed itself to be muzzled or cooperated with the government. The record of the world's largest Socialist party during the war was a sorry one, at least in the eyes of a radical pacifist like Nicolai.

Thus the handful of pacifists who remained steadfast, standing aloof from the stirring spirit of the August days and denying themselves the emotional release so vividly described by Herr Haenisch, were lonely men indeed. Unsupported by the feeling of solidarity that comes from belonging to a party, a national movement, or a religious group, they had only their personal conviction to sustain them. Bourgeoisie and proletariat, Christian and Jew, intellectual and peasant, the academic community and the uneducated—all were united in an upsurge of patriotism akin to the fervor of medieval crusaders. To keep a cool head amidst the torrent of highly colored tales of victory and heroism, to hold out against the pressure from friends, colleagues, and perhaps family, took strength of character. The man who has nothing to oppose such a tidal wave but his rational mind and does so is admirable.

Nicolai was such a man. How did he, a member of the German middle class of the Wilhelminian age, come by his heretical opinions? What was his background, what experiences shaped his character, what drove him to risk his career for a hopeless cause? We must attempt to answer these questions before resuming the story of his quixotic battles.

NOTES

1. Werner Sombart, "Die Anderen und Wir" ("The Others and Us"), in *Das Eiserne Buch*, ed. George Gellert (Hamburg: Gebrüder Enoch, 1915). This collec-

tion of patriotic effusions was typical of the time. It included contributions from such notables as the emperors of Germany and Austria; Field Marshal Von Hindenburg; Grand Admiral Tirpitz; the writers Gerhart Hauptmann and Thomas Mann; the philosophers Rudolf Christoph Eucken, Georg Simmel, and Wilhelm Wundt; the theologian Adolf von Harnack; the scientist Ernst Haeckel; the composer Max Reger; and the painter Max Liebermann.

2. *Ibid.*

3. See his *Deutschland oder England* (Munich: Süddeutsche Monatshefte, 1914).

4. "Das Schuldbekenntnis," *Die Zukunft* 28, no. 22 (February 1920):247ff.

5. Quoted by O. Nippold in *Der deutsche Chauvinismus* (Stuttgart: Veröff entlichung Verband für Internationale Verständigung, 1913).

6. This and the quotations that follow are from *ibid.*

7. Quotations are from contemporary pamphlets in the Zentralbibliothek, Zurich.

8. Quoted by Nippold, *Der deutsche Chauvinismus.* Before the war Thoma was a frequent contributor to *Simplicissimus.*

9. Konrad Haenisch, *Die deutsche Sozialdemokratie in und nach dem Weltkriege,* 4th ed. (Berlin: C. A. Schwetschke, 1919).

II. THE MAKING OF A REBEL

4. A Family of Rebels

"We utterly reject the charge of being unpatriotic. Those gentlemen understand patriotism as approval of the government's policy, but *we mean by patriotism the fight for everything that in our opinion is wholesome for the fatherland, regardless of how the government of the moment feels about it*." The words might have been Nicolai's in the war of 1914–18, but in fact they referred to another war, Bismarck's war against Austria, and were written in June 1866, one week after the start of hostilities, by Nicolai's father, editor of the staunchly democratic weekly *Die Verfassung* (*The Constitution*). The defiant italics were his answer to Bismarck, the head of the "government of the moment," who was riding roughshod over Liberal opposition to a war against fellow Germans. The "fatherland" was not yet a united Germany but the Kingdom of Prussia, a conglomerate of territories which had been acquired over the years by the Hohenzollerns and which was about to be rounded out handsomely by the annexation of the Kingdom of Hanover, the Grand Duchy of Hesse, and other valuable property. The "gentlemen" who had cast aspersions on the writer's patriotism were Bismarck's underlings, who had ordered the press to cease all criticism, a demand which, as the editorial drily commented, "puts us in a bad spot." Worse yet, the government was putting pressure on the newspapers to publish articles designed to inspire the *Volksgeist*, the martial spirit of the public. "How?" asked the writer. "There is no awakening the enthusiasm of the people with articles written on command."

The editorialist, Nicolai's father, was not the man to be cowed by Bismarck. In the last two months alone, two issues of *Die Verfassung* had been confiscated for voicing objectionable opinions. The first issue carried a satire on the issuance of twenty-five million thalers in new paper money to finance the impending war. The scenario included four beneficiaries of this windfall, Geheimrat Wichtigmaier ("Mr. Big Shot"), Kommerzienrat Rupfmaier ("Mr. Pick-Em-Clean"), a Hoflieferant Schnappmaier ("Mr. Grabby"), and a trigger-happy young lieutenant of the Guards, all happily singing the praises of Bismarck as the author of the measure. The second recalled the prediction of the revered statesman Baron Karl vom Stein on the eve of the disastrous battle of Jena that Prussia would disintegrate unless she abandoned her autocratic ways. The parallel was obvious.

Nicolai's father, Dr. Gustav Lewinstein, was a veteran of the revolution of 1848, a former professor of chemistry who had turned to political journalism, an irreconcilable foe of Bismarck, and—before his marriage to a Christian girl—a Jew. The reason for his conversion had been strictly personal: his father-in-law had insisted on his being baptized before he would consent to the marriage. Gustav did not change his unmistakably Jewish family name, but his son, the offspring of a mixed marriage who grew up as a Protestant, did. At the age of twenty-three Georg Lewinstein, with his father's consent, became Georg Friedrich Nicolai.

Gustav Lewinstein, a native Berliner who fought on the barricades in 1848, returned to the city of his birth to help defend constitutional government against Bismarckian autocracy. In 1866, at the height of the constitutional crisis in Prussia, he boldly defied the most powerful man in Europe, risking his freedom and his modest capital in the process. Unlike most Liberals, he did not change his tune in the face of Bismarck's successes, nor did he later succumb to the blandishments with which the victor sought to win over his erstwhile opponents. He viewed the new empire with a jaundiced eye and never ceased to mourn the democracy Germany might have been. To the end of his days, the place of honor in his home was occupied by the scene of the capitulation of the fortress of Rastatt to Prussian troops, painted in jail by his friend Otto von Corwin, the leader of the unsuccessful uprising of the Badensian democrats in 1849.

Thus the political ideas to which the young Nicolai was exposed were decidedly unusual. It would have come as a shock to most Germans of his generation to be told that once there had been a flourishing democratic movement in Germany, so completely had Bismarck's triumphant *Realpolitik* erased the memory of 1848 and of the great constitutional battle that lasted from 1862 to 1866. Having ignored the constitution by collecting taxes to build up the army, against the wishes of the parliament, Bismarck, the victory over Austria safely in his pocket, obtained passage of the so-called Indemnity Bill, by which the same parliament retroactively sanctioned four years of unconstitutional taxation. Eager to advance the unification of Germany under the now inevitable aegis of Prussia, the hitherto unshakable opposition collapsed. It was impossible to argue with success. Bismarck had won the contest of wills and destroyed the last vestiges of democracy which the revolution of 1848 had left behind.

It was a decisive moment in German history, and Gustav Lewinstein and the small band of diehards with whom he stood recognized it as such. Commenting on the passage of the Indemnity Bill, *Die Verfassung* foretold the consequences of this act of political expediency. "There can be no German unity unless it is based on law and liberty. If it is not, we have this to say: a unification of Germany that leads to suppression of freedom and subjection of the people to a privileged caste would not be worth a single drop of blood."[1] Most of the former Liberals, now, significantly enough, calling themselves National Liberals, carried the sacrifice of principle to its logical conclusion by becoming pillars of the regime and ultimately Bismarck's dupes. Lewinstein foresaw this outcome. "Bismarck," *Die Verfassung* had said on the eve of the Austrian war, "is the most decided enemy of the Liberals, and never can this party make peace with him, even if he should hold out his hand. For he believes that all authority belongs to the rulers and none to the representatives of the people."[2] The result of the Bismarckian solution was that Germany, while developing into a great industrial nation, was kept in a straitjacket of authoritarianism, paternalism, and caste privilege. As Nicolai would learn to his sorrow, the end of the First World War found the Germans without a political tradition that would allow them to govern themselves rationally. Democracy was in bad odor, having never been experienced except as fear of the machinations of presumably corrupt and power-hungry politicians. The men of 1848 and 1866 were forgotten.

Those men, nevertheless, had fought the good fight, and Gustav Lewinstein had been in the thick of it. As was to be expected from a youth of eighteen who combined in his person the attributes of a bourgeois, a student, and a Jew, he had thrown himself into the March Revolution body and soul, and he remained a "Forty-Eighter" all his life. As a young Jew he embraced the liberal cause with special ardor, for it was the cause of emancipation. Having become thoroughly assimilated, the Jews of Prussia resented the many restrictions imposed on them after they had been granted citizenship in 1810. It was not as Jews but as Germans aspiring to brotherhood and freedom that they took part in the struggle. Liberalism was the natural creed of a bourgeoisie whose rights had been trodden underfoot by the anachronistic regimes of the Reaction. The divine right of kings had ceased to be self-evident, to say nothing of the government's right to the taxes required to maintain royal courts and armies. The students were in the forefront of the fight against absolutism, rebellion against authority being a natural tendency of youth. The universities could not be sealed off against the liberal tide. Hegel, Prussia's official philosopher, had taught that the state was the *ultima ratio* of history and that the individual had no need of political freedom since he derived his freedom from the state, represented by the person of the sovereign, but this freedom offered no protection against arbitrary arrest. Nor did it seem plausible in an age of rising expectations that the dialectic process should have reached its ultimate perfection in the Prussian state, that thesis, antithesis, and synthesis had halted their march in the Restoration, or that the Creator had aimed at nothing higher than an efficient bureaucracy. The students of Lewinstein's generation were the most radical and political that ever filled the lecture halls of German universities and the beer gardens to which they repaired after classes.

For a brief moment the March Revolution seemed to have triumphed. The jails were opened, censorship was lifted, and a constituent assembly was elected to implement the royal promise of a constitution. The king stood bare-headed before the bloodied corpses of the freedom fighters, and a few days later, when the troops were withdrawn, rode through the streets under the protection of a citizen's militia, draped in the tricolor. The events had an ominous resemblance to the beginnings of the French Revolution. But 1848 was not 1789, Frederick William IV was not Louis XVI, his queen was not Marie Antoinette, and the Berliners were not Parisians. Though no less adept in building barricades, at heart they were peaceable and forgiving. They did not know what the English and French revolutionaries had known: kings were an untrustworthy breed whose blood alone could seal their promises. They allowed the king to go to Potsdam, where, under the protection of his officer corps, he began to have second thoughts. Soon the troops returned, and when General Wrangel's troops surrounded the Constitutional Assembly, the representatives of the people quietly went home. Still, the revolution had not been altogether in vain. The king promulgated a constitution of sorts, an amnesty was declared, and censorship was relaxed. In the newly created Prussian parliament the Liberals gained a majority and were able to defy the royal will, and it was not until Bismarck took the reins that the gains of 1848 were all but completely erased.

Being young and resilient, Gustav Lewinstein temporarily abandoned politics and turned to science. He studied chemistry under the great Robert Bunsen in Breslau and must have shown exceptional promise, for after he had obtained his doctorate in Berlin in 1856, Bunsen, who meanwhile had moved to Heidelberg, called him there as Privatdozent (unsalaried university lecturer). This was no small honor. Heidelberg was then a Mecca for chemists, boasting such names as G. R. Kirchhoff, Emil Erlenmayer, and August Kekulé. The young Dr. Lewinstein became codirector with Erlenmayer of the university's chemistry laboratories and was soon entrusted with the task of editing, jointly with Kekulé and the renowned mathematician Moritz Cantor, the prestigious *Kritische Zeitschrift für Chemie, Physik, und Mathematik.*

A speech defect kept him from lecturing and restricted him to the laboratory. Whether this was the sole reason, or whether the lure of politics was too strong, he abandoned his scientific career a few years later in favor of political journalism. Perhaps the double handicap of being a stutterer and a Jew made it too unlikely that he would ever become a tenured professor. For a time the newly hatched journalist worked for liberal newspapers in southern Germany, but that region had comparatively tolerant regimes. The challenge was Prussia, where Bismarck was battling the parliament over the issue of the budget. At stake was the constitution. Lewinstein returned to Berlin to found his own newspaper and attacked at once.

He exhorted the Liberals to guard the most sacred of parliamentary rights, that of budget approval. He reminded the king of his oath to the constitution. He warned Bismarck that ministers could be brought to trial for unconstitutional acts. He protested a ruling of the Obertribunal, Prussia's highest court, which deprived two Liberal deputies charged with slandering Prussian judges of their parliamentary immunity. "This," he wrote, "endangers the constitution as well as the administration of justice." No elected representative could legally be prosecuted for remarks made in a parliamentary debate. "Much has happened that we deplore, though nothing that cries out more powerfully to those who govern us, 'Stop on the path you are treading,' than this latest decision of the Obertribunal." *Die Verfassung* was thereupon confiscated, but Dr. Lewinstein, undaunted, brought out a special issue which opened with the declaration: "We do not feel justified in passing silently over an event of such importance for the constitutional development of civic life."[3]

This was the moment Bismarck chose to commit the reluctant king to the war against Austria and to close the obstreperous Diet. *Die Verfassung* reminded him that the proper remedy against parliamentary opposition was not to close the Diet but to dissolve it and call new elections. It was clear, the lead article of 3 March 1866 said, that he had no hope of gaining a majority and was therefore postponing the test of public sentiment until the fall in hopes of a military success before then, but war was a terrible thing, "and no people dare forget its rights over it"—a warning that might have changed the course of German history, had it been heeded. "Constitutional battles are also a kind of war, and that war must be accepted and fought out by the representatives and by the people, for our honor is at stake." A week later *Die Verfassung* raised the fundamental issue. "The king has the right to declare war, but not if the representatives of the people find it unjust or deem it to be against the interests of the country. That is the meaning of the parliament's right to pass on the budget." The

Fig. 5. Dr. Gustav Lewinstein, Nicolai's father, ca. 1866.

writer was breaking new ground, for the Prussian monarchy rested on its army, and to tell a Hohenzollern king that he was not free to use it as he saw fit was to intrude upon his most sacred preserve. But Bismarck bided his time, the Diet remained closed, and preparations for war continued.

When the archenemy of democracy suddenly called for a national parliament, *Die Verfassung* objected because "the experience with Bismarck in Prussia shows that he has no intention of giving such a parliament any real power." The leopard could not change his spots overnight. An all-German parliament had been the Liberals' dream, but Bismarck's proposal was nothing but a ploy to conceal the failure of his policy. "He knows that the rights connected with suffrage are harmless, but he errs grievously if he thinks that the profound antipathy of the German people will suddenly turn into affection."[4] This was wishful thinking of the kind Lewinstein's son would indulge in fifty years later, when he predicted that the "real Germany" would awaken once the power of the military was broken. But Lewinstein's diagnosis was correct: in Bismarck's empire the Reichstag would never have any real power.

In June 1866, when the Austrian war finally started, the press was ordered to cease all opposition, an order that became pointless almost immediately, for Austria was defeated in less than three weeks, but Lewinstein rose to the challenge. Using a tactic worthy of his son, he complied with the order by blandly reporting it under the eye-catching headline "There Is To Be No Opposition," thus exposing the attempt to intimidate the press. The authorities were not fooled. They told him to print a "rectification" to the effect that it was not opposition as such which was forbidden, but that "so cutting an opposition as *Die Verfassung* continues to manifest cannot be tolerated, and that it is therefore in the interest of the paper for its editorial board to subject itself to a significantly greater degree of self-restraint."[5] Lewinstein duly printed this order with the comment that the Herr Polizeipräsident was making a very fine distinction between simple and "cutting" opposition. The press, he added wryly, was in a dilemma when the government changed course, as it had done when Bismarck appropriated the opposition's program with his call for a national parliament. Who was inconsistent here? What was opposition?

It was a losing battle. *Die Verfassung* was confiscated once more for saying that a peace that did not bring internal reform was a rotten peace. It was cool to Bismarck's request for the Indemnity Bill. The admission that the government had violated the constitution and needed the forgiveness of the parliament was a moral victory, but was worthless unless it led to internal peace. What was needed were reforms in the ministries of Justice, Interior, and Education; jury trial for certain offenses; curtailment of the powers of prosecutors; an end to the baronial jurisdiction still prevailing in the east; separation of church and state; and permanent recognition of parliamentary control over the budget. It was the classical Liberal program. Significantly omitted was the demand for abolishing the three-class suffrage which disenfranchised 80 percent of the population, namely, the workers and peasants. Liberals and Conservatives were united in regarding the franchise for "the people" as dangerous and in their abhorrence of Marxist and Lassallean socialism, to which the disenchanted proletariat was turning. Lewinstein's revolution had aimed at political rights for the bourgeoisie, not at social change, and he never progressed in his thinking beyond the Liberal ideology of 1848.

The final crisis of *Die Verfassung* came when the government reneged on its promise of amnesty for political "crimes," offered by Bismarck in return for the Indemnity Bill. When several alleged offenders were brought to trial, the paper accused the minister of justice of twisting the king's solemn word. As the responsible editor, Lewinstein was indicted for insulting a government official, found guilty, and sentenced to prison. He appealed, and on 11 April 1867 the higher court handed down the final verdict: the lower court had erred in finding that the editorial in question had by implication called the minister a liar and hypocrite, for, as the defendant had correctly argued, it had merely pointed to the factual discrepancy between word and deed. The tone had been restrained, and the passage on which the original verdict was based had not been cited by the prosecutor, nor had the defendant been examined on this point. Having

Fig. 6. Dr. Lewinstein, ca. 1898.

been scrupulously correct thus far, the appeals court then executed a logical somersault which enabled it to avoid outright acquittal of a man who plainly deserved punishment. The defendant was not guilty of insulting the minister, but he *was* guilty of violating paragraph 32 of the Press Law. "The accused denies having written or read the offending editorial, and there is no proof or even likelihood that he did. We therefore find him guilty of negligence and change his sentence from an obligatory jail term to a fine." He had the choice of paying twenty-five thalers or serving fourteen days in jail.[6]

With this anticlimax Lewinstein's career as political journalist came to an end. *Die Verfassung* had already ceased to exist. On 25 March 1867 a simple notice informed the readers that this was the last issue. No explanation was given for the abrupt termination, and none was needed. The constitutional crisis that had been the raison d'être for a paper that called itself "The Constitution" was over. The great attempt to find a liberal solution for a united Germany had failed, and the faithful were deserting the cause. Bismarck, the Machiavellian autocrat, would make the new Germany in his image. One can only guess Lewinstein's feelings as he cleared out his desk and paid his fine, and one cannot help wishing that he had admitted the "crime" with which he was charged, though we have no reason to doubt his testimony that he neither wrote nor read the editorial. While it is hard to see how the editor of a small weekly could have been unaware of an important article on the front page, to lie on this point would have been to betray his most cherished beliefs, an act not in keeping with the upright character to which friends and foes testified until the end of his life. He was one of the few who remained faithful to the Liberal cause, and he was soon elected to the Central Committee of the Progressive party, to which the decimated Liberals now rallied. In 1870 he was among the signers of a proclamation demanding—on the heels of the victory over France—that the parliament of the united Germany be given the right to be consulted before the monarch could declare war. To demand such a concession from a government flushed with victory was the sign of a stout heart. Gustav Lewinstein was a fighter for lost causes.

After the demise of *Die Verfassung*, Lewinstein became a free-lance writer for technical trade journals and eventually editor-in-chief of the *Deutsche Tabakszeitung*, the organ of the tobacco industry (Fig. 6), a position he held until his death. His obituary in Berlin's *Vossische Zeitung* credited him with having helped to protect the industry against excessive taxation. In his spare time he wrote a book on the history of alchemy and chemistry. He cultivated the memories of the past and quietly nursed his grudge against the present. He corresponded with other old Forty-Eighters, both those who had remained in Germany and those who had emigrated, but he never again took an active part in politics. He was a gentle, modest man with a genuine gift for friendship. Forty years after his departure he was remembered in Heidelberg as "a well-known local personality," according to the *Heidelberger Zeitung*.

Before his death Gustav Lewinstein had the satisfaction of finding himself understood by his son Georg. For his seventieth birthday in 1899 he received a filial tribute of rare warmth in the form of a poem written in Heidelberg by the young medical student. It began conventionally enough. I alone cannot join you on this happy occasion, it said, but here in Heidelberg I am walking in your footsteps, where you studied and worked, drank the wine of the country, walked in these valleys, and

> dreamed the happy dreams of future triumphs,
> Your mind aglow with fervor and devotion.

Your generation's noblest aims
Unfolded here in joyous visions.

The echo rang through many years thereafter,
In which the times took on a different face,
New idols cast their spell upon the nation,
And pomp and martial splendor ruled the day.
The youth that followed you succumbed
To brute reality's compelling call,
And even old and trusted comrades
Stood smiling in the victor's camp.

The hopes of yesteryear are unfulfilled,
The time of greatness did not keep its promise.
Beneath the purple robe it covered lies,
Ashamed to show the world the dismal truth.
Instead of brilliant sun and lightning flashes
It gave us cold and dreary days of rain.
The youthful struggle for ideals
Is ebbing in Lucullan banquets.

You did not win your fight, admit it freely.
The younger generation took its turn,
Oblivious of their elders' aspirations
And bold ascent from false romantic dreams.
But hope and dreams will never die.
The sun continues in its stately path.
And therefore no regrets today!
For every age will have its men.

For when a raging storm blows through the forest
And in its path leaves death and devastation,
Amidst the splintered trunks of fir and birch
The rugged oak alone defies the havoc.
And when a people trembling bends its back,
The man of courage stands before our eyes.
Though all the nation lost its faith,
Not even Bismarck shook your will.

He was proud of his father, the young poet said, a man who never bowed
or bent, whose colors were for all the world to see, who never shied from
a fair fight. The highest bliss under the sun, he ended, paraphrasing
Goethe, is to be one's own man, contemptuous of the herd, standing alone
and looking with serene detachment upon the hurly-burly of the world.
"You are such a man, and therefore hats off, you modern people!"

It was not great literature, but rather—despite its Homeric metaphor
and its pathos—a piece of "occasional poetry," to be read aloud at a family
dinner when the plates have been cleared away and only the wine glasses
are standing on the table for a final toast. Yet coming from a son who had

81

often defied his father's authority and whose convictions were far more radical than those of the old Forty-Eighter, it was a deeply felt tribute from one man to another, the salute to a life in which ideals had counted for more than success. It was also a perceptive summation of a defeated generation, and in such lines as "You did not win your fight, admit it freely" or "The time of greatness did not keep its promise" it attained a tragic quality. It was, moreover, a view of the contemporary scene few members of the smug and prosperous middle class of the time would have shared or were capable of sharing. Except for the gentle skepticism of the novelist Theodor Fontane and the furious onslaught against the complacency of the Philistines of Nietzsche—both contemporaries of Lewinstein rather than of his son—there is little to suggest that German writers at the turn of the century had the insight to detect "the dismal truth beneath the purple robe." Stefan George might have written that line, but he lived in a different world.

Nicolai's mother was far more radical than his father. If he clung to his past, she had all but completely broken with hers. Marrying a Jew had been one of the rungs on the ladder of her emancipation, but she had not stopped there. Husband and wife made a united front when it came to the children, but otherwise Elise Lewinstein, née Michaelis, went her own way. Hers was by far the stronger personality and the more original mind.

In 1870, as a young woman en route from her East Prussian home to England, she stayed in Berlin long enough for Gustav Lewinstein to fall in love and propose marriage to her. She declined and went on to England, where she remained for a year as governess to an aristocratic family. Gustav, a man not easily discouraged, repeated his proposal in writing, and a correspondence began. Elise had been attracted by the urbane, scholarly ex-Privatdozent, whose views on life and politics seemed to match her own. In Berlin, away for the first time from her provincial hometown of Königsberg and alone among strangers, accustomed to keep a tight rein on her feelings, the young woman had been distrustful of her instinct. Then too, Lewinstein was the first Jew she had ever met. She promised to reconsider her decision after her return, which took place sooner than originally planned. After she had seen her suitor again a number of times she decided, in her sober, reflective manner, that she would become his wife. For a girl of her background it was a drastic step that threatened to cut her off from her own kind, and in the end did. Her father consented to the marriage on condition that the groom be baptized, but most of her friends turned away. On this point she never had any regrets.

Lewinstein himself accepted baptism without qualms. Unlike politics, religion was not a matter of conscience for him. Having shed the trappings of orthodox Judaism in less than one generation, German Jewry had become more German than Jewish in its outlook. For many Jews it was immaterial whether they went to the synagogue or to church, or to neither, for that matter. To belong to a religion that was perceived as alien in the German cultural landscape was a handicap. "Judaism is not a religion but a misfortune," Heine said, and called the baptismal certificate "the admission ticket to European civilization." It was indeed that, although it entitled the bearer only to standing room in the gallery. Still, conversion had its practical advantages in an age when anti-Semitism was still based largely on religious prejudice rather than on the racial theories of a later, more barbaric time. Thus the apostates were by no means stigmatized by their former coreligionists. In general, baptized and unbaptized Jews retained the same outlook, occupied a similar position in society, and moved in the same sphere. It was as if many who had not yet been baptized knew that they might follow those who had, if and when—as in the case of Gustav Lewinstein—a powerful motive presented itself. For the fiancé of Elise Michaelis, as for the young Heine half a century earlier, adopting the Protestant faith was "an act of indifference," not a betrayal.

Elise was born in 1844 in Königsberg, the cradle of the Prussian monarchy, the city of Kant, and a stronghold of Lutheran orthodoxy and also, more recently, of a sturdy Liberalism. Her mother died early, and her father, a teacher in a secondary school (Oberlehrer), remarried soon afterward. Stepmother and stepdaughter did not get along, and Elise started to go her own way at an early age. Left to her own devices, she developed a passion for reading which persisted all her life. (In later years, when her eyesight had begun to fail, she employed a companion to read aloud to her for several hours every day.) As a young girl she read all of Shakespeare, both in English and in German, and devoured every book she could lay her hands on, including "forbidden stuff." (One wonders what the "forbidden stuff" was: Boccaccio, Rabelais, and Voltaire? *Tom Jones* and *Tristram Shandy*? Or Stendhal, Balzac, Dumas, and Dickens? Did Elise read *Madame Bovary*? Did she know the new heretics in German theology and philosophy David Friedrich Strauss and Ludwig Feuerbach? Had the writings of Karl Marx penetrated as far as Königsberg?)

But the future mother of the encyclopedist Nicolai was by no means a bookworm. In the autobiographical sketch she wrote in old age, she described her adolescent self as giddy, bent on amusing herself even in school, devious in her ways, and notorious among her friends for her "wild capers." It was the same mixture of intellectual passion and frivolity which her son Georg would later display (though failing in school, he often sat up nights devouring Kant, Karl Marx, or Henry George, but he was also just as likely to be chasing after girls or gambling). Elise as a female in the Victorian age was more restricted in her choices—one wonders what her "wild capers" amounted to—but apparently she did the best she could. She loved social life, danced all night long with army officers, and for a time was the belle of the ball, according to her own testimony.

As she matured, these attractions began to pall, and she withdrew from the gay young crowd of Königsberg as from a circle to which she did not belong. At home the conflict with her stepmother made her feel unwanted. She retired to her room and her books, but she was dissatisfied with her life and herself and felt isolated and useless. The only person to whom she felt close was her grandmother, Jeannette Nicolai Kiepke, aunt of Otto Nicolai, composer of *The Merry Wives of Windsor*, whose name her son Georg later adopted. She passed through a spiritual crisis in which she renounced the strict Lutheran faith of her ancestors; in the end she abandoned religion altogether. Casting about for a purpose in life that would be in keeping with her strong sense of independence, she studied and took examinations for a teaching career. As she recalled later, this was an unheard-of step for a marriageable female at a time when the emancipation of women was just beginning and genteel German girls were expected to be models of domesticity.

When she married, she gave up her plans for a career, though not her independence or her aspirations. The marriage was not a success. For her as for her husband, much of its attraction had been the expected sharing

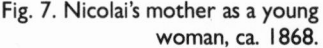

Fig. 7. Nicolai's mother as a young
woman, ca. 1868.

of intellectual and political interests, but she soon found herself disappointed. Fifteen years younger than Gustav, burning with intellectual passion and receptive to new ideas, she found him fixed in his thinking and uninterested in social problems or in the ethical and psychological insights of the great writers of the age, Dostoevski, Tolstoy, Ibsen, and Zola. His hostility toward socialism grew in proportion to the interest she took in it. He was, she wrote later, a Liberal of 1848 vintage who "rejected everything that was not old-time democracy." He refused to discuss or even read the books from which she drew her spiritual nourishment. In her own words, she soon found herself living side by side with a stranger whom she respected but with whom, except for the children, she had virtually nothing in common.

With characteristic clear-sightedness, she accepted the situation and set about building a life of her own. "I lost interest in the pleasures of bourgeois life and turned to the young intellectuals and idealists," she wrote. The house became the center of a circle of men and women, mostly young, who were searching for new solutions to problems which neither liberalism nor the Bismarckian state could solve. These problems were social rather than political and concerned the structure of the family, the rights of women, the burdens of the poor, alcoholism, child welfare, divorce, and the encroachment of machines on human lives.

The outstanding member of the group was Franz Oppenheimer, a physician and a pioneer in the young science of sociology. Others were Oppenheimer's sister Paula, who later married the poet Richard Dehmel; Dehmel himself; Hedwig Lachmann and her future husband, Gustav Landauer, the apostle of "nonviolent revolution" and an anarchist in the tradition of Proudhon and Kropotkin; and August Bebel, the leader of the Social Democratic party and a staunch opponent of Bismarck. Given the deep gulf that separated the middle classes from the Socialists in Bismarck's Reich, these were radical friends indeed for the daughter of a Prussian Oberlehrer from Königsberg. Small wonder that her husband would have nothing to do with them.

Women of Elise's generation had been denied access to higher education. Now, as a married woman, she satisfied her hunger for knowledge by attending courses at the university and taking adult education classes on a wide variety of subjects, from philosophy to jurisprudence. Frau Lewinstein became a familar figure in university corridors and lecture halls and cultivated the friendship of the professors. She went to the museums and art exhibits. But she was no mere bluestocking. The theater was one of the "pleasures of bourgeois life" she had not forsworn. Elise was a passionate theatergoer, a devotee of the "moderns" (Ibsen and Gerhart Hauptmann in particular) as well as of the classics. Her circle of friends included the great actor and matinée idol Josef Kainz.

As her children grew older, amateur theatricals, tableaux vivants, magic lantern shows, charades, and dances were frequent events in the Lewinstein home. Under their mother's tutelage, Georg and his sister Eva became expert puppeteers and, later, ardent theatergoers. Above all, Frau Elise enjoyed outings of the kind so charmingly described in the novels of Theodor Fontane, festive occasions with hampers of food and wine and a "Kremser" (a large open carriage typical of Berlin) carrying as many as twenty guests to picnics by one of the many pleasant lakes near the city. Her children, "who were educated with much freedom," went along on these excursions. Whether her husband did, she does not say.

The marriage produced two offspring: Georg, born in 1874, and Eva, born a year later. Despite their estrangement, husband and wife saw eye to eye about their children's upbringing. As Elise wrote later, in her peculiarly detached manner, the children were handsome, lively, and headstrong, "a joy to behold and difficult to live with, the terror of the neighborhood." Georg was especially gifted, "and I taught him reading and many things not taught in school that later were more interesting to him than school subjects." As an old woman she sketched this remarkably objective portrait of her (by then) famous son:

> George was so wild and hard to control that he was sent to boarding school at an early age because I did not want him to become alienated from his mother. In the seventh grade he fought a pistol duel. No one was hurt, but the minister of education barred him from all the schools in Prussia. "Now I have no choice but to go into the Bohemian forest and become a robber," he said when he heard of this decision. He was sent to another boarding school at Gotha [in the Duchy of Saxe-Coburg], but this move was likewise unsuccessful. Georg tried too hard to educate his teachers, and they did not like it. As a last resort he was sent to a school in Alsace, where he finally graduated. After many trials and tribulations he at last became professor in Berlin. I thought this was a safe harbor, but, on the contrary, it was to be the main catastrophe of his life.
>
> He had changed his name with his father's consent, and on my advice adopted that of his great-grandmother, a relative of the composer Nicolai. The manifesto he wrote shortly after the outbreak of the war antagonized many professors because it was especially sharp in its criticism of scholars and scientists for not being objective and truthful. I stand entirely by my son, but I cannot deny that he talked too much about his pacifism, and in places where it was not at all appropriate—for example, in the presence of military men and people opposed to his views. For this reason he was demoted by his military superiors and made a simple private, a thing that was especially hard for him, who was so little capable of subordinating himself. Thus there were many conflicts in which I could not always side with him.[7]

Elise Lewinstein died at the age of eighty-four. Her attempt to avoid alienation from her son had failed for reasons beyond her understanding. She had tried to be a modern mother, relying on her ability to stimulate the boy's interest rather than on discipline, but he had never ceased to be rebellious, and she had never ceased to be critical of him. The woman who had lived side by side with a stranger for thirty years had no illusions about her son. Her pragmatic mind reduced the great moral issue for which he sacrificed his career to a question of temperament, and in this she was wrong. But her unblinking diagnosis was correct: Nicolai was not only a fighter for a noble cause but a fighting cock, whose feathers were ruffled by the mere sight of an opponent. He was also, she might have added, the true child of his parents, a rebel born of rebels and the product of a home where *Zivilcourage*, a virtue sadly lacking in a nation accustomed to taking orders from above, was highly prized, and where no authority was ever accepted on faith.

NOTES

1. 8 September 1866. *Die Verfassung* is the principal source for this chapter. Bound volumes for 1866–1867 are among the Nicolai archives preserved by Frau Katz. Dr. Lewinstein was its editor in those years.

2. *Ibid.*, 29 April 1866.

3. *Ibid.*, 10 February 1866.

4. *Ibid.*, 27 April 1866.

5. *Ibid.*, 30 June 1866.

6. All quotations are from the Nicolai archive.

7. *Das Leben je nachdem es ist.* This unpublished autobiographical memoir of Elise Lewinstein's was written in about 1924, when she was eighty. The manuscript is in the Nicolai archive.

5. Cuckoo's Egg*

Born on 6 February 1874, Georg grew up in an age when child psychology had not yet come into its own. Authority rather than understanding was the cornerstone of the family. Gustav and Elise Lewinstein might be more tolerant or more enlightened than most of their contemporaries, allowing their offspring more freedom and treating them more nearly as equals than was customary, but when it came to principles they shared the attitudes of the solid German middle class to which they belonged. Children were small adults whose behavior could be controlled by reason and whose character must be molded by wholesome influences at home and at school. They were expected to obey their parents, to be well-mannered, to respect adults in general and teachers in particular, and to do their homework conscientiously and well. If they failed to live up to these expectations, they were reasoned with, admonished, and, if need be, punished. People might laugh at *Max und Moritz*, Wilhelm Busch's pair of juvenile mischief-makers perpetually at war with the stuffy order of the adults; in the real world offenses against that order were no laughing matter. Children who failed to respond to parental discipline were declared "unmanageable"—a term signifying an inborn and incorrigible flaw in the child's character rather than parental inability to cope with the problem—and sent away to boarding school.

This is what happened to Georg. At eleven we find him at the boarding school of a Dr. Möller at Wulkow, a little town in the province of Brandenburg. We do not know what act of disobedience triggered the decision to send him away, nor does it matter, for clearly it was only one of a long series of incidents. Too little is known about Georg's early childhood to trace the roots of his rebelliousness. If his many transgressions were mere attention-getting devices, did he have reason to feel neglected? If anything, he and his sister received too much parental attention, but it may not have been the right kind to satisfy their emotional needs. Gustav and Elise lived in an adult world to which they were willing and even eager to admit their offspring—this was the measure of their "progressiveness." They educated their children, they read and talked to them, but they did not laugh or play with them. The difference in age—Gustav was approach-

*The principal source for this chapter is a collection of letters from Gustav and Elise Lewinstein and from Eva Lewinstein-Blos, Nicolai's sister, as well as from various friends and acquaintances of Nicolai's. They cover the period 1885–1895. Dates, when not indicated in the letters or by postmarks, were determined either from the context or from pencil notations of the year added by Nicolai to many letters in later years. A second source is a collection of letters from Nicolai (then Georg Lewinstein) to his sister, written in the same period and made available by Frau Ruth Katz, daughter of Eva Lewinstein-Blos.

ing sixty when Georg was sent away to school—was in itself a formidable barrier. And although the parents presented a united front, the children could not have failed to sense that they were living in a loveless marriage.

If the purpose of boarding school was the rehabilitation of the youthful offender, the experiment was a failure. Georg was not really a juvenile delinquent; his behavior would raise few eyebrows nowadays. He was headstrong, self-centered, and quick-tempered, physically and mentally precocious, handsome and extraordinarily gifted (Fig. 8). Aware of his superiority, he felt that he was above the rules applied to ordinary mortals, a kind of juvenile superman. He accepted Wulkow as a means of escape

Fig. 8. Nicolai at age nine, ca. 1883.

from the nagging of his parents and caused as much trouble in school as he had at home. The nagging. of course, continued by mail. The Lewinsteins took turns bemoaning the consistently bad reports from Dr. Möller and vainly tried to make their wayward son feel guilty about the grief he was causing them. Papa was in poor health; every setback in his condition was blamed on the news from Wulkow. "You caused me so much worry that I was sick for two days," the old man would write. "No, you cannot make the trip with us, much as I would have enjoyed having you, because you are so inattentive and ill-behaved in school." That was the tenor and those were the themes of a steady stream of parental missives. Georg should eat the unappetizing fare served by Frau Möller: "It won't hurt you to eat milk soups; they are good for you." Rowing was a dangerous sport: "Be careful on the water." Money was not to be squandered: "I am sending postal stamps; what do you want ten or twenty marks for?" There were complaints about the boy's failure to write, his forgetfulness, his carelessness, his lack of consideration for others—a catalogue of petty misdemeanors magnified into grave crimes by a frustrated father. Mama was equally unhappy, though her reproaches had a gentler ring; she appealed to Georg's better nature rather than trying to play upon his guilt feelings: "We couldn't see you because Papa has received so many unfavorable reports. When will you become reasonable? Some day, of that I am certain! You are only hurting yourself. How much I would enjoy having you here!"

But whether the parents enjoyed their son's company or not, they denied themselves almost every opportunity to do so. For years he was regularly punished by not being allowed to come home for holidays. "Did you make use of your vacation to catch up on your studies?" Papa inquired, thus rubbing salt into an open wound. Georg had no intention of catching up on his studies. During his four years at Wulkow he remained indolent, inattentive, lazy, and disrespectful to his teachers. The truth is that he was bored, the classic case of the gifted child who finds himself in a dull environment.

Neither the curriculum nor the teaching methods of the "Humanistic gymnasium" of the time were designed to arouse the student's interest. All he was offered in the lower grades were rules to be mastered or facts to be memorized: Latin grammar, without a hint of the poetry and power of the language; stereotyped mathematical formulas, to be learned by rote and repeated on command; Greek and Roman history, presented as a succession of battles and heroic feats by impossibly noble characters. For the young Georg all this was meaningless. He was interested in ideas, ready to test his mental powers in debates with his intellectual peers rather than dutifully accepting the pronouncements of his schoolmasters as the ultimate wisdom. Though he was emotionally immature, his mind was far ahead of his years. The boy who was always at the bottom of his class and who repeatedly failed to be promoted was a voracious reader of books that would have taxed the intelligence of educated adults. If genius can be equated with intelligence Georg was a genius or at least had the makings of one, but neither his parents nor his teachers made allowance for this gift of the gods. On the contrary, the unceasing parental disapproval must have dampened the boy's high spirits, while the school's decision to make him repeat several grades only increased his boredom and killed what little interest he had in the proceedings. It was a vicious cycle from which the educational practices of the time offered no escape.

Georg found other outlets for his vitality. Endowed with a strong physique, he was passionately fond of rowing, swimming, hiking, ice-skating, and, later, skiing, then a novel and exotic sport. He had a natural talent for drawing which he would cultivate all his life. He enjoyed working with his hands and while at Wulkow took up wood-carving. Later on he learned bookbinding, experimented with photography, collected weapons, played in amateur theatricals, and became an expert in making and handling marionettes for puppet shows.

He also took an early and intense interest in the opposite sex and had his first sexual experience at the age of fourteen, while still at Wulkow. Liesel K., "The First," as she appeared in a list of his conquests many years later,[1] may have been a servant in Möller's household, a barmaid at the local tavern, or a peasant's daughter from a nearby farm. The choices were limited at Wulkow, and the ambience did not favor romance.

In 1889, fifteen-year-old Georg left Möller's establishment for Schwedt-on-the-Oder, residence of the Margraves, minor vassals of the kings of Prussia, and site of another boys' school, directed by a kindly gentleman named Dr. Eickhoff. Perhaps the transfer was the result of a specific offense; perhaps Möller despaired of his unruly student. Eickhoff, in any event, had no better luck than his predecessor. Having already repeated two grades, Georg was placed in the lower third form. He was the oldest boy in his class and, of course, the most difficult to handle. Toward the end of the school year it was once more doubtful whether he would be promoted. In the end he was, but by then his anxious parents had other things to worry about.

With the advent of puberty Georg had gotten still further out of hand. He tried to prove his manhood by drinking, gambling, betting at the races, and showing off in every possible way. "Mama is upset," Eva wrote from Berlin, "about your breaking through the ice skating on the Oder." Georg had led a group of his classmates on a forbidden skating expedition and, being the fastest and boldest, outdistanced the others until the treacherous crust gave way and he almost drowned. Papa supplied the sermon for the occasion: "Once again you risked your life without thinking of your promise to me. Your friends ran away instead of rescuing you. That's how it has always been: your comrades laugh at your wild behavior, but in the end you are the scapegoat." Courage was a moral rather than a physical attribute, the old man reminded his son on another occasion, when Georg had been caught lying. "There is no excuse for secretiveness or lying. You always boast of your courage. Well, remember that lying is cowardice." And why did Georg always associate with the worst elements in his class? As for drinking, "it is still a little early for *Kneipen*" (organized beer parties of fraternity students not ordinarily attended by boys not yet admitted to the university). "I am not opposed to a glass now and then, but how you can stand drinks for the whole gang is more than I can fathom." Papa was beginning to mellow, but he continued to worry about expenses: "I am glad that you had a good time at the races. I have no objection to an occasional bet on the horses, but you must stay within the limits of what you can afford."

Georg's demands for money or for things that cost money were indeed becoming a problem. "Your many wishes are unreasonable," Papa complained; "I have to earn my living the hard way." Lewinstein's income was modest, and keeping Georg in boarding school meant financial sacrifices for the family. But the young man was interested in clothes. "No, you can't have another suit so soon after buying the last one," Papa wrote. Georg's confirmation was approaching, and he intended to be dressed exactly right for the occasion, but he had to settle for something less resplendent. "I have already bought black cloth for your confirmation suit," his father informed him. "It is preferred over blue. Don't feel too bad. You don't need a top hat; a black bowler will do, a chemisette, and white gloves. Frau Eickhoff can go shopping with you." Books were another large item on Georg's list of wishes, and though they might be more desirable than clothes or gambling losses, they still cost money. There was in any case no point in stuffing one's head with things which—in the opinion of his father at least—Georg did not understand. Were not his letters full of misspellings unworthy of a boy who aspired to get into the second form?

Although there was no letup in the complaints from home, and although Georg continued to teeter on the brink of failure in school, he began at last to take an interest in some of his classes. "You are reading Homer," Papa noted with approval. "I am happy that you got good marks on your German theme." Georg had also done well on a Latin test but needed tutoring in mathematics. In his leisure time he read Goethe, Kleist, and even Karl Lachmann, the great philologist and colleague of Jacob Grimm. By now it was obvious that he had a brilliant mind, making it all the more deplorable that he seemed incapable of making sustained effort. "You have everything a person can desire," his mother wrote on the occasion of his sixteenth birthday, "health, youth, talent, looks. But apply them correctly—that you will not do, for that you lack the energy. I am terribly afraid you might not pass, because if you don't, Papa will not let you study at the university." This was the ultimate weapon; in the eyes of an educated German middle-class family, it was a fate worse than death for a boy not to have a university education, not to become a Herr Doktor, to have to "go into trade." The threat would be used again and again in the coming years, not without effect.

But it was not failing grades that put an abrupt end to Georg's career at Schwedt. He was expelled from the gymnasium and—by a ministerial decree—from the entire Prussian school system for having fought a duel with pistols. Except for the ritualistic fencing with sabers that was part of the fraternity tradition, dueling had long since been outlawed throughout Germany. Grown men on rare occasions and in the utmost secrecy might still settle questions of honor by this method, and the authorities usually closed both eyes if the offenders happened to be members of the officer corps or the nobility. For boys of high-school age to fight a duel was quite another matter, especially when they bore names that were far from aristocratic. Stern disciplinary action was clearly in order.

The reason for the duel is lost in the mists of time. Given Georg's explosive temper, any provocation might have served. There was no better way to prove one's manhood than an *affaire d'honneur*. The romantic appeal of a duel, combined with the feudal code of honor that had remained a Prussian ideal, made for an almost irresistible temptation, especially if the quarrel was about a girl. But if in fact Georg was the challenger he may have had more serious provocation. Someone might have made a derogatory remark about his obviously Jewish name. By 1890, anti-Semitism had become widespread among middle- and upper-class Germans. Since it was already aimed at the so-called Jewish race rather than the Jewish religion, a Lewinstein would be a likely target, even if he was the son of a Gentile mother and reared as a Lutheran. Georg would be doubly vulnerable because he could not identify himself with the proud tradition that served the unbaptized descendant of the Chosen People as a shield. Only his name tied him to that tradition, and the name was in conflict with the role he played as a non-Jew. Against an anti-Semitic insult he could put forward only his worth as an individual, to be proven by his courage on the field of honor.

There is indirect evidence for this speculation. Surely a more frivolous reason for the duel would have brought endless recriminations from a father who earlier had repeatedly reminded his son of his promise not to risk his life. But this episode is shrouded in silence. The parents may have been embarrassed by the exposure of an open but hitherto unmentioned secret: the apostasy of the father and the defection of the mother, whose burden had now fallen upon the son. Gustav Lewinstein and Elise Michaelis, the Jew and the Prussian, had broken a taboo that was no less potent for being denied by a supposedly enlightened society. If Georg had fought a duel to vindicate his identity as the scion of a mixed marriage, his parents would have had to forgive him and perhaps even secretly condone the act. As for Georg himself, whom fate had placed in a society whose values excluded Jewish culture, he must have undergone an identity crisis at some point in his adolescence. The outcome was foreordained: he had no choice but to be a German. But it would have been out of character if he had turned his back on the problem and denied his Jewish ancestry by changing his name—as he later did with his father's consent—without giving proof that the choice was dictated by his free will, not by cowardice. A duel in defense of his ancestral name would have been the best proof possible.

The duel itself is easy to imagine. All the formalities must have been observed, and in fact it was probably the formalities that mattered the most: the formal challenge, delivered by beardless but deadly serious seconds; the setting of time and place; the choice of weapons, probably from Georg's own collection; and finally the secret rendezvous at dawn at some remote spot on the edge of the woods. Nobody was hurt, but somebody must have talked. The authorities acted swiftly. Georg was remanded to the custody of his parents, while his opponent ran away and was arrested in Cairo on his way to German East Africa. Georg let himself be persuaded to finish his education. Since every school in the state of Prussia was now closed to him, he was sent to the Ernestinum, a famous boys' school in the Grand Duchy of Gotha (Fig. 9).

Gotha was a great improvement over Schwedt. The duke, who was also the patron of the school, was a liberal prince in the tradition of Goethe's protector, the duke of Weimar. The Ernestinum, in Nicolai's own words, "was one of the few institutions of learning that had not yet fallen prey to the new German conformism of the imperial age, one in which the spirit of German humanism, with its enthusiasm for all things beautiful and especially for classical antiquity, was still alive." Had there been more schools like it, he wrote forty years later, Germany's history would have been different. There the aim was not to produce obedient servants of the state but to stimulate young minds to unfold, each according to the individuality of the student. The faculty included a number of distinguished scholars, among them a Latin professor "whose vociferous enthusiasm for

Fig. 9. Nicolai at age seventeen, 1891,
while at the Ernestinum.

Horace could inspire even the most prosaic of spirits" and a Greek professor "who taught his pupils how to study and gave them an inkling of the meaning of scientific inquiry." There was a young physicist whose experiments were as rigorously designed as those offered in any university course, and "the fat Sch., who lectured on the touchy subjects of German literature and history without grossly embellishing them."[2] But the outstanding faculty member was Kurd Lasswitz, already renowned as a philosopher and author of an original work on atomic theory, and later to become famous through his science fiction novel *Auf zwei Planeten (On Two Planets)*.[3]

A genuine friendship, which outlasted the school years and came to include their families, sprang up between the mature scholar and the brilliant young student. Lasswitz was the first original thinker Georg had met in the flesh and probably the first of his teachers to treat him as an intellectual equal. The impact of his moral philosophy on the future author of the *Biology of War* is unmistakable. Lasswitz's Martians possess not only a superior technology—*On Two Planets* anticipates interplanetary travel, spaceships manned by astronauts, space stations, weightlessness, radio, radar, the utilization of solar energy, and other inventions too numerous to mention—but moral and intellectual superiority over the inhabitants of Earth. On Mars, war is looked upon as both immoral and stupid. The squabbles of the European powers become absurd in the face of a Martian expedition equipped with irresistible weapons, though the weapons are strictly defensive, designed only to force the semicivilized earthlings to make peace. Mars is governed by a League of Nations composed of states with the most diverse forms of government, all coexisting peaceably. Morality is based on wisdom; free will is identical with intelligent behavior. The Martians have resolved the Kantian dilemma: enlightened self-interest and the Categorical Imperative are one and the same thing for them.

Lasswitz's utopia did not appear in print until 1897, but these ideas were germinating in his mind long before, and Georg, who for a time was a boarder at his house, became well acquainted with them. In the setting of the new Imperial Germany, they were almost subversive. The generation which had fought the Franco-Prussian War and celebrated "Sedan Day," the anniversary of the victory over Napoleon III, as the highest national holiday regarded war as a positive ideal. The early encounter of the future pacifist with a teacher who saw in war the relic of a primitive barbarian past was a providential circumstance.

For the present, however, neither the congenial atmosphere of the Ernestinum nor Lasswitz's lofty ideas had the slightest effect on Georg's behavior. While his intellect grew prodigiously, he remained rebellious and emotionally immature. He quarreled with most of his teachers, including Lasswitz. Only his father's reminder that his room and board had been paid in advance kept him from moving out of Lasswitz's house in the middle of the term. The next teacher with whom he boarded soon gave up. "You can't hold it against a teacher," Papa wrote, "if he refuses to board someone who will not abide by the house rules." In fact, Georg boarded with a succession of teachers, none of whom was willing to put up with him for long. For one thing, they found him too argumentative. "If you argue with Professor Kampen," the worried Dr. Lewinstein warned him, "you can't expect decent grades, which you need if the [Prussian] minister [of education] is to let you return to Berlin." But the teachers were the enemy, and baiting them was Georg's favorite pastime. He was becoming expert at finding their weaknesses. "One may indeed argue the propriety of influencing the students through Latin exercises," Papa conceded when his son objected to a professor's attempt to inject his political opinions into the interpretation of Latin texts, "but for a student to express his opposition through deliberate mistakes in Latin is hardly wise." One suspects that a young man capable of such subtleties had the best of his teachers in many an argument.

Not content with displaying what he considered his intellectual superiority, Georg cultivated an arrogant and supercilious manner. "The teachers, dear Eva, are becoming more impertinent every day," he wrote to his sister and only confidante in the family.

> Our professor now imagines that I would take notice of him outside of school hours. I was at the opera, sitting opposite a charming young lady. As a young man who loves beauty as an aesthetic pleasure, what was I to do but look across at her during the intermissions, using opera glasses to heighten the enjoyment? In back of her sat Ewald. Both looked ethereal to me, he in the literal sense of the word—that is, like the air that one sees through—but the next day he complained to the principal that I had stared at him the entire evening.

Georg was not merely trying to impress his adoring sister with his cleverness, he was expressing his contempt for the authority Ewald represented.

With arrogance went self-righteousness. He would never apologize: he was never in the wrong. "I feel bad about your relations with Dr. Rosenstock," Papa sighed, "but you are at least partly to blame. You should have asked his forgiveness at your return, to remove the tension, as I told you. Did you? I suppose not." The old man's guess was correct: the conflict with Rosenstock dragged on to the very end. But Georg's conduct reflected more than conceit and self-righteousness. He was beginning to show an indifference for the feelings of his fellow humans that bordered on cruelty. "Your behavior toward your Professor Gilbert was quite inhumane," Papa reproached the then eighteen-year-old; "you should have respected his grief and attended his wife's funeral, no matter how you felt about him."

It was the same story at home. In addition to the usual laments about Georg's poor grades, recklessness, extravagance in money matters, and sexual escapades, the parental letters were filled with anguished cries. Was there no love in Georg's heart? His rare visits at home invariably ended in ugly scenes. His parents might have failed him when they sent him away at an early age, but they loved him after their fashion and eagerly waited for a sign that their love was returned. The prodigal son accepted the fatted calf as no more than his just due, wreaked havoc in the orderly world of the little family, provoked bitter arguments with his father, his mother, and even his sister and her friends, and returned to school, leaving in his wake anger, bewilderment, and frustration. "I am sorry your visit ended in disharmony," Mama wrote after a Christmas vacation:

> You were objectively in the wrong, but worse yet, even if you had been right you should have yielded in deference to the love of your parents. Beyond right there is a higher power, love, of which you have never partaken. You always do as you please, you are never considerate of us. I enjoyed having you this Christmas; now, for the

sake of a petty thing, you destroy everything. Why? Do you like yourself better this way?

Even Lotte, she reported, a girl whose friendship with Georg his parents evidently approved, had been moved to ask, "Doesn't he know that one can do things for love, for the sake of pleasing another?"

It must have been a stormy Christmas. Several weeks later Papa wrote his son a birthday letter that came from the depth of a wounded soul.

> I write with a sad and heavy heart, having no other wish for you than that fate may spare you the disappointments and failures which you so wantonly create. You are as harsh toward your parents as if you were determined to alienate us as you have alienated all your boyhood friends. I shall not hold up to you all the pain you have caused us nor the sacrifices we have made for you, but I remind you that I am an old man.

Georg was unmoved, and the emotional bond that tied his parents to him finally snapped when his father had another serious heart attack. He was old enough to be responsible for his actions, he knew the precariousness of the old man's health, and yet he continued to provoke ugly scenes. In a letter as bitter as any son's mother could write, Mama drew the consequences:

> There is no choice but to make sure by not letting you live with us that there is no repetition. I say nothing of my own misery. *I* shall not die of your doings; I am too healthy, I am sorry to say. Since no improvement on your part is to be expected, we must all suffer the consequences. For your parents and for Eva this is very painful. As for you, you won't miss us.

The incident itself had been trivial, an argument over a key Georg had appropriated when someone else needed it. He had insisted on his right to keep it. "I know you well," his mother wrote, "but there is one thing I don't know: do you really believe yourself to be in the right or do you merely pretend? In the first case I must doubt your intelligence, in the second you have no heart."

If Georg had no heart, he had everything else: keen intelligence, insatiable curiosity, an observant eye, an excellent memory, wit, charm, good looks, an athletic body, and an inexhaustible fund of energy. Like a young dog sniffing the morning breeze and straining at the leash, he was ready for every pleasure life had to offer, now, today, here. School was a necessary evil, to be endured for the sake of the future but not to be taken seriously and on no account to interfere with his freedom. He drew his knowledge from sources of his own choosing, and for a time he nourished the wildly impractical plan of leaving the gymnasium altogether and preparing himself for the university with his own resources. He shrugged off the conflict with his parents, secure in the knowledge that he could count on their support, no matter what.

His demands grew every month. He wanted new skates, new clothes, books and more books, money for trips, for theater tickets, for fencing, dancing, and elocution lessons (from a "former court actress!"), to pay his gambling debts, buy wine, entertain girls. If the money was not forthcoming he charged his purchases to Papa's account, bought things on credit, or pawned his overcoat or watch. He liked to travel in style, giving Papa ample grounds for complaining that a boy his age did not have to live "like a grand seigneur," staying at the Vier Jahreszeiten, Munich's fanciest hotel, when his mother had been content with a modest pension near the railroad station.

These were golden years for Georg, full of all the contradictions of adolescence. Childish naiveté mingled with serious thought, rebellion with a sense of order, and youthful escapades alternated with the quest for clarity. He was—or wanted to be—both a dandy and a philosopher on a park bench, both a daredevil and a detached spirit who looked upon the doings of ordinary mortals from the Olympian height of his intellect, a despiser of the crowd and at the same time a seeker of approval and applause. Alternately he played the strong silent male and the dazzling raconteur, the social critic and the rake. In one and the same letter to Eva—to whom he confided "even the craziest things"—he pokes fun at the scramble for partners at his dancing lessons, describes an afternoon spent in the school lock-up, laments the lack of money with which to buy books by Schopenhauer and Lassalle, and lists his wishes for Christmas. When the command is given, he writes, "every boy rushes toward the ladies, pushing and shoving. One literally falls into a girl's lap. I take my time, getting there last and usually getting the best, if not the best-looking, dancers, but isn't that the purpose of the exercise? And what stupid conversation! But I am making progress."

He was locked up for playing hookey, he reports, "because while going for a book during recess I met Ella and decided to let school be school. I told the teacher that I had a headache. The best remedy was the fresh air in the park, but there I met a professor who turned me in." The imprisonment had been most enjoyable. "Ella sent chocolates. Fritz T. and I were locked up together, and we sang and danced until the custodian appeared and locked us up properly, after much argument. Then I rang for pen and ink to decorate the walls with quotations from Goethe, Heine, and others, all thoroughly opposed to studying." Finally he composed a Latin essay on "de optimo temporis usu" (the best way to spend one's time), which had made the teacher, a devout Christian, very unhappy. "I started with 'vita nostra brevis est' and ended with 'gaudeamus igitur,' having concluded that as long as we are faced with eternal death we might as well use life to have as much fun as possible."

But among the books he asks for in the next paragraph are the works of Kant and Karl Marx, Henry George's *Progress and Poverty*, Theodor Hertzka's *Laws of Social Evolution*, Aristotle's *Athenian State*, a complete edition of Plato, the annotated Lucretius Carus, and essays on Thomas More, all heavy fare, none on the school's list of suggested reading for the second form.

Books were his passion. He read them, collected them, had them bound, even learned the craft of book-binding himself, designed covers and a bookplate, and bought first editions. At sixteen, he badgered his parents for the complete works of Kant. "There is no need for Kant now," Papa objected "just to skim through and impress people with your erudition. Wait." But he gave in. Still, he knew his son: Georg tried to dazzle Eva with such formidable Kantian terms as "the unity of transcendental apperception," taken completely out of context for the sole purpose of showing off. But he had grasped its meaning, though he gives it an unexpected twist. "Let yourself be enlightened," he said grandly.

> This transcendental unity applies not only to transcendental ethics (although you wouldn't understand that term either, and I wouldn't know how to explain it to you, nor do I have the time), but in a more general sense this desire for unity is uniquely human, the ultimate, the most satisfying thing. If you want fulfillment you must allow for this desire, you must subordinate everything to a particular viewpoint, and you will see how the whole world will then give you greater pleasure.

If the fifteen-year-old Eva was impressed by her big brother's profundities, his mother was not. "We gave you Kant for Christmas because you claimed to understand and appreciate him, but you show not the slightest evidence of a Kantian sense of duty." For Frau Elise, the Categorical Imperative had a practical meaning.

For the most part, Georg's letters to Eva were less intellectual than the one just quoted. He describes a country fair "with lots of merry-go-rounds and glider rides," which he enjoys; otherwise his interest is mainly in the Pfefferkuchen, for culinary reasons, and in the peasant boys and girls, "for psychological reasons." He asks Eva to make a blue silk cap for him and gives detailed instructions, enclosing a sketch to make sure that she gets them right. He has other jobs for Eva with equally precise instructions. She is to write a letter on behalf of a fictitious "Aunt Marie" to provide him with an excuse for skipping school on Sedan Day. He specifies the text:

> Dear Georg, you know that at my age I can't make the voyage to Frankfurt in one day, must travel in short stages, would like to stay in Weimar, which I want to see in any case, and since it is nearby and you have the day off because of Sedan I ask you, dear Georg, to assist me a little bit, as I am unfamiliar with Weimar. I arrive there at 10.45; Uncle tells me that you should be able to meet that train. I shall expect you then for certain and hope you won't leave me in the lurch, your loving Aunt Marie. P.S. If you can't make it, write immediately.

Eva is to copy this "touching plea of an aunt's heart that should melt the most hardened principal's resistance" and mail it back at a specified time, for "it must arrive neither too soon nor too late."

It was not the last time that Georg would specify the exact wording for letters that others were to submit on his behalf, though ostensibly on their own initiative. In his battles with the army during the war he would use a Reichstag deputy, a sympathetic historian from Danzig, his own wife, the old astronomer Wilhelm Förster, and even Albert Einstein in a similar way. It was best to leave nothing to chance.

Helpless old Aunt Marie served her purpose. On Sedan Day Georg went hiking in the Harz mountains, "paid a social call"—a discreet reference to the real object of the stratagem, which was to see a girlfriend—and returned on the night train, arriving in Gotha at 6:58 A.M. "What luck! Class started at seven. I was just in time to rush there, a trifle late perhaps. You see, I am making good use of my time." *De optimo temporis usu*!

The theater was his other passion, shared by Eva, who was so stage-struck that she talked of becoming an actress. Her worried parents had to enlist Georg's help in dissuading her. But Eva was allowed to come to Gotha to act in one of the amateur theatricals her brother directed. Georg also acted in his own productions, hence the elocution lessons. His only friend at the Ernestinum was Alex Moldenhauer, another theater buff; he wanted to quit school for the stage and eventually ran away to become an actor, borrowing a hundred marks for his escape from Georg. When Alex's brother Willy needed a libretto for an opera, Georg's text—in rhymed verse—brought compliments from Moldenhauer *père*, a critic with a jaundiced eye indeed. Georg was thoroughly familiar with both the classical and the contemporary theater; he could recite whole scenes from Karl Gutzkow's *Uriel Acosta*,[4] not to mention *Faust, Hamlet,* Schiller's *Don Karlos*, and *Nathan the Wise*. But the gods of his generation were Ibsen and Gerhart Hauptmann, and to see their plays he had to go to Berlin. This being possible only during vacations, and the theater at Gotha offering a very limited repertory, Georg made frequent trips to the nearby towns of Weimar and Erfurt.

The purpose of these excursions was not always strictly artistic. Sometimes the leading actress was more interesting than her role. Resplendent in his "bicycle costume," armed with a huge bouquet, Georg once pedaled to Erfurt to see Clementine von Winterstein (obviously a stage name) and bought an expensive box seat. Undeterred by the amused looks of the audience, he sat conspicuous in splendid isolation through the first act. During intermission he sent the flowers backstage with his card. To his delight, he was allowed to see the lady to her lodgings, "a little surprised that she came unescorted and lives by herself." It seems that he was rewarded for his pains, for "on the way back, although moon and stars were in hiding, my mood after a few bottles of champagne was such that I could have embraced the whole world—though I was none too happy when I succeeded in that experiment. Damn the pesky cobblestone that brought me to a pitiful fall! Arrived here at dawn."

Next he reported that he had run an old lady over with his new "veloci-pede," which he bought, against the express wish of his parents, for the exorbitant sum of five hundred marks, but "thank God, she isn't going to die, so spare me the sermon à la Lasswitz." The old lady was seriously injured, and Papa had to settle her claim. His parents had been shocked by the extravagance of the purchase in the first place. To afford it, "we would have to eat dry bread for months," Mama had written. "I don't know what you intend to do about it; we can't pay." An angry Papa had added: "See how you get out of this scrape!" He relented, as always, though he had to draw upon his savings. Apparently, he was moved by Georg's offer to use his own money or, rather, the money he had received from home to pay his membership dues to the Goethe Society. For Georg,

Fig. 10. Greetings from a friend on Georg's twentieth birthday, indicating his interests: drinking, dueling (the pistol), velocipede, painting, skating, gambling (the playing cards), bowling, and Kant and Homer.

the lover of books and a bit of a snob, this was a real sacrifice. Mama, too, was willing to forgive. "The bicycle will give you much pleasure. It is better than a heap of Goethe's works, but be careful!"

Being careful, of course, was not Georg's intention. Owning a bicycle served much the same purpose for a boy of his time as owning a sports car or a motorcycle would for the adolescent of a later generation: showing off a shiny piece of machinery, arousing the envy of one's peers and the admiration of the girls, and enjoying the sense of power that comes with speed. "Since I ride like a madman," he informed Eva, "my usual place is the ditch, though my instructor says I have a natural talent. Heaven knows what all I am supposed to have a natural talent for, but with all of them I don't seem to get any farther than ordinary mortals." (As so often in these letters, his boasts are tempered by a refreshingly ironical view of himself.)

Georg on his velocipede was indeed a menace. His next victim was a classmate's sister's favorite pug. Then he put his own life in jeopardy by racing a train to an unguarded crossing, cutting across the tracks seconds ahead of the locomotive, and causing the terrified engineer to pull the emergency brake. Proud to be the center of so much attention, he accompanied the train to the station, where he identified himself to the stationmaster. Papa, who had to pay the fine, thought it a stupid thing to do. Undaunted, Georg made plans to ride his bicycle all the way to Berlin, armed with his pistols in case of a nocturnal attack. Papa vetoed the project on both counts.

Although Papa called his bicycle costume tasteless and ridiculous, Georg decided to take a photograph of himself in front of his machine, surrounded by his other sports paraphernalia (including a pair of skis he made himself), and, for good measure, a dog he had somehow acquired. Given the cumbersome equipment of the time, it was a formidable undertaking, and it ended in disaster. He lugged the bicycle upstairs, darkened the window with black cloth, placed his reflector on top of a cabinet, and positioned himself and the dog in front of the camera, bulb in hand. But the animal would not hold still, and in the commotion the skis came crashing down, ripping the drapes off the window and overturning the tripod.

His next subject, a girl, was more cooperative than the dog, patiently waiting while Georg fussed with the magnesium lamp, which never went off. He complained to Eva: "The chemist had given me the wrong stuff. My giant reflector swept a bottle of arrack from the cabinet and I spilled kerosene all over myself while trying to fill my little red lamp in total darkness." Georg did not tell his sister that his subject had been a girl. The total darkness had served a purpose. Nine months later the poor thing reminded him of what she no longer considered an amusing or exciting incident. She had given birth to a little girl, but she had steadfastly shielded the father's identity from her irate parents, blaming a traveling salesman for her pregnancy. The heartless Georg returned this kindness with insinuations that he had not been the only one to enjoy her favors, a charge which she indignantly denied. "How can you ask who the father is? That is what has hurt me the most. Yes, I may have flirted with others, but the only one with whom I forgot myself was you." She recalled the preliminaries, just as Georg had described them to his sister. "Actually, it happened in your room the day you insisted on taking my picture and the magnesium bulb failed to go off, remember?" But then "we shared a time of happiness. No one shall ever know. I am deeply unhappy and want to die, but please write me once more." She did not die, but soon afterwards the baby did.

The girl was a petite bourgeoise, daughter of respectable parents; while she was socially far beneath a student from Ernestinum, she was not a "loose woman." There could have been no question of marriage. In the social climate of the times it was permissible for young gentlemen to satisfy their sexual urges with girls of the people without taking responsibility for the consequences. The line between the upper and middle classes on the one hand and the common folk on the other was sharply drawn. Young women of good family were generally unavailable for premarital sex, being expected to enter holy matrimony in a state of innocence or at least virginity. Lower-class girls were more accessible, some because they lived more natural and spontaneous lives, and some because a *Verhältnis*, an affair with a gentleman, carried certain benefits, tangible or otherwise, and some simply for love. But it was they who paid the price if something went wrong. These were the realities, accepted by everyone, even by the gentle Theodor Fontane, whose recent novel *Irrungen und Wirrungen* dealt with such matters in a contemporary setting. Georg had nothing to fear even if the girl had talked. His slur on her moral character was therefore entirely gratuitous, another sign of his utter lack of feeling for others.

Georg took his pleasure where he found it, and he did not have to look far. Nor did he have to limit himself to girls of inferior social status. Already irresistibly attractive to women of every class and age, he cared little whether he seduced a chambermaid or a well-brought-up young lady. He never passed through the stage of romantic idealization of the fair sex that was typical of the age. It was not the Eternal Feminine that attracted him, but the temporal, the carnal. His sexual appetite was enormous. All women were made for love, or at least for pleasure, all possessed bodies miraculously designed to still the insatiable hunger of the adolescent boy, and, for all he knew, all might be willing to do so.

It mattered little that girls, even the educated ones, were not his intellectual equals, were in fact generally rather silly creatures who gave themselves airs and talked about the most inane things. It was not for their conversation that he sought their company. The realm of the mind, as far as he was concerned, was clearly a male preserve, accessible to females— if at all—only as a reflection transmitted by a higher intelligence such as his own. What would they ever know of Plato and Aristotle, of Kant and Schopenhauer, of Karl Marx and Henry George, or, for that matter, of the real meaning of Ibsen and Tolstoy? But his knowledge of these mysteries served to impress the girls. Admiration by susceptible young females was something he appreciated and quickly recognized as a basic ingredient of his success, whether it was directed at his derring-do or at his intellect. They might not understand the ideas he tossed out, but they responded instinctively to the elementary masculine force behind them, perhaps more strongly than to the reckless juvenile feats with which he tried to impress them. Venturing out on the frozen wastes of the Oder, racing a train to a crossing, skipping classes for the sake of parading one's girl through town in broad daylight, even dueling with live ammunition—these were ways of showing off which the adolescent wisdom of the girls could see through and write off. But when Georg talked about a book or a play, about causality, psychology, or socialism, these young middle-class girls, accustomed to the blend of gaucheness and swagger of future Herr Doktors and Herr Leutnants sensed the fire of his personality and lowered their defenses, showing that intellect can be a potent weapon in the arsenal of seduction.

Georg possessed other weapons, of course—good looks, physical courage, boldness, and self-confidence. Soon he acquired an attribute which has ever been a most powerful stimulant to the imagination of virtuous females: a bad reputation. There was no lack of parental warnings. "Be careful in your dealings with Ella," Mama wrote. "We have no objections to talk and poetic exchanges, but you should avoid the wrong tone and stay out of trouble. I hope you are staying on the narrow path of decency. She will not be the only girl to imagine more than exists. You should develop a method."

Georg had a method, but it was not one that Mama would have approved. Papa was more realistic. "I believe you are already prone to sexual excesses," he wrote. "It is your duty to keep the house unsullied. You gave your word. It is just as irresponsible to let any old strumpet come to your room as it is to try to seduce the maid. You must make a promise not only to others but to yourself that you will reform, otherwise you will sink to the lowest level of morality. And think of the practical consequences!" It was good advice and, like all of Papa's admonitions, went unheeded. The incident to which Dr. Lewinstein referred—obviously not the first of its kind—was somehow hushed up, apparently with the approval of the principal, who had taken a liking to the most difficult but also most promising of his pupils, and Georg continued in his evil ways. He did learn to avoid scandals, however.

In the face of the young man's countless transgressions, it is easy to lose sight of the less spectacular process of intellectual maturation which took place during these turbulent years. Nicolai the scientist, the brilliant thinker and critic of the contemporary scene, did not appear on the stage like Minerva springing from the head of Jupiter. The foundations of his encyclopedic knowledge were laid at Gotha, though the stimulus came from within rather than from the school, which he continued to ignore as best he could. We know what kind of books he read, sitting up nights when he was not drinking, gambling, or whoring. His passion for the theater sprang from the same source. It was not only entertainment he sought but truth, the truth of Shakespeare, Schiller, and Ibsen, truth about human nature. At bottom he was already an intellectual, a believer in ideas, a worshiper of great minds.

Some of the letters to his sister show this side of him. Only someone who had seriously thought about the place of the individual in modern society could have written what he wrote her on her seventeenth birthday in 1892:

> You are now seventeen. I don't want you to change, though by all means improve yourself, perfecting but retaining your personality. There is nothing more beautiful than a fully realized individuality. Of course, this is often overrated and viewed from a purely aesthetic viewpoint, as by some writers who glorify the formation of a personality in conflict with the whole social order—and indeed every strong character excites our admiration—but from a moral viewpoint it lacks all foundation in today's world. I must point this out to you, for your self-sufficiency and your contempt for every kind of opposition or obstacle, while essential where your true self is at stake, must not be outwardly visible and must never be a mere matter of style. Believe me, who has passed through all this and makes himself pretend that he is above all such things and yet has been underneath and in the middle—for to be above one must have control, and that means both using them and submitting to them. Contradiction? But that's how it is.

Though the expression becomes garbled at the end, the meaning is clear and remarkable enough for an eighteen-year-old who publicly gave himself Byronesque airs: strive to develop your personality, but subordinate yourself to society in a world where everyone is dependent on everyone else.

Where Eva was concerned, Georg behaved responsibly. She was the only human being he truly loved, perhaps because she was like him in many ways, only gentler and more introspective. He was troubled by what he called her "remoteness" and earnestly tried to draw her out of herself. The effort was unnecessary. Eva had a large circle of friends, danced a great deal, acted in amateur theatricals, and went on the country drives Frau Elise loved to arrange for her own friends. Like Georg, she was a voracious reader. Ibsen, Tolstoy, and Turgenev were her idols. Though she was as much of an intellectual as a girl in the 1890s was allowed to be, she enjoyed life to the fullest. Still, her brother saw dangers ahead. He expressed his concern in criticizing one of her letters.

> You should write everything you think and feel, otherwise one senses the gaps and remains dissatisfied. But *that* you are not willing to do with your experiences, harmless as they are. Ninety-nine percent of them remain hidden in your bosom, and that is the worst, not by any means because your letters become less valuable, but because you yourself become less of a person and more unhappy. Mankind has become as one family, and one cannot escape this reality without taking on a burden. Look, my darling, this letter has become more serious than I intended, but I really think that in your remote manner there lies a danger for you. I cannot tell you in every detail what kind of danger it is, but you read Ibsen and perhaps love him. Just think what he would say about you. But that is what you don't understand yet. You don't see what is immoral in Ibsen's Nora and

Eina Ellida, only their noble and beautiful side, and that's what is so terribly pernicious. They too don't speak out, they pretend. Beware of admiring such people. But you do it only too readily, and for that reason you should not read Ibsen.

Whether or not Georg understood his sister, his analysis of Ibsen's feminine characters was perceptive and wholly original, the product of a mature mind.

Unfortunately he showed no such maturity in his own life. After four years at Gotha, within sight of the final examinations, he managed to get himself expelled once again. He was now twenty and far too old to conform to rules designed for younger boys, and he had refused to obey the command "lights out." When Dr. Rosenstock, his old enemy, insisted, he threw him down the stairs. "Too bad it had to happen like this," one of his "foster mothers" wrote after his sudden departure. Like every woman in whose house he had been a boarder, she liked the handsome, quick-witted boy. She was sorry that he was not accepted at nearby Eisenach. But Georg could not hope to be accepted anywhere within a radius of a hundred miles. Prussia was closed to him, and the fiasco should have been the end of any academic dream he had nurtured. His father had threatened often enough to make him go into trade. But whether the old man could not bring himself to disappoint his own hopes for his son or whether Georg's powers of persuasion once more carried the day, a last desperate effort was decided upon, probably through the intercession of his mother, a woman with many friends in educational circles. One of them, the principal of the gymnasium of the small Alsatian town of Hagenau, agreed to accept the troublemaker as a favor to Frau Elise.

For ordinary Germans to be sent to Alsace in those days was somewhat like being sent to Siberia, though it was the political rather than the physical climate that was hostile. The annexation of Alsace-Lorraine by Germany was resented by a population that had lived under French rule for more than two hundred years and thought of itself as part of the French nation. This resentment was kept alive by the clumsy way in which the Germans, disappointed by the reluctance of the Alsatians to rejoin the Fatherland and suspicious of sabotage and treason, administered the province. Alsace was given neither autonomy nor statehood, and, because of the rivalry between Prussia and Bavaria, it was not incorporated into either of those states. Rather, it was declared a *Reichsland*, a national preserve of second-class citizens. In Paris the statue representing the city of Strasbourg on the Place de la Concorde was draped in black, and the mourning was scarcely less intense among the Alsatians themselves.

It was this charged atmosphere that Georg entered. He was, of course, no ordinary German. On the principle that "the enemy of my enemy is my friend," he quickly became a lover of all things French. "Are you learning French, or is it considered unpatriotic?" his mother asked. The answer was yes on both counts: he threw himself into the language in part because it was considered unpatriotic. Chauvinism was running high on both sides of the Rhine. On the German side, France was widely regarded as a dangerous enemy plotting revenge and at the same time as a degenerate and wicked nation abhorrent to every decent German. There was no better way for a nonconformist like Georg, reared in a climate of hostility to Bismarck's Reich and expelled from more than one German school, to show his feelings than to embrace the French-Alsatian cause.

There was, of course, a positive side to his conversion. Georg was far too susceptible to ideas and style not to respond to French influences. France was a libertarian republic, not a near-absolute monarchy run along outmoded lines by a feudal class. The Rights of Man had been proclaimed here a century ago and were still respected. The Paris Commune of 1871, mourned by left-leaning German intellectuals like Georg's own mother, was a thing of recent memory. The great sweep of French literature had carried the ideas of Flaubert, Zola, and Renan across the frontier. French Impressionists had revolutionized painting, French fashions set the style, French politics were turbulent and exhilarating. Life itself—at least in Paris—was freer, more adapted to human desires and less to rigid codes of behavior, than anywhere else on the Continent. The same quality of life that drew Henry James's inhibited American characters to Paris appealed to Georg, and he would remain a francophile all his life.

His stay at Hagenau was brief and relatively peaceful. He had come for the sole purpose of meeting the requirements for graduation, and whether he was sobered by the knowledge that this was his last chance or whether he had truly matured, he behaved himself, studying hard and cultivating the friendship of the principal, a Dr. Heyer, and his daughter Magda. After only one semester he passed the *Abitur*, the final examinations, and was ready for the university at last. He was in his twenty-first year.

I have described these stormy beginnings in detail because they give many clues to the complex and contradictory personality of the man who would later challenge the German war machine, sacrificing a brilliant career as a scientist and member of the Establishment, and who did so in a needlessly offensive manner. Nicolai was driven by egomania as much as by principle, giving vent to a deep-seated hostility toward the country whose product he was and whose idealized image he nevertheless held sacred. At twenty-one he had not yet proved himself, and there was nothing to indicate an aptitude or even an interest in natural science or medicine. His bent seemed to be toward social philosophy, political history, literature, the theater. But he was clearly destined to play a role in human affairs, perhaps as a creative force, perhaps as a rebel, or perhaps as both.

His great intellectual gifts, in combination with his reckless courage and his aggressive instincts, would make him a formidable character. Virtually all the external influences which shaped that character were of a kind that would create severe stress, tension, and insecurity. His parents were too old and too rationalistic for the young boy, and also too embittered, standing as they did outside the fellowship of patriotic Germans that dominated the scene after 1870. Bismarck was a bitter taste in their mouths, the monarchy a cruel anachronism, the flag an abomination. The mother associated with Socialists, people whom the Kaiser had branded enemies of the state; the father silently disapproved. Georg absorbed all this from his earliest days. With whom could he identify? Was he even a German, Georg Lewinstein, son of a Jewish father who has abandoned the faith of *his* fathers? Must he, could he, defend himself against anti-Semitic provocations?

Did anybody love him? His parents preached to him, sent him away to boarding school, rejected him (or so he must have perceived it). He rebelled, partly by refusing to study, partly by overt acts of disobedience and violence. He was expelled again and again, branded as an undesirable in his native Prussia, rejected by the system as well as by the family. He sought other outlets, in sports, in manual skills, one of them valued by parents who equated worth with academic education. He read, and was told that he was too young to understand what he read. Not surprisingly, he had few, if any, friends. He became arrogant, domineering, patronizing, indifferent. Very early he discovered his power over women, a power at once mental and physical. He used it to satisfy his sexual urge and to dominate, not to communicate with human beings. Emotionally he was an empty shell, selfish, indifferent, cruel, but his mind was superb and led him into higher regions. He could not love, but he could worship the spirit. He would come to despise human beings while embracing the ideal of humanity.

NOTES

1. A notebook used by Nicolai during his travels in Russia in 1931 contains two lists of his sexual conquests, one alphabetical, the other chronological. There are some 106 names, with brief notations for each, neatly cataloguing the person and the circumstances involved.

2. Quoted from the manuscript of Nicolai's unpublished autobiographical novel, *Herr der Erde* (1928).

3. Lasswitz was appointed to the faculty of the Ernestinum by the duke of Saxe-Gotha in 1876. He is mentioned in *Herr der Erde*, and the Nicolai estate has letters from him to his pupil. His famous book *Auf zwei Planeten* first appeared in 1897 and went through many editions. (The original German version was reissued in Frankfurt, with a preface by Wernher von Braun, in 1969.) Though its success was based on its imaginative science fiction, its emphasis was on social and cultural criticism, as indicated by the subtitle, "A Utopian Novel."

4. *Uriel Acosta* portrays the struggle of Spinoza's teacher against the rigid orthodoxy of the Jewish community of Amsterdam, a *Toleranzdrama* in the tradition of *Nathan the Wise*. Until the advent of Hitler it was a standard in the German theatrical repertory.

6. Unconditional Satisfaction

With the graduation certificate at last in his pocket, Georg announced his decision to study medicine. The choice must have come as a surprise to his parents, and perhaps to the young man himself, for his interests during the formative years at Gotha had seemed to lie wholly in the realm of the humanities and social sciences. The Ernestinum had offered little in the way of natural science, and the reading he had done on his own had given no hint of a bent in that direction. Papa was probably relieved that the *enfant terrible* with the penchant for Kant, socialism, and sex was choosing a solid career, even if it meant supporting him for another four or five years. But what were Georg's own motives? He was too egocentric, too lacking in humility and compassion, to be prompted by a burning desire to allay the sufferings of his fellow men. He was also too much of an intellectual to be swayed by the material rewards of a medical career, though he was by no means averse to them when they were to be had.

What attracted him to medicine was, no doubt, its scientific side, the challenge of exploring uncharted territory. Medicine was a frontier that attracted the best minds, much as physics would draw the academic elite of the atomic age. The turn of the century was a time of discovery and excitement, of almost unlimited opportunities for those who knew how to use the new tools of research. It was an age when every effort was likely to pay off; one had only to dig diligently in order to find gold. But what of Georg's intellectual life? What of Kant and Goethe, Thomas More and Schopenhauer, what of socialism, what of the theater? For him these would have been meaningless questions. The gulf between science and the humanities was not yet as wide as it would become; scholars on both sides still thought of themselves as belonging to the same indivisible Republic of Letters. The growing demand for specialized knowledge was narrowing the horizon of the average medical student, but a far-ranging mind like Georg's could still encompass the two cultures. He would not have felt that in becoming a scientist he was cutting himself off from the fellowship of humanists.

The first order of business was selecting the locale. German universities being state institutions with uniform standards, the student who could afford it could move freely from place to place until it was time to settle down. For the first semester or two, his choice would depend less on academic excellence than on the amenities a school had to offer. Georg chose Königsberg, his mother's home town. Its university, Kant's alma mater, boasted a splendid medical faculty. The town was handsome and comfortable, its attractiveness enhanced by the proximity of the Baltic and the moors and forests of East Prussia. It was not a student town like Heidelberg or Göttingen, where the undergraduate was the cock of the walk, but life would be less expensive there, and Georg could board with the Kunzes, his maternal relatives. For his economy-minded father, this was no doubt the deciding factor, and Georg went along. He seems to have been fond of his Prussian cousins, solid, sensible, hospitable people who—for once—did not bring out his quarrelsome nature. One attraction of life with the Kunzes was the Bärenapotheke, the "Pharmacy at the Sign of the Bear," owned by the elder Kunze and located on the ground floor of the family dwelling. Here the young medical student spent hours browsing among the shelves; observing; helping customers as they came in with their prescriptions, complaints, and small talk; learning something about the pharmacopoeia; trying his hand at grinding powders with mortar and pestle; and measuring, weighing, and mixing liquids. It was a useful experience for a future doctor and an idyllic interlude in an old-fashioned setting.

Another attraction was Georg's cousin Elisabeth, a handsome, intelligent girl his own age. The relationship seems to have evolved into a brief love affair, but that in turn evolved into a life-long friendship, one that was to have a decisive influence on the girl's future.[1] It was the first of many similar relationships in which he was both lover and teacher. Though incapable of love in the sense of surrendering himself, Georg was not insensitive to the spiritual needs of women. He always saw himself as the dominant male, but in that role it was his gift to stimulate and fertilize the feminine mind. His conquests were not complete if they did not include the realm of the intellect. Perhaps he tried subconsciously to prove himself superior to his intellectual mother, the one woman he had never been able to impress. Be that as it may, he treated Elisabeth as a disadvantaged equal who needed his help, and indeed she was underprivileged when it came to education, just as his mother had been, for the universities were still virtually closed to women. Georg opened the doors to the world of ideas for her, and he did so without being patronizing. We have her testimony in a letter written almost twenty years later, when she had at last gained admission to the university. "I may be unfair to my alma mater, but everywhere I see connections between the things I hear or read and the things I learned from you, whether it be in English, as with *Othello* or other Shakespeare plays, or in German, as with the "Prometheus" fragment [of Goethe], or in church history, as when Saint Francis is being discussed." The instruction had taken place on walks or picnics, on boat or sleigh rides, at dances, at the theater, or during quiet evenings at home. Granted that this was an advantage over classroom conditions, the young medical student had achieved a success that professional educators might well envy. Clearly he had not abandoned the humanities.

But as always, his behavior was full of contradictions. The intellectual who acted as mentor to a sensitive girl was capable of crude antics of the kind one might expect from an ordinary medical student who tries to convince the world that he is tough and cynical, inured to the horrors of the anatomical theater and able to look at death with the cold eye of the scientist. Drinking from a skull was a typical manifestation of this mentality. Georg went a step farther: he made himself a wallet from the skin of a cadaver. (Elisabeth's reaction to this blend of bravado and bad taste is not recorded.)

Shakespeare, Goethe, and Saint Francis notwithstanding, Georg plunged into fraternity life with gusto. Here was a setting in which many of the things he had done earlier in defiance of school regulations and parental admonitions were seen not only as legitimate but as praiseworthy. He was invited to beer-drinking sessions, asked to observe saber practice, initiated into the rituals and the jargon of the brotherhoods, and wooed in many gratifying ways. In Königsberg, a city with a strong tradition of liberalism, his Jewish name was no obstacle.[2]

When he returned to Berlin in the spring of 1895 to continue his studies, he promptly joined a local fraternity known as Freie Wissenschaftliche Vereinigung (Association for a Free Science), or FWV.[3] Soon he was deeply involved in FWV affairs. Fraternity life was not merely a matter of good fellowship: it was a battleground of student politics where serious clashes were common events. Brilliant, quick-thinking, and aggressive, Georg was a natural leader in this setting. The fraternities represented a peculiarly Teutonic form of institutionalized *machismo*, the outlet for the pent-up energies of a generation whose political ambitions had been thwarted when Bismarck forcibly united the nation and destroyed the Liberal opposition. What was left to fight for? The universities were no longer hotbeds of rebellion, but on the contrary obedient defenders of the state, in return for its generous support and protection. Who would bite the hand that feeds him? All that remained of what had once been a struggle for academic and political freedom was the ceremonial claptrap. The fraternity offered a setting in which young males could act out their aggressions, cultivate their vanity, indulge their clannish instincts and prejudices, and flaunt their archaic notions of honor. Each had its colors, its motto, its ornamental initials, and its special salutation. The fraternity man in full regalia for ceremonial occasions was a wonder to behold, with his embroidered cap and gold-trimmed velvet jacket, his multicolored sash, snow-white breeches and shiny knee boots, standing stiffly at attention, his gloved hand resting on the pommel of his dress sword.

Each fraternity had its regular meeting place, usually a tavern, where the brothers sang the traditional student songs, argued about university politics, plotted alliances and moves against rival factions, and above all consumed huge quantities of beer. Beer was the lifeblood of the student movement. Drinking was a complicated ritual, requiring constant attention and a large capacity. Freshmen were obliged to drink themselves sick at the whim of the seniors. There was "beer honor" and there were "beer scandals," duels in which beer was the weapon and the object was to drink one another under the table. Drinking before the command was given, spilling beer, or leaving a few drops in the bottom of one's glass were crimes for which there were fixed penalties. All this childishness was codified in a quasi-official *Bier Comment*, a booklet the newcomer did well to memorize at once. It was forced gaiety, frequently interrupted by hiccups and trips to the men's room to empty bladders or stomachs, but compliance was a matter of honor.

Another matter of honor was bravery on the dueling floor. The *Mensur* was a scheduled ordeal which every member of a *schlagende Verbindung* ("dueling fraternity") had to undergo. The opponents used naked sabers but no protective masks. To flinch was to betray cowardice. Cuts were sewn up in such a way as to leave the most conspicuous scars possible, which were coveted symbols of manliness. Sabers were also used in "heavy" duels in which insults were settled. Pistol duels, though long since outlawed, were still occasionally fought, and as recently as 1888 an FWVer had been killed in such an encounter. Fraternity men were a touchy lot, always ready to take offense and forever embroiled in petty quarrels that could be blown up into matters of honor. Challenges were common and more likely to be accepted than not, for to apologize was to show weakness. The man who chose to face the consequences would in due course receive a formal visit by his adversary's second to arrange time and place for giving "satisfaction," provided he was *satisfaktionsfähig* (acceptable as an honorable opponent). Whether he was and whether the challenge was appropriate were matters for a court of honor to settle. Georg, who had been through a duel at fourteen, saw nothing objectionable in these tribal customs.

The fraternities, though representing only a minority of the student body, dominated the academic scene. While generally patriotic to the point of chauvinism and consciously or subconsciously anti-Semitic, they were for the most part nonpolitical. The exception was the Verein deutscher Studenten (V. d. St.), a hate group dedicated to the elimination of all Jewish students from German universities. (Strangely enough, anti-Semitism did not fall under the government's definition of political matters, and the V. d. St. was not only allowed to flourish but at its founding received a congratulatory message from Bismarck, who was not anti-Semitic himself.)

Unorganized or "free" students lacked all representation in university affairs—not that it mattered much. The only function in which students were allowed a voice in Prussian universities was the management of the *Lesehallen*, or reading rooms. At Berlin the Lesehallen elections therefore assumed a large symbolic meaning and were hotly contested. Free students were those who could not afford the expense of belonging to a fraternity, who for various reasons chose not to join, or who were not wanted—Jews, baptized or not, and a sprinkling of socialists, teetotalers, and females.

The FWV was formed in 1881, a year after the V. d. St., for the express purpose of combating the latter's raucous and often violent anti-Semitism. Its founder, Max Spangenberg, and many of its early members had been Gentiles, old-time Liberals repelled by the barbarism of a movement bent on bringing intolerance into the hitherto peaceful and outwardly united student body. They wanted to restore the tradition of tolerance, humanitarianism, and idealism that had culminated in the revolution their fathers had made in 1848. Among the FWV's honorary members were two of the greatest representatives of that tradition, the historian Theodor Mommsen and the pathologist Rudolf Virchow, both great scholars, Liberals of the old school, and former parliamentarians. "Anti-Semitism is the signature of the times," Virchow had said in his inaugural address (duly reprinted in the FWV newsletter) as rector of the University of Berlin. Mommsen had publicly castigated Treitschke, the apostle of the new nationalism, for his strident anti-Semitism.

The FWV also aimed at promoting the scientific and social interests of its members by sponsoring lectures and debates, as well as outings and dances. Its name, so different from the Latinized tribal names of most fraternities, such as "Germania," "Borussia," "Normannia," and the like was a program in itself. The FWV aimed at a general education of equal interest to future doctors, lawyers, teachers, and engineers. The lectures dealt with such varied topics as "Ancient Mexican Civilization," "Platonic and Early Christian Communism Compared with Modern Socialism," "Schopenhauer," "Social Self-Help," "Suicide," "Prostitution," "Civil Marriage," "The Nature of Honor," and "Heredity." It was a program of high intellectual content for a fraternity, equaled only by that of Sozial-wissenschaftlicher Verein, a group formed for the study of social problems. That group, however, had been denied a charter, for to the authorities the very words "social" and "sociology" smacked of socialism, and that *was* politics. In the words of Herr Pfleiderer, a theologian who was rector at the time, "students should be content with cultivating love of fatherland and idealism, and stay away from social and political questions," otherwise dilettantism would become rampant. In other words, academic youth, the future leaders of the nation, should remain ignorant of public business, which the government alone was competent to handle.

The FWV had narrowly escaped the fate of the would-be social scientists. The police, alerted by a well-informed V. d. St., had dissolved the founders' meeting on the grounds that it was "political." Only the quick thinking of Max Spangenberg saved the day. He raced to the rector's office and persuaded him to approve the charter before he got wind of the police action. Thereafter the FWV had been careful to stay out of politics, as the Prussian government understood the word. But it was militant, the lofty character of its educational program notwithstanding, and the enemy was the V. d. St. and its anti-semitic propaganda. The strategy was to oppose it on every front—in the Lesehallen elections, in public debates, in a perpetual war of handbills, by demanding equal representation at official ceremonies, and by making common cause with more tolerant fraternities whenever possible. Informers infiltrated the opposing camps, one group outbid the other for desirable meeting halls on such special occasions as the Kaiser's birthday, and the masthead of the FWV newsletter carried the warning "Strictly Confidential!" It was war. The war had turned bloody in 1888, when a member of the V. d. St., one Eichler, challenged FWV brother Blum for calling anti-Semitism a disgrace to the student body. Blum, a Jew, accepted and was fatally wounded. Eichler, son of a Protestant minister, was tried before a jury and sentenced to two years imprisonment in a fortress—the minimum for the crime and a more honorable penalty than an ordinary jail term—but the authorities were upset and threatened to dissolve both fraternities.

Blum need not have died had not the FWV adopted a policy of "unconditional satisfaction." In truth, dueling went against the innermost convictions of most FWVers, and many resigned in protest, but the rest felt that they could not afford the stigma of cowardice. The FWV having become predominantly Jewish (inevitably Jews and people like Georg Lewinstein, who were lumped with the Jews because of their names, gravitated toward the last bastion of tolerance, while the number of Gentiles dwindled as it became known as "that Jewish fraternity"), they were determined to prove themselves every bit as brave and sensitive in matters of honor as their Teutonic brethren. They even debated whether the FWV should maintain its own stock of weapons, but this resolution was decisively defeated. They chose instead to rely on the arsenal of the Sprevia, an all-Jewish fraternity whose posture was even more militant.

Born as they were of rejection and intolerance, these organizations of untouchables did their utmost to imitate their tormentors. As so often happens to those who fight fire with fire, they had become indistinguishable from their enemies and thereby showed that they possessed physical courage but not the courage of their convictions. They would not rely on moral and intellectual weapons (although, to be fair, to do so would have been ineffectual in the prevailing climate). The FWV needed the respect of the other fraternities for its missionary work among the heathen. It could get that respect only by displaying the kind of courage that the others understood. Its members thought of themselves as Germans among Germans, students among students. Theirs was the tragedy of a century of assimilation that ended with Hitler's Holocaust.

The assimilation was complete: the FWVers had their own Kneipen, swilling beer with the best of them in keeping with all the rules of beer honor. They had their colors, blue (for fidelity), red (for liberty), and white (for truth); their song and their motto, "Unity and Right and Honor," were taken straight from "Deutschland über Alles," the old battle cry of the Liberals that had become the national anthem. They too sent delegates in full regalia to academic ceremonies and funerals, celebrated the anniversary of the founding of the Reich, and toasted the Kaiser on his birthday. And, of course, they had their regular saber practice, for it would never do to cut a poor figure on the dueling floor, and their own court of honor.

This, then, was the fraternity Georg Lewinstein joined at twenty-one. It reflected and magnified the split in his own personality, reaching out in one direction toward high intellectual ideals and plunging with gusto in the opposite direction into noisy brawls and childish rituals. It intensified rather than allayed the identity crisis that beset him, for like him it had no choice but to be German without being accepted as such.

Georg quickly established himself as a leader in its affairs. In June 1895, the newsletter carried the announcement of his membership; by November he was on the executive committee; by December he had been elected president; and by January he was the FWV representative for the Lesehalle, holding the exposed position that had proved fatal to Blum. It was Georg Lewinstein who proposed the toast "for Kaiser and Reich" on the emperor's birthday that year.

To toast the Kaiser was a strange thing for the son of an old-line democrat and a socialist mother to do. Perhaps the newly elected president was merely indulging his vanity. He soon remedied the lapse by failing to show up for the FWV's celebration of the twenty-fifth anniversary of Bismarck's Reich. The absence of the chief officer on such an important occasion so embarrassed his fraternity brothers that they voted then and there to censure him, whereupon he submitted his resignation. This was not what they had expected. Unpredictable and irascible as he was, they admired and needed him. The very next day in extraordinary session they explained their vote: Brother Lewinstein had every right to stay away from a celebration that offended his principles. Not for his absence had they censured him, only for failing to appoint a substitute. Georg relented and graciously allowed them to reelect him on the spot. For the time being his leadership was unchallenged.

The business that next faced the president was the threatened defection of the FWV affiliate in Heidelberg, founded by the Berliners four years earlier in hopes that it would be the first of many to spread the gospel of tolerance far and wide. But the Heidelbergers had gone their own way. In the more liberal climate prevailing in the state of Baden, anti-Semitism was not an overriding issue. Unlike the parent fraternity, where Jews far outnumbered Gentiles, the FWV of Heidelberg had maintained a reasonable balance between Christians and Jews. Feeling no pressure, it was no longer militant, nor was it willing to bear the stigma of militancy attached to the Berlin FWV.

The Heidelbergers had approached the matter gingerly, suggesting merely that the affiliation should be optional for each member instead of compulsory for all. When Berlin played deaf, the suggestion grew into a demand, but the reasons for the demand were not given. It was the turn of the now thoroughly suspicious Berliners to demand an explanation. One Otto Driesen finally let the cat out of the bag. The Berlin FWV was almost 100 percent Jewish, he wrote in a twenty-seven page letter to Georg, whereas Heidelberg had one-third Gentiles. In Heidelberg, as in every German university, prejudice against the Berlin FWV was growing. "They say in Munich, 'FWV—that's the Jewish fraternity that makes so much noise at the Lesehallen elections.'" The proctor at Heidelberg was reported to fear unrest if not outright scandal from a fraternity that was tied to the notorious FWV of Berlin, and to doubt that the local affiliate was not also "progressive, socialist, or in any way political."

The Berliners felt betrayed. Their offspring was turning against them, or at least deserting their cause. Swallowing their pride, they made one last desperate effort to keep the errant sheep in the fold. This was not a trivial student quarrel: the idea of a nationwide student movement for tolerance was at stake. Letters were written, representatives were sent to Heidelberg, and the alumni were asked to mediate, but all in vain. In the end Georg, who as president had maintained a statesmanlike posture throughout, wrote a stiff note, and the affiliation was formally dissolved, with much bitterness on both sides. In their anger the Berliners passed a resolution calling for the expulsion of any brother who maintained friendly relations with the apostates, a resolution hotly debated and vetoed by

Georg, whose best friend and future brother-in-law, Edwin Blos, was a Heidelberg alumnus. But the dream of a broad movement for tolerance, spreading from university to university, was dead.

For Georg the lesson was clear. He stood and would continue to stand for tolerance and reason, but if tolerant and reasonable people, many of them Jews themselves, abandoned the struggle because of general anti-Semitic prejudice, then Jews and bearers of Jewish names could not be effective standard-bearers. For the son of a baptized father and a Gentile mother, "Lewinstein" was nothing but an obstacle and a burden. It was at this time that he decided to change his name.

It is important to understand his motives. Not being a Jew and having no emotional ties to Judaism, he was not an apostate. He was shedding a label that had no meaning for him, an inconvenience at best and an albatross around his neck at worst. Henceforth he would fight his battles without having to defend that label. His record had proved that he had the courage of his convictions where convictions were at issue. The man who later sacrificed everything for his ideals was not a crass opportunist in his youth, nor was he so regarded by his family or his friends. He obtained the express consent of his father, that obstinate man of principle; he remained a member in good standing of the FWV; and it seems that his fraternity brothers did not lose their respect for him. His mother later drily recorded in her memoirs: "Georg found his paternal name inconvenient." It was she who suggested Nicolai, after her relative Otto Nicolai. It was no doubt because the composer of *The Merry Wives of Windsor* was the only famous member of the family that she made the suggestion, rather than because of any special affinity for music on Georg's part; one of the few gifts he lacked was a musical ear. At any rate, Georg readily agreed. All he wanted was a new identity. The name, with its faintly exotic Russian sound, suited him perfectly. However, to change one's name without changing one's environment is awkward. Georg solved the problem by going abroad during the winter of 1896–97 and returning in the spring as Georg Friedrich Nicolai. As such he resumed his studies in Berlin, as such he was reinstated in the FWV, and as such he would fight his battles.

Where had he been in the meantime? In Paris, of course, the Paris of Zola and Sarah Bernhardt, the capital of republican France and in his eyes the true capital of the West, the center of Europe, the center of freedom, of pleasure, of the modern age. France was having her own wave of anti-Semitism just then, but it had not crested. Dreyfus was a prisoner on Devil's Island, but as far as the public knew he was there as a convicted traitor, not as a Jew. The army's covert anti-Semitism had not yet surfaced as the cause of the miscarriage of justice that would tear the nation apart. Paris was calm, beautiful, and joyous, a paradise for the senses and a beacon for the spirit. That in any case was Georg's view, though few Germans of his generation shared it. To them, France was the hereditary enemy and Paris was a wicked city. The French were unreliable, temperamental, and undisciplined. Their food and wine were good, but they drank absinthe and had abominable morals. The politics of their parliamentary republic defied understanding. Their music lacked the vigor of German music; their art was devoted to such unheroic subjects as still lifes, ballerinas, and picnics in the country; their science was declining; their sense of order and authority had atrophied since the days of the great Napoleon. To study in Paris was unworthy of a German student.

For Georg, most of France's alleged vices were virtues. "I immediately felt at home on this pavement," he wrote to Eva soon after his arrival in October 1896.[4] He took a small apartment on the Left Bank at 142 rue du Bac, and decorated it with a scroll of the "Marseillaise," posters of Sarah Bernhardt, maps of Paris, theater programs, wine bottles, knickknacks and flowers. "The most pleasant disorder reigns all around me, but it is— untranslatable in French—*gemütlich*." He perfected his French and soon was writing his letters to Eva in that language. Arriving at night, he stepped from the station into brilliantly illuminated streets teeming with people who were celebrating the visit of France's new ally, the tsar of Russia. The Parisians were giving Nicholas and Alexandra a tumultuous welcome, and Georg was swept up in the general delirium. "These are not people who—like ours—allow themselves to be told where they may go, where they may work, how to amuse themselves and how to vote," he wrote to Eva.

> In my first moment on French soil, at the railroad station, instead of the familiar "It is forbidden to cross the tracks," I read "Les voya-geurs sont priés . . . ," and that is no mere formula. Of course there are rules and prohibitions, but that police tutelage which makes a nation so petty and un-self-reliant is absent here. But then, this people has learned to govern itself; there still exists here a collective will and a collective impulse that creates its own order without much effort.

He watched the people of the quartier arrive at the local square and, find-ing the illumination inadequate, rush off to raid another neighborhood for wreaths and Japanese lanterns. "The police watched peaceably, so unlike German order."

Georg roamed the streets, went to the races, danced at Bullier's *bal des étudiants*, and visited shops, factories, and hospitals. He attended political gatherings, including one from which he was expelled as a "sale Prussien" ("dirty Prussian") and another in which the socialist orator, in the excite-ment of predicting the downfall of capitalism, smashed the table and was rewarded by deafening applause. "I like the intensity of French politics, but not the result," he commented cryptically. He made contact with so-cialist students and wrote reports on their doings for a Belgian socialist student newspaper. Did he see himself as a successor to Heine or Karl Marx in Paris? Probably not, for politics was only a spectacle for him there. Such political ideas as he did absorb were Fourierist and Proudhon-ian and no doubt shaped his later critical attitude toward Marxism.

French medicine fascinated him. "Though I came here only to spend my energies in the delights of Paradise, to live with joy in my heart and in my flesh," as he confided to Eva, he went faithfully to the Salpétrière four times a week to hear the successor of the great Charcot lecture on psy-chiatry.

> The amphitheater is old, badly lit, and uncomfortable, but it always reminds us of the man who first demonstrated here the mysteries of an unknown science. It takes me an hour to walk here. There being no check at the entrance, the public is very mixed, for these long causeries about the intimate recesses of the soul attract not only first-rate physicians but artists as well, actors and painters who come to see the hallucinators and witness the searing cries of ecstasy and the delirious harangues from which they derive inspiration for their art.

The description evokes a scene by Daumier, with gaslights bathing the tortured features of the possessed in the pit, shadows from above softening the sharp profiles of the actors on the benches. Ten years earlier, Sigmund Freud sat in this amphitheater watching Charcot himself banish the terrors of hysteria with his hypnotic commands. For him it had been a revelation, the opening of a gate leading to the dark recesses of the subconscious mind. The young Nicolai saw the demonstrations mainly as theater, his reverence for Charcot notwithstanding. Some day he would write a scorching critique of psychoanalysis, rejecting it as "unscientific," no matter how brilliant some of Freud's insights might be.[5] In his rationalist universe there would be no room for the soul.

French medicine in general was much to Georg's liking. "It is a pleasure to watch a French professor at the bedside," he reported.

> He chats casually with his assistants and with the patient, he jokes and laughs, and all chime in gaily. If one didn't know that it is a matter of life and death one might think one were at a soirée, all the more because everyone is immaculately attired—especially the professor, who (a bit of coquetry to my way of thinking) wears the rosette of the Legion of Honor in his buttonhole. Only when he bends down to examine the patient does his face turn serious, and one realizes from his anxious, searching expression that here too on these wards young doctors are taught a science built on love of humanity and devotion to work, that in the great medical men of France the same powerful urge to help and to understand is at work as elsewhere.

"Elsewhere" meant the German clinics, with their more formal atmosphere. At this stage Georg was given to ready generalizations, and his enchantment with all things French mirrored his rebellion against all things German.

His interest in French medicine, however, was not allowed to interfere with the "delights of Paradise." He went to Monte Carlo, where he was lucky at the roulette tables, returning with what an envious friend called a small fortune. His knowledge of both the language and the French way of life increased by leaps and bounds, mainly because within the remarkably short span of three weeks after his arrival a young woman named Emilie moved into his apartment at 142 rue du Bac. Life took on the quality of *La Bohème*, except that this Rodolfo was not poor and his Mimi, far from being a consumptive, was a robust young woman who taught him the art of cooking as well as the art of love. There were little improvised dinners at the apartment where the guests sat on pillows or horizontally placed nightstands and sang Provençal songs, before moving on to a café at midnight.[6] For the first time in his life Georg was totally happy, finding his mind and his senses in harmony with his environment. "Free at last from restraints," he wrote to a friend at home. "I never noticed that you were much inhibited in Berlin," the friend replied, "or that you suffered under the 'harsh discipline' of your parents." But it was a matter of attitude. At home Georg was in a constant state of rebellion. Here in Paris, for the first and perhaps only time, he was not swimming against the stream. For a time he seriously considered staying in France for good. He returned home a confirmed francophile, and his attitude toward the war of 1914 was profoundly influenced by his Parisian experience.

But he put that experience behind him, like a too beautiful dream that has nothing to do with reality. It is not the fact that he returned to Berlin that is surprising but the fact that on his return Georg Friedrich Nicolai took up the same life he had left behind as Georg Lewinstein. Resuming the presidency of the FWV, he allowed himself to be drawn again into endless petty student quarrels: who had insulted whom by refusing to shake hands, who had slapped whose face first, who was or was not *satisfaktionsfähig*, which court of honor was competent to pass on what grievances, which fraternity was the proper keeper of weapons for whose duel? Was Brother Wolfson behaving correctly or not in refusing satisfaction to Herr Köhler, who had insulted—shades of the martyred Brother Blum—not him personally but the editorial board of the socialist students' magazine, of which Wolfson was a member? Was Herr K. to be believed when he claimed that he had challenged Herr W. only in order to bring the matter before a court of honor? Could an FWV court of honor settle a dispute involving a member of another fraternity, or was a mixed court called for?

Brother Nicolai, the free spirit from the Left Bank, not only took this nonsense seriously but seemed to relish it. The thinker about society and socialism, the admirer of Charcot, the bohemian and lover of Emilie enjoyed his power in the fossilized world of the fraternities. He spent much time arbitrating between quarreling brothers, serving as go-between in disputes with other fraternities or as second in "heavy" duels, presiding over courts of honor, and exchanging stiff formal notes with challengers. He also fought his own duels, losing quantities of blood and acquiring conspicuous scars, much to the disgust of his Parisian friends. "You have too much *esprit* to pander to these barbaric customs which the civilized world disapproves," a young publisher names Dujol scolded him. "One does belong first to one's country, whose customs often have the force of law, but you, innovator, apostle of intellectual and social renewal, you owe it to your cause to set an example. You are brave and never *reculez l'épée à la main*" (the phrase conjures up a dashing Cyrano defending Roxane's honor, rather than a saber-wielding fraternity man on the dueling floor), "but it is braver still to spurn certain obsolete customs and to disdain *les appréciations rétrogrades de la société routinière*" ("the backward attitudes of an indifferent society"). The contrast between this glimpse of the young Nicolai in Paris as the prophet of a new age and the role he resumed in Berlin as voluntary prisoner of the arachaic system he had just escaped is tantalizing. His identity crisis was not yet resolved, only deferred. He had succeeded in becoming a German and was acting out his Germanness at the very moment when he was about to become a European.

Meanwhile, *Candidatus medicinae* Nicolai was a man to be reckoned with in student affairs, much admired for his forthrightness and bravery and acquiring a reputation for fairness that extended beyond his own fraternity. With his powers of persuasion he was able to bring about reconciliations between the bitterest enemies and avert needless bloodshed. "After the court of honor over which you presided I consider you honorable and impartial," an engineering student named Zinn wrote him. "Only as the result of your persuasion did I shake hands with Wolfson, though the affair has probably ruined my good name beyond repair." It was a quarrel with his own fraternity that put an end to Georg's role as an arbiter and ultimately led to his departure from Berlin. Once again he found himself repudiated by his brothers for taking a more radical stand on a political issue than they would abide, but this time the breach was beyond repair. The fracas was triggered by what should have been a happy occasion, the university's celebration of Theodor Mommsen's eightieth birthday. Revered as a scholar by all and as a Liberal by the dwindling minority of democratic Germans, Mommsen was an honorary member and patron saint of the FWV. His jubilee on 30 November 1897 was the fraternity's day of glory. Elaborate preparations were made for the ceremony in the great hall of the university. Rector, faculty, and student delegations appeared in full regalia. As president, Nicolai delivered the eulogy on behalf of the fraternity that could claim the great man as its own.

It was a task to Georg's liking, for at heart he was a hero-worshipper, and Mommsen was a hero he could worship with a free heart. He was the foremost living historian of a country that honored its historians, an innovator who had broken new ground in many areas of historical scholarship, a brilliant yet totally honest writer dedicated to the defense of human rights. Mommsen the revolutionary of 1848 had sacrificed more than one position for the sake of his liberal convictions; the sheer weight of his accomplishments had finally overcome official hostility, and he was given a chair at the University of Berlin. Mommsen the man of action was for many years a member of the Prussian Diet and later of the Reichstag; he refused to make peace with the triumphant Bismarck of 1866 and stood up to Bismarck himself in 1882, calling the chancellor's tariff policy a fraud. As a result, he stood trial for slander and won his case against Europe's most powerful man. Mommsen the leader in the fight against anti-Semitism and bigotry had publicly castigated Treitschke as the most popular bigot of academia. In short, Mommsen was the embodiment of that ideal Germany which the young Nicolai believed in and which the author of *The Biology of War* would defend against the successors of Bismarck and Treitschke.

We can imagine the young man at the rostrum, handsome, self-assured, proud to be the spokesman for liberal youth, speaking with the fire of conviction. There is no record of the text of his speech, but we can surmise its tenor from the events that followed. Whether he had planned to seize the golden moment or whether he was carried away by his emotions, he evidently shocked the audience with his republican sentiments. The Mommsen he eulogized was not merely the illustrious author of the *Roman History* but the scholar who had stepped from the ivory tower into the political arena, a living model of *Zivilcourage* and integrity, Bismarck's adversary and still, at eighty, a champion of democracy. The speech was not pleasing to official ears. The rector, Gustav von Schmoller, a political economist with—for the times—relatively liberal views,[7] professed to be offended and demanded an apology from the FWV for the objectionable remarks of its president.

The fraternity, perhaps no less shocked and certainly no less surprised, hastened to comply, convinced that once more its existence was at stake. Without consulting Georg, a delegation called the rector and convinced him that the FWV did not share the radical opinions of its president, and that, in fact, it had no political opinions at all. Schmoller was easily pacified. His personal reaction to the speech had been less negative than the official position he had to take as rector of a Prussian university (that at least was the impression he conveyed to Georg's mother, unaware that Frau Lewinstein, an old acquaintance, took a special interest in a student named Nicolai). As far as the university was concerned, the incident was closed with the FWV's apology.

For Georg, the incident was far from closed. Not without justice, he considered the apology an act of betrayal. "I am told," he wrote stiffly,

> that someone had apologized in the name of the FWV to His Magnificence Herr Schmoller for the speech I gave at the celebration. I take the liberty of duly inquiring whether this information corresponds to the facts and if so, whether the person in question acted on behalf of, or with the subsequent approval of, the fraternity. Such action—for the fraternity to disavow the man it has elected as its president, even if the election was a foolish mistake—seems to me improper to such a degree that there must be some misunderstanding. I ask the honored fraternity for a factual statement, all the more urgently because until the above-mentioned information reached me I had the same feelings toward the brotherhood as in the days before the ties that bound me to it were ruptured, whereas an affirmative reply to the above question could not fail to elicit the appropriate response.

Behind the stilted prose, typical of the style in which matters of honor were treated in fraternity circles, Georg concealed a towering rage. He had already resigned from the FWV. Upon receiving an "affirmative reply"—Brother Ewer, his successor as president, thinking perhaps of the reversed founder Max Spangenberg's example in a similar emergency, rushed to Schmoller's office and apologized, and the executive committee promptly endorsed the action—Georg dropped the formal pose and hurled coarse insults at the entire fraternity. The next day three of the brothers challenged him to "heavy" duels, but Ewer was not among them. Herr

Nicolai was obliged to decline to duel unless Herr Ewer chose to fight or was expelled from the FWV: Ewer was a common coward who deserved to be horsewhipped. Georg repeated this insult in a registered letter and, when this brought no results, demanded the convening of a court of honor within two weeks. Otherwise, "I consider the matter settled," meaning that a fraternity that harbored a coward like Ewer was not worthy of his attention.

This tempest in a teapot was rapidly becoming a major scandal, a source of embarrassment to the FWV and a cause of glee to its detractors. Reluctant to wash its dirty linen in public or to disavow its new president—whose continued silence had indeed caused eyebrows to be raised—the fraternity asked another fraternity, the Sprevia, to mediate. Georg ignored the Sprevia's summons, insisting on a court of honor of his own choosing and within the specified time. The FWV ignored this ultimatum, whereupon Georg broke off all further communication, declaring the entire fraternity to be not *satisfaktionsfähig* and leaving his would-be challengers to the contempt of the public. To a brother who urged him to reconsider, he wrote: "I no longer wish to use the intimate *Du* customary between fraternity men. I forgo a critique of your letter because I do not wish to leave a fraternity to which I have belonged for three years with a nasty word." But this noble prose crumbled before his rage: "What I refrain from saying to you I shall not repeat to third parties, of course, but I shall no longer be able to defend you against the people who are calling your actions those of cowardly *Lumpen* [his first draft read "whining curs"] without spine or conscience, willing to betray their elected leader." He was imposing this "restraint" upon himself "not by any means because I fear the consequences or even consider them undesirable, but solely out of loyalty to the FWV, to which you, gentlemen, have the undeserved honor to belong."

The break was complete. In refusing to give satisfaction to people whom he had publicly insulted and whose concept of honor demanded that they clear their names in combat, Georg had rejected not only his fraternity brothers but the entire code of behavior of student society in which he had been so deeply involved. He was quitting the game because the rules no longer suited him. He had put himself beyond the pale. That was certainly how his friends viewed the matter. "Your rejection of challenges which you yourself have provoked is beyond my understanding," the FWV alumnus Dr. Wilhelm Caspari wrote. He was not surprised that Georg found it difficult to admit being in the wrong,

> but never did I imagine that you would not stand up for your cause with your whole person, that you would shirk your obligation, while on the other hand you lack the moral courage to admit that you are in the wrong. I do not understand your reasons. If you had addressed your insults to Ewer and Wolfson you could have kept the matter on a personal plane, but you preferred to address your insults to the entire fraternity. You knew, moreover, that it could not handle the matter on such short notice.

Caspari reminded Georg of his own insistence on proper protocol in a similar case. "Farewell. It is with deep regret that I end an old friendship. Thank you for what you have been to me all these years." Other friends wrote in a similar vein. A girl even returned a poem Georg had written to her, saying, "For the sake of your honor, I assume that you did not know what you were doing." Georg was paying a stiff price for his stubborn pride.

The girl was right: he had lost control over his reason and thought of nothing but revenge. "I consider it my duty to inform Ewer of your threats," a mutual friend wrote him, "and at the same time protect you against the excesses of your own temper." The warning was in vain. Georg was in a state of pathological rage that bordered on insanity, one of several such episodes, in the first of which, at Gotha, he had thrown poor Dr. Rosenstock down the stairs. Toward the end of the winter semester of 1897–98, Georg Friedrich Nicolai, otherwise a satisfactory student, was expelled from the University of Berlin for "having caused great bodily harm to a fellow-student."[8] The record does not show whether the victim was the disgraced Ewer or another of Georg's many *bêtes noires*, nor does it matter. The real victim was Georg himself. The "excesses of his own temper" threatened to destroy him.

He was finished with fraternity life, with his friends, with student honor, with causes. His sanity returned. In the spring he left for Heidelberg, determined to concentrate on his studies. A new and entirely different phase of his life was beginning. The years between his graduation from a school for problem students and his expulsion from the University of Berlin were crucial, not because Georg matured to any significant degree but because he became involved in causes—the battle against intolerance, the socialist question, the European idea, the "true" Germany as personified by Mommsen—that forced him to make choices. These choices were curiously ambivalent. He stood against anti-Semitism but he abandoned his Jewish name; he embraced the French way but returned to Germany to conform more than ever to the Teutonic code of conduct; he revered intellectual greatness but resorted to abusive language and physical violence. His intellectual development was still outracing his emotional maturation.

NOTES

1. Elisabeth Kunze's correspondence with Nicolai, preserved in the Nicolai archive, extended over more than forty years and proved a useful source of biographical data. She became a teacher in Königsberg and was dismissed from her post in 1933 for refusing to give the Hitler salute.

2. For example, a Jewish Königsberger, Eduard von Simson, was professor of jurisprudence at the university, president of the all-German Frankfurt Parliament in 1848, and leader of the delegation that offered the Imperial crown to the king of Prussia the following year.

3. This account of German student politics at the end of the nineteenth century is

based on a unique historical source, the collection of the monthly newsletters of the FWV, *Monatsberichte der Freien Wissenschaftlichen Vereinigung*, from the first issue of June 1887 to No. 71 of October 1897. It is supplemented by material drawn from reprints of speeches, announcements of special events, fraternity regulations, songbooks, and the like, and by letters from friends and Nicolai's drafts of his replies. All are found in the Nicolai archive.

4. The letters to Eva Lewinstein-Blos written in the winter of 1896–97 were made available by her daughter, Dr. Ruth Katz.

5. *Analisis del Psicoanalisis a la luz de la psicología fisiológica* (Buenos Aires: Editorial B, 1953). See Chapter 24 below for discussion of this work.

6. A notebook in the Nicolai archive entitled "Georges et Emilie, 142 rue du Bac," a household account, reflects the bohemian domesticity of the couple from November 1897 through February 1898.

7. Von Schmoller was a *Kathedersozialist*, that is, an academic socialist opposed to socialism but advocating state intervention to achieve social reforms. His election to the office of rector was a gesture in defense of academic freedom, then under ultraconservative attack.

8. Nicolai's certificate of attendance (in the Nicolai archive) bears this notation. I was not allowed to examine the transcript of Nicolai's file in the archives of Humboldt (formerly Royal Friedrich Wilhelms) University.

7. Ascent with Detours

Nicolai's ouster from the University of Berlin was a blessing in disguise, a drastic but effective cure for his obsession with honor and image. The childish quarrels and false starts of the fraternity years were behind him as he packed his bags for Heidelberg, determined to make a fresh start in new surroundings. At the age of twenty-four he was at last beginning to find himself. The curve of his life now rose steeply. Little more than ten years after his expulsion, he would be one of the brightest stars of the faculty of medicine, lecturing in the very amphitheaters from which he was now barred. It was not that he suddenly became ambitious. His career, impressive as it was, would be the framework for the unfolding of his many-sided personality, not an end in itself. He was capable of working harder than most of his colleagues, but work was play for a man possessed of Georg's brilliant mind and boundless energy, a means of gratifying a universal curiosity rather than a process of plodding toward success. Each of his many interests was a challenge to be mastered rather than a mere hobby. Science fascinated him, but so did the humanities, so did political and social affairs, so did the theater, chess, photography, every kind of sport from skiing to sailing, so did feminine psychology—in short, the whole of life. He would never let his career interfere with the enjoyment of his mental and physical gifts; he did not have to, for he was one of those rare people whose every moment is fertile, whether they are working, playing, or seemingly doing nothing.

During the last turbulent semester in Berlin he had somehow managed to pass (with flying colors, needless to say) the *Physikum*, the basic examinations required for admission to the clinical courses. At this point a change in locale was common practice, even under normal circumstances. Georg chose Heidelberg, where the political climate was more liberal than at any Prussian university and where his record as a troublemaker was no obstacle. The ancient Ruprecht-Karls University had an outstanding faculty of medicine, the setting was delightful, he would be welcome in the homes of his father's old friends, and his sister Eva, about to marry his own best friend, Edwin Blos (Fig. 11), would soon be living in nearby Karlsruhe. It was spring and Georg arrived in an exuberant mood, happy to have escaped the overheated atmosphere of Berlin, ready to make up for lost time, and eager to savor life in all its fragrance.

His medical studies progressed without a hitch and he was able to graduate two years later, in the spring of 1900. Among his teachers were such outstanding men as the psychiatrist Emil Kraepelin, the neuroanatomist Franz Nissl, the neurologist Wilhelm Heinrich Erb, and the pathologist Julius Arnold, all names enshrined in the pantheon of medical science. Georg attended classes conscientiously, but did not confine himself to the obligatory courses. He found time to audit lectures on experimental psychology, criminal psychology, higher mathematics, a course entitled "Darwinism as *Weltanschauung*" (Darwin's ideas were still hotly debated at the turn of the century), and, for good measure, an altogether extracurricular seminar, "Italian Studies," held by the distinguished medievalist and Dante scholar Karl Vossler. It was a strenuous program for a medical student and a rich and varied diet for the most voracious intellectual appetite.

But for Georg the university offerings were not enough. In the fall of 1898, the theater page of the *Heidelberg Tageblatt* began to carry reviews by a new but obviously knowledgeable critic who signed himself "N." or

Fig. 11. Eva Lewinstein-Blos and Dr. Edwin Blos, ca. 1898.

"Ni." Georg struck up an acquaintance with the director of the Stadttheater, who told him that the newspaper needed a critic. He promptly offered his services and, despite his lack of credentials, convinced the editor that he was the man for the job. The arrangement proved eminently satisfactory to both parties and continued until Georg reluctantly left Heidelberg, at which time he bequeathed the critic's desk to another amateur, his friend Otto Buek, then a philosophy student. For the editor it was a stroke of luck, for the medical student turned drama critic was one of the most

126

competent reviewers ever to write for a provincial newspaper. For Georg it was a source of free theater tickets and a small honorarium but, above all, an opportunity to indulge his passion for the theater. He was no ordinary amateur, having imbibed his love for the stage almost with his mother's milk. As noted above, he and Eva had been ardent puppeteers writing their own plays, designing the sets and costumes, handling the marionettes, and supplying the voices. When they were old enough, they were taken to plays as often as the family budget would allow. As adolescents they had been the stars of many amateur theatricals. Eva had been thoroughly stage-struck, and Georg had mastered the techniques of the "great" and the "little" embrace, stage fencing, and falling on his knees with aplomb. At home Theodor Fontane's theater column in the *Vossische Zeitung* was avidly read and every performance and every play expertly discussed.

The Heidelberg Stadttheater was a far cry from the stages of Berlin, but the young critic approached his task with enthusiasm. His reviews—fifty in all, over a year and a half, encompassing drama and comedy, folk plays, operettas, and even an opera or two—were little gems, thoughtful and scholarly or light-hearted and witty, enthusiastic or sarcastic, depending on the play.[1] Not for nothing had he read Fontane, the greatest German theater critic, who had raised reviewing to an art form, combining subtle irony and an easy informal style with an unfailing instinct for quality and a profound understanding of the possibilities and limitations of the stage. Georg was not a mere imitator of Fontane, however; his style was his own and his ideas and observations were original. If the stage is a mirror of society, the critic must be social critic, psychologist, moral philosopher, and literary judge all in one. Georg felt at ease in each of these roles. He diagnosed the strengths and weaknesses of the plot, exposed the psychological core or the social implications, discovered nuggets of theatrical gold in the dross of contemporary comedy, and judiciously bestowed praise and criticism on the cast. The pithy style of *The Biology of War* is foreshadowed in these essays, and here and there we get a glimpse of the future critic of the war in the philosophical asides of the youthful theater critic.

Not surprisingly, the son of Frau Elise was a champion of women's rights, in principle if not in practice. He commented caustically on a play by the popular Berlin playwright Adolf L'Arronge, entitled *Hasemann's Daughters*:

> Once again we are told that the education of emancipation-minded ladies is useless in matrimony, and that boiling potatoes and knitting socks are the things that count—next to love, of course, which is the main ingredient. L'Arronge seems to think that love rests on domesticity. When one of Hasemann's daughters, who had enjoyed a higher education in music and other fields, founders in her marriage to a man she has wed without love, old Hasemann, in order to save his younger daughter from a similar fate, begins to instruct the latter in the art of boiling eggs and other housewifely skills. Well, perhaps it helps. But since at the end the marriage is happily salvaged, we

may hope that love and education are compatible after all, no matter what popular playwrights may say to the contrary.

"N." was critical of authors who contented themselves with cheap effects instead of exploring the psychological depths of their characters. Ludwig Fulda, a minor star then rising on the literary horizon, had written a play about a group of bachelors whose friendship comes to an end when they marry. According to Georg's synopsis, it was an attempt to show that in spite of the best intentions these wives were bound to destroy the ties joining their husbands because they came from different social backgrounds:

> The task of describing how people who are trying to come close to one another succeed only in becoming more and more estranged, simply because they do not understand each other, is worthwhile but difficult. For Fulda it was too difficult. The pleasing talent of the amiable storyteller fails him when it comes to giving a psychological foundation to social differences. It is not, as he would have us believe, the fact that these women are different which causes the men's friendship to break up, but, on the contrary, the fact that they are all alike, that in spite of the most diverse background all of them are quarrelsome, touchy, gossipy females. That three persons, each of whom goes into a crying spell over the most innocent remark, cannot possibly live in harmony for any length of time is a banality for which we did not need proof from Herr Fulda's pen.

But Georg had a kind word for Fulda's style. "Not for nothing has he been translating French masterpieces for many years, thereby acquiring a fluidity of language and grace of style which at this moment is almost nonexistent in German literature." The statement betrays a concern with aesthetic values well beyond the grasp of ordinary drama critics, let alone medical students. Who but an enthusiast would have known that Fulda's achievement was the translation of all of Molière's plays?

Ibsen, revered both as a dramatist and a social reformer by Frau Elise and her children, was still a controversial author at the turn of the century. A performance of *The Enemy of the People* gave Georg a chance to rise to his defense. "A *Tendenzstück* [play with a message], I heard people say on the way out, and for such critics that seems to exhaust the subject." Yes, Ibsen's plays carried a message, but was that necessarily a fault? "It is only because of the flood of inferior works in which good intentions must stand for accomplishment and the moral message replaces literary talent that we have come to despise the genre. But we need only think of Molière to remind ourselves that excellent plays can have a message." The surge of the action and the subtle characterizations of Ibsen's men and women were the mark of a powerful dramatist: "We cannot allow the effect to suffer from the fact that the playwright was not content with portraying human beings as such, but wanted to tell us something of his own hates and loves, that he shows us the victory and defeat of ideas that have occupied a lifetime of his thought." Later the great reformer became resigned to the necessity of lies and conventions, but "here he still steps forth with youthful vigor, although already with less vehemence than when he wrote *Pillars of Society* five years earlier." Georg knew his Ibsen, and his judgment has stood the test of time.

The theater as a vehicle for social ideas was a recurrent theme of these reviews. Georg returned to it in his discussion of Hermann Sudermann's *Die Ehre (Honor)*.

> Sudermann rarely allows us to forget that he belongs to a generation of believers in heredity, not unlike Ibsen in this respect. But whereas the latter always stresses individuality and tries to show how the uniqueness of every person is molded by his ancestry, Sudermann sees the individual solely as a type and product of his class, whose actions are predetermined by age-old traditions and inbred notions. It turns out that this conception is very serviceable for dramatic purposes: as the individual steps out of his class he is exposed to the—for him—incomprehensible prejudices of the opposite class. It is in this struggle, in trying to cope with these new forces, that Sudermann's heroes triumph or perish. Thus he emerges as the dramatist who has most effectively dealt with modern class strife.

Unlike most critics, Georg found no fault with the happy ending, in which the lowly commoner from the rear building becomes the business partner of the wealthy nobleman who occupies the main house, "for gold is a very real power, and if one writes about the class struggle one must perforce show how in most people's eyes a sack full of gold becomes the best justification for undesirable racial or social qualities." On the other hand, Arthur Schnitzler's *Liebelei*, the story of a seduction that ends in death and suicide, displeased Georg because the innocent sensuality of the beginning was belied by the gruesome ending. If, as the girl's father in the play is made to say, his daughter was not to be blamed for tasting the fruit of happiness from the tree of life before becoming an old maid, then Schnitzler should not let her be destroyed by her love. "If that really was [his] message, he should have shown us how Christine overcomes the guilty passion of her youth and becomes an honest and useful member of society in the end." At this stage Georg was a moralist in his own right.

Lessing's *Nathan the Wise*, the classic fable of tolerance between Christian, Muslim, and Jew, moved the young critic to deplore the decline of public sentiment since the Age of Enlightenment. "The well-beloved verses of the first German dramatist, once memorized by every schoolboy, sound almost like a tale from *A Thousand and One Nights* today," he wrote wistfully. In Lessing's day the Germans had been receptive to the ideal of universal brotherhood, but Nathan, "the most perfect representative of this vanished world," would be an anachronism in modern Germany, "where tolerance has given way to the notion that both the individual and the group must place the sharpest emphasis on their racial and national origin if they want to flourish." In condemning nationalism as a disruptive force, the future author of *The Biology of War* was sounding the theme that became the leitmotif of his indictment of German militarism: war is evil not only because it destroys lives and cultural treasures but also because it severs the bond between human beings that makes them human.

A farce about a nouveau riche manufacturer's encounter with the old nobility generated a sociological aside in a lighter vein. "To talk about literary merit or the lack thereof seems as inappropriate as talking about the value of tinsel," Georg wrote. But the play had served its purpose of amusing the public, "and indeed it was not the worst fare we have been offered lately." Throwing barons together with crockery-makers was the stuff of comedy, "and the rising as well as the declining class could provide splendid comical figures if the characters had life, but that, alas, is lacking in all of them."

The personality that emerges from these clippings is surprisingly mature, considering Georg's stormy history. He comes across as a man of parts, a critic with a flair for style, a gift for satire, a good understanding of human frailty, a wealth of knowledge, and a clear sense of values. We must remember, moreover, that he wrote these reviews as a medical student, with his left hand, as it were, and that his future achievements lay in fields other than literary criticism. While there is little connection between these essays and his later stand as a militant pacifist, they betray the same far-ranging intellect and the same humanism that informs *The Biology of War*.

Soon after his arrival in Heidelberg, Georg fell in love for the first and possibly only time in his life. Olga, blond, blue-eyed, and fair-skinned, was a Russian Jewess who, like so many of the Russian intelligentsia, had fled the oppressive tsarist regime. For once Georg faced a woman—other than his mother—who was his intellectual equal rather than a sex object, a proud and passionate spirit rather than an adoring female. Her brand of socialism was considerably more radical than his, and their nights were divided between lovemaking and stormy arguments over the way to improve the world. Georg welcomed the Tsar's call for an international peace conference, but Olga saw it as a sham. Her friends in St. Petersburg and Moscow were being dragged to Siberia in chains. A gradual transition to a socialist order, as advocated by moderate German Social Democrats, might be possible in a civilized country; in backward Russia a violent revolution was needed. The lovers did not convert one another, but Olga's vivid tales of life in a police state opened Georg's eyes to a reality he had hitherto ignored, for she was not an unkempt, wild-eyed revolutionary, but a beautiful, intelligent woman of his own class. Olga also taught him Russian—he was always eager to learn a new language—while he helped her with German. He was a tender and solicitous lover. When Olga fell ill he was at her bedside day and night. Later he persuaded Eva to let her convalesce at her house in Karlsruhe. When she suffered a relapse, he took her to Berlin to consult the famous Professor Gerhardt. He introduced her to his mother, although this did not mean that he intended to marry her. As a modern woman Frau Elise was tolerant of "free love," and in due course Georg brought many of his mistresses, including married women, into her circle.

The relationship with Olga ended with his departure from Heidelberg, but like most of her successors she remained his devoted friend for life, while he—unlike his usual self—remained romantically attached to her memory until he saw her as a married woman in St. Petersburg seven years later. He wrote to the woman who was then his mistress that she had been both the Venus of the Hörselberg and Saint Elizabeth to him.[2] He also compared her to a silver sphere which in his mind he had polished until all the spots and roughnesses were gone. "When he was alone," he wrote, describing his state of mind during the intervening years, "he placed it on an altar and knelt before it, and whenever he felt sullied he thought of his pure silver sphere, and whenever he felt that he was about to succumb to frivolousness and skepticism, he was grateful and glad of the weight of the load he carried with him, for he believed in his silver sphere." Never again would he be so romantic.

To all appearances Georg was now intellectually mature, emotionally stable (or at least capable of genuine love), and socially responsible, to judge by his graduation as a physician. But appearances were deceptive. In the little town of Osthofen, where he served briefly as locum tenens for a former fraternity brother, he seduced his colleague's sister and was challenged to a duel by the irate brother. Although an overt scandal was somehow averted, he left Osthofen under a cloud. Next he went to Karlsruhe for a surgical internship at the municipal hospital at which his brother-in-law was an attending surgeon. Here Olga's sensitive lover proved himself capable of downright coarseness. While living in the Blos house he insulted a female guest, boasting that no woman could resist him and reinforcing his boast with suggestive remarks and obscene gestures. This time there was an open scandal, for the scene took place in a restaurant and ended in a brawl that attracted the police. Georg refused to apologize, whereupon the deeply embarrassed Eva forbade him her house. Considering himself the aggrieved party, he demanded that Edwin should resign from the hospital staff so as to spare him, Georg, awkward encounters, and he enlisted the ineffectual Otto Buek as his go-between. The episode is so ludicrous as to suggest a temporary mental derangement, which was indeed Edwin's diagnosis. The quarrel was settled somehow, Georg left Karlsruhe soon afterward, and the apparent fit of insanity did not recur, but his hair-trigger temper continued to embroil him in countless clashes.

From Karlsruhe he went to Leipzig as unpaid assistant to the renowned physiologist Ewald Hering. Here he behaved like a model young academic, alert and hard-working, helpful in the laboratory, respectful toward his elders, attentive to the ladies, and friendly toward his colleagues. He lived in a pension run by an impoverished baroness and had a placid affair with a young Englishwoman named Marian Hogg, from whom he learned English, as he had learned French from Emilie and Russian from Olga (he was always ready to reap practical benefits from his *affaires de coeur*) and whom he squired to the Gewandhaus concerts, chamber music, recitals, sedate garden parties, and soirées at professorial homes. We learn that the violinist Joachim, Brahms's friend and interpreter, played in Leipzig that year. We hear of picnics and walks in the woods, of bicycle rides, tennis, and rowing on the Pleisse river—once the boat capsized and Georg's white flannel trousers lost their crease—in short, of a genteel life pleasantly divided between recreation and work.

Hering, whom posterity would honor as the discoverer of a vital respiratory reflex, was the center of a group of brilliant young scientists. Drawn into this circle, Georg, though already licensed to practice medicine, temporarily abandoned his plans for a career in that field. As an experimental scientist he would be able to indulge his intellectual curiosity without having to deal with human lives. He called himself *studiosus rerum naturalium* and took courses in zoology, comparative anatomy, and general chemistry (one of his professors was the great chemist Wilhelm Ostwald) in preparation for a doctoral degree in zoology. Hering assigned him the task of measuring the speed of transmission of electrical impulses in the olfactory nerve of the pike, an arcane project which, however, would advance knowledge of bioelectrical phenomena. Apart from mastery of physical and physiological theory, it entailed working with delicate instruments and provided a good background for Georg's later research on the electrocardiogram. The excursion into zoology was a detour but not a waste of time, for it broadened his scientific horizon. He would always consider himself a biologist who applied the general principles of his science to the special case of the human organism, rather than as a mere practitioner of medicine. In the end he used his thesis for a doctorate in medicine. On 26 February 1901, the University of Leipzig bestowed the coveted degree on the twenty-seven-year-old candidate. The printed dissertation bore the dedication "For my parents in gratitude." A milestone had been passed.

Georg's career in academic medicine was now assured. Hering, who could open many doors for him, gave him a letter testifying to his "exceptional ability." Hering's son, himself a professor of physiology at Prague, offered him a paid position, and inquiries came from Halle and elsewhere. But Georg was not ambitious. His career could wait. Confounding the expectations of his well-wishers, he declined all offers and went to the Orient for an indefinite stay.

It was a strange decision for a man who was already several years older than were most of his colleagues at the same stage in their careers. Did he still have doubts about his vocation as a scientist? Did he have an irresistible urge to see the world before settling down to a workaday life? Did he want to break out of the stifling political atmosphere of Wilhelminian Germany? Had he planned the voyage long in advance, or was he acting on a sudden impulse? Whatever his reasons, in the summer of 1901 he sailed as ship's doctor on the *Prinz Heinrich*, pride of German Lloyd's East Asia fleet, destination Hongkong, with stops at Colombo, Penang, Singapore, and Saigon. His subsequent travels took him into the interior of China, to Japan, the Sunda Islands, and the Philippines.

For a European, the Far East was then very far away indeed. It was the world of Joseph Conrad and Rudyard Kipling, dominated by the white man but utterly alien and mysterious. The fastest ships took many weeks for the voyage. Transportation on land and on local waters was slow and often hazardous. Accommodations were generally primitive, the food was apt to be tainted, and tropical diseases were ever-present threats. The streets of the cities teemed with beggars, emaciated coolies, drawers of rickshas, litter carriers, and vendors of every commodity from hashish and opium to amulets and incense. The poorest of Europe's poor were kings compared with the pitiful creatures who thronged about Georg's ship in every port. Orientals seemed little better than animals to the average westerner; they were potentially dangerous, as the recent Boxer Rebellion had shown, but docile enough when kept firmly in their place. They were useful and indeed indispensable human beasts of burden who worked for a pittance and subsisted on a handful of rice, while the Europeans enjoyed luxuries which at home only the very rich could afford. It was the age of unabashed colonialism.

How did the future pacifist and humanitarian reconcile his ideas about the brotherhood of man with his impressions of a world in which the "colored" races lived in degradation and poverty? When he arrived in 1901, the Boxer Rebellion was very recent history. The western powers had crushed it with the utmost brutality. Georg must have been aware of these atrocities, for August Bebel, his mother's friend, had condemned them in a thunderous speech before the Reichstag. We may assume that Georg, the disciple of Lessing and Kant, condemned them no less strongly, but unlike Bebel, he was not opposed to colonialism in principle. As a child of his time and class, he took the superiority of the white race for granted, and everything he saw in the East only strengthened this prejudice. Every inch the European, dressed—as a surviving photograph shows him—in immaculate white linen and a tropical helmet, he peered through his pince-nez with curiosity but no compassion at the surging mass of brown and yellow humanity (Fig. 12). He was, as he later confessed to Romain Rolland, incapable of feeling any sense of kinship with these Asiatics, as if in their poverty and servility they belonged to a different species. Then and for years afterward, to be human meant for him to be civilized in a narrow Western sense which included cleanliness, order, dignity, and a state of consciousness that could rise above superstition and fear. He knew that Orientals—the Chinese in particular—had created great civilizations in the past, but he could not fit their wretched descendants into his scheme. The brotherhood of man ended at the gates of Asia.

He attended a performance of Saint-Saëns's *Samson et Dalila* at the Grand Théatre Municipal of Saigon, where the program carried the notice "natives must be properly attired." He enjoyed the hospitality of Dutch plantation owners and made love to a Mefrouw. He bought ivory and jade, art objects and exotic weapons, for he had money—we shall presently see how he earned it—and we may safely assume that he tasted all the pleasures the Orient had to offer. But he also made strenuous trips into dangerous territory—the interior of China was infested with bandits, warlike Muslim tribes lurked along his route through the hills of Sumatra between Deli and Toba—to carry medical and dental instruments, bacteriological supplies, and mail and messages to remote outposts. He set up a portable laboratory for the study of marine animals in the Sunda Sea. He learned what he could about tropical diseases, consulted with medical missionaries, lent a hand with surgical operations, took photographs of his hosts and their wives and children, and generally made himself useful to the isolated Europeans in the hinterland. "We shall always remember you fondly," a German missionary wrote from Swatow, where he had spent Christmas in the family circle.[3]

Georg's finest hour came when cholera broke out among the coolies in the steerage of an island steamer on which he was traveling. Identifying himself as a physician to the panic-stricken captain, he took charge, tending to the dying, supervising the burials at sea, organizing a quarantine system, and calming passengers and crew. Inevitably, he contracted the

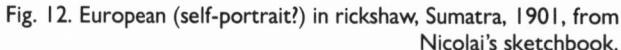

Fig. 12. European (self-portrait?) in rickshaw, Sumatra, 1901, from Nicolai's sketchbook.

disease himself and became gravely ill. His bravery earned him a citation and spread his name throughout the foreign settlements and missions of the East.

But this heroism was dictated by the physician's code of ethics rather than by the humanitarian's love for his fellow creatures. In other circumstances Nicolai had no qualms about using his medical skill for a less humane and more profitable purpose. To supply cheap labor for the plantations in the Dutch East Indies, it was customary to round up Chinese coolies in the mainland ports, trick them into accepting contracts which they did not understand, and ship them off like so many head of cattle. The mortality from malnutrition, disease, and overwork was so high that the Mynheers found it cheaper to pay a physician for screening out the unfit at the port of embarkation than to pay for their transportation and upkeep and shipping of corpses back to the mainland. For the young globe-trotter, it was literally a golden opportunity. He devised a screening procedure that was as simple as it was ingenious. Stationing himself at the gangplank, he asked each man as he walked past him to shake his hand, rejecting those whose grip was too feeble. His employers were pleased with the results, for they paid him a handsome twenty thousand francs for a few months' work. Back in Leipzig, Marian Hogg was shocked. "I am very interested in what you write about the coolies," she wrote. "I don't quite understand how they are 'bought.' Don't they know where they go when they come aboard? It is very sad that such things exist. I also fail to understand how you, who is so enthusiastic about civilization, can speak about it as if it were quite natural that so many human lives must be sacrificed to it. Have you any skin left after shaking so many hands?" But neither his hand nor his conscience bothered Georg, who thought it only proper and fitting that Chinese coolies should sacrifice their lives to enable the Dutch to build a Western civilization in the islands. It would be an exaggeration to compare his role to that of the infamous Nazi doctors who supervised the "selections" at Auschwitz, but the fact remains, as Marian clearly saw, that he had allowed himself to become part of an inhumane system.

Being restless and inquisitive and finding himself in demand wherever he went ("I could have settled in many places," he later wrote Eva), Georg had the makings of a perennial traveler. In the late summer of 1902 he left Singapore, once more as a ship's doctor, intending to go to England and then to America. But in Genoa he received word that his father was dying. He left the ship and went by train to Berlin, arriving just in time to be at the old man's bedside before he died. He had long since made peace with his father. Like many rebellious sons, he had come to admire him once the grounds for conflict between them had disappeared. Unlike his mother, who never ceased to challenge and criticize her son, his father had become a tolerant parent, somewhat in awe of his brilliant but erratic offspring but pleased with his outward progress and content to let him be. He had long ago retired from the political wars and had become an avuncular figure who could have stepped from the pages of a novel by his contemporary Theodor Fontane. His son was genuinely saddened by his death.

Georg's globe-trotting days were over. Although his mother was provided for, his presence was needed as executor of the will. He came into some money himself, but it was clear that he would have to find a paid position. While in the Far East he had kept in touch with his friends in Leipzig, among them Anton Tschermak, a brilliant young physiologist who had since moved to Halle. Impressed by Georg's ability, Tschermak recommended him to Julius Bernstein, head of the Physiological Institute at Halle. After many delays the appointment was approved by the Ministry of Education—the same ministry that had barred Georg Lewinstein from the public schools of Prussia—and on 1 April 1903 Dr. Georg Friedrich

Nicolai became second assistant to Professor Bernstein at an annual salary of nine hundred marks. "Are you becoming ambitious at last?" asked Marian Hogg, his no longer platonic mistress.

Georg had climbed the first rung on the ladder of success, but he was still not ambitious. Halle was a dull provincial town with few attractions for a world traveler. His first assignment, taking inventory of the apparatus in the laboratory, was not inspiring. He found that he disliked his chief, and the hoped-for collaboration with Tschermak failed to materialize. No sooner had he arrived at Halle than he began to look for a position elsewhere, preferably in Berlin, not so much because of the greater opportunities for advancement as because life there was more to his taste. Once more Tschermak came to his aid by recommending him to Wilhelm Engelmann, director of the Physiological Institute of the University of Berlin. On Tschermak's advice, he made "personal reasons" his excuse to the annoyed Bernstein for leaving, and presented himself to Engelmann. The stratagem worked: by the end of the year Georg, now almost thirty, returned to the university that had expelled him six years earlier, now as an Assistent at a prestigious institute.He had climbed the second rung of the ladder.

His quick intelligence, combined with an almost infallible memory, insatiable curiosity, manual dexterity, and a truly astonishing capacity for work, so impressed his new chief that within the year he sent Nicolai to the Fourth International Congress of Physiology at Brussels, where he mingled with the scientific elite of the world. Nicolai was chosen to report the proceedings, a signal honor for a young and still untried scientist. To breathe the air of an international gathering, where national prejudices were buried and the finest minds from every corner of the earth joined in a common purpose and treated one another with exquisite courtesy, was a decisive experience for the future opponent of war between civilized nations.[4]

Georg's course was now firmly set. He joined the medical and the physiological societies of Berlin and soon became a familiar figure as presenter and discusser. He organized a select journal club, devoted not only to the physiological literature but to such arcane topics as radiation physics, physical chemistry, and experimental psychology. Always eager to broaden his knowledge, he attended a seminar in theoretical physics given by Max Planck, the father of quantum physics. At the Institute he taught (for a fee from the participants, as was the custom) a course in physiological methods, for which he prepared an exquisitely illustrated manual (Fig 13).The science of electrocardiography was then in its infancy, and he spent much time designing and testing new apparatus, corresponding with colleagues about details, and arguing with suppliers over specifications and costs. Once again he was burning the midnight oil, for apart from all these activities and the pursuit of pleasure, which included chess, boating, tennis, and a flourishing love life, he wrote, for several specialty journals, comprehensive annual reviews of the literature that would have taxed the capabilities of an expert: his survey of the field of nerve and muscle physiology for the year 1906 contained no fewer than 562 references.

The young Assistent was quick to recognize the importance of the electrocardiogram as a diagnostic tool for heart disease, at a time when clinicians relied on such primitive methods as percussion and auscultation.

Fig. 13. Drawing for Nicolai's physiological manual, ca. 1904.

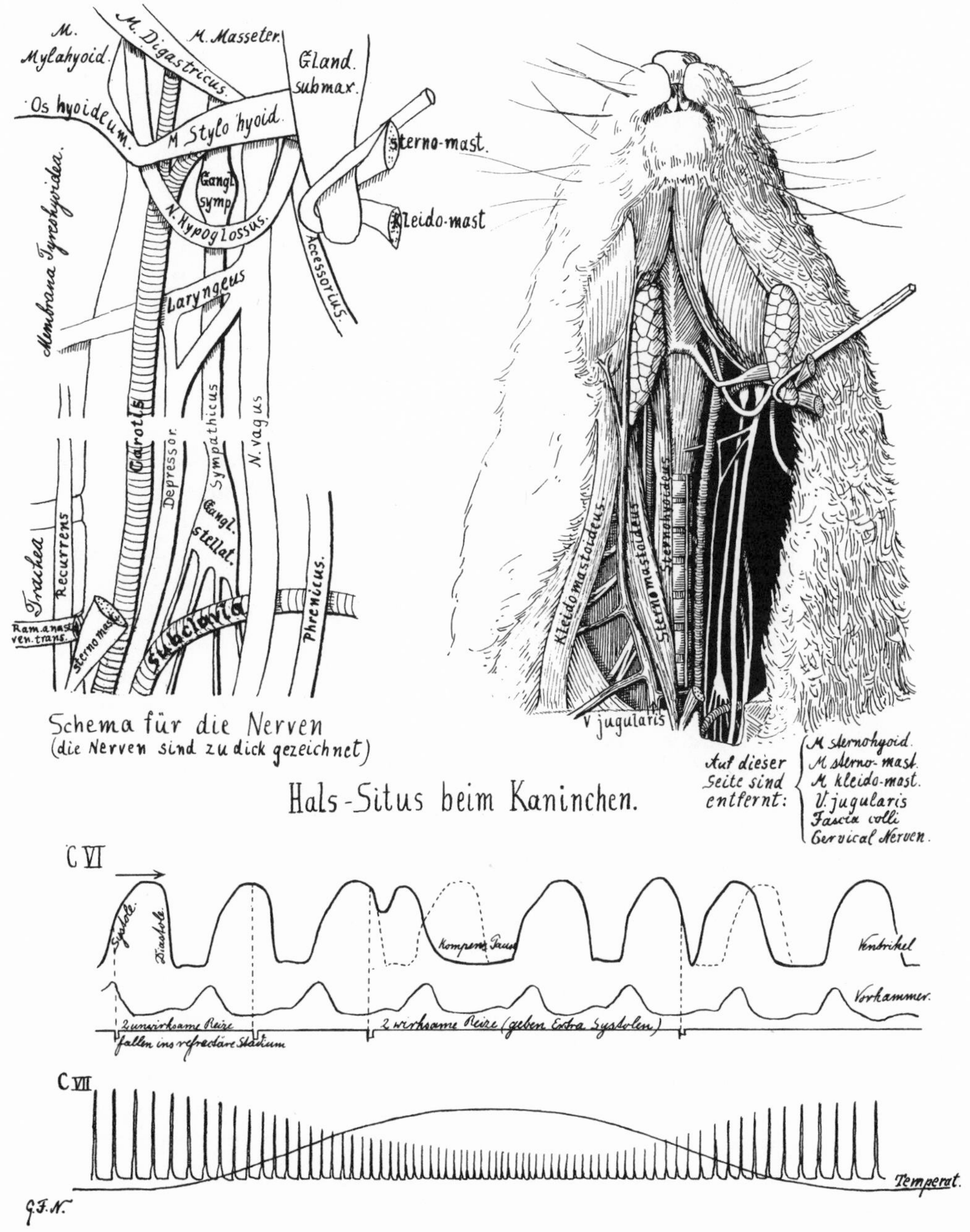

Hals-Situs beim Kaninchen.

The instrument had just been developed by the Dutch physiologist Willem Einthoven, whose laboratory at Leyden was a Mecca for electrophysiologists and already a center for clinical research.[5] Georg spent six weeks with Einthoven and returned with a fund of first-hand knowledge that put him ahead of almost all of his German colleagues. It was not long before Friedrich Kraus, professor of medicine and director of the Second Medical Division of the Charité Hospital, enlisted his collaboration. The result was a dual appointment in physiology and medicine which enabled him to rise to the top of his profession within a few years.

But once again intellectual curiosity prevailed over ambition. In 1906, Nicolai obtained a leave of absence and went to St. Petersburg to work for six months with Pavlov, one of the great scientific geniuses of the age. Pavlov, who had received the Nobel Prize in medicine two years earlier for his classic studies of the secretory functions of the digestive tract, had recently begun the studies of the conditioned reflex on which his fame rests today. As yet the full significance of that discovery was not clearly perceived, not even by Pavlov himself. Georg, who always had his ear to the ground, failed to mention it in a tribute he wrote for the master's birthday in 1905, even though he had assisted in the surgical preparation and training of Pavlov's dogs at the Physiological Institute in Berlin (Fig. 14). This omission is all the more significant in view of Georg's interest in experimental psychology. Once in St. Petersburg, he saw immediately—and perhaps more clearly than the cautious Pavlov himself—that the conditioned reflex was the key to the learning process and the physiological basis for the association of ideas in human psychology. By using physiological methods, Nicolai wrote many years later, Pavlov had placed psychology on an objective basis and demonstrated the essential unity of body and mind. To the mature Nicolai, Pavlov seemed to be one of the two most creative scientists of recent times; the other was Darwin. The young Nicolai sensed this greatness; his experience in Pavlov's laboratory was a decisive one, not because it determined the direction of his own work but because the man's genius left an indelible mark on his mind. "You are always happy when you can truly look up to somebody, and that does seem to be the case with Pavlov," Georg's mother commented perceptively.

Whereas Pavlov devoted the rest of his long life to the methodical study of the conditioned reflex, Georg, a more mercurial personality, abandoned the field soon afterward, though not until he had made some observations of his own which show that he would have made a splendid experimental psychologist had he chosen to persevere. Throughout his life his view of the human psyche was Pavlovian (many years later he returned to the field and devoted himself to the creation of an "Institute of Psychogenesis" in Chile). In 1906, on his return to Berlin, he extended and refined Pavlov's experiments, showing that dogs could learn to distinguish a circle from a pentagon if they were first taught to discriminate between a circle and a square, and that they could recognize a given pitch even if the tone was produced on an unfamiliar instrument or in combination with other tones. He observed that the flow of saliva ceased after the first few drops if the tone had the right pitch but the "wrong" tonal color, "as if the stimulus of the correct tone first reflexively produced a response but was then recognized as something different after all, because of the wrong overtones." Bolder than Pavlov, he took these findings as evidence of "that complexity of the interlocking of individual reflexes which we generally tend to call a psychic process." In 1907 this was a daring conclusion.[6]

Georg's stay in St. Petersburg came at a turbulent moment in Russian history. He arrived in February 1906, during the interval between the bloody suppression of the October riots and the convening of the first Duma. His sympathies, of course, were with the revolutionaries. As he wrote to his current mistress, Johanna Wolff, in Karlsruhe, he was "a little envious of the Russians"; "if the students should fight, I could not remain

Fig. 14. Sketch of "Pavlovian" dog, ca. 1906.

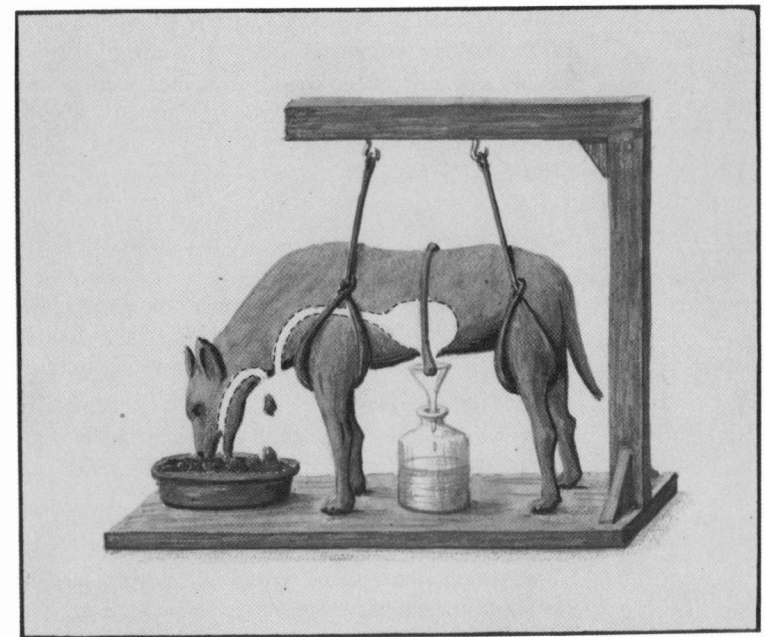

a spectator." But the city was quiet, and he explored the little taverns, watched the services at Saint Isaac's Cathedral, visited the art treasures of the Hermitage, played chess with Russian acquaintances, dazzled his colleagues at the Institute by presenting a paper in Russian, and saw Olga again. She was now the mother of a little boy, "for whom I begin to have avuncular feelings." He was living in style once more, having borrowed a large sum from his mother, much to Johanna's disgust. He capped his stay in Russia with an extended voyage to the Arctic, Arkhangelsk, Murmansk, and Vardö, ostensibly to conduct studies of the northern fauna—as he had conducted studies of the tropical fauna of the Sunda Sea—but actually because he wanted to see that remote and lonely part of the world. He spoke of the excitement of the white nights in Lapland, in whose wastes he remained for many days while awaiting the ship that was to take him back to civilization. He returned in leisurely fashion by way of Stockholm and Copenhagen, where Johanna, a married woman, joined him for a two weeks' cruise along the coast of Norway.

Like the roundabout return, the entire visit to Pavlov's labratory was in a sense a detour, but like his earlier detours—the nocturnal readings of Kant and Marx at Gotha, the semester in Paris, the venture into theater criticism, the excursion into zoology, even the love affairs with a Frenchwoman, a Russian Jewess, and an Englishwoman—it had greatly expanded his horizon. He had been a student or associate of some of the greatest scientists of the age, including Virchow, Hering, Ostwald, Planck, and Pavlov, to name only a few. He himself had become a respected scientist, teacher, author of serious publications in his field, and master of the most advanced physiological techniques then available. His knowledge of the scientific literature had become encyclopedic, his knowledge of the humanities scarcely less so. He spoke or was able to read half a dozen modern languages, to say nothing of Latin and Greek, and he had seen a large part of the world. Few men were ever so saturated in Western civilization. Small wonder that he felt called upon to oppose the suicide of that civilization in 1914.

NOTES

1. These reviews are quoted from a volume of newspaper clippings labeled "Georg Friedrich Nicolai, 'Heidelberger Theater Journal des Heidelberger Tageblatts, zusammengestellt von Luise [?], 1898, 1899, 1900," in the Nicolai archive.

2. Nicolai's reference is to the feminine symbols of profane and sacred love in Richard Wagner's *Tannhäuser*.

3. The description of Nicolai's Far Eastern travels is based on correspondence and memorabilia preserved in the Nicolai archive.

4. International congresses were still a novelty at the turn of the century, and attendance at them was comparatively modest. The Fourth International Congress of Physiology took place in Brussels from 30 August to 2 September 1904. There were 255 scientists in attendance: 92 from the host country, Belgium, 45 from France, 25 from Germany, 23 from Great Britain, 22 from Italy, 11 from the United States, 8 from Austria, 8 from Switzerland, 6 from the Netherlands, 5 from Russia, and a sprinkling from other countries. The program included some of the great names in physiology: Barcroft, Einthoven, Embden, Loewi, Richet, and Sherrington.

5. Since it was as impractical to bring the delicate string galvanometer to the bedside as to transport patients from distant sites to the laboratory, in 1904 Einthoven devised an ingenious method for obtaining electrocardiograms in other hospitals: he used the city telephone system to transmit the signals generated by the patient's heart over a distance as great as several kilometers.

6. This account of Nicolai's experiments is based on his article "Das Lernen der Tiere auf Grund von Versuchen mit Pawlows Speichelfistel," *Zentralblatt für*

Physiologie 22, no. 11 (1908):1–3. His book *Die physiologische Methode zur Er-forschung der Tierpsyche* (Leipzig: Ambrose Barth, 1907) dealt with the technical aspects of the Pavlovian experiments. While Nicolai was clearly aware of the psychological implications of the conditioned reflex even in 1907, he never accepted the philosophical consequences of behaviorism. "Pavlov's marvelous yet simple experiments tell us much about our psyche," he wrote in 1946 at the age of seventy-two (these quotations are from his article "El Mecanismo psiquico explicado por doble inervación a la Base de las Experiencias de I. P. Pavlov," published in February of that year; the author's name is given as Jorge Nicolai). "They not only afford convincing evidence for the theory or association . . . but they give us valuable hints about the foundations and origin of our psychic life. Of course, the real foundation, the fact that we possess a consciousness capable of perceiving what is going on in our body and especially in certain parts of our brain, remains as enigmatic as ever." Later in the article he elaborated on this statement: "The reflex is essentially an objective phenomenon which acquires its ultimate subjective character in man only by virtue of the fact that our consciousness is able to contemplate and interpret it. The objective relationship between the reflex and the environment is not altered by the fact that it becomes the object of our contemplation." Since man has no way of knowing reality except through sensations, that is, reflexes caused by external stimuli, it follows that "the reflex as the link between the contemplating consciousness and the indirectly perceived reality is the closest objective phenomenon that can still be studied by objective methods." Rationalist though he was, Nicolai respected the ultimate mystery of the human mind.

8. A Need for Great Deeds

The brightest years of Nicolai's life fell into the era which later generations, looking through the rose-colored spectacles of nostalgia, would call "the good old times" but which even contemporaries consciously or subconsciously perceived as the golden age of Europe. It was good to be alive, especially if one was young and vigorous, attuned to the spirit of the times, and fortunate enough to belong to a privileged class. By the time the war drove him into conflict with his society, he had achieved all the things by which worldly success is measured and all the satisfactions of which his nature was capable. In the process he offended sundry people with his unconventional behavior, his unorthodox politics, and his hubris, but these shortcomings were excused in an age that tolerated or even admired eccentrics. "When I am old you will be a Geheimrat and an original," Johanna predicted in 1908, "for I believe absolutely in the sincerity of your convictions, and if today you cause objections with some of your views, later on people will be pleased with them as expressions of originality." Without the war her prediction might well have come true. In the spring of 1914, when the renowned Professor Nicolai married the daughter of Carl Busley, a man of wealth and a pillar of society, he was well on the way to a Geheimrat's title, and, with the possible exception of his ever-skeptical mother, none of the distinguished guests attending the wedding banquet at the Hotel Adlon (Fig. 15) could have foreseen that within the year he would be a quasi-prisoner at Fortress Graudenz, charged with harboring subversive ideas.

For the time being, the convictions of which Johanna spoke were little more than private opinions flamboyantly expressed. He was a pacifist, of course, which was almost tantamount to treason in Wilhelm II's realm, and he professed to be a socialist, which was even worse, but he was not actively involved in either movement. The world was at peace, governed by great powers whose statesmen seemed to know their business and whose polished diplomats exuded confidence and spoke French, the language of educated people everywhere and a symbol of the unity of civilization. There were always expeditions against fractious natives in remote tropical countries, but colonial wars did not count, for the earth rightfully belonged to the white race by virtue of its self-evident superiority. The chauvinist clamor on both sides of the Rhine could be shrugged off as empty noise, and who could take the quarrels of backward Balkan peasants seriously? Had there not been two great international disarmament conferences at The Hague, was there not an International Peace Bureau in Bern, did not the Nobel Committee each year solemnly award a peace prize, and—if worse came to worst—had not the socialist parties of every country vowed to refuse to take part in a capitalist war? The Kaiser's antics were worrisome, but Georg found them amusing. When "Willy" and "Nicky," the "Autocrat of all the Russias," met on their yachts off Björkö to sign a friendship pact (which their ministers promptly nullified), he parodied the imperial embrace, forcing the petite Johanna to climb on a chair so that he could throw his arms around her in mock solemnity. He was content to leave the cause of peace to earnest pacifists, starry-eyed idealists like Bertha von Suttner and Alfred Fried, and experts on disarmament or trade like Ludwig Quidde or Norman Angell.[1]

To be both a socialist and a professor in Germany was almost a contradiction in terms, but Nicolai was both. He never joined the party and had no taste for the proletarian life, but he made no secret of his views. He

Fig. 15. Program for Nicolai's wedding, 20 May 1914.

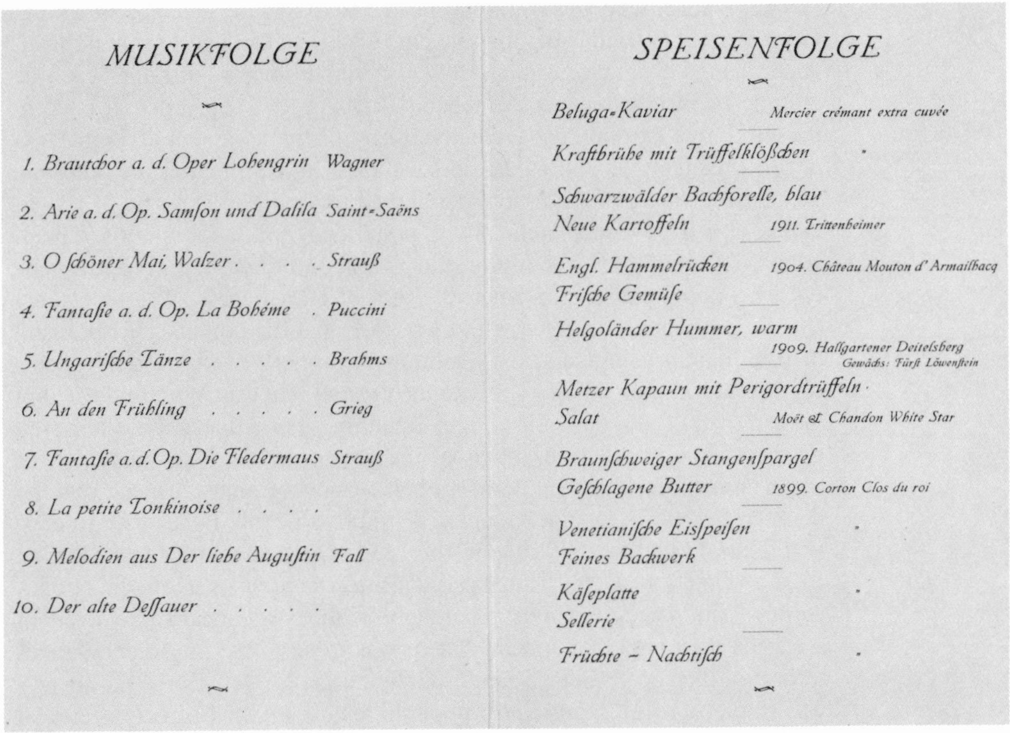

MUSIKFOLGE

1. *Brautchor a. d. Oper Lohengrin* Wagner

2. *Arie a. d. Op. Samson und Dalila* Saint-Saëns

3. *O schöner Mai, Walzer . . . . Strauß*

4. *Fantasie a. d. Op. La Bohéme . Puccini*

5. *Ungarische Tänze . . . . . Brahms*

6. *An den Frühling . . . . . Grieg*

7. *Fantasie a. d. Op. Die Fledermaus Strauß*

8. *La petite Tonkinoise . . . .*

9. *Melodien aus Der liebe Augustin Fall*

10. *Der alte Dessauer . . . . .*

SPEISENFOLGE

Beluga-Kaviar Mercier crémant extra cuvée

Kraftbrühe mit Trüffelklößchen

Schwarzwälder Bachforelle, blau
Neue Kartoffeln 1911. Trittenheimer

Engl. Hammelrücken 1904. Château Mouton d' Armailbacq
Frische Gemüse

Helgoländer Hummer, warm
  1909. Hallgartener Deitelsberg
    Gewächs: Fürst Löwenstein

Metzer Kapaun mit Perigordtrüffeln
Salat Moët & Chandon White Star

Braunschweiger Stangenspargel
Geschlagene Butter 1899. Corton Clos du roi

Venetianische Eisspeisen
Feines Backwerk

Käseplatte
Sellerie

Früchte – Nachtisch

attended socialist rallies and even marched in "Sozi" parades, perhaps more to shock his hidebound colleagues than because he put any faith in demonstrations. He was in fact repelled by the quasi-military discipline of the German Social Democrats and by the dogmatic rigidity of Marx and Engels. His thinking had gone through several phases since he had sat up nights reading their writings as a pupil at the Ernestinum. In Paris he had become acquainted with the French variants of socialism—Fourierism, Saint-Simonism, and the anarchistic individualism of Proudhon—and the last had particular appeal for him, no doubt because it was the antithesis of the despised barracks spirit of the Prussian state. Later he flirted briefly

143

with the "National Social" movement of Friedrich Naumann, the former Protestant pastor who vainly tried to interest the workers in a Christian alternative to the godless materialism of Marx and Lassalle. He attended some of its meetings, read Naumann's magazine *Die Hilfe*, and found himself in agreement with Naumann's message that a joint effort of all classes was preferable to class war as a means of achieving the classless society.[2] But the flirtation did not last long. To the relief of his old friend Otto Buek, now a "private scholar" with radical views, Georg concluded that this joint effort was a chimera pursued by well-meaning dreamers. The propertied classes would no more divest themselves of their riches than the great powers of their armaments. As Proudhon said, "property is theft," and thieves did not voluntarily disgorge their loot.

Thus Georg, who was by no means averse to owning and enjoying property, reverted to socialism, and to its most suspect form at that: anarchism. Anarchism, of course, was not a well-defined dogma but rather a vague attitude of protest against the inequities of the existing order. It encompassed at one extreme the violent activism of the assassins of Tsar Alexander, President McKinley, and other public figures, and at the other the gentle philosophy of a Kropotkin and the unworldly utopianism of a Landauer. Georg, whose anarchism was nonviolent and purely philosophical, admired Kropotkin as a fellow scientist-turned-political-thinker and a martyr for a noble cause. Landauer, the soul of humaneness, was a personal friend. But while he agreed with these men that the voluntary association of free human beings and the abolition of property were desirable goals for the future, they did not apply to the present. He was more interested in the removal of all constraints on his freedom—particularly those imposed by the state—than in the details of the new order. He was anarchist, or rather nonconformist, by temperament, and we may suspect that he flaunted his views to shock, annoy, or impress people rather than to convert them. "I had to think of you," his always critical mother wrote him in 1908, "when I read that Roosevelt considers anarchists as the most dangerous criminals, who must be fought with every means. So even in America they are condemned." There was in any case no urgency about reform of the social order. Seen through bourgeois eyes, European society was stable, a solid, hierarchical pyramid resting on the bedrock of eternal principles, at whose apex an enlightened or at least responsible class ruled by virtue of tradition and wealth, while the toiling masses at the bottom could improve their lot by steady work and proper respect for their betters rather than by listening to socialist agitators. The German middle classes, though they lacked political power, had little to complain about, for they had both money in the bank or under the mattress and hopes for the future, being the bearers of progress and possessors of the greatest treasure of all, a higher education.

As a socialist in principle and a democrat, Georg might object to the inequities of this system, but as an academic person he was its beneficiary and an ardent champion of the culture to which it had given rise. Science, for him the most valuable product of that culture and, like the French language, a bond between civilized nations, was bringing about a revolution more momentous and more beneficial to mankind than any political revolution. Science was the bringer of light, to which all the evils of man's past—hunger, poverty, and disease—must yield. Already the causes of malaria, cholera, yellow fever, tuberculosis, and syphilis were known, and controlling them was only a matter of time. Laymen might not grasp the significance of the equally important advances in theoretical physics— Rutherford's and Bohr's new models of the atom, Planck's quantum mechanics, and Einstein's portentous equation of energy and matter—but the blessings of Marconi's marvelous invention were obvious to all. For Georg, who kept abreast of all these developments, the spirit of the age found its perfect expression in the recently created Nobel prizes, those for physics, chemistry, and medicine, rather than the Peace Prize, which had gone to such unlikely pacifists as Theodore Roosevelt and Elihu Root.[3]

Progress in technology was equally gratifying to a man who thought about the evolution of mankind. Distances were shrinking, speedy trains and sleek ocean liners linked nations and continents, subways and electric streetcars provided cheap and rapid transportation, and the telephone and wireless telegraphy bridged time and space. The ancient dream of Icarus was at last coming true. In 1896, Otto Lilienthal, inventor of the glider and a friend of the Lewinsteins, whose flights at Johannisthal the young Georg had witnessed, crashed to his death, but in 1900 the first Zeppelin rose over Lake Constance, in 1903 the first heavier-than-air flying machine left the ground at Kitty Hawk, and in 1908 Blériot flew across the English Channel in less than thirty minutes. In a world where everybody was becoming everybody else's neighbor, surely war was an anachronism.

But technology had not yet overpowered the comfortable human dimensions of the past. In Berlin coachmen in their old-fashioned cylinder hats and greatcoats still watered their nags at cast-iron pumps and fed them oats from canvas bags. Streetcleaners and sparrows were as busy as ever, for horse-drawn vehicles still outnumbered automobiles. Voyages abroad were major undertakings, requiring elaborate preparations and much bulky luggage. The traveler had time to become adjusted to changes of climate and customs. The telephone might be a practical invention, but lovers, friends, husbands and wives, parents and children still conveyed their feelings and thoughts to each other in long handwritten letters. The pace of life was increasing but not yet frantic. Families were close-knit, though the lines between the generations were clearly drawn. Old people were old and dignified; children were seen but not heard.

Relationships between the sexes were governed by a strict code. Georg's experiences with women, married or otherwise, suggest that this code was honored in the breach as often as in the observance, but a veil of secrecy was drawn over the beds of Wilhelminian society, no doubt adding to the pleasure of their occupants. Golden opportunities for the mingling of the sexes came each winter at the great public balls, where men and women in masks and constumes could shed their identities. Divorce was almost unheard of in "good" families, and illegitimacy was mostly a problem for lower-class women. Georg, who sired his first illegitimate child at eighteen, had several more, among them a son named Georg Wolfgang, whose self-effacing mother, Else Lenz, addressed him as "Herr Professor" and darned his socks and mended his shirts for years afterwards. He in turn gave her a small income and saw no reason to keep the matter secret.

Sports, except for tennis and ice-skating, were a male preserve, as were the professions, by and large. Women depended for their education and entertainment on books and adult education courses. In Germany the works of foreign authors—Anatole France and Romain Rolland, Tolstoy and Gorki, Shaw and G. B. Chesterton, Conrad and Kipling, Dreiser and Upton Sinclair, Jack London and Selma Lagerlöf—were read as quickly as they could be translated, and many women were able to read Dickens and Maupassant or even Dante in the original. Men were less inclined to spend their valuable time with books. Georg, who read Stendhal, Poe, Dostoevski, and Conan Doyle and discussed Hofmannsthal's poetry with Johanna, was an exception. But both sexes devoted many pleasant hours to the theater, opera, and concerts, of which there was a plethora not only in Berlin, Dresden, and Munich but in most provincial cities. Visits to museums and art exhibits formed an equally important part of German middle-class culture.

Nor were the simple pleasures of life neglected. Everywhere there were parks and playgrounds with foot and bridle paths, benches for the weary and ponds with rowboats, excursion steamers, tennis courts, and skating rinks. Lakes and quiet pine forests in easy distance from Berlin beckoned to nature-lovers, bathers, and hikers. At the end of the journey they would find a beer garden or a little country inn where coffee and *Kuchen* with whipped cream was served under chestnut trees.

This then was the golden age in which Georg lived and felt at home. In 1909, at the youthful age of thirty-five, he had been admitted to the charmed circle of professorial privilege. The year before he had been called to Naples to supervise the installation of an electrocardiograph at Anton Dohrn's world-famous marine biological institute (and had spent six enchanted months exploring the beauties of Italy). In an era when many saw German medicine as the best in the world, Nicolai was coming to be regarded as a leading medical figure. With his chief and protector Kraus, he had written the first authoritative textbook on the electrocardiogram. As *Oberarzt* (senior physician) at the Charité, he held a prestigious post at Berlin's most prestigious teaching hospital. He had charge of all diagnostic services, including X-rays and, of course, electrocardiography. Doctoral candidates sought his counsel or worked under his tutelage, making him the head of a "Nicolai school" which upheld his theory of the electrocardiogram against the great Einthoven himself. He insisted respectfully but firmly that his interpretation of the electrical waves measured by the instrument, which he designated A, J, and F, in contrast to Einthoven's P wave and QRS complex, was the correct one. (Though he buttressed his view with impressive historical, physiological, and clinical observations, time has sided with Einthoven.) In addition to lectures and demonstrations for medical students, he gave a general course on the interplay between human evolution and the development of tools as extensions of man's natural organs, a far-ranging inquiry combining biology, anthropology, and history. It was this course, used as a vehicle for expression of pacifist ideas, which aroused the ire of the authorities after the outbreak of the war and served as the preliminary expression of the ideas of *The Biology of War*. Nor was this all. An enthusiastic sportsman himself and also a champion of carrying education beyond the cloistered halls of the university, he held classes for laymen on the benefits and hazards of sports. With funds wangled from the municipality of the borough of Charlottenburg, he created and directed a sports laboratory, the first of its kind in Europe, for the study of the effects of exercise. Last but not least, he operated a lucrative private diagnostic laboratory in partnership with the distinguished biochemist Leonor Michaelis.

This is not the place for a description of Nicolai's scientific contributions, though they deserve a niche in the history of medicine. If we mention one particular set of papers, it is because they reveal both his mastery of a difficult mathematical problem and his razor-sharp polemical style.[4] They deal with the behavior of elastic membranes, which were used by physiologists to measure blood pressure and the like. A certain Professor O. Frank had developed a mathematical model from which he deduced that such membranes assumed a paraboloid shape when distended. Georg challenged this conclusion: "I wish to show by means of a specific example how far one can stray from the truth if one approaches a biological problem from a purely mathematical angle." Some day it would be possible to describe every biological phenomenon in mathematical terms, wrote Nicolai, but at present the complicated formulas in vogue among biologists served only to hide their ignorance of the facts. "The example seems instructive to me, firstly because the problem at hand for once is strictly physical and therefore solvable with relative ease, and secondly because the author is one of the ablest physiological physicists and probably far more experienced in physical-mathematical problems than I." After this disclaimer, Georg took his gloves off. Frank's figures happened to be wrong, "but the question whether the calculations are correct or not is less important than the question whether one should calculate at all, or whether it would not be better to have a look." Georg had done so, taking actual photographs which clearly showed that the shape of the distended membrane was not paraboloid but spherical.

His professorial dignity offended, Frank issued an angry rebuttal, insisting on his theory and charging his young colleague with lack of respect. The argument threatened to deteriorate into one of those absurd academic quarrels in which rank and professorial authority outweigh facts. But Georg stood his ground. It was regrettable, he wrote in his response, that Herr Frank had answered his factual article with personal arguments, for the issue was simply whether or not his theory was correct. Nicolai's experiments had proved that it was not, but "since Frank seems to distrust my experiments and generally to place little value on empirically observed facts unless they can be arrived at by deduction, I have turned to the qualified representative of theoretical physics here in Berlin, a man whose competence in mathematics and theoretical physics even those who might not wish to accept *me* as a competent judge of Frank's papers must concede." That man had authorized him to state that he considered Nicolai's results correct, "that he shares my view that the problem can only be solved experimentally, and that he therefore agrees with my criticism of Frank's work." The man's name was Max Planck! The hapless Frank was not heard from again. But it was not the personal triumph that mattered to Georg. It was the victory of experimental science over scholasticism.

With growing fame came material rewards. Nicolai's patients included not only the Prussian aristocracy but the crowned heads of some of the many principalities of prerevolutionary Germany, august personages who not only paid well but bestowed medals and ribbons on the famous heart specialist. His socialist convictions did not keep him from accepting invitations to the hunt or to a game of poker from barons, or to tea at the Hotel Kaiserhof from their wives. He was called in as consultant in the case of the empress, who suffered from heart trouble and was a voluble talker, whose flow of words he interrupted with the terse command, "kindly take your clothes off, Your Majesty"—an anecdote retold with relish among his friends. Once he examined His Imperial Highness the crown prince. By 1909 he was prosperous enough to move to a spacious house in a refined old neighborhood, Kronprinzenufer 4, where he also had his office and laboratory. Fräulein Elsbeth van Kampen, a spinster who had once briefly been his mistress, served as his secretary, accountant and housekeeper. His income enabled him to buy a châlet called the Dobel in the Black Forest (looked after by another ex-mistress), keep a sailboat on the Wannsee, which at Johanna's suggestion he christened *The Charmante*, collect rare editions, surround himself with fine furniture, travel first class, and frequent the best hotels and restaurants.

Nicolai was thus already a well-to-do man when he improved his fortunes by marrying Friederike Busley a scant three months before the outbreak of the war. The bride, one of the volunteer social workers with whom his mother surrounded herself, was intelligent, warmhearted, and deeply in love with the dashing groom but was neither young enough nor beautiful enough to attract such a connoisseur of feminine charm as Georg. We must conclude that he married her for her money. The engagement was brief and Friederike was apprehensive. Her mother sent ten thousand marks as a wedding gift. The newlyweds moved to a twelve-room apartment in the fashionable "New West," with access to a garden, cellar, and attic and special facilities for Georg's X-ray machine and electrocardiograph (Fig. 16) The annual rent came to eight thousand marks. Georg himself designed the furniture.

He now had everything a man might wish for: a devoted wife, a satisfying profession, recognition, wealth, social position, good looks, health, and a still brighter future. These were the things he sacrificed when, only a few months later, he defied the authorities. As a man of the world he was no more cast for the martyr's role than was Thomas à Becket, a pleasure-loving companion of the king before he became an austere defender of the Church. He was not liable to military service, nor was he morally obliged to raise his voice against the war, as might behoove a pacifist of record. Other pacifists remained silent or, like Albert Einstein after the fiasco of the "Appeal to the Europeans," realized the futility of overt opposition and contented themselves with working behind the scenes for an early peace. Strength of conviction alone, therefore, does not explain the reckless abandon with which Georg threw himself in front of the military juggernaut.

The answer to the puzzle is as complex as the man himself, a tangle of contradictory ideas and emotions shaped by a unique constellation of personal experiences and historical circumstances. In tracing Georg's early history we have encountered many clues to the nature of these contradictions: his having grown up in a home where the prevailing national ideal was bitterly rejected; his rebellion against parents and school; his pro-

Fig. 16. The Nicolais in their apartment in Berlin, June 1914. (After his Russian trip he affected Russian peasant blouses at home.)

longed identity crisis; the conflict between his precocious intellect and his urge to prove his masculinity equal to that of his peers; his possession of a mind too spacious to be contained by the traditional barriers separating fields of knowledge to which ordinary mortals must be limited, and his irascible temper, bordering on the pathological. We must now examine the attitudes of the mature personality toward the men and women in his life and toward the German nation at large.

Up to now, Nicolai had behaved on the whole like an ordinary person in his everyday life; he was a hard worker and a difficult colleague, but otherwise a pleasant enough fellow who liked his creature comforts, enjoyed a good cigar, played a good game of chess and a fair game of tennis, kept a dog, dressed well, and generally conformed to society's expectations.

He was well on the way to becoming the proverbial absent-minded professor, always mislaying or forgetting things. He might have to rewrite a paper two or three times because he had lost the manuscript, and he was apt to miss an important conference because he was playing a game of chess. He arrived in St. Petersburg in the middle of the Russian winter without his overcoat, forgot to cancel appointments, and left practical matters to his mother, his mistresses, or Fräulein van Kampen. "You see, Georg, I knew right away that you would not be here for the move," Frau Elise complained in a typical letter. "At least answer my questions. You spoke of leaving the Goethe here. Am I to store your curtains? Can I keep the chaise lounge? The book shelves in the attic? What about the keys? I take care of everything to the best of my ability, only you must answer right away." He probably never did.

His room at the Physiological Institute (where he was entitled to live and which he painted a scandalous red) was in perpetual disorder unless cleaned and rearranged by female visitors, who also brought flowers, pictures, and knickknacks. His working habits were equally untidy. "I hope your visit [to Einthoven's laboratory in Leyden] has made a deep impression on you," an exasperated older colleague wrote him. "You will understand now what order means in a laboratory."

But the portrait of the lovable distracted professor has a darker side. Forgetfulness in a young person is a form of egotism, the subconscious expectation that others will look after him. Georg, however, was not merely forgetful or careless; he was inconsiderate of other people's feelings, especially those of women, and of his mother in particular. He was not a loving son, nor indeed was Frau Elise a doting mother, but in an age when filial devotion was taken for granted she had grounds for complaint. He seldom came to see her and seldom wrote when he was away. "You know that you had promised to come yesterday," she wrote bitterly on one of many such occasions. "It was wrong to make me wait all evening. I had made a good dinner. You have a telephone everywhere; at least you could have called. I was all the more anxious to see you because I had just received a letter from Edwin and no one was here to read it to me. I am sending it along, for I think you would be interested in your ailing sister, after all. I would so have wanted to talk to you about her." As a rule Frau Elise, always unbending in her peculiar Prussian coolness, clothed her feelings in sarcasm rather than pathos. "Thanks for your cards. I imagine you wrote a lot from Vardö, for there you were bored while waiting for the ship." Returning from one of her own trips—she, too was a great traveler and, despite her poor eyesight, ventured as far afield as Moscow and Paris—she let Georg know that she had no illusions: "And then I arrive in Berlin, where you must be tenderly awaiting me," she wrote from Riga. "As far as things here are concerned, you will be most interested in E's well-being." "E" was Georg's dog. Sometimes she let her anger show. "You needn't trouble to come to the station," she wrote him once. "Since I don't know when you can come to me, I shall come to *you* Thursday to find out when you are coming." Kindred spirits at bottom, both cold and unsentimental to the core, mother and son were forever locked in a battle of wills. Instead of admiring him as other women did, she was critical; instead of marveling at his spectacular success, she always expected him to crash in midflight. He in turn deliberately provoked her by his conduct and his extreme views. Having been reared in the strictest Prussian discipline, she had raised her children in the deliberately permissive way. "And yet a firm hand would have been better," she wrote as an old woman: "I

Fig 17. Nicolai's mother in later life.

saw this too late, for my children were exceptionally strong natures who would not have been harmed by parental constraints."

If Georg felt challenged by his mother, it was because she was his mother, not because he accepted her as an intellectual equal. His attitude toward women was one of unrestrained male conceit and egotism. Grafted on his natural inclination to treat them as sex objects was his firm belief that they were intellectually, emotionally, and even biologically inferior to men. "The fact that I don't know anything about mathematics doesn't necessarily prove that women are atavistic remnants of the past," Johanna protested once. But Georg would have agreed with Nietzsche, who said, "If a woman has scholarly aspirations, there is usually something wrong with her sexuality." In Georg's own words, "Women who are productive are not true women; women consume rather than produce." To which Johanna replied, "Nonsense," quoting Emerson's saying, "In the realm of the spirit we change our sex every moment." She added that men were not merely active and women passive, and that "even you are not pure maleness, for you have an artistic temperament." Georg claimed that women could not think in an orderly fashion. "You must learn that they *can*," she insisted. He said that men suffered more than women. She disagreed. Some women felt the frustration of their physical desire more strongly than some men, she asserted. She had witnessed the grief of mothers, the despair of young girls; she herself had lost a brother when she was fifteen. "Where do you get your ideas?" she asked. Rousseau had said, "Le sentiment vaut mieux que la raison et les grandes pensées viennent du coeur," which she paraphrased, "The light of reason shines on us all, but the fullness of the heart no one can give us." But Georg, unshakably rationalist and conscious of his power over women, remained wedded to his Nietzschean clichés.

We must look closely at his relationship with women, for his reckless defiance of the Prussian military sprang from the same source as his attitude toward the opposite sex, a bottomless egocentricity akin to megalomania. He saw himself as a superman who single-handedly could stop a world war with the power of his intellect. In his autobiographical novel the thinly disguised hero acts out his fantasy of stopping all wars by means of a tiny atom bomb of his invention. The device is so difficult to detect that he is able to plant one under every world capital, all of which he then threatens to demolish unless all nations disarm. The title is significant: "Herr der Erde," "Lord of the Earth." There is no need to describe his countless erotic adventures. Utterly promiscuous, he slept with seamstresses and titled ladies, shopgirls and bluestockings, but he was most attracted by intellectual women, evidently because it was with them that he could assert his superiority most dramatically. Their lack of a comparable education gave him the edge and allowed him to shine in the role of the masterful teacher, even while exploiting their emotional and sexual vulnerability.

Johanna was the most remarkable of his lovers, a strong personality and a keen observer, whose letters combine the intensity of passion with the clarity of hatred. Seen through her eyes, he embodied every aspect of the male principle: Abélard and Don Juan, Faust and Mephistopheles, thinker and rake, the sentimentality of a Werther and the ruthlessness of a Marquis de Sade, chivalry and boorishness, the refinement of a connoisseur of the higher things in life and the crudeness of an oriental potentate. Johanna was a recently married young woman whom Georg swept off her feet. She became his unwilling slave, but she never lost her incorruptible judgment. "My beloved misfortune," she prophetically called him at the very beginning. Only a few months after meeting her at Eva's house in Karlsruhe, he asked her to accompany him to Russia, and although she declined she did join him on the Scandinavian cruise afterward. She was petite, dark, passionate, unconventional, and furious to find herself, after a brief and turbulent affair for which she had sacrificed her marriage to a devoted, sensitive husband, only a member of his harem. A highly intelligent, literate woman who considered herself emancipated, who wrote plays, gave poetry readings, worked for a newspaper, championed women's causes, traveled alone, and had strong sexual urges, she fiercely resented Georg's refusal to treat her as an equal. Yet she could not bear to give him up, not even when he deliberately flaunted his other mistresses before her. "I shall never do you the honor of being jealous of anyone, and certainly not of your little girls," she told him contemptuously. But she *was* jealous. "A man who tells the woman who is ready to give him everything that he does not wish to deprive himself of 'the general erotic atmosphere in which he lives' cannot extinguish love, only devalue it," she wrote. Devalued, she clung to it nevertheless.

She alternately poured impassioned love, rage, maternal tenderness, and biting sarcasm over him. "If you would gather your illegitimate brood around you, you'd make a splendid *pater familias*," she taunted him, and deplored his "forgetfulness," which had "somehow" resulted in the pregnancy of one of his technicians. She scolded him for staying up until dawn, for drinking whisky before noon, and for playing tennis in the midday heat. "You could have been Nagel's successor if I had been your adviser," she chided him. "You think bigger than the others who have petty minds but succeed in their career." She accused him of cruelty but rallied to his side when her most hated rival committed suicide: "The thought that I wanted her and you both dead now fills me with horror." Was Georg's indifference the cause of the woman's suicide? We don't know.

Wounded by his coolness, Johanna cries out: "Sometimes I feel as if I were under your experimental knife and you do nothing but observe how the poison is acting." But she is perceptive herself. "What would cure your strange rootlessness?" she asked, and supplied her own answer. "I believe that if you succeeded in making an important scientific discovery, your need for great deeds would be satisfied." She had put her finger on the root of the rebelliousness that would bring him to a Prussian court-martial. Although he would achieve success, he would always feel himself capable of greater things. Perhaps he would have been satisfied if he had discovered insulin or penicillin or split the atom, not because he craved fame but because it would have made him the benefactor of mankind. He had a need for great deeds.

And yet Johanna, like Marian Hogg, like every intelligent woman who loved him during those years of ascent, accused him of indolence, even while complaining that he worked too hard. Some of this indolence was pose; he often assumed a melancholy air, expressing a sense of futility, boredom, or despair and talking of abandoning his career. From Raïssa, the second of his Russian lovers, we learn that he had tears in his eyes when watching a Chekhov play. But his dissatisfaction with himself was genuine, precisely because he had an exalted opinion of himself. In "Herr der Erde" he would describe himself as a universal genius, "perhaps the most thoroughly educated man of our century." He did not care if people called him an indolent Epicurean, "all the less because these people were not entirely wrong. If one has a fault one cannot deny and is not willing to correct, one must for the sake of one's self-respect call it a virtue." But by then he had known defeat and resignation. In his thirties he had a "need for great deeds," for he knew that he had not yet lived up to his powers.

Johanna made another diagnosis. "You are not passionate, only sensual," she tells him when his ardor cools and his love-making becomes routine. Again and again she rails against his unshakable male conceit. "Have you never known an experiment that failed?" she counters when a play of hers receives bad notices. Furious at his patronizing remark that she will change and end up thinking like him, she asks: "Have you no sense of mutuality?" They discuss books, plays, paintings, politics, and philosophy, he tells her about his experiments, but never does he acknowledge her intellectual equality.

She is equally resentful of a morality that gives men sexual freedom while denying it to women, of Georg's promiscuity, of his matter-of-factness in bed, most of all of her own feminine nature which makes it impossible for her to "separate body and soul." She cries "because the man to whom I give myself has a woman every week, no matter who," because he takes her "as if she were the one from day before yesterday or day after tomorrow, not knowing what it means for her to have waited, waaaiii-ted since October. Oh the devil, rather starve than find misery in the act of love!" She is contemptuous. "How do I make 'demands' on you?" she asks. "The three-hundredth sermon on the serving role of women and all that! Permit me to pass over the generalities in silence. How little use you have for the wholeness of a human being!" Georg made light of such complaints, hers and those of other women. "To correspond with you is like a conversation with the deaf," Johanna once wrote. But he would not let her out of his clutches. The relationship lasted more than six years.

Johanna's was an extreme case, the sexual enslavement of a remarkably intelligent woman. But the pattern was always the same. Georg stimulated, awakened, possessed, and then debased and humiliated his lovers. He put his mark on them for life, so that indeed they found themselves thinking like him. "Outwardly I have come to resemble you," wrote Susi Rosenberg, who for a time shared his favors with Johanna. "Well, dearest Georg, you are my beautiful past that never was the present. You take nothing and give only unconsciously. You leave the most precious part of a woman unloved. Why am I going to school? Because I can't be a woman." And Raïssa, whom he induced to study medicine in Freiburg, was surprised when she passed her examinations. "My self-confidence is restored. You had discouraged me so much that even now I don't have the faith in myself I had before I met you." Georg exacted a terrible price for his attentions. Johanna was right when she accused him of being more interested in power than in pleasure. It is one thing to clothe one's philandering instincts in Nietzschean rhetoric and another to destroy those whose love we accept.

But it is time to turn to the intellectual foundations of Georg's "great deed." His hubris sprang from his awareness of his mental powers. Reared in an environment that placed a premium on intellectual achievement, the precocious boy was conscious of these powers at an early age. Able to solve the most difficult problems with his reason long before he was mature enough to be troubled by the uncertainties that lie beyond reason, he was destined to become an uncompromising rationalist. The world was a solvable problem, if only one was intelligent enough and had enough facts to solve it. Inevitably, he turned to science, the tool of reason par excellence, the key to the physical universe and ultimately to human behavior as well. The faculty of reasoning was the unique product of human evolution, a biological phenomenon and therefore susceptible to scientific analysis. But it also freed man from his biological past and allowed, indeed obliged, him to take his evolution into his own hands. Science made him truly the master of his fate. Henceforth morality, both public and private, must be in harmony with the evolutionary self-interest of the species *homo sapiens. Sapiens*! Man must live up to that most human of his attributes by discarding or at least controlling those instincts which he recognized as harmful remnants of the past. Pacifism was the logical consequence of the insight that war was such a remnant. In a society that still glorified war this was heresy, but it was the gospel the scientist must preach at any risk.

But if Georg's pacifism was the credo of the scientist, he preached it arrogantly. Although he could be charming in conversation, he also easily became overbearing and abrasive. "Drop the schoolmasterish tone in our personal contacts," a member of his journal club once wrote him. "Do not infer from my silence that it is acceptable to me. I am grateful for your advice and instruction in scientific matters, otherwise you are not entitled to use this tone." If lesser minds failed to see what was perfectly obvious to Nicolai's superior intelligence, whether it was a matter of science, politics, history, or personal relationships, they were "idiots," an epithet he bestowed freely and without regard for the consequences on anyone who disagreed with him. Most of his classmates, teachers, fraternity brothers, and colleagues were idiots. Adapted to the Spanish idiom in which he talked and wrote as an exile in Latin America, "idiótico" was still his favorite expression in his old age. It was idiotic to make war in a world whose resources sufficed for all mankind. The General Staff was idiotic not to seek peace after the defeat on the Marne, when it was plain that the enemy would outstrip Germany in a long war. Georg's transfer from Graudenz was precipitated by his remark that it was idiotic—as well as criminal—to sink the *Lusitania* and to use poison gas. It was idiotic to draft him as a private when the country needed doctors. Dr. Böse was an idiot for assigning him menial tasks and jailing him without proper legal grounds. And so an ad infinitum.

Superior intelligence coupled with an aggressive temperament was at the root of his hubris. But the vehemence of his protest against the war points to a deeper, more specific cause. It was a protest against Germany, or rather against the Germans, and it was all the more vehement because it sprang from the love-hate feelings that are nowhere stronger than among members of the same family, who know each other too well and detest one another's faults because they share them. Like Goethe, Heine, Nietzsche, the gentle Hermann Hesse, and the not so gentle Heinrich Mann, Nicolai was a German who felt ill at ease in his German skin. It was Goethe who said half seriously that the Germans should be scattered over the face of the earth like the Jews, for only in exile were they bearable. Nietzsche charged his countrymen with "every crime against civilization in four centuries" and wanted to be remembered as the arch despiser of Germans. Heine in his voluntary exile in Paris cried out that all things German affected him like an emetic, and that even his own poetry at times disgusted him because it was written in German. Nicolai hated the political anachronism of Bismarck's Reich and despised the mass of his compatriots who felt at home in it, obedient subjects who wanted to be governed from above instead of governing themselves, and who confused voluntary acceptance of discipline with freedom.

But Georg's alienation from German society went beyond politics, for political mores determine style and manners. The breath of the French Revolution had not touched Germany, and in rejecting its spirit the nation had also rejected the *savoir vivre*, the common sense and the realism that France contributed to Europe and that Georg valued so highly. "You are a German with a German hatred and cosmopolitan sentiments," Johanna observed. For him, the skepticism of Voltaire, the passion of Delacroix, Victor Hugo, Zola, the subtle psychology of Stendhal, and, yes, the frivolity of Montmartre and the bohemian verve of the Left Bank were ingredients of the European spirit no less essential than the legacy of Goethe and Beethoven, Helmholtz and Virchow. But that spirit could not thrive in a country presided over by a swan-helmeted, swashbuckling romanticist like the Kaiser. The perception of reality was bound to suffer as long as the conduct of a modern industrial society was governed by the myth of divine right and the code of honor of an obsolete warrior caste. In that make-believe world the sober forces of the machine age were disguised by heroic symbols; the present was smothered under the claptrap of the synthetic past. Human behavior was idealized as the struggle between the powers of light and darkness—virtue, chivalry, and duty against lust, greed, and villainy—instead of being taken for what it was, a blend of courage and cowardice, love and hatred, hope and fear, the sublime mingling with the ridiculous. In his time Nietzsche deplored the lack of psychologists among the Germans. As far as Georg was concerned, there were still none.

As might be expected, he overshot the mark. He missed no opportunity to criticize his countrymen and all their works, though his remarks were often intended merely to shock and provoke his listeners. At heart he loved his country, but contemporary Germany was a caricature of his ideal. His mother, a loyal German in spite of her own dissent from the existing order, was the butt of his sharpest barbs. Happy to learn that he admired Pavlov, she found it necessary to add, "Only it should not make you unjust toward the Germans." When he was in Naples she wrote: "It is really too bad that you were born a German. I can believe that you like Italy. There even the occultists, whom you call idiots in Germany, meet with your approval." In 1908, when Count Zeppelin made a triumphant aerial progress over southern Germany, Frau Elise asked: "Why are you so annoyed with Zeppelin? The papers are full of his praise and he is making great voyages with his dirigible, so it can't be all bad." At Kiel, as we learn from Johanna, Georg was severely critical of the German fleet, another source of national pride. "I wish it were night," Johanna wrote on another occasion, "and I were lying on the divan and holding my Bubi in my arms after he has finished his daily anti-German sermon while his entourage listens to his wisdom." Her casual irony gives us a vivid glimpse of Georg's obsession.

The same obsession, thinly disguised as an attack on Prussian militarism, pervades *The Biology of War*. Georg was far too intelligent to expose his flank by making overt anti-German statements during wartime in a book addressed to the public at large. But the soundness of his argument and the loftiness of his humanitarian ideals could not entirely conceal his hostility. His military superiors sensed this animus when they accused him of harboring "anti-national" views. The spirit, not the letter, of his book would later cause his academic colleagues to expel him from their ranks for the same reason. Try as he might, master of linguistic subtleties that he was, the depth of his unspoken feelings betrayed him.

We are at the end of our exploratory voyage. The attempt to trace the hidden emotional and intellectual roots of Georg Friedrich Nicolai's heroism is a rewarding if not always pleasant task. If we knew less about the private man, the public figure would be more attractive, though less understandable. He was a hero nevertheless.

NOTES

1. Quidde, a leading German pacifist, was attacked by Nicolai in 1919 for being too moderate. In 1924, however, he was tried for treason for exposing the secret rearmament plans of the Reichswehr. The British economist Angell also advocated pacifism, but on economic grounds. The two shared the Nobel Prize for Peace in 1933.

2. In 1904 Nicolai was on a walking tour with the young Theodor Heuss, Naumann's editorial assistant and devoted disciple (see letters in the Nicolai archive).

3. Root, who as United States Secretary of War from 1899 to 1904 had been criticized for tolerating brutality by U.S. troops in the Philippines, shared the Nobel prize with Roosevelt in 1912.

4. The details of the Nicolai-Frank controversy are taken from two papers by Nicolai, reprints of which are in the Nicolai archive: "Die Gestalt einer deformierten Manometermembran, experimentell bestimmt," *Archiv für Anatomie und Physiologie* 3 (1907):129–40; and "Noch einmal die Franksche Paraboloidmembran," *Zeitschrift für Biologie* 50 (1907):456–58.

III. THE BELLIGERENT PACIFIST

9. Ovid on the Shore of the Baltic

The tribulations of MKW (Militärkrankenwärter, or medical corps orderly) Nicolai during the two years he was stationed at Danzig were a blend of tragedy and trivia, sacrifice and selfishness, the sublime and the ridiculous. Far from resigning himself to the inevitable, he fought the battle against militarism not only on the lofty plane of ideas but in the humdrum setting of the barracks. While secretly pursuing the all-important matter of his book and exploring new projects for the cause of peace, he carried on a day-by-day guerilla war against the system into whose power he had fallen. Every officer, every former colleague in uniform, and every non-com on the post was as much an enemy as the unseen powers in Berlin and at General Headquarters. No incident was too trifling to serve as a cause for complaint; no challenge was ignored; no opportunity to provoke official eyes and ears was overlooked. Clearly Nicolai enjoyed these skirmishes, but he was also eminently practical and averse to unnecessary suffering. Through an unbroken succession of petitions and protests he tried to escape from the net in which he was caught or to obtain special privileges from the very people he was doing his best to annoy. Actually he was not treated harshly, in part because he was known to have influential friends, especially among Progressives and Social Democrats in the Reichstag, and in part because, even after his fall from grace, he was still a distinguished colleague and member of the Establishment whom the army doctors regarded with a mixture of awe and embarrassment. These men were on the whole decent, intelligent people who found themselves pushed into the role of callous disciplinarians by the rebelliousness of their subordinate. To a later age, inured to the horrors of the Third Reich, the methods used in dealing with undesirable elements in Wilhelminian Germany appear quite humane.

After being inducted into the Landsturm on 1 April 1916, the new recruit was given two weeks of basic training, consisting of drill in the morning and "instruction" in the afternoon. He was then assigned to the Sanitätsamt, the central health authority for the military district. His superiors must have racked their brains for ways to keep this unusual private occupied, for he was provided with pencils, empty ledgers, a ruler, and a bottle of glue, and told to rule blank pages and paste newspaper clippings. From this stultifying activity he shortly graduated to the task of checking accounts and reviewing medical records. This proved to be a mistake, for he promptly discovered billing errors and, worse, impermissible entries in the medical records. He was able to point a finger at an army doctor who had misused his authority to send a politically undesirable convalescent to the front. "Recalcitrant, therefore fit for field duty," the obviously angry physician had written on the chart—a slip of the pen which betrayed an attitude secretly shared by many of his colleagues. Enlisted men who failed to show the proper deference or were suspected of socialist or pacifist leanings were liable to find themselves certified as healthier than they were, as long as the record did not show the examiner's bias. As consultant cardiologist in Graudenz, Nicolai had been able to rescue some of these victims. Now, as clerk in the health service of the same command, he was in a good position to spot such cases. He was hurriedly transferred to what his superior hoped would prove a less sensitive post.

His next assignment was to the bacteriological laboratory. Here MKW Nicolai, lately codirector, with no less an authority than the renowned biochemist Leonor Michaelis, of a sophisticated diagnostic laboratory in Berlin, had to assist an untrained corporal in drawing blood specimens and performing tests for venereal disease, urinalyses, and other menial chores. For the time being he was denied ordinary privileges, such as furloughs or the right to buy his own food. Confined to the post, he ate in the enlisted men's hall, slept in the barracks, polished his own boots, and stood at attention whenever the occasion demanded it.

Nicolai did not like being a private. Not only was his every fiber in rebellion against the constraints of military discipline, but he was shocked to find himself suddenly on the wrong side of the deepest gulf dividing German society, that between the *Gebildeten*, the educated elite, and the common people, a gulf which his most fervent belief in democracy did not enable him to bridge. Consciously he might frown on class distinctions based on privilege and property, though he would have considered it self-evident that even in Utopia only educated people were fit to govern. Subconsciously he shared the *Bildungsdünkel* of his caste, the conceit with which those who possessed a classicial education and an academic degree looked down on those who did not, well-to-do and poor alike—in a word, the *Ungebildeten*. Now as a lowly orderly, he was being treated as one of them, and he resented it deeply. It was one thing to risk one's liberty for one's convictions, and another to be stripped of one's professorial dignity.

Nicolai was not the only one to be shocked by the turn his career had taken. In the Wilhelminian social hierarchy, the degradation of a physician and a university professor was a jolt to the system and a cause for indignation. Paradoxically, it was a Socialist, the Reichstag deputy Georg Davidsohn, who brought the case to public attention. Nicolai must have alerted him of his plight within a day or two after his forcible induction, for barely a week later, on 7 April 1916, Davidsohn laid the matter before the Reichstag.[1] The moment was auspicious, for that august body happened to be engaged in exercising its only constitutional right, that of approving the budget, and on this day was debating various appropriations for the War Department. Although approval was a foregone conclusion, the government was anxious to avoid conflict with the Social Democrats, whose left wing had already parted company with the more docile majority and was ready to use this opportunity to air its grievances against the army.

A Majority Social Democrat with an ingratiating manner, Davidsohn related the Nicolai case in a low key, as if trying to avoid offending Herr Von Wandel at the government table, to whom, as acting minister of war, he was addressing his remarks. Perhaps he hoped to accomplish more in backstage conversation, for—like many fellow Socialists—he maintained excellent confidential relations with important government officials whom it was his duty to oppose publicly. The renowned professor, he said, had been denounced while at Graudenz by "physicians under his command" (sic) who objected to some of his comments on the conduct of the war. A "noble gesture" on the emperor's part had seemingly settled the matter, but no sooner had Nicolai resumed his lectures in Berlin than he was exiled once more. The members of the House knew the story thus far, for it had been in every newspaper. What they did not know was the sequel. Asked to take the oath on his arrival in Danzig, Nicolai had refused, both because he was a conscientious objector and because as a physician under contract with the War Ministry he was not obliged to do so. As a result, this man was now a private, forced to eat army food and to submit all his writings to the military authorities, "who, needless to say, understand less than nothing" of scientific matters. "That, gentlemen, is the case of Herr Doktor Nicolai, professor at the University of Berlin and now an orderly. Such occurrences would be impossible if there were a little less nervousness in certain places." The deputy concluded his remarks by citing another example of "nervousness," the indictment of the archivist Dr. Wittmann, who had insulted the honor of the German army by writing, in a private letter, "As a Catholic I regret and condemn the atrocities in Belgium and northern France; as a Christian I deplore the misery of the war."

If there was something ludicrous about Davidsohn, presumably a class-conscious representative of the toiling masses, reproaching the army for forcing a professor to insult his bourgeois palate with rations that were good enough for common soldiers, it escaped the attention of his listeners. As for nervousness, Von Wandel showed no trace of it. He shrugged off the complaint as being in the competence of the Generalkommando in Danzig, which, regrettably, had not yet furnished the War Ministry with the records. He was equally bland in his reply to Cohn and Stadthagen of the Socialist Working Conference, a radical rebel group on the left wing of the party, who were less considerate of the army's feelings than was Davidsohn. According to Dr. Cohn, army rations were far from good enough for the common soldier, especially when compared with the food served at officers' clubs. He had no hope of changing the class character of the German army during the war, he said, but he wished to air a long list of grievances on behalf of enlisted men, including the poor quality and preparation of meals, the insulting language and physical abuse they had to endure, the shortness of leaves and scarcity of railroad passes, delays in granting medical discharges—especially to men suspected of being Social Democrats—and the recent curtailment of the right of appeal.

It was a familiar ritual. Championing the cause of the common soldier was tantamount to criticizing the army, and criticizing the army was both unpatriotic and in bad taste. Only men of the extreme left would stoop so low, but they were beyond the pale in any case. To let them speak at all was to prove that parliamentary freedom did exist in Germany. The national parties sat by disapprovingly, and the regular Social Democrats kept a wistful silence. In the end the leftist resolutions would be defeated, the debate would be cut off, and obstreperous deputies like Karl Liebknecht, an outcast shunned even by his own party, would be called to order and eventually silenced.

And so it came to pass on this day. But the presiding officer was not without finesse. Before calling on Von Wandel to defend the government, he asked the Reichstag to join him in a message of gratitude and good wishes for Field Marshal Von Hindenburg, "strategic genius and liberator of East Prussia," on his fiftieth anniversary as a soldier. The deputies rose as one man, and with this patriotic interlude the atmosphere was cleansed. The caviling of the uncouth men of the Left had been put into proper perspective, and Von Wandel could speak in the mild tones of a father explaining to his children that wicked or thoughtless people sometimes interfere with the Lord's design. The debate was thereupon closed—over the lone objection of Liebknecht—and sections 4 to 43 of the budget, "War Ministry, Sundry Expenditures," were declared approved without even the formality of a voice vote.

In this setting Davidsohn's tame protest was a mere pinprick. Still, the army, possibly because of his intercession, made the last attempt to come to terms with its problematical MKW. That at least was Nicolai's interpretation of a broad hint, dropped by his drill sergeant, to the effect that he might yet be reinstated as a physician if only he would take the oath, a mere formality after all. Nicolai pretended not to understand, and when his commanding officer formally repeated the request, he refused indignantly, declaring that he was not one to make deals in matters of conscience. On the contrary, he challenged the legality of his induction and submitted protest after protest to the Sanitätsamt, demanding that they be referred to "higher authorities" through channels. They were not. He then asked for leave so that he might consult his legal counsel in Berlin. This request also was denied. The eminent professor remained an orderly.

For a man as articulate as Nicolai, it was as hard to be deprived of the right to express his opinions as it was to have lost his freedom of movement. He was now effectively muzzled. But a last chance to make his voice heard came unexpectedly in October, when *Neue Jugend* ("New Youth"), a recently founded publication with pacifist tendencies, asked for a contribution for its almanac from the already legendary dissident. Nicolai immediately accepted, disregarding the prohibition imposed on him. The contributors to the almanac were the cream of the intellectual opposition to the war in Germany and Austria, among them the writers Franz Kafka, Franz Werfel, and Heinrich Mann, the poet Else Lasker-Schüler, and the artists George Grosz and Oskar Kokoschka. The novelist Leonhard Frank and the anarchist philosopher Gustav Landauer were personal friends of Nicolai; Else Lasker-Schüler had once been his lover; Friedrich Wilhelm Förster was the son of the cosigner of the "Appeal to the Europeans" and a pacifist in his own right, as was the writer Annette Kolb, daughter of a French mother and a German father. Censorship being what it was, overt opposition was out of the question, but the very names of the authors amounted to a program of subversion, and indeed *Neue Jugend* was suppressed almost immediately. Nicolai's contribution did not even see the light of day.[2]

"Barbarus hic ego sum" was the theme of his message. The quotation from Ovid's *Tristia* was not wholly appropriate, for in its entirety the line, written at Tomi on the desolate Black Sea coast, where the wrath of Augustus had banished the Roman poet, was the ageless lament of the exile condemned to live among uncomprehending strangers: "Barbarus hic ego sum, quia non intelligor ulli" ("Here I am a barbarian, for no one understands my speech"). Nicolai was stationed on German soil, and if he was not understood it was because his arguments fell on deaf ears, not because his speech was not perfectly intelligible to his superiors. But the point of comparison was the degradation of a civilized human being at the hands of a brutish tyranny. "Here in Kashubia," he wrote, "I felt at first like erstwhile Ovid in Tomi, but the Roman exile had the advantage of camping among backward Dacians and could take comfort in the thought that his fellow Romans at home were more civilized, whereas I am living among my own countrymen."

What were his complaints after six months in uniform? Ovid, he said, could take his sorrow to the shore of the eternal sea and forget the annoyances of his existence at the sight of the majestic waves, whereas a private in the German army was not free to visit the lovely Baltic beaches, except with the written permission of his captain. Ovid had probably been able to choose his attire, whereas the German soldier was forbidden to wear dress shirts, stand-up collars, kid gloves, and yellow boots, the symbols of upper-middle-class status that officers were privileged to display. The private was forced to have his hair cut to regulation length, trim his beard, and submit to countless picayune rules designed "never to let him forget that he belongs to a band of heroes." He must spend his entire day in a state of vigilance lest he forget to salute some passing non-com. Even at mealtime, in the very act of lifting a spoonful of soup to his lips, he must jump up and stand at attention. Were these the right measures for instilling the fighting spirit into the defenders of the fatherland? Or were the innumerable regulations intended as reminders of their lack of freedom, devised because the authorities had come to realize that in the twentieth century, "the century in which communications and technical advances have made universal brotherhood a necessity, peaceful citizens can make good soldiers only if their free will is broken"?

Nicolai did not tell the *Neue Jugend* that he was making every effort not to be a good soldier. In the testimony given at his subsequent court-martial, his superiors spoke with feeling of his many derelictions. In a spit-and-polish environment he took pains to appear sloppy. The former dandy let his hair grow long and sported an untidy beard. His boots were not shined, buttons were missing from his uniform, and a cigarette dangled from his mouth. Athletic in civilian life, he now affected a slouching posture, protesting with his body as well as with his spirit. He was often late for reveille. Off duty, he violated regulations by wearing mufti and failing to salute officers. On duty, he had his nose in a book whenever he was not otherwise occupied.

Trivial as his grievances were, Nicolai succeeded in giving them a symbolic twist: the indignities he suffered were offenses against civilization, committed by a despotic regime bent on enslaving the basically peaceable masses in order to wage war. He had discovered that the common man was deprived of his human rights by military law. "In judging our army impartially," he wrote, "we tend to lose sight of the fact that the German soldier must be regarded as legally disenfranchised. He can neither marry nor have a tooth pulled without the consent of his legal guardian, the captain, also known—for this very reason—as the father of his company." But since men in their forties could hardly be classified as children, it followed that they were considered as subhuman, in other words, as animals, a fact that went far to explain the liberal use of barnyard language in Prussian barracks. Those who would ban the use of such language as offending dignity or delicacy were wrong, for it expressed nothing more than the plain truth. The "infamous and barbaric" laws of the Prussian army were originally designed for twenty-year-olds but were presently applied to mature men, fathers and providers. If men who, after decades of teaching, had the right to consider themselves mentors of youth were forced to snap to attention before the greenest officer candidate and take his abuse if he found fault with their posture (Nicolai could not have been more obvious), then one might think that ultimate despotism had been reached.

But such was not the case. The height of despotism, Nicolai asserted, was the arbitrary manner in which regulations were applied. Since every waking moment in the enlisted man's life was hedged in by some sort of prohibition, every move he made without express permission amounted to a violation of some rule or other and made him liable to punishment at the whim of his superiors. The average soldier would get by because his officers would wink at trifling offenses, but the "difficult subordinate"—another reference to the writer's own case—could expect no such leniency. *He* was made to obey the rules in all their strictness and had no recourse against tormentors who could claim that they were merely following the book, even though they acted maliciously. Thus applied, the law became a device for punishing nonconformists. The German soldier was bound to develop a slave mentality unless he was endowed with truly heroic powers of resistance. But Nicolai refused to give up hope for a better Germany. "I have never belonged to those who consider this nation hopeless," he wrote, implying that there were ample grounds for despair, "and I have never believed that August 4 [1914] could be the culmination of the German spirit." Even in "darkest Kashubia" he was waiting every day for the awakening of the new Germany, which was in truth the old Germany, "that now legendary union of humane spirits which we love as our fatherland, and which—once it becomes reality again—all men worthy of being called humans will love."

To inflate his grievances into a great moral issue was a tour de force only an egomaniac could have achieved. While the war was devouring a million lives (1916 was the year of Verdun and the Somme), Nicolai was airing the real and imaginary wrongs committed against his person. But there was a connection between the caste system and militarism in Imperial Germany. As he saw it, men were going to their deaths because they had been taught *Kadavergehorsam*, the blind obedience of cattle going to the slaughter. Readers of *Neue Jugend* would appreciate his argument, he knew, because, quite apart from the war, they hated Prussian-German militarism as an all-pervading, arrogant, stultifying, and ultimately deadening force. The distaste of the radical intelligentsia for the anachronistic warrior caste was of long standing, and the war had aggravated this distaste. Nicolai was touching a raw nerve.

His message ended on a frankly seditious note. The name *Neue Jugend* implied a program, he wrote. "I do not know you and I do not know whether your goals are my goals. But the word 'new' seems to indicate a desire to turn away from today's values." What he had to say on that subject could not be said in public, "not even in the cautious language of scientific formulations," but in due course the truth would prevail, proclaimed perhaps in brutal form by men of action, the soldiers in the trenches. "And if you really are the new youth that is bound to come some day as the vanguard of the new humanity—if you are not just another clique of literary aesthetes—then you will do without encouragement from me what the world expects of you and what cannot yet be said today." His meaning could not have been plainer, and he was surprisingly optimistic if he expected the censor to pass such inflammatory language. He was also less than candid in pretending not to know the personalities or the goals of *Neue Jugend*. Perhaps he did not know the actual names of the contributors to the almanac, being isolated in a military environment at Danzig, but he must have been aware of the nature of the venture. The editorial office was in fact housed in his own deserted apartment on Rankestrasse 34 in Berlin, and Heinz Barger, the young publisher, was making his home there, taking care of Nicolai's valuable furniture and, alas, periodically falling behind in the rent. Whatever the nature of this connection, it speaks for Nicolai's reputation as a war resister that the impecunious Barger went to the expense of having his "open letter" typeset in the face of overwhelming odds against its publication.

It was indeed a bad time for independent spirits. The authorities no longer tolerated even the most veiled criticism. Liebknecht, deprived of his parliamentary immunity, was in the penitentiary for denouncing the war at the May Day demonstration. The Bund Neues Vaterland, a group of very respectable people working quietly for an early peace, had been suppressed, and its courageous secretary, Lilli Jannasch, was likewise in jail. With Hindenburg and Ludendorff now at the helm, the military had tightened its grip on the nation and embarked on a fight for total victory. The indecisive chancellor was already little more than a figurehead, and the Kaiser himself was rapidly fading into the shadows. Coerced by the High Command, the Reichstag was about to pass the Patriotic Auxiliary Labor Law, which made every male between the ages of sixteen and sixty liable to compulsory labor. The war had become total. In this climate Nicolai's attempt to make his voice heard was doomed to fail. Save for the copies of *The Biology of War* that were smuggled across the Swiss border the following year, none of his writings reached German readers until after the collapse. The letter to *Neue Jugend* was resurrected as part of Nicolai's collected essays in 1921.[3] By then the Prussian army was no more, though its spirit lived on.

In fairness to the army, it must be said that Nicolai was his own worst enemy. What he called chicanery was often little more than an attempt to maintain a minimum of discipline. The treatment he complained about no

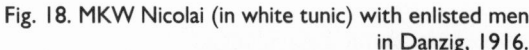

Fig. 18. MKW Nicolai (in white tunic) with enlisted men
in Danzig, 1916.

doubt at times was influenced by the loathing his superiors felt for a pacifist, but more often than not he gave them ample provocation. His unmilitary bearing was calculated to make him look like a walking protest (Fig. 18), and he openly belittled his superiors in front of the other enlisted men. He aired his political views freely wherever and whenever he found an audience. His tone had not changed since the fateful luncheon at the Königlicher Hof in Graudenz; if anything, it was sharper. Germany bore the sole guilt for the war; her conduct of military operations was criminal; the use of poison gas would bring well-deserved retaliation; submarine warfare would fail of its purpose and bring America into the war on the enemy side; the German fleet had turned tail at the battle of Jutland, the battle Germans were hailing as a triumph over the British navy. The men of the High Command—the revered pair of Hindenburg and Ludendorff—were idiots. The military situation was hopeless, the political outlook worse.

Faced with such provocations, Nicolai's superiors had little choice. Nevertheless, the strictures on his activities were gradually relaxed, he was granted substantial privileges, and it was not until the spring of 1917 that official patience was exhausted and he was called to account for disciplinary offenses.

Far more important, of course, than the unending fight against army regulations was the fate of the still unpublished *Biology of War*. The matter was always on his mind. It was at the root of his troubles with the military and touched his personal life profoundly, poisoning family relationships and destroying his career. It alone justified his sacrifices. The existence of the manuscript had remained a secret. It had had nothing to do with his removal from Graudenz or his subsequent demotion. Those measures he had drawn upon himself by his scathing tongue and his uncompromising attitude. Meanwhile, he had used his reprieve in Berlin during the winter of 1915–16 to find a publisher. With the return of his friend Thesing from the western front, the problem seemed solved. Thesing's firm, Verlag Naturwissenschaften in Leipzig, a respected publishing company specializing in scientific books, was the ideal nest in which to hatch the political cuckoo's egg, with its learned title. As a fellow pacifist, Thesing could be counted upon to keep the project a secret in the hope that the publication would present the censor with an accomplished fact. Nevertheless, he must have known that he was taking great risks. It was not to be expected that a government which had refused to let Nicolai lecture before a small audience (on his return from Graudenz sixty persons had registered for the forbidden course) would allow him to put the same subversive ideas before a much larger public through a book. Since May 1915, moreover, preventive censorship had gone into effect, and a publisher who submitted an unacceptable book risked not only the loss of his investment but a fine or even a jail sentence.

Nicolai's own situation was even more precarious, for since his induction he was under orders to abstain from political utterances and to submit his writings, political or otherwise, to the commandant at Danzig. He could only claim that these orders did not apply to a book that was already in press. Both he and Thesing may have banked on the chaotic state of censorship in wartime Germany. This function was exercised independently by each of the twenty-odd Generalkommandos into which the country was divided, and it happened not infrequently that one censor would pass a publication that a colleague in another district would have banned. Nicolai's book stood no chance in Prussia, but since it was to appear in Leipzig, a Saxon censor might let it get by.

The galley proofs had begun to arrive in Danzig in April 1916, at the very time when Nicolai was undergoing basic military training. He hid them among other papers and began to show a remarkable zeal for his clerical duties, seizing the opportunity to do his proofreading under the very noses of his superiors. He was pleasantly anticipating the stir the book was bound to cause when, early in May, his new commander, Generaloberarzt Böse, sent for him and demanded the manuscript. He answered that the manuscript was not in his possession. This was the literal—but only the literal—truth and did not fool Böse. A few days later Böse, according to Nicolai's blow-by-blow account, detained him in his office in a "suspiciously prolonged conversation," while a certain Dr. Kschicho searched the room in which Nicolai kept his papers and in which he had spent such an inordinate amount of time recently. The galleys were found and he was arrested on the spot, placed under guard, and held incommunicado.

The arrest was of doubtful legality, but Böse wanted to teach his slippery excolleague a lesson by keeping him locked up for a while. Not even Frau Nicolai, who had recently joined her husband in Danzig, was allowed to learn what had happened, for she might alert his influential friends in Berlin. But Böse had not reckoned with his prisoner's resourcefulness. Although a guard was posted at the door round the clock, Nicolai succeeded in smuggling out a letter, which was delivered to the minister of war the next morning. By one o'clock that afternoon he was a free man, freer than before his arrest. Böse, impressed with the magical power of his subordinate (the order for the release must have arrived by telegram), became positively obliging. He granted Nicolai permission to leave the post until ten o'clock that evening. He informed him that henceforth he was free to live in town and buy his own food. Evidently Davidsohn's intercession had done some good after all. But Nicolai received formal orders to desist from further clandestine attempts to publish his book; Thesing was given an official warning; the plates were impounded.

What made this setback especially galling was the fact that the authorities had been alerted by a person in Nicolai's family circle, none other than his father-in-law, Geheimrat Busley. Nicolai was too proud or too embarrassed to publicize this fact. In his later public account of his wartime experiences[4] he referred to the informer merely as an official of the Schichau Yards who had entry to his home; in a letter to Pfemfert written immediately after his arrest, however, he left no doubt, describing his betrayer as a man of means, a Geheimrat and personal friend of the Kaiser who lived in Berlin and was responsible for negotiating contracts between Schichau and the navy. This could only be Busley, the general representative of Schichau Yards, which just then was feverishly producing submarines.

Busley, an impressive man with bushy eyebrows, aquiline nose, walrus mustache, and jutting chin (Fig. 19), was a naval engineer, an authority on ships' engines, and a technical adviser on naval matters to the Kaiser, whom he had often accompanied on his famous northern cruises. He was naturally conservative in politics, an ardent monarchist, and a staunch patriot. The pacifist views of his brilliant but obviously demented son-in-law were anathema to him. Sometime during the preceding winter in Berlin, Nicolai had discussed the plans for his forbidden book in Busley's presence at a family dinner. The older man roared his disapproval and announced that he would take drastic action. Asked whether he would at least read the book before condemning it, he declined indignantly. "*We* are painfully earning our living from the war," he had said, according to Nicolai, "and this fellow writes for peace!" The two equally strong-willed men faced each other in a cold rage. Busley, who two years earlier had

Fig. 19. Carl Busley, Nicolai's father-in-law.

consented to his daughter's marriage to a rising star whose eccentricities were outweighed by his success, now saw his son-in-law as an enemy of the fatherland who must be prevented from spreading his defeatist poison. Nicolai, who had condescended to marry Friederike Busley for the sake of her generous dowry, now felt that he had torn the mask of patriotism from a member of the ruling class and exposed the hideous face of the war profiteer. He was not altogether unhappy, for the episode was grist for his mill, but he had not expected his own father-in-law to turn informer. "One gentleman less," he wrote bitterly to Pfemfert. The break was permanent. Soon afterward Busley made a new will, which excluded his son-in-law from any inheritance and even forbade him to handle any of the assets that would come to Friederike. Nicolai's principles were beginning to cost him dearly.

He was not entirely unprepared for the eventuality that his book might be confiscated. Several copies of the manuscript were circulating among friends in Germany, and two were somewhere in Switzerland, one smuggled out by the writer Leonhard Frank and the other carried out in the official pouch of a sympathetic diplomatic courier of the Reich. Nicolai had made good use of the past winter in cultivating his connections in the capital. After the war he spoke contemptuously of "men in high places" who had been willing to smuggle books and letters across the border and slip him confidential information from the Foreign Office and even the War Department, but who lacked the courage of their conviction, "men who assured me of their sympathy over a bottle of Burgundy in the privacy of their homes but would not return my greeting *Unter den Linden*." For obvious reasons he never identified these helpers, though there is no doubt that they existed. They might not have shared Nicolai's extreme views, but they were intelligent and well informed, and as high-ranking civil servants and professional diplomats they understood the weakness of Germany's military position and secretly opposed the do-or-die policy of the High Command and its rabid Pan-German followers. But in the face of what the chancellor himself privately called the "mad political unreason of blind emotions," a profound sense of frustration pervaded the upper echelons of the government. "It is truly a miracle," the chancellor's aide Kurt Riezler confided to his diary, "that the German nation does not founder on this dilettantism in which it has an unshakable faith because it wears a uniform."[5] Nicolai could not have said it better. Riezler's prophecy that in defeat "a Germany with mortal physical wounds will be wholly confused spiritually" might have been lifted from *The Biology of War*. But publicly these men had nothing to say. The High Command was omnipotent and infallible. *Zivilcourage*, a virtue highly prized by Nicolai, was not the forte of Germany's civil servants. Nicolai had many sympathizers and few supporters.

Once the last chance for publishing his book in Germany had vanished with the confiscation of the plates, Nicolai alerted his intermediaries in Switzerland to go to work. He then took an additional precaution. A Swiss publisher might be beyond the reach of the German authorities, but the author was not. To let a work appear abroad that had already been declared subversive at home was to invite retribution. Accordingly, he wrote a letter to Pfemfert to serve as proof that the manuscript was already abroad and that its fate was beyond his control, in case he should be called to account.[6] It was an ingenious piece of deception, meant for official eyes but written in a conspiratorial tone, as if he did not want it to fall into official hands. With a show of indignation he describes the search for the galley proofs and his arrest (of which he had already informed Pfemfert in an earlier, truly confidential letter). But his lot is easier now, he continues sanctimoniously, and he may well be satisfied with the outcome of the affair, were it not for his fear that the already circulating copies of the manuscript may fall into the wrong hands.

> My book has now been confiscated, and that troubles me greatly, of course, for I have reason to believe that two of the copies are in a foreign country and that the work might conceivably be published there, perhaps in a distorted form and with all sorts of errors, and that would be bound to create a very bad impression.

Ostensibly his was the case of a fussy author, but that was not all:

> Unfortunately I see no way of preventing this eventuality. The only person who might help is not likely to cooperate, for, apart from the fact that I have no way to communicate with him, I am told that R. has meanwhile become very anti-German, a most regrettable development, to be sure. I am not at all certain, moreover, that he knows the whereabouts of the manuscript.

The identity of the mysterious "R." would not be hard for the authorities to establish. He was quite obviously Romain Rolland, the French pacifist, living in voluntary exile in Switzerland. Rolland was in touch with Einstein and with Pfemfert himself. He exercised an enormous moral authority in pacifist circles of every country. Many German sympathizers wrote to him or, if they were able to do so, made the pilgrimage to his place of refuge at Vevey. Hermann Hesse, Franz Werfel, Stefan Zweig, and many other German intellectuals were his friends. Young writers sent him their articles and poems. Though attacked as a Germanophile in France, he abhorred German militarism and made no effort to hide his feelings. It was thus entirely plausible that Nicolai, who from the beginning had hoped to see a French edition appear simultaneously with the German original, should have tried to enlist his help. The allusion to his alleged anti-German bias would not be misunderstood by Pfemfert, who was himself sending copies of *Aktion* to Vevey. It was calculated to show Nicolai in the pose of a good German patriot, should it become necessary to produce the letter in court, for the risk of communicating with a citizen of an enemy country was considerable. On the other hand, that Nicolai did not at the moment know the whereabouts of his brainchild was true. He had entrusted the manuscript to his couriers and left the details to their discretion, so that he was somewhat in the position of a man on a desert island who has placed a message in a bottle and hopes that somebody will find it.

As it happened, Rolland had no knowledge of the manuscript. By coincidence he first heard of Nicolai within a day of the latter's letter to Pfemfert. On 14 May 1916 he recorded in his diary the visit of the young German poet Alfred Wolfenstein, a cofounder of *Aktion* and intimate of Pfemfert, and who was thus well informed about Nicolai. "Wolfenstein told me of a great independent in Germany who deserves to be famous as an equal of Liebknecht but who, strangely, has been kept out of the public eye," Rolland wrote. Nicolai was one of the men "whose name Germany will be happy to remember at a later time," he prophesied.[7] The prophecy remained unfulfilled. Like many educated people of his time, Rolland overestimated the power of rational thought. He believed that the intellectuals of Europe were destined, like high priests, to proclaim the truth to a humanity that only needed to hear it to be converted. In this he was at one with Nicolai.

Being published by unauthorized persons abroad was not the only danger Nicolai pretended to fear for his book. Pfemfert should know, the letter continued, that he had been approached in the street by a stranger, a soldier whose uncle owned a print ship in Königsberg, who had requested one or two chapters for a clandestine German edition. He had refused, but others "who might possibly be holding galley sheets or manuscripts" might get the same idea. His concern, he wrote, was for the distortion that would result from piecemeal publication. By themselves certain chapters would have a "purely inflammatory" effect because of the absence of balancing chapters in which he spoke of "Germany's true mission." "And you know," he added piously, underlining each word for the potential benefit of the judge advocate, "how much I abhor purely agitatory effects." Wasn't it deplorable that the authorities saw only the antimilitaristic tendency in a book intended to strengthen Germany's prestige? Its conciliatory message would be lost unless the book were published as a whole. Unlike the preceding letter, which as usual was to be destroyed immediately, Pfemfert was to keep this one for future use, and this final instruction should dispel any doubts about its real purpose.

Having protected himself as best he could, Nicolai set about to accomplish the very thing he had expressly repudiated. While his friends abroad quietly explored the prospects for an edition in Switzerland, he made every effort to bring excerpts of his book before the German public. Dropping the pose of the pedantic author who insists on the integrity of his text, he authorized Pfemfert to publish several chapters that could pass for scientific articles, such as "The War Instinct" and "War and the Struggle for Survival," in *Aktion*. Strangely enough, this piece of effrontery in the face of a ban on all of his writings did not cause a ripple at the Danzig Commandatura. As for the censors of the Generalkommando in Berlin, they either accepted the scientific titles at face value without reading the essays or failed to grasp Nicolai's argument. In the latter case they were singularly inept, for the political overtones of seemingly technical statements were unmistakable, as when the writer says that modern war causes a negative biological selection by eliminating the young and healthy while protecting "the blind, deaf-mutes, idiots and hunchbacks, the scrofulous, the insane, the impotent, the paralytics, epileptics, dwarfs, and freaks." Was it the biologist or the pacifist who noted that modern battle conditions were causing an unparalleled accumulation of mental and nervous disorders?

Perhaps the censors in Berlin allowed *Aktion* to exist as a showpiece for the freedom of the German press, for Pfemfert was not afraid to show his colors. He took delight in displaying for his readers the most violently anti-German passages from Nietzsche's *Ecce Homo* in order to refute the claim that the philosopher had been a German patriot and the embodiment of the Prussian spirit. Was it necessary, he asked, to enlist the ghost of the man who had written, "It is my ambition to be known as the despiser of Germans par excellence?" Were there not enough defenders of the fatherland among living intellectuals, for example, Thomas Mann and Gerhart Hauptmann? *Aktion* had mourned the death of a Frenchman, Charles Péguy, "who lived for humanity and fell for the grotesque idea which his compatriots call the national honor."[8] The writer did not have to spell out his opinion of his own compatriots' notion of national honor. In the midst of the war, whole issues of *Aktion* were filled with the writings of enemy nationals, among them André Gide, Paul Claudel, and Maxim Gorki. "Whence such freedom under a censorship that at other times can be quite tyrannical?" Romain Rolland asked. "Is it because the powers-that-be are not worried about these intellectuals, knowing that their public is muzzled, that they cannot direct opinion as in France?"[9] There was much truth in this observation. The oblique attack on militarism and nationalism of this handful of German intellectuals took place on the lofty plane of ideas, and neither the censors nor the public made the connection between ideas and reality. As in the days of Goethe and Schiller—and during and after the Hitler era—the German bourgeoisie conceived its intellectual treasures as a sort of heavenly currency, a hedge against reality, rather than coin in the practical world.

But not even *Aktion* could risk publishing certain chapters of *The Biology of War*, and Nicolai resorted to another subterfuge. He persuaded the aged Wilhelm Förster to issue one of the most inflammatory chapters as a brochure. The distinguished astronomer agreed, insisting only that some of the most seditious language be deleted. "This is a chapter from a book which for various reasons cannot be published as yet," he wrote in a brief preface of his own. "Deeply moved by the entire argument of the author, whom I count among my friends, I have undertaken—despite minor differences of opinion—the publication and distribution of this chapter and sign my name to it in the profound conviction that this proclamation can contribute to a reasonable attitude among friends and enemies alike."[10] Living in the small village of Bornim near Potsdam, Förster, a known pacifist and father of Friedrich Wilhelm Förster, whose own pacifist activities had begun to arouse official displeasure,[11] was sure to be under surveillance. He made a poor conspirator in any case, his realm being the heavenly spheres rather than this insignificant planet. The plot was discovered and the brochure seized before it could be distributed. Förster was not prosecuted. The authorities chose to treat him as the unworldly victim of a clever malefactor and were satisfied with a deposition which later supported the case against Nicolai.

Undaunted, Nicolai made one last attempt to bring at least the existence of his book to the attention of his compatriots. An anonymous brochure, inspired, if not written, by him, recounted his efforts and provided a table of contents.[12] This time the Commandatura took notice. Nicolai and his wife, "who was entirely innocent of the affair," were brought in for questioning. They were released for lack of proof, but it was clear that there was no longer any hope for reaching the German public, and Nicolai turned his boundless energy to other projects.

Meanwhile Orell Füssli in Zurich had become interested in the manuscript, which had come to it through Leonhard Frank. Before offering a contract to an author with whom he could not communicate, the publisher wrote to Thesing in Leipzig in order to clarify the complicated question of publication rights. Thesing was the owner of the impounded plates and did have a valid contract. His mail was also being controlled—he had just published a pacifist book, *Deutsche Jugend und der Weltkrieg* (*German Youth and the World War*), by the younger Förster—and as a result Nicolai received a formal order from Major General Von Pfuel, commandant of Danzig, enjoining him from publishing *The Biology of War* abroad. This was what he had been waiting for, and he was ready to make the most of it. He replied in writing that he would regret it "if my book were to be printed abroad in what may turn out to be a badly done or incomplete version, but that I could do nothing about it, nor would I, for I consider its publication to be wholly in the German interest." If this was outright defiance, he knew that this time he had the upper hand. It was an undeniable fact that he could not stop a foreign firm from publishing his work even if he wanted to, and of course he did not want to. As the author he could protest against an act of apparent literary piracy, but in the first place he knew that Orell Füssli would recognize the protest as a sham, in the second place he could secretly countermand his instructions, and in the third place he had already laid the groundwork for the claim that he was the innocent victim of circumstances. The fact that copies of his manuscript had long been circulating in Switzerland was his trump card. Not even the Generalkommando could expect a foreign publisher to pass up such a juicy plum as an antiwar book by a persecuted German professor.

The Generalkommando found itself in a dilemma. It did not want to produce grist for the enemy's propaganda mills by making a martyr of a man who was beginning to be known abroad as a fighter for peace and whose book was bound to create a sensation, but neither could it ignore the gauntlet Nicolai had flung down. In an attempt to handle the matter as gingerly as possible, a staff officer named Captain Kuse was delegated to talk things over with Nicolai. Both men found it advantageous to affect a causal manner and to pretend that they were having a friendly chat between gentlemen about an unfortunate occurrence that could surely be resolved on the social plane (at least that was Nicolai's version at the subsequent court-martial). The captain told him, "to my surprise," he testified, that his book was being printed in Zurich, and asked him "almost in passing in the course of a conversation that touched on many things" whether he would write to Orell Füssli to stop the publication and return the manuscript. He demurred, saying that these were not his wishes but the army's and that at most he could write that he had been ordered to make the request. Kuse replied that that would suffice and that he should submit a copy of the letter to his superiors. He even dropped a hint that the Generalkommando would have preferred to ignore the matter altogether but felt compelled to take some sort of action after receiving an inquiry from its counterpart in Leipzig. "In short," Nicolai told the court, "I had to conclude that the request was not an official order. Certainly the word 'order' was not mentioned."

For Nicolai the distinction between a request and an order was no mere technicality. He was trying to establish the fiction that in writing to Orell Füssli he was honoring a gentlemen's agreement, rather than obeying an order. For the same reason he phrased the note which accompanied a copy of his letter to the commandant's office in the style of a polite business communication: "Referring to our recent conversation, I take the liberty of sending you a copy of the letter I posted today to the publishing house of Orell Füssli of Zurich." Böse, attuned to the subtleties of his subordinate, was quick to object to the unmilitary tone of this note but could do nothing about the letter itself, which was safely on its way to Zurich. As a stickler for military etiquette, he returned the note with his corrections. "Referring to our recent conversation" should read "According to verbal orders," and "I take the liberty of sending you" should be changed to "I submit the enclosed copy," he replied, but he knew that he had been outwitted. At the trial Nicolai was able to turn the tables on him. He complied, he said, "in the sincere belief that this was a mere formality, but in view of subsequent developments I can only conclude that it was a deliberate attempt to trick me into recognition of an order."[13]

For the moment the battle between Nicolai and the Prussian army resembled a duel with finely pointed rapiers. Both sides were fighting according to the rules of the art, Nicolai because he enjoyed the game and the army because of its regard for a protocol that stemmed from the dusty chancelleries of a distant century. Anyone wondering why the almighty Generalkommando should bother to "trick" a plain soldier into acknowledging an order instead of making him obey it unconditionally did not understand Nicolai's equally obsolete conception of his rights. "It is clear," he continued his deposition, "that such an order would be a monstrosity. I could not even remotely imagine that the captain, a man who gave an impression of absolute refinement, would expect me to commit the immoral act of writing a letter contrary to my convictions and expressing an opinion I did not hold." That would have amounted to "nineteenth-century despotism at its worst."

Whether ordered or requested, the controversial letter was a masterpiece of insolence. In technically correct fashion it conveyed the exact opposite of Kuse's intent.

> The Generalkommando, at whose request I write this letter, has informed me that you have inquired of the firm of Dr. Thesing in Leipzig whether you could publish my book in case it did not appear in Germany. At the same time the Generalkommando has informed me in the most emphatic manner that an imprimatur in Germany is out of the question for the duration of the war. I wish to state that the decision does not rest with the publisher but solely with me, and

at the moment not even with me but with the Generalkommando, to whose authority I am subject. It has ordered me to tell you that I do not wish the book to be published and to request the return of the manuscript. As things stand I must obey this official order, as I am doing herewith. Speaking for myself, I would add that, much as I would like to see my work appear under the auspices of your internationally renowned firm, I would naturally regret it if the book were to be printed—as is inevitable—on the basis of an as yet incompletely revised manuscript and without my own corrections. Therefore, in case you decide to publish the book in spite of this prohibition (which, of course, neither I nor the Generalkommando could actually prevent), I appeal to your sense of fairness to give the reader a suitable explanation to the effect that the author had no part in its preparation, perhaps best by reprinting this letter.

The victim was toying with his oppressors. The last thing the Generalkommando wanted was to see this letter published as a preface to the book—which was now certain to appear. If Orell Füssli had entertained any doubts as to the author's real wishes, they were now erased. Nicolai had exploited the opening the "refined" Kuse had given him. He had obeyed his instructions to the letter, but he had mailed his missive without waiting for the wording to be approved.

The authorities were squeamish about interfering with freedom of thought or, rather, about admitting to such practices, but Nicolai had left them no choice. The Generalkommando called a court-martial. The preliminaries dragged on for months. The trial was held on 16 February 1917 by order of the Commandatura Danzig. The charge was violation of paragraph 28 of the Press Law of 4 May 1874 and of paragraph 9b of the Articles of the State of Siege, the first covering the printing of the brochure under Förster's name and the second the impending publication of *The Biology of War* abroad. In finding the accused guilty on both counts, Major Witte, the presiding judge, refused to consider the merits of the work or to go into the reasons for the original confiscation, "since it is not for the court to question orders given on the basis of the Articles of the State of Siege." The court asserted its competence, inasmuch as the accused had been under the jurisdiction of the Commandatura at the time of the confiscation. According to paragraph 30 of the Press Law, confiscation by a military commander had the same force as a court order. Reprinting of objectionable passages from a confiscated book was forbidden under paragraph 28, and violation of this injunction in full knowledge of the ban was punishable. It was an open-and-shut case, for the defendant had shown his awareness of the illegality of his action by not using his own name for the brochure.

The charge of violating paragraph 9b of the Articles was more difficult to prove, if only because the book itself had not yet appeared. It was established, however, that Major General Von Pfuel's order of 11 September 1916 had enjoined the defendant, under penalty of a fine of fifteen hundred marks, from publishing his book anywhere, at home or abroad. When the defendant claimed that he was not in a position to comply, the witness Kuse had tried to persuade him not to disobey an official order. Kuse—on this point the witness's version agreed with Nicolai's—wished to give the interview an unofficial character by talking to the defendant as one educated person to another. He had permitted him to tell Orell Füssli that his letter was the result of orders, but he had added repeatedly and emphatically that the wording must convey the writer's sincere wish to have the manuscript returned. The defendant had agreed to this stipulation, saying, "If I promise to get it back, I shall write in such a way that the recipient will return the book or at least be aware that I *want* it back."

The court's problem was that Kuse in his innocence had declared himself satisfied with this ambiguous statement. But, going straight to the heart of the matter, it ruled that the accused had acted in direct violation of both the commandant's order and Kuse's instructions when he had asked for the return of the manuscript and yet made it obvious that he would be only too happy to see his book published, adding insult to injury by pointing out that the Generalkommando was powerless. Had he not had the impudence to instruct the publisher to print his letter? His argument that the manuscript had not been in Orell Füssli's possession when the commandant issued his prohibition and that he had not known its whereabouts was irrelevant. It was indeed likely that it had not been in Zurich at that time, "but it is wholly immaterial whether Orell Füssli had the manuscript or not. The Supreme Censorship Office and the commandant had the definite suspicion that it was. The order of 11 September was issued on that premise. The accused had to obey without regard to his private opinion. . . . As his letter shows, he acted in exactly the opposite sense. His intention to induce the firm of Orell Füssli to publish the book if the manuscript was in its possession is unmistakable on the evidence of the letter."

The court was willing to note the fact that the accused had no prior criminal record, Witte said, in setting the penalty; however, the country was at war. In such a time, when everybody without regard for his profession must submit to the laws of the land, the accused, an educated man and a soldier, had disobeyed orders issued in the interest of public safety. He was therefore sentenced to pay a fine of seven hundred marks for violating paragraph 28. By rights a prison sentence was called for on the second count, but the commandant's injunction spoke only of a fine. An additional fine of five hundred marks was therefore in order, the total being determined by paragraph 79 of the Penal Code. As supreme magistrate, Von Pfuel appealed his surprisingly lenient verdict on the grounds that the law knew only jail sentences for violators of paragraph 9b of the Siege Law and that a stiffer fine was called for if such a sentence were not imposed.

Nicolai did not think of appealing. He had achieved all but complete victory. The law being what it was, he had received an eminently fair trial, especially if one considers that the court was composed entirely of officers on the post who were aware of his reputation as a troublemaker. Whether or not the verdict was influenced by fear of international repercussions, the procedure had been correct and the sentence lenient indeed. Nicolai was never again brought to trial on charges involving his writings or pacifist utterances, not when *The Biology of War* finally appeared a few months later, not the following winter, when he circulated a clandestine pamphlet, *Grundlagen der deutschen Politik* (*Foundations of German Policy*), a frankly political and highly inflammatory piece which the authorities were able to trace to him. After the war he would say that they had been afraid to prosecute him and instead resorted to chicanery in a deliberate attempt to crush his spirit.

Except for this first court-martial, Nicolai's well-publicized troubles with the army stemmed from disciplinary offenses. It would be no exaggeration to say that he was not the victim but the aggressor, deliberately

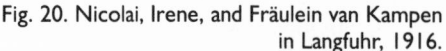

Fig. 20. Nicolai, Irene, and Fräulein van Kampen in Langfuhr, 1916.

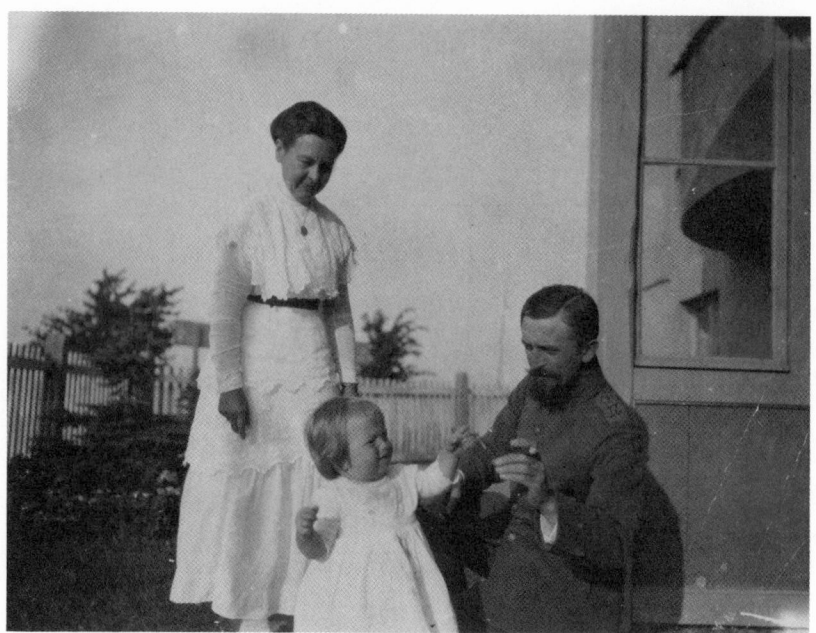

testing official patience. The truth is that after the first few weeks his life in Danzig settled into a fairly comfortable pattern. He was living in the suburb of Langfuhr (Fig. 20), where he had been joined by his wife and one-year-old daughter, Irene, and by his secretary of many years, Fräulein van Kampen, who in her neat handwriting copied the innumerable petitions with which he bombarded the authorities and who took care of his still voluminous correspondence. He had access to the city library, received frequent passes for the beach resort of Zoppot, and wangled furloughs to go to Berlin, to the Black Forest, and to Bonn, where he was the pampered guest of a doting mother-in-law. (Friederike's parents were divorced, and Frau Busley sided with Nicolai against her husband.) After the first six months, he was allowed to practice medicine in town in his spare time, provided that he reported punctually for duty on the post, a provision he violated only too frequently. Thereafter, patients with illustrious names like the Countess Von Kleist-Retzow, née von Wrochen, came to Danzig to consult the eminent orderly. One grateful patient offered to supply him with geese or, failing that, with goose grease, a precious commodity in wartime. He played chess with a local devotee of the game who was so impressed that he asked him to write a book for chess lovers. Nicolai toyed with the idea. He also toyed with the affections of the girls in the laboratory, dazzling them with his Berlin manners, his knowledge of laboratory procedures, and his bold political notions. He seduced at least one of them, the daughter of a retired officer. He had a talent for making his martyrdom as pleasant as possible.

NOTES

1. See the protocol of the session of 7 April in *Proceedings of the Reichstag, Thirteenth Legislative Period*, vol. 2; an unbound reprint of the protocol is in the Nicolai archive.

2. Nicolai's open letter was separately printed but was not included in the volume. The last page of the almanac carries this notice: "We intended to include a letter to the editor from Professor G. F. Nicolai. Solely in the interest of the writer's personal safety, it was decided to refrain from publishing the already printed text." The Nicolai archive contains a copy of *Der Almanach der Neuen Jugend auf das Jahr 1917*.

3. See *Aufruf an die Europäer, gesammelte Aufsätze zum Wiederaufbau Europas*, edited by Hans Wehberg (Leipzig: Verlag der Wiener graphischen Werkstätte, 1921). The collection contains political essays written from 1914 to 1920.

4. *Ibid.*, p. 102.

5. Quoted in Margret Boveri, "Im Dienst der Macht: Kurt Riezler," *Merkur* 28, no. 12 (1974):1144–58.

6. A handwritten draft of this letter, dated 25 May 1916, is in the Nicolai archive.

7. See his *Journal des années de guerre 1914–1919: Notes et documents pour servir à l'histoire morale de l'Europe de ce temps*, ed. Marie Romain Rolland (Paris: Albin Michel, 1952), p. 102.

8. Quoted in *ibid.*, p. 289. *Aktion*'s comment appears in the issue of October 24, 1914.

9. *Ibid.*, p. 435.

10. *Deutsche Freiheitsliebe* (*German Love of Freedom*), p. 1. The brochure, which carries no date or publisher's imprint, is in the Nicolai archive.

11. The younger Förster was in disfavor during the war for publishing an article critical of Bismarck. After the war he was driven from his professorship of history at the University of Munich as a "pacifist traitor." For further details see Chapter 15 below.

12. The pamphlet, *Über ein Werk der Wissenschaft* (*About a Work of Science*), has a preface signed "Wenige deutsche Europäer" ("A Few German Europeans") and dated 2 May 1916. A copy is in the Nicolai archive.

13. The correspondence concerning publication of *The Biology of War* and the transcript of the court-martial proceedings are quoted from documents in a folder labeled "Heeressachen" ("Army Matters") in the Nicolai archive.

10. Professorial Ethics

Although life in Danzig had become tolerable, Nicolai had ample cause for bitterness. His sacrifices amounted to nothing less than the destruction of his career and his personal life. He was banished to a provincial city, demoted to the rank of private, forced to perform menial chores, and subjected to a humiliating discipline. His scientific productivity was at an end, and his financial situation was a shambles even after he was allowed to supplement his military pay (twelve marks and forty pfennigs a month) with the income from his part-time practice. While maintaining a household in Danzig he had to pay the rent for his Berlin establishment, which came to eight thousand marks a year. The lover of the good things in life—which those who could afford them could enjoy even in wartime—was reduced to a life of Spartan simplicity, the brilliant conversationalist was muzzled, the gregarious man-about-town was isolated, and the connoisseur of women had to be satisfied with naive provincial girls. After his bout with rheumatic fever in 1915, he was not in good health, but his numerous requests for convalescent leave or transfer to a milder climate fell on deaf ears. He was bored and restless. The people of Danzig by and large shunned him, for he was too radical even for those who had begun secretly to wish for peace. It was embarrassing, if not dangerous, to be seen in his company. The blight had touched his family when his father-in-law betrayed him. His wife and his mother in Berlin stood by him, to be sure, but they were only women and only doing their duty.

Perhaps the hardest blow was his estrangement from Friedrich Kraus, his chief of many years and one of the few men he loved. On 30 June 1916 Nicolai received a registered letter informing him that the direction of the Charité, "upon recommendation of Geheimrat Kraus," had terminated his appointment as first assistant at the II. Medical Clinic. The mention of Kraus's name was a formality, required because the Charité, founded by a Prussian king and therefore administered by the army, was a university hospital. Nicolai's dismissal had been ordered by the War Ministry, but Kraus had to be consulted, as head of the service. He agreed in the hope that thereby he might salvage Nicolai's academic appointment. Nicolai refused to believe that Kraus had done such an infamous thing. He wrote to him by return mail, asking for confirmation. Kraus answered no less promptly.

As I have already written in detail to Professor Einstein [in academic circles Einstein was evidently regarded as Nicolai's protector], the main concern will be that you keep the *venia legendi* [lecturing privileges]. With all the material against you in the files of the Charité and at the Ministry, nothing can be done in the matter of the hospital. I advise you to take no steps in that direction. I have tried very hard to protect you, not only in this affair but in general. Unfortunately, you went your own way. I can only disapprove the business in the Reichstag and many other things. But I believe that you have done nothing dishonorable and therefore can remain a member of the academic community. And you are paying a harsh penalty. But a medical position, where you have to work with men who represent an *entirely different* viewpoint—that is simply impossible. Do not doubt my goodwill. What you have done in recent days, often against my well-meaning efforts, has taken a heavy toll of my nervous system. In hopes of a better time.[1]

Nicolai lashed out furiously against what he saw as a betrayal. He attacked not only his chief's complicity in a punitive measure aimed at his pacifist principles, but the man himself.

Into the medieval grotesque with whose unintentionally comical aspects the military is trying to lighten the general tragedy for me, your letter has brought the first personal discord. It signifies the irrevocable loss of a human being whom I had respected for ten years. You once told me how unhappy you were that as an academic teacher in one of the most eminent positions in Germany, you did not leave behind a school of your own. When I hinted at the time that this entailed a certain moral responsibility and a feeling of mutual respect, you were annoyed. As you know, I have continued to be loyal to you and to defend you when others charged you with forgeries, plagiarism, broken promises, etc., because I believed that these acts were only a consequence of your temperament, but that, deep in your heart, love of truth—or, more precisely, of science—was alive and that you might err at times in your choice of means but that your goal always remained the furtherance of knowledge. Now you have killed this faith, for, though you did not answer the only question I asked in my letter, it is precisely this eloquent silence which dispels all doubts.

It is nothing new for the Prussian government to fight politically undesirable adversaries by destroying their scientific careers, but it *is* new for the holder of a scientific post to lend his hand to such dirty work and—so it seems—even to push himself forward by taking the initiative. The glory of having taken the first step and thus leading the "new German" a little farther along the road to perfection is one that nobody will begrudge you.

As for me, permit me to say that I am sad, not only for the good name of Germany but for you personally, for I am willing to believe that this thing has "taken a heavy toll of your nervous system," for you do believe in science after all—at least in your own way—and you must feel instinctively that you have now buried your whole life under the rubble. Your attempt to deceive yourself through the patronizing tone of your letter is in vain, for you know quite well that such phrases must sound ridiculous coming from one who is actually doing things he expects to hurt another person.

Kraus, professor of medicine at the University of Berlin, was a superb clinician, a great teacher, a fair-minded and humane chief, beloved of his students and respected by his colleagues. He had spotted Nicolai's genius and brought him to the Charité, furthered his career, and smoothed over the conflicts arising from his protégé's quarrelsome disposition. It was Kraus who obtained the coveted professorship for him, Kraus who sent him to the palace to attend the most august of cardiac patients, the empress of Germany. Chief and assistant had collaborated on scientific papers, and the book *Das Elektrokardiogramm*, a major achievement, bore the names Kraus and Nicolai.[2] This order should have been reversed, for Nicolai's was undoubtedly the far greater contribution. As department chairman Kraus was the absolute ruler of his realm, in the European academic tradition, and could claim credit for the publications of his staff. But it was Nicolai who brought to the subject the requisite knowledge of both theory and experimental techniques—experience gained in the laboratories of Hering, Engelmann, Einthoven, and Pavlov, a talent for tinkering with delicate machinery, and the familiarity with the literature provided by his voracious reading. (Indeed, he would later flatly assert that he was the sole author of the book.) The allusion here to his defense of Kraus against the charge of plagiarism, however, harks back to another matter entirely, a prewar episode, the details of which are now obscure, in which Kraus was accused of plagiarizing the work of a Viennese scholar named Goldstein.[3]

Justified or not, this attack on his chief's personal and professional integrity can, of course, only be explained by the strain under which Nicolai was laboring at the moment. His scathing criticism of Kraus's role in the matter of his dismissal, on the other hand, hit the nail on the head. A kindly man, genuinely fond of Nicolai, Kraus had acted with the best intentions, hoping that by taking the initiative he might avert more serious action by the authorities. But in so doing he had sacrificed an important principle: he had made himself an instrument of the state in the punishment of a colleague for a political offense. He had put *raison d'état* above academic freedom.

Kraus remained uncomprehending in the face of Nicolai's fury. Like almost all professors of his generation, he took it for granted that his first duty was to the state as his employer and "the embodiment of the general will," as Hegel had put it, rather than to his conscience as an individual. Nicolai, the son of a professor who had fought for freedom on the barricades in 1848, had put that conscience ahead of the general will when he invoked the right to dissent from the government's war policy. In doing so he was adhering to a tradition that had long ceased to exist, if indeed it had ever existed. Eighty years ago the academic community had meekly accepted the dismissal of the "Seven of Göttingen," among them the brothers Grimm, for protesting the abrogation of the constitution by the king of Hanover. The German universities, Jacob Grimm said on that occasion, "should be extremely sensitive and concerned about everything, good or evil, that happens in the country. If it be otherwise, they will cease to fulfill their traditional purpose."[4] It was to be otherwise. Before Bismarck the professors had been liberals. Under the impact of his success they had a change of heart. All but a handful turned into obedient or even enthusiastic supporters of the new state, civil servants rather than guardians of liberty. Having accepted Bismarck's prescription for Germany and having been given a privileged position in the new order, they considered themselves free because they had—or thought they had—no grounds for complaint. A few men of the stature of a Virchow or a Mommsen remained in opposition; the rest became indifferent to the great issues that had moved their fathers.

Since then, professorial freedom of conscience had been challenged only once, in 1898, when the Prussian Ministry of Education asked the Philosophical Faculty of the University of Berlin to open proceedings against a colleague, the mathematician Leo Arons, for the crime of being a Social Democrat. Arons was also a Jew, but that was not yet a crime, merely an aggravating circumstance. The faculty demurred and, when the minister insisted on Arons's dismissal without a proper faculty recommendation, lodged a protest against government interference in academic affairs. Even after the Prussian Diet passed an ad hoc law, the infamous Lex Arons, empowering the government to step into the case, the professors acquitted their colleague, finding him an honorable man and a brilliant scholar. But when the authorities asserted that it was the mission of the university to prepare students for service to state and church and that an avowed socialist was by definition unfit for this task, the guardians of academic freedom quietly gave in.[5]

Nicolai's case was very similar to that of Arons. Although not a card-carrying Social Democrat (and as such ipso facto regarded as an enemy of the state by Wilhelminian authorities), he did hold subversive views and insisted on his right to voice them. No one questioned his qualifications; on the contrary, like Arons, he was regarded as a scientist and teacher of the highest promise. Nor, as Kraus had expressly certified, was there doubt as to his moral fitness, the only grounds other than politics which in Kraus's eyes could disqualify a man from holding an academic position. He was fired because he was a pacifist and had said so publicly. It was true that the post from which he was removed was a hospital post not directly part of the university, but the affiliation of the Charité with the university, and Kraus's position as both chief of medicine and professor made his highest-ranking assistant an academic person whose dismissal for political reasons a truly independent spirit would not have condoned, let alone abetted. The fact that Kraus did not share Nicolai's views had no bearing on the issue. The case illuminates a central problem of German history, a flaw in the way the German academic leadership conceived the meaning of freedom.

In all its bitterness, Nicolai's letter became a ringing profession of his creed. "The picture can hardly be so distorted," he wrote,

> that you could say that I was "paying a harsh penalty." Evidently you have the wrong idea of the situation. You are probably unaware of your misconception, for you take the wrong view of your own good-natured indolence and hardly see what lies underneath. Did you think I was repentant? Had resigned myself or was currying the favor of the crowd once again? You are not a connoisseur of men or

enough of a friend to cover this intellectual deficit by sympathetic understanding.

But this much ten years of collaboration should have told you about me: that such things as are now being done to me cannot seriously disturb my peace of mind. They have taken my work away from me. Well and good, I accept that—inwardly too—with all its consequences. At last I have the leisure I have for years longed for. And I can assure you that I am making the most of it. Inwardly free through external coercion—I don't know whether you are capable of understanding that, but if you had even a faint notion, the surgeon general would envy the MKW. For your own sake I can only hope that later, when the time comes that is bound to come, you will have formed a similar concept of what is *adiaphoron* [incorruptible] in life and what is not.

If, incidentally, your concern regarding my teaching appointment is meant as a hint that you and those who think like you are about to take my academic privileges away from me, I accept that too with equanimity. For me there will always be a place on this mother earth. During the past few weeks I have already received an offer from a foreign university, which I declined for the time being because I still believe that some day when wind and sun are not arrayed on the wrong side and we can cross swords in a fair fight there will be enough idealism left in Germany to cope with all enemies of the spirit. That is my patriotism.

And one more thought regarding what seems to me the most fantastic part of your letter: You write, verbatim, "I believe that you have done nothing dishonorable." I want to tell you that I for my part do not consider it honorable to hurt one's political opponent by crippling him economically.

Kraus was free to make use of this missive in any way he wished, Nicolai went on. He had written only in self-defense and "because I considered it my duty to make you aware of the reason why the salutations at the beginning and end of my letter no longer express my true feelings but have become mere conventional formulas." However, he ended the letter: "Asking you once more to believe that this letter was extremely hard for me to write, I am . . . ," etc.

Nicolai was not a respecter of men. He reserved his affection for those few who, he believed, combined superior intelligence with integrity of character, such as Ewald Hering, his first great teacher, Pavlov, Einstein, and, for a time, Rolland. Kraus belonged to this select group, and the ferocity of Nicolai's attack stemmed from a wounded heart. At the very nadir of his fortunes he had been betrayed by the man to whom he had felt closest. But Kraus, whatever his conception of academic freedom, was an extraordinarily decent human being. He answered the uncalled-for attack on his personal integrity by defending his part in his colleague's dismissal as a mere formality in circumstances beyond his control, but he also undertook the hopeless task of supporting the protest which Nicolai—against his advice—had sent to the Ministry. Kraus had already gone there on his own and had been told that it was best to let the matter rest, a clear hint that even more drastic action would be taken if a formal appeal were to be made: Nicolai's teaching privileges would be abrogated. But Kraus was able to report that these privileges would not be touched, "at least not on the basis of your doings thus far."

Kraus then went even farther, offering to advance Nicolai a year's salary out of his own pocket, stipulating only that "you don't consider it as another 'underhanded trick,' a humiliating gesture, or the like." As to the picture Nicolai had drawn of his character, "I have long been able to believe that I was one of the few who had influence over you, a *good* influence. I was not always successful in my attempts to bring you along in keeping with your ability, to help you over many a shoal, to mitigate the consequences of your impulses and the vicissitudes of your intellectual and emotional temperament. For you at least I have done more than I promised." In the face of such magnanimity Nicolai's wrath evaporated. "Your unexpected offer," he replied, "has given me great pleasure, and I am far from seeing it as anything but the friendly remembrance of former days. If I nevertheless decline with thanks, I must ask you to believe that it is not a matter of personal animosity. But I feel that the wrong which has been done to me by the state can only be remedied by the state (or by persons in official positions), not by a kindly private person."

The letter ended with Nicolai's offer to withdraw his name from the list of contributors to Kraus's *Handbook of Medicine*, an offer which Kraus rejected "as a matter of course." It was this very project Kraus would use a few months later as a pretext for requesting Nicolai's release from the army on the grounds that it required his presence in Berlin. The army, no doubt aware that Nicolai was behind the request, did not grant it. By asking Kraus to intercede for him at that juncture, Nicolai shows that he looked upon the older man as a kind of father who could be forgiven for clinging to erroneous beliefs and who in turn could be expected to forgive the outburst of a temperamental child. That Kraus was willing to do so after all that had passed between them shows how fortunate Nicolai was. Even at the height of their quarrel, Kraus wrote him: "I must insist on my right, acquired over so many years and far from shaken by recent events, to be regarded as one who has your interest at heart, even though he disagrees as strongly as ever with your political views and disapproves your actual conduct."

As a bizarre postlude to his dismissal, the business office of the Charité demanded that Nicolai return his salary for the month of November 1914 because, "according to information received from the military administration," he was already on the payroll of the War Ministry at that time. The Prussian fiscal machinery had continued to function with its customary efficiency. Nicolai, whose noble ideals did not prevent him from paying close attention to money matters, challenged this claim and registered a counterclaim for back pay for the three months preceding his dismissal, on the grounds that during that period he had received only a private's wages. The fiscal authorities, surprisingly, acceded to this demand and paid the requested amount—after deducting 112 marks and 50 pfennigs for its own claim. So ended Nicolai's career as a civilian employee of the State of Prussia.

NOTES

1. The exchange between Nicolai and Kraus consists of handwritten letters from Kraus and carbon copies of Nicolai's replies; the period in question is July and August 1916. The letters are preserved in the Nicolai archive.

2. *Das Elektrokardiogramm des gesunden und kranken Menschen* (Leipzig: Veit, 1910). The page proofs of the book, with corrections in Nicolai's hand, are in the Nicolai archive.

3. In an article written in 1920 by Nicolai's attorney during the battle with the academic senate of the University of Berlin (and clearly inspired by Nicolai himself) the following passage occurs: "In 1917 Geheimrat Kraus seized upon the unjustified degradation of Professor Nicolai—to whom he owed so much, who had written his book for him, and who had been his sole defender when he so brazenly plagiarized the Viennese sociologist [sic] Goldstein—to deprive him of his laboratory, which was Professor Nicolai's creation." For the background of this matter, see Chapter 16 below.

4. Quoted in N. P. Bleuel, *Deutschlands Bekenner, Professoren zwischen Kaiserreich und Diktatur* (Bern: Scherz Verlag, 1968), p. 26.

5. See *ibid.*, pp. 49–51, for details of the Arons affair.

11. The "Politics of the Classics"

Nicolai's statement to Kraus that he was making good use of his enforced leisure was no idle boast. In the spring of 1916, almost immediately after his induction, when it became clear that the duties of a laboratory assistant would leave him with much free time on his hands, he embarked on a new secret undertaking. Much to the annoyance of Dr. Schwer, his supervisor, he began to spend his unoccupied moments in the laboratory reading and annotating the works of Kant and Fichte. Schwer could not very well complain, for he had to admit that Nicolai, an old hand at every laboratory procedure, was a fast and reliable worker who finished his assignments well ahead of schedule. Nor could he object to the choice of his reading matter, for in Prussia it would have been absurd to call the inventor of the Categorical Imperative or the inspirer of German youth during the Napoleonic wars subversive. But in the context of the present war, some of their ideas were in fact highly subversive (had not Kant written a manifesto on Eternal Peace, and Fichte in his youth flirted with the French Revolution?), and it was to this side of the great philosophers that Nicolai addressed himself. His seemingly innocuous readings were part of a project which, at Pfemfert's suggestion, he intended to call the "Politics of the Classics."

Thwarted in his attempts to make his own voice heard, he conceived the plan of publishing selected writings by classical authors to show that the thinkers whom the nation revered as its spiritual guides were devoted to universal brotherhood, liberty, and tolerance, rather than to the narrow nationalism imputed to them by chauvinist professors. The implication was clear: the classics would have condemned the present war, and with it the regime that had led Germany into it and now refused to make peace, and the classics could not very well be suppressed by the censor. To Pastor Steudel, a fellow pacifist in Bremen, Nicolai wrote: "I consider it impossible that men like Fichte should be forbidden today, but read his 'Reflections on the Attitude of the Public Concerning the French Revolution,' read Jean Paul's 'Peace Sermons for Germany' and many of his other writings, and you will see that we need to add nothing, but can let these men speak for us." The idea was in the air of confronting the Germans with the political views of writers whose collected works, bound in half-leather, were found on the bookshelves of every middle-class home. The intelligentsia, which could not speak in its own voice, hoped to borrow their voices to impress a people that prided itself on its respect for the classics. Nicolai worried greatly that someone else might have the same idea, and indeed Kurt Hiller's *Das Ziel* for 1917–18 offered excerpts from Schiller, Fichte, Schopenhauer, and—for good measure—Voltaire, but Nicolai had no cause for alarm. To publish a series of volumes on political morality and other austere topics by long-dead authors was poor business for any publisher, no matter how idealistic.

Nicolai in his youth had steeped himself in the writings of Kant and his successors, and the liberal tradition he absorbed from his parents had given him a view of German literature that was almost unique among his contemporaries. He saw the writers of the classical age not as august spirits hovering on an abstract Olympus, whose divinely inspired words floated down to earth to provide suitable material for lectures and banquet speakers, but as men of flesh and blood speaking out against the tyranny, prejudice, ignorance, and complacency which they saw around them. Germany's classical age extended from an era of absolutism to a reign of darkest reaction, and in one way or another the writers of the period had to come to grips with the issues of freedom, personal dignity, and the brotherhood of man in a climate of political oppression. These had been the themes of Lessing and Schiller. Herder proclaimed a universal religion of humanity. Kant was a republican, a pacifist, and an advocate of world federation. Georg Büchner fled for his life, and Heine went into voluntary exile in France. Goethe criticized the German national character and political institutions, neither of which had changed much since his death. In Metternich's and Frederick William III's realm, Fichte's patriotic writings had been forbidden for ten years after Waterloo. These facts were not taught in the state-supported and state-supporting schools of Imperial Germany, but Nicolai was well aware of them. An avid reader with a phenomenal memory, he had stored away every event and every utterance that supported his conception of a German humanism opposed to power, oppression, and bloodshed, not only in the exalted realm of ideas but on the practical and political plane. For him classicism was a living force, a fire that had fed the Revolution of 1848 and had since been banked but not extinguished by the Realpolitik of Bismarck and his successors.

The interpretation of German classicism as a revolutionary movement was a Nicolaian tour de force, the idealist's view of Idealism. One could find rebellious passages in the vast literature of the period, but a literary tradition concerned with the concrete goals of social and political justice, such as existed in France, had never taken shape. Germany's classic writers were more nearly comparable to the lofty French dramatists of the seventeenth century Corneille and Racine than to Voltaire, Montesquieu, Rousseau, or Condorcet. The thrust of their work had been nonpolitical, and for the most part they had accommodated themselves to the governments under which they lived. Nicolai was pursuing a chimera that he desperately wanted to have a life of its own. His contemporary Heinrich Mann saw the lack of a fighting tradition much more clearly. "The spirit that governs France is not the ethereal ghost we know hereabouts," he wrote in "Geist und Tat," an essay that was then being reprinted in *Das Ziel*. In Germany, "where so much thinking is done," no one could say that "the forces of the nation have ever been gathered to transform insights into deeds. Neither the abolition of unjust power nor the liberation from the claims of a faith turned absurd has ever been an actual goal."[1] Still, German authors by and large had been libertarian and cosmopolitan, and Nicolai hoped that their political ideas, for the most part unknown to the public or glossed over by their modern interpreters, would furnish potent

191

ammunition to dissidents like himself. He was not so naive as to think that ideas could stop the armies on either side; he was thinking of the need for reeducating a stultified and brutalized nation once the emotional orgy of the war had ended. He wanted to prepare the Germans for the inevitable letdown, for the day when, according to Kurt Riezler's secret prophecy, "a mortally wounded Germany will be suffering from utter spiritual confusion"[2] and when he hoped the nation would again be receptive to its true heritage.

For these reasons, Nicolai believed that the time to act was now, not after the war. Germany, he wrote to Steudel in February 1917, would be either completely victorious or utterly beaten: "It will then be proved that even today, in the twentieth century, the brutal power of arms can lead to success. Who then will be listening to those of us who are saying, 'it must not come to this'? One cannot wish for this kind of success, for then it will be too late for Germany, and in case she will rely on the sword and conduct Realpolitik for as long as we live, and longer." But if—as he foresaw—Germany were defeated,

> and we then step forward with our ideas about the universal brotherhood of man, will it not be logical for the others to say, "Well, now that you are on your knees, now that you see that force is not the way, now you appeal once more to your old ideas from the times of your great classics"? Then the enemy will say, "We no longer believe you, for not of your own free will did you elect this viewpoint but—like felons caught in the act who see that they have failed to accomplish their ends by violent means—you now try to talk your way out with all kinds of beautiful phrases, 'We did not mean it that way.'"

The forecast was accurate. When Prince Max, the last imperial chancellor, sued for armistice and offered to abide by the Wilsonian principle of self-determination, as though that had been Germany's aim all along, Woodrow Wilson refused to believe his "beautiful phrases." The switch from Ludendorff's military dictatorship to a peace-loving democracy was too abrupt to be credible.

The obstacles to the launching of the "politics of the classics" were enormous. As time went on, MKW Nicolai had less leisure to devote to the project. Schwer realized the real purpose of his studiousness and forbade him to read while on duty (thereby giving him the opportunity to complain that he was being persecuted for reading Kant and Fichte). The texts he needed were not always available, especially the unpublished writings of the Prussian reformers of the Napoleonic era, which were at the Royal Library in Berlin. The task was too large for one person, and Otto Buek was enlisted to do some of the legwork. Even off duty Nicolai had little time, for now that he was allowed to practice medicine he needed to do so to shore up his sagging personal finances. But the main obstacle was the lack of funds. Knowing that no publisher would risk his capital, Nicolai decided to create his own corporation. The officers were to be himself, Buek, and, he fondly hoped, Einstein. Pfemfert, who enthusiastically supported the project, was to be editorial director. The capital was to be raised from wealthy sympathizers. Seldom has a business venture begun under less favorable auspices or with less qualified partners. The most sanguine person could not have hoped that excerpts from dead classics would become best-sellers in wartime Germany. None of the prospective officers had business or publishing experience. Nicolai was sitting in Danzig under strict surveillance, severely restricted in his movements; Buek was poor as a church mouse and most impractical, barely able to cope with everyday life. Pfemfert was a radical, likely to frighten away the rich backers Nicolai hoped to attract, and Einstein had as yet given the others no commitment to join them.

Nicolai estimated that at least thirty thousand marks were needed, but since this sum would be eaten up by the first two publications, and since financial returns, if any, were not to be expected for some time, it was better to start with twice that amount. Early in January 1917, shortly before the start of his court-martial, he managed to obtain a three-day furlough in Berlin, where he ran from person to person with his scheme. Einstein was cool to the idea but willing to contribute the modest sum of five hundred marks. The attitude of Elsa Einstein, his cousin and future wife, was more encouraging. She was a patient as well as a personal friend of Nicolai, she found the project exciting, and she promised to interest another cousin, a wealthy businessman named Moos. Moos, a cautious man, agreed to put up ten thousand marks if Nicolai could raise the rest.

When Nicolai returned to Danzig he had already obtained tentative commitments for another ten thousand. He had seen Woycech Korfanty, a member of the Reichstag for a Polish district. Korfanty had no love for Prussian rule and often sided with the left-wing socialists in opposing a war whose successful outcome would perpetuate German rule over the Polish minority. He offered to form a syndicate to raise the ten thousand marks. A cavalry captain, one K., who was apparently a pacifist despite his martial title, signed for five thousand marks, and there were vague promises from others.

In view of the fact that he had only three days, Nicolai's success as a fund-raiser was impressive, but he soon saw that his collaborators were more a hindrance than a help. Pfemfert's first meeting with Moos was a debacle, for the editor of *Aktion* did not conceal his socialist views, and Buek was not the man to repair the damage. Korfanty had gone back to his district. The business of the syndicate would have to wait. Nicolai had counted on Elsa Einstein to keep the wavering Moos in line, if possible with moral support from Albert. Albert, however, had had grave misgivings from the start. He had given Nicolai, as an introduction to another potential donor, a calling card which read, "I have suggested to Herr Professor Nicolai, with whom I am personally acquainted, that he call on you, for you will certainly be sympathetic to an enterprise he has called into being." Though noncommittal this was bound to be helpful, coming from Einstein. But within a few days Einstein had changed his mind. "Dear Nicolai," he wrote, since you left I have turned your plan over in my mind. I consider the matter completely hopeless and likely to cause you much annoyance and disappointment. Imagine how we shall face the people you now wish to approach, if things go awry. We must not indulge in illusions about the chances of the enterprise. Only a tiny number of people concern themselves with writers of the past in these agitated times; the latter remain undisturbed in the libraries. I believe moreover that Herr Buek should not be burdened with a task which even the most energetic person cannot handle. As likable as this man is in other respects, his meek and despondent manner makes him absolutely unsuitable for carrying out such a mission. Do not feel offended by this frank expression of my opinion. My conviction is so firm that silence would be insincere.[3]

Clearly Einstein was more realistic than Nicolai. He was also aware of the latter's frustration and agitation, which alone could explain his frantic pursuit of a hopeless cause. Nicolai chose to ignore this well-meant advice. On 22 January, he wrote to Elsa Einstein, "The publishing company whose germ seemed to blossom so well under your aegis *must* succeed; a great deal depends on it." He was still optimistic. Buek and Pfemfert, too, had rosy visions and were thinking up names for the series, such as "The New Europe" or "The Mountain", the latter favored by Pfemfert as an allusion to the Jacobin "*Montagne*." But Buek's next letter brought the bad news of an altercation between Pfemfert and Moos. Nicolai upbraided his friend severely:

You can imagine that I was not exactly overjoyed with your letter. I will say nothing of the fact that unfavorable circumstances have arisen, but I think that it is precisely when circumstances are unfavorable that one must work all the harder. In this respect I only want to say to you that in principle Moos should have no dealings with Pfemfert but only with you, and that it is therefore wholly wrong if you are informed about Moos through Pfemfert. Once again you have allowed the initiative to be taken out of your hands, and exactly what I feared has happened, namely, that P.'s radicalism has scared M. off.

Evidently Nicolai had not lost his psychological acumen altogether. To Buek's question whether he should continue to work on his editorial assignments, he answered with an emphatic yes. Nicolai's own two volumes were as good as ready:

If yours were farther along, we could proceed quite differently, I think. But of course if we carry the idea for months or even years without giving birth we cannot be surprised if others are quicker. That is not unfair competition but simply the way of the world, and perhaps the proper way. And how do matters stand with regard to the money? Have you approached anyone? Have you been negotiating? When I was doing the negotiating, more than half the amount was firmly promised, and I had only three days!

Poor Buek defended himself valiantly. "Dear Georg," he answered,

> your reproaches are quite unfair and based on such erroneous prem-
> ises that I must refute them one by one. It was not I who presented
> Pfemfert as editorial director, but you. If Pfemfert's views made
> Moos gun-shy, that is not my fault. You yourself expressed the wish
> that I bring M. and P. together, and I did so the next day, in keeping
> with your instructions. M., incidentally, had categorically demanded
> to see P. At our meeting everything was settled jointly. There was
> nothing to indicate that M. was annoyed and intended to withdraw.

Buek then reported another calamity: Korfanty had been unsuccessful.
As for Moos's defection, the news had come to him out of the blue through
Pfemfert, who in turn had it from Frau Einstein and her daughter Ilse,
who had come to see him on behalf of their cousin; Moos himself had not
seen fit to inform Buek. "According to our understanding I was not to see
M. again until the list of contributors was complete. There is thus no
question of letting the initiative be taken out of my hands." He could take
no further steps, Buek said, "especially because my ties to the Einstein
family are not so close that I could go to see them and try to change their
minds." His feelings would not be hurt if he were relieved of his task, for
he had few rich friends among his acquaintances. "If you are counting
only on me, the outlook is very dim indeed." Buek at least knew when he
was beaten.

Nicolai at once became conciliatory. He had not meant to criticize his
friend, but only to let him know that he should have kept Moos more
firmly in hand. He should not throw in the sponge. The important thing
was to complete the editing (he himself had been working on the project
six hours a day since his return from Berlin), as a completed text would
be like money in the bank if it became necessary to approach an established publisher. Nicolai had completed the collections of Jean Paul and
Fichte and was working on Kant. He was also compiling the various declarations of human rights: the English Bill of Rights, the American Declaration of Independence, the *Droits de l'Homme*, *Le Tiers État* of Sieyès,
Lafayette's *Resolution*, and the German Declaration of Basic Rights of
1848, a powerful collection, of whose existence most Germans were probably unaware.

It was a grandiose conception, all the more impressive when one re-
members that Nicolai was neither a historian nor a political scientist and
at the very moment faced a court-martial that required his full attention. If
exposure to the noblest political documents of history could cure political
sickness, his approach should have succeeded. "The more of these documents we complete, the more successfully we can act some day when
circumstances become more favorable," he exhorted the faint-hearted
Buek. "Believe me, this labor is not wasted, even though it may appear to
you that way now. Times change, and what matters is to be prepared for
the changes."

But it was Einstein, the convinced pacifist, the cosigner of the "Appeal to the Europeans," the man Nicolai revered above all others, who administered the coup de grace. To Nicolai's renewed plea he replied on 17 February, the day after the court-martial at the Danzig Commandatura, no doubt unaware of the coincidence that would sharpen the pain of his letter:

> Dear Nicolai:
>
> Nothing is so difficult as to turn down Nicolai. The man who is so sensitive in other respects that the growing of grass is a loud noise to his ears seems almost deaf when the noise involves a refusal. In the face of this enigma science resorts to a dubious explanation: lack of attention. I therefore raise my voice with the strength of a young bull just reaching maturity and say—shout—solemnly, passionately, "No!" (The music stops, two bars rest, followed by an elegiac *piano*.)
>
> Reasons and justification: it is one of the inalienable human rights that a man is permitted to keep a considerable number of hobby-horses, depending on his temperament. But human rights also include the right of refusing to run alongside when one's dear neighbor rides his hobbyhorse. You therefore have every right to plant stale cabbages, fertilize them with modern manure, and sell them personally in the market. *I* have the right to stay away and devote myself exclusively to my own hobbyhorses. That is how it shall and must remain. With the plea that you take this into lasting and consequential consideration, with best regards, your A. Einstein.[4]

Nicolai kept his answer factual. "For two reasons I return once more to the matter of the publishing company," he wrote Einstein on 26 February: "the first that it is of practical importance, as you will see; the second is that I would not like this business, in which apparently a number of misunderstandings have played a part, to become a permanent difficulty between us." Despite this conciliatory opening, however, he firmly rejected Einstein's position. "I do not for a moment deny your right to withdraw from an agreement you have come to regard as undesirable, but I do deny your right to do so without at the same time doing everything in your power to make sure that you cause no unnecessary damage to the other party." Moos, according to his own statement, withdrew only after receiving word from Einstein that the latter had "thoroughly reflected on the matter and decided to withdraw because he did not think that the goal could be attained in the manner proposed by Professor Nicolai." He himself had not known that Einstein had abandoned the project, "only that you had serious objections. On the contrary, after receiving your cousin's [Elsa's] letter, I asked you specifically whether you had any intention of withdrawing, and you did not reply to my question, but only enumerated the objections you had to the plan in general." He had assumed, Nicolai continued, that the agreement with Moos was firm—"and it was your and your cousin's initiative, respectively, that led me to Moos." Einstein must know that he was in no position to plan the venture on any other basis. "You must therefore admit that if Moos, following your example, first agreed and has now been induced by you to withdraw (which he has every right to do, since he never made a legally binding commitment), the whole business may fall flat because of what you did." And while Einstein's participation was no longer needed or even wanted, Nicolai went on, Moos was still wavering and might yet be swayed by a statement from Einstein to the effect that he considered the plan a poor investment but the cause worthwhile. Nicolai ended with an oblique plea: "Incidentally, I would like you to know that the manuscripts for Kant, Fichte, Herder, and Jean Paul are ready for printing. I really think you would be utterly delighted if you were to read them and lend your earnest support in bringing these works to the German people. The objective knowledge of what our classical authors—albeit under different conditions—thought of Germany's politics can only be useful, whatever one's point of view, assuming that one considers the truth to be a desirable goal. And that, I am convinced, we both do."[5]

Einstein's note, though humorous, had come as a painful shock to Nicolai, but Einstein had not meant to give offense. "In rereading your letter," he replied,

> I regret the ungracious simile concerning your efforts to bring out the writings of the classics, which I used in a moment of high spirits. You should consider it as nothing but a coarse joke. Objectively I want to add that there can be no question of my wanting to hurt the enterprise. I dissuade no one who would participate without me. It is only that I do not wish Herr Moos to go along *exclusively for my sake.* Such a sacrifice on the part of a relative and personal friend would embarrass me. Kindest regards, to your wife as well, from your old A. Einstein.[6]

The relationship between Einstein and Nicolai was the comradeship of two men fighting for the same cause, rather than a personal friendship. Einstein, who moved to Berlin only months before the outbreak of the war, may have signed the "Appeal to the Europeans" because he was not yet aware of the intransigence of the German professors. He did not again speak out publicly during the war, preferring to work behind the scenes. He justified his silence on the grounds that he was after all a Swiss citizen and quasi-guest of the German government (though he was, of course, German by birth). He had resigned himself to the fact that the war must run its course and that Germany's purpose could not be changed "by the weapons of the mind":[7] "Those who consider men like Nicolai to be utopians do so with honest conviction." Facts alone—by which he meant defeat—would teach the Germans that the use of force was unprofitable in the long run.

Nicolai, who believed in the "weapons of the mind" and knew himself to be at one with Einstein in the struggle against militarism, was at a loss to understand such detachment. His truth, like that of Giordano Bruno, existed only as long as he was willing to burn for it, while Einstein—at that time at least—like Galileo, saw only eternal verities that needed no corroboration. Einstein's pacifism later carried weight because he was the author of the Theory of Relativity, while Nicolai achieved such greatness as he did by putting his person on the line in a battle he knew he could not win.

Einstein's cordial note allowed the relationship between the two men to remain what it had been. Nicolai respected the great physicist too much to let a misunderstanding come between them, and Einstein clearly admired the courage and constancy of Nicolai's purpose. He took a tolerant, slightly amused, but always sympathetic view of Nicolai's quixotic character, but he gave him what support he could. As Kraus's letter suggests, others saw him as Nicolai's protector. Rolland had the same impression, which was also shared by Einstein's friend Heinrich Zangger in Zurich, who had been told that Nicolai was on the verge of collapse and asked Einstein what could be done to help him.[8] But in the matter of the publishing venture, Einstein remained adamant.

Moos was permanently lost to the project, and the "politics of the classics" never got off the ground. Buek continued to report nothing but failure, and the last mention of the subject is in the form of an almost casual inquiry from Nicolai to Pfemfert in May: "Whatever happened to our publishing company?" But the presses in Zurich were rolling. There was nothing to do now but wait.

NOTES

1. Quoted in Heinrich Mann, "Geist und Tat," reprinted in *Der Aktivismus 1915–1920*, ed. Wolfgang Rothe (Munich: Deutscher Taschenbuch Verlag, 1969), p. 24. This essay was originally published in *Pan* in 1910 and reprinted in *Das Ziel* in 1916.

2. Kurt Riezler, quoted in Margret Boveri, "Im Dienst der Macht: Kurt Riezler," *Merkur* 28, no. 12 (1974):1155.

3. Einstein to Nicolai, n.d., Nicolai archive.

4. Einstein to Nicolai, 17 February 1917, Nicolai archive.

5. Nicolai to Einstein, 26 February 1917, Nicolai archive.

6. Einstein to Nicolai, n.d., Nicolai archive.

7. Einstein to Romain Rolland, 22 August 1917, quoted in Otto Nathan and Heinz Norden, eds., *Einstein on Peace* (New York: Schocken, 1968).

8. Zangger to Einstein, n.d., Nicolai archive.

12. Burlesque in Field Gray

In the spring of 1917, when *The Biology of War* at last reached the world, its author was once again embroiled in a court-martial, this time for insulting and threatening his superiors. It was a tempest in a teapot—or rather in an inkwell—but it cost him a prison sentence. Streams of official ink flowed, scores of witnesses were heard, and the accused covered reams of paper with arguments worthy of a Talmudic scholar,[1] but to no avail, for his position was untenable. Never was the contrast between his brilliant intellect and his uncontrolled temper more strikingly apparent than in the farcical struggle that now ensued.

The villains of the piece, inevitably, were Drs. Böse and Schwer, the former the senior medical officer at Danzig, and the latter the supervisor of the laboratory to which Nicolai was assigned. Lesser roles were played by a Dr. Momber, a chemist whom the defendant called an *agent provocateur*; Private Lemanczyk, an orderly whose Polish name concealed a good Prussian heart; Fräulein Rohlfing and Fräulein Schreiber, laboratory technicians who had succumbed to Nicolai's charms; their older colleague Frau Zipfel, who had not; and sundry extras such as scrubwomen and landladies who might have overheard damaging remarks.

For a curtain-raiser, Nicolai was arrested on a charge of insolence, brought by Schwer, and placed in solitary confinement for three days. He had taken exception to Schwer's order forbidding him to read while on duty. "Never in my entire military career have I seen anybody who does not occupy himself in some such manner," he had protested to the hospital administration. "Depending on his tastes, one man will read the newspaper or discuss politics; another looks after his private professional interests or visits friends in other departments; still others study for their exams, read novels, or tend to their personal correspondence. I happen to devote myself to Fichte." The administration could not have relished this candid picture of the routine in a Prussian army hospital. Nicolai's request that he be allowed to pursue his studies, "all the more because I am accustomed to intellectual activity, cessation of which would be especially painful, considering the work I am required to perform," was rejected. He thereupon made a point of showing his boredom openly. After finishing his daily chores (he charged that Schwer purposely assigned him the most unpleasant tasks, such as sputum and stool examinations), he would sit at his bench with a vacant stare, arms folded across his chest, disdaining to make a show of being busy when Schwer entered, hoping to goad him into some rash act that would show him in the role of a long-suffering subordinate put upon by a capricious overseer.

He soon had his wish. One morning in April, Schwer entered the laboratory in an exceptionally bad humor. The girls hastily bent over their microscopes. Nicolai, conspicuously unoccupied, stood in the middle of the room, disdaining to bestir himself. The following dialogue, later sworn to by four witnesses, then took place. Schwer asked, "Have you nothing to do?" Nicolai replied "No." Schwer said "In that case I shall report to the Generaloberarzt that you refuse to work." Nicolai answered "Bitte!" Under the circumstances *Bitte* (literally, "please") could only mean "suit yourself" and was no doubt uttered in the most insolent tone of voice Nicolai could muster. It was improper in any case, for military etiquette called for *Jawohl*, "Yes, sir," when a private was spoken to by an officer. Schwer took it as the insult it was meant to be and went straight to Böse. Before nightfall Nicolai was a prisoner again.

He took the three days of arrest calmly, much as in his boyhood he had taken his confinements in the school lockup, but instead of ribald Latin graffiti or flippant verses for his lady love, he now composed the first of a long series of protests against the injustice that had brought him there. No sooner had the cell door shut behind the turnkey than he began drafting a formal complaint against Böse for overstepping his authority and failing to give him a proper hearing. He whiled away the rest of his time memorizing Greek verb forms, solving mathematical problems, measuring the exact dimensions of his cell, and calculating its volume to the last cubic centimeter. A pencil drawing which he kept as a memento shows in painstaking detail the interior of a Prussian military prison cell, complete with washstand, basin and pitcher, a single chair, and a cot. Standing on the raised end of the cot is the prisoner himself, in fatigues, craning his neck for a glimpse of freedom through the skylight (Fig. 21).

Nicolai's complaint against Böse was exquisitely clever, childish, and wholly ineffective. His reply to Schwer had been no more than factual, he wrote, for there *had* been nothing for him to do after he had completed his assignment for the day. It was beneath his dignity to pretend to be busy whenever the chief came in. Having directed a laboratory himself, he felt obliged to make Schwer aware of the state of affairs in his domain, for nothing was worse for the morale of the staff than to have time on their hands. After this oblique insult, he went on to state that Schwer had deliberately distorted his meaning when he accused him of refusing to work. As for saying "Bitte" when Schwer threatened to report him, it was true that "Jawohl" was the correct response, but that would have been out of place, for logical as well as grammatical reasons: logical, because it would have meant admitting the justice of the accusation; grammatical because Schwer had used a phrase that could not be answered with yes. In the heat of the moment he had not paused to reflect on the propriety of the word, but even after giving the matter serious thought he still felt that "Bitte" was the only suitable reply, for in the face of an unjust charge he had wanted to show that he welcomed the opportunity to clear himself.

The Sanitätsamt, which received the protest, was not interested in either logic or grammar. Recognizing Nicolai's intent to rub salt in Schwer's wounds, it not only rejected the complaint but added an extra hour to Nicolai's daily duties as punishment for the new insolence. Nicolai appealed to the Generalkommando in Danzig and to the surgeon general of the army. The latter gave him the satisfaction of reviewing the case and stipulating that Schwer's charge that he had refused to work was indeed unfounded, adding, however, that "this does not change the fact that Nicolai behaved improperly toward a superior and therefore deserved punishment even if mitigating circumstances are recognized. His unmilitary and unseemly conduct has been established once more through the testimony of the eyewitness Sanitätssoldat Lemanczyk, who was interrogated upon my orders. I therefore reject the complaint of the MKW Nicolai as unfounded."

Nicolai was delighted, for no less a personage than the surgeon general had walked into his trap. If, as he now wrote, in a petition addressed this

Fig. 21. Pages from Nicolai's notebook with sketches of his cell and mathematical notations.

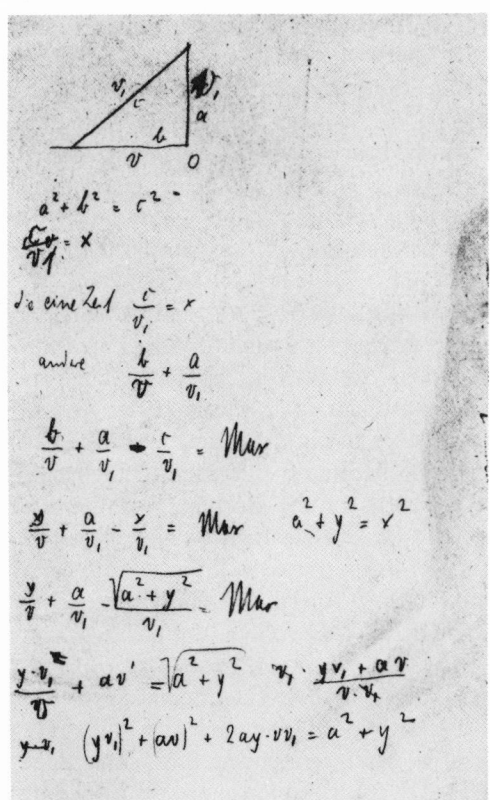

time to the Kaiser, Schwer's charge was factually baseless, the only remaining grounds for his arrest was the use of "Bitte," which was after all "the most polite word in the German language." True, he had uttered it in an excited tone of voice, but Lemanczyk could not have testified that it was a sarcastic tone, and in the face of Schwer's crass insult one could hardly blame a man for showing some emotion. In effect, then, he had been jailed for being momentarily unable to control the vibrations of his vocal cords, and whether that was a crime was a question he would gladly submit to any court of justice on earth.

We have no record of the Kaiser's response to these hairsplittings. The supreme warlord had other things to worry about in the closing days of June 1917. Five months of unrestricted submarine warfare had failed to "bring England to her knees" as the German militarists had prophesied; in the meantime, the United States had entered the war. General Nivelle's spring offensive had been beaten off, but the battle of Flanders was now raging. Russia had ceased to be a military threat, but the Russian Revolution had put dangerous ideas into the heads of the German socialists. The great strikes of April showed how restive the workers had become during the terrible "hunger winter" of 1916–17. Chancellor Bethmann-Hollweg's fall was imminent; Ludendorff's shadow was growing longer; victory was as remote as ever; and the prospect of yet another winter of war frightened even the High Command. In this situation the fact that the complaint of a mere private who, in the official view, was plainly a crank could stir the military bureaucracy all the way up to the surgeon general, if not to the emperor, shows the concern for correctness and formal justice that was part of the Prussian tradition. For his part, Nicolai, in forcing the army to admit that he had been punished for no other crime than failure to control his vocal cords, had achieved a triumph which, as a latter-day disciple of Voltaire, he relished more than an official apology: the *reductio ad absurdum* of military discipline through irony. It was worth three days of solitary confinement.

He was still drafting complaints about Schwer, Böse, and the surgeon general when the army struck back. Acting on a report by the now thoroughly incensed Schwer, Major General Von Pfuel as supreme magistrate of the Commandatura ordered an investigation, or rather a fishing expedition designed to catch enough evidence to put the troublemaker behind bars for good. The accuser once again became the accused, charges and countercharges flew through the air, and soon the machinery of the military bureaucracy was humming with the contrapuntal themes of justice and discipline. Nicolai was fighting for his rights with the tenacity of a bulldog, while the army was determined to squash the obnoxious raisonneur once and for all. This time the matter was serious: the charge might be treason.

The fishing expedition yielded a meager catch. The attempt to convict Nicolai of subversive or treasonable activities failed abysmally, and once more he had the best of his adversaries. Kriegsgerichtsrat Pusch, the judge advocate in charge of the pre-trial hearings, heard the witnesses named by Schwer as able to testify to the suspect's political opinions. According to Dr. Knoch, brought from Graudenz for the occasion, Nicolai had praised the valor of the Allied troops, belittled the victories of the German fleet, questioned the superiority of the German air force, and declared that Reuters, the British news agency, was more trustworthy than Wolff's, its German counterpart. Dr. Momber testified that the suspect was hostile, "or at least unfriendly," to the German cause, but he could offer no details other than that he had heard him say that the destruction of towns by the retreating German army was an act worthy of savages, and that Böse and Schwer were to be pitied for their stupidity and would have cause for regret once the war was over. Private Lemanczyk was more helpful, asserting that Nicolai was a dyed-in-the-wool republican, for he had overheard him applaud the Russian Revolution (Nicolai was referring to the moderate republican phase under the Provisional Government headed by Prince Lvov) and predict that after the war the German people, too, would throw off their shackles and join the brotherhood of man. Nicolai had not openly called for the overthrow of the monarchy, but he had explained to Lemanczyk and others that this was President Wilson's goal, and that it would be achieved, for Germany would lose the war.

Deta Braun, a laboratory technician, knew nothing of such talk, but Helle Freymann, another technician, had heard statements that "must offend any good patriot's ears": the Hohenzollerns must step down; the war cannot be won; the revolution will not stop at the Russian border. Fräulein Rohlfing, the only witness placed under oath at this stage—her tender feelings for the defendant had not escaped official notice—admitted that she had heard him express satisfaction over the events in Russia, though only because they would hasten peace. Frau Zipfel, who had no love for Nicolai, reluctantly conceded that she had heard nothing of a detrimental nature; neither had MKW Schülke and the two scrubwomen, Frau Piastowski and Frau Naujoks.

It was hard to draw up an indictment from such testimony. Judge Pusch had hoped to convict Nicolai of treasonable or seditious activities, but all that could be shown was that he held undesirable opinions. Nicolai, however, had taken no chances. He still had influential friends in the Reichstag and other high places. On 18 May Pusch received a stern warning from Berlin:

> The War Ministry has been reliably informed that the Magistrate of the Danzig Commandatura has initiated inquiries concerning Professor Nicolai which bear on the following questions not referred to in the files:
> 1. Whether Nicolai habitually commits lèse-majesté.
> 2. Whether he has treasonous tendencies.
> 3. What his beliefs are.
> 4. How he expresses them.
> It has also been stated that he has been forbidden to cultivate social relationships with the laboratory personnel outside the hours of duty.
> An immediate reply is requested.

The War Ministry was remarkably well informed, and it is not hard to guess by whom. The fact that Nicolai received a copy of this document speaks for itself. Schwer had indeed warned his subordinates against associating with "that fellow" Nicolai on a social basis, and Böse had called on Miss Schreiber's father, a retired Prussian officer, to caution him against letting the girl be corrupted by a man whose conduct placed him beyond the pale and whose persuasiveness made him especially dangerous to impressionable young females. Reports of these goings-on had come to Nicolai, and naturally enough he made the most of them, complaining to Berlin about this interference in his private life.

Nicolai had been giving a running account of developments to his old friend Davidsohn, the Reichstag deputy, and Davidsohn had a conduit to the war minister. He was on the best of terms with Generalarzt Schultzen, the minister's adviser for medical affairs. Davidsohn was also a member of the Budget Committee which had to pass on the ever-larger requests for funds to conduct a war that had long ceased to be popular with his working-class constituents. Like the other deputies of the Majority Socialist delegation, Davidsohn was a frustrated pacifist with feelings of guilt about supporting the war effort. He was also completely under Nicolai's spell and allowed himself to be ordered about like an errand boy. At the start of the hearings, Nicolai asked him to make representations "at suitable levels." Now he complained: "the only effect of your earlier steps was to extend the scope of the interrogation to include questions about lèse-majesté, treasonable activities, and the like." If the deputy was to take any further steps, "they must, of course, not amount to intervention in a case pending before the court, but only suggest to the minister of war that he should take the trouble to find out how the charge has arisen. Thus far I have received no answer to my question who denounced me." If every private who griped about his officers were put on trial "no soldier would be walking around as a free man these days."

Nicolai had another horse in his stable, Progressive deputy Struve. He had asked both him and Davidsohn to testify at his trial, hoping to prove that the War Ministry had assured them of its concern over his treatment at Böse's hands, but Davidsohn had begged off lest his delicate relationship with the military be exposed. Nicolai saw the danger at once. "Belatedly," he wrote to Struve, "I have come to doubt the wisdom of asking you to testify concerning remarks that were probably made to you in confidence. I have withdrawn your name from the list of witnesses." He also told Davidsohn that he would be excused "though I should be very glad if you came over for the hearing." He would get a firsthand picture and might yet volunteer to testify. "Of course, you must be our guest." If he had not already paid a visit to the War Ministry, he might also suggest that the minister send an observer. Davidsohn, a cautious man, declined the invitation. The fact that it was issued speaks not only for Nicolai's eagerness to drag him into the trial—at this point he was genuinely worried that he might receive a stiff sentence—but also for conditions at his home in the suburb of Langfuhr, which were comfortable enough to entertain a house guest of the stature of a Reichstag deputy. The invitation throws a curious light on a letter written shortly afterward to another influential personage on Nicolai's behalf, calling him "the physician most harmed by the war" and suggesting that the recipient inquire at the Norwegian embassy as to whether the Nobel Foundation might make a loan to this sufferer for the cause of peace.[2] The sufferer never lost sight of the practical side of life.

The warning from the War Ministry caused Pusch to beat a hasty retreat. He explained that the reports given to him had made it necessary to investigate the questions listed in the memorandum, but that there had been no intent of inquiring into the beliefs of the accused. The charges regarding Nicolai's anti-German views would be quashed and only his insulting behavior toward his superiors would be at issue. Nicolai had won the first round.

The second round was a tie, in a manner of speaking. An indictment was duly drawn up on 19 June charging Nicolai with insulting Böse and Schwer and with denying them the respect due them by threatening them. The court-martial convened with Pusch in the role of prosecutor and in due course found the accused guilty as charged, imposing a jail sentence of five months. An impartial bystander might well have wondered, however, who was on trial, the MKW or his superiors. Utterly unrepentant, Nicolai contended that any disrespectful remarks he might have made were the result of the extreme stress under which he labored because of the unceasing chicanery of his superiors. He also offered to prove that their behavior had been stupid indeed. It was stupid to keep a skilled physician occupied with menial chores; it was stupid to make a martyr of a dissenter; it was stupid to deprive a man of his legal rights. He challenged the impartiality of the court and the credibility of witnesses who manifestly had been coerced by the very persons who were pressing charges against him. He managed to introduce into the trial record a memorandum purportedly written by the Danzig historian Walther Gräbner, which listed his grievances in minute detail and which, as he took pains to inform the court, had been placed in the hands of Reichstag Deputy Struve, who in turn had passed it on to the minister of war and was giving it the widest circulation in the capital. He also intimated that it was because of their unfairness to himself that Böse and Schwer had been transferred from their posts even before the trial had begun, Böse to the naval station of Wilhelmshaven and Schwer to the East Prussian garrison of Allenstein.

Böse and Schwer thus found it necessary to defend themselves against Nicolai's charges in lengthy written depositions. Böse admitted that he had called Nicolai's conduct in the "Bitte" incident insolent and had said that he would not shake hands with him. He still thought that a man with subversive opinions who refused to take the oath of loyalty to his king was socially unacceptable. He had not called him a fellow without a country or a man with whom he would not want to be seen in the street, though he might have told Fräulein Schreiber, "who came to me of her own volition some weeks ago and protested in tears that she in no way sympathized with Nicolai's views," that he would not walk down the street in his company, for he considered his proselytizing despicable. Nicolai had shown his true colors, said Böse, in the statements he had made upon his arrival in Danzig and in his refusal to take the oath. As physician-in-chief, he had a duty to keep an eye on the man, especially after Schwer reported that he was "spinning an intellectual web" around some of the girls in the laboratory. Had Nicolai not returned from Berlin to tell his listeners that the situation there was even worse than in Danzig, and that the blackest mood reigned at the Foreign Office? People with limited ability to form their own judgment had to be protected against such poison, and it was for this reason that Böse had enlightened Geheimrat Rohlfing about the man his daughter admired. Rohlfing had been grateful and volunteered to give his errant child paternal advice. As for Fräulein Schreiber, Böse had found it sufficient to remind her that she was the daughter of a high Prussian officer.

Answering Nicolai's statement and Gräbner's memorandum point by point, Böse denied that morale was low in the bacteriology laboratory. Nicolai's claim that he had defended his superiors against a resentful staff "because we were not evil men but simply did not know better" was patently absurd. Using expressions like "fathead" and "idiot" to describe one's officers, not once but repeatedly, is hardly a sign of concern for staff morale. Nicolai should not have been excluded from a staff outing for which he had paid his share of the cost in advance, but that had been a "procedural error," and Böse had said that the black sheep should have been allowed to come along. Yes, he might have told the non-com to see that Nicolai had his hair cut. He had occasionally but not habitually referred to him as "that fellow." He might well have shown surprise when his subordinates inadvertently addressed Nicolai as "Herr Professor," for he could not allow the stature of a dangerous political agitator to be increased in the minds of "simple folk." Böse had always spoken of and to Nicolai as "Militärkrankenwärter." He had not acceded to Kraus's request for Nicolai's release because the man's conduct scarcely entitled him to special favors. It was true that he had granted prolonged leaves to Momber and another man, but it was not, as Nicolai charged, time given them to work on their doctoral dissertations but time for important research projects, as certified by the director of the Chemical Institute. The fact that these projects might help the two men obtain their doctoral degrees was purely coincidental, Böse stated. Doctoral dissertations, moreoever, often possessed special scientific merit. The allegation that a third man was allowed to work on a patently useless project involving grasshoppers was an example of Nicolai's tendency to twist facts to suit his purpose, a tendency which the earlier court-martial had amply demonstrated. It so happened that a plague of locusts threatened the food supply not only of Turkey, Germany's ally, but that of the entire Near East, and Sergeant La Baume had been detailed to help combat this danger.

Böse's attitude had been that of a man bending over backwards in the face of constant provocation, he stated. He had given Nicolai permission to practice medicine with the proviso that he must not neglect his military duties to do so. He could not very well give him carte blanche to be late for duty whenever it suited him, especially because Nicolai was notorious for his tardiness and for flimsy excuses such as a breakdown of the streetcar. Nicolai was the only physician under his command to complain that he could not look after his patients if he had to report to the post at a fixed time. If Böse had indeed used a special yardstick for a man so patently bent on disrupting discipline, it was because leniency had failed. It was as though Nicolai, perhaps relying on his influential friends and relatives (Böse must have been unaware that Geheimrat Busley had broken with his son-in-law), was trying to see how much provocation his superiors would tolerate. Böse's attitude had been guided not by personal animosity but by his desire to maintain discipline and protect his subordinates against subversive ideas, he concluded, and "therefore I believe that my actions concerning MKW Nicolai have been governed by my duty to the state."

One can almost hear the sigh of relief with which the Generaloberarzt closed his memoir. Whether or not his transfer had anything to do with Nicolai's complaints, he was rid of a responsibility that had taxed his endurance. He had been saddled with the most difficult subordinate in the armed forces. Far from being a martinet, for the sake of peace he had closed both eyes to many of Nicolai's peccadilloes, excusing his conduct on the grounds that he was *weltfremd*, ignorant of the ways of the world, and assigned him to non-coms known for their calm temperament and experience in handling new recruits. He soon regretted his strategy, however, for he was not a bad psychologist. "Like a red thread, countless petitions and complaints run through the by now greatly swollen Nicolai file," he wrote, "and in addition to these written documents he has made many verbal requests and protests. From all this an unprejudiced observer must gain the impression that he is dealing with a crank, albeit a highly talented one." It was his superb intelligence that made him dangerous, for "he knows how to throw out seemingly casual remarks and tell the most fascinating stories with which to spread the poison of his internationalist and in these times subversive ideas and to influence less critically inclined persons and draw them into his intellectual sphere." Böse's sketch was remarkably perceptive.

Schwer supported his chief. Böse, he wrote in his rebuttal, enjoyed the respect and affection of his subordinates and the citizenry of Danzig. Nicolai's attempt to drag the name of such a man through the mud proved his malice. Schwer too, felt compelled to refute every charge made by Nicolai and Gräbner, though he was far more bitter than Böse, for he had borne the brunt of Nicolai's attack. He denied having refused letters of recommendation to the technicians who sided with Nicolai, but admitted having stopped the agitation that began behind his back after the "Bitte" incident, when the troublemaker tried to gather signatures for his petition to the emperor. These goings-on had so disrupted the laboratory that he was indeed forced to threaten the removal of the "disturbing elements," whereupon Frau Zipfel had expressed, "in the name of every technician in the laboratory," her sincere regret concerning a situation which, though not maliciously, they had helped to create. She had amplified this apology by explaining that "Nicolai, sad to relate, exerted an almost hypnotic influence on some of the employees," but that these weak souls had withdrawn their signatures once they realized the gravity of their offense. Speaking for the entire staff, Frau Zipfel had assured him that they would henceforth avoid Nicolai. Schwer had been pleased with this outcome, for two of the girls, Fräulein Rohlfing and Fräulein Schreiber, had been so completely under Nicolai's spell and had been seen with him so often on and off the post that the entire staff had been scandalized.[3] Schwer passed over the abrupt dismissal of the girls, who were evidently considered beyond redemption even before the court-martial. When they consulted Nicolai, he was ready with a petition for them to submit to the Kaiser. His draft, thoughtfully prepared with blank spaces for the names, personal information, and date, stated that the undersigned had been employed at the fortress hospital since (blank) and had always rendered satisfactory service.

> Suddenly I received my dismissal notice effective 15 July, allegedly for reasons of economy. Since no consideration was given to seniority, since the accompanying circumstances suggest that the dismissal was brought about by personal and political factors, and since, moreover, my personal honor is being attacked and I am the daughter of [blank], I herewith request cancellation of the notice or reemployment in another capacity.

The writer then related that "Herr Professor Nicolai" was working in the same laboratory as the writer:

> We technicians benefited from his medical help, frequented his home, and were especially appreciative of the far-ranging instruction he gave us in laboratory subjects. For reasons beyond my knowledge, the military authorities ordered us to cease this relationship but reversed themselves when Professor Nicolai protested. We were thus well within our rights in continuing the relationship, but when the authorities learned that we had shown our gratitude by embroidering a pillow for him, Dr. Böse scolded us harshly and Dr. Schwer told us afterward that "those who stick with Professor Nicolai will be fired."

Some of the girls apologized, the draft went on, but the undersigned saw no reason to do so, believing that they had the right to choose their friends as they saw fit.

The authorities must have recognized Nicolai's fine hand in this petition. In any case, the appeal went for nought. The girls had to leave Danzig and found positions with the Medical Corps in German-occupied Romania, where Fräulein Rohlfing almost died of typhus. One wonders how these daughters of "good Prussian families," reared in the traditions of the Hohenzollern monarchy, reacted to Nicolai's ideas. Encountering his overpowering personality must have meant a complete upheaval in their thinking. At first—as Böse correctly said in his memoir—they were shocked by his radical opinions, only to embrace them with the fervor of the convert once they dared to think the unthinkable. War was evil and obsolete, pacifism was salvation, a new day was dawning for mankind, and Nicolai was its prophet and a "Herr Professor" to boot. He was also handsome, virile, and knowledgable in the ways of pleasing women. Small wonder that Böse and Schwer feared for the spiritual welfare of the laboratory staff.

Ghostwriting for the girls also served Nicolai's own purposes and was typical of his stategy. The Gräbner memoir was also written by him. Here the ostensible author (Gräbner) protested that he did not share the political views of the man (Nicolai) whose rights he wished to defend. He then recounted the innumerable wrongs suffered by the victim of a cruel, insensitive, and unintelligent apparatus, from the transfer to Graudenz to the "Bitte" incident and the trivia of life in the laboratory at Danzig: "Every witch-hunt, every personal quarrel, amounts to a waste we can ill afford, a squandering of our strength and a danger to the true Germany." It was time to put an end to this waste and place the professor where his skills could be used effectively. The Gräbner memoir may have contributed to the War Ministry's intervention in the pretrial hearings. It did serve to draw out Böse and Schwer. Böse recognized it as Nicolai's handiwork and the court ignored it as biased. (The Generaloberarzt did not know that the draft bore extensive corrections in Nicolai's hand and that the final copy was typed on Nicolai's typewriter, no doubt by Fräulein Van Kampen.) Its real author stayed in the army and remained an MKW.

The verdict nevertheless took cognizance of each of Nicolai's counter-charges, including his allegation that Böse and Schwer instigated the pro-ceedings solely in order to head off an inquiry into their own misconduct, and that the War Ministry tacitly admitted their guilt by transferring them to other posts. The court certified that they had behaved correctly at all times, even though repelled by the "peculiar political views of the ac-cused." Nicolai was mistaken, said the court, if he thought that he was entitled to unlimited privileges. Nor was it true that he had been specifi-cally enjoined from reading Fichte. (The court was evidently sensitive to the casting of aspersions on the intellectual standards of the officer corps.) He had simply been told to stop using working hours for his private busi-ness. Schwer had tried to interest him in research, but he had always rejected these suggestions. He had been assigned to microscopy rather than bacteriology because of his careless handling of infectious material. As for the transfers of Böse and Schwer, the court flatly stated that they had nothing to do with the case at hand.

The sworn testimony of thirteen witnesses had proved that the accused had been treated with a leniency "almost exceeding permissible limits." His conduct had been such as to "grievously damage the authority of his superiors." He had created currents of discontent that inferfered with the functioning of the laboratory. His claim that he had counseled peace was patently false. "Nevertheless the court assumes that in assessing the pun-ishable acts of the accused the stipulations of Paragraph 98 of the Military Penal Code are applicable, for it is apparent . . . that the accused had talked himself into the erroneous belief that he was the victim of malicious misuse of official authority. The court therefore considers both the insults and the threats to have been made under the impact of this emotional imbalance." The court was even willing to consider all of the individual offenses to have resulted from a single decision by the accused. He was punishable nevertheless, for as an intelligent, highly educated man he could be expected to behave correctly, whereas in actual fact he had caused a serious erosion of discipline. A sentence of five months was appropriate, Paragraph 98 notwithstanding.

Did the extraordinary leniency of the verdict stem from the court's awareness that Nicolai had friends in high places, or from a genuine in-sight into his paranoia? In either case, admirable patience and fairness had been displayed. Nicolai, of course, did not see it in this light. For him the outcome was a victory of sorts. He immediately appealed, and laid the groundwork for the next court battle, intending to take the offensive this time. Meanwhile he planned to enjoy the amenities of Danzig. Life had become quite tolerable, now that Böse and Schwer were gone. His duties were light; his practice was blossoming. He had found people who would listen to his ideas. Above all, *The Biology of War* had come out in the midst of the trial, and although he had not seen the reviews, he knew that it was creating a sensation abroad.[4] Was he perhaps a candidate for the Nobel Prize for Peace, he wondered.

NOTES

1. Throughout this chapter quotations from the court-martial proceedings of 19 June 1917 and related correspondence are taken from the court-martial transcripts and letters preserved in the Nicolai archive, "Heeressachen" ("Army Matters") folder.

2. This letter is quoted from a copy in Nicolai's handwriting in the Nicolai archive; neither the writer nor the intended recipient is identified.

3. The two young women had embroidered a handsome satin pillow with an artistic design representing malaria parasites in red corpuscles, which they tenderly presented to the professor who had taught them hematology, parasitology, and other things. This remarkable object, which Nicolai kept to his dying day, is now in the possession of the Feldmann family of Santiago, Chile, where this writer saw it in 1972.

4. The first mention of the appearance of the book occurs in a letter from Nicolai to Leonhard Frank dated 26 June 1917, a week before the conclusion of the court-martial: "The only thing new is the fact that I am entangled in a number of trials which are partly in a preliminary stage of investigation, partly in the process of being appealed. This I did not dream when we said goodbye. I confess that I never imagined that such things were even possible. Meanwhile, as I see from a notice in the *Neue Zürcher Zeitung*, the *Biology* has come out. I would be interested to know what you think of it and what others are saying. The only response I have had thus far were a few lines from Professor Forel." Auguste Forel was one of the leading pacifists of the period; like Nicolai, he was a scientist and social reformer as well.

13. The Breaking Point

The Biology of War made a profound impression on those of Nicolai's contemporaries who saw it. Reviewers in the neutral countries, accustomed to raucous propaganda and unreasoning hatred from the intelligentsia of the belligerent nations, were generous with their praise for a work that supported the cause of humanism and sanity with powerful scientific arguments and suggested a rational basis for the reorganization of the civilized world. It was "a work of fundamental significance," Paul Seipel wrote in the *Journal de Genève*, "the noblest work that has appeared in these terrible war years," Romain Rolland added in *Demain*.[1] The *Neue Zürcher Zeitung*, German-speaking Switzerland's foremost newspaper, devoted almost the entire front page of its Sunday edition of 17 June 1917 to a review which—though the writer pointed out Nicolai's occasional tendency to lapse into "malicious pamphleteering"—praised it as "a good book, strong, pitiless, spacious, spiritual, and demanding, a work that belongs to the future and to those who believe in the human being of the future because they themselves carry a piece of that human being in their breast." The *Zürcher Post* called it "a brave, richly informative, stimulating book, a work that will in all probability belong to the future." Nicolai was "one of the few whom the coming times will honor," Ellen Key wrote.[2] His book was "an overwhelming document," Ivan Goll said in the *Gazette de Lausanne*, "an outcry of truth, a work that will outlast the times for which it was written." It was to be expected that Alfred Fried's *Friedenswarte* would welcome the potent ammunition Nicolai had provided for the pacifist cause, but even a sober observer of military affairs like the *Allgemeine schweizer Militärzeitung* waxed rhapsodic: "No reader of this work, at least none who reads it without prejudice, will put it aside without the feeling that it was written by a man who as bearer of mankind's ideal of brotherhood will lead the way into the future of the world's nations." The *Basler Nationalzeitung* went even farther: "one is almost tempted to say," its critic wrote, "that the World War was not entirely in vain if it gave rise to this book."

Even in Germany and Austria a few editors took notice of the forbidden book. Noting that it had been "conceived in pain in the face of the greatest catastrophe," the *Kölner Tageblatt* called it "the spiritual bridge to the future beyond the war, built by human reason." Theodor Wolff, the editor-in-chief of the nominally liberal *Berliner Tageblatt*, a man whose intelligence was greater than his courage, refused to review an officially outlawed book, but the *Tageblatt*'s competitor, the *Vossische Zeitung*, whose tradition harked back to the spirit of Lessing was willing to take its chances on the censor. Up to now man had been silent, Adolf Koelsch wrote in the issue of 7 September:

> One becomes conscious of this fact in all its shamefulness, now that he begins to speak and write, abandoning his silence and shouting.

Such a shout, the voice of the downtrodden and tortured man, spiritual man, forward- and backward-looking man, is the book Georg Fr. Nicolai has just permitted Orell Füssli of Zurich to publish. This man, who held the rank of professor of philosophy [sic] at the University of Berlin, has proved once before—as is known from the proceedings of the Reichstag—that he belongs to that admirable group of people who stand ready to answer with their persons for their cause and who follow the path of their convictions even if it leads to jail. This book is a courageous restatement of his faith in his cause, which is the cause of openness to the world, of cultural humanism, of the future.

The *Literary Annals* of the Dürerbund asserted that "war has never been put beyond the pale of civilization in a manner so thorough, so gripping, so entirely free of prejudice, as in the *Biology of War*, which actually is far more than its title indicates; it surveys the biology, philosophy, sociology, and history of all socioorganic phenomena connected with war."

Paul Kammerer, in the Viennese journal *Der Morgen*, called Nicolai's work "perhaps one of the most magnificent books of all time." Jacob Feldner, a young idealist who was among the students attending the lectures which led to Nicolai's removal from the University of Berlin in 1915, wrote in *Neue Bücher*: "Only the wisest will dare criticize this book. We, his former pupils, have only the task of thanking him. The author has suffered degradation, banishment, insults, and disgrace, but the most vicious persecution did not keep him from fighting on. His greatest achievement is the book we now hold in our hands." Nicolai had cleansed the name of German scholarship, sullied by the mouthings of thousands of noisy chauvinist intellectuals, said Feldner: "If the message of this book reaches the world as quickly as did that of the Ninety-Three, the blots will have been erased and the escutcheon of German science will shine again."

In the face of so much enthusiasm, it was not unreasonable for Nicolai to hope for the Nobel Peace Prize, which had not been awarded since 1914. Clearly, *Biology of War* ranked with the best efforts of earlier pacifists like Bertha von Suttner or Alfred Fried, who had been so honored, and the circumstances under which it was written and published gave it a unique moral weight. For Nicolai, who was appealing his prison sentence for insolence toward Prussian army officers at the time, the thought of being plucked from this situation to Christiania, to receive the Nobel Prize from the Norwegian Storthing at a solemn session, combined the pleasure of a dream fulfilled with the sweet taste of revenge: it would be a worthy reward to him and at the same time a slap in the face of the German militarists.[3] The prize money would also help his finances: maintaining the household in Danzig-Langfuhr, with wife and child, secretary and maid, required more money than a catch-as-catch-can medical practice was bringing in, and his military pay of twelve marks and forty pfennigs a month barely covered his postal expenses.

It was a time of waiting and frustration. Not until August did Nicolai see a copy of his book, for he was still under strict surveillance, and the few copies smuggled out of Switzerland were hard to come by. "Only to let you know that here in Danzig several people have ordered—and received—the *Biology of War* from their bookseller," he wrote Franz Pfemfert impatiently: "If it can be done by provincial bookstores, people in the capital should be able to do as well." Pfemfert should put an announcement in the Mail Box of the *Aktion*, said Nicolai, and he must not forget to mention that the author had recently been sentenced to five months in

Fig. 22. At ease in Danzig in the summer of 1917.

prison (Nicolai was not above making capital out of his as yet unconsummated martyrdom).

To Theodor Wolff, that timid liberal, he made an urgent appeal:

> When your Mr. Zeiz was here, he told me that you refused to review the *Biology of War*, for reasons of censorship. Your editorial policies are none of my business, but since I am anxious to see at least a mention in one of Germany's leading liberal newspapers, I take the

liberty of giving my reason: the book is much read in Switzerland, as proved by the number of copies sold and the many enthusiastic letters I have received. It is now being translated into English and Dutch, and people will not understand why this book—which at most may be criticized for being *too* German, *too* caught up in German ideology—is not mentioned by any German liberal newspaper. As far as I know, it has been reviewed thus far only by Socialist papers. I consider the government stupid for suppressing it out of fear of pacifism, for it would be an excellent propagande device at a time when German propagandists are so busy. But it would also seem stupid to me if our liberal newspapers joined in this boycott. At a time when, as surely you know better than I, regardless of victories on the battlefield, the battle for free thought—I say "free" in order to avoid the word "liberal"—is being decided perhaps for centuries to come, at such a time the few intellectuals who have identical or similar goals should close ranks; otherwise, we make it too easy for our adversaries.

This plea fell on deaf ears.

But the fate of the first edition of *Biology of War* no longer really mattered to Nicolai. A perfectionist, he was unhappy about the minor flaws, inadvertent omissions, misplaced headings, wrong dates, and missing references which he discovered in the printed text. Now that the success of the book was assured, the task of preparing a second edition became urgent, all the more so if it were to be considered by the Nobel committee. "I seize the opportunity to write an uncensored letter," he wrote to his Swiss publisher when he found someone willing to take contraband mail across the Swiss border,

> to tell you of the extraordinary pleasure you have given me by publishing my book. Now I know that at least some people abroad can hear what not a few here in sealed-off Germany are thinking. That alone would satisfy me, apart from my hopes for commercial success, of course. I would like to know whether a second edition is in sight, in which case you should use the corrected copy which will reach you by the same route as this letter. As grateful as I am to the unknown editors for their surely not inconsiderable pains, I have found much to criticize as to details.

The obstacles were formidable. Communication with the foreign publisher was tenuous at best, Nicolai's own mail was read by the censor, his time was not his own, his resources were limited, and, having been court-martialed once for violating the press law, he was placing himself in serious danger by taking an active part in the preparation of a new edition. None of these considerations stopped him, however. The revision took precedence over everything, even the preparations for his legal appeal against the latest court verdict.

But on 19 September, before he had made much progress, an unexpected blow fell: by order of the War Ministry, effective immediately, he was transferred from Danzig to the little town of Eilenburg near Leipzig, in the jurisdiction of the Fourth Army Corps. Nicolai was thunderstruck. He had never ceased to agitate for a change of scenery, but he had Berlin in mind, not some God-forsaken hole in provinicial Saxony. If he could not be in Berlin, he wanted to remain in Danzig.

Ironically, the transfer was the result of his own backstage maneuvers and those of his politician friend Davidsohn, to whom he immediately wrote an irate letter. But this time Davidsohn was unsympathetic. "I hope your husband has taken himself *peacefully* to his new post," he wrote to Frau Nicolai, who stayed behind to pick up the household. "Had I known that the well-intentioned transfer order would not be issued till the last moment, I would have informed Professor Nicolai, for the War Ministry had notified me some time ago" (for a Social Democrat, Davidsohn's re-

Fig. 23. "Boredom." Silhouette by unknown artist.

NICOLAI IN EILENBURG.

lationship with the military was indeed excellent), "but as things stand I would recommend that your Herr Gemahl take a look at Eilenburg first— not that he has any choice. Perhaps things will turn out to be tolerable, perhaps he will get permission to practice there, etc. Under today's conditions, moreover, the Saxon air might be much healthier for your husband than that of Prussia. He might even get a medical officer's pay, and for that reason, too, it is advisable for him to rein in his understandable impatience. To plead for him to be allowed to stay in Danzig after moving Heaven and Hell to get him transferred *out* of Danzig goes against my grain, after all."

Nicolai failed to see the humor of the situation. Once more he was deprived of his income, for he did not receive a medical officer's pay, he was not allowed to practice medicine until five months after his arrival, and it was difficult to build up a clientele in a small town under any circumstances. "In this God-forsaken hole there isn't even a decent chess player," he complained. Surveillance of him was again strict. Food was harder to come by than in Danzig, where friends had supplied him with such treats as fats, sugar, and tea. "The proximity of Leipzig sucks the

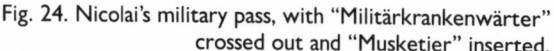

Fig. 24. Nicolai's military pass, with "Militärkrankenwärter" crossed out and "Musketier" inserted.

countryside dry," he wrote Eva. Worst of all, he had nothing to do (Fig. 23). Even the drudgery in Dr. Schwer's laboratory was preferable to complete idleness. With his transfer he had been reclassified—illegally, he claimed—from medical orderly to rifleman in the infantry (Fig. 24), and once more his superiors devised meaningless chores for him.

It was in this black mood that he wrote to Leonhard Frank in Switzerland:

216

I have had no news from you or anyone on the outside for a long time; are you all on vacation? And waiting is so hard for me. I wrote you a few times (those letters, too, may not have arrived) and thanked you for your efforts on behalf of my book. I shall have to be in your debt once more, because I herewith ask you to take care of the second edition as well. I am not well off here in the hinterland, have no permit to travel, no books, no friends or letters, no knowledge of what is happening in the world, living here quite alone, and yet they see to it that I don't have leisure for my work. Senseless duties—now I am allowed to trace, with ink, lines that others have drawn with pencil. They try to torment and break a man. But unfortunately they will not succeed. I have sat serenely with bread and water when they locked me up. I draw my [ink] lines with serenity, thinking that it will get better and that the future will be different. At first I hoped that others (colleagues or politicians) would take an interest in my case or that a foreign university would approach me because they felt an obligation to counteract this senseless waste. Now I hope for nothing and live as I imagine the hermits of old must have lived. At bottom I owe the military a great deal: one can be a civilized human being even in slaves' chains.

Such resignation was uncharacteristic, and it did not last long. Eilenburg had one advantage over Danzig: it was closer to Berlin. Nicolai's friends could come to see him (and bring news, messages, mail that could not be entrusted to the postal service, and food parcels). Buek came for Christmas, and Ilse Einstein, Albert's future stepdaughter, who had become his ardent admirer, was a frequent visitor. Through her, Nicolai made contact with a young Polish woman named Fanja Lezierska, who supplied him with the clandestine pamphlets of the revolutionary underground movement Spartakus. Far from having nothing to do, he now faced three projects: his legal appeal, set for 18 December; preparation of the new edition of his book; and the writing and distribution of some clandestine pamphlets of his own.

The hearing took place in Danzig, which permitted him to return in triumph to the scene of his martyrdom and to stop in Berlin en route for consultations with his lawyer and various influential friends.[4] He had no intention of serving his jail term; on the contrary, he was determined to even the score with the army, feeling that he had the upper hand now that his book had made him famous. He attacked at once, using the Supreme Military Tribunal as a forum for his charges against Böse and Schwer, his accusations of entrapment against the witness Momber, his catalogue of the judicial and procedural errors of the lower court, and a lecture to the army on how to treat educated privates. But the mainstay of his strategy was his claim that Böse had received instructions from his superiors in Berlin to treat him with greater consideration, proof, Nicolai argued, that the War Ministry recognized the injustice of which he had been the victim. It followed that Böse had, first, exceeded his authority, second, violated explicit orders, and third, made concessions to decency only as the result of intervention from Berlin.

This convoluted logic, oddly enough, was effective, for it was based on an embarrassing fact: the cozy relationship between Generalarzt Schultzen, the war minister's special adviser, and the Social Democrat Davidsohn, a relationship neither party was anxious to expose to the light of day. Nicolai intended to exploit his knowledge of that relationship, notwithstanding the fact that he had benefited from it, and at his insistence Dr. Schultzen was summoned to Danzig as a reluctant witness whose testimony provided the ammunition he needed.

Dr. Schultzen began his testimony by stating categorically that no orders concerning the treatment of Nicolai had gone from the War Ministry to Dr. Böse. Nicolai maintained that such an order did go to Danzig. Schultzen, being under oath, was visibly uncomfortable. "Not an order as such," he answered evasively: "Not until the summer of 1917 did the War Ministry issue instructions to the Generalkommando, which I am not in a position to discuss at the moment. They did not deal with the way the accused had been treated." This tantalizing bit of information no doubt referred to the order to Judge Advocate Pusch to quash the charges of lèse majesté and treason.

Nicolai's spirits rose. He asked, did the witness recall the following:

> After Messrs. Böse and Klauer [Böse's representative at the Commandatura] had testified that they had not been influenced from above, I traveled to Berlin and a few days later visited the Reichstag. I was talking with several deputies, Mr. Struve, Mr. Davidsohn, some members of the Center, and others whose names were unfamiliar to me, when Generalarzt Schultzen entered the room. Mr. Davidsohn went over to meet him. The conversation took place in such a way that I and the other gentlemen could hear it. When the witness was told that Messrs. Böse and Klauer had denied under oath having been subjected to pressure, he said: "I am acquainted with Herr Klauer. I don't happen to know Dr. Böse. I cannot believe that Herr Klauer would perjure himself."

Schultzen indignantly denied the insinuation that in vouching for the veracity of Klauer he had meant to impugn that of Böse. As to his conversation with Mr. Davidsohn, he testified that he might have said that the truth would come out in due course, but not that Dr. Böse had been ordered to be kinder to Nicolai. Challenged once again by the defendant, the witness admitted having told Davidsohn that "if everything you tell me is true I would not hesitate to call it objectionable." He recalled adding that "such matters are apt to be embroidered." He had never said that he considered the treatment Nicolai had received improper: "After all, the accused was a complete stranger to me."

Evidently Dr. Schultzen had not been aware—nor could he have imagined in his wildest dreams—that the medical orderly in the Reichstag building in Berlin, chatting with a group of deputies and eavesdropping on his conversation with Davidsohn on the very subject of his case, was Nicolai. Schultzen admitted on the stand that he had promised Davidsohn to intervene if the necessity arose, but it had not, he said. He further admitted that he had had to report personally to the acting minister of war, one Herr von Wandel, but that he had had nothing to do with the order that had actually gone out, for he had been ill during the period in question.

Nicolai spoke up again: "I request that the statements of Herr Dr. Schultzen be recorded verbatim. It is clear that there has been interference with the present trial as well, and that the desired result has been achieved." The prosecutor objected strenuously: the sole question before the court was whether the accused had insulted his superiors or not. Therefore there was no need to inquire whether Dr. Böse had received instructions to change his treatment of the accused. Schultzen, asked by Nicolai's counsel whether he considered the demotion of a university professor to the grade of medical orderly an appropriate response to the refusal to take the oath, declined to give an official opinion. His private view was that a physician who had proved himself unworthy of his profession need not be employed as a physician thereafter. He could not be more specific without knowing all the facts.

The courtroom drama reached its climax when Dr. Schultzen was forced to admit that the order to mitigate the hardships of which Nicolai had complained did indeed constitute intervention by the War Ministry, and, moreover, that it had been issued on May 5, 1917, that is, *after* he had recovered from his illness: "Before that date no intervention on behalf of the accused took place, as far as I am aware." He might have talked about proper treatment of subordinates in general, he said, but the Nicolai case had never been remotely touched upon. Nicolai leaped into the breach: "Why, then, did the Herr Generalarzt give members of the Reichstag the opposite impression?" Schultzen, his credibility shaken, replied lamely: "I have already stated that I have been asked about this case so many times that I can no longer remember the details. Whatever I may have said was always based on the premise that the facts were as represented. I must deny ever having said that I or the War Ministry have actually intervened." He also stated that Dr. Böse's transfer, as far as he knew, had been in no way connected with the Nicolai case. Did the accused actually claim that it had been, the prosecutor asked incredulously. Nicolai responded, "I consider it very likely." The witness Schultzen then asked to be excused. There being no objection from either party, he was released from what was undoubtedly the most unpleasant ordeal of his career. Nicolai had won another skirmish.

He had every reason to be pleased with the outcome of his appeal, but he was not yet fully satisfied. "What now?" he wrote to Davidsohn, knowing that the deputy would be furious at having been duped by his friend the Generalarzt.

> I think I have done my duty; now do yours. I have blasted the interesting confession from the beautiful soul; now you should make use of it. The gentleman was there in person; that was the most important part of the trial. You can imagine what a red face he had when he was forced to answer my questions. The judge interrupted me to say that they were irrelevant. I said no indeed, for I wanted to prove that I was surrounded by a tissue of lies and that this was part of that

tissue, and that settled the matter. The penalty was reduced from five months in jail to six weeks of *Mittelarrest*, with the unofficial comment that the latter was chosen to avoid creating a criminal record, and that's the end of this business. They told me the sentence was immaterial in any case, for I would not have to serve it. You see, one never knows. But I think the untruthful denial by the embassy in Bern—though unsuccessful and published only in the *Zürcher Post*—had something to do with the outcome.

The last remark was a reference to a statement issued by the German embassy in Switzerland to the effect that the original court-martial had sentenced Nicolai not to five months in jail but only to a fine of seven hundred marks, a transparent attempt on the part of the government to minimize the impact of the verdict on public opinion abroad. But although he now knew that he would not have to serve five months or, for that matter, any time at all in jail, Nicolai had no intention of letting himself be robbed of his martyrdom. He had been sentenced to five months, he insisted in a complaint to Secretary of State Richard Kühlmann, the official who had jurisdiction over embassies. The fact that a higher court had later reduced the sentence was immaterial: he was entitled to an official retraction of the denial by the ambassador. Once again he was successful. On orders from the Foreign Office, Ambassador von Romberg issued a rectification to the Swiss press, and in due course Nicolai was notified of this action by Generalkommando Magdeburg.

Davidsohn was impressed. "My most respectful congratulations upon the dramatic reduction [of the sentence], which amounts to almost complete vindication," he wrote. "We shall cut through the 'tissue' in good time." But Nicolai had no intention of letting the easy-going politician off the hook. His victory over Schultzen and the War Ministry could be used to weaken the power of the military. Was not Davidsohn a member of the Appropriations Committee, and did not the Army depend on the good will of the Social Democrats at budget time? The deputy must not be allowed to drop the matter. For a year and a half Schultzen had told him that he was looking out for his protégé, said Nicolai, but things had only gotten worse. "Now I give you sworn proof that Schultzen has lied to you, for he has testified that he never wrote to Danzig on my behalf; that is a fact," Nicolai complained. "Thus you and I—but especially you—were lied to by a representative of the government, and I assumed that something will happen now and that you would rouse yourself to energetic action, but I have been waiting a month and a half already, and nothing *is* happening. My case is unimportant in itself, but it is a symptom of arbitrary military power, and I still expect that you and your party will fight against such arbitrary rule, even if it forces you to oppose the government with which you are now on such cordial terms."

There was no action, now or at any time. Davidsohn, though angry at Schultzen for making a fool of him, was a cautious politican and a good party man. Increasingly unhappy about their inability to stop a war which was now plainly revealed—by the negotiations with the Russians going on at Brest-Litovsk—as a war of conquest, the Social Democrats had no desire to upset the precarious balance between their loyalty to the government and the war-weariness of the masses by precipitating a crisis over an outsider like Nicolai. Davidsohn chose to treat the business with Schultzen as a personal matter. He confronted the Generalarzt in private and was told that the assurances he had been given earlier were made in jest, he reported. Joking with a Reichstag deputy was as bad as lying, Nicolai fumed, but Davidsohn temporized. He would wait for the budget hearings to play his cards most effectively. The budget hearings were postponed until after Easter. By then Nicolai had more pressing problems.

The visit to Danzig had been profitable in several ways, apart from the triumph in court. The *Danziger Zeitung* took notice of it in a sympathetic article entitled "A University Professor as Orderly," in which Nicolai's earlier tribulations were retold tongue-in-cheek. "Of course, he acquitted himself very well, and so it is not surprising that the orderly often knew better how to treat the patients than the physician who was his superior," the reporter wrote. Many charming anecdotes are told in Danzig about the professor who always had his nose in a volume of Kant or Fichte, even on the streetcar or the hospital ward, arousing curiosity and getting himself involved in odd conversations. He quoted Nicolai's assertion that the *Biology of War* had helped the German cause, although in his, the reporter's, opinion, "it does not fit war time, even though it refers less to the present war than to the history of war." The article was obviously inspired by Nicolai himself, but the fact that it could appear was a sign that times had changed.

As a further indication of the change in atmosphere, Nicolai was invited to address the Philosophical Society of Danzig. He spoke on the risky topic "German humanism and German militarism." Herr Post, the president, gave him a warm introduction, the audience was friendly, and Herr Post's brother, who owned a country estate, looked after his material needs. He returned to Eilenburg in good spirits, laden with packages of butter, eggs, chocolate, and tea.

From now on Nicolai was no longer merely fighting his own battle. Inspired by his triumph over Schultzen, he began to think about the role he might play in weakening, if not actually bringing down, the wartime government of Germany. He was now a sort of power, a moral power, to be sure, but not entirely negligible, and he saw more clearly than most Germans the weakness of the military and political situation of the Central Powers in the fourth year of the war. What could he do to hasten the inevitable collapse of the regime? As in a game of pick-up-sticks, dislodging a single stick at the bottom might suffice. If the Social Democrats were too timid to use the power of the purse, the Independent Socialists at least had ceased to support the war effort, and to their left was the untested strength of Spartacus, the underground movement founded by the now imprisoned Karl Liebknecht, with which Nicolai was in touch through Ilse Einstein's friend Lezierska. But Nicolai was interested in peace rather than revolution, for the Spartacists were revolutionaries first and pacifists second, and he went his own way.

The facts are shrouded in obscurity, but it was probably the Spartacus underground that helped him to mimeograph and distribute a pamphlet, highly subversive, in official eyes, entitled *Six Facts as a Basis for Judging Today's Power Politics*.[5] Written in the winter of 1917–18, it was in effect a call for civil disobedience, "a distress signal of the German conscience," as he called it. The "six facts" were that the Germans did not know their true situation; that the nationalist notion of the German fatherland was false; that a greater fatherland, Europe, already existed; "that this war has been fruitless; that there is a duty of professing one's beliefs; and that the longing for peace is today the most wide-spread phenomenon in Europe." Therefore the Germans had the right to act in the manner "most conducive to the happiness of Germany and of Europe." As Schiller had written, only freedom of thought could have saved the Spain of Philip II, and "only freedom of thought could have saved Russia from the terrible spasms that tear her apart today."[6] For the same reason "anybody who loves Germany and wants to look beyond the end of the current budget period" must now demand that the spirit of deceit, "which today is rife as never before in German lands," be destroyed root and branch. Unhappily, the educated people, the natural leaders, no longer lead "but allow themselves to be led without resistance by force and the power of suggestion."

So that his argument would not remain purely academic, Nicolai made a specific proposal: "We must demand that our government offer peace under one single condition: the formation of a general congress of all civilized states with complete sovereignty, in which each state is represented according to the number of its inhabitants." This congress would decide and arbitrate all questions raised by the war, on the basis of self-determination of peoples. It was Woodrow Wilson's League of Nations before Wilson. Nicolai did not say how the existing national states could be made to give up their sovereignty, but then neither did Wilson.

If Nicolai expected an aroused public opinion to affect the decisions of the German High Command, which at this very moment was preparing for the gigantic spring offensives of 1918, he was mistaken. There was no such thing as "public opinion" in wartime Germany, nor could there be, for the demi-gods Hindenburg and Ludendorff were infallible as well as omnipotent. They had ignored the Peace Resolution of the belatedly sobered Reichstag,[7] and only weeks before the collapse they would force Secretary of State Kühlmann out of office for merely hinting that peace negotiations might be desirable. The more desperate the situation, the less the voices of reason were heard. Nicolai's statement that "we Germans do not know our true situation" was all too true. As for his pamphlet, it had no chance of reaching the public, for it was illegal and as dangerous to distribute as the issues of *Spartakus* Lezierska was smuggling to Eilenburg.

The government, of course, knew of *Six Facts*, for Germany was teeming with informers and it was easy enough to keep Nicolai under surveillance. If he escaped punishment, it was because he had become a power whom it was best not to challenge openly. He had successfully defied Prussian military justice, published a subversive book abroad while in the power of the Army, caused two of his superiors to be transferred, bested a Generalarzt, forced a retraction from an imperial ambassador, and, for all the authorities knew, might indeed be a candidate for the Nobel Peace Prize. All this was an outrage, but there seemed to be no remedy.

Nicolai may have thought of taking the offensive at this point. Among his papers is an extraordinarily interesting letter which suggests that he was ready to use political dynamite against the government. On 5 January 1918 he wrote to a Mr. Alexander Bloch in Berlin. "Thank you for sending me the address," he begins, in a conspiratorial tone:

> Will you write the following letter to the gentleman:
> "Dear Sir, in connection with a pending lawsuit I have been told by a reliable source that you have exact information as to the monies Herr Lenin received from the German government at the time [of his voyage through Germany in a sealed train]. Since I would rather not summon you as a witness, and rather not get involved myself at all, I ask you kindly to let me know what you know about this matter."
> If I wrote this myself, the person would know who the reliable source is, and there would be complications which I would like to avoid.[8]

Why was Nicolai interested in the arrangements between the German government and Lenin? The matter had nothing to do with his own case. His trial had just ended, and no additional lawsuits were pending against him. The "reliable source" whom he wished to protect may have been one of his Spartacist contacts, though it could equally well have been someone at the Foreign Office opposed to Ludendorff's reckless pursuit of the war. But who was the gentleman who knew the details of the transaction? Was it the enigmatic A. L. Parvus-Helphand, the wealthy socialist sympathizer whom the German government used as a go-between in its dealings with Lenin in Zurich?[9] The fact that the German government had sent Lenin across Germany in a sealed train was common knowledge, but the details, especially the fact that money might have changed hands, were a closely guarded secret whose disclosure would be a serious embarrassment to both parties, particularly to the Imperial Government as the upholder of the feudal order. If Nicolai intended to publish this information abroad, he was playing with fire.

We do not know whether Bloch provided the desired information. At any rate, Nicolai's life had begun to revolve around the fate of the second edition of his book. The revised manuscript was ready by the end of November 1917. The problem was how to get it across the border to the Swiss publisher. The effort engendered a farcical cloak-and-dagger conspiracy which lasted nearly six months, involved many false starts and far too many people, gave rise to more than one narrow escape, and succeeded only because of the laxity of the border authorities and the almost incredible incompetence of the censors. Besides Nicolai's sister Eva Blos, who served as a listening post in Karlsruhe, his lawyer, Viktor Fraenkl, in Berlin, a Professor Hönn, then in Konstanz, a casual acquaintance of Eva named Frau Maria Müller, and a complete stranger in Munich named

Rosie Goldschmidt all were enlisted. All were utter amateurs in the plotting business.

Eva wrote innumerable letters in disguised handwriting under the code name Mathilde to a fictitious Else (Frau Nicolai), in which the manuscript was "the child" whose placement with its proper "guardian" was causing concern. Hönn, who was somehow connected with the Foreign Office and could cross the border without being searched, was to take the child out of the country once he received it from Rosie, to whom in turn it was to be delivered by Frau Müller, who would get it from Eva, who had it from "the father." The plot was beset by the most ludicrous mishaps. Rosie was to be notified of the impending arrival both by letter and by telegram, but mysteriously both were sent to the wrong address and arrived too late. "I hope the package will reach me without trouble, I have done what I could to make sure," the good soul wrote Nicolai on 11 December. But on 16 January she had to report a near-tragedy: "Once more the package; I sent it to Hönn in Konstanz upon receipt of the telegram, from whence he was to take it with him, but before it got into his hands it was opened under martial law and—returned to me! I took the liberty of opening it, only to see if it was intact. As best I can tell everything is in order, only the outer seals were broken and official stamps applied." Evidently Rosie was as innocent as the customs officials who had re-sealed the contraband package and returned it to the sender. "Sorry about the mishap; I am surprised that Hönn did not anticipate this possibility." But there was another possible carrier, a Herr Wachsmuth, though he would not be going to Switzerland until the end of February: "You may prefer to have me return the package, let me know where to send it."

Rosie's tale was sad indeed, Nicolai replied: "If necessary, wait for Wachsmuth. You have done so much, I hesitate to impose further on you, but in the next few days a Mrs. B. who has been 'over there' will call on you. Do what she advises." "Mrs. B." was Eva Blos, who had been in Davos in the Swiss Alps to visit her husband, recuperating in a tuberculosis sanatorium. Nicolai's concern for Rosie's safety was touching but insincere. "All I care about, Rosie, Wachsmuth, or the Consul, is to get the package across; *I* can do nothing, for my mail is censored," he wrote to Frau Müller, forgetting that this letter, too, could be read by the censor. The "consul" was Herr Hegi, the Swiss consul in Munich, whose help Nicolai had been naive enough to solicit. Hegi, needless to say, declined, as he was honor-bound to do. Poor Rosie advised that she had found Nicolai's letter on her return from a long absence and had handed the package back to Frau Müller: "She also has your letter and that of your sister. Have heard nothing from Professor Hönn; I myself will not be back until mid-April. I should very much have liked to help you, but I am restricted in what I can do. After the bad luck with the package I no longer feel secure."

In the meantime, contact with Orell Füssli in Zurich had been made through Fraenkl in Berlin. Nicolai now became "Dr. Wirtz," author of a book on the grain economy of Switzerland. Fraenkl drew up a formal contract between the fictitious Wirtz and the real publisher, which both parties solemnly signed, its doubtful legality notwithstanding. Orell Füssli requested photographs of Herr Wirtz for the new book and was able to report that the firm had sold the rights to an English translation. A Swedish edition was also under way, but nothing could be done until the manuscript was safely across the border. Inevitably, communications with Zurich became garbled, misunderstandings cropped up, tempers flared, and the entire project was in jeopardy.

It was Eva, with her common sense, who diagnosed the problem. "I even had a telegraphic inquiry," she wrote her brother in mid-February. "Why doesn't Friederike travel, or Fräulein van Kampen? I am unable to. But you are used to having others do everything." A few days later she scolded him again: "I don't understand. There were two ways, and you have tried neither. Now eight weeks are lost. I constantly urge personal contact; that means a trip." She was becoming angry: "Well, have you done anything, made inquiries about the whereabouts, or whatever else? That would be the least if one counts on the Nobel Prize. I am disgusted. If I had known *that*, I would have traveled immediately in December. I know you. At the moment I have no energy; only the most ordinary sense of duty keeps me going. But now perhaps you really will get the Nobel Prize."

Eva had pricked Nicolai's soap bubble. He had deceived himself about the matter of the Prize, mistaking his own hopes for reality. "*I* was not the one who brought up the question of the Prize," Eva wrote to Friederike on 23 February. "You optimists, you wrote me of your hopes, and I entered into the spirit of the thing. That is all I know. But I don't cherish such exaggerated hopes. In fact I have no hopes at all, and yet at the bottom of my soul I know that *you* will not perish. You will manage somehow."

Eva was right: Nicolai was disappointed but not discouraged. It would have been nice to get the Nobel Prize—and it might happen yet—but the important thing was the publication of the *Biology of War* in the form in which he wanted to see it: two scholarly volumes, one dealing with the historical aspects of war, the second with the philosophical issues, fully annotated and carefully edited, with a handsome photograph of the author and an eloquent introduction by none other than Romain Rolland, his French brother-in-arms.[10]

But the manuscript did not get to Switzerland until May 1918, and then it got into the wrong hands. Instead of being delivered to "O. F." (Orell Füssli) in Zurich, it was placed in the hands of the well-known Swiss pacifist Nippold in Thun, probably by Leonhard Frank. Nippold was a logical choice, for Nicolai himself earlier had sent him a copy of his pamphlet *Six Facts* (which Nippold did not publish until the author was safely beyond the reach of the German authorities). However, Nicolai had since learned of Nippold's connection with the violently anti-German Freier Verlag of Bern, a publishing venture organized by German refugees and thought to be financed by French and British sources. Nicolai wanted nothing to do with this clique and its backers. He regarded its activities as in bad taste and treasonable. His own attacks, as he was at pains to stress again and again, were directed not against the German people but only against the present militaristic-autocratic regime in Germany. He was profoundly upset when, in September 1918, the Freier Verlag brought out *Six Facts* in an unauthorized edition with a laudatory preface by Nippold.

There was further cause for concern when "Lili," a new fictitious character who had joined the cast of conspirators, reported from Basel that "the youngest of your brothers, whom you don't know as yet, was sent to Thun; I can't tell you the name of the recipient; Edwin knows." Evidently, "Lili," too, was a rank amateur at the conspiratorial game. Would the censor not find it strange that a man did not know his own brother? Edwin, of course, was Nicolai's real brother-in-law, still convalescing at Davos; the "youngest brother" was a new courier, and the anonymous recipient was Nippold. "Unfortunately, the brother was not told what to do with the child, and the gentleman with whom it is now boarding does not know whether Georg would take offense at its being placed in a public boarding-house" (the reference is to the Freier Verlag). A few weeks later "Mathilde" (Eva) reported that "Professor N." (Nippold) had received the package. She had made inquiries, and wondered whether he was not "too radical for Georg and might hurt him." She had been told that he was a loudmouth and always looking for rewards "from the other side." Warming to her improvisation, Mathilde-Eva elaborated: "If Georg wants to have nothing to do with the other family, he might be displeased with N.'s attitude. His child is well taken care of and too well brought up to be thrown together with those fresh, ill-mannered children. Georg must let us know above all whether N. should act as guardian. Georg does not need his protection; he is bigger. Under no circumstances should N. be allowed to act in an official capacity, as he did with the older child" (the "older child" was *Six Facts*, then in Nippold's custody).

After so many harrowing experiences Nicolai must have been relieved to receive a concise message from Fraenkl in Berlin, dated 18 May: "In the matter of Professor Wirtz, the manuscript has arrived in the proper hands." But the ending was anticlimactic. The publication of the second edition of the *Biology of War* (Nicolai called it the "*Originalausgabe*," the original edition, the only version whose authenticity he recognized, as he had no hand in the preparation of the older and by now famous edition of 1917) was delayed until 1919, by which time the war was over and, as he wrote in the preface, "events have meanwhile left the words behind." His hope that now at last his countrymen would become acquainted with the work remained unfulfilled. The boycott to which the *Biology of War* was subjected in postwar Germany was to prove no less effective than its earlier suppression by the authorities during the war.

Meanwhile the situation in Eilenburg had deteriorated. The pipeline to the War Ministry through Davidsohn was now broken. Still trying desperately to obtain a transfer to Berlin, Nicolai applied to the newly accredited Russian ambassador, Joffe, for an appointment as embassy physician. "In view of my former clientele and my friends at Russian universities, I might not be entirely unknown in Russia," he wrote in his application. He also mentioned that he had worked for a prolonged period of time in Pavlov's institute at St. Petersburg and had "some competence" in the Russian language. It was an ingenious idea, but the request would have to come from the embassy; his own application would carry no weight with his superiors, as he knew only too well. The scheme came to nought, notwithstanding the strenuous efforts of the faithful Otto Buek and a Miss Baumgarten of the Russo-Polish Relief Society. Joffe was not interested, and if he had been, the Prussian Army would not have given its approval.

Nicolai was becoming claustrophobic. He had now been in Eilenburg for almost nine months, without permission to travel, with no one to talk to or even to play chess with, cut off from the world, deprived of all but a few books, living in close quarters with his wife, his secretary, and a three-year-old daughter in whom he took little interest. Under these circumstances it was almost a relief to find himself in conflict with the authorities once more. In his capacity as infantryman he suddenly received orders to report for drill with sidearms. It was, as he later claimed, the Army's way of punishing him for having written *Six Facts*, a means of accomplishing by chicanery what legal action had failed to do. He refused to obey this "immoral order," which he called a violation of his rights as a physician under the Geneva Convention and the Military Code. It was also, he claimed, a breach of the promise made to him by the Minister of War to employ him "in keeping with my particular skills." His conversion from orderly in the Medical Corps to rifleman in the infantry had been illegal to begin with, but, he said, he had not objected "in order to keep the peace." For two years he had performed his duties without having to bear arms. Now he was forced to submit a formal protest to the minister.[11] All he wanted was to be transferred back to the Medical Corps.

The request was denied out of hand. The commanding officer at Eilenburg, unlike Dr. Böse in Danzig, was not a psychologist willing to listen to the logic of a strange but interesting mind; he was a simple soldier and a strict disciplinarian who expected his orders to be obeyed, War Minister or no. "For three weeks," as Nicolai later described the situation, "the contest of wills—the issue of whether the saber-rattling-monomaniacal commander or I would have the last word—formed the chief entertainment of the garrison." Finally the commander called his officers together and "in front of the assembled warriors" ordered the obstreperous rifleman to report for drill with regulation sidearms the next morning. Nicolai smiled and "regretfully declined." The colonel, also smiling, gave him until the next morning to think it over.

It was the breaking point. "The question was," Nicolai wrote, "did I want to persevere and—like the one and only Liebknecht—go to the penitentiary, or did I, like so many of my friends, seek freedom? There was no other choice." The only train to Berlin left in three hours. He thought of Socrates, he said, "who in obedience to bad laws drank the cup of hemlock," but also of Martin Luther, who fled his persecutors in order to complete his great work, the German Bible, in the safety of the Wartburg. But Socrates had been an old man: "Had he been as young as I, he would have taken the ship his friends had readied to sail to golden freedom on the islands." He, Nicolai, had done his share for the cause. The *Biology of War* had carried his message to the world. There was nothing more he could accomplish by sitting in the regimental jail at Eilenburg. His rights had been trampled under foot. Furthermore, he had never taken the loyalty oath; therefore his escape could not be called desertion.[12]

By nightfall he was on the train to Berlin, pressing himself into the darkest corner of the poorly lit third-class compartment. He knew where he would find shelter: at Haberlandstrasse 36, where Albert Einstein lived on one floor and his future wife, Elsa, lived on another with her daughters Ilse and Margot. Ilse, a spirited, idealistic young woman to whom Nicolai had become a romantic hero (she had visited him repeatedly in Eilenburg, and it was she who had transcribed his protest to the War Minister and carried it to Berlin), would be thrilled to have a role in his escape.[13]

From this unlikely hideout he wrote a last letter to the War Minister. Typical of Nicolai was the fact that it was neither a petition nor a protest but an ultimatum: if the wrong done to him was not redressed within four weeks, he would find ways to leave the country. He expected the threat to carry some weight. To have the famous Professor Nicolai turn up in a foreign capital as an escapee from Prussian militarism would be a serious embarrassment to the German government and grist for the propaganda mills of the Allies. But a Prussian Minister of War could not be expected to negotiate with a deserter, and did not do so. When no answer was forthcoming within the specified time, Nicolai considered himself a free man. His ordeal was over—or so he thought.

NOTES

1. These and the other quotations from contemporary reviews of *The Biology of War* were taken from clippings and excerpts in the Nicolai archive. The general background for this chapter was drawn from "Letters from the Eilenburg Time," also collected in the Nicolai archive.

2. Ellen Key (1849–1926), a Swedish educator, feminist, and pacifist, wrote *The Century of the Child* (1900) and *Women in the World War* (1918).

3. In 1935 the Nobel Peace Prize was awarded to the German pacifist and antifascist Carl von Ossietzky while he was an inmate in a Nazi concentration camp. He accepted the prize and died later in the camp. Awarding the Peace Prize to Nicolai would have been a challenge to Wilhelm II's regime not unlike that which the award to Ossietzky posed to Hitler. However, for unknown reasons, Nicolai was never considered for the prize.

4. This account of Nicolai's court-martial before the Oberkriegsgericht (Supreme Military Tribunal) in Danzig on 18 December 1917 is taken from the transcript of the proceedings preserved in the Nicolai archive, "Heeressachen" ("Army Matters") folder.

5. The pamphlet, *Sechs Tatsachen als Grundlage der heutigen Machtpolitik*, appeared in an authorized version in Copenhagen in September 1918, was reissued as No. 2 of the imprint "Revolutions-Bibliothek" by Verlag Gesellschaft und Erziehung in Berlin in 1919, and was included among the Nicolai essays collected and published by Wehberg in 1921. The unauthorized edition arranged by Nippold was published by Der Freie Verlag, Bern, in 1918.

6. The reference is to the famous line in Schiller's drama *Don Karlos*, "Sire, geben sie Gedankenfreiheit."

7. This "Peace Resolution," adopted on 19 July 1917 by a coalition of Centrists, Progressives, and Social Democrats, called for a negotiated peace without annexations. It was first opposed, later ignored, by the High Command.

8. The authenticity of this document is further substantiated by a draft of the letter in Nicolai's handwriting, which breaks off with the words "what amount Herr Le____." I cannot identify Alexander Bloch.

9. Alexander Lazarevich Parvus, alias Helphand (1867–1924), a Russian-born Jew, served as intermediary between the German Social Democrats and the Russian revolutionaries and as organizer of Lenin's underground magazine *Iskra*. It was rumored that he led the Petersburg Soviet in the 1905 Revolution. During the war he offered his services to the German ambassador in Constantinople and eventually received large sums for distribution to Russian revolutionaries. There is no proof that Lenin himself received money, but some of his close associates, notably the Austrian Marxist Karl Radek (who was allowed to board the famous sealed train at the German border), are known to have been given ample funds by the Imperial Foreign Office.

10. The second edition of *The Biology of War*, published by Orell Füssli in 1919, carries Rolland's introduction in its original French and in German translation, a potent gesture of pacifist solidarity.

11. A copy of the draft of Nicolai's protest to the Prussian Minister of War, in Ilse Einstein's handwriting (independently verified from other documents), is in the Nicolai archive.

12. Nicolai describes the final events at Eilenburg in the pamphlet *Warum ich aus Deutschland ging* [Why I Left Germany], published in Copenhagen in 1918, which was later incorporated in the collection of his essays edited by Wehberg under the title "Eine Episode aus meinem Kampf mit dem Militär."

13. The story that Nicolai took refuge in the Einstein house on Haberlandstrasse is told by surviving relatives and was repeated to the writer by Margot Einstein in an interview at Princeton, New Jersey, in 1972.

14. Citizen of the World

In the early morning hours of 20 June 1918 two biplanes bearing the insignia of the German air force were warming up at the military air field at Neuruppin in the province of Brandenburg, some fifty kilometers northwest of Berlin, one an F16, the other an Albatross. The crew of the F16, consisting of an officer candidate named Adam and a Corporal Haase, was ready for takeoff. In the Albatross the pilot, one Corporal Silberhorn, was anxiously peering into the darkness for a mysterious civilian who was to be his navigator on the flight across the Baltic to neutral Denmark. The three men were members of a Spartacist cell at the air base who had decided to desert. Unable to find a fourth for their risky enterprise, they made inquiries among their political friends in Berlin and learned that there was someone who was looking for a way to escape from Germany and was willing to share the dangers of the flight. He would not reveal his identity in advance. The deserters understood and agreed to take their chances on a stranger. They may have thought that Liebknecht himself had escaped from the penitentiary and would be their passenger.[1]

At last a tall man appeared, wearing dark glasses, collar turned up, hat pulled down over the eyes. After giving the password and being provided with goggles, gloves, and a warm overcoat pilfered from a storeroom, he hoisted himself aboard, and the two planes took off into the dawn, headed for Copenhagen and freedom. Only en route did the mysterious passenger reveal himself to Silberhorn as Nicolai, wanted by the military police for insubordination and desertion.

This was not Nicolai's first attempt to leave the country. The logical place to go was Switzerland, the traditional haven for political refugees from Germany and home of his publisher, Orell Füssli. He attempted to cross the Swiss border on foot but ran into a German patrol and was arrested forthwith. As luck would have it, he was taken before a sympathetic elderly officer who seemed to know who he was and released him with the warning not to go near the border again at night, for the woods were teeming with patrols and police dogs. Later that day he met a smuggler who showed him a safe escape route, but he chose to return to Berlin, unwilling—so he said afterward—"to leave my fatherland pursued by police dogs."

The thought of making an escape in an airplane appealed to Nicolai, not only because of the novelty and the sensation it was bound to create but because of the symbolic character of such a daring gesture. Escapes on foot, by train, by automobile, or by boat were humdrum everyday occurrences, Nicolai thought.

> Then it occurred to me that the youngest child of our modern technology, the airplane, had been originally intended by its optimistic inventors to fly over those frontiers which one could not step over.

I was intrigued by the thought of restoring this nation-uniting device, so shamefully misused in the war, to its true purpose, at least somewhat—to use this blood-stained instrument at least once for peaceful purposes.

It was also an efficient means of escape, although risky. Nicolai had his ear to the ground and soon, from an officer in the air force whose identity he never revealed learned of the would-be deserters at Neuruppin. Denmark suited his purposes perfectly. Contact was made, and a few days later he was in the cockpit of Silberhorn's Albatross. It was an exhilarating experience, heightened by the sense of danger from the anti-aircraft batteries along the Baltic coast. "With the red sun rising in the East, the blue sea churning below, a few white bursts of shrapnel exploding around me, I last saw Germany framed by the colors of the liberating tricolor, he wrote, "which, let us hope, will soon be her colors also, for the tricolor is not only the flag of France but the symbol of every noble struggle against medieval feudalism and the rule of arrogant Junkers."

The strange passenger must have been able to read the instruments on board the Albatross and to chart the course correctly, for the aircraft made an uneventful landing near the Viderslev gas works on the outskirts of Copenhagen. The F16 was less fortunate. A storm blew it off its course and forced it to land on German territory. Somehow the pilot persuaded the supply officer at the depot near Kiel to let him have thirty liters of benzene, but this was not enough for the flight to Copenhagen, and the plane had to land again on the island of Langeland in the southernmost part of Denmark.

The arrival of two German warplanes in distant parts of the kingdom within hours of one another aroused grave apprehensions: this could be the beginning of another attack on a neutral country; the "deserters" could be spies for the German air force. The two men in the Albatross were taken into custody in Copenhagen: the pair on Langeland were brought there under guard the following day. Nicolai and Silberhorn spent the night in the Nytorv jail and were questioned the next morning by a prosecutor of the Seventh Criminal Court. Nicolai's claim that he was a well-known German scientist and author of *The Biology of War* left Prosecutor Thorup unconvinced. He had no papers to prove his identity and, with his saber scars and monocle, looked like a Prussian officer. It occurred to Nicolai that there was a Danish colleague who might identify him. The man was brought to Nytorv but had no recollection of having met Nicolai. As a last resort the prisoner was subjected to a series of questions requiring knowledge of anatomy and physiology. When he passed the test with flying colors, he was accepted as the authentic Professor Nicolai, and his ordeal was over. He was conducted to the Hôtel d'Angleterre, where he received reporters and dined in style.

The daring aerial escape from Ludendorff's tightly guarded realm was an international sensation of the first order, reported with glee by the French and British press and with outspoken admiration by the newspapers of Scandinavia and other neutral countries. Public sentiment in the

Nordic countries on the whole favored the Allies rather than the Central Powers, but everybody, whether pro-Entente, pro-German, or neither, opposed the war, and few sympathized with German militarism. Denmark, which had suffered more from the war than her northern neighbors, was the center of a strong pacifist movement, and Nicolai could be sure of a cordial reception there.

From Villeneuve Romain Rolland sent greetings. The German pacifists in Switzerland were electrified. In Berlin, the Einstein family was jubilant. Ilse Einstein composed a ballad in many verses, sung to the accompaniment of a lute, in which she extolled Nicolai's heroic feat.[2] The German authorities, on the other hand, took a dim view of the matter. Nicolai's apartment in Berlin was searched, several of his acquaintances were questioned, Corporal Silberhorn's fiancée was arrested, and Frau Nicolai was enjoined from exercising power of attorney for her husband. For the time being no public announcement of the flight was made, and when Nicolai's case came up once more before the Reichstag, the war minister avoided the issue. It was more embarrassing for the minister than for the fugitive, as Nicolai noted from Copenhagen. But even the tightest censorship could not keep the news from leaking out, and when it did, the government declared Nicolai insane in absentia. This strategy was used against other prominent opponents of German war policies;[3] apart from its usefulness as a propaganda device, it reflected the view of the military faction that anyone opposing the war must indeed be mad.

All this was to be expected, for Nicolai had broken the law and in the technical sense was guilty of desertion. His own position was that *his* rights had been violated. Though he participated in the theft of government property, the airplanes were undamaged, and he had seen to it that they were promptly returned to Germany. As for his flight, it was in reaction to an overt breach of the law on the part of the War Ministry. He was still willing to give the war minister a chance to redeem the honor of the military by restoring him to his rightful place in the Medical Corps and rescinding the order for his arrest. He would wait eight weeks before making a public statement, he told Count Brockdorff-Rantzau, the German ambassador in Copenhagen, whom he had gone to see the day after his arrival. The count, an intelligent man and an able diplomat, was pleasant, even sympathetic, but noncommittal. He well remembered the embarrassment Nicolai had caused his colleague Baron Romberg in Bern. The War Ministry for its part ignored the offer, as was to be expected, but Nicolai kept his word and for eight weeks refrained from issuing a statement.

In the meantime, his life was pleasant. A few days after his arrival he became the guest of the wealthy banker Axel Valentiner at his handsome summer cottage on Tibirke, where he was pampered by Valentiner's wife, ate the good Danish food, smoked his host's good cigars, played with the little Valentiner daughter, picnicked with the family at the beach, and generally enjoyed the change from the constant battle and hardship of the last two years.

Despite his silence on the subject of his flight, he was the object of friendly attentions from the press, Scandinavian groups interested in promoting peace, and publishers. His first project was the preparation of a Danish edition of the *Biology of War*. An enterprising Copenhagen publisher, Steen Hasselbalch, eager to capitalize on the publicity generated by the spectacular escape, offered him a substantial advance. A translator was soon found, and *Krigens Biologi* appeared in record time, followed almost immediately by a Swedish edition. The book sold well in both countries, and Nicolai was now also able to draw the royalties due him from Orell Füssli in Zurich. By the time he left Scandinavia five months after his arrival his bank account totaled seven thousand kroner, a tidy sum for a man who arrived a penniless refugee.

But money was incidental to Nicolai's mission. His spectacular gesture, along with his established reputation as an advanced thinker, had thrust him into the role of one of the world's foremost pacifists. At this moment he was virtually the only German whose views on the future peace carried weight among the neutrals and—he hoped—among Germany's enemies as well, for here was a man who had not been tainted by association with German imperialism, who had steadily and openly opposed the war and urged a peace without victors, and who was even now urging his government to negotiate with the Allies while Germany was still strong enough to negotiate. Though muted by censorship, his had been the only voice in Germany to call for a League of Nations even before Wilson proclaimed his Fourteen Points, the only voice to protest the brutal peace terms imposed on the defeated Russians at Brest Litovsk, the only credible voice to call for the reconciliation of Europe while Europe was bleeding from a thousand wounds. He could claim to represent all the peace-loving elements in his country, for, as he now wrote from Tibirke, "precisely because I did not belong to any one party, I came in contact with the most diverse individuals and groups: members of the Progressive and the Center Party, 'Imperial' and Independent Social Democrats, Spartacists and rebellious intellectuals, malcontent officers and dissatisfied civil servants, despairing clergymen and shame-filled journalists, but above all with soldiers from the front and soldiers at home."[4] More than anyone else he had probed the conscience of wartime Germany. In mid-July Ludendorff unleashed the last of the great German offensives of 1918, and a few days later Marshal Foch for the first time pierced the German front at Villers-Cotterêts: the handwriting was on the wall, but inside Germany few people knew the truth and none were in a position to influence the course of events. Nicolai saw himself as the spokesman for a muzzled and fettered nation.

His position was precarious, however, for in attacking the government he became vulnerable to the charge of treason. There were those, especially among the German refugees in Switzerland, whose desire to bring about the downfall of Ludendorff's dictatorship led them to accept French and British money and to call openly for the total defeat of their fatherland. The most notorious of these cliques was the group associated with the *Freie Zeitung* at Bern, a publication of the Freier Verlag financed by French capital. Its hatred of all things German was expressed as violently as the most venomous anti-British propaganda of the early war years, such

233

as Lissauer's "Song of Hatred." "People of France! Your hatred is not strong enough!" one of these expatriates, a certain Dr. Roesenmeyer (strangely enough, like Lissauer, he was a German Jew) had written. "Shed your illusions and face the naked truth: you are up against a nation that has surrendered to the Devil . . . , a nation that gives its allegiance to the most satanic, the most infamous, the most ferocious, the most hideous gang of criminals the world has ever known. . . . Arm yourself, O French people, with that deadly hatred that shrinks from nothing. . . . Cease to see human beings in today's Germans!"[5]

Nicolai wanted nothing to do with these "pacifists," whom he regarded as unscrupulous adventurers or misguided fanatics. He made it clear that he did not want Germany's destruction or even an Allied victory, but rather the overthrow of the military regime as a precondition of peace, a peace without victors, a genuine reconciliation of Europe. "I am now a man without a country; I stand on this earth a free man, a German citizen of the world," he declared proudly. The world was ripe for peace after four years of futile slaughter, but no one seemed to know how to bring it about. He, Nicolai, "citizen of the world," was taking the first step "because I consider it necessary that somebody step forward and make a beginning."

The belligerents on both sides ignored this call to reason, as they had ignored the pope's attempts to mediate, the "Appeal for an Honorable Peace" of the women of Scandinavia, Henry Ford's Peace Ship, and, for that matter, Lenin's and Trotsky's call for an end to the war on all fronts in the fall of 1917. In the summer of 1918 the Allies could smell victory in the air, although Ludendorff refused to admit to himself and to the powerless civilian government that the cause was lost. As late as 9 July he had forced the dismissal of Richard von Kühlmann, the secretary of state, for hinting that channels of communication between the belligerents would somehow have to be opened if the war were ever to end. The German conservatives were as rabid as ever in their determination to fight on. "As our valiant sword has brought us peace in the East," their leader, Kuno Count Westarp, told Kühlmann in the Reichstag, "so our good sword will have to bring us peace in the West." And still later, on 27 August, only a month before the collapse, the Germans wrung new and still more cruel concessions from the defeated Bolsheviks. Under these circumstances a defeated Germany could expect no mercy, and Nicolai, who knew that the defeat was imminent, was as anxious to preach moderation to the Allies as he was to bring his own countrymen to their senses.

The response in the neutral countries was heartening. Invitations to speak came from all over Scandinavia. Nicolai was the guest of the archbishop of Upsala, of the great Swedish physicist and Nobel laureate Svante Arrhenius, of the socialist mayor of Stockholm, Carl Lindhagen, of Christian Lange, the secretary of the Interparliamentary Union,[6] and of writers, clergymen, and businessmen throughout Denmark, Sweden, and Norway. But he sought an even wider audience. Immediately after his arrival in Copenhagen, he contacted Romain Rolland, Nippold and Alfred Fried in Bern, and Shaw Desmond, a British pacifist of Irish descent, in England. Each of them was to contribute an article to *Das werdende Eu-*

ropa ("The Evolving Europe"), an international magazine for peace and reconstruction which he intended to launch forthwith. The notion of a Frenchman, a German, and a Briton joining forces while their countries were at war was a bold one, which he expected to impress the war-weary nations of Europe. The editorial board included some of the most respected names in Scandinavia: the famous Danish author Georg Brandes, the even more famous polar explorer Fridtjof Nansen, the Swedish feminist and pacifist Ellen Key, the editor of the Norwegian newspaper *Samtiden* Gerhart Gran, as well as Arrhenius and Lindhagen. The magazine's motto, inspired by Ellen Key, read "neutral toward the belligerents, passionately partisan for Right against Might." Nicolai could well be pleased: a more distinguished panel would have been hard to find. His own position as a leader of international pacifism was firmly established.

But time was of the essence. Nicolai decided not to wait for the promised contributions of Rolland and Desmond. The first issue of *Das werdende Europa* would carry only a message from his Danish colleague and fellow-pacifist Nyrop, contributions from Fried and Lindhagen, and, as the lead article, his own account of the reasons for his flight, entitled "Why I Left Germany." The efficient Herr Hasselbalch promised to have the proofs ready within a few weeks, but the printing was delayed, and the magazine did not appear until 15 October, by which time Germany was suing for an armistice and much of its impact was lost. The first issue turned out to be the last one, for it became clear that Nicolai would soon be returning to Berlin.

"Why I Left Germany" (Fig. 25) had an unhappy fate. An advance copy somehow reached London and was published in the *Times* even before Nicolai's own magazine appeared. As his enemies would later assert, this circumstance proved that he was collaborating with the British. Equally embarrassing was the fact that Nippold, to whom Nicolai—forgetting his earlier misgivings in connection with the manuscript of *The Biology of War* the previous winter—had sent a copy, had turned it over to the notorious Freier Verlag. Nicolai protested vehemently but was powerless to stop the publication of it in Bern. Through no fault of his own, he had fallen into bad company. His image as a "good German" was becoming somewhat tarnished. Inevitably, his motives were misconstrued by both sides.

Nor was this all. In the hope of bringing his message of reconciliation to the people of France, he received two emissaries from the French legation in Copenhagen, who came ostensibly to sound him out on the possibility of a French edition of *The Biology of War*. The French had belatedly come to the realization that Nicolai's writings made splendid material for their propaganda against the militarist *boches*. To Nicolai himself, the pacifist message of his book was as valid for French as for German militarists. Not until his visitors made him an offer of five thousand kroner for the French rights did he see that he was to be a pawn in the propaganda war against Germany. He wanted no part of it. "You are authorized to publish *The Biology of War* and to make such use of 'Why I Left Germany' as you may see fit," he wrote to the French minister in Copenhagen

235

in a confidential letter, but he refused to accept any money: "If you have really set aside the amount that was mentioned to me, MM L'Herbier and Chiqurouet should be given half of it as compensation for their efforts. You may wish to give the rest to the Red Cross of your country."

While this potentially embarrassing episode remained secret, a public gesture from Moscow caused him a far more serious problem. It was a

Fig. 25. Cover of a pirated edition (1918) of the pamphlet *Why I Left Germany*. It reads: "Open Letter/to the unknown person who holds the power in Germany"; the publisher is listed as the Union of German Democrats Abroad.

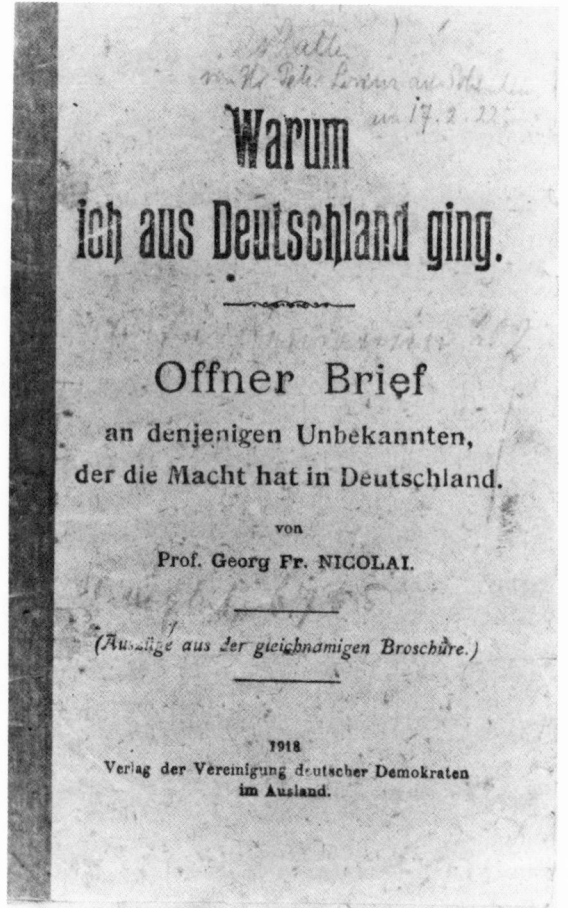

decree signed by L. B. Kamenev, president of the Moscow Soviet and one of Lenin's closest associates, conveying on "the German citizen Georg Nicolai all the rights of the citizens of the United Socialist Republics of Russia, effective 30 September 1918." Nicolai was a "bourgeois" who had made no secret of his opposition to Bolshevism, based on his unshakable conviction that the world—and Russia in particular—was not ready for socialism and that violence on the part of Russian revolutionaries was no better than violence on the part of capitalist or militarist regimes.

The history of the decree remains obscure; the fact that it was made is certain. Romain Rolland, who learned of it from an item in the Soviet publication *Nouvelles de Russie*, which appeared in Bern, noted with ill-concealed dismay: "Nicolai has asked to be naturalized as a citizen of the USSR. The Central Executive Committee has sent him its acceptance in the following terms: 'Comrade! Having examined your request for admittance to the family of Russian citizens, the Central Executive Committee of the Moscow Soviet of Workers and Peasants decrees. . . .'"[7] As was his custom with items of interest to him, Rolland copied the text verbatim in his diary without having verified it. It is virtually certain that Nicolai's alleged request for Soviet citizenship was a Bolshevik propaganda invention, designed to exploit the defection of the famous pacifist for the benefit of the young Soviet regime. In the difficult year 1918 the Bolsheviks were still striving for Western understanding and support, especially among Germans, for revolution in Germany was deemed vital for the success of the revolution in Russia and elsewhere. It is possible that Kamenev may have thought that a man who had escaped from the Reich with the help of Spartacists was a Spartacist himself and would seek the protection of the Bolshevik government, Spartacism being looked upon in Russia as the German equivalent of Bolshevism. What is more probable is that, having decided to claim Nicolai for the Bolshevik cause, Kamenev considered it essential that the initiative should appear to have come from the victim of imperialism rather than from the Soviet government. Unsolicited offers of citizenship to prominent Western sympathizers were accepted Soviet practice, and truth was an expendable commodity. At about the same time Romain Rolland himself was surprised to receive a nomination to the newly founded Socialist Academy of Social Science of Moscow.

Nicolai was a man who conscientiously preserved every document pertaining to his life. His collection of papers contains no record either of his application or of Kamenev's decree. Many years later, when he applied for a visitor's visa for the Soviet Union, he reminded the Soviet authorities of their offer of 1918, hoping to facilitate the cumbersome bureaucratic procedures connected with the admission of Westerners to the Workers' Paradise, but he made no mention of having applied for—let alone accepting—Soviet citizenship. Furthermore, such an offer could hardly have appealed to him at a moment when he expected the downfall of the regime in Germany to be imminent and hoped to play a role in the German revolution, a revolution he believed would be non-Bolshevik and non-violent.

At any rate, Nicolai rejected Kamenev's overtures and publicly pointed to his opposition to terror from whatever quarter, the Russian Revolution having just then entered a particularly violent phase. He issued a denial to the Scandinavian newspapers, but the story appeared in the German press—in October censorship was relaxed in the wake of the "Revolution from Above," a hastily instituted process of "democratization" triggered by Woodrow Wilson's refusal to treat with an authoritarian regime—and was accepted at face value by his friends and foes alike. Like Kamenev, the German newspapers assumed that the companion of Spartacist deserters was a Bolshevik sympathizer, and the clever wording of the Soviet decree did nothing to dispel this notion. "The Moscow Soviet of the only proletarian republic in the world greets in you, comrade fellow-citizen, a bold and indefatigable fighter for the peace of the peoples," it declared. "May your forthright decision openly to abandon the bourgeois world in order to take your place at the side of the oppressed and exploited set an example for all our hesitant brothers, poisoned as they are by the breath of imperialism. The Soviet Republic needs upright, brave, and honest citizens. Welcome, Comrade!"

Nicolai paid little attention to this matter. Nothing was farther from his mind than abandoning the bourgeois world; on the contrary, he wanted to save Western civilization, which was after all a bourgeois civilization, from the consequences of the real war that was still raging on the battlefields of France. He was working feverishly on the next issue of his magazine, which was to contain articles by Romain Rolland, Nippold, Ellen Key, and the Swiss chemist and Nobel laureate Hermann Staudinger, as well as an essay of his own entitled "Theoretical and Practical Possibilities of a Coming Peace." It was the twelfth hour, he wrote, not only for Germany but for a Europe that could not recover from the war unless the Allies refrained from revenge and concluded a just and durable peace with the enemy. Therefore the war must stop now, before Germany was utterly crushed. The statesmen of the Entente must be made to understand that an anarchist postwar Germany would constitute a grave danger to European civilization. The solution lay in a union of European nations ("which, of course, must include all those states whose culture derives directly or indirectly from Europe"). The Entente was an alliance of four-fifths of humanity (though the union, it was true, was forged for the purpose of fighting a war). It only needed to be expanded and adapted to the purposes of peace. Let the League of Free Nations be founded now, today, Nicolai urged. Then invite the states with whom you are still at war to join. The time for words was past; the mutual distrust had become too deep. Deeds alone could save the world now. It was useless to wait until the war was over: "The house is burning now; now is the time to extinguish the flames!"[8]

But events were bypassing Nicolai. The second issue of *Das werdende Europa* never appeared. Pacifist thought counted for nothing in the colossal upheavals that marked the end of the war. History was being made in Washington, London, and Paris, not in neutral Denmark, and by politicians and generals, not by visionaries. Even Wilson could not prevent the peace from becoming what Nicolai had feared it would become: the seeds of another war. On the whole, Nicolai's Scandinavian episode was a failure, the romance of the flight and the early glow of praise and fame notwithstanding. His prophecies had come true, but would there be a place for him in Germany now, or would he have to pay a price for his reckless disregard of his compatriots' notion of loyalty to the Fatherland?

NOTES

1. The account of Nicolai's flight to Denmark in June 1918 is based on the following sources: contemporary reports in the Danish press (*Politiken* and *Berlingske Tidende*), preserved in the Nicolai archive; Nicolai's own account in *Warum ich aus Deutschland ging* (Copenhagen: Steen Hasselbalch, 1918); various entries in Romain Rolland, *Journal des années de guerre 1914–1919: Notes et documents pour servir à l'histoire morale de l'Europe de ce temps*, ed. Marie Romain Rolland (Paris: Editions Albin Michel, 1952); testimony given in *Nicolai* v. *Wilamowitz-Möllendorff* in 1922 (see Chapter 19); and letters from Corporal Silberhorn's mother, written in 1919, in the Nicolai archive.

2. This anecdote was related to the author by Miss Margot Einstein, Einstein's stepdaughter, in Princeton, N.J., several years ago.

3. Nicolai was in good company. Other "madmen" included Prince Karl Max Lichnowsky, the last German ambassador to the Court of St. James before the war, whose secret memoir "My Mission to London," which was widely circulated in German military circles, attempted to dispel the myth that Britain had engineered the war. Wilhelm Muehlon, another victim of the policy, was the Krupp director privy to the secret preparations for war early in July 1914; he went to Switzerland in 1916 and there revealed the details of the Kaiser's "blank check" to the Austrian government and other matters.

4. *Warum ich aus Deutschland ging*, p. 23.

5. Quoted in Rolland's *Journal des années de guerre 1914–1919*, p. 1628, from a brochure in French of 1918 whose English title is "What France Can Expect If She Lets Herself Be Deceived by Germany."

6. The Interparliamentary Union was founded in 1888 as a sort of forerunner of the League of Nations and aimed at promoting peaceful cooperation between nations. Lange received the Nobel Peace Prize in 1921 for his services to the Union.

7. *Journal des années de guerre 1914–1919*, p. 1634.

8. This summary of Nicolai's planned essay is taken from a draft in the Nicolai archive.

IV. THE PROPHET IN HIS FATHERLAND

15. A Touch of Greatness

Germany in defeat was a derelict vehicle hurtling downhill through the darkness. For more than four years there had been total censorship not only of military but of all political and social news which—in the view of the German High Command—might have an unfavorable effect on the morale of the people. What forces had been stirring in the dark? Was the revolution of 9 November a mere prelude to Bolshevism and civil war, like the Russian Revolution a year earlier? Was the reactionary officer corps strong enough to restore the monarchy or impose a military dictatorship on a nation that had neither the experience nor the will to govern itself? Was there hope for the rebirth of the democratic spirit of 1848, long smothered in blood and iron? Seen from abroad, anything seemed possible, now that military control and been removed.

Nicolai, waiting impatiently in Scandinavia, forecast the fall of the monarchy. "Instincts have been aroused," he had said before a Swedish audience on 1 November, "men are armed, accustomed to violence, aware that they are the masters. Soon the others will have to flee, as we had to flee."[1] But by "we" he meant only the handful of pacifists like himself who had taken refuge abroad, intellectuals without a political program or a following at home, not hard-headed revolutionaries with a plan of action. In this group there were no Lenins or Trotskys. Nor could Nicolai find a single established political figure in Germany who was not compromised by his record during the war. "Four years of deceit must now be paid for," he warned. "The people have no leaders in whom they can believe."

It was true enough. The military propaganda machine had assured the public almost up to the last minute that victory was certain, and those who knew better had kept quiet. "There is no way to snatch victory from us," the vice president of the Prussian Diet told the deputies in August, only days before British tanks broke through on the western front. With Russia knocked out of the war and forced to make huge concessions at the Peace of Brest Litovsk and German armies in France and Belgium, in Poland, Lithuania, and the Ukraine, such assurances had sounded convincing. What had gone wrong?

Clearly it was time to question the judgment, if not the honesty, of the supposedly infallible generals who insisted on total victory. Their noisy civilian supporters the Pan-Germans, who had clamored for the annexation of Belgium and of vast Eastern territories as the price of a "German peace," had lost all credibility. But the liberal press, too, had played the game. Few could have faith now in the great *Berliner Tageblatt*, which—one month after the entry of the United States into the war on the side of the Entente—asked its readers to "acknowledge gratefully how much better off we are than the island of Britain, as it drifts toward famine." The *Vossische Zeitung* greeted the American declaration of war with a sneer:

"The Americans can't come over, for they can't swim across and they can't fly across—there is no other way." And its editor-in-chief, only weeks before the final collapse, proposed in all seriousness an alliance of Germany with France and Russia against the "real enemy," England. The Social Democrats were tarred with the same brush, for despite their ideological commitment to pacifism and to the solidarity of the international proletariat, they had first sanctioned the war as necessary for the defense of the Fatherland and then closed their eyes when its offensive character became undeniable. In Nicolai's eyes they, too, were among the deceivers of the people.

Events proved him right. The widely cherished illusion that Germany would be allowed to rejoin the family of nations as an equal in a new world order based on Wilson's Fourteen Points had already been shattered by the reality of the armistice. The Reich was now utterly at the mercy of its enemies, and not a single public figure with a record of opposition to its military rulers could plead its cause before the victors. "We were Utopians," Nicolai said in Göteborg on 8 November, "laughed at, killed by silence, imprisoned, persecuted, driven from the country. Who are the Utopians now?" It was time for the prophet to return to his fatherland, not to seek political power (that notion never seems to have entered his head) but to alert his confused countrymen to the realities of their plight. Surely they would listen to him now.

On 25 November he took the ferry across the Baltic from Gedser to Warnemünde, uncertain whether he would be arrested as a deserter or welcomed as a hero on German soil. But the border officials were merely correct, and he was allowed to proceed to Berlin, where his arrival went almost unnoticed in the general turmoil.[2] As he reported to *Dagens Nyheter*, the Danish newspaper from which—with his eye for an opportunity—he had procured an assignment as a correspondent, he found the city outwardly unchanged. The streetcars were running, the bureaucracy was functioning as always, theaters and concerts were as well attended as in the good old days, there was a great demand for speakers on every subject from the League of Nations to Free Love, and those who could afford it were preparing for Christmas. Not even the ravages of the Spanish flu seemed to have much of an effect on public attitudes.

But what of the revolution on which Nicolai had pinned his hopes? The conscience of the "real Germany" would rise up; "the sword of vengeance hangs over the unholy seducers of the people," he had told his Scandinavian audience. But the revolution, far from being the glorious dawn of a new era, was a dreary business, the unexpected and unwanted byproduct of a sailors' mutiny that blew the decrepit old regime away and left a vacuum to be filled by uninspired functionaries.[3] Not a hair had been harmed on the heads of the seducers of the people, no blood had been shed for liberty, no crusade had been started in the name of justice. The Kaiser and the Crown Prince had escaped abroad, presenting the spectacle of Prussian officers deserting their troops, as Nicolai's supporters would later remind those staunch patriots who accused *him* of desertion. The Social Democrats served as reluctant caretakers of the government. Their leaders, by striking a revolutionary pose, had succeeded in rallying the bulk of the proletarian masses behind the party banner, but at heart they were mortally afraid of their own followers. For them, as for the frightened bourgeoisie, the sight of soldiers roaming the streets and ripping the epaulets from officers' tunics was painful to behold. They were concerned more with maintaining law and order than with creating a new society. The revolutionary Workers' and Soldiers' Councils (the Räte, equivalent to the Soviets), which for a fleeting moment held the power in their hands, had elected the Social Democrat Friedrich Ebert head of the provisional government, unaware that this representative of the workers hated the revolution more than he did capitalism or imperialism.

It did not take Nicolai long to grasp the situation. "There has been a 'revolution' in German lands," he wrote contemptuously, "and a few dozen thrones have been toppled. Instead of Wilhelm of Hohenzollern we have Fritz Ebert to rule us, and those who saw a danger in the last of the dynasty may rejoice that someone else has taken his place." But, he added, those who understood that "the royal puppet" had been nothing more than the plaything of Krupp and the other powers behind the scenes would ask themselves "how the realities of life have changed."[4]

They had changed very little indeed. When Nicolai returned to Germany, it seemed at least that the rule of the military was ended. The once all-powerful Ludendorff was hiding in Sweden, and his colleagues on the General Staff were staying out of the public eye, but appearances were deceptive. On 10 November, the very day of his election by the Räte, Ebert accepted the secret offer of the High Command—still ensconced at its wartime headquarters in Belgium—to protect his shaky regime against the revolutionary masses whom the Räte represented. To Ebert the Räte—whose actual aim was the non-violent transfer of power from the old ruling class to a government of the people and whose strength soon proved to be illusory—were as odious as they were to the military. His desire to save the institutions of the good old days coincided with the determination of their members to regain control, and he was willing to pay the price. Unknown to the public, the counterrevolution began barely twenty-four hours after the revolution itself took place. The stage was already set for the Terror, but the Terror would come from the reactionary Right, not from the revolutionary Left.

Meanwhile there were the dreaded Spartacists, the only real revolutionaries on the horizon, but even they had no concrete plan of action, nor had they succeeded in gaining control of the Räte as Lenin had gained control of the Soviets. Their leader, Karl Liebknecht, a man much admired by Nicolai for his integrity and personal courage,[5] was no Lenin, no leader of men, no organizer, not even a thinker. He was the only member of the Reichstag to vote against the war credits as early as December 1914, and he spent more than two years in prison for shouting "down with war, down with the government" at a May Day rally in 1916. Just released from the penitentiary, he had become the living symbol of the revolution and the bogeyman of all right-thinking citizens, including his former comrades among the Social Democrats. From abroad, Nicolai had called him the only honest man in Germany, asserting that his steadfast opposition to the war made him uniquely qualified to negotiate with the Allies and urging that "because of his undoubted popularity" he be invited to join the government, "even if he were to ruin the country."[6] Now he was having second thoughts, for he did not share Liebknecht's enthusiasm for the "dictatorship of the proletariat." The Spartacus program, drafted by Liebknecht's associate Rosa Luxemburg, expressly disavowed violence as "a method necessary in bourgeois revolutions" and abhorrent to the proletarian revolution, "which has no need of these weapons because it is fighting institutions rather than individuals and does not enter the arena with naive illusions whose collapse it would have to avenge in blood."[7] But Nicolai only needed to look at Russia for proof that the noblest of proletarian revolutions could not avoid violence.

Actually, the danger of a Spartacist dictatorship on the Bolshevik model was remote. On 9 November Liebknecht, flanked by red flags, tried to proclaim a Socialist People's Republic from the balcony of the imperial castle. To head him off, the Social Democrat Philipp Scheidemann immediately rushed to the balcony of the Reichstag to proclaim *his* version of the republic, which was, in effect, the old firm doing business under new management. Scheidemann's action had been an improvisation, but it served its purpose. Liebknecht was checkmated before the game had begun.

What then had the revolution accomplished? It was apparent to Nicolai—though perhaps not to most Germans—that the new, nominally Socialist rulers had no intention of tampering with the capitalist system which, according to Socialist theory, was the ultimate cause of all war. Feudal privileges had been abolished, but it would take time for ordinary people to think of themselves as the equals of any of their fellow-citizens. After centuries of unquestioning obedience to the Obrigkeit, the Germans did not take readily to freedom. In revolutionary France men and women of all classes had called one another "citizen." In Germany even this symbolic revolution failed to occur. Aristocrats, officers, bureaucrats, and professionals all continued to use their traditional titles. That was a matter of style, but in a revolution style matters; it mattered to Nicolai, who as a student had admired the egalitarian manners of the French. Far more serious was the fact that the new regime allowed the real sources of power—the administrative apparatus, courts, schools, and universities—to remain in the hands of its enemies. The civil servants, judges, professors, and schoolteachers, monarchist and nationalist to a man, continued to draw their salaries without a day's interruption. Nicolai was scandalized: "as for the old bureaucracy," he wrote in the addendum to *Six Facts*, "it is firmly in the saddle and through passive resistance thwarts even the most modest attempts at reform on the part of the new ministers." Even the propaganda officers, undercover agents, and censors of the old regime were still in business, he noted.

He had good reason to be concerned. For the moment the forces of reaction were lying low, but they were biding their time, waiting to take revenge on the man who had raised his voice against the cultural elite of

Germany, the war-resister and deserter Nicolai, traitor not only to his Fatherland but to his class.

Still worse in the eyes of a believer in republican virtue was the patent dishonesty of political life in Germany. Freedom of the press was great, Nicolai wrote in the addendum, but "the effectiveness of this freedom is quite limited. The entire phalanx from the *Post* [an extreme right-wing daily that would soon attack him viciously] to the *Vorwärts* [the official organ of the Social Democratic Party] is fed lies and money by the government and by powerful business interests. What chance is there for the impoverished proletarian press? It lacks the means of supporting its own news services, while the news releases of the government are virtually all false or at least biased."

He was hardly exaggerating. So effective was the manipulation, suppression, and falsification of news by government and press alike that in the months to come the public laid the large-scale massacres and the many individual murders of real and suspected Spartacists at the doorstep of the victims, not that of their well-organized right-wing killers. Everyone knew that the Reds were bloodthirsty monsters whose "bestiality"—a standard term in the vocabulary of the press—called for merciless retaliation. Nicolai had his own sources of information, among them his friend E. J. Gumbel, who was to become the historian of the Terror. Gumbel personally investigated hundreds of killings and found that almost all the bloodthirstiness was on the Right. He reported 314 assassinations by right-wing elements as opposed to 13 by Reds. Thousands of workers were massacred by regular troops and mercenaries of a regime that called itself Social Democratic, and the public, haunted by the fear of Bolshevism, condoned or even applauded the slaughter.[8] "Worst of all is the fact," wrote Nicolai, "that already the nation wants to rely on this machinery of lies, for when one points to a falsehood the answer is 'Well, what of it?' in nine cases out of ten and 'Well, thank God!' in the tenth." His faith in the "real Germany" was badly shaken: "Our generation, I fear, is beyond hope."

Still, he clung to his romantic ideal. "Only in another age, when today's youth has grown up—only then will that new Germany for which the world is waiting be reborn." How this could happen with control of the schools firmly in the hands of reactionaries he did not say. He was a critic, not a leader, a voice crying in the wilderness, not a soldier of the revolution. But as a critic he had few equals. "If there is one fact that the revolution has laid bare in present-day Germany," he observed, "it seems to be this: it is not imperialism and militarism, not capitalism and bureaucratism, which are bankrupt, but socialism and above all the old German idealism."

On 10 December the dependable Ebert paid the first installment on his secret debt to the generals by greeting the returning troops marching through the Brandenburg Gate as "heroes unbeaten in the field." The highest official of the republic was contributing his share to the "stab-in-the-back" explanation for Germany's defeat, the myth that was used by every enemy of the republic from Hindenburg to Hitler. The Army's secret plan to use the troops to "clean up" the capital had to be abandoned, however, for its formations had melted away by nightfall. The Terror had to be postponed because the men were anxious to get home by Christmas.

On the same day Nicolai, in his capacity as foreign correspondent for *Dagens Nyheter*, interviewed the foremost of the intended victims of the "clean up," Karl Liebknecht.[9] The two men had much in common. Both had courage, both were idealists and convinced pacifists, both were famous—or notorious— and both were disenchanted with the revolution and disgusted with the new regime. They agreed on the goal of a socialist society, though not on the method of achieving it. Nicolai rejected Bolshevism as a violent and untimely solution and a threat to human rights. The Spartacus movement, while ostensibly keeping its distance from the Russians and stressing its democratic character, in contrast to Lenin's dictatorship, was becoming hard to distinguish from outright Bolshevism, Nicolai felt.

Liebknecht was candid with the man who had fled Ludendorff's Germany in the company of members of the Spartacist movement and had been offered Soviet citizenship by Lenin's close associate. Bolshevism, he answered, was "the consequential realization of socialism." Did the Spartacists believe in the use of force? "Yes, force is necessary to combat force; force is needed to carry the inert masses along." Did the Spartacists intend to make common cause with foreign Bolsheviks? "Yes, we believe in the victory of the Internationale." How did other Social Democrats look upon Bolshevism? "There *are* no other Social Democrats." Pressed for a better answer, Liebknecht said that "the majority Socialists hate us and the Independents envy us but lack the courage to follow us." Did he expect a counterrevolution? "The counterrevolution is here already, and—what is worse—it is represented among us proletarians [it should be noted that Liebknecht held a doctorate in law] by the 'Imperial' Social Democrats [i.e., loyal subjects of the Kaiser]. The war criminals should be tried by a German court, but this will not happen. They will be brought before an international tribunal, which will find them guilty and then pardon them, 'for they knew not what they did.'" His message to the peoples of the world was to "tell them we love all our brothers as we love ourselves. We not only *want* peace among nations, we *are* peace." As for the future of Europe, "socialism will triumph, though perhaps only after a long period of brutal reaction, perhaps not until long after we have been murdered."

Discounting the stereotyped rhetoric, Nicolai was impressed with the human qualities of his interlocutor. The man whom the press had portrayed as a fiend seemed a sincere idealist who was being controlled by events instead of controlling them, a gentle human being who used the language of the New Testament and saw himself as a sacrificial lamb. "From a purely human point of view," he wrote a month later, when the Ebert government had already declared open season on Spartacus and Liebknecht had only a few more days to live, "the Spartacists with Liebknecht at their head are probably the most valuable personalities of this revolution. Their view that the moment is ripe for the realization of a socialist society is an understandable but nonetheless fatal error. It is the views, not the men, that one must combat, and the weapons must be objective and intellectual, not slanderous and violent."[10]

Even as he wrote these lines, regular troops and mercenaries were firing on revolutionary workers who, without waiting for directions from the Spartacists, had seized newspaper offices and railroad stations. Liebknecht had been remarkably accurate in his diagnosis: the counterrevolution was already in progress. With complete indifference to Nicolai's "purely human" values, the new defense minister, Gustav Noske, nicknamed "the Bloodhound," unleashed the terror known as Spartacus week.[11] One of the few voices raised in protest was Nicolai's. He went into the streets to see for himself what was happening, and wrote: "He who takes the trouble to make actual contact with the proletarians in their struggle against the government of Ebert and Scheidemann and to observe them in battle and among themselves, as some of us have done, knows that this is no rabble." Were they the scum of the earth because "they risk their lives for ideals taught them by those who are having them massacred today"? Were they "bandits" because they took the dictatorship of the proletariat seriously? "They consider themselves—perhaps justly—as the most consistent defenders of those socialist principles which their leaders have preached to them for half a century." They were victims of "criminal and deceitful agitation." Who could blame them for accepting Russian money when they had been taught to believe in international solidarity? The guilt belonged to the "hypocrites and criminals," the party leaders who "for decades have hammered all these beautiful slogans into the brain of the masses." He decried "the grotesque fact that once again [as in the war] proletarians are fighting proletarians," and he warned that "if Spartacus should succumb today," it would rise all the more irresistibly tomorrow.[12]

It was easy to misconstrue or distort Nicolai's meaning. His enemies portrayed him as a "Red," a Communist sympathizer. In reality his defense of Liebknecht and his followers reflected the Voltairean outrage of a free spirit who protests the muzzling—and now the killing— of opponents with whom he disagrees but whose rights he respects. His sympathies were with Spartacus not as a program but as the underdog. Inevitably, a sense of social justice made him sympathetic to socialist causes—as it did H. G. Wells, G. B. Shaw, Bertrand Russell, Albert Einstein, Romain Rolland, and many other European thinkers of his generation—but he regarded socialism as an idea whose time had not yet come. "Decent people accept the *spirit* of socialism as a matter of course," he asserted, "but socialism as a *party program* remains debatable." Nothing good could come of attempts to impose it by force, as the Russian example had shown, for it required prepared minds. It was no accident that the German revolution was failing, for "the masses are not internationalist, revolutionary or socialist, but nationalist, conservative, and petit bourgeois." As for the Russian Revolution, it had disproved Marx's theory of the foreordained non-violent overthrow of the capitalist system by the progressively impoverished proletarian masses (his *Verelendigungstheorie*). Lenin's seizure of power, according to Nicolai, confirmed the old utopian beliefs of Rousseau and Fourier, who regarded the masses as always passive and dependent on the initiative of a small elite.

It was Nicolai's mastery of socialist theory and history that made him a formidable critic of socialist groups and at the same time exposed him to the charge of being a Red, for surely a man who spoke their language and knew their sources as he did had to be tainted. Being able to quote chapter and verse, he could play the referee in the heated disputes then taking place between the disunited socialists. Speaking at a meeting in late December 1918 called by the Bund Neues Vaterland to reconcile these differences, he castigated Social Democrats, Spartacists, and independent Socialists with sovereign impartiality. The Social Democrats had forfeited the right to govern in the name of the people, he said, for they had betrayed the Internationale in 1914 and the revolution in 1918, and "it would be madness to think that capitalism can be overcome by a movement that is not international and revolutionary." He was not passing judgment, "only stating facts," he claimed, and he proceeded to illustrate his point with passages from Marx's *Critique of the Gotha Program* and Engels' *Origin of the Family*. The Spartacists—in December they were still a force to be reckoned with—were "true socialists" who deserved praise for their unwavering idealism. Unfortunately they were using the wrong means at the wrong time, though no one should be surprised that the war had given rise to violence and destruction. "Those who really believe in themselves and their theory must fight for it tooth and nail and—I hate to say it—with machine guns." He saw no future for the Independents, who had left the majority Socialists solely because of their support of the war, dismissing them with the terse comment, "the war is over; they will disintegrate," a prediction that would shortly come true.[13]

It was at once Nicolai's weakness and his strength that he kept aloof from political parties. His posture was that of the incorruptible critic who combines a radical sense of justice with a thorough knowledge of socialist theory, passionate idealism with the objectivity of the historian who can take the long view. Such men rarely influence the course of human events, though for a brief moment they may illuminate the stage with the flame of their intellect. In the French Revolution he would have been on the side of the ardent spirits of the Gironde, visionaries like Condorcet, Brissot, Vergniaud, and Madame Roland, who gave a lasting splendor to the cause for which they died, and like them he would have been destroyed by the forces of unreason. But in the gray, uninspired setting of this German revolution visionaries had no role to play, not even that of victims allowed to die gloriously on the guillotine. The few intellectuals who ventured into the political arena, men like Nicolai's old friend Gustav Landauer or Kurt Eisner, briefly prime minister of Bavaria,[14] died a mean death at the hands of brutal killers.

The nearest thing to the Gironde was the Bund Neues Vaterland, mentioned above, a small group of enlightened men and women who braved the general hysteria in 1914 to urge an early, sane peace; after being outlawed it came together again after the war to work for the republic, for social justice, for the reconciliation of Europe. These were Nicolai's own aims, and he immediately joined the Bund and became one of its most active members. The Bund, despite its luminaries,[15] was an experiment bound to fail. It was not a political organization aiming at power but rather a loose grouping of highly individualistic personalities united by a common, vaguely socialist philosophy, an elite with a sense of noblesse oblige that led nowhere. For example, it described itself as a working group like the Fabians in England, dedicated to the creation of a German socialist republic but opposed to class war, "since even democracy and socialism are but means to an end," that end being the "free development of each personality and its untrammeled unfolding on the basis of a truly spiritual and moral culture."[16] This strange blend of individualism and socialist ideas would naturally appeal to Nicolai.

It was the Bund that sponsored the meeting of the three socialist parties at which Nicolai played referee. After the brutal murder of Liebknecht and Luxemburg by right-wing elements in the army on 15 January 1919, almost the only voice raised in protest was that of the Bund. Nicolai was charged with drafting the resolution. "We consider Karl Liebknecht and Rosa Luxemburg courageous and honest fighters for their ideas, even though we believe those ideas and above all the methods of putting them into practice to be erroneous," the document began.

> We are profoundly saddened that such deeds are possible in our young Republic, but still more profoundly saddened by the fact that wide circles approve and rejoice over them. Voices in the press and among the public at large testify to a grave loss of moral sensitivity. Liebknecht's case [Rosa Luxemburg's fate was still in doubt] demands impartial justice, for which we hope and are willing to wait. But we must protest against the pogrom-like spirit that prevails against Spartacus, tearing Germany apart and reminding us of the chorus of hate against our enemies in 1914. We expect that at least intellectual circles will take a stand and not allow hatred and vengefulness to grow beyond all bounds.

The notion that an intellectual elite could stem the tide of fanaticism was part of the creed by which Nicolai and his fellow-idealists lived. It was naive, yet far less naive than the belief of the small-minded men in power that the decay of political morality could safely be ignored. An unbroken line leads from the murders of Liebknecht and Luxemburg, Gustav Landauer, Kurt Eisner, Erzberger, Walther Rathenau, and untold other victims of the Weimar period to the horrors of the Third Reich. Nicolai had laid his finger on one of the ultimate causes of the Germany tragedy.

The Bund's resolution, duly printed and distributed as a handbill, caused hardly a ripple. The "intellectual circles" remained silent, the murderers went unpunished, and the formula "shot while trying to escape" became the official formula to describe political assassinations. As if trying to protect the public against some horrible contagion, the government sealed off the streets through which the simple funeral procession of Liebknecht and thirty-two of his comrades was to move toward the ceme-

251

tery. Cannons and machine guns, manned by soldiers in battle dress, were placed at strategic points. The coffins—Liebknecht's bearing a scarlet bow—rode on plain trucks, one inscribed "Fruit for Sale" and the owner's name. Harry Kessler, who managed to get a glimpse of the cortege and recorded these details in his diary, called the contrast between the ragged proletarian mourners and the heavily armed troops of the Socialist government symbolic of the state of the revolution. It was an accurate observation: under the efficient direction of the Social Democrat Defense Minister Noske the massacres of revolutionary workers increased in the months that followed. The right-wing press took courage and began to call openly for the assassination of those who deserved to die for the crime of being republicans, pacifists, internationalists, or Jews. Nicolai, who, in the eyes of his enemies, was guilty on all four counts, would soon find himself on such lists.

In his case character assassination was the preferred method, though in time his life would be threatened as well. The history of his fight for peace, tolerance, and democracy is interwoven with the details of the campaign of slander and spite that was mounted against him. At the very time when he was approaching the height of his influence as a European thinker he was harassed, insulted, threatened, and deprived of his livelihood. His abrasive personality and unprofessorial manner made him an inviting target.

His ordeal began with a pinprick. He had taken a modest apartment on Uhlandstrasse, installed his wife and child, arranged to share the office of another physician, and announced the resumption of his practice in the newspapers. At a time when many physicians were returning from the war this was routine, but the rabidly chauvinist *Deutsche Tageszeitung* refused to print the notice and seized the opportunity to remind its readers of Nicolai's shabby war record. "Disgraceful advertising by physician," the headline read. Nicolai demanded a retraction. When none was forthcoming he threatened to sue for libel, then decided to let the matter drop.

Next he asked to be reinstated in the hospital position he had lost during the war, counting on the new socialist government of Prussia to grant his request as a matter of course. But the Charité, an ancient institution originally established as a military hospital and—though long since converted to civilian use—still administered by the Army, was still under the control of the same minister of war whom Nicolai defied before his flight to Denmark. The request was denied out of hand. By an ironic coincidence at this time another official of the same War Ministry asked him, "as one of the leading Germans, whose voice is heard at home and abroad," to intercede with the Allies for the release of the many German war prisoners still detained in enemy camps. It was a case of the right hand not knowing what the left was doing. "The unfortunate fact that the German government on its part detained Russian prisoners after making peace with Russia is no reason for me not to condemn most emphatically a similar practice on the part of the Entente," Nicolai responded. There were, however, "certain practical difficulties." The War Ministry should first disavow those who had been responsible for the unlawful detention of the Russian prisoners; then the Allies might listen to pleas for the release of the German prisoners. The advice could not have endeared him to the minister, who himself had sanctioned the detention of the Russians, but Nicolai was not one to resist the temptation of rubbing salt in an opponent's wounds.

Things were not much better at the University of Berlin: on 31 January 1919 the faculty of medicine considered a resolution to deprive Nicolai of his teaching privileges. The motion was narrowly defeated, but the faculty unanimously disapproved his promotion to the rank of professor extraordinary, a step recommended by his ever loyal chief, Geheimrat Kraus. The new minister of education, the Social Democrat Konrad Haenisch who had already approved the promotion, wavered in the face of faculty opposition. As an outsider and a socialist to boot—he was reluctant to interfere in faculty matters and Nicolai had to remind him that he owed his position to a revolution whose supposed aim it was to "create a freer and morally stronger educational system." The professors' objections were political in nature and should be overridden," he wrote. "For four years I have suffered the consequences of my convictions to the fullest extent. My scientific, social, and economic position is in ruins because I fought for things that are part of the creed on which the present regime bases its right to exist." This blend of genuine pathos and barely concealed sarcasm proved effective. Haenisch, a timid but decent man, remembered his socialist conscience and stood by his decision. As his later actions would show, Nicolai had made a deep impression on him. The professors were furious but, for the moment, powerless.

Although he had won the skirmish, Nicolai did not resume his lectures at this time. He knew that his victory had only aggravated his colleagues, and as for the students, he could gauge their mood from their noisy and often violent demonstrations against "un-German" professors. He became deeply pessimistic and for the first time thought of leaving Germany for good. The chair of physiology at the University of Zagreb, formerly Agram, in the new state of Yugoslavia was vacant, and he had reason to hope that it would be offered to him. The offer never came.

To make matters worse, the anti-Semitic press, which by now had discovered his ancestry, began to circulate reports of his imminent departure for Posen (Poznán), a former Prussian province now part of Poland, whose large Jewish population associated it in the minds of German readers with the image of the ghetto. The stories were made of whole cloth, richly embroidered with libelous details, and progressed to a full-scale campaign of lies. It was a fitting move, said a newspaper called, of all things, "Truth" (*Die Wahrheit*), "for, as we learn from our readers, Herr Nicolai comes from Posen and his real name is Abramowicz." This Nicolai-Abramowicz was an impostor whose lectures had been lifted verbatim from the stolen notes of a recently deceased Professor Schulz; he had been forced to leave Berlin when the dead man's family brought suit. "If the Poles want to take this fine gentleman off our hands," said another newspaper, "we shan't begrudge them this 'German' acquisition."

Nicolai filed away such articles in his usual methodical way as they arrived from his clipping service, and ignored them. He had larger battles to fight. The desire to escape to Zagreb had been a fleeting weakness. The times were out of joint, and he, the "Great European," as Romain Rolland had called him, had both the obligation and the ability to help with the task of putting them right. One must begin by facing the facts, Nicolai thought: one must recognize that the revolution was merely political, not social, a skirmish, not the real battle. The masses must be told the truth: conditions are not ripe for the establishment of a socialist society. They will understand that they must be content for the moment with the republic such as it is, combat the counterrevolution, and create a genuine democracy with absolute freedom of speech and other guarantees of human rights. Above all, violence must be abandoned as a method of settling conflicts and the pacifist creed must be adopted as the foundation of all political actions, domestic or international. In Germany this would mean the creation of a peace party strong enough to counteract the existing political parties, all of which had used force and deceit in the pursuit of their interests. On the international plane, a League of Nations with power to enforce the peaceful settlement of all conflicts was needed.

This was the language of reason, and Nicolai was not so naive as to think that an appeal to reason could of itself be effective. Not even the most destructive and most pointless war in history had sufficed to bring the nationalists to their senses. But had not the war also shown that men were willing to make enormous sacrifices for an idea, even if it was the wrong idea? Surely the materialistic view of human nature was too narrow. What was needed was the element of faith, a passionate belief in a great cause. That cause was pacifism. As a rationalist Nicolai saw the problem as one of applied psychology. Pacifism was not a mere matter of disarmament treaties; it was a profoundly revolutionary idea, "perhaps the most revolutionary one the world has ever known." To implant it in the consciousness of the people, "to bring about a transformation of the mass psyche, must be the foremost task" of the pacifist movement, he told the delegates of the German Peace Society, in his capacity as keynote speaker at its first postwar meeting in Kassel.

But psychology was not enough. The greatest idea was doomed without an organization to propagate it. The pacifist message was simplicity itself and could be brought to people of every political and religious persuasion, the middle class as well as the proletariat. This would be the mission of the peace party. By its very existence such a party would force all other parties to align their policies with the general interest, for it would give the voters a yardstick with which to measure the performance of the traditional politicians: "We only ask that the moral imperative should become a regulatory force." But the sphere of action of the new party would not be restricted to the political arena. It would make its influence felt in schools and churches, in the press, the theater, the universities, every area of public life: "If this comprehensive effort should fail, if we have deluded ourselves, if history rejects the lessons of truth and follows a different scheme, then we will have to submit. But the very power of our idea lies in our rock-like conviction that it only needs to be forthrightly stated in order to triumph."

Unfortunately, much more was needed—for instance, financial backing and political strength, neither of which was to be found in pacifist circles. Industrial and financial leaders were not interested, there being no profit in moral imperatives, and the political parties had other concerns. The three socialist parties were all nominally pacifist, but the Communists—as the Spartacists now called themselves—were going their own way, the Social Democrats had sold their souls to the devil by becoming the partners and the shield of the reaction in the civil war now raging, and the Independents were struggling for survival. The Center Party represented the Catholic Church, while the Democrats—whose leading lights included men of the caliber of the sociologists Max and Alfred Weber, Walther Rathenau, and Hugo Preuss, the author of the Weimar Constitution—owed their fleeting success to middle-class fears of the Reds rather than to enthusiasm for democracy. To the right of the Democrats, pacifism was a dirty word, the creed of cowards and traitors.

Also unfortunate was the fact that the pacifists themselves were far from united. Most of them were intellectuals rather than practical politicians, individualists who quarreled among themselves like prima donnas at an audition. Nicolai was no exception. At the very meeting in Kassel at which he was cheered and his resolution proclaiming the aims of the Peace Society adopted, Nicolai himself demanded the exclusion from the presidium of the revered veteran pacifist Ludwig Quidde because he had not been radical enough in opposing German war aims. When the delegates refused to expel Quidde, Nicolai resigned and forbade the publication of his keynote speech by the society. There were pacifists on the right and on the left, pacifists national and international, Christian and Freethinking pacifists, pacifists who wanted to abolish the Army and pacifists who wanted to keep it, pacifists who held Germany alone responsible for the war and pacifists who considered the Entente equally guilty, pacifists absolute and relative, and on the fringe of the movement hovered diverse sectarians who wanted to write their pet ideas—anti-vivisectionism, abolition of the death penalty, adoption of Esperanto, and the like—into the platform. Recent converts were snubbed by the oldtimers, while those converts accused the Old Guard of having lacked courage during the war. A bitter feud broke out between the temperamental and opinionated pacifist Kurt Hiller, who advocated a merger with Clarté, a group founded by the French antiwar novelist Henry Barbusse, and those who had other ideas about international cooperation. Cliques and splinter groups were forming, dozens of new magazines were founded, and the peace movement resembled nothing so much as a bevy of Byzantine theologians debating the three persons of the Trinity.

Nicolai occupied a unique position among these squabbling factions. No one could challenge the credentials of the man who had openly defied the government during the war, no one could question his integrity or his foresight, and no one could match his energy and devotion to the cause. The *Biology of War*—though few of these pacifists had read it—had established his reputation as an original thinker and powerful writer. He was the most spectacular figure among the pacifists of his day.

What were his chances of success? He surveyed the field, listing the individuals, newspapers, and magazines sympathetic to the cause. Categorizing the names in his usual methodical manner, he found little comfort in the numbers but could console himself with the diversity and stature of the potential peace party candidates: Albert Einstein, of course, and the old Geheimrat Wilhelm Förster, the third signer of the ill-fated "Aufruf an die Europäer" ("Appeal to the Europeans") of 1914; the Göttingen mathematician David Hilbert and the sociologist Max Weber, the legal scholar and liberal politician Walter Schücking and the historian F. W. Förster, son of the astronomer and a prominent pacifist in his own right; the writer Heinrich Mann and the journalists Hellmut von Gerlach and Wilhelm Herzog, both staunch personal allies of Nicolai; the redoubtable feminist Helene Stöcker and the grand old lady of socialism Clara Zetkin; and a sprinkling of aristocrats like Count Arco and former military officers like Hans Paasche and H.-G. von Beerfelde.[17] If such a diverse and outstanding group of people could be pacifists, it should be possible to convert the ordinary citizen, but in his heart Nicolai knew that "as a class the bourgeoisie is not only antisocial, which is its privilege, but anti-pacifist as well, which shows that it has a guilty conscience. It no longer trusts in the power of the word, only in cannons and machine guns."

Despite this insight, however, he threw himself body and soul into his missionary work as if the fate of the movement rested on him alone. The record is all the more striking if one considers that he had to tend to his personal affairs, rebuild his medical practice, and defend himself against the constant attacks of his enemies. He was in great demand as a speaker, debated any and all comers at public meetings and in clubs and in private homes, wrote for newspapers and magazines, drafted resolutions and manifestoes, translated important articles from abroad, carried on a voluminous correspondence, and traveled wherever he was assured of an audience. He joined Wilhelm Herzog as co-editor of Herzog's new newspaper *Die Republik*, contributed articles to both *Vorwärts* and *Die Freiheit*, the official organs of the majority Social Democrats and the Independents, respectively, and on occasion even to the bourgeois *Berliner Tageblatt*. His essays appeared in the American magazine *The Nation*, in Maximilian Harden's still influential *Die Zukunft*, and in Siegfried Jacobsohn's ultra-liberal *Die Weltbühne*. When Max Reinhardt staged Romain Rolland's drama *Danton* in Berlin, it was Nicolai who wrote the program notes paying tribute to the great French pacifist. No task was too small for him, and no self-respecting editor in the liberal camp could ignore him.

He spoke in Hamburg and Bremen, Göttingen and Braunschweig, Stuttgart, Kassel, and Münster, in small towns and often at rallies in Berlin. On each occasion he tailored his message to his audience—"Pacifism and Science" or "The Obligation of the Intellectuals" for educated listeners, "The Moral Tasks of the Proletariat" for workers. Often the hall was invaded by nationalist rowdies who terrorized the audience or attacked the speaker, while the police either stood idly by or kept out of sight altogether. To chose a topic like "The War Guilt" and cite an array of facts incriminating the imperial government was to invite attacks with rubber truncheons and brass knuckles, if not revolvers and machine guns, but Nicolai refused to be intimidated. In a talk entitled "Solace in Tears" he deplored the Treaty of Versailles because it undercut the efforts of the embattled German pacifists, but he added that a peace dictated by Germany would have been equally unjust. Freed from the yoke of militarism at last, the Germans could now turn away from war forever. His most terrifying message was contained in the title of the talk "Between the Wars," in which he foretold the next world war.

If the intellectual passion of one man could have awakened the German people from its mood of aggressive self-pity, Nicolai would have succeeded. But unlike Hitler, who played on the most primitive and irrational impulses of the mass psyche, Nicolai was appealing to man's rational nature, demanding thought instead of offering emotional release, using finely honed arguments instead of rabble-rousing rhetoric and eye-filling spectacles, asking for a difficult, reasoned kind of love rather than unreasoning hate. Hitler, of course, was the better psychologist.

While Nicolai was battling for the soul of the German people, the fate of Europe was decided at the Paris Peace Conference, where pacifists had no voice despite the noble efforts of Woodrow Wilson. Germany was excluded, but there was still hope that she would be admitted to the League of Nations, on which the new international order was to be built. Another burning issue was the future of the Second Internationale, the only established organization that stood for an international principle. Both issues were to be aired at international Socialist conferences at Bern, Switzerland, in the spring of 1919. In his triple capacity as a "leading German," a man known to have urged the creation of a League of Nations before the defeat, and an impartial but sympathetic critic of socialism, Nicolai was invited to both congresses.

Reporting in *Die Republik* on the Socialist congress, he was sharply critical of a resolution, passed after the departure of a small radical minority for Moscow to found the Third Internationale, expressing confidence in the German Social Democrats and thanking them for having made the revolution. It smelled of backstage maneuvering by the Scheidemann clique, Nicolai wrote, showing his contempt for the "imperial" socialist who had gotten on so well with the old regime during the war and was now prime minister of a republic that was engaged in wholesale massacres of workers. Since it was now clear that the German comrades had no intention of carrying out a social revolution, "it would seem reasonable to conclude that the others don't want socialism either." "The indolent masses who today seek shelter under the chicken wings of the Socialist Party will fall apart like jelly if their support should be needed some day, for socialism gives them no incentive to fight." Once more Nicolai saw farther ahead than the politicians.

He showed more enthusiasm for the League of Nations, which he saw as the only hope for the abolition of war and the eventual rehabilitation of Germany. It was not yet apparent that the Wilsonian promises which had persuaded the Germans to surrender would be broken. As an official spokesman of his delegation Nicolai did his utmost to pave the way for

Germany's admission to the League. He made an impassioned plea before the plenary session of the Bern conference, persuading his German fellow-delegates to adopt a resolution repudiating the invasion of Belgium, a gesture which, strangely enough, the new German government had failed to make. As head of a three-man commission elected to report on the explosive issue of Germany's war guilt (his colleagues were the well-known pacifist and Reichstag deputy W. Schücking and the ex-general Max Count Montgelas, a recent and in his opinion unreliable convert to pacifism with whom he soon parted company[18]), Nicolai forced the adoption of a declaration which he read before the assembly on 12 March:

> In view of the fact that the Central Powers rejected the proposal, made first by Serbia and subsequently by the Tsar, to submit the dispute to arbitration by the Hague tribunal, and the further fact that the declarations of war against Serbia, Russia, and France emanated from the Central Powers, the Germans present at the international conference for the League of Nations make the following statement: it is in the interest of the German people as well as of the League of Nations that the question of the responsibility for setting in motion and prolonging the war be aired by introducing in evidence before a German court all documents in the German archives, and that the guilty persons be held accountable.[19]

The declaration was both a triumph of Nicolai's leadership and a pyrrhic victory. It split the German delegation—twenty-eight approving, four disapproving, and two abstaining—for while it did not explicitly saddle Germany with the sole responsibility for the war, it implied as much and was so understood by all concerned. Nicolai and his radical supporters, battling the unreconstructed German militarists, were convinced that a frank admission of German guilt was needed to overcome French and British distrust; for the moderates, this was treason. It was not yet possible for historians to discern the deeper causes of the catastrophe, the competing national interests in an age of European nationalism and imperialism. Nicolai himself later denied that he had called Germany the sole culprit. His efforts at the conference were an exercise in futility, in any case. The shape of the League of Nations was decided in Paris, not in Bern, and Germany was excluded.

The visit to Switzerland did provide welcome relief from the harassment at home. Nicolai found sympathetic audiences in Zürich, and Geneva, and Neufchâtel. He called on Auguste Forel, the grand old scientist and pacifist of Yvorne,[20] and on Romain Rolland in his self-imposed exile in Villeneuve. Rolland has left us a penetrating description of the man whom he called "Le Grand Européen" during the war:

> He impresses me as a very intelligent man, solidly cast yet flexible, supple and capable of further development; in no way sentimental, no more sensitive than necessary, virile without an ounce of femininity, essentially a rationalist and an experimentalist, burning with the small hidden flame of the *frondeur*, the gambler, suggesting strange

adventures. His face in profile with the ruthless curvature of the nose is somewhat reminiscent of a bird of prey, and indeed this humanitarian . . . does not belong to that group of people who allow themselves to be eaten. He would rather be among those who do—or could have done—the eating. If he has not done it, it is because reason dominates his hidden nature. In any case, his face bears the traces of the brutal sights it has witnessed in the course of his adventures among men.[21]

Romain Rolland was a good observer. In the midst of his efforts on behalf of humanity, Nicolai was indeed looking out for his own interests. From the modest Berlin apartment he had taken on his return from Scandinavia he soon moved to large and luxurious quarters on Kurfürstendamm. He kept a close account of his speakers' fees, the honoraria for his articles, and the royalties from the sale of the *Biology of War* (the second German edition had at last come out but was doing poorly, but the Danish, Swedish, and English translations were selling well), with which he supplemented his income from his medical practice. He saw to it that the rent for the Dobel, his property in the Black Forest, was paid on time, invested money in various business ventures, and even registered a patent for an invention to reduce the size of X-ray films. As before, he had the help of the faithful Fräulein van Kampen. He had resumed his philandering ways with a vengeance and spent his free time with a succession of mistresses. Rolland, who was not privy to these details, was struck by his manifest lust for life. Comparing him to another recent visitor, Albert Einstein, "who denies himself the simplest luxuries . . . because others are suffering from want of everything," he noted that "Nicolai has no qualms whatsoever about protecting himself and his own against deprivation. He thinks: 'Try to rescue your fellow-men, but if they insist on drowning themselves, don't drown yourself with them, stay alive!'"

The encounter had nevertheless been cordial. Face to face at last, the two most outspoken opponents of the war, the one a francophile German, the other a germanophile Frenchman, were conscious of the symbolic significance of their encounter at the very time when, in Paris, Clemenceau was seeking vengeance. They also discovered, as they talked deep into the night over a bottle of wine or walked on the shore of Lake Geneva, Nicolai without an overcoat, his jacket unbuttoned in the March breeze, explaining that he was used to rough weather and never felt cold, that they liked one another personally.

There was work to be done. Rolland showed his guest the draft of a manifesto entitled "Appeal to the Intellectuals of the World" or, more grandly, "Déclaration de l'indépendence de l'espirit," a call for the founding of an "Internationale of Intellectual Workers," and Nicolai agreed to translate and disseminate it in Germany. Both men had an unshakeable faith in the power of the word and believed in the mission of the intellectual elite. One might think that Nicolai's experience would have discouraged him from promoting yet another manifesto, considering the fate of the "Appeal to the Europeans" of 1914, the failure of the protest against Liebknecht's murder, and, most recently, the indifference with which his call for "The Reconciliation of Europe" in *Die Republik* had been received by the German public. But this time it would be different. The moral authority of Western civilization, represented by the greatest minds of the time, would stand behind this appeal to the conscience of mankind. Three outstanding personalities would be asked to head the list of signers. Names were discussed for England, Bertrand Russell (who had proved his pacifism in a British jail), Norman Angell, and George Bernard Shaw "if he consents"; for the United States, Upton Sinclair; for Italy, Benedetto Croce; for Austria, Stefan Zweig; and for Norway, Fridtjof Nansen. Rolland himself and Henri Barbusse would represent Frances Nicolai and the maverick aristocrat and writer Fritz von Unruh, Germany.[22]

The manifesto recalled the unity of Western civilization that had existed before the war: "Intellectual workers, fellow spirits scattered throughout the world, separated for five years by the armies, the censorship, and the hatred of warring nations! At this hour when the barriers are coming down and the frontiers are reopening, we call on you to restore our brotherly union and make it stronger and more durable than before." Creative minds, scholars and artists alike, had allowed themselves to become tools of hatred and degradation. It was time to shake off the bigotries of nationality, race, and caste: "We know no peoples, only the People," a single and universal mankind, "the People that suffers, struggles, and stumbles, and rises again, always advancing in sweat and blood along its rugged path, the People that is Everyman, brother of us all."

These rolling Gallic phrases inspired Nicolai. He put his heart into the translation and brought forth a German version worthy of the original. But this was only the beginning of his labors. To obtain the signatures of Germany's cultural leaders was a Herculean task that required a blend of diplomacy and moral authority and, above all, a grasp of the personalities and idiosyncrasies of people of varied background, people who were smarting from defeat, humiliation, and privation. At the outset Nicolai decided to ignore the universities, knowing that the overwhelming majority of their faculty would reject even the noblest document if it bore the name of the man who had attacked the Ninety-Three. But there were other people who had been silent until now, neither chauvinists nor pacifists, neither heroes nor martyrs, men and women who had suffered from the spiritual isolation of Germany and who now were experiencing guilt feelings or a sense of inferiority. The preachings of the German pacifists could only reinforce these feelings. Rolland, a Frenchman revered in Germany, with Nicolai's help was opening a door to the world. His manifesto invited the German intelligentsia to rejoin the republic of letters in the company of such figures as Bertrand Russell, Benedetto Croce, Rabindranath Tagore, Georges Duhamel, Jane Addams, and Selma Lagerlöf.

Assisted by his wife and Fräulein van Kampen, Nicolai sent out a thousand copies of the manifesto with self-addressed postcards for signature and comment. He persuaded a number of newspapers to publish the entire document. He catalogued and analyzed the responses and published the results with his commentary.[23] Of those whom he approached directly, 496 responded favorably, an additional 611 were recruited by recipients of the original mailing, and more than a thousand volunteered their signatures after reading the manifesto in the newspapers. It was an impressive success for a man whose first manifesto had found only two signers and whom his own colleagues regarded as a renegade.

The signatures make fascinating reading, almost a *Who's Who* of the Weimar Republic. Among the writers whose names are still remembered were Hermann Hesse and Heinrich Mann (but not his brother Thomas), Max Brod, Franz Werfel, Stefan Zweig, Arthur Schnitzler, Fritz von Unruh, and Emil Ludwig. The poet Ernst Toller, until recently a member of the ill-fated Bavarian Räte regime, returned his endorsement with the dramatic notation "currently Fortress-Prison Eichstätt, Bavaria." From the new republic of Czechoslovakia came the signature of the composer Jaromir Weinberger.

Albert Einstein signed, of course, as did a small number of distinguished scholars, among them the mathematician David Hilbert, the sociologist Alfred Weber, the philosophers Hans Driesch and Hans Vaihinger, and the biochemist Otto Meyerhof. The pacifists of record buried the hatchet long enough to support this call for international solidarity: the Försters, father and son; Alfred Fried of the *Friedenswarte*; Nicolai's allies Gerlach, Gumbel, Wilhelm Herzog, and Hans Wehberg[24] and his adversaries Kurt Hiller and Ludwig Quidde; Harry Kessler, "the Red count," currently ambassador to Poland; the former naval officer Hans Paasche; the Alsatian writer and pacifist René Schickele; and the aristocratic gentleman-jockey Kurt von Tepper-Laski, who was a founder of the original Bund Neues Vaterland.

As a group, musicians were the most enthusiastic signers, evidently because their art was the most truly international. Among them was Arthur Nikisch, the conductor of the Berlin Philharmonic, the Leizpig Gewandhaus, and much earlier, the Boston Symphony Orchestra; his rival Felix von Weingartner, one of the Ninety-Three who had seen the light; the violinists Willy Burmester and Arnold Rosé of the famous Rosé Quartet; the pianists Eugen D'Albert and Artur Schnabel; the Austrian composer E. W. Korngold; the singer Lilli Lehmann; opera stars, a prima ballerina, and several influential music critics.

The other arts were represented by Lyonel Feininger and Walter Gropius, of the Bauhaus in Weimar, and by Käthe Kollwitz, beloved for her moving portrayals of human suffering. The clergy, on the other hand, made a poor showing. A few ministers but not a single theologian of stature signed the call for the reconciliation of Europe. Even the great theologian Ernst Troeltsch refused to lend his name. The Catholic hierarchy remained silent, perhaps because both the author and the translator of the manifesto were suspect of heresy. Among Jewish thinkers only the great religious philosopher Martin Buber responded.

Politicians were equally cool. It was still risky to agree with a Frenchman on anything, especially—after the publication of the peace terms of Versailles—on rapprochement with the enemy. Only three major figures, none currently active in government, were willing to sign: Walther Rathenau, the future foreign minister; Hugo Preuss, the architect of the Constitution, whose brief tenure as minister of the interior ended with the resignation of the entire cabinet in protest against the terms of Versailles; and the courageous Gustav Radbruch, a future minister of justice but then professor of jurisprudence at Kiel.

It was not only theologians and politicians who shied away from signing the manifesto. The brilliant and sensitive writer Ricarda Huch wrote that she had no use for "those who stretch out their hands while kicking us with their feet," in effect blaming the pacifist Rolland for the cruelty of the revanchist Clemenceau. Karl Kraus, the eccentric Viennese satirist, declared that "no temptation is strong enough to lure me into any kind of cultural endeavor that has the support of Wilhelm Herzog," thus putting a petty literary feud above the greater cause. And the classicist and translator of Homer Ulrich von Wilamowitz-Moellendorff, an ultrapatriot and sworn enemy of Nicolai, replied, "The request for me to appear in such company is no doubt the result of a mistake."

Not all the refusals were scurrilous or capricious. Many objected to the phrase "We know no peoples, only the People" as an affront to their national pride, and even the ardent pacifist and francophile Heinrich Mann made his signature contingent on the phrase being stricken. Nicolai classified the opposition in two groups, those who were unwilling even now to "make a human gesture of atonement for the inhumanity of the war" and those who regretted their earlier espousal of militarism but could not bring themselves to admit that "premature pacifists" like Nicolai and Rolland, "who opposed the war while it was going on, had been right. Going beyond such general statements, he published the names of individual refusers, quoting their replies and adding his own pithy comments. Of those who objected to the international flavor of the appeal, he said scornfully: "Evidently they want a League reserved for Germanic humanity." To the diehard patriots who were already calling for revenge, pointing to Versailles as proof that it would have been better to fight to the last man than to accept the peace terms, he said, "No one ever suggested *losing* the war, only making peace while there was still time." Such sarcasm was not likely to make his cause more popular, but he found it irresistible, and in any case he saw the refusers as lost to the cause. A few more enemies did not matter.

He had to admit that the Allies, by imposing conditions that were bound to create new hatred, made a fatal mistake at Versailles—the treaty had been published by the time his manifesto began to circulate in Germany—though he commented that "it might be good for the [German] people to experience on its own body what it had planned to do to others." But it was difficult to preach reconciliation when the victors insisted on revenge. He shared the general despair, noting that shortsightedness was not a German monopoly: "Whether or not Germany bore the guilt for the last war, the responsibility for the *next* war will rest with the other side."

This crusade for Rolland's manifesto was made Nicolai the voice of Europe's intelligentsia in Germany, and the voice of the finest elements of German culture in the European community, now almost drowned out by the shouts of hatred and rage. He had mobilized impressive support for an idea that was still novel and almost revolutionary to a nation taught to believe in the power of the sword and the survival of the fittest. His call for the renunciation of force, whether domestic or international, had at last been heard in Germany, albeit only by men and women of good will, not by those who were terrorizing the country. Although he was not alone in his struggle, he had done more for the cause of peace and sanity than any other German.

His efforts were in vain, for in a country where political murder had become commonplace, the "weapons of the mind" on which he relied were inadequate. He was defeated by the very evils he had denounced as the cause of the German tragedy: the worship of power, the habit of obedience to authority, the absence of a democratic tradition, and the lack of an informed public opinion. The unexpected loss of the war only exacerbated these tendencies. Psychologically, the Germans could not cope with postwar reality. Nicolai's inexorable logic infuriated them. He was lucky not to be physically maltreated, as Gerlach and Gumbel and Maximilian Harden were maltreated, or killed, like his fellow-pacifist Hans Paasche and so many others. But he would soon be driven from the country, and his enemies would see to it that his very name was forgotten. The coming age belonged to Hitler.

NOTES

1. Excerpts from Nicolai's speeches in Sweden in November 1918 are from handwritten notes in the Nicolai archive.

2. The account of Nicolai's return to Berlin appeared in the Danish newspapers *Dagens Nyheter* and *Politiken*.

3. This account of the revolution of 1918 closely follows that of Sebastian Haffner, *Die verratene Revolution* (Bern: Scherz Verlag, 1969). In contrast to the traditional view (see, for example, Erich Eyck, *A History of the Weimar Republic*, Science Editions [New York: John Wiley, 1967]), Haffner argues convincingly that the revolution eluded the control of the Spartacists, whose largely rhetorical threats provided the pretext for the counterrevolutionary terror, and that the Workers' and Soldiers' Councils aimed not at Bolshevik dictatorship but at the orderly and peaceful transfer of power from the old regime to the elected representatives of the people.

4. Quoted from the addendum to Nicolai's *Sechs Tatsachen als Grundlage der heutigen Machtpolitik*, ed. O. Nippold (Bern: Freier Verlag, 1918).

5. Sebastian Haffner (*Die verratene Revolution*) appraises Liebknecht as an idealistic dreamer, rather than a ruthless revolutionary, which agrees with the picture drawn by Nicolai in his hitherto unpublished account of his interview with Liebknecht on 10 December 1918; see n. 9 below.

6. G. F. Nicolai, "Liebknecht und der Friede," *Politiken*, 18 October 1918, reprinted in *Aufruf an die Europäer, gesammelte Aufsätze zum Wiederaufbau Europas*, ed. Hans Wehberg (Vienna: Verlag der Wiener graphischen Werkstätte, 1921).

7. From "Programm des Spartakusbundes," cited in *Völker hört die Signale. Der deutsche Kommunismus 1916–1966*, ed. Hermann Weber (Munich: Deutscher Taschenbuch Verlag, 1967).

8. Gumbel, a mathematician, published his well-documented reports on right-wing terrorism in postwar Germany in *Zwei Jahre Mord* (Berlin: Berger, 1921), with a preface by Nicolai. He was later driven from the University of Heidelberg by Nazi students.

9. Quotations are from a questionnaire in English bearing the notation "for Desmond" (a reference to Shaw Desmond, a prominent Anglo-Irish pacifist) and Liebknecht's answers as jotted down in German by Nicolai during the interview. The interview seems to have remained unpublished, perhaps because of the rush of other political developments. The fact that Nicolai could make contact with the hunted Spartacist leader indicates a measure of trust in him not accorded to bourgeois reporters. The name Sonia Liebknecht (whether sister or wife is not known) appears in Nicolai's records in a context suggesting an intimate relationship.

10. From a typewritten manuscript in the Nicolai archive entitled "The Necessity of Combating Bolshevism with Intellectual Weapons" ("Die Notwendigkeit, Spartakus mit geistigen Waffen zu bekämpfen"), evidently intended for dissemination by the Bund Neues Vaterland.

11. Noske, a Social Democrat and member of the provisional government, issued the notorious Noske Shooting Edict calling for shooting on sight any person carrying arms, which order served as the justification for thousands of murders.

12. The above quotations are also from the "Necessity of Combating Bolshevism" typescript.

13. Quotations are from Nicolai's handwritten notes in the Nicolai archive.

14. Eisner, a "coffeehouse intellectual" who proclaimed the republic in Bavaria on 7 November 1918 and became prime minister of its Räte government, was assassinated three months later, two days after resigning from office.

15. Among the members were Count Harry Kessler, well known as a social critic; he was named German ambassador to Poland the following year. His diaries (*Tagebücher 1919–1937* [Frankfurt-am-Main: Büchergilde Gutenberg, 1971]) form a prime source for historians of the 1918 revolution and the Weimar period. Other prominent members were Ernst Reuter, a Social Democrat later in exile during the Nazi regime, who was to be lord mayor of Berlin during the Berlin airlift following World War II; E. J. Gumbel, the historian of the Terror; Carl von Ossietzky, a well-known writer who was editor of *Die Weltbühne* in the years just before the Nazi takeover in 1933 and then Nobel laureate for Peace in 1935, an award which, as mentioned above, he received while in a concentration camp; Helene Stöcker, an officer of the German Peace Society and delegate to the League of Nations Conference in Bern the following year, where she voted with Nicolai on the War Guilt Resolution; and Magnus Hirschfeld, a physician known for his studies of human sexuality and the moving force in the reactivation of the Bund.

16. Quotations are from the bylaws of the Bund, undated but ca. November or December 1918, in the Nicolai archive.

17. Herzog until 1915, when it was suppressed, edited *Forum*, a pacifist magazine. In 1918, he founded the newspaper *Die Republik*, which was "dedicated to the defense of the revolution, the Internationale, humanity" and bore as its motto

words from Pascal: "justice and power must become one, so that justice may become powerful and power just." Herzog's "Internationale" was not the political organization but the *geistige* ("intellectual") community. Clara Zetkin was to be a co-founder of the German Communist Party and member of the Reichstag on that ticket in 1920. Georg Count Arco, a director of the Telefunken Company, was a liberal member of the Bund Neues Vaterland. Hans Paasche, son of a vice-president of the Reichstag, a naval officer who became a pacificist after reading the Lichnowsky memoir (see Chapter 14, n. 3, above), was jailed for his views. Released in November 1918, he took an active part in the Revolution. Hans-Georg von Beerfelde, an officer attached to the General Staff, like Paasche was converted to pacificism by the Lichnowsky memoir, for whose unauthorized distribution he was responsible. He too was jailed and released in November 1918. Elected president of the Berlin Räte, he was stripped of this office three days later in the confusion of the power struggle between radicals and moderates.

18. Montgelas was in disfavor for his criticism of the Battle of the Marne and the slaughter of Ypres and his opposition to the bombing of open cities. As military governor of Cambrai, he was dismissed for "excessive justice" toward an alleged saboteur. He became a vocal pacifist and, with Schücking, edited the first collection of German documents concerning the diplomatic antecedents of the war. Montgelas, as Nicolai had suspected he would do, later abandoned his pacifist beliefs and reverted to type.

19. The text of the declaration appeared in French translation in the *Journal de Genève* of 19 March 1919 under the title "Un Aveu de la culpabilité allemande."

20. Forel, though one of the leading pacifists of the period, is best known for his classic study of the ants of Switzerland, for the second edition of which Nicolai wrote the preface.

21. Rolland, *Journal des années de guerre 1914–1919: Notes et documents pour servir à l'histoire morale de l'Europe de ce temps*, ed. Marie Romain Rolland (Paris: Albin Michel, 1952), p. 1766.

22. Unruh, a Prussian officer who turned pacifist during the war, described the hell of Verdun in his novel *Opfergang*.

23. *Romain Rollands Manifest und die deutschen Antworten* (Charlottenburg: Mundus Verlagsanstalt, 1919). The Nicolai archive contains the complete file with the responses.

24. Wehberg, a jurist and authority on international law and disarmament, was drafted into the army as a private because of his opposition to the invasion of Belgium. After the war he wrote a book, *Als Pazifist in Weltkrieg*, which he dedicated to Nicolai, whose personal friend he became. In 1921 he published a collection of Nicolai's essays.

16. Excommunication

From the ideal of universal brotherhood it was but a step to the ugly reality of postwar Germany. Murder and mayhem, perpetrated by frustrated nationalists and tolerated, if not encouraged, by an impotent government, became commonplace in the dismal winter of 1919–20. Pacifists, Socialists, Jews, foreigners, and advocates of accommodation with former enemies—all were fair game. The courts were blind to crimes committed in the name of patriotism, the universities turned into strongholds of reaction, and the Army stood aloof. By March of 1920 the Right considered the time ripe for the coup d'état later known as the Kapp putsch. Government buildings were seized, the extremist Kapp proclaimed himself chancellor, Ludendorff and Hitler (the latter as yet only an obscure spy for the military) rushed to Berlin, and the cabinet fled south. The putsch foundered on the general strike it provoked, and the frustrated forerunners of Nazism reverted to individual acts of terrorism. Their time had not yet come, but their spirit pervaded the air. Men of good will might well despair of the future.

It so happened that on 11 March, two days before the putsch, the Social Democratic paper *Vorwärts* gave its readers a summing up of the most recent horrors. At Königsberg a republican teacher was horsewhipped by army officers. At Baden-Baden the Jewish student Kahn was fatally shot. In Berlin and in Bremen members of the Allied High Commission were roughed up by nationalist rowdies. In the Ruhr district troops disrupted an amateur theatrical performance staged by a labor union, assailing cast and audience with whips and truncheons, shooting, throwing stink bombs, and—for good measure—arresting those who rushed to the rescue. A pacifist rally organized at Osnabrück by Nicolai's ally Hellmut von Gerlach was invaded by more than a hundred thugs of the notorious Free Corps Lichtschlag, shouting insults at pacifists, Jews, and other "vermin." A young man named Knüppe was shot while trying to stop the intruders, and the killer walked away under the protection of his comrades. All this, the *Vorwärts* noted, was just the harvest of the last two weeks. To list every act of terrorism of the past winter would require more space than the editor could spare. A few striking examples would have to suffice.

Item: at a pacifist gathering in a Berlin suburb the speaker and the presiding officer—again the intrepid Herr von Gerlach—had been beaten almost to death by Pan-German ruffians and members of the dread Marine Brigade, the group which staged the Kapp putsch.
Item: a young fanatic, emulating Count Arco, who was idolized by nationalists as the murderer of Eisner, tried to assassinate Finance Minister Erzberger.
Item: at Arco's trial his fellow-students from the University of Munich turned out en masse to demand his release. Even the rector openly de-

clared his sympathies for the murderer. A lone dissenter who objected to such pronouncements as unbecoming the highest official of the university was thrown out of the student assembly, and Professor Max Weber, the great scholar, was howled from the rostrum for condemning Arco's crime.

Item: in Berlin Albert Einstein, though world-famous for his relativity theory, was the target of anti-Semitic student riots.

Item: Nicolai, the noted pacifist, had to abandon his lectures in the face of violent demonstrations.

If the *Vorwärts*, a paper serving a working-class readership, gave so much coverage to goings-on in academia, it was because the universities harbored the most dangerous enemies of the republic.[1] Working hand in glove with the right-wing press, faculties and students alike openly defied the government. Attacks on men like Weber, Einstein, and Nicolai were challenges to the authority of the Social Democratic regime. Nicolai, as the most flamboyant of these personalities, became the center of the most serious controversy. The attempt to drive him out of the university was the most vicious and the most sustained, giving rise to the suspicion of collusion between students and academic authorities and threatening to embroil the Ministry of Education in an ugly fracas.

The ordeal began in January. After winning the battle for promotion to professor extraordinary, Nicolai waited almost a year before resuming his lectures. He had been busy spreading the gospel of pacifism, but he had also hoped that the political climate would improve as the bitter memories of the war receded. Far from improving, however, it deteriorated, most of all in the universities. But at heart Nicolai still considered himself primarily a scientist and a teacher and now saw nothing to be gained from waiting any longer. He therefore submitted to the rector's office the titles of two courses for the winter semester, one a lecture series on the topic "Brain and Soul," the other a practical bedside exercise, "Introduction to Clinical Medicine," to be held at the Charité, where in happier days he had been second in command under Kraus. The announcements did not find their way into the university catalogue. An oversight, said the rector, but no one else's announcements had been omitted. He had to settle for the assurance that the notices of his courses would be prominently displayed on the university bulletin boards.

His opening lecture was set for 12 January 1920. He could hardly have chosen a less propitious moment. A rail strike was paralyzing the country, delaying the return of German war prisoners from Allied camps and causing new resentment against labor and its sympathizers. Restive crowds demonstrated in support of the strikers. The next day eighty thousand people gathered in front of the Reichstag, threatening to invade the building and impose their will on the parliament. Troops fired into the crowd, killing or wounding forty-two persons. The government seized the opportunity to suspend the left-wing press on the grounds that it had incited the disorders in an attempt to overthrow the legal authorities. In his coming battle with the university, Nicolai was thus deprived of the support of newspapers friendly to him, while the extreme right-wing press remained free to attack him.

Nicolai's confrontation with the students, most of whom were rabid nationalists, was a public event.[2] He was too well known to slip quietly back into his former role of professor of medicine. To most of the students he was an archvillain and embodiment of everything that was rotten in Germany. To the few souls who believed in the brotherhood of man he was the shining defender of a new faith. Both sides were ready for the occasion. The right-wing press had fanned the flames for weeks. "The notorious Professor Nicolai-Lewinstein considers himself fit to be a teacher of German students," said the *Deutsche Zeitung*. "We have been demanding for some time that his colleagues should get rid of him; otherwise, the students should take matters into their own hands." On 13 January, the day after Nicolai's first lecture, the same paper reported that "the German-thinking portion of the student body has given clear and unmistakable expression to its feelings about the deserter."

The "German-thinking" students had needed no such urging, however. Reinforced by thugs whom no one could have mistaken for academic youths, they came in droves, many of them in their wartime uniforms and brandishing their service revolvers or army knives, intent on teaching the "deserter-professor," as the right-wing press called Nicolai, a well-deserved lesson. But the other side had not been idle. Alerted by the German Peace Society, whose leaders were understandably worried about the safety of its most notorious member, the small Socialist Students' Union mobilized its forces. As a result, on the day of the lecture the rowdies found every seat in the lecture hall occupied by grim-faced supporters of the intended victim. Momentarily taken aback, they milled about in the corridor, trading insults with the audience within while they revised their strategy. Although no university police were in sight, the presence of so many able-bodied opponents made brute force seem inadvisable, and Nicolai escaped his friend Gerlach's fate of being manhandled. His arrival, in fact, was greeted with stormy applause by his admirers, but before he could begin to speak the rioters burst into the hall with shouts of "swine, traitor, miserable coward, deserter, scum of the earth." This invective was followed by an ear-splitting cacophony of sirens, police whistles, house keys, and pocket combs. Finally a former air force lieutenant, one Stuckardt, called for silence and "in the name of German academic youth" demanded to know how the professor pleaded to the charges of treason and desertion. Face to face with the younger generation in whom he had placed such high hopes, Nicolai earnestly tried to explain the beliefs that had brought him in conflict with the rulers of wartime Germany. But the rowdies had not come to be converted. As the *Deutsche Tageszeitung* described the scene, "the deserter-professor was asked politely to interrupt his lecture and defend himself against the charges. The melodramatic and self-serving arguments with which he tried to represent himself as a hero precipitated lively manifestations of displeasure, for German youth does not judge on the basis of talmudic sophistries. It accepts as heroes only men who have the courage to stand up for their actions with their persons."

A less biased source might have given Nicolai credit for the courage it took to brave the "lively manifestations" of the ruffians. He stood his ground, vainly trying to make himself heard above the pandemonium. At last one of the pacifist students rose and urged him to "end this disgraceful spectacle and stop dignifying the insults of these louts by further responses." The intruders refused to leave the hall, and the ugly scene continued until Stuckardt—thinking, no doubt, that he had hit upon an exit line that would make good reading in the next day's *Deutsche Tageszeitung*—called on "all good Germans" to leave. This proved to be a tactical error, for Nicolai's supporters remained firmly in their seats and once more burst into applause when it seemed that the enemy was routed. They rejoiced too soon: the enraged patriots stationed themselves at the doors and sang "Deutschland über Alles" and "Die Wacht am Rhein." Drowned out by these raucous voices, Nicolai acknowledged defeat and abandoned his lecture.

The next day a similar scene took place at the Charité. The corridors were teeming with senior medical students determined to keep the "deserter-professor" from defiling a German clinic. A delegation told the administrator in Nicolai's presence that it would not listen to a traitor and would use force against him if necessary. Kraus, as chief of the medical service, sent a senior staff member to remind the future doctors that they were in a hospital and must not disturb the patients with violent demonstrations. The future doctors replied that all possible consideration would be given to the sick, but that the planned action would have to be carried out, come what may. Kraus bowed to the inevitable and ordered the lecture canceled.

For Kraus, as for Nicolai, it was a bitter moment, ending a relationship of almost twenty years. Recognizing Nicolai's brilliant promise, from the beginning Kraus had protected him against professional jealousies (and against the excesses of his own temper). He had made him his primary assistant and obtained the professorship for him. Their names were linked as co-authors of a book that became a standard text for a generation of physicians. The dedication with which they had proudly presented the work to the profession in 1910 had read, "for the opening of the new building of the II. Medical Clinic," the very building from which Kraus was now forced to banish his former disciple. He himself was completely apolitical and had always deplored Nicolai's involvement in various "causes" as an aberration in an otherwise outstanding scientific career. During the war he had gone to great lengths to protect Nicolai's academic appointment and had even offered to lend him money when financial difficulties threatened. After the war he recommended him for promotion against the wishes of the entire faculty. He still believed that Nicolai's place was in medicine and had looked forward to his return to the Charité, but now these paternal hopes were dashed.

The prodigal son, for his part, was unrepentant. According to the *Post*, another right-wing newspaper, he stood by "in a pose of deliberate rudeness," his hands in his trouser pockets, "hurling coarse insults" at the students. The veracity of the *Post* is doubtful, but Nicolai had ample grounds for losing his composure. It was clear now that the rioting was part of an organized campaign and that his cherished academic career was at an end.

On mature reflection, however, he took the view—at least this was his public stance—that the students were idealistic young hotheads "led astray by a press campaign without parallel" but who should be treated with leniency. He was mistaken: these students, many of them military veterans who had returned to school mature in years, if not in wisdom, knew perfectly well what they were doing. Their demonstrations, far from being spontaneous outbursts of youthful anger, were part of a campaign to destroy him. The spirit for which he stood was unacceptable to the "German-thinking" elements who dominated the student body in the Weimar Republic and who would give their allegiance to Adolf Hitler a decade later. Nicolai's very presence in a German university was an affront. His ideals—pacifism, social justice, democracy, international unity, tolerance, reason—were seen as poisoned arrows aimed at the heart of the already bleeding Fatherland.

Nicolai underestimated the depth of these feelings. He was too much of a rationalist to comprehend that the very notion of pacifism was an outrage to young men who had risked their lives for their country and whose most cherished experiences had been the camaraderie and the shared danger of the trenches. The concept of non-violence ran directly counter to the hallowed customs and traditions of "student honor," an ideal which—as he knew so well from his fraternity days—rested on personal valor and had to be upheld in individual combat. War between nations was no less a matter of honor than receiving "satisfaction" on the dueling floor. A pacifist was a man without honor, a coward who ran from a fight. Nicolai had not only offended the national spirit with his pacifist utterances but had actually fled the country when it appeared that he would have to fight (so the right-wing press portrayed his flight to Denmark).

Nicolai's internationalism was no less despicable than his flight in the students' eyes, for it undermined the pride in the uniqueness and superiority of the German people which had been proclaimed so loudly and so long in the universities, the pride that had sustained the educated middle class during the war and was sustaining it now in defeat. To be a good German meant to be "national," that is, anti-international. Now more than ever German patriots gloried in the conflict between the misunderstood, outnumbered, betrayed yet spiritually unconquered and unmatched Fatherland and the treacherous, degenerate world outside. Besides, it was both humiliating and useless to curry favor with former enemies: the Treaty of Versailles had shown what international good will was worth.

This frustrated nationalism blended easily into the volkish ideology, which in turn rested on the pseudoscientific doctrine of racial purity. As far as the students were concerned, Nicolai was a Jew. Anti-Semitism, feeding on the military defeat, the economic misery of the middle class, and the overcrowding of the universities, was even more vicious now than in his youth. The Jews were the "un-German" body in the midst of the heroic German people; they were crass, commercial, cowardly parasites draining away the nation's life blood. It mattered little that they, too, had fought in the trenches or served their country as best they could: they were the perfect substitute for the enemy. Nicolai, now unmasked as the son of the Jew Lewinstein (or Löwinstein, as the anti-Semitic press affected to spell the name), was an ideal target. "Nicolai—Jewish spirit—Versailles Treaty!" one young idealist exclaimed in a letter to the *Deutsche Zeitung*.

Then, too, Nicolai was an avowed democrat in a nation where democracy was the bitter fruit of a revolution in which these students —unlike their grandfathers in 1848—had played no part and which threatened their image of themselves as an elite destined to lead the nation. Democracy was an unwanted import from the despised West, foreign to the romantic soul of the German people, which drew its strength from the mystical union with its God-given sovereign. In a democracy there was no room for heroes, no outlet for that loyalty of brave men to their leader which passed for a uniquely German virtue. A president in top hat and morning coat was a poor substitute for the martial splendor of a Prussian king. Parliamentary squabbling was unedifying and ineffectual compared with the incisive rule of the old authorities. Democracy meant weakness, lack of discipline, dirty politics. Imperial Germany had been power and glory, order and prosperity; the republic had brought humiliating defeat, chaos, and poverty. Most students—and most professors as well—longed for the return of the monarchy. At the University of Berlin, according to a decree issued by the rector, the anniversary of the revolution was to be commemorated not as a holiday but as a day of atonement, for "on that day the nation unmanned itself."

Lastly, Nicolai was known to lean toward socialism, the very antithesis of the "national" spirit which students had a right to expect from their professors. Their attitude toward one of the major political currents of the century was one of total rejection based on total ignorance. Not only were they unfamiliar with socialist theory, but, as sons of the middle and upper classes, they had no contact with workers and knew next to nothing about their social problems or political ideas. When Messrs. Noske and Haenisch called on the students for help against the revolutionary masses, many rushed to arms—and some distinguished themselves by acts of exceptional brutality—in the conviction that the proletarians must be kept in their place and that the state must be defended even if it were in the wrong hands. Thus Nicolai flunked every test by which the majority of the students judged their professors.

His young adversaries knew how to exploit their victory. Barely a week after the riots they held a meeting at which they went through the forms of debating three alternatives: disciplinary action against the rioters; hearings, with Nicolai and Stuckardt as the principal witnesses; or a demand for Nicolai's immediate suspension. The last motion won by an overwhelming majority[3] and was promptly forwarded to the rector and Academic Senate for action. Nicolai was now in deep trouble. The rector, the ultraconservative historian Eduard Meyer, who called the revolution the unmanning of the nation, was his bitter enemy.[4] The rioters could take Meyer's support for granted (if, indeed, he had not secretly approved their action beforehand or even inspired it, as skeptics would charge) and had only to wait for the victim's next move. If he played his cards right, Meyer could exploit the students' formal demand to rid the university of this renegade foisted on it by a Socialist Minister of Education. Publicly, however, he struck a pose of stern objectivity, for as rector he could hardly condone a flagrant breach of student discipline. Nicolai was still a faculty member in good standing, after all, and as professor extraordinary he was exempt from the jurisdiction of the academic authorities and could be removed from his post only by the minister of education.

While pondering this obstacle, Meyer posted a notice on the bulletin board announcing that he had assured Professor Nicolai of the full protection to which he was entitled under the statutes of the university: "However, in view of the essential relationship of mutual trust between teachers and students it seems wiser to me—and to Professor Nicolai—to refrain from coercive measures. Rector and senate will examine the Nicolai case [not the case against the rioters] and report the results of the investigation to the student body as soon as possible." Meanwhile, the students should refrain from further actions and seek to restrain the press, "insofar as it is in their power," from further publicity about the matter.

Nicolai was slow to recognize the threat concealed in this bland message. Instead of calling for punishment or even censure of the disturbers of the peace, it implied that he, the aggrieved party, was to be the object of an investigation whose results would be submitted to *them*. Though he had ample grounds for suspecting skulduggery, he clung to his faith in the German academic tradition, the priceless legacy of the Humboldts, of the Brothers Grimm, of Helmholtz, Virchow, and Mommsen. He was undisturbed by the coolness with which the rector responded to his request for protection. The facts of the case were undisputed; therefore, the "investigation" could only be a device to calm the troubled waters. In due course, he believed, both rector and senate would rally behind a colleague, the students would be gently but firmly reprimanded, and the whole affair would blow over. As a friendly reporter remarked, Nicolai was "touchingly naive." He posted a notice of his own on the bulletin board announcing the postponement of his lectures "until a later date."

Nevertheless, Nicolai did pay a call at the Ministry of Education, counting once more on the Socialist administration for support against the reactionary academic establishment. But the education officials were loath to expose themselves to the charge of tampering with the autonomy of the universities. Undersecretary Carl Heinrich Becker, himself a distinguished scholar and former university professor, was sympathetic but expressed the view that matters of student discipline are best left to the academic authorities. Nicolai had no choice but to deal with the rector.

Meyer, who had made no attempt to conceal his hostility, now changed his tactics. He requested a second meeting, at which, according to Nicolai, "he was like a different person, greeting me with 'my dear colleague' and offering apologies, for he had known me only from the *Deutsche Tageszeitung*, but now that he had looked into my record—which showed that my conduct had been justified, inasmuch as I had openly refused to take the oath to the colors and suffered the consequences of that refusal for three years—he could see that from a moral standpoint I could not be called a deserter." When Meyer offered him the protection to which he was entitled in any case, "I accepted gratefully," Nicolai reported, "and did not smell a rat until he demanded that I agree in advance to accept the verdict of the senate." The rector assured him that "the whole thing was a mere formality intended to provide a legal basis for arbitration by the Senate, and that differences in political opinion would not be allowed to become an issue." He shrewdly clinched the argument with the suggestion that "surely I preferred to be rehabilitated by my peers, as he was certain I would be." Nicolai succumbed to these blandishments, but as soon as he signed the agreement, "His Magnificence quickly regained his earlier reserve."

This account, which Nicolai made public shortly after the senate had rendered its verdict, was borne out by the events that followed and was never challenged by Meyer. Evidently the rector was not above using deceit and flattery to achieve his purpose, that of tricking Nicolai into submitting his case to "arbitration" by a hostile body that had no jurisdiction over him.

Nicolai was not completely blind to the rector's design, however. He had been foolish, he wrote afterward, to deprive himself of his right to appeal to the minister, "who alone was legally competent and, as I knew, sympathetic to me, and to put myself into the hands of a corporation in which, as I knew equally well, I did not have a single friend." It was one of Nicolai's rare understatements: nowhere was he more cordially detested than among the academics. Here, on his own ground, among his peers, he was among his real enemies. Four of the men who were to sit in judgment over him were among the signers of the Manifesto of the Ninety-Three of October 1914 and as such had been the objects of his sharpest criticism.[5]

The official machinery began to move with uncharacteristic speed. The first public hearing took place on 23 January, less than a week after Nicolai's second interview with the rector. In the manner of a prosecutor addressing the jury, Meyer opened the proceedings with a statement that should have dispelled any illusions Nicolai might still harbor about the heirs of Virchow and Mommsen. The issue before the senate, Meyer said, was whether Nicolai's actions during the war had harmed the German Reich, in other words, whether the charges of treason and desertion leveled against him could be substantiated. Taken by surprise, Nicolai objected that this was a political question that had no bearing on his fitness as a professor of medicine and as such had been expressly excluded from the agenda which had been agreed upon. The response, however evasive, must have satisfied him, for at the next hearing two days later he signed a formal protocol affirming his willingness to "submit to the decision I have requested from the senate regarding my fitness as a university teacher, and to accept whatever consequences might flow from the decision with respect to my relationship with the institution." He furnished copies of his wartime writings, prepared a point-by-point rebuttal of the charges, and agreed to the transfer of his files from the War Ministry, the Foreign Office, and the Ministry of Education. He was ready for another "Nicolai Case."

Why did he let himself be drawn into this suicidal game? He was known the world over as Germany's most outspoken pacifist and would not shrink from the confrontation with the relics of a bygone era. Moreover, he was convinced that he would win his case on its merits. As far as he was concerned, the trial (for by now the proceedings had evolved into a trial in which he was facing a kangaroo court without benefit of legal assistance) must focus on the issue of academic freedom. He had the right to follow his conscience in matters unrelated to academic affairs, and the question of whether his conduct had been detrimental to the national interest was indeed "political" and therefore inadmissible. For that matter, he was prepared to argue that the Manifesto of the Ninety-Three had done infinitely greater harm to the German cause than anything he himself had written. The only point at issue, he wrote, when he finally withdrew his consent to the proceedings, was "whether I had done anything unlawful or contrary to the general rules accepted by decent people." His so-called desertion was legally moot, for he had never been prosecuted by the military and, in any event, a general amnesty had been proclaimed for offenses connected with the war.

The faculty senate made a show of thoroughness and objectivity, but the outcome was never in doubt. The senators scrutinized the *Biology of War* and Nicolai's other wartime writings, probably for the first time. They studied his voluminous files at the War Ministry and the confidential reports of the German embassies on his activities as a fugitive in Scandinavia. They even heard witnesses, among them Dr. Klauer, Böse's successor at Danzig, who described Nicolai's last court-martial. They also invited student representatives to "testify," although clearly the only thing they could contribute was their prejudice. The fact that the students had broken the laws of the university was ignored: these young ruffians were now Nicolai's accusers. Professors and students were working together, the younger generation supplying the brawn and the older the brains. As the *Welt am Montag* said, youth provided the "mindless brutality" and age the "diplomatic cunning" needed to destroy the victim. "We have to admit," the commentator wrote sarcastically, "that there is such a thing as academic solidarity."

That solidarity became even more obvious during the Kapp putsch, which erupted just days after the conclusion of the trial. At the request of the "Herr Chancellor" (the usurper Kapp), Rector Meyer closed the university while a student named Biertimpel—who, with Stuckardt, was one of the ringleaders of the anti-Nicolai riots—rallied his comrades in support of the rebel government. (A few months later the rector presented Biertimpel with a handsome six-volume edition of the history of the University of Berlin, perhaps as a reward for yeoman service during the putsch, perhaps for his role as a ringleader and "witness" against Nicolai.) In the fall Biertimpel was sought by the police as an embezzler of student funds, but the discovery came too late to discredit him at the trial.

While the senate gathered information, the right-wing press, ignoring the rector's pious plea for silence, stepped up its campaign against Nicolai, charging that he had written his anti-German book in the safety of a foreign country, that he had been in England during the war and furnished valuable information to the enemy, that he had spread anti-German propaganda in Scandinavia, that he had incited German soldiers to desert, that he was a Soviet citizen. Did not the British drop leaflets with the caption "what a famous German professor has to say" over the German lines at Armentières to induce the troops to lay down their arms? He was, in short—to quote the *Deutsche Tageszeitung*—one of the "insiders who stabbed the German Army in the back with their daggers and poisoned darts." On top of everything else he was a common thief who had stolen clothing, leather boots, and goggles from a military depot for his flight to Denmark.

This last charge came in a signed letter from retired Captain Hermann von Wilamowitz-Möllendorff, press officer at the air base where Nicolai began his flight. His father, a professor at the university, was Germany's leading classicist and a signer of the Manifesto of the Ninety-Three. (It was he who had returned Nicolai's invitation to join in Romain Rolland's call for the reconciliation of Europe with the caustic notation that surely the document had been sent him by mistake.) Scurrilous as it was, Nicolai could not afford to ignore this charge. He sued the captain for libel, a risky thing to do, for under German law the defense was not restricted to proving the relevant facts but was free to introduce any and all testimony that might discredit the plaintiff. The suit dragged on for two years and became a source of frustration and expense to Nicolai.

Nicolai, however, would not be intimidated by these attacks. He continued to speak in public with his accustomed vigor. Even the best republic would be wasted on a nation of slaves, he told a rally called on 29 January to debate the topic "republic or monarchy." In an interview for the *Daily News* of London—he was still an international figure, and the bizarre "trial" had attracted the foreign press—he put his finger on one of the ultimate causes of his troubles. If the Entente had shown even a spark of understanding for the situation in Germany, he told the reporter, the reawakening of chauvinism could have been avoided. Versailles had been a terrible blow for the advocates of reconciliation. "I can hardly blame my students for shouting me down. My feelings are those of despair rather than anger."

Meanwhile the senate investigation was grinding toward its foregone conclusion. In his instructions to the jury on 18 February the rector once more stated that the verdict should be based on its judgment as to whether or not Nicolai had undermined the German war effort. At last Nicolai saw that he had been tricked and that neither the gentleman's agreement with Meyer nor his objection at the start of the trial would be honored. He registered a verbal protest and the following day formally retracted his consent to the hearings. "There can be no doubt," he wrote, that "the question as to what is harmful or useful for the state is a purely historical (or, for contemporaries, political) problem." His conviction that the former rulers of Germany had harmed the nation was as valid as the view that *his* actions were injurious, "and this is no less true because one party calls its own political views patriotic and those of its opponent unpatriotic." But all this was beside the point, "since in my special case *any judgment of a political nature* invalidates the very foundation of these proceedings. I did not appeal to the senate or recognize its competence until you had assured me that all political aspects were to be excluded." Otherwise these hearings were a total waste of everyone's time, for "since all members of the senate disagree with me on what is harmful or useful for the state, any political evaluation of my case would ipso facto be tantamount to my condemnation." He did not wait for the outcome but departed early in March for speaking engagements in Switzerland and was still abroad when the verdict was rendered.

Just before this blow fell, there was another one. On 27 February Frau Nicolai gave birth to a son, named Charles Isaac Sven Otto Romain, Charles after his father's French colleague the physiologist pacifist Charles Richet, Isaac probably after Newton, Sven after some Scandinavian friend, Otto after the composer and original bearer of the name Nicolai, and Romain, of course, after Romain Rolland. It soon became apparent that the child was afflicted with mongolism and would never live up to the promise of his names.

One week later the senate published its verdict, a lengthy document entitled "In the Matter of the Students' Protest against the Teaching Activities of Professor Extraordinary Dr. Georg Friedrich Nicolai." It began with a solemn disclaimer: "It goes without saying that no political considerations were allowed to affect the fact-finding, the deliberations, or the conclusions reached; the sole purpose was to establish whether Professor Nicolai had committed acts that are incompatible with the position of an academic teacher and with the dignity of the university." The conclusion was that he had. The senate was forced to agree with the students that he was both a deserter and a traitor.

There could be no question that Nicolai was a deserter in the technical sense, even if he had acted on the assumption that as a physician he was exempt from bearing arms: "Objectively his conduct in this respect does not appear justified. Precisely because he, as he says, for historical reasons never believed in a German victory, he was duty-bound as a 'good German' to do his part for the hard-pressed fatherland, wherever he was placed." If, as he claimed, his rights had been violated by the military, he should have waited until the end of the war "instead of pursuing his personal interests amidst the terrible distress of the nation." If he deplored the lawlessness attributable to the war, how then could he join common deserters in breaking the law? The only circumstance in his favor was the fact that the military authorities, by taking "half measures" instead of punishing him as the professors thought he should have been punished, had allowed his "awareness of the immoral nature of his desertion to become dulled."

When it came to the crime of treason, no mitigating circumstances could be adduced. Nicolai's wartime writings and speeches sufficed to convict him. It was not the pacifist tenor of the *Biology of War* which was objectionable but rather the numerous statements disparaging Germany, many of them borrowed from enemy propaganda or, worse, suitable for use as enemy propaganda. Had Nicolai not repeated the enemy's charge that all Germans welcomed the war? Had he not called the rumors of atrocities allegedly committed by enemy soldiers a threat to the moral health of the German people, while saying nothing about the rumors of German atrocities that were allowed to poison French and British minds? He had fulminated against the chauvinism of the German press but remained silent on the subject of chauvinism in the enemy camp. He had professed outrage at Germany's attempt to cut Britain's lifeline by submarine warfare but found nothing to say about the inhumanity of the hunger blockade of Germany. He had asserted that millions of Germans approved the introduction of cholera and plague bacilli into enemy countries. His attitude was all the more reprehensible because his writings had appeared abroad, the senators asserted, ignoring the fact that Nicolai had made determined efforts to publish the *Biology of War* at home and that he had not been at liberty when the book finally appeared in Switzerland.

The clearest proof of Nicolai's anti-German bias was to be found in his condemnation of the invasion of Belgium. "Belgium is prostrate and cannot fight back," the verdict quoted from the *Biology of War*. Why then had he not protested the cruel treatment of Germany by the Allies when he had the opportunity to do so in 1919 in the addendum to *Six Facts*? Why had he objected to Bethmann-Hollweg's dismissal of the guarantee of Belgium's neutral status as a scrap of paper, but said nothing when Wilson's Fourteen Points were reduced to so many scraps of paper at Versailles?

The senators did not explain how Nicolai's failure to protest actions taken by the Allies after the war related to the charge of treason during the war, nor were the facts correct. No one had been more outspoken in condemning the Treaty of Versailles than the man who during the war had warned against the dangers of a complete victory by either side. "Make peace while the scales of power are perhaps not yet too unbalanced," he had written on 10 October 1918 in an open letter called "A Warning at the Twelfth Hour." Before 1918 permanent peace would have been impossible, he said, "because it would have been a German-dictated peace." After 1918 it would be an Entente-dictated peace. The victory of 1919 would corrupt the Allies, as the victory of 1870 had corrupted the Germans, "and once Germany lies crushed on the ground, the nations of the Entente will not take the trouble to raise her up again." Even in the midst of this controversy, in the *Daily News* interview, and many times before that, he had denounced the shortsightedness of the Versailles Treaty.

"But the most inexcusable fact," the report continued, "is this: Professor Nicolai, pointing to himself as an example, dared to tell soldiers at a base hospital that 'the only honorable way was openly to refuse to serve and to take the oath.'" That was a clear incitement to disobedience and desertion. Lastly, the reports from the embassies in Scandinavia indicated that Nicolai's speeches there, far from winning friends for Germany, had been highly detrimental to the cause of the Reich. French and English newspapers had seized upon his statement that Germany's desire for war was the principal cause of the war. Copies of his pronouncements had been handed out to German prisoners of war in French camps. "Morally this support of our enemies during the war can only be called treason, even though the facts may not suffice for prosecution under criminal law, and notwithstanding the circumstance that they would fall under a general amnesty."

In conclusion, the senate held that Nicolai had "gravely sinned against the moral principles of right and honor," violated "the fundamental concept of the law itself," and acted contrary to "the ideal of the community per se as a binding contract among social beings." He was guilty because "in the hour of need he coldly abandoned those to whom he belongs, from whom he has received all his mental and physical assets, with whom he should have worked and fought. From a safe port he put poisoned weapons in the hands of their enemies, with whom he chose to make common cause." It was therefore the unanimous opinion of the senate that Professor Nicolai was unworthy of continuing his teaching activities at the university.

This tortuous reasoning would not have stood up in any court of law, not even in a German court. But this was not a verdict arrived at after due process; it was an excommunication. The high priests had driven the desecrator of their cult from the temple. The insult to the Ninety-Three, Germany's academic elite, had at last been avenged.

NOTES

1. For background information on the political attitudes of students and professors at German universities in the Weimar era, two studies, both with extensive bibliographies, were consulted: H. P. Bleuel and E. Klinnert, *Deutsche Studenten auf dem Weg ins Dritte Reich* (Gütersloh: Sigbert Mohn Verlag, 1967), and H. P. Bleuel, *Deutschlands Bekenner, Professoren zwischen Kaiserreich und Diktatur* (Bern: Scherz Verlag, 1968).

2. The following account of the events at the University of Berlin and its proceedings against Nicolai is based on the official report issued by the rector and academic senate under the title *Der Fall Nicolai* (Berlin: Friedrich-Wilhelms-Universität Tagebuch no. 1816, 1920), on Nicolai's formal rebuttal, printed as a brochure, *Richtigstellung des Urteils des Senats*, in Berlin in 1920, and on contemporary newspaper clippings from the Nicolai archive. The author was denied access to the archives of Humboldt University in East Berlin, repository of the files relating to Nicolai's academic appointment and trial.

3. In the student elections a month later the volkish national group captured 1,857 of 2,600 votes cast, as compared with 210 for the Democratic Union, 184 for the Socialists, and 143 for the Jewish minority.

4. Meyer was a signer of the Manifesto of the Ninety-Three of 1914 and the War Aims Declaration of 8 July 1915. The declaration demanded annexation of vast

territories and support for the admiralty's call for unrestricted submarine warfare. After the war he was author of a declaration of German university professors protesting the extradition of the Kaiser to "a partisan court installed by hatred and vengefulness."

5. Eduard Meyer and three influential members of the twelve-man academic senate, the theologians Adolf Harnack and Reinhold Seeberg, and the physiologist Max Rubner.

17. The Rebuttal

Konrad Haenisch was a decent man and anything but a flaming radical. An old-line Social Democrat, he belonged to the revisionist wing which rejected revolution in favor of gradual reform and education. In 1914 he happily surrendered to the intoxicating spirit of national unity, rejoicing that he and his comrades were no longer pariahs but part of the brotherhood of the nation. Later he would say that national and Socialist ideals had never been conflicting ones for him. As a journalist and bookseller he was the nearest thing to an expert on cultural matters in a party that, when the revolution swept it into power, had long been excluded from the domain of higher learning. Thus he was appointed Kultusminister (minister for religious affairs and education) for the State of Prussia and in that capacity had to deal with the universities. The expulsion of a professor whose promotion he had authorized only a year ago was a challenge to his authority as well as personally distasteful to him.

Wilamowitz-Möllendorff set the tone by declaring publicly that Haenisch was an ignoramus in the arts and sciences and unfit to occupy the ministerial chair. The professors refused to acknowledge that times had changed and that the universities must change with them—that war, defeat, and revolution had transformed the society in which they had been part of the ruling elite into a new and uncertain order. At first they meekly awaited the housecleaning to which their new masters seemed committed. When it did not take place, the old arrogance returned quickly. No one was going to interfere in academic affairs; no one was going to open the universities to the lower classes, liberalize the curriculum, force Socialists or Jews onto the faculties, or tamper with professional privileges.

Haenisch, who tried to accomplish these things through persuasion and conciliatory gestures, expressing his hope for "the gradual creation of a new intellectual aristocracy on the foundation of democracy and socialism," was indeed unfit to be minister of education.[1] He was a naive idealist who lacked the ruthlessness to deal with the recalcitrant professors. He reprimanded Professor Träger of Marburg for telling his students that there was no hope for the German people until it repudiated the republic and all its works, but he did not dare relieve him of his post. The right-wing press seized on the affair to brand him as a tyrant and violator of academic freedom, but the professors knew better: they saw him as a paper tiger whom they could safely defy.

Haenisch watched the proceedings against Nicolai from afar, hoping to avoid direct involvement. Rector Meyer claimed to have kept him informed, but his reports must have been misleading, for Haenisch was as slow to get the drift of the hearings as Nicolai had been. The verdict, made public on 9 March and hastily posted on the university bulletin board, took him by surprise. Although he, too, disapproved of Nicolai's conduct in wartime, he was appalled by the bigotry of the senate which had over-stepped its authority and at the same time ignored the critical issue of student discipline. He clearly perceived the threat that would hang over every dissenter from the nationalist gospel if the decision were allowed to stand, and this time he acted quickly and forcefully. Within twenty-four hours he issued a decree annulling the verdict.

A group of students, in grave violation of academic discipline, had pre-vented Professor Nicolai from lecturing, the minister wrote, and Nicolai, "with my approval," sought the protection of the senate, but the latter, instead of protecting the freedom to teach, had violated its own principles by rendering a political verdict. It could not punish anyone for acts cov-ered by an amnesty decreed by the people's elected government; as a purely administrative body, it was not competent to render a political judg-ment; and it did not have disciplinary power over a professor extraordi-nary. "Its verdict therefore has no legal validity whatsoever." The argu-ment that Nicolai had voluntarily accepted the senate's jurisdiction was worthless, since he had rejected it as soon as the investigation moved from the academic to the political arena. While deploring the students' unlawful conduct, the senate had ignored the fact that the rector had been unable to maintain academic discipline. "In light of this fact and in the interest of academic freedom—which must be preserved under all circumstances—I feel obliged to protect Nicolai in the exercise of his duties, should he desire to continue his teaching activities, and to safeguard the academic order within the university with every means at my disposal."[2]

The affair was now a cause célèbre, hotly debated in newspapers and magazines throughout the country, with echoes in the foreign press as far away as Paris and Madrid. Predictably, the left-wing domestic press was outraged by this monstrous intolerance toward a political dissident, though most commentators were careful to express their disapproval of Nicolai's wartime actions. It was the principle that mattered. Had not these same German professors applauded conscientious objectors in the enemy camp, men like Bertrand Russell and Norman Angell, who had gone to jail for their beliefs? "These people have learned nothing and forgotten nothing," one editorialist noted. Another asked how members of the Ninety-Three could sit in judgment over their critic. *Die Freiheit* called it sheer hypoc-risy: "With this verdict the academic senate has condemned itself before the whole world. It has proved that its intellectual and moral level is lower than that of the Tsar's henchmen during the worst reaction in Russia. Even the Tsar's lackeys never dared to strike at the pacifist teachings of Tolstoy (which Nicolai proclaims in altered form), as the lackeys of kaiserism are doing in republican Germany." From Zurich came the comment that the "reactionary students and professors have caused irreparable damage to the prestige and the future of Germany; in Madrid *España* observed that the ideal for which Nicolai was crucified was vastly more noble than the narrow patriotism of his persecutors. Even the cautious *Berliner Tageblatt*, while deploring the acts committed by Nicolai "in his justifiable hatred of the war," suggested that the wartime utterances of many professors, including Rector Meyer, in favor of annexations and blindly nationalistic, had hurt the German cause severely, "and about *them* no senate has anything to say."

The same press praised Haenisch for his firm stand, qualifying its applause only with doubts as to whether he would bolster his brave words with deeds in the face of the onslaught now to be expected from professors and students alike. "We can only hope that he remains steadfast and does not shrink back after the first bold start, as on former occasions," said *Die Freiheit*. With the verdict against Nicolai monarchist Germany had thrown down the gauntlet against the revolution: "should the real battle now be joined, in other words, should Nicolai insist on his rights and the minister keep his promise to protect him with every means at his command, the resulting struggle will be interesting to watch, and its outcome will be of more than symptomatic importance for Germany's future." "All we can say to Herr Haenisch," the article ended, "is, 'little monk, little monk, thou goest on an arduous errand.'"[3]

On this point the right-wing press agreed. Haenisch's intervention on behalf of a traitor repudiated unanimously by senate and students was so grotesque, the *Schlesische Zeitung* declared, that his removal must be demanded. "You want to maintain order in the institutions of higher learning? Try it!'" sneered *Die Gegenwart*. Haenisch had shown an utter lack of understanding of the spirit of German academic youth. "Nicolai is finished, and no ministerial decree can protect him," one newspaper said. Did Haenisch plan to send troops into the university to shield a man whose moral corruption made every good German nauseated? Let him be under no illusions, the *Deutsche Tageszeitung* warned: "He has reached the point where there is no longer room for compromise." The Nicolai Case had become the Haenisch Case.

This time Haenisch did not hesitate. The day after he had annulled the senate verdict, he spoke his mind to a reporter. The Nicolai case was only one in a series of similar incidents, and "our institutions of higher learning are the most dangerous centers of the counterrevolutionary movement today." The danger was all the more serious because it was there that the civil servants of the next generation were created, those whose ideas would determine the future of the country. The reasons for "this most regrettable phenomenon" must be explored, he said, for "in contrast to the revolutionary era of 1848 almost the entire academic world is in the reactionary camp today." He, Haenisch, was averse to punitive measures from the depth of his soul, but overt reactionary attacks such as the Träger affair and the Nicolai Case would not find him wanting in determination. If the pacifist students were to accuse Rector Meyer and his colleagues of having hurt Germany with *their* political utterances and then rioted against these respected scholars, he would protect them just as he was now protecting Nicolai. He would tolerate terrorism neither from the Left nor from the Right.

The hollowness of these brave words was dramatized the next day by the Kapp putsch. In the early morning hours of 13 March Captain Ehrhardt's Marine Brigade marched through the Brandenburg Gate and the government fled. When the putsch failed four days later, Haenisch returned to his office unscathed but shaken. The illusion of his power had vanished. Most students had openly sided with the rebels, and Rector Meyer had declared his allegiance to "Chancellor" Kapp.

In the wake of the putsch a new wave of the "White Terror" swept the country. Its victims were once again the workers, who alone had risen to the defense of the legitimate government. Thousands were rounded up and hundreds were shot. In the punitive expeditions, which the reinstated Socialist government sanctioned in the interest of reestablishing "order," student volunteers distinguished themselves by acts of brutality. The worst of these was the murder of fifteen workingmen from the little Thuringian town of Bad Thal by a detachment of student militia from the University of Marburg. The men were seized at random, marched off for a "court-martial," beaten to a pulp, and shot in small groups along the road.

Haenisch rose bravely to the occasion, demanding punishment for the "cowardly murder gang of Marburg." He would soon have to eat his words. It was his duty to stand up for the students when their honor was being impugned, he was told; as "their" minister he had betrayed their trust. Student representatives from all over Germany met in Marburg and resolved unanimously to protest his conduct. The rector and the senate of Marburg University declared their solidarity with the killers. The latter were tried and acquitted by a court-martial. Later the case came before the civilian court of appeals at Kassel for a jury trial, but the prosecutor himself moved for acquittal.

Haenisch now beat a hasty retreat. The workers were understandably suspicious of reactionary students, he explained, but the students' viewpoint was equally understandable. They were tied to the old Germany with a thousand bonds, "steeped in the Hohenzollern tradition, in the monarchic ideal as such, in the spirit of the oath to country and colors." He would not ask them to "burn today that which you revered yesterday." Unlike the "average pacifist," he knew that the war had been a great spiritual experience for them, and he respected "the old Germanic loyalty of the liege to his lord" which bound them to the imperial family or the lesser dynasties. But they must accept the "transvaluation" of the national idea. He then apologized for his remarks about the killers of Marburg. The students rejected the apology and formally censured Haenisch in the sharpest language for his "irresponsible attacks." He apologized once more, publicly retracting his "harsh expressions."[4] The rector and senate of the University of Berlin meanwhile rejected Haenisch's annulment of the verdict against Nicolai and found that the rector had indeed maintained student discipline and that the senate did have jurisdiction over the matter because it had not concerned itself with crimes that might fall under a general amnesty "but solely with moral worth, which no amnesty can touch." The charge that academic freedom had been violated was utterly rejected: "The Herr Minister may rest assured that no one guards and protects the priceless treasure of academic freedom more faithfully than [signed] Rector and Senate of the Friedrich-Wilhelm-Universität." The triumph of the Right in the universities seemed complete.

The authors of this statement saw to it that this blend of insolence and hypocrisy was given wide publicity, but when the dust began to settle, Haenisch returned to the attack. On 27 April he sent a message to the Prussian legislature: "If the academic authorities had misgivings about Nicolai's fitness as a faculty member, they had the right to initiate disciplinary action against him." The opportunity to do so had arisen, Haenisch pointed out, when Kraus sponsored his promotion, but at that time only formalistic objections were raised, not questions about his moral qualifications. "The Ministry must unconditionally insist," he concluded, "that any action against Nicolai stay within the bounds prescribed by law. For this reason we could not accept the decision of a court of honor as binding even if both parties were willing to abide by it, an assumption which, incidentally, has been challenged by Professor Nicolai." The same statement appeared as an unsigned article in the semi-official *Deutsche Allgemeine Zeitung*. In a general statement to the press Haenisch took an even firmer stand: "Under no circumstances can we tolerate a situation in which academic youth, with utter disregard for academic discipline, takes it upon itself to act against a professor who had incurred its displeasure."

Meanwhile, the object of this controversy was traveling through Switzerland, where he was interviewed, fêted, and listened to with rapt attention by packed halls of students (he had come at the invitation of the Comité des Conférences Universitaires) and the general public. To the Swiss, who were both puzzled and alarmed by the resurgent madness in the Reich, he was the representative of a new and saner Germany. On this trip Nicolai gave the speech entitled "Between the Wars," perhaps his finest piece on the mission of pacifism.[5] He was as critical as any of his detractors with respect to the peace terms imposed on Germany at Versailles, but unlike them he had not advocated a "German peace" to be imposed on the world if Germany won the war. This gave him a moral authority which they lacked. We know, he said, that Versailles is not an eternal peace, for it is not a peace of justice and reconciliation. The details of the treaty were unimportant. What did it matter who owned Alsace, the Tyrol, Fiume, or Danzig? "We know that peace comes not when frontiers are moved," he said, "only when they disappear." The sad lesson of Versailles was that "the national state has shown itself to be as flawed as the dynastic state." Nothing but the abolition of national sovereignties could avert future wars. He recognized that his dream of a powerful League of Nations was not the solution, for it would not stop civil war, a phenomenon which had become almost constant in Russia and Hungary and recurrent in Germany, while Ireland was perpetually suppressed: "We are getting into the habit of violence and lawlessness." Trotsky welcomed the war because he wanted revolution; Nicolai "opposed the war from 1914 on because I did *not* want revolution in Germany." At this point socialism was a leap into the dark, but it was clear that the materialistic view of history was wrong, "for we obey instincts, and instincts are apt to be selfish and brutal." Mankind believes in force. "This is our guilt; this is my view of the war guilt. The historical details can be left to the diplomats, generals, kings, and officials. To change, we must repent; each of us must bear his share of the guilt; every country, including Germany, must face up to its responsibility." The task of the pacifists was not to take sides but to sweep the arena clean, to fight against lies and violence. "We need faith; our only salvation lies in mutuality. Persuasion is better than force; the weapons of the mind are superior to firearms." This was indeed the Tolstoyan creed, updated and buttressed by political facts. But Nicolai closed on a pessimistic note: "Perhaps it is too late, perhaps we can no longer rid ourselves of the bloody spirits the war has conjured up."

The news of the senate verdict enraged him. "The 'facts' established by this honorable body are untrue without exception," he said in a preliminary statement released in Switzerland, "deliberate lies insofar as the senate knew the record, careless slander insofar as it failed to carry out its obligation to examine it."[6] The charge that he had furnished weapons to the enemy while safely abroad was absurd, for the writings to which the senate referred were published while he was in the German army. The charge that he had incited soldiers to desert was one that "I encountered for the first time when I read the 'verdict.' I was not even asked about it in my 'interrogation,' and I am very curious to know in whose brain this lie was hatched." And the assertion that he had made common cause with the enemy was unsupported by any evidence. Nicolai was more blunt than Haenisch in explaining why his colleagues waited a year before attacking him: "The silence of these worthies is not surprising, for the debate over my promotion fell into that part of their lives which began with the 9th of November [1918, the date of the revolution] and inhibited, at least temporarily, the brave expression of their convictions." Then no one knew which way the wind was blowing, but now, "when at least nine or ten thousand students are behind them," the professors had rediscovered their principles. And even then, instead of keeping their promise to settle his case quickly, they had dragged the verdict out "until the bombastic champion of professorial daring stood at the gates of Berlin." The implication that the rector, if not his other attackers, had had advance knowledge of the plans for the Kapp putsch was unmistakable.

The agitation against him had orginated among the professors rather than among the students, Nicolai charged, and for this reason he had never really been angry at the students. But "the Herr Professors in their reply to Einstein, who had asked them to support me, excused their silence on the grounds that *their* students would likewise riot," and that was inexcusable. Cowardice and lack of conviction were inborn character traits, but "in my opinion the wisdom and self-respect of men brought up to be scholars should have kept them from exhibiting these traits in all too public a manner."

Nicolai was confident of winning, for the Germany he still believed in, Kant's and Goethe's Germany, was bound to triumph "over all those elements which the French unflatteringly call *boche*." (A worse insult to the rector and his supporters was hard to imagine.) But he could not afford to settle for a moral victory this time. Even before his return from Switzerland he announced his intention to ask that criminal proceedings for malicious defamation of character be instituted against Meyer et al. This step was unprecedented in the annals of German universities. To take a quarrel between academic colleagues to the courts, even if it had already been aired in the press, was to violate the gentleman's code which governed the professorial club and by which he was expected to abide. A rector, almost by definition, could not be guilty of a criminal act; both his office and his person were sacrosanct. If further proof of Nicolai's unfitness to teach were needed, he had now furnished it. Even men who secretly deplored the verdict felt that he had put himself beyond the pale.

Furthermore, his chances of winning a legal battle in a German court were nil. The judiciary, taken over intact from the old regime, had no love for pacifists, democrats, or socialists. The judges and prosecutors shared the attitudes of their academic brethren in the universities where they themselves had studied law. Protected by a doctrine of "judicial independence" under which judges could not be removed from office, they sided openly with the enemies of the republic, closing their eyes to the most brutal crimes committed in the name of patriotism while handing out harsh punishments to offenders of a leftist persuasion.[7] Nicolai had nothing to hope for from the guardians of the law, least of all when challenging the representatives of the only institution that had survived, untouched, the downfall of the old order. Not surprisingly, the prosecutor refused to press the case, and Nicolai eventually sought redress in civil court, where, of course, his chances were no better.

Meanwhile the battle over the senate verdict was still raging in the arena of public opinion. Upon his return to Berlin in April Nicolai issued a formal point-by-point refutation of the verdict. Published as a pamphlet, it was addressed to the minister of education for transmittal to the senate.[8] In the manner of a trained lawyer, Nicolai challenged both the formal and the material basis of the verdict. As a matter of law the senate was not competent to try him. The validity of the entire procedure rested on his consent, given with the express stipulation that political issues would be excluded. The stipulation had not been respected. When it became clear that he had been tricked into a political trial, he had withdrawn his consent, and therewith the legal basis for a verdict had collapsed. As for the material aspects of the case, he contended that the charge of desertion was legally moot, for while he had in fact deserted, his induction into the army had itself been unlawful. Nicolai was not merely defending himself but was staking out a claim as the leader in the battle against a law-breaking state. To his contemporaries this claim must have appeared as sheer impudence, if not lunacy. As for the moral side, "I have broken no oath, and it is an act of incredible temerity and the height of prejudice to place me— as the senate has done—on a par with common deserters, men who *have* broken their oath, and to saddle me with 'the burden of society's contempt.'" Though the senate had found a mitigating circumstance in the lenient attitude of the military, which might have encouraged him in his reprehensible conduct, "I refuse to accept such charity. Those who do not know, respect, and revere [this principle] do not belong in a university."

All of the quotations from his writings to show his anti-German bias were distortions, "and nearly all are crude, inexcusable falsifications."

Where he was quoted as saying "every German loved and glorified the war," the actual text read "nearly everybody loved the war." Nor had he accused "millions of Germans" of approving germ warfare, but only two individuals, whose names he did not give.

He was attacked for not protesting the Entente's disregard of Wilson's Fourteen Points, but the *Biology of War* was written long before Wilson announced them: "Although I am flattered by the confidence the verdict places in my prophetic gifts, I can hardly recognize a charge based on them, at least not until science has shown them to be attributes of normal persons." The senate seemed to think that he should have expressed "the requisite indignation" in a specific piece of writing, the Addendum to *Six Facts*, "but they seem to disregard the fact that this piece appeared in April 1919, when it was really impossible to predict what would remain of the Fourteen Points." He showed that every quote was inaccurate, taken out of context, or freely invented. "With such methods one can prove anything. 'Give me three lines from any person, and I can have him hanged.' But that was said by Fouché, and he was a French police minister, not a German professor." The senators were unable to find anything suitable, and, "in order to give at least the appearance of having found something," produced "nine distorted or falsified quotations," despite the fact that it is a matter of "professional pride" to scholars to quote accurately.

The charges relating to his wartime actions were equally untrue, Nicolai's pamphlet went on. The gravest was the claim that he had incited soldiers to mutiny or to refusal to take the oath of loyalty. On the contrary, he had told men who "under the guise of pacifism asked me for medical certificates in hopes of avoiding military service" that this was the way of cowards and that, if they were sincere, "the only decent thing to do was to refuse both oath and service outright." The charge was especially perfidious because it made a farce of his entire philosophy: "I, who expressly refused to take the oath so that I might not have to break it some day, and who because of this respect for the oath have suffered much—I am supposed to have incited others to break their oath!" Why had he never been questioned on this charge? And in a footnote he added that he was one of the few Germans who had broken no oath. "One half broke theirs on 9 November 1918, the other half on 13 March 1920, many perhaps on both occasions."[9]

It was true that his writings had been circulated in England and France and that isolated passages had been used for enemy propaganda, but he was as helpless against their misuse by foreign chauvinists as he was against those German chauvinists who extracted passages to serve their own ends. The *Biology of War* had been banned in France no less than in Germany, "for it is a book that attacks every chauvinism and every imperialism on earth." As for his purportedly treasonous activities in Scandinavia, he asked for the pertinent reports from the German embassy on which the accusations were based in order to reply. In reality, he wrote, he had gained Germany many friends in Scandinavia, and the testimony of prominent Scandinavians could be obtained to prove this assertion.[10] "In short," he concluded, the charge of anti-German activities would be justified "only if one were to identify Germany with those who use her name as a shield for brutality, lies, and villainy. Those alone did I and do I attack."

Nicolai closed with a ringing plea for freedom of thought. The senate had called its philosophy a self-evident truth. If so, "then indeed I no longer belong to the community of humans, but neither, in that case, would Luther and Galileo, nor would the men of '48 and the thousands of believers in the social concept of life, from Rousseau to those who took part in the November revolution."

As far as the senate and the academic community at large were concerned, however, this refutation might as well never have been written. The University of Berlin, represented by Rector Meyer, would no longer communicate with Nicolai directly. In the language of a later era, he had become a "non-person."

NOTES

1. For details of the struggle between Haenisch and the universities, see H. P. Bleuel, *Deutschlands Bekenner, Professoren zwischen Kaiserreich und Diktatur* (Bern: Scherz Verlag, 1968), pp. 126–27, 139–41.

2. The text of Haenisch's statement is included in the rector's official report, *Der Fall Nicolai* (Berlin; Friedrich-Wilhelms-Universität Tagebuch no. 1816, 1920).

3. The writer is quoting a remark of the rough-and-ready Landsknecht leader Georg von Frundsberg to Martin Luther, on Luther's departure for Worms to face Emperor Charles V.

4. Haenisch's controversy with the student organizations is described by H. P. Bleuel and E. Klinnert, *Deutsche Studenten auf dem Weg ins Dritte Reich* (Gutersloh: Sigbert Mohn, 1967), pp. 75–78.

5. The manuscript of "Zwischen den Kriegen" is in a collection of postwar speeches by Nicolai in the Nicolai archive.

6. The statement was published in the *Neue Schweizer Zeitung* in March 1920 and was reprinted in Zurich the same year as a pamphlet, *Professor Nicolai und die deutschen Professoren*, by Buchdruckerei Genossenschaft Schweizerischer Sonntagsblätter.

7. Details of these practices are found in H. Hannover and E. Hannover, *Politische Justiz 1918–1933* (Frankfurt-am-Main: Fischer Bücherei, 1966), passim.

8. *Richtigstellung des Urteils des Senats* (Berlin: Privately printed, 1920).

9. The dates refer to the German revolution of 1918, when the professors broke their oath to the king, and to the Kapp putsch, when those who declared for Kapp broke their oath to the republic.

10. The Nicolai archive contains letters from Georg Brandes, Gerhart Gran, Carl Lindhagen, and others which support Nicolai's contention.

18. The Road to Oblivion

Nicolai still had a loyal ally in the minister of education. Haenisch was incensed by the rector's failure to acknowledge Nicolai's refutation and even more incensed by his failure to discipline the rioters. In his report to the legislature he went so far as to accuse him of complicity: "Academic authorities which allow [acts of lawlessness] to occur without taking disciplinary countermeasures, conteting themselves with expressing vague disapproval, become partners in the crime." This was strong stuff. Meyer, who read the press accounts of Haenisch's remarks but was unaware of their official character, lodged an angry protest demanding the retraction of the "absolutely unfounded and totally distorted" allegations. Becker, Haenisch's second in command, to whom the protest was addressed, was unmoved. Since the remark was part of Haenisch's report to the legislature, it was impossible to accede to the demand for "corrections." As for the facts, "the differences between us regarding the interpretation of the procedure agreed to in discussions at the ministry are indeed considerable." Becker went on to quote an earlier communication in which he had said that no unbiased observer could fail to recognize the enormous difference between the alleged purpose of the hearings, as originally announced by Meyer, and the actual conduct of the trial.

But Meyer insisted that the minister had approved the procedure. He again rejected the charge that political issues had been injected into the trial and asserted that the verdict was a moral judgment, requested by both parties and binding on both. The fact that Nicolai had retracted his consent was not mentioned. The Senate had accomplished its task, and that was that.

It was a stand-off, but face-to-face discussions did follow, and both sides adopted a more conciliatory position, at Nicolai's expense. On 26 June, more than three months after the publication of the verdict, Haenisch issued a new decree, in which he conceded that the Senate might have acted in good faith, even though "it could have recognized that Nicolai's protest removed the basis for arbitration." He was satisfied that all parties had acted on the basis of honest convictions. His earlier criticism had been directed not at the integrity of anyone involved, but solely at errors of judgment. If and when Professor Nicolai wished to resume his teaching, however, "I am confident that the senate will take every care to assure that it remains undisturbed." Conciliatory language had been skillfully combined with an unmistakable warning.

The rector posted this decree on the university bulletin board with a postscript of his own. The university had at all times recognized its duty to protect academic freedom. The senate's hands were clean. "If, as hinted in the ministerial decree, Herr Professor Nicolai should resume his lectures after all, I shall ask the students to refrain from disturbances of any kind, and I am confident that they will obey this warning, avoid any new conflict, and add to the dignity of the university by conscientiously respecting the law." Meyer was anxious to give the appearance of bowing to the minister's authority, partly because after the failure of the Kapp putsch he had no hopes of getting rid of him, partly because he wanted to head off Nicolai's threatened lawsuit. He was in any case certain that Nicolai would never lecture at the University of Berlin again. After a last perfunctory letter signed jointly by Meyer and all members of the Senate, reaffirming their original position, the exchange came to an end.

But Meyer did not let the case rest there. The entire correspondence on the matter, together with the text of the senate verdict and a final defiant commentary, was printed and circulated as an official document to the officials of every university and polytechnic institute in Germany. With this move Meyer outmaneuvered the minister, spread the tale of Nicolai's disgrace to the farthest corners of the country, and made certain that no other institution would give shelter to the outcast. The document ended with a masterpiece of innuendo: "Should Nicolai violate his promise [to abide by the senate verdict] and, with the support of the ministry, insist on his formal right to lecture at the university, the latter cannot prevent him, and the rector is forced in his official capacity to do everything possible to avert disturbances on the part of the students."

This dubious accommodation between ministry and university pleased no one. The attacks on Nicolai in the press reached a new peak. The senate verdict was, if anything, too generous, the *Deutsche Zeitung* complained:

> Certain implicit views are not acceptable to the students, for in contrast to the vast majority of their professors they think in terms of race rather than nationality. Thus, if the verdict speaks of [Nicolai's] duty as a "good German," volkish students must object strenuously. Nicolai has never been a German; therefore he cannot have been under any oblication to act as a good German, even though he was beholden to the host nation whose hospitality he enjoyed in good times and whose civil rights he claimed.

Nicolai was not the only object of such attacks. In May F. W. Förster, son of the co-signer of Nicolai's *Appeal to the Europeans* and himself a leading pacifist, was forced to resign from the faculty of the University of Munich. As the liberal paper *Börsenkurier* commented at the time, "academic chairs will soon be filled only by men who can prove their qualifications at nationalist gatherings." Albert Einstein, Jewish, a pacifist, the author of an abstruse, "talmudic" theory, unprepossessing in appearance, was another obvious target. National Socialism was not yet an organized political force, but its spirit was very much alive, and nowhere more so than in the universities.

Among the attacks on Nicolai was that of the *Deutsche Zeitung*. The newspaper had discovered that his writings had been distributed among German prisoners of war in French camps and, worse, that they were used even now in the French-occupied Palatinate as ammunition in the battle over the war guilt question. The paper quoted the respected historian Hermann Oncken as condemning "these rootless pacifist deviates whose pronouncements on the war guilt issue serve as propaganda material for our enemies." Even the trade magazine of German book publishing joined in, rejecting an advertisement for Nicolai's *Six Facts* because "we do not consider it our task to participate in the dissemination of works intended to debase the German Army and its former leaders."

Nicolai had good reason to be dissatisfied with the results of Haenisch's intervention, for academic Germany had branded him as a traitor and deserter. Somehow rector and senate must be forced to rescind the verdict and restore his good name. It was a matter of survival as well as honor, for referrals to his already declining medical practice were bound to fall off if this reputation became accepted, but the question of honor was uppermost.

The way to settle such a question was to force one's opponent to apologize publicly or to fight, as fraternity member Nicolai knew well. Dueling was no longer in fashion, but for the rector to ignore the insults Nicolai had heaped on him, calling him an *agent provocateur* and a dishonorable man, was unthinkable. Yet Meyer could afford to ignore them, for Nicolai was no longer *satisfaktionsfähig* (i.e., the sort of person who could demand "satisfaction" in a duel). In the face of Nicolai's continued provocations he wrapped himself in disdainful silence. Legal action was Nicolai's only recourse, no matter how dim the prospect of success.

His first attempt to obtain redress through the courts was an abysmal failure. The chief prosecutor rejected his demand for a public suit against Meyer et al. out of hand, basing his decision on the records of the senate hearings. Nicolai's attorney asked to see the file but was refused on the grounds that this required the consent of the senate, which would not be forthcoming. It was a strange ruling, his lawyer noted, for under the Constitution an official was entitled to see his file. It was in fact a clear indication that the law was working hand in glove with the professors. Undaunted, Nicolai petitioned the minister of justice, as the authority of last resort, for access to the file, again without success. He then instructed his attorney to bring suit against the rector and the twelve senators in civil court.

The threat of a libel suit troubled the rector, not because he was afraid of losing but because it was undesirable to have the university dragged through the courts. Nicolai's attorney, the distinguished jurist Emil Schweitzer, was a dangerous opponent. The senate verdict had accomplished its purpose, and nothing was to be gained from another battle. Perhaps the trial could be avoided. The new rector (Meyer's term of office had expired) thought so, and two emissaries approached Nicolai with the suggestion that he drop his suit in return for a "revision" of the verdict—that, at least, was Nicolai's explanation of why he did not press his demand for a public suit and delayed his private suit. His version was challenged later by the university's judge advocate, but he was a man obsessed with the truth, and the story is plausible. Under a peculiar statute of limitations in German law, a public suit involving libel had to be instituted within three months. If Nicolai could be induced to let his complaint lapse, the university would be off the hook. For whatever reason, he did let the public suit lapse and delayed the private suit for some time. If he did so in the expectation of a *quid pro quo*, he was headed for another disappointment.

By the time the trial finally got under way in December, Nicolai's opponents had consolidated their position. The senate verdict had been reprinted in the official organ of the Berlin student body, thus becoming even more deeply embedded in the public record. The rector had released the correspondence with the ministry as an official document bearing the clearly prejudicial title The Nicolai Case and had circulated a secret letter to every institution of higher learning in Germany and Austria, containing excerpts from the very files that had been denied to Nicolai and his attorney. His actions were neither necessary to uphold the verdict nor honest in terms of the accommodation reached with the ministry. Nicolai might well have said, with Dr. Johnson, "patriotism is the last refuge of a scoundrel." Another blow came on 27 July, when the representatives of the various student organizations at their annual meeting in Göttingen passed a formal resolution declaring Nicolai unworthy of being a university teacher. Young and old, vocal or silent, the German academic community was united in their rejection of the dissenter and all he stood for.

Nicolai had his defenders, but none of them belonged to the academic establishment. "I seek that one just man (not even the ten for whose sake Sodom and Gomorrah were spared) who will make German scholarship honest again," Nicolai wrote a year later. "An inquiry into this murky business would have to come about if only a single determined individual connected with a university strongly insisted on it."[1] Apart from the Socialist press only Alfred Fried and the equally seasoned pacifist Ludwig Quidde took a public stand. In an article entitled "The Nicolai Case in Its International Significance" Fried called the verdict "an intellectual debacle of as yet unforeseeable dimensions." Already the moral credit of Germany's intellectuals had shrunk more than the gold reserve of the treasury, he wrote. Nicolai was one of the few men listened to with respect abroad. The day would come when the German people would erect monuments to such men. Singlehandedly this dissident had breached the wall of hatred for Germany; the senate had helped to close that breach. Nicolai's "excommunication" would only increase his prestige abroad, "but for the German people this product of academic shortsightedness will once again mean increased hatred, distrust, and, in the long run, unemployment and hunger."[2]

Quidde's act was one of extraordinary selflessness. At Kassel the year before, Nicolai had demanded his ouster from the presidium of the Peace Society, and resigned in protest when the motion failed. However, in the face of the students' action at Göttingen, Quidde put his feelings aside to castigate both the students and the senate whose verdict had inspired their resolution. "Within the pacifist movement I am separated from Professor Nicolai by the sharpest differences, both factual and personal," he began. The senate verdict had led him to read, "for the first time, I am ashamed to admit," the *Biology of War*. He had expected to find in it vicious anti-

German propaganda, "things that I, too, find exasperating, that could drive even a pacifist into the nationalist camp." He had found nothing of the sort. The book showed how widely the reality differed from the propaganda of the German government. It had been a necessary response to the disastrous Manifesto of the Ninety-Three, whose authors had destroyed the credibility of Germany's intellectuals with their patriotic lies. "Such men are sitting in the senate of the University of Berlin. Mindful of their sins against Germany's reputation, they should hang their heads in shame and refrain from pronouncing judgment on a work which, even if erroneous in some details, was a necessary and meritorious reaction against— let us be kind in our choice of words—their folly." The students' resolution at Göttingen showed what devastating effects the verdict had exerted on the morality of the younger generation. "German youth, instead of remaining faithful to its mission of defending freedom of thought, allows its conscience to be violated and joins in the cry of 'Crucify!'—a shameful spectacle, doubly shameful for the senate of the University of Berlin, which bears the chief responsibility for it."[3]

Fried's and Quidde's were isolated voices. The outlook for pacifism in Germany was bleaker than ever before in this frightful summer of 1920. Political murder had long since become commonplace, but the victims had been chiefly the leaders of the revolutionary Left. Now it was the turn of pacifists and other "traitors." The Kapp putsch had failed, but its spirit was very much alive. In May, Hans Paasche, a former naval officer turned pacifist, was assassinated. "There is less safety for political dissidents in Germany today than in the most disreputable South American republic or in the Rome of the Borgias," Harry Kessler wrote in his diary, commenting on the fact that Hellmut von Gerlach, his and Nicolai's friend and fellow-pacifist, had canceled a speaking engagement and was thinking of leaving Berlin because of threats against his life. "After Paasche, Gerlach is next in line," someone close to the terrorists had told an acquaintance of Kessler.[4] The mathematician Emil Gumbel had been beaten and would have been killed had he been at home when the assassins came to look for him. Germany was a very dangerous country for pacifists, the *Journal de Genève* observed from abroad: "Ebert's republic is hardly friendlier than Wilhelm II's monarchy, which at least did not allow them to be put to death by soldiers."[5]

If men like Paasche, Gerlach, and Gumbel were fair game, Nicolai— an outcast whose crimes included, besides pacifism, desertion, and treason, descent from a Jewish father, association with leftists, the writing of anti-German books, scathing criticism of the academic establishment, and now a legal challenge to the dignitaries of the University of Berlin—was in grave danger. Thinly veiled calls for his assassination began to appear in the extremist press. While any prospect of his resuming his role as professor of medicine had now vanished, he remained highly visible in his role as militant pacifist, offering an irresistible target, if not to assassins, then at least to raucous nationalist demonstrators.

On 5 July the Union of Pacifist Students held a meeting with Nicolai as invited speaker. Much in the manner of the rioters of January, nationalist intruders, led this time by the law student Silvio Conti, invaded the hall. Conti's motion to deny the floor to Nicolai was roundly defeated, but it took more than half an hour to restore order. The familiar ritual ensued: finding themselves outnumbered, the troublemakers marched out shouting "All decent Germans, follow us!" They later returned in sufficient strength to break up the meeting. The irony of the scene was recognized by the *Vorwärts* in a wry comment on the foreign descent of the ringleaders: "It is of interest to know who the leaders of the nationalist students are. Last semester it was Herr De la Chevallerie; this semester it is Silvio Conti and his brother Leonardo. These are the 'decent Germans.'"

Barely a week later Nicolai was back at the university for yet another struggle. Somehow a Socialist student group obtained the rector's permission to hold a meeting in the main auditorium devoted to the twin topics of pacifism and socialism. The invited speakers were Nicolai and Georg Ledebour, a fiery orator, the old lion of the Socialist delegation in the Reichstag, now an Independent. For a professor—even an ex-professor—to share the platform with a representative of the proletariat was in itself an affront; to do so within the grounds of the university was a further insult. But the ultimate provocation was the presence of the proletarians themselves. Attracted by Comrade Ledebour's name, they came to the auditorium by the thousands, overflowing into the hallways and causing the frightened rector to call in the security police. Predictably, nationalist students attempted to disrupt the meeting. Blows were exchanged, stink bombs were thrown, and the usual patriotic songs were sung to drown the speakers out, but the patriots were no match for the muscular comrades. As *Die Freiheit* proclaimed the next day, "for the first time the proletarian will was imposed on that bulwark of the reaction, the university." The rector had the yard cleared, and the speakers could proceed in "comparative peace." The discussion, however, was again drowned out by shouts and whistles, though not before the audience had unanimously adopted a resolution calling for the reinstatement of Nicolai.

The two speakers were by no means in agreement. Nicolai again voiced his opposition to all forms of violence, including class war and revolution, which he called "social war." True socialism must come through education, persuasion, mediation, and public enlightenment. Ledebour disagreed sharply, taking the classical Marxist position that the privileged classes would never voluntarily relinquish their privileges. Forcible expropriation and dictatorship of the proletariat were the only means of arriving at socialism. It was an amicable disagreement, for the two men were in accord about their ultimate goals, and Nicolai finally confessed that he had abandoned his stubborn optimism, that pacifism, too, could be realized as a policy only with a proletarian class at the helm of government.

This concession was more than a gesture to his proletarian audience or his fellow-speaker. Thoroughly embittered by his treatment at the hands of academia, Nicolai was turning his back on the middle class as the preserver of German culture. The bourgeoisie, he believed, had abdicated its historical role. Instead of welcoming its liberation from the yoke of militarism, it longed for the martial discipline of former days; instead of building a democratic society, it remained addicted to the Byzantine claptrap of the monarchy; instead of seeking reconciliation with the family of nations, it retreated into dreams of revenge. It was indifferent to the needs of the working class and made no attempt to bridge the gulf that separated it from those uneducated masses. It had become the breeding ground for chauvinism, anti-Semitism, and obscurantism, and nowhere were these attitudes more thriving than in the universities. German scholarship, the finest flower of bourgeois culture, was yielding a poisonous fruit. He, who had tasted of it, was now experiencing its deadly side effects. By contrast, the workers were by and large sensible and realistic. They had been the mainstay of the war effort and were the true pacifists. They might lack a higher education, but they had a firm grasp of the social issues of the day, they were open-minded, and they were the only group in German society that had remained free from the taint of anti-Semitism and jingoism. Their leaders had betrayed them, but their survival as a disciplined force amenable to reason offered the sole hope for the future.[6] This did not mean that Nicolai accepted the doctrine of the dictatorship of the proletariat, though he never explained how he expected to proletariat to become the ruling class without a revolution, which he abhorred as both unnecessary and ineffective. His approach to socialism was fuzzy, moralistic, and utopian, closer to the revisionist than to the revolutionary wing of the movement, yet embracing neither.

This mass meeting at the university marked the end of Nicolai's career as a public speaker in Germany. Although the resolution demanding his reinstatement was gratifying, he knew that nothing could come of it. He had won a pyrrhic victory: the rector announced that henceforth the university would be closed to all political gatherings. The student representatives passed—against the votes of the Socialist minority—a motion disapproving the events connected with the Nicolai-Ledebour rally and demanding that outsiders be barred from the premises. While this might seem to be a step toward peace within the citadel, its real intent was to affirm the insular character of academic institutions. The university existed for the students, a privileged group, not for the uneducated masses. Talk of opening the institutions of higher learning to the workers was dangerous Socialism. A motion to censure Haenisch for his remarks about the Marburg "murder gang" was narrowly defeated, not because it would not have passed but only because the text of his statement was not available at the time of the motion. In the same spirit the student Biertimpel, at this time still in good standing, was reprimanded for sending to every German university the announcement of a vote of no confidence against Haenisch and a demand for his replacement by an "expert." Neither the minister nor Nicolai could take much comfort from these goings-on. Nicolai could only wait for the long-delayed libel suit against the former rector and his colleagues to get under way.

NOTES

1. *Die Zukunft* 29, no. 48 (27 August 1921), p. 255.

2. Alfred H. Fried, "Der Fall Nicolai in seiner internationalen Bedeutung," *Die Weltbühne* 16 no. 15 (8 April 1920):389–92.

3. "Nochmals der Fall Nicolai," *Berliner Tageblatt*, 11 August 1920.

4. See Harry Count Kessler, *Tagebücher 1919–1937*, ed. Wolfgang Pfeiffer-Belli (Frankfurt-am-Main: Büchergilde Gutenberg, 1971), p. 225.

5. *Journal de Genève*, 3 June 1920.

6. This summary of Nicolai's views on the bourgeoisie and the proletariat is culled from newspaper reports of the joint Nicolai-Ledebour rally at the University of Berlin on 12 July 1920 and from the draft of a speech, "The Moral Tasks of the Proletariat," in the folder labeled "Pacifist Speeches" in the Nicolai archive.

19. On the Legal Merry-Go-Round

It was one of life's small ironies that the lawsuit that pitted the outcast against the academic establishment was entered into the court records as *Nicolai vs. Cohn*, an astronomer named Cohn, a member of the senate, being first in the alphabetical list of defendants. To see a man named Cohn at the head of the list of upholders of patriotism must have confused Nicolai's "German-thinking" enemies, who may have wondered whether this was a quarrel between two Jews.

For Nicolai, winning his legal battle had become an obsession, and the outlook was anything but favorable. When the court convened at last on 16 December 1920, attorney Emil Schweitzer's petition to the minister of justice asking for access to the record of the senate hearings was still unanswered. On 1 October Meyer, now the ex-rector, publicly stated that the senate's verdict was final and that the Nicolai Case was closed. The defendants' strategy was clear: they would force the plaintiff and his lawyer to grope in the dark.[1]

Schweitzer attacked at once. A month before the trial opened he published an article in *Die Weltbühne* accusing the custodians of the law of collusion with the academic authorities in an attempt to conceal the true facts. He reasserted Nicolai's claim that, "for reasons of collegiality," when the university's emissaries approached him with the prospect of a revised verdict, he allowed the criminal charges against Meyer et al. to lapse. He, Schweitzer, had respected this agreement, although he did not like it: "I was loath to remain silent, because I do not like to remain silent when I see an honorable man wronged. I was content to remain silent because the truth behind the senate verdict must be so devastating for its authors that I would have been pleased—in the interest of all German scholars—to leave the guilty parties an opening for a decent retreat. For there can be no doubt that the verdict against Nicolai is a tissue of untruths and distortions."

He then examined the legal aspects of the case. Rector Meyer had told the minister of education that the verdict was a "private opinion" rather than an official judgment. "I accuse the former senate, whose members include jurists, of having played a false game not only with Nicolai but with the minister as well." In claiming that all parties had agreed to abide by the verdict, Meyer had glossed over the fact that Nicolai had withdrawn his agreement to accept the authority of the senate. The senate had acted like "a shady business firm holding a customer to a contract signed in a thoughtless moment." Any lawyer knew that Nicolai's consent was not binding, said Schweitzer, yet the distinguished jurists who sat in the senate had condoned this flagrant breach of the law. But the worst disgrace was the fact that the senate had treated its political opinions as a moral imperative, and then denied that its judgment was a political one. "I know the tune and I know the words," Schweitzer exclaimed. "Since Bismarck's day Socialists and Centrists have been accused of besmirching Germany's image abroad. But until now all these conservative and national-liberal politicians have never had the audacity to claim that such attacks were nonpolitical. That hypocrisy was to be reserved for the Berlin senate." Nicolai had chosen his counselor well: Schweitzer was as articulate, as abrasive, and as passionately devoted to the cause of justice as was his client.

In his preparatory brief Schweitzer asked the court to find the senate verdict legally invalid because Nicolai had not submitted to such a judgment but merely asked the protection of the senate against the rioters, because the senate lacked disciplinary powers, and because the verdict had been annulled by the education minister. At the trial he extended the motion and asked the court to rule that the defendants, as private persons, had no right to render a disciplinary judgment, and that it enjoin further dissemination of the verdict.

Defense attorney Beer declared that he would not do the plaintiff and his counselor the favor of entering into the substantive aspects of the case. The court had neither the authority nor the means to verify the factual basis of the senate verdict. Nor was this a proper civil lawsuit as defined by the statute governing the powers of courts. In any event, this court lacked jurisdiction over the defendants, all but one of whom resided outside its district. Finally, legal considerations aside, it was "*a priori* impossible" for university professors to make false assertions in an official verdict.

None of the defendants saw fit to appear. Nicolai submitted in evidence his printed refutation, then protested Beer's argument "in very temperamental language," as the right-wing *Tägliche Rundschau* put it with unaccustomed understatement. Schweitzer called attention to the fact that the minister had not disciplined Nicolai for publicly accusing university officials of lying and fabricating evidence. The minister, too, he said, was aware that his client was the victim of gross injustice. Schweitzer rested his case on the dual argument that the senate verdict constituted an improper exercise of authority and that it was full of untruths. The court took the case under advisement and adjourned until 20 January 1921.

Press coverage was rather scanty and, on the whole, restrained this time, perhaps because there was no decision to report, perhaps because just then the case was overshadowed by other sensations, such as the Bad Thal murder trial, which had reached the court of appeals in Kassel. A Bavarian newspaper predicted that "student youth will never and under no circumstances accept such a professor, regardless of whatever legal considerations may guide the court's decision." *Die Freiheit* used the occasion to remind its readers that ex-Rector Meyer, the principal defendant, was the protector of the infamous Biertimpel, one of the ringleaders in the anti-Nicolai rioting, now convicted of embezzlement, and that the senate had taken its stand with the mob led by this man.

Nicolai's patience was being sorely tested, for there was a further postponement of the trial until 24 February. Meanwhile the "battle of the files," as the newspapers called the struggle for access to the senate records, was being waged with increasing heat. The minister of justice at last responded to Schweitzer's petition of 18 August, perhaps because the delay had become embarrassing. He no longer objected to releasing the records, he said, since his colleague at the ministry of education had notified him that *his* department had no objections. The prosecutor, however, told Schweitzer that the records had been returned to the university, and, as before, the rector refused to let them see these files. Schweitzer filed a formal complaint with the minister of education, pointing out that the records were the source of damaging quotations used by the rector in his secret circular to other universities, the dissemination of which the lawsuit was designed to halt. (Indeed, the obstruction of justice was so crass that even the hostile *Tägliche Rundschau* was moved to observe that "Herr Haenisch may well find that the petitioner has a rightful claim.")

Haenisch was helpless, as the records were no longer at the university but once more in the custody of the justice department. He notified the minister of justice of Schweitzer's desire to examine them. When Schweitzer went to the ministry of justice to do so (by now it was May 1921, and *Nicolai vs. Cohn* had long since been decided and the decision appealed), he was turned down again. He protested in writing against "the coordinated sabotage of my client's rightful interests by certain subordinate authorities." (He should have included the minister of justice himself among the saboteurs.) But the farce was nearing an end. On 23 May, nearly a year after his first request to the rector, Schweitzer was informed that the records were no longer part of the prosecutor's files, and that there was concern about the fact that in the interval his client had brought suit against the former rector and senate, for the records contained information pertinent to that suit. (This was, of course, precisely why Schweitzer and Nicolai wanted them.) The records were now in the custody of the minister of education, the two were told. Schweitzer knew when he was beaten. The Prussian bureaucracy had shown itself highly efficient at being inefficient.

The postponement of the trial allowed Nicolai to accept an invitation to lecture from the students of the University of Zurich. The *Neue Zürcher Zeitung* greeted him as the "bold scientist whose ideas, proclaimed when he stood alone, are now the common property of many." It was his "immortal feat" to have retained his scientific clarity amidst the raging war fever. In Lucerne a newspaper welcomed "the famous pacifist, whom our readers will be interested in meeting, now that his lawsuit is about to be decided in court." Once again he had made the leap from pariah to celebrity. He returned to Germany rested and ready once more to face the enemy.

It was upon his return that he learned of the printed circular disseminated by the rector as the official record of the senate findings. Angrily he demanded that Steckel, the new rector, transmit a copy of his refutation and a new rebuttal to the recipients of the circular. In that rebuttal he developed the argument on which he would henceforth base his strategy: "It is not my fault if these questions touching upon my honor are as yet unresolved. In the enclosed memorandum [the refutation] I have refuted the charges point by point, using sharper language than I can repeat here. In doing so I was confident that the professors would either repudiate my insults or retract theirs. They have done neither." "Not only did I give the senators ample opportunity to proceed against me, but I have instituted a lawsuit to have the verdict set aside. In doing so I was aware that from a purely legal standpoint the admissibility of the suit was doubtful, but I assumed that the senators would be happy to prove before Prussian judges that I was wrong in accusing them of untruthfulness. But there, too, they seek to evade me in every way possible." Hiding behind procedural and technical details "they will not defend themselves against the charge of lying." They had even refused to repeat their accusations in court. "This may be procedurally correct, and in certain circles it may be no dishonor thus to shift the center of the controversy, but it certainly goes against all academic traditions."

This document was written well before the trial resumed. Nicolai evidently expected to lose the court battle, but his real purpose was to challenge his opponents' facts and methods. His only hope of smoking them out lay in an attack on their honor. They could ignore him as a convicted felon, they could ignore the press as beneath their dignity, but they could not ignore a challenge to their honor. If an unbiased body of scholars were to demand an accounting of their machinations, the truth would have to come out and his good name would be restored. This was another miscalculation, of course, as Steckel nipped his plan in the bud by refusing to transmit the material Nicolai had sent him.

For the next stage of the trial Schweitzer submitted a lengthy brief stating, among other things, that the injury inflicted on his client by the senate was indeed a proper subject for a civil suit, for the defendants had represented their verdict to the minister as a private opinion and could therefore claim no greater immunity than, say, the governing board of a private club. Though fully aware of the legal irrelevance of the verdict, they had fostered the impression that it was an official document. Beer's contention that they had acted in an official capacity and could not be sued as private citizens must therefore be rejected, as must the assertion that the suit offered no basis for fact-finding by the court. Nor could the defense claim that a cease-and-desist order was inappropriate if it were proved that the defendants were in fact guilty of an improper act.

In addition Schweitzer obtained an opinion from Geheimrat Heilberg, an expert on political law attached to the superior court of Breslau. Heilberg was asked two questions: was the senate verdict nonpolitical or did it contain political arguments, and, if so, were such arguments, when used by a court of honor, compatible with freedom of conscience and did they constitute a threat to the political freedom of professional men? His answer was that the verdict *was* political and that the arguments *did* constitute a threat to individual freedom. Were Nicolai's attempts to influence public affairs a subject of discussion in the verdict, and were they decisive for the outcome, Schweitzer asked Heilberg. They clearly were, said Heilberg, and the senate's claim that it had excluded political considerations was untenable. Whether or not Nicolai's writings were correctly quoted, his criticism of Germany's conduct of the war was a political evaluation, just like the opposing view in the verdict. Even the incitement to desertion, if true, reflected Nicolai's political judgment: "The verdict states that such acts would have led to Germany's destruction. But this shows precisely that the question is one of differences of political opinion, regardless of whether the charge itself is true." Heilberg's conclusion must have startled the senate: "No unprejudiced student of history will deny that revolutions and counter-revolutions, which from the viewpoint of prosecuting attorneys are nothing but a series of grave crimes, have become starting points for a new and burgeoning life for many a nation." This was not an endorsement of Nicolai's views but merely proof that "even a crime that leads to the destruction of one's own state can be an important political act."

As for the political freedom of professional men such as doctors and lawyers, Heilberg pointed out that their conduct was regulated by boards dealing with violations of professional ethics in the manner of courts of honor. However, the Prussian law of 1851 stated that "political, economic, or religious beliefs can never be the concern of a court of honor." The bar association fell back upon this principle in 1889, when it refused to discipline an attorney for publicly shouting "Hurrah for International Social Democracy." It reaffirmed it ten years later with the declaration that a lawyer was entitled to participate in politics "even if it advances the cause of socialism." In short, the senate had acted improperly by condemning Nicolai for his political beliefs. Its verdict was a grave threat to the freedom of thought of professional persons and to political freedom in general.

The hearing on 24 February brought no surprises. The small courtroom was filled with spectators, mostly Nicolai's supporters. As before, the defendants were absent. The three-man court heard oral arguments. Schweitzer and Beer engaged in a heated exchange, the former demanding that the defendants be placed under oath, the latter challenging the admissibility of the entire lawsuit. Nicolai reiterated his contention that his consent to the senate proceedings had been obtained under false pretenses. He had let the criminal suit of the previous summer lapse because he had been told that the verdict would be revised. It was not true that the prosecutor had refused to take action. "I must accuse the distinguished senators of lying." The ministry of education had made the same accusation: "The picture is so clear that it should be easy for the court to decide for the triumph of justice."

Schweitzer stressed the fact that his client had been assured that political issues would be excluded from the hearings. The judge pointed out that the minister had left the judgment up to the senate. "Unfortunately," Schweitzer replied, "the senate has denied us access to its records. Nicolai had no inkling that *his* conduct would be the subject of an inquiry when he complained about the rioting of the students." Citing the Heilberg opinion, he accused the senate of rendering the worst kind of political verdict. Even Karl Liebknecht, when sent to the penitentiary for high treason, had not been condemned by his peers; the bar association had recognized the political character of his motives. "I consider the verdict of the senate a tissue of 'untruths,' to avoid a sharper term, designed to destroy a man."

The spectators burst into applause and were sternly rebuked by the judge. Beer, summing up for the defense, replied that in the end it did not matter how the senate had arrived at its verdict, that Rector Meyer represented one view of the world, Nicolai another. Meyer's was the correct one, of course, and the only thing that mattered was that it should triumph.

Commenting on this departure from legal reasoning, Emil J. Gumbel, who was covering the trial for the *Deutsche Montagszeitung*, called Beer's remark an open invitation to a political verdict, "but we hope that Prussian judges will not render a second political judgment." He should have known better, for his investigations of right-wing terrorism had given him more than a taste of Prussian justice in the republic. On 11 March the court rejected Nicolai's suit, ostensibly on the grounds that his dispute with the senate was not a proper matter for litigation. Contrary to his claim, said the court, the defendants had acted not as private persons but as a public corporation charged with settling the conflict by the education minister, the plaintiff, and the students. The dissemination of the verdict by the rector was not in itself an illegal act. The plaintiff had belatedly objected to the introduction of political issues, but the defendants rightfully claimed that the verdict dealt solely with the moral qualifications of a faculty member. A cease-and-desist order was not needed, for if in fact the verdict contained deliberate untruths, it would be a proper cause for a criminal libel suit rather than a civil suit. (The court conveniently forgot that the public prosecutor had rejected Nicolai's demand for just such a suit.) For these and other reasons the plaintiff's complaint must be denied in its entirety, said the court, and the plaintiff must bear the cost of the trial.

The court had adopted Beer's argument in full. The battle was lost, but the war was not over. Nicolai promptly announced his intention to appeal and, this time, to sue for damages as well. He then left for an "antimilitarist congress" at the Hague to act once more as spokesman for German pacifism. On his return, he renewed the demand for disciplinary action against Meyer and company which had been rejected earlier by the minister of education on the grounds that a civil suit was pending. That objection having been removed, Nicolai argued, a hearing by the minister was now his only means of confronting the allegations which the senate refused to substantiate in court, while, in the meantime, the minister should reinstate him in his teaching position. But Haenisch had no taste for another defeat.

From now on Nicolai's main effort was to draw the professors into a direct confrontation. He denounced them publicly whenever he could, clinging to the hope that a strong enough provocation would force them to respond. He made new enemies, among them the editor of the *Berliner Tageblatt*, Theodor Wolff, the same timid liberal who had been afraid to review the *Biology of War*, and whom he now accused of abetting liars by refusing to print a comment "from a highly respected source" urging an impartial inquiry to determine who was lying, Nicolai or his opponents.[2] He found an ally in Stössinger, the editor of the socialist *Die Freiheit*, who called Wolff's refusal a grave violation of journalistic ethics. *Die*

Freiheit would keep up the battle for the truth, "since the bourgeois press will not do so, until the tainted professors come out of hiding, even if journalists of Theodor Wolff's ilk continue to shield them."

He found other allies. The League of Pacifist Students demanded that Meyer and the former senators either refute Nicolai's insults for the sake of their honor and that of the university or retract their verdict. The ploy only succeeded in endangering the career of these young idealists. Rector Steckel called their president, a young man named Medding, on the carpet and threatened to dissolve the League or even expel its members unless the letter was withdrawn. It would not be dignified by an official response. Nothing could force the senators to reopen the Nicolai Case. Nicolai was incapable of insulting them: "German professors are above such things." It would do Nicolai no good to sue again, for the court would deny him the right to establish material facts. In effect, Steckel was admitting that Beer's retreat into legal technicalities at the trial reflected the university's desire to avoid exposure of the machinations by which the senate had tricked Nicolai into agreeing to the hearings and doctored the evidence against him (at least that was Nicolai's interpretation of Medding's written report of the interview). Any court, Steckel told Medding, would take the position that twelve respected German professors, among them a famous jurist, would never resort to slander, that Professor Meyer was incapable of acting like an *agent provocateur*, and that it would take the court less than half an hour to convict Nicolai of libel.

Nicolai then asked Maximilian Harden to publish an "Open Letter to the Academic Teachers of Germany" in *Die Zukunft*. Harden, whose flair for the sensational had been balanced recently by his instinct for self-preservation, hesitated. "I don't see how [the letter] can lead to unpleasantness for you, Herr Harden," Nicolai wrote him. He had not asked him to take sides, only to bring the matter before the public. "There are no Brutuses or Zolas in the land of the linden and the oaks. I am riding alone toward adventure, I only want a chance to show my *panache*." Nationalist students had asked him how he dared to call the rector a liar and told him that they would report his remarks to Meyer himself. "I told them that they could give me no greater pleasure, for if the rector still refused to sue me they could see for themselves that something was rotten."

Harden yielded and printed the open letter with a postscript disavowing any intent to take sides in the controversy, "which Professor Nicolai seeks to keep from silting up." He had always considered it his duty to "open the door to someone who finds no outlet for his grievance elsewhere, even a person of lesser intellectual stature than the author of the *Biology of War*." Nicolai retold his story, "not by any means to convince [the reader] of the justice of my cause, but to call attention to the fact that for almost two years university professor Meyer has let himself be called a liar and *agent provocateur* by university professor Nicolai without so much as batting an eyelash or responding to my suit." Either he was a slanderer who did not belong in a university or the Thirteen were.

He got at least a slight reaction to this latest attack. The judge advocate of the university, one Herr Wollenberg, who as such was a permanent member *ex officio* of the senate, wrote Harden. The senate had never offered to revise the verdict in return for Nicolai's dropping the criminal libel suit, he asserted. Nicolai was elated. At least the enemy had entered into a debate over a fact, even if it was a secondary one. "The professors would have been smarter to keep silent," he wrote Harden, "for this kind of rebuttal basically constitutes an admission of their guilt." Now they could not object to the introduction of factual evidence and reject his complaint on purely formal grounds when the case went to appeal.

Wollenberg's rebuttal was distributed to the press, and Nicolai pounced on this additional chance to nail the enemy. The emissaries who had conducted the negotiations for the senate were officials of the ministry who could verify his story. Again *Die Freiheit* was a friend in need. "It is high time that the Senate responds to Nicolai's demand that he be sued for libel," it declared, "so that at last this worst of scandals can be resolved. The German people cannot allow its academic teachers to imitate the formula used by the perjured [French] generals in the Dreyfus Affair, 'la question ne sera pas posée.'" The question would have to be asked and answered.

The hapless Herr Haenisch felt that he had done enough. Nicolai had become a thorn in his flesh. He turned down yet another request for disciplinary proceedings against the senate or against Nicolai himself, demanded by Nicolai on the grounds that it continued to disseminate a verdict which he, the minister, had annulled. He saw no reason to take such action against either party so long after the case had been officially closed. He had "sufficiently reprimanded" the senate for its disregard of his ministerial directive, he claimed, and he reminded Nicolai that the ministry had participated in the protracted negotiations of the summer of 1920 intended to reach an "amicable settlement."

It was now January 1922, and Nicolai was preparing to leave Germany. When Haenisch turned him down, he went to the prime minister of Prussia, Otto Braun. Braun coldly replied that the case fell into the purview of the minister of education, and there the matter ended. Politicians and bureaucrats were weary of Nicolai's ceaseless nagging. The appeal to a higher court was still pending, but Nicolai knew that he had no chance of winning. The great controversy had indeed " silted up."

There was still another bit of legal unpleasantness ahead. On 24 February 1922, after many delays, Nicolai's other libel suit, the action against the former air force captain Wilamowitz-Möllendorff, came to trial before the municipal court of Charlottenburg.[3] At issue was the defendant's article, written at the height of the agitation surrounding the student riots of January 1920, accusing Nicolai of the theft of articles of clothing. The courtroom was packed once more. The Bund Neues Vaterland had alerted ten foreign correspondents, as well as the local press, to the significance of the trial in Nicolai's struggle against the university.

The captain acknowledged authorship of the article. The seizure of the airplanes, he said, might be considered merely misuse of government property, since they were eventually returned, but the theft of clothing had involved burglary and amounted to a felony. The flight had been planned by a political group close to Nicolai—Spartacus—to enable him to spread anti-German propaganda abroad. He was the intellectual author of the enterprise, which foreign diplomats had called a blow to the prestige of Germany's armed forces and which had resulted, the captain wildly claimed, in the death of several hundred thousand German soldiers. There had been no connection between the publication of the article and the events at the university.

Schweitzer, again at Nicolai's side, challenged this last statement immediately. Had the article not ended with a direct reference to his client's unfitness as an academic teacher? Nicolai called the captain's testimony complete fiction. As press officer of the air force, he could have had no factual knowledge of the flight. Witnesses for the defense, including the commanding general of the air force and the inspector of the air base at Neuruppin, where the venture began, testified that it was "generally assumed" that Nicolai had chartered the flight, but conceded that all they knew was hearsay. Everybody thought that the articles in question had been forcibly removed from an iron locker. But the witness Haase, who participated in the escape, told a different story. The would-be deserters needed a fourth man, and a "friendly couple" from Berlin told him of a gentleman who wanted to leave Germany but who would not reveal his identity until they reached Copenhagen.[4] Nicolai appeared at the air base in dark glasses at four o'clock in the morning, as instructed, and knew nothing about the preparations for the flight.

After four hours of deliberation, the court found the defendant guilty, in accordance with paragraph 185 of the civil code. The article clearly revealed libelous intent, as the testimony yielded no evidence that Nicolai was the intellectual author of the flight. The court nevertheless held that the defendant had acted entirely in good faith, since the official reports available to him created the presumption that Nicolai was the author of the plan. The court was unanimous in its opinion that the plaintiff had participated in a act of desertion in wartime. He was therefore gravely compromised in the eyes of the nation and could not claim the full protection of the law to which an "intact person" was entitled. The defendant was fined two hundred marks, and the plaintiff was given the right to publish the verdict in the *Deutsche Tageszeitung*, where the libelous article originally appeared.

Nicolai lost far more than he had gained with this verdict. The court was forced to rule against the captain on technical grounds but exonerated him morally. Two hundred marks was a token fine, barely the equivalent of one dollar at the current rate of exchange. It also administered a gratuitous slap in the face to the injured party. The nationalist press was jubilant, although "for the patriotic elements among the German people Professor Nicolai had long since been proved guilty," as the *Deutsche Zeitung* commented in a typical editorial. The Socialist press came to the opposite conclusion. It was not Nicolai who was compromised, *Die Freiheit* declared, but the court. The militaristic madness was not yet cured. The trial had illuminated one of the darkest chapters of the war. "If Professor Nicolai did indeed desert, he did so for the cause of humanity. If Wilhelm of

Hohenzollern, Ludendorff, and the others had, for the same reasons, drawn the consequences *he* drew a few years earlier, things would be different in Germany today." *Die Neue Zeit* called the verdict "peculiar in more than one respect." "It seems that the revolution still has not penetrated the consciousness of the overworked judges. There is no other explanation for the strange mildness of the judgment."

The most detailed report came from an "occasional contributor" to the *Prager Presse*, a liberal German-language newspaper in Prague. This writer analyzed the trial in depth, recounting how defendant Wilamowitz had demanded the introduction of the senate files into the record in order to denigrate Nicolai's character, and how Schweitzer had protested that, much as he would like to see those files, the motion was nothing but an attempt to obstruct the proceedings. He, Schweitzer, knew from years of bitter experience that the senate would never part with the files, being fully aware that they contained deliberate lies and lacked a proper foundation. The readers of the *Prager Presse* also got a summary of Schweitzer's argument that the libel suit ignored the captain's charge of desertion because it involved a political act beyond the competence of any court. The Kaiser had been similarly accused of desertion and had refrained from legal action, apparently for the same reason. Nobody could be surprised, the reporter concluded, that a nationalist judge had condemned Nicolai's pacifism and the flight that was its outgrowth. That he had nevertheless found against the libeler, however gentle, the reprimand was a small but welcome step forward: "This first public trial in this matter, forced by Professor Nicolai—albeit after two years of waiting—is by no means a rehabilitation of the Prussian bureaucracy, which continues to prove that it has learned nothing since the revolution, but it is, perhaps, a beginning." This "occasional contributor" was none other than Nicolai himself.[5] It was perhaps the last and possibly the only time that he could laugh at his enemies.

NOTES

1. Principal sources for this chapter are a file labeled "Universität-Kultusministerium" and a collection of contemporary newspaper clippings, both in the Nicolai archive. The file contains copies of the various legal briefs filed by Nicolai's attorney; the petitions to the several ministries; the correspondence with Rector Steckel; the expert opinion by Justizrat Heilberg; the exchange with Maximilian Harden concerning publication of Nicolai's open letter in *Die Zukunft* and related matters; and the report of the pacifist student Wolfgang Medding to Nicolai concerning his meeting with the rector, as well as official copies of the judge's verdict.

2. In all likelihood, the "highly respected source" was Albert Einstein, for later, in an open letter to *Die Zukunft* of 27 August 1921, Nicolai refers to Wolff's refusal to print a letter by Einstein.

3. The following account of the libel suit against the younger Wilamowitz-

Möllendorff is based on an extensive file in the Nicolai archive containing, among other things, the official transcript of the Charlottenburg court's verdict.

4. Haase's testimony and Nicolai's agreed: Nicolai stated that he learned of the would-be deserters from an officer of his acquaintance whose name he could not reveal even after all this time.

5. A typewritten draft of the report in the *Prager Presse* with corrections and insertions in Nicolai's hand and a notation in Fräulein van Kampen's hand is in the Nicolai archive. Additional correspondence there indicates that Nicolai had a standing invitation to contribute articles of interest to this newspaper.

20. Farewell to Europe

While the prophet was struggling for survival in his own land, his star was shining more brightly than ever in foreign skies. Nicolai was an honored guest in Holland, Austria, Switzerland, even France. Leading Scandinavians wrote Nicolai testimonial letters regarding his activities in their countries during the war. Visitors came from Germany and abroad to ask his advice on the tasks of pacifism in these trying times or simply to pay homage to a martyr of the movement. Translations of the *Biology of War* appeared in Russia, Finland, Romania, Argentina, and Japan.

Why did his ideas find their strongest echo in these particular countries? The war between the most advanced nations of Europe had had a profoundly shocking effect on the others, who were accustomed to look to Europe for cultural and spiritual guidance. European civilization, that splendid edifice which the rest of the world had admired and imitated, had collapsed like a house of cards before the barbaric forces of nationalism and militarism. The promise of unending progress had ended with death and destruction, poverty and famine. What hope was there for mankind now? The question was especially distressing for many Eastern Europeans, South Americans, and Orientals, who had looked to Germany. A humane, orderly society had given way to anarchy and brutality. Was this the meaning of German philosophy and science, music and art, discipline and efficiency? These were, of course, the very questions Nicolai had been asking.

Among Nicolai's visitors was the young Romanian writer Eugen Relgis.[1] The time was July 1921, the place his consulting rooms on Kurfürstendamm. For the visitor, who had translated excerpts from the *Biology of War* into his native language, it was a solemn occasion. For him Nicolai was an innovator, larger than life. As Marx had replaced utopian with "scientific" socialism, so the biologist-evolutionist Nicolai had replaced utopian with scientific pacifism. His logic was simple but compelling: biology was the key to man's future, and biological imperatives were forcing the human race to seek alternatives to war. Like Galileo he had challenged an established dogma, the pseudo-Darwinian dogma of war as an instrument of natural selection, but unlike Galileo he had not recanted. While waiting to meet him, Relgis wrote, "I imagined the man of the future, seeing him alternately as a titan dominating the machines and as a sort of demiurge with a gigantic brow, reclining in an armchair and poring over a yellowing folio." He reverently describes the setting: "In the waiting room. The author of the *Biology of War* is attending his cardiac patients. I have time to order my thoughts, like a fisherman arranging his lines, looking meanwhile at the walls and bookcases that testify to the travels of a savant." The room held a collection of art objects and exotic weapons—tribal spears, sabers, yataghans, ancient firearms. "In a glass showcase a pale Buddha smiles in divine beatitude amidst other

Indian and Chinese statuettes, mementos of a voyage to the Far East. Various English lithographs evoke Dickens. A recent photograph of the professor reveals the torment—traces of the lynching, one might say— that he had endured at the hands of that academic youth which so often has been the most potent tool of the Reaction. How could students attack the man who had proclaimed the unity of civilization in the midst of a fratricidal war?"

At last the visitor is ushered into Nicolai's study:

> a room lined with books, tables piled high with journals and manu- scripts, cabinets filled with shiny instruments. I am greeted by a tall, slender man dressed in a chestnut-colored velvet jacket. A vigorous, silent handshake. While we exchange a glance of recognition I espy over his shoulder in the adjoining room a skeleton decorated with a broad sash extending from the clavicle to the pelvis. The savant had adorned it with the colors of some regiment, the colors of killers. Its sarcastic grin dominates the table at which he has given shape to ideas for which solitary minds the world over have waited.

The conversation quickly turned to the deplorable state of the world. Would the younger generation rally to the cause of peace? "We are too few," said Relgis, "but I feel that this epoch belongs to us. The army of tomorrow, the vanguard of the intelligentsia, is girding for battle." "Ah, the intellectuals!" said Nicolai. "I know, so many have betrayed humanity, so many have succumbed to inane 'ideals,'" Relgis conceded. "Here in Germany their number is legion," Nicolai went on: "Colleagues from the laboratory, companions in the struggle against ignorance and disease in former days, they and so many others—all have contributed to the slaugh- ter in the name of their 'ideology.' Words have a terrible power."

During the war, Nicolai continued, his courage had been sustained by the belief that he was speaking for every human being. Now he was dis- couraged. In the wake of defeat German nationalism had entered into its most vehement phase.

"Those are the death throes of spent passions," said Relgis. Nicolai asked again: "where are our intellectuals?" "But we have the masses with us," said Relgis. The masses were well intentioned, Nicolai conceded, but they needed leaders who were dedicated to the welfare of mankind rather than to a single nation or class. Nothing less than the survival of the spe- cies was at stake. It was the overriding duty of "men of wisdom" to fight the "evil traditions" of the past.

Making allowance for a bit of posturing on the part of the great man, we may accept Relgis's description of Nicolai's state of mind in the dismal summer of 1921 as accurate. His public stance was as pugnacious as ever, but before this sympathetic listener he let his guard down and showed his profound disillusionment. "In the muted light I observed the fine, ener- getic features of the man who launched the *Appeal to the Europeans*," Relgis wrote, "a somewhat haggard face, tired from the exertions of med- itation, the temples graying, a legacy of the war and the stubborn effort to defend his honor against the nationalist mob."

309

Yet at bottom Nicolai remained hopeful. In the long run humanity could not be deflected from its path by the antics of short-sighted reactionaries. As a creature capable of reason man had the power to shape his destiny, to take over where evolution had left off, to throw off the shackles of the "evil traditions of the past." History and biology provided better guideposts than "all those simple ethical, philosophical, and aesthetic notions based on intuition," he told Relgis. The bold minds who could show the way were few in number and would always be attacked as enemies of society. "Nevertheless, humanity is moving forward. Those who see only the present with its tragic lies may scoff, but the human mind progresses, always becoming receptive to larger, more creative, more humane ideas. Civilization has developed faster than morality; machines can be perfected more quickly than human beings." One must make allowance for man's tribal heritage, "but the race of Cain must disappear."

To make this happen, a world-wide organization was needed. However, when Relgis mentioned Romain Rolland's "Internationale of the Mind" Nicolai smiled skeptically. Rolland's comrade-in-arms had become disillusioned. "Each of us," he said, referring to the intellectual avant-garde, "has been in love with Utopia at one time or another. How many of us have discovered that humanitarianism in general and the 'internationale of the mind' in particular are mere dreams that 'practical men' smile at?" For his part he was putting his faith in science and technology, especially the latter, for "it imposes on the peoples of the world new relationships that will crack national frontiers and political boundaries."

Nicolai's dismal view of the contemporary scene was more than a pose, but his own unhappy experiences did not cloud his vision. His mind was too spacious, his vitality too irrepressible, his self-esteem too robust. In the midst of his dogged battle for his personal honor he remained a force to be reckoned with in the larger battle against bigotry and chauvinism. Nor did he let the threat to his existence interfere with the enjoyment of life, as witness the spacious apartment in which he received his visitor, the collection of oriental art and exotic weapons, and the impressive library. Relgis, invited to stay for dinner on his second visit, described the dining room as large, "with gilded ornaments," where he and his host (Frau Nicolai remained invisible and Irene curtsied shyly from the doorway) ate at a massive table "that had served the great dignitaries of yore at opulent banquets." Martydom and luxury were not necessarily incompatible.

Dignitaries now boycotted the famous heart specialist. "That fellow should have his face slapped," his former patient the crown prince, now an exile in Holland, was reported to have said when told of his activities. But new patients made up for the loss of the prewar clientele, some of them perhaps thrill-seekers who used their complaints as a pretext to meet the notorious dissident in person. Women saw a romantic figure in the handsome doctor who had braved the anti-aircraft batteries to fly to freedom and preach the gospel of peace. On balance, the publicity surrounding his case probably helped rather than hurt his practice.

His financial situation was thus far from desperate. In addition to medical fees he received royalties from the foreign editions of his book, honorariums for lectures and articles, and interest on loans he had made to friends or relatives. He always kept an eye open for opportunities to invest his money. In April 1921, undaunted by his recent defeat in court, he signed a contract with Hans Schwann, a wealthy businessman and, incidentally, an ardent pacifist, which made him a silent partner in the latter's wholesale paper company. His investment of 120,000 marks—still a tidy sum in 1921—entitled him to a third of the net earnings, with the option to become a full partner.

He still played chess with a passion. He wrote articles on a wide range of subjects: a review of his fellow pacifist F. W. Förster's account of *his* battle against militarism; a history of the swastika, "which today fools' hands smear on lavatory walls" as the emblem of anti-Semitism, but which in ancient times had been the universal symbol of the sun; a report of an exhibition of Frans Masereel's powerful Expressionist woodcuts portraying the horrors of the last war; a critique of the noted biologist Jakob von Uexküll's theories concerning the nature of cellular life; and a humorous but erudite history of occultism from Cagliostro and Swedenborg to the latest medium beguiling Berliners with fraudulent tricks.

Then, always, there were women to relieve the tedium. His relationships with them entailed intellectual as well as physical seduction, casual and almost mechanical on his part but shattering for his partners, most of them good German *Hausfrauen* with the social and political prejudices of their class. For them the encounter with a real pacifist, a radical thinker, and a man who had been banished from the company of decent people was indeed a thrill; he pushed them into a world of unfamiliar ideas. But the experience left them uneasy in the environment from which they came. For his part he needed women to still his unabated sexual appetite, but in none of these passing liaisons did he find other satisfaction. As for his wife, Friederike was approaching middle age and was stigmatized as the mother of a defective child. She was too useful to him to be discarded, and home, with his son Otto underfoot, was a constant reminder of irksome obligations. Irene, though a bright, affectionate child, was little more than an occasional plaything for her morose father. Nicolai was not cut out for family life.

He needed a challenge to his intellect; he found it in the Theory of Relativity. As a scientist he understood that he had witnessed a revolution—the toppling of Newton's eternally secure universe—that dwarfed the political quarrels of his contemporaries. Accordingly, he set out to master the mathematical complexities of Einstein's great discovery. The result of his labors was nothing less than a film entitled *The Foundations of the Relativity Theory*, with script and supervision by himself. He had been long interested in popular education and had sensed, earlier than most of his contemporaries, the value of motion pictures as teaching aids, especially in a subject that had so much to do with motion. The time was ripe. Though Einstein had only recently returned from a triumphal visit to

311

America and England and was being acclaimed by all but the most benighted anti-Semites and chauvinists, few people understood the meaning of his work.

In October, Nicolai signed a contract with the German financier Simon Guttmann, who was to supply the capital and act as intermediary with Colonna Films Ltd., in whose studios the film would be made. The plan called for two versions, one for the general public, the other for scientific audiences, to be accompanied by lectures given either by Nicolai or by his old friend Otto Buek. Although the venture was above all a labor of love, it also promised substantial material rewards.[2]

Nicolai was in his element, writing the narrative, making his own drawings, consulting with the experts on lighting effects, and supervising the actual filming. It was to be a film of interest to anyone with a basic knowledge of physics, though hardly to the man in the street. It began with a simple introductory sequence showing the fall of an object, first from a stationary automobile, then from the same vehicle in motion. It ended dramatically with the British expedition to the tropics to photograph the Hyades during the solar eclipse of 29 May 1919, photographs which confirmed Einstein's postulate that light was deflected by the gravitational pull of the sun. Nicolai might well be satisfied: he had presented a dry and difficult subject in a lively and interesting manner. With the "relativity film" he became a pioneer in visual education.

For some reason he had not mentioned the project to Albert Einstein, who was in Berlin at the time and with whom he was on good terms. The film was shown in Berlin in the spring of 1922 and in New York later in the same year, but in spite of favorable reviews it did not fare well. At home it was boycotted as the work of a notorious traitor. There were recurrent squabbles over the franchise between Colonna Films and Guttmann, to whom Nicolai had given power of attorney. Worst of all, Einstein, who was absent from the city at the time of the first showing, publicly disclaimed any connection with the project on his return and expressed his unhappiness with its title.[3] Someone connected with Colonna had made unauthorized use of Einstein's name in an effort to promote public interest in the film. Nicolai, too honorable to capitalize on his relationship with Einstein, was horrified but powerless to repair the damage. He was on the way to Argentina by then and had left matters in Guttmann's hands. Guttmann, equally appalled, terminated the contract with Colonna and sold the partnership's rights to a financial group. Nicolai's share, paid in installments providentially pegged to the American dollar, came to about five thousand dollars, not what he had hoped for but not a bad settlement under the circumstances.

Nicolai's love affair with the Relativity Theory did not end there however. A few years later, in exile, he wrote a book on the subject, examining the perception of space and time as a function of the biological characteristics of the human brain and tracing the concept of the universe from Kepler and Newton to Lorentz and Einstein. It was a veritable storehouse of scholarship, ranging from Greek philosophy to modern physics and biology. This time there was no material reward, only the gratification of

Fig. 26. "God before the throne of science," Nicolai's drawing with his notes for a talk. In these notes he says: "Man pushes the responsibility for his acts onto that transcendental God whose will is unfathomable. God permits war, God protects property, God opposes the new understanding of the human world, God as the embodiment of a past morality hinders the new morality." This God, he says, is "the product of dreams, fears, superstitions, and anthropomorphic notions of nature." Science, having itself transformed the world, had the right to ask whether this old God should not also be transformed.

an intellectual passion, for Nicolai was a true believer. For him science was still man's best hope. The recent war surely was a temporary aberration, a madness that would eventually yield to reason. For him the link between science and universal brotherhood was self-evident. If the world was in a sorry state, it was because men did not act in accordance with the insights science could provide, in the moral as well as in the physical sphere (Fig. 26).

The hostile judge who presided over Nicolai's libel suit against Captain Wilamowitz-Möllendorff would argue with unconscious irony that Nicolai was not an "intact person" in the legal sense; as a real person he was not only intact but growing. In the disastrous year 1921 he lived as if his existence were not in danger, writing, lecturing, traveling, making sexual conquests, giving interviews to foreign journalists, looking after his patients, investing his money, and moving as an equal among equals among the intellectual vanguard of the Weimar Republic.

In these circles he was accepted as an enlightened thinker, a fascinating conversationalist, and a man of the world. A society which acclaimed— or at least tolerated—a Bertold Brecht, a George Grosz, a Walter Gropius, and a Kurt Weill had room for a Nicolai. His strange dual role as villain to some and hero to others mirrors the split in the ranks of the German intelligentsia between Right and Left, traditionalists and rebels, nationalists and cosmopolitans—between the phalanx of academic insiders and the chaotic forces in search of new values outside the universities. As a scientist in the academic tradition Nicolai was a special target for the hatred of his colleagues. Had he not been a professor, he might have been ignored by the guardians of the German soul as merely another despicable intellectual.

While the timid bureaucracy and the equally timid liberal press had now abandoned him, however, he still enjoyed the support of the pacifist and socialist press. Prestigious magazines like *Die Weltbühne* and *Die Zukunft* still offered him a forum. Above all, the Bund Neues Vaterland, that remarkable collection of personalities whom he considered the true elite of Germany, stood by him to the end. Those closest to him were men who were themselves on the proscription lists of the proto-Nazis: the valiant Captain von Beerfelde, the historian of the Terror Gumbel, the veteran of many disrupted pacifist rallies Gerlach, and Hans Wehberg, the expert on international law.

Wehberg, too, had paid the price for his pacifism by being drafted into the Prussian army as a private. The book in which he described his wartime ordeal, *Als Pazifist im Weltkrieg*, was dedicated to Nicolai, a gesture of solidarity for which he was expelled from the alumni association of his fraternity. He now reaffirmed that support by placing before the public a collection of Nicolai's essays, *Aufruf an die Europäer*, most of which, suppressed by the censor or published in Scandinavia during the war, were unknown in Germany. "To acquaint the German reader with the writings of this controversial figure is an urgent task," he wrote in his introduction. With admirable objectivity he distinguished between the man and his achievement: "Nicolai's personality, which can make collaboration with him difficult, has caused much antagonism even among pacifists, and I have often felt that even in those circles he is not judged fairly. This is all the more deplorable because Nicolai is one of the greatest pacifists of all times and all nations." It was easy to forget how much courage it had taken to stand up to the rulers of wartime Germany, Wehberg wrote, "but some day when the future is brighter and one can look at the pacifists of the earliest days from a distance, the name Nicolai will shine ever more brightly. It will not be forgotten then that *one* man in Germany, five minutes before midnight, had the immense courage to protest against the mili-

Fig. 27. Orell Füssli's 1921 advertisement for *The Biology of War* in a German book trade paper, indicating the boycott of the book in postwar Germany: "Attention! There seems to be a purpose beyond the refusal of various bookstores to fill orders for the well-known book *The Biology of War* by Professor Georg Nicolai on the grounds that it is out of print, namely, to smother it in silence. We therefore state once again explicitly that any and all orders will be filled promptly from our stock."

Zur gefl. Beachtung!

Ⓩ

Es scheint eine gewisse Tendenz darin zu liegen, daß von verschiedenen Sortimentern das bekannte Buch

Die Biologie des Krieges

Betrachtungen eines Naturforschers den Deutschen zur Besinnung

von Prof. **Georg Nicolai**
Privatdozent a. d. Universität Berlin

Erste Orig.-Ausgabe * 2. Auflage
:: 2 Bände geheftet 170 Mark ::
In einem Band gebunden 200 Mark

auf Bestellung hin als vergriffen bezeichnet wird, um dasselbe

totzuschweigen!

Wir weisen deshalb wiederholt und ausdrücklich darauf hin, daß jede eingehende Bestellung von unserem Auslieferungslager prompt erledigt wird.
Alle Bestellungen an C. Cnobloch, Leipzig.

Verlag: **Art. Institut Orell Füssli**
· **Zürich.**

tary regime by his deeds and to unfurl the white banner of pacifism in that grave hour."

This was high praise indeed, though ineffective. Few Germans had read the *Biology of War*, the work for which Nicolai had sacrificed his career (Fig. 27), and fewer yet would read the little volume so eloquently presented by Wehberg. Wehberg's prophecy did not come true, though at the time it must have been balm for Nicolai's wounds. Wehberg himself eventually, after laboring fruitlessly as Alfred Fried's successor as editor of the *Friedenswarte*, left Germany to work for the League of Nations. For the Wehbergs, Gumbels, and Nicolais, for all the independent spirits who resisted the tide of chauvinism, racism, and irrationality that swept postwar Germany, the future held three choices: exile, suicide, or the concentration camp.

If Wehberg was an ally in the battle against unreason, Nicolai's guiding light was Einstein. He revered him above all living men as a genius whose name, like Newton's, would be remembered when all the other German professors were forgotten. The brief rift between the two men had long since healed. Both were pacifists, democrats, advocates of non-violent socialism; both were targets of chauvinist and anti-Semitic attacks. A sense of comradeship in the face of the common enemy sustained their otherwise casual friendship. Their paths crossed frequently, their wives were on cordial terms, Nicolai was Frau Einstein's physician, her daughter Ilse had remained his friend and admirer. Albert himself, ever gentle and generous, was tolerant of—and perhaps a little amused by—Nicolai's quixotic forays, while Nicolai acknowledged the wisdom of Einstein's serene attitude toward the passions and foibles of human beings. "You and I say the same things," he told Eintstein, "but when you say them you seduce people; when I say them I make them angry."

The occasion for this remark was the visit of Anatole France to Berlin. After receiving the Nobel Prize in Stockholm in December 1921, he stopped there expressly to meet the two most famous German pacifists, Einstein and Nicolai. The encounter was recorded by the writer's traveling companion, François Crucy, a reporter for the *Petit Parisien*. Einstein, first to arrive, expressed his admiration for the Frenchman, a confirmed socialist and (except for an acute attack on patriotism during the war) pacifist. Nicolai in turn paid homage to the writer who seemed to embody the spirit of Voltaire. France was pessimistic, "saddened by human stupidity." Einstein was more hopeful: the military were no longer in control of Germany, most people everywhere wanted peace, and "what good intentions fail to accomplish, dire necessity will." Here Nicolai broke in with a question: "Do you think then, M. France, that human reason is the sole factor capable of ameliorating the human condition?"

France evaded the question: "I have long dreamed that it might become one of the principal forces, and I have followed its progress with passionate hope, in spite of many disappointments. You, whose greatest writer placed such a high value on intelligence and reason, cannot blame me." Nicolai was pleased with the reference to Goethe, and said so. "Alas," France said, "my ignorance of the language keeps me from coming as close to the poet as I would wish, but the thinker belongs to the world." Einstein confessed his lack of enthusiasm for Goethe. "He is too—rational? No, no, too—optimistic? No, that's not it either. Too detached? Yes, detached. He dwells on Olympus. I admire him from afar; when I approach him more closely I do not find him human enough."

Crucy observed that Einstein was deeply moved by the encounter with Anatole France, whereas France could find no rapport with the physicist but immediately entered into a lively exchange with Nicolai. Harry Kessler, to whom Crucy described the meeting, suggested that France, the skeptic, had too little in common with Einstein, whom Kessler called a deeply religious man: "As if Jehovah had suddenly called on Voltaire." By contrast, in Nicolai, the francophile and rationalist, the Frenchman recognized a kindred spirit. He was in any case indifferent to science and refused to be overawed by Einstein. "As I understand it," he told the *Figaro* after his return to Paris, "he has found a theory which is as new as Laplace's was in its day, although the two were very different. But at bottom *c'est toujours la même chose*." Yes, Einstein was a pacifist, "though not as energetic a proponent as Dr. Nicolai, a renowned scholar who entered the army as a high-ranking physician and left it as a plain orderly. But then, he protested against the sinking of the *Lusitania*. The great Einstein dreams of the stars; therefore our petty concerns are of little interest to him."

Nicolai had a better understanding of Einstein, as a scientist, as a pacifist, and as a human being as well. When Nicolai left Germany, soon after their meeting with France, Einstein gave him a signed photograph which he treasured for the rest of his life (Fig. 28). They saw each other again, first in Córdoba, during Einstein's visit to Argentina in 1925, then at Einstein's residence in Caputh, near Berlin, in 1931, when Nicolai was on his way to the Soviet Union, and they wrote to each other for decades.[4] But the relationship was never a close one or one of equals. When Nicolai, then an octogenarian, spoke at the University of Chile on the occasion of Einstein's death, he described the relationship in these words:

> I have been asked to participate in this homage to Einstein because I was thought to be his friend. I can lay no claim to this honor, neither in the sentimental sense nor in the sense that we shared a conception of the world. I was simply an admirer of the man whose unique genius added to our understanding of the universe and to the progress of science. A single moment—in truth, a historical moment—brought us together, a moment in which we experienced the same inescapable sense of our duty to mankind.

Einstein, he said, was a man who

> remained true to his belief in humanism, who from the height of his wisdom judged the passions of the world with impartiality and died revered by that world. For in spite of everything there is such a thing as justice, and men have felt—perhaps without completely understanding why—that he was one of the geniuses of humanity who

must not be judged by the part he played in the quarrels of the world but by the essence of his contribution to the progress of our species. And for me, in all my misfortunes, he has always been the greatest source of strength, because in that unique moment which perhaps gave a certain value to my life I could feel myself united with the greatest of my contemporaries. For that is what Einstein was.[5]

But in the difficult year 1921 the moral support of Einstein and the other brave souls of the Bund Neues Vaterland was not enough. As the year progressed Nicolai had to admit that his prospects in Germany were dis-

Fig. 28. Einstein's gift upon Nicolai's departure
from Germany in 1922.

mal. He had fought the good fight against insuperable odds, he had gone farther than most of his companions, he was still fighting, for that matter (it was when he was making his most furious efforts to force his adversaries into a confrontation), but he knew that he was beaten. Pacifists were fair game in Germany. On 26 August 1921 Erzberger—a marginal pacifist at best but a marked man because he had signed the Armistice—had been assassinated. It was only a question of time: Nicolai's turn would come. His hope for a call from a university within the German academic orbit— Prague perhaps, or one of the Swiss or Austrian schools—had not materialized, perhaps because he was too controversial a figure, or perhaps because he had been away from academic medicine too long. Every exit seemed blocked.

A *deus ex machina* had appeared the previous spring, in the shape of Enrique Barros, a recent graduate and self-appointed emissary of the Universidad Nacional de Córdoba in Argentina. The students there had recently staged a successful rebellion against the faculty, in which—as often in such situations—legitimate protests against unsatisfactory teaching conditions escalated into attacks against the academic establishment as such. Since they identified their professors with the old order discredited by the war in Europe, they were naturally pacifist and sympathetic to democratic and even socialist revolutions. Barros, a young firebrand who had led the rebellion at Córdoba, saw Nicolai as the perfect man to revolutionize the ossified faculty: comparatively young, modern, unconventional, famous as a fighter against reactionaries and at the same time a renowned scientist and brilliant teacher. Would he come to Argentina?

Córdoba was a backwater in a backward country, remote from the center of Nicolai's European universe, but it was a port out of the storm that threatened to engulf him. A contract for two or three years would allow him to return to Germany when the atmosphere cleared. It would be a leap in the dark, but he was accustomed to take chances. As a German professor he would be well received in a country in which many of the revolutionaries of 1848 had settled. Then too the mere fact that he, a pariah at home, was wanted there spoke in its favor.

Still, Nicolai hesitated. As late as November he had told France's friend Crucy that he would remain in Berlin even if he did not regain his teaching position. "I do not want to abandon my patients," he had added, "and even less my followers, who are threatened because they stand by me. These young men and women, who recently demanded from the academic authorities an explanation of my expulsion, have been asked to withdraw their petition on pain of being expelled from the university themselves." These were, of course, rationalizations, as Nicolai had done nothing whatsoever to restrain his young disciples, and as for his patients, Berlin was full of capable physicians. The truth was that he was reluctant to bury himself in a provincial town in Argentina, perhaps even more reluctant to return to the quiet life of a professor of physiology. His old chief Kraus had warned him that he would lose interest in medical research once he had tasted the excitement of the political arena, and he was right.

The summer of 1921 had brought one more triumph for Nicolai. The

Women's International League for Peace and Freedom, meeting in Salzburg under the chairmanship of Jane Addams, offered him a prominent place on its program. As a romantic figure, an impassioned speaker, intelligent and handsome, he was the center of attention. He chose three topics, "The Development of Man's Social Instincts," "The Advantages of Mutual Assistance as Opposed to the Struggle for Survival," and "The League of Nations as the Sole Remedy against War." A cordial relationship sprang up between Miss Addams, the great American humanitarian, and

UNE AFFAIRE DREYFUS EN ALLEMAGNE

Le professeur Nicolaï au ban de l'Université

Le professeur **Georg** Nicolaï, auteur de la *Biologie de la guerre*, qui n'est pas encore traduite en notre langue, connu surtout en France pour sa sensationnelle évasion en avion de l'Allemagne impériale et **guerrière** en compagnie d'officiers antimilitaristes, est actuellement l'objet d'une criante injustice de la part des nationalistes allemands, qui valent les nôtres.

On ne lui pardonne pas son opposition irréductible à la guerre. On n'a pas oublié qu'il fut, avec le physicien Einstein et l'astronome Forster, l'un des rares Allemands

LE PROFESSEUR NICOLAI
(Croquis de F. Després.)

qui protestèrent contre les étranges prétentions des « 93 intellectuels ». On le lui fit bien voir, en l'excluant, en 1919, par un vote unanime de l'Université — dont il était pourtant un des plus brillants professeurs.

Fig. 29. From an article in *L'Humanité*, 29 August 1921.

Nicolai, the great German pacifist. As WILPF was a women's organization, Frau Nicolai was also invited but was held back at the Austrian border for lack of a proper visa. Her husband consoled himself with one of the French delegates. The admiration of the delegates, the lovely surroundings, the excellent Austrian cuisine were all exhilarating.

Fig. 30. Leningrad edition of *The Biology of War*.

At home, however, the pressures were mounting. Nicolai's open letter to *Die Zukunft*, published at this time, produced no response, nor did a resolution passed in October by the Berlin chapter of the German Peace Society demanding "clarification of the Nicolai Case." The hour of decision was at hand, and Barros' offer was still open. Nicolai inquired about

321

a leave of absence and was told that his (by now illusory) appointment would be kept open for two years. On 21 January 1922 he signed a contract with Rector Francisco de la Torre of the Universidad Nacional de Córdoba, represented by the Argentine consul in Berlin. In return for performing the usual duties of a head of a department of physiology he was to receive a monthly salary of five hundred gold pesos, an advance of two thousand gold pesos for moving expenses, and a guarantee for the same amount if the contract was not renewed at the end of three years. From a material viewpoint it was a good arrangement. Nicolai began Spanish lessons (from an attractive young woman, of course) and began to select the books, furniture, and instruments for Córdoba. His wife would stay behind to wind up his tangled affairs. She would join him later if he found the situation in Córdoba to his liking.

To the very last he maintained his role as a champion of peace. Less than three weeks before signing the contract with Córdoba he was in Paris as an emissary of the Bund Neues Vaterland, one of three men sent to establish rapport with French moderates. It was an important mission. French bitterness over the devastation of northern France and the not entirely baseless suspicion that Germany was secretly rearming was the chief obstacle to the reconciliation of Europe at that moment. A rapprochement between the former enemies was needed if Germany were to be admitted to the League of Nations. In December 1921 the Bund sent Harry Kessler, its most cosmopolitan member, to Paris for exploratory talks. The obstacles were enormous. In Germany a right-wing newspaper had called on patriots to shoot members of the Bund on sight because the Bund's secretary had urged economic cooperation with France and had warned that Germany must abandon her secret plans for rearmament if France was to withdraw her troops from the Rhineland. Reason was treason. In France things were not much better. The Ligue des Droits de l'Homme had to face irreconcilables like Clemenceau, who thought that there were twenty million Germans too many. Against this backdrop of hatred, the Bund and the Ligue agreed on an exchange of visits.[6]

Nicolai's participation was a foregone conclusion, for he was one of the few Germans who could hope to be believed when in France he spoke of a reconciliation. As he warned in 1918, there were no public figures who were not compromised in French eyes by their support of the war. He was indispensable, even though it was known that he would be leaving Europe shortly. His fellow delegates were Hellmut von Gerlach, the president of the Bund, and Lehmann-Russbüldt, its secretary. (Einstein, another unimpeachable pacifist, was to be the fourth but was unable to come at this time.) The delegation left for Paris early in January 1922.

Not even Einstein could have overcome the loathing of French nationalists for all things German. *L'Eclair* asked why "the theoretician of the non-existence of time has not come, so that he can demonstrate the non-existence of our ruins and of the void of our economy." Nicolai, who received the most attention from the press, did not fare much better. Noting that he had once studied in Paris, *L'Eclair* discounted his profession of love for France: "Behind the monocle a steely eye fixes the void, looking at nobody and nothing. A long scar runs across his cheek, proof that after frequenting the Quartier Latin he 'studied' the saber in some Munich beer hall. Today he is famous, yet only yesterday he was fêted at the court of Potsdam." It granted that he had refused to take the oath and had paid the price, but his assertion that the French as victors were now responsible for peace bordered on insolence. As for Herr von Gerlach, who exhibited a placard with the words "Nie Wieder Krieg!" ("Never Again War") to prove the existence of pacifism in Germany, and Lehmann-Russbüldt, "a big blond lout without distinction," they were no doubt sincere, but unimpressive, *L'Eclair* wrote. "These are three republicans, that is to say, the most reliable friends we have in Germany. *Pauvres de nous!*"[7]

But in pacifist and socialist circles the trio was well received. The *Journal du Peuple* turned its irony on the French chauvinists. "Yesterday," the reporter wrote, "I saw barbarians, three of them—a horde!" They were exceptional men, "who have neither hated nor killed, who refused to deny their ideals when Poincaré and Wilhelm II said 'you shall hate, you shall kill!' They appear before us in the splendor of their barbarism. Barbarians? Human beings!" Nicolai called himself a citizen of the world first, a German second. He had never ceased to love France, but his love had matured: "In my youth I was seduced by the grandeur of Napoleon. Today I know that the true conquests are those of the spirit. Today I admire Voltaire." He reminded the audience of his calling: "For the physician all men are equal." Had not Victor Hugo said, "La porte d'un médecin ne doit être jamais fermée"? Was he, as a German, not justified in telling the French that they as the victors bore the responsibility for the future, inasmuch as he had told his own countrymen the same thing when *they* expected to win?[8] Thus reported, the warning seemed entirely proper. The socialist *L'Ere Nouvelle* was equally friendly, calling them "not *boches* but citizens of the world and beyond that, heroes." There was no better word to describe men who had risked their lives for their ideas, ideas which were "ours, they very principles of the French Revolution, the rights for which the Entente fought against the Central Powers."

But there was work to be done. The visitors and their hosts drafted a carefully worded joint declaration which called for Franco-German cooperation not only among industry and labor but among intellectuals, scientists, and artists; it called for bilateral disarmament, opening of the archives, binding arbitration by the League of Nations, and acceptance by Germany of its obligation, both moral and legal, to repair the damage in northern France. The Ligue and the Bund jointly were to devise a program of counterpropaganda against the chauvinist and imperialist tendencies in both countries.

Unlike many well-meaning manifestos of the period, the joint declaration was a major achievement, the first step toward a genuine peace, even though it was to prove premature. Victors and vanquished had spoken with one voice. Though Poincaré, who was about to become premier again, would send troops into the Ruhr within a year, a powerful sector of French public opinion had been mobilized for reconciliation with the former enemy. In contrast to the Bund Neues Vaterland, the Ligue des Droits de l'Homme was a large and influential organization and could command the support of leading politicians, intellectuals, and labor leaders. Unlike Germany, France was not so polarized that right and left, nationalists and pacifists, middle class and labor did not speak the same language. On the subject of peace, professors and even generals could agree with union leaders and Communists. When the joint declaration was ratified in May, on the occasion of the reciprocal visit of the Ligue to Berlin, it bore the signatures of past and future French prime ministers, of professors at the Sorbonne, of Anatole France and General Maurice Sarrail, commander of the Third Army at the Battle of the Marne. At the time it seemed that Nicolai and his fellow delegates had rendered the world a service.

Nicolai met Madame Curie, the physicist Paul Langevin, former prime minister Paul Painlevé and former minister for armaments Albert Thomas, his own colleagues Charles Richet and Emile Gley, the historians A. Aulard and Charles S. Seignobos, and virtually the entire avant-garde of the Université de Paris.[9] To breathe the air of Paris, to encounter, in the political salons connected with the Ligue, the intellectual and scientific elite of France, was a truly extraordinary experience for a man whom his colleagues at home shunned like a leper. Here he was an honored guest "the illustrious friend of Einstein and Anatole France," as Emile Vandervelde, the Belgian Socialist leader who came to Paris to witness the occasion, called him. For *L'Humanité* he was "the unforgettable author of the *Biology of War*, one of the finest books of the tragic epoch soiled with the blood of fifteen million Europeans." *Le Peuple* coupled his name with that of General Sarrail, the victor of the Balkan campaign that gave the coup de grâce to the Central Powers. In a setting described by Vandervelde as "a friendly house in Paris well known to every Socialist in Europe, where many memories evoke the shadows of Victor Hugo, Michelet, and Victor Considérant," the French general and the German pacifist discussed war and peace. "I asked myself," Vandervelde wrote, "who did more to bring Wilhelm II down, the soldier with the victor's laurels on his brow or the savant in his laboratory who had the courage to pit his judgment against everybody else's and bore the stigma of an enemy of the people for defending the conscience of humanity."[10]

In France, as in Germany, the peace movement was spearheaded by the Left. Even the Communists received the bourgeois pacifists from the other side of the Rhine. "Nicolai is not exactly a Communist," said *L'Humanité*, whose editorial offices he had been invited to visit, "but his faith in humanity makes him infinitely sympathetic and close to us. He declared himself greatly impressed by the cultural concerns of the French Communists whom he has met thus far. An intimate dinner brought Nicolai together with most of our staff. During the dessert cordial toasts were exchanged between Nicolai and our secretary, Amédée Dunois."[11] Evidently the staunch anti-Communist Nicolai could forgive French Communists for being Communists because they were French. As opposed to the Russian and German variants, Communism in his beloved France was bound to be civilized.

But he was more interested in Paris than in politics. "However one may feel about the value of joint declarations for the reconciliation of the peoples," he wrote, "the temptation to see Paris again after the war was so great that I happily accepted the invitation." He wandered through the city and found it almost unchanged: "The two-wheeled carts rumble through the streets, men walk about in their blue smocks, victuals and articles of clothing are sold on the sidewalks, and the bookstalls along the quais—unlike those in Berlin—are as well-stocked as ever. As always, old houses are torn down everywhere, but the character of the city resists change. The method is still the same: the worker stands with bravura on some piece of masonry and hacks away at the wall on which he stands."[12]

He talked to strangers on park benches, in little restaurants, at the Café de la Régence, the Mecca of chess players, telling everybody that he was German—not that it was necessary, as his accent and his face gave him away—without encountering any hostility. On the contrary, he was asked to join the chess players and invited to share a bottle of wine: "We played chess all night and forgot that the nasty conflict between Germans and Frenchmen even exists." Such contacts were more important than those between intellectuals, he asserted, "for they proved without exception that the hatred fanned by the press on both sides had not taken root among the people." He was nevertheless pleased with the intense involvement of French intellectuals in politics. He was pleasantly surprised to find members of the Sorbonne and the Institut de France at the dinner given by *L'Humanité*, "the Bolshevist newspaper of France," as he called it. In Germany such a gathering would be unthinkable. There intellectuals were excluded—or excluded themselves—from politics, to the detriment of public life. The Germans, Nicolai wrote, had been driven into the slaughter under the slogan "You shall rule the world—or at least Baghdad," whereas the French were told that they were fighting for humanity, for justice and peace—also slogans, to be sure, but important just the same.

And then it was over and Nicolai was plunged once more into notoriety. The lawsuit against Wilamowitz-Möllendorff was in the future and it was time to prepare for his journey. His impending departure spurred his supporters to a last desperate action. They organized a public meeting, to which ex-Rector Meyer and his colleagues were invited to defend themselves against the charge of malice and lying and to retract their verdict. None appeared. On 22 March, four days before Nicolai's departure, at a Bund Neues Vaterland meeting, speeches were given by his close friend Heinrich Dehmel, the poet's son, and by Hans Wehberg and his lawyer Emil Schweitzer. The meeting then adopted the following resolution for transmittal to the Prussian Diet: "Immediately before Professor Nicolai's departure for Argentina the assembly of the Bund Neues Vaterland has once more considered the so-called Nicolai Case. After hearing testimony, we conclude that Professor Nicolai has suffered gravely thereby. The assembly therefore urges the Prussian Diet to re-examine the matter."[13]

The effort was in vain. Four days later Nicolai sailed from Bremerhaven on the Stinnes liner S.S. *Köln*. "On 26 March Professor Nicolai took ship for Argentina," Gerlach wrote sadly in the Viennese magazine *Die Wage* a few weeks later: "Honored abroad, he is cast out by his countrymen."

After recounting again the details of the battle with the university, Gerlach pointed out the personal tragedy: "Now Nicolai had had enough. As an academic teacher he had been paralyzed. As a human being he saw himself thwarted in the battle for his rights. As a man of science he was profoundly ashamed that almost no German scientist dared to take his side openly in this battle, which was also a battle for the honor and freedom of science. He has turned his back on the fatherland which he loves with all his heart."

German pacifism had lost its most valiant fighter.

NOTES

1. He recorded his impressions of the meeting in *Georg Fr. Nicolai, un sabio y un hombre del porvenir*, a collection of essays begun in 1921 but not published until 1949 (Buenos Aires: Ediciones Reconstruir, 1949). A new Spanish edition was issued in 1965, after Nicolai's death, in his memory, by Ajica, a Buenos Aires publisher. Relgis had translated and published excerpts from the *Biology of War* as *Biologia Razboiului* (Iasi: Editure Vista Romanesca, 1920) before this visit to Nicolai. He later emigrated to Uruguay and carried on a correspondence with Nicolai for the next four decades. The quotations in the text are from pages 23–27 of the 1965 edition of Relgis's book on Nicolai.

2. Nicolai was to receive 10 percent of the net proceeds, half to be paid on a current basis, the other half when earnings reached 100,000 marks. A supplemental agreement provided for a bonus in case a franchise in the United States was arranged. A separate contract between Nicolai and Buek assured the latter of a share of the net earnings. Additionally, a fee for the lectures was provided for both men. Originals of the contracts pertaining to the film drawn up among Nicolai, Guttmann, Colonna Films Ltd., and Buek are in the Nicolai archive. Ronald W. Clark, in his *Einstein, the Life and Times* (New York: World Publishing Company, 1971), p. 290, refers to the film as made by "a Professor Nicolai and a Herr Kornbaum [Kornblum]"; apparently he was unaware that this Nicolai was the author of the *Appeal to the Europeans* mentioned elsewhere in his book.

3. The title of the film is so clearly Einsteinian that the public would assume that Einstein was either the author or, at least, closely associated with the project, and it appears that the film company deliberately fostered this idea. Clark refers to Einstein's disavowal of the film's authorship (*ibid.*). In the Nicolai archive there is a letter from Guttmann to Frau Nicolai of 29 July 1922 in which he mentions "questionable incidents such as the unscrupulous action of the management [of Colonna Films] which provoked Professor Einstein's statement."

4. During World War II Einstein tried to obtain the release of Nicolai's illegitimate son Arne and his mother, Elly von Schneider, a close friend of Ilse Einstein, from a French internment camp. In turn Nicolai, who by then had found a permanent haven in Santiago, interceded with the Chilean authorities on behalf of a refugee recommended to him by Einstein. In 1941 Nicolai asked Einstein for help with a mathematical problem involving the application of Pascal's triangle to a biological issue, explaining that he had been unable to reach the French mathematician Émile Borel, who had been arrested by the Nazis. In 1953 Georg Lenz, another of Nicolai's illegitimate sons, on behalf of his father sent Einstein some of Nico-

lai's scientific papers and reminded him of the priceless gift Einstein had given him long ago: a signed copy of his book on the relativity theory.

5. The typewritten manuscript of this address is in the Nicolai archive.

6. Founded to protect the French Republic at the time of the Dreyfus Affair, the Ligue had 120,000 members, as compared with the handful of Bundists or even the 15,000 members of the German Peace Society. A brochure giving a full account of the joint effort of the Bund Neues Vaterland and the Ligue, by Otto Lehmann-Russbüldt, appeared, entitled *Die Brücke über den Abgrund* [The bridge over the abyss], in 1922.

7. *L'Eclair*, 6 January 1922.

8. *Le Journal du Peuple*, 6 January 1922.

9. The list of public figures involved in the talks with the German delegation also included Deputy Joseph Paul-Boncour, later prime minister; Deputy Pierre Renaudel; and Ferdinand Buisson, former minister of education and at this time president of the Ligue. Other notables were Professors Victor Basch, Charles Gide, and Leon Brunschvig of the Sorbonne.

10. Writing in *Le Peuple*, 8 January 1922. Victor Considérant, a French economist, was a disciple of Fourier.

11. *L'Humanité*, 9 January 1922.

12. These and the following quotations are from a typewritten manuscript fragment, "Reise nach Paris," in the Nicolai archive.

13. A copy of the resolution is in the Nicolai archive.

V. TEACHER OF A CONTINENT

21. El Gran Europeo

"Now you are on your way to South America," Friederike wrote, "enjoy the boat ride and the chess, Spanish books and conversation, shuffleboard, theatricals, political discussions, and the bar!" But the voyage of the S.S. *Köln* to Buenos Aires was not the pleasant ocean voyage she envisaged. A German ship in the 1920s was a microcosm of the hatreds and tensions of the homeland. Politics seeped into every conversation, every gesture, every glance. Thrown together at close quarters, people whose paths did not normally cross—monarchists and republicans, militarists and pacifists, Gentiles and Jews—made poor traveling company. Their formal upbringing had taught them to use manners not so much to bridge social or political differences as to inflict slights and subtle insults. Besides Nicolai, the passenger list to Buenos Aires included a Professor Alfonso Goldschmidt, a political economist who had also received a call to Córdoba, and his wife; Frau Elly von Schneider, a friend of Ilse Einstein; and Herr Von der Drosse, an ex-major in the Prussian Army.

We have no record of the major's reasons for the voyage, but Argentina was a haven for former military officers and other nationalists who found the Weimar Republic uncongenial. What is known is that he was an unreconstructed monarchist whose loyalty to the House of Hohenzollern had survived the Kaiser's unheroic flight to Holland. Frau Von Schneider's purpose, on the other hand, was unequivocal. As she had proclaimed before all the world, Frau Nicolai not excepted, she was making the voyage in order to be impregnated by the great man. Nicolai obliged, perhaps adhering to the principle of paternal selection which he would later advocate in a treatise on eugenics. As a connoisseur of women he could have had no other reason, for Elly von Schneider was a plain, bony, graceless woman who prided herself on intellect and an unsentimental approach to life. In any case the bargain was consummated in business-like fashion. Nicolai accepted a measure of financial responsibility for the offspring-to-be but declined to bind himself in any legal way. Neither party seems to have doubted that it would be a son, as indeed it later proved to be.[1] If the presence of a female traveling companion other than Nicolai's wife shocked the delegation from Córdoba that came to welcome him at the pier, its members were too polite to say so.

For Nicolai the "idyll" with Frau Von Schneider was a mere interlude in the more serious drama which took place aboard the S.S. *Köln* and which did not end when the boat docked in Buenos Aires. The officers of the German Merchant Marine, many of them with long service in the Imperial Navy, yielded nothing to Herr Von der Drosse in their loyalty to the old regime, and the captain of the *Köln* was no exception. The German shore had hardly vanished from sight when the Imperial black-white-and-red flag was hoisted. Nicolai demanded that it be hauled down forthwith and replaced by the black, red, and gold colors of the republican Merchant

Marine. In demanding that it be taken down he was entirely within his rights, but it was not until he threatened the captain with legal action that it was done, and his action attracted the displeasure of the fashionable passengers. His popularity did not improve when he organized a collection among the passengers on behalf of the starving women and children of Russia and when he remained seated and protested audibly at the end of the first gala dinner, when Major Von der Drosse proposed a toast to "His Majesty, our beloved Kaiser." Nicolai and his party were the only ones to keep their seats, but, as he later told Argentinian reporters gleefully, the example took hold among the more timid republicans, and each time Von

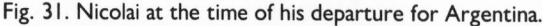

Fig. 31. Nicolai at the time of his departure for Argentina.

der Drosse toasted the Kaiser thereafter, the numbers of persons who remained seated increased.

The defenders of the old order had their revenge. When the *Köln* docked on 20 April, those gathered on the pier were startled and dismayed to learn that Nicolai and Goldschmidt were detained on board and denied entry into Argentina.[2] Whether the captain or Herr Von der Drosse had cabled ahead to warn the authorities or whether—as the *Diario de La Plata* reported—a mysterious woman who had demanded to speak confidentially to the official in charge of the pier was responsible, the immigration service was adamant in its refusal to let the two men go ashore.

The Liberal and Socialist press of Buenos Aires reported the incident under headlines such as "A Disgrace," "A Deplorable Blunder," and "An Irritating Injustice." *La Vanguardia*, after giving a resumé of Nicolai's career, predicted that the shameful and unprecedented act of the immigration service would arouse the ire of every citizen. Goldschmidt figured only incidentally in the entire account. Where both men were named, it was always *Nicolai y Goldschmidt*, but then Nicolai was famous in Argentina.

The only explanation the surprised professor had been given as to why he was being detained, *Vanguardia* reported, was that these were orders from above. Many of his friends boarded the ship but were not allowed to speak to him, as if he were "un apestado" (a leper), and only one person succeeded in even catching a glimpse of him. The orders had originated with the director of the immigration service himself. "Nicolai is not an ordinary immigrant," said *Vanguardia*, forgetting again the hapless Goldschmidt, "but a guest of the Republic, a man of science coming here not on his own initiative but at the invitation of the University of Córdoba, and this man is forbidden to disembark in the rudest manner and without being told the motives behind an order that is at best fitting for savages governing a republic of Zulus." Determined to find out why, the reporter braved the "ferocious" guards of the *Köln*, but by then it was midnight, and "*Nicolai y Goldschmidt*" had gone to bed, so he pieced his story together from the other passengers. A German nationalist plot was suspected, for the right-wing German-language paper *Deutsche La Plata Zeitung* had published, before the arrival of the ship, a complete passenger list from which the names of the two men were missing. *Diario de La Plata* interviewed the immigration authorities, who lamely excused their action on the grounds that the Argentine consul in Berlin had failed to issue a visa to Nicolai. "We all know who he is," the commentator said; "The law is being violated, for with a contract from the University of Córdoba he needs no visa." *El Zonda* called for a protest by the academic youth of Argentina to save the national honor.

The next morning Dr. Stuckert, a Swiss-Argentine from the School of Engineering at Córdoba, sent by the university as a member of the official welcoming committee, arranged for the release of the distinguished arrivals, though not without difficulty. *Diario de La Plata* described his interview with Señor Remigio Lupo, the director of the immigration service. "I have a strong suspicion amounting to virtual certainty," Lupo said, that "Nicolai and Goldschmidt are secret agents of the German Bolsheviks." Apparently, the thought that Bolshevik agents would not tip their hand by organizing a collection for starving Russians and making themselves otherwise conspicuous had not occurred to Lupo, whose sympathies were evidently with the Von der Drosses of the German community. "But the contracts were approved by the highest authorities," Stuckert objected. "The secretary of foreign affairs and the minister of public instruction gave their blessing, and the arrangements were made through the Argentine embassy in Berlin." Lupo stuck to his guns: "All the same, I have before me a denunciation to the effect that they are Bolsheviks. Once before there

333

was a similar case involving a professor who was later unmasked as an agent of the 'Maximalists'" (a then-popular term for the Bolsheviks as proponents of the "maximal" goals of socialism). Stuckert insisted that Nicolai and Goldschmidt were in Argentina in an official capacity. After long argument, Lupo eventually gave in, on the understanding that Stuckert would hold himself responsible for their conduct.

Thus, as the ward of a stranger, the "Great European" stepped ashore, already a center of controversy. The hatred of his countrymen was accompanying him to the New World: the long arm of the nationalist Reaction was the most international of political creatures. Once again, however, his own actions on shipboard had added fuel to the fire. Friederike, who had no illusions about him, was depressed when she read a distorted account of the contretemps in a Berlin newspaper. "I understand that you were arrested before landing," she wrote her husband. "Are things going to be the same over there as they were here? Can there not even be an ocean voyage without fighting? I had hoped otherwise." She was reluctant to report on the latest developments in the court battle against the academic senate, she told him, "for these dreary squabbles ruin all more profound thoughts."

Her husband was undaunted. He was coming to Argentina as a celebrity. The clumsy interference of the immigration authorities only gave his arrival wider publicity and brightened his martyr's crown. He was well known in professional circles for his prewar scientific contributions, when German scholarship served as a model for countries like Argentina. The *Biology of War*, although not yet translated into Spanish, was famous there, if only because of the drama surrounding its publication, and his spectacular flight to Denmark by airplane had captured the Latin imagination. The eminent Spanish physiologist Pi Suñer had recently spoken at the Colegio Nacional Mariano Moreno on the subject "two pacifist physiologists," Richet of France and Nicolai of Germany. In a country where French cultural influences were also strong, the writings of Romain Rolland had added luster to his name, and it was widely known that Anatole France had come to Berlin to meet Einstein and Nicolai. The expulsion from the University of Berlin, described in Argentina as "persecution by the implacable Junkers," was fresh in everyone's mind as a monstrous insult to justice and academic freedom. The general feeling was that to have attracted such a man to an Argentine university was an honor for the country.

After the oppressive atmosphere aboard the *Köln*, Nicolai greatly enjoyed the attention and honors that were now heaped on him. He gave interviews right and left, shrugging off the obnoxious Señor Lupo as a petty clerk who had merely followed orders, calling for an investigation of the monarchist conspirators who engineered the denunciation, clarifying his political stand, giving his views on developments in Germany, and, for good measure, promising *Vanguardia* a series of articles on his friend Einstein's theory, to be written in terms his readers could understand. His first care was to repudiate the label of "Bolshevik." "The cry 'Bolshevik!'" he said prophetically, "is the war cry of reactionaries everywhere against liberals." He had been a republican under the monarchy, and "although I served as physician at the Imperial court, there was no reward large enough to make me change my mind. I was republican when the Kaiser's Reich shone in the brilliance of its arms and the splendor of its victories. When the ship [the *Köln*] sailed, I was the only one to protest the Imperial flag and was therefore accused of being a Bolshevik, but I was only doing what was legally proper, and because of my protest the colors of the Republic were flown."

Despite his own experiences he was optimistic about the future of German democracy, pointing to the decrease in the number of assassinations as a hopeful sign. As for himself, he was both nationalist and internationalist, he said, reverting to one of the themes of the *Biology of War*, German in cultural matters—but only if free from the taint of chauvinism—and international in political matters. "What is German culture?" he asked. "All nations have their culture, more often than not older than that of Germany. It was mainly under the influence of foreign cultures that Germany developed her own." However, these alien influences reached their highest flowering in their "German phase," he claimed: Charlemagne was the founder of a "German" academy; Bach was the heir to Italian, French, and English music; Mozart was the composer who brought Italian opera to perfection; Kant was the assimilator of European philosophy. Germany's historical mission was to merge these various currents of European civilization. It was the Nicolaian credo, a mixture of nostalgia for a Germany that never existed (except as an ideal distilled from the creativity of individual geniuses) and the arrogance of a man who believed the environment that had formed him to be the center of the universe.

Nicolai made these pronouncements in a Spanish that the reporters variously described as "correct" and "somewhat slow but perfectly idiomatic." Those who added that he had "only a slight German accent" were being polite to the distinguished newcomer, for his pronunciation was—and would remain—atrocious, an ear for language being one of the few gifts denied him. Still, handling these interviews was quite an achievement for a man who had only begun to learn the language a few months earlier. Receiving an endless stream of visitors at all hours, in the lobby, in the dining room, or in his suite at the Hotel España, he was thoroughly at ease. The reporters, accustomed to Creole formality and expecting a German professor to be pompous, found his forthright manner refreshing. One of them, pleasantly surprised at being received without having to cool his heels in the anteroom, described him as "a different breed of scientist from those we have known, tall, broad-chested, ruddy-cheeked, resembling an athlete more than a scholar."

When asked for impressions of his new country, Nicolai cagily gave a conventional answer: "The European is awed by the sight of Buenos Aires. The splendor of this metropolis makes him realize that Argentina is worthy of being compared with the most advanced countries of the world." Nicolai was playing the game of *cortesía* to perfection. But this shrewd reporter wanted to probe more deeply: "Córdoba, Doctor, has the reputation of being one of the most clerical cities in America." Nicolai shrugged impatiently. "He realizes that we have pushed the conversation onto slippery and delicate terrain," the reporter wrote. "But he answers the question with unsurpassed eloquence: he opens the shutters of the balcony overlooking the Plaza San Martín, and, as if on command, the bells of a hundred churches sound the Angelus, the somber shadows of dusk close about the opaqueness of a hundred tall belfries—and the shutters close again in response to a vigorous motion." The reporter dropped the subject, but his shafts were well aimed. Nicolai would find the shades of the Jesuit past in Córdoba harder to shut out than these bells.

For the moment, however, breathing the cosmopolitan air of the capital and enjoying himself in the role of "Man of the Day," as the *Revista Atlantida* called him, he was unworried by the prospect of yet another battle in a provincial city on the opposite edge of the pampa. He and Goldschmidt lingered in Buenos Aires for another week, fêted and lionized by the press, the academic community, and the liberal elements of the German colony, the descendants of the Forty-Eighters. The two celebrities were guests of honor at a welcome at Aue's Keller, arranged by the German Republican Association, whose president, a Herr Lindemann, told an overflow crowd that this occasion alone justified the existence of his group. The so-called leading circles of the German colony had chosen to ignore the two scholars because of their pacifism and their faith in democracy, he said. The hostility of their colleagues toward the emissaries of a new Germany was finding an echo here. Even the Wissenschaftlicher Verein (the local scientific association), organized to foster German-Argentine cultural ties, had snubbed them, making a mockery of the ideals of its adopted country. Thunderous applause greeted Nicolai's improvised response, which the *Argentinisches Tageblatt* called worthy of being published just as it was given.

The events at the keller were fully reported by *La Prensa*, Argentina's most influential newspaper, and by its competitor, *La Nación*. The latter shared with its readers a visit to its offices by "Dr. Jorge Federico Nicolai." A few days later it carried a full-page cartoon, "The Adventures of Professors Nicolai and Goldschmidt in Argentina" (Fig. 32), which, taking its cue from the quip of Vanguardia about the republic of the Zulus, showed the travelers at one end of a giant telescope and a group of naked savages at the other, with the travelers exclaiming, "the Argentines are *muy simpático* but very, very big," while the Zulus, peering suspiciously at the diminutive Europeans, were saying, "these foreigners are exceedingly small. We better investigate them!" Readers of the German-language newspapers sent in welcoming letters and even poems in praise of the warrior for peace. Apart from the right-wing readers of *Deutsche La Plata Zeitung*, only an illiterate could have remained unaware of Nicolai's presence in the city.

The crowning event was an *acto academico*, with which the Faculty of Economic Sciences of the University of Buenos Aires honored the visitors (Fig. 33). It is worthy of note that the main address was given not by a professor but by a student, D. Enrique Siewers, president of the Centro de Estudiantes de Ciencias Economicas, who greeted the two "maestros" in the name of the young sciences of Argentina. In calling Nicolai a man "in whom our youth reveres the man of science and the spirit of liberty," Siewers was speaking the language of the *Reforma*, the student movement which, after stormy beginnings in Córdoba, had swept the country and indeed the continent and was then at the zenith of its power in Argentine universities. The terms "science" and "liberty" had a very specific meaning for this audience: they were two cardinal points in the *reformista* program, which aimed at nothing less than the complete reshaping of institutions of higher learning. "Science" meant original research, first-hand inquiry, experimentation, and technical competence, rather than mechan-

Fig. 32. *La Nación* (Buenos Aires) cartoon, 4 May 1922.

Aventuras de los profesores Nicolai y Goldschmidt en la Argentina

ical regurgitation of the contents of textbooks by professors and students alike; it meant application of the scientific method, rather than scholastic tradition, the *universidad laboratorio* in place of the *universidad claustro*, the cloistered atmosphere in which higher education traditionally took place in Argentina. "Liberty" stood for many things, from exalted ideals to release from the drudgery of examinations, from simple rebellion against authority to carefully thought-out plans for student participation in the governance of the universities. Each listener knew—or thought he knew—exactly what was meant by the two catchwords. It was Nicolai's first encounter with the living forces of the *Reforma*.

The ceremony closed with a speech by Alfredo Palacios, a leading figure among Argentine intellectuals and academicians and a man of great integrity and courage. He had returned the medal of the Legion of Honor to the French government because he disapproved of its treatment of the workers. He had already made a name for himself in parliament and at the university, and he was one of the few academic leaders to embrace *Re-*

Fig. 33. Reception at the University of Buenos Aires in honor of Nicolai and Goldschmidt. Alfredo Palacios is seated at the far right, next to Nicolai (*Revista Atlantida* [Buenos Aires], 2 April 1922).

Los profesores Nicolai y Goldschmidt, de la universidad de Berlín, acompañados del decano de la Facultad de Ciencias Económicas, del Dr. Alfredo L. Palacios y de otras personas que concurrieron a la recepción ofrecida en dicha Facultad en honor de ambos sabios alemanes.—En los círculos: izquierda: Dr. Goldschmidt, invitado por la universidad de Córdoba para dictar un curso de economía. — Derecha: Dr. Nicolai, que dictará en la misma universidad un curso de fisiología.

forma. His accolade was a measure of the expectations aroused by Nicolai's arrival in Argentina. Palacios asked the guests of honor to forget the bad moments which the bureaucracy had caused them, and to remember instead that "a few yards from the ship on which they were detained there stood the youth and the entire Argentine nation, eager to receive and embrace them, to begin spiritual communion with these great representatives of new ideas and of science." The visit of a professor of physiology in transit for Córdoba hardly called for such language: in reality, Nicolai was being received as a hero and a prophet.

In *Facundo* (1845), a classic known to every educated Argentine, Domenigo Faustino Sarmiento, writer, educator, statesman, and patron saint of Argentine liberalism, described Córdoba in the 1840s. He dwelt on the charm of the great Paseo Sobremonte, broad, shady alleys of plane trees and weeping willows surrounding a large pool, enclosed by a high wrought-iron fence a block long on each side, with huge gates at each corner, "so that the square has the air of a gay prison where one circles endlessly around an attractive Greek pavilion resting immobile in the pretended lake." In contrast, the real prisons of Córdoba, designed for the live burial of heretics, were hidden. They extended for miles underneath the city, radiating outward from the chapterhouse of the Jesuit fathers. Every block of the inner city harbored a seminary, a monastery, or a nunnery. Every family furnished a priest, a monk, a nun, an acolyte, and a choirboy to the Church. "Strolling through the town," Sarmiento wrote, "we come to the famous University of Córdoba, founded in 1613, in whose somber cloisters eight generations of doctors of sacred and profane law have spent their youth." He went on to quote the spiritual director of the Jesuit university as deploring the influence of Aristotle, which corrupted the purity of the school's theological teachings. According to Sarmiento, the university had produced "not a single writer who did not acquire a new education in the European tradition in Buenos Aires afterward." The city had no theaters, no opera, no newspapers, no printing presses. Drawing-room conversation revolved around processions, saints' days, nuns' vows, examinations, and doctoral degrees. It was hard to know how much this had influenced the spirit of the people, said Sarmiento, but "one only needs to observe how the Cordobese keeps his eye to the ground and shuns the view of the horizon. His universe extends no farther than four blocks from the market square." Córdoba was one single monastery, its plaza a fenced-in cloister, its university a seminary "where everybody wears soutanes or cardinals' robes," and the medieval scholasticism taught there "a solidly fortified and buttressed wall protecting the students against any thoughts not related to text and commentary." He added ironically "Córdoba has no idea that there are other things in the world beside Córdoba. True, it has been rumored that there is a place called Buenos Aires, but if such rumors are given credence, which is by no means always the case, one is promptly asked: 'Does it have a university, how many convents are there, and does it possess a plaza like ours? What would be the good of anything else?' "

Córdoba was the refuge of the Spaniards during Argentina's struggle for independence.

> Persecuted everywhere else, they were at home here. What traces can a revolution leave in a people educated by Jesuits, shielded against nature, art, and science? What soil for revolutionary ideas, those offspring of Rousseau, Mably, and Voltaire—if perchance they should stray into the Spanish catacombs while roaming through the

pampa—what soil for such ideas can there be in brains so uniquely conditioned to resist everything new? What stirrings can they awaken in these minds which—like their plaza—harbor at their center an immobile idol surrounded by stagnant water that prevents every approach?

Before he left Córdoba, Nicolai copied these passages, which no doubt served as a model for his own satirical farewell to the city five years later. The *spiritus loci* ridiculed by Sarmiento was still alive. But at the time of his arrival he had grounds for optimism, for *Reforma* was triumphant, and he was its hero.

There had been some changes since Sarmiento's day. Fanciful fountains and *jeux d'eaux* had been installed in the artificial lake in the center of the Paseo Sobremonte, little motorboats darted gaily on its surface, and at night bengal lights illuminated the scene. The university was no longer run by the Society of Jesus but had become a state institution, the Universidad Nacional de Córdoba. The Cordobese could choose from two newspapers, the arch-conservative *Los Principios* and the progressive *La Voz del Interior*. The town now boasted, if not a theater, at least a cinema, but until the advent of the student rebellion the living and thinking habits of the citizens had remained much the same as in Sarmiento's day. Though the Plaza San Martín was dominated by the equestrian statue of the Liberator, the churches and convents were as numerous and as powerful as ever. Life flowed slowly; the quiet houses and sun-drenched patios seemed to invite contemplation. No one had much difficulty earning a living, but then expectations were not high. The strongest influence was an old-fashioned family spirit, reinforced by the Creole sense of dignity. Women, according to the connoisseur Nicolai, played a minor role outside the home. Svelte in their youth but plump after the first child, they made good mothers and housewives, but their restricted lives, "somewhat influenced by the memory of the Arabian harem, rarely give rise to a stirring of the emotions."

It was foreordained that the rebellion should have begun at Córdoba, for while discontent was nationwide and the movement spread like wildfire to every university in Argentina, conditions here were more archaic than anywhere else. The young *reformistas* were idealistic, intelligent, and articulate, and their writings give a vivid picture of the intellectual dry rot that afflicted the *Docta y Santa*, the "Learned and Holy," as the university was called, either reverently or sarcastically, depending upon the speaker.

The sorest spot was the law school, heir to the original Faculty of Theology and guardian of its tradition. Until 1918 it continued to teach sacred and profane law, with emphasis on the former and open disapproval of such incursions by the state into the latter as civil marriage. Under the name of "public ecclesiastical law" it forced upon the students "professions of a faith that was incompatible with the spirit of a university," according to Arturo Orgaz, one of the rebels, who himself later became a professor.[3] Philosophy of law courses did not go beyond the ideas of the university's founder, Padre Trejo y Sanabria. The history of government followed an obscure and obsolete text. The library was in a state of neglect and bespoke an "insuperable incapacity for culture and a lack of concern for the living present." The professors covered the prescribed information as if they were dealing with elementary school pupils. The lectures were based on texts "embodying the sum and substance of all that can be known, so that nothing was left to the initiative of the student, since the professor himself lacked curiosity and the desire for intellectual renewal." Examinations followed an inflexible routine: what seemed to be "fluency and spontaneity was only rote and mediocrity: servility of the intelligence, dogmatism of knowledge, death of science, sacrifice of culture, the academic lie."

Writing in the year of Nicolai's arrival, Orgaz sketched a class as it had been before *Reforma*—the boredom of the students and the pomposity of the professor who takes an interminable time with preliminaries intended to impress his listeners. When at last he speaks, the students wait for "the revealed word of an arcane science, the secret essence of truth, the magic formula, the dazzling and persuasive initiation into the sacred mystery of the law." They all are hopeful, for

> young minds are given to hope and adventure, and believe, class after class, that this will be the day on which the professor will begin the happy initiation into his teachings, the truth as he understands and feels it, and once this is done there will come the happy marriage of spirit, industry, enthusiasm, and frank cordiality between master and disciples. But the days go by in unbearable monotony and the year ends without this man, who appears to be—or ought to be—the mentor, illuminator, and shaper of young minds, having guided, instructed, or created anything but a muddle.

Orgaz was not exaggerating. All contemporary witnesses agree that the Faculty of Law was a bastion of obscurantism and incompetence, "protecting the student against any thought not related to text and commentary," as Sarmiento had said. But things were no better at the Faculty of Medicine, where future physicians were taught by the "oratorical method," that is, without the use of cadavers, actual patients, or experimental animals. As Nicolai's Córdoban sponsor Enrique Barros wrote in 1924, the pretentious motto of the Jesuit founders, "ut portet nomen meum coram gentibus" ("let My name be carried to all the world"), was a cruel irony in a school where no research was conducted, where radium and deep X-ray therapy were still unknown, where anatomy was taught as it had been in Vesalius's day, and where the faculty had not helped save a single life during the recent terrible typhoid epidemic, when the citizens were dying "like the masses of an Asiatic slum." Thus it was only natural that the faculty would resist—and, if need be, sabotage—the *reformistas'* attempts to import European professors who would make local deficiencies all too apparent. Barros charges that in one instance the already confirmed appointment of a biochemist was canceled by a secret telegram from Buenos Aires sent at the instigation of the dean.

Law students and medical students, determined to obtain a modern education from competent teachers, thus became the prime movers of the *Reforma*. They objected to the medieval discipline of the classroom, the forced attendance, and the frequent examinations. Feeling themselves full-fledged citizens of the Republic of Letters, they protested the total absence of student representation in the governance of the *Docta y Santa*. But most of all, they resented the influence of the Church: in university affairs the archbishop was a dominant figure and defeated every effort at modernization. Anticlericalism was one of the roots of the movement, and when the students finally took to the streets, their battle cry was *Frailes, No!* ("No Priests!").

The first stirrings occurred in 1916, in response to the Church's prohibition of a lecture on comparative religion. Liberal elements founded Córdoba Libre, an organization whose first act was to invite the anticlerical Dr. Palacios to address its members. Subsequently it established a "people's university," which the government was forced to recognize, where classes of practical interest were offered in an academic setting. The groundwork was thus laid for an attack on the main bastion of tradition. After some desultory student demonstrations, a committee "pro *Reforma*" was formed to make plans for the reorganization of the university. When its plans were ignored, the committee proclaimed a general strike of the student body. "Animated by an irresistable impulse toward progress, the youth of Córdoba finds itself in conflict with its ancient and decrepit university," its manifesto of 31 March 1918 declared. The strike was neither an outburst of youthful anger nor a rebellion against the "desirable discipline of work and study," it said. On the contrary, the students aspired to live "the full life of the intellect in an environment of true scientific freedom, taught by modern instructors free from dogmatic prejudices." Then, on a stronger note: "We are the rising generation that must fight for the progress of our fatherland, capable of shaping its destiny in the family of modern societies. We are the spirit of the present and the future—and this university has the audacity to educate us for the past and to mold our brains to be fit for the archives of history!"[4]

Now transformed into the Federación Universitaria, a national organization and a power to be reckoned with, the committee asked the government to intervene in the student's dispute. Vaguely alarmed, President Yrigoyen sent a high-ranking official to Córdoba as an *Interventor*, with executive power. Underestimating the seriousness of the situation, the official instituted a few token reforms and departed. The new rules did not prevent the old guard from engineering the election of one of their own to the office of rector over the students' candidate. When the election results were announced, pandemonium broke out. In the elegant, wood-paneled eighteenth-century *salón de grados* and the adjacent cloister books flew through the air, chairs were overturned, chandeliers and French doors were smashed, and furniture was tossed into the street. An attempt was made to overturn the huge statue of Padre Trejo y Sanabria, the university founder, which dominated the cloister, and its pedestal was covered with improvised posters. The students then declared the day "the day of the advent of the new university" and deposed the new rector.

The clerical party was shocked and outraged, and the town was now completely polarized. "Córdoba the illustrious and learned, the traditional, the cradle of culture and thought, mother of famous classics is in mourning," *Los Principios* cried. A "committee for the defense of the university" was hastily formed to organize a "mitin de desgravio a la cultura córdobese" (roughly, "rally to restore the honor of Córdobese culture"). In the words of *Los Principios*, "venerable matrons and beautiful maidens, packing the streets and the balconies along the route of the parade, bestowed the prize of their smiles, their applause and their flowers on the knights of culture."

The *reformistas* responded by formally seizing the university buildings, planting their flag atop the Casa de Trejo, and proclaiming themselves the governing authority. They appointed students as deans of each faculty and even proceeded to hold examinations—which, to everyone's surprise, several candidates failed. The army was mobilized, and the governor of the province ordered the police to lay siege to the administration building and starve the rebels into subjugation. But the headquarters of the Federación were across the street, and the beleaguered students were supplied with bread, fruit, and canned food via an aerial route. At last the soldiers stormed the buildings and took the occupants into custody at their regimental barracks.

The Yrigoyen government, far away in Buenos Aires, did not understand the nature of the conflict but did now realize that things had gone too far. A second *intervención* had already been requested by the rebels themselves. The new mediator, a Dr. Salinas, minister of justice and public instruction, was greeted enthusiastically and proceeded to remedy the grievances laid before him. The statutes were amended to give the students a voice in university affairs. As a result, the professors and other officials of the old regime resigned en masse, their positions were declared vacant, elections were held by the students, and new authorities filled the empty posts. They took office in a solemn ceremony, at which Salinas made a speech calling the rejuvenated university a monument to the educational and scientific progress of the nation and of the entire continent: "You are now in possession of the reconstructed University of Córdoba," he said. Before departing, he went to the local office of the Federación and in a storm of applause signed the register. It was a complete victory.

All this was very recent history when Nicolai arrived, and the *reformistas* were still in full control, although the forces of the Reaction were quietly regrouping. The rector, Dr. Francisco de la Torre, had been elected by the students, as had the majority of the Consejo Superior, the university governing body. Without their concurrence neither Nicolai nor Goldschmidt, the latter an avowed Marxist, could have been appointed. But the full measure of student power is evident in the way in which Nicolai's appointment had been brought about. Barros had stepped onto the balcony in 1918 to proclaim the seizure of the university; after graduating he went to Germany to study under the famous pathologist Ludwig Aschoff in Freiburg. There he had taken it upon himself to recruit faculty for the "new university."[5] Nicolai, along with Eugene Debs, Albert Einstein, and Bertrand Russell, was named in the Federación's Manifesto of 1920 as one of the persecuted apostles of freedom and peace. To bring such a man to Córdoba would be a crowning victory. And thus, upon the sole recommendation of a young man who barely a year ago was an undergraduate, the *Docta y Santa* gave Nicolai a three-year contract.

The appointment was unprecedented, not only because no official or faculty member had ever laid eyes on him or, for that matter, had read anything he had written, but also because it circumvented the normal hiring process, the *concurso*, an open competition in which a candidate would give sample lectures, submit an essay, and otherwise prove his qualifications. A *professor contratado* (under contract), moreover, was almost unheard of, and the fact that Nicolai was reimbursed for the cost of his trip, guaranteed his return fare, and paid a handsome salary only made the scandal worse, in the eyes of the old guard.

As for Nicolai, the fact that he embarked on his venture simply upon the word of a young graduate student is a measure of his desperation. In Europe he had no other option. Unaware of the scientific reputation—or lack thereof—of Córdoba, he may have been attracted by its romantic past. In any case, he was hedging his bets, as evidenced by the guaranteed return fare, the leave of absence from the University of Berlin instead of resignation, the installation of a locum tenens in his practice, and—unlike Goldschmidt—the leaving behind of his wife. In his prime at the age of forty-eight, he was not ready for the contemplative life and had no intention of spending the balance of his years in a South American backwater.

If the newcomer had reservations, Dr. De la Torre had none. Perhaps he was more idealistic and more naive in his appraisal of the reactionary forces than a rector should be. In his welcoming address he defended the appointment of foreigners.[6] A great effort was needed, he said, to liberate the university from the yoke of religious and philosophical dogmatism. Metaphysics, however spiritually satisfying, must give way to scientific inquiry, which alone could bring understanding and remedies for the world's problems. The university must be modernized and "for that purpose we must turn to teachers from abroad." It would be a grave mistake to "let ourselves become irritated and wrought up under the cloak of misconceived national pride and self-sufficiency." Paris took pride in having attracted a Metchnikoff and a Madame Curie; the United States was looking for scientists wherever it could find them; the venerable University of Heidelberg, which had meant so much in the lives of Nicolai and Goldschmidt, began its existence with a faculty of Frenchmen, among them the great jurist Hugo Donnellus. What better time than this era of transition to attract the talent that Europe could not retain.

The rector then went on the offensive. Leaping from the Middle Ages to the modern era and expressing a central theme of *Reforma*, he said that science had the task of investigating all problems, even the most immediate ones, "call them love or justice, that are at the heart of the moral and physical tranquillity of society." It could not remain aloof from any aspect of life. "It is in this spirit that we have looked for men of positive science, and we present them today in the persons of Professors Nicolai and Gold-schmidt. One in the field of biology, the other in economics, they have searched for the truth with the means of their craft, and, notwithstanding their widely divergent point of departure, both have arrived at humane and intellectually sound conclusions." Biological insights had led Nicolai to oppose the slaughter of war, while Goldschmidt sought solutions to that most human of problems, the struggle between capital and poverty. "*Ciencia y amor*," science and love, Dr. De la Torre proclaimed in a strangely modern juxtaposition, "these, my young friends, are what they will offer to guide your spirit and your work." In a separate tribute to the author of the *Biology of War* he amplified his thought: "Science and love, yes! We seek love in the man of science as well. For the sake of love he sacrificed his comfort, his social position, his fortune; not the love of the proselytizer or the hypocrite but the understanding and disinterested love that transcends national and class barriers for the sake of human happiness. To the law of desolation Professor Nicolai opposes the scientific principles of peace and life."[7]

The Rector, too, was speaking the language of *Reforma*. Argentine students had been awakened from their indolence by the war, much as American students would be awakened from theirs by the war in Vietnam. The European culture from which they had taken their values had destroyed itself in a bloody orgy whose purpose they could not fathom. It was time to return to humanity, to abandon militarism, to reconcile nations and classes, to adopt new values. "The universities have come to be the faithful mirror of these decadent societies which are pledged to offer the sad spectacle of senile immobility," the famous manifesto of 21 June 1918 had said. Love, human warmth, personal involvement, social conscience— these were the things that the academic youth of Argentina demanded from the universities and from society at large.

Following the *acto academico*, held with Spanish punctilio in the *salón de grados* (Fig. 34), the new professors went across the street to the headquarters of the Federación to celebrate and fraternize with the students on their own ground. The setting—a dark, narrow, octagonal courtyard illuminated by torches, dominated by a balcony that served as a speakers' tribune (Fig. 35), was packed with a crowd that overflowed into the street. For the students it was a moment of triumph, the symbol and substance of their victory. These men were the first of *their* men, the new breed of teachers for whose sake their long battle had been fought. The welcome was delirious.

Edmundo Tolosa, the president of the Federación, castigated the reactionaries, who "present to the illustrious guests of our university the shameful spectacle of odious nationalist narrow-mindedness and who had the audacity to cast aspersions on these outstanding scholars." He was referring to the resignation of three members of the Consejo Superior to protest Nicolai's and Goldschmidt's appointments. In addition, the conservative students, taking their cue from *Los Principios*, which had questioned the academic qualifications of Goldschmidt, were demanding an investigation. Goldschmidt, it seemed, was not a "real" professor but had only taught adult education classes at the Lessing Hochschule in Berlin. In the eyes of the *reformistas* it was no disgrace to teach outside the sacred precincts of the university: on the contrary, as the "people's university" had proved, their program called for the opening of higher education to all classes and especially to the workers. The universities of Latin America had traditionally served only the privileged classes, the sons of landowners, doctors, lawyers, and merchants. *Reforma* aimed at changing all that. In this respect, too, Nicolai conformed to the ideal of the rebels. He himself had lectured at that very Lessing Hochschule before the war. (Later he would become a prime mover of the Colegio Libre de Estudios Superi-

Fig. 34. The Salón de Grados at the University of Córdoba, scene of Nicolai's inaugural lecture.

ores, a true "people's university" created—largely for his benefit—in Buenos Aires and Rosario.)

The guests of honor at the Federación celebration ignored the scurrilous attacks. Goldschmidt brought greetings from Barros, who was still abroad. Then Nicolai, *El gran Europeo*, stepped onto the balcony, a commanding presence, tall, erect, his monocle sparkling in the light of the torches. "I have come to Córdoba for one reason only," he told the hushed crowd, "namely, because the Revolution of 1918 took place here, and I see in this academic youth not only a tradition but a hope for that which must come." He had expressed the same hope in his message to the Neue Jugend in wartime Germany, he said, but the new generation of Germans had let him down. The Russian Revolution, which at first had seemed to be the wave of the future, had turned into a dictatorship from which he expected little, his sympathy for starving women and children notwithstanding. The United States of President Harding and the speakeasy was an unlikely place to rebuild the world. But here, in this remote corner of South America, he had found a young generation that seemed worthy of

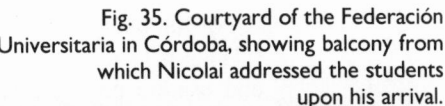

Fig. 35. Courtyard of the Federación Universitaria in Córdoba, showing balcony from which Nicolai addressed the students upon his arrival.

his faith, seekers of new goals yet respectful of culture, enthusiastic yet serious, rebellious yet conscious of their ultimate responsibility.

The moment was deceptive. The enthusiasm of the students would fade as they got their degrees and went out to earn a living; the ingrained conservatism of the Cordobese would reassert itself; the reformist administration would succumb to the old guard, the impetus of the movement would be wasted in intrigue, backbiting, and foot-dragging, until at last it vanished as if swallowed by a quagmire. Nicolai and Córdoba were incompatible. He was bound to come in conflict with the inertial Establishment, and his young supporters could only aggravate that conflict. With his speech from the balcony he had publicly chosen sides in the battle between *reformistas* and traditionalists, and the latter would never forgive him. Once more he had become controversial even before he had assumed his new role.

For his inaugural lecture he chose the grand theme "¿Qué es la Vida?" ("What is Life?"), delivered in the grand manner. It was the sort of elegant and erudite performance that a Latin audience would appreciate, filled with references to the Bible, Goethe, Montesquieu, and, of course, in a Spanish setting, Calderón's *La Vida es Sueño*. It was also a thorough and masterful review of current biological knowledge. In passing he criticized some well-known contemporary biologists for letting irrational or "metaphysical" notions creep into their thinking. Such notions were the obverse of his faith, not in science, which is infallible, but in the scientific method as applied by scientists, who are not. The touchstone of the scientist is his willingness to abandon today's theory tomorrow if it can be disproved: *Scientia fluctuat nec mergitur*—science has its ups and downs but never goes under—was Nicolai's motto. The inaugural lecture was an unqualified success.

His regular classes were no less successful. Well attuned to the *reformista* creed, he began with a question: what is the purpose of holding classes today? Lectures were relics of the Middle Ages, when books were hard to come by. With the invention of the printing press, the universities remained unchanged. The students got nothing from their teachers but what they had already read in their textbooks. They could look up the number of red corpuscles or the chemical composition of the blood. "The true purpose of having classes must be for us to give you something that is not in your texts," said Nicolai. This meant, first, demonstrations and experiments, second, the imparting of "a little love for the subject, a little love on which to base the humanitarian profession you have chosen as your life's work." He then plunged into a technical discussion of the circulation of the blood. He was a superb lecturer, lively and entertaining as well as concise, combining mastery of his subject with showmanship. He performed dramatic experiments in the classroom and illustrated his points with beautiful freehand drawings on the blackboard (Fig. 36). When presenting an important idea he would retrieve the monocle that was dangling on his chest and fix the class with a triumphant stare. The students were entranced.

His colleagues loved him less. At first both town and gown lionized him, but the honeymoon was brief. Except for a few enlightened spirits, Córdoba found the Great European uncongenial and overbearing. He in turn found them staid, provincial, and ignorant and took no pains to conceal his feelings. He had the support of the students, the few *reformistas* on the faculty, and the liberal *La Voz del Interior*, which gave a great deal of space to university affairs. He quickly formed friendships with a few like-minded persons—above all Gregorio Bermann, a young psychiatrist of great promise and a leading theoretician of the *Reforma*, a man of wit and personal culture and the only Córdobese with whom he would remain on close terms for decades. He returned to the pastimes of his first exile in Graudenz—chess, horseback riding, hunting in the nearby sierra. As for the ladies, circumstances did not favor liaisons between a distinguished

Fig. 36. Nicolai's "examples of organic colonies." His blackboard drawings were equally elegant.

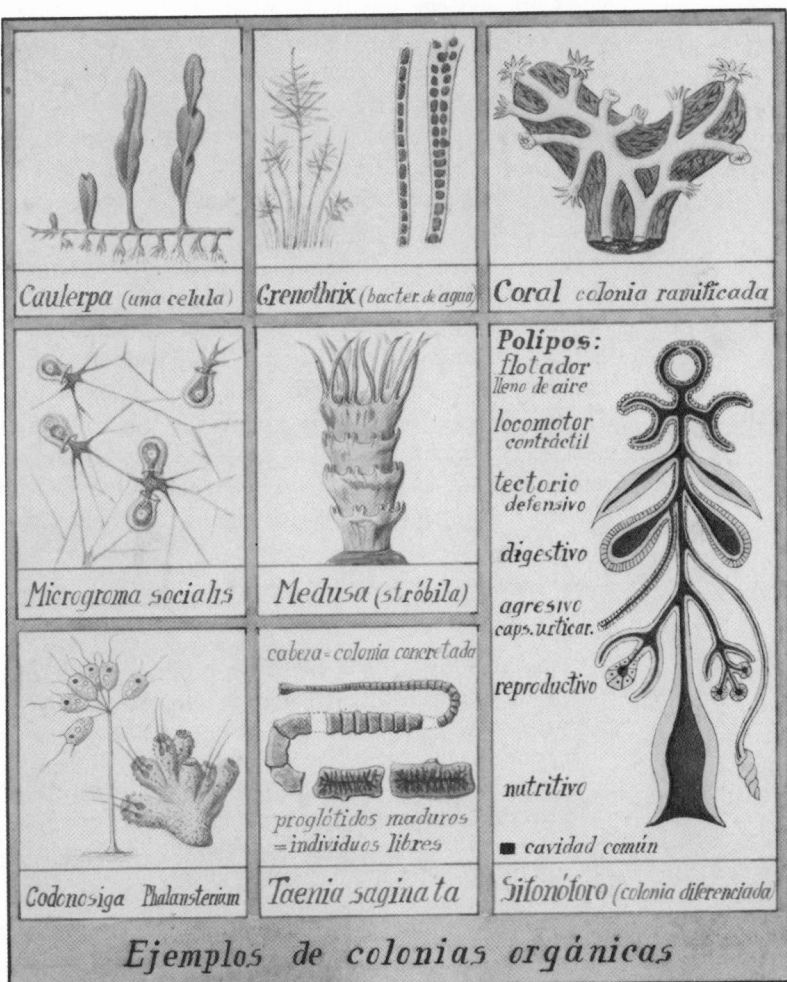

foreigner and the local belles. In Córdoba even a Nicolai had to be conventional, at least in this respect.

If he had intended to resume his disrupted research, he was slow to start. The university laboratories were woefully antiquated and underequipped. Part of his time was spent in building a consulting practice, for even as *profesor contratado* he had to supplement his income. This was an evil of which the rector had spoken in his welcoming address: a system which paid token salaries to full professors and none to the rest of the faculty forced everyone to earn money on the side. The development of a properly paid full-time faculty was one of the aims of *Reforma*. Nicolai's salary of five thousand pesos was the envy of his colleagues and a fortune for an exile from inflation-ridden Germany, but it was not enough. He meant to rebuild his fortune and live in style. He would accept privation when necessary for the sake of his principles; otherwise he enjoyed the good life and was always keenly interested in money. But he was a prodigious worker, and if he was unproductive, it was because he was at loose ends. He had been in the thick of battle and had confronted the great issues of the times. He did not admit it to himself, but Kraus' prediction had already come true: he was lost to the laboratory. As time went by, his mind was more and more occupied with the grand concepts of science. His mission henceforth would be that of a thinker and critic, not that of a scientist at the laboratory bench.

His heart was still in Europe, though the news from home was far from good. Friederike put up a good front, but there were things she could not conceal. "I am trying to live up to your instructions," she wrote, "but it is difficult because of the inflation." Georg had left specific directions for the family budget, but "things are now twice as expensive as when you left. The dollar now stands at 390 marks; an egg costs 6 marks and 10 pfennigs." The locum tenens was unsatisfactory. There was trouble with the rent control office. As for Otto, "sometimes I am seized with horror at the sight of him, imagining that I am being stared at by the reproduction of all the Mongolian idiots I have seen, then again for weeks I see him as a tender, roguish little fellow." She had no illusions about her absent husband:

> Judging from the letters you don't write, I imagine that you live untroubled in the old manner. No one here has heard from you in seven weeks. Still, in this environment you are held to be the founder and protector of a bourgeois idyll in which little people can unfold themselves undisturbed. Since I know that this confining life need no longer oppress you and that you are in a free country where you can indulge every chaotic urge, I pursue my simple, orderly life with an easier mind. Make a happy life for yourself and remember your fellow human beings sometimes.

She must have thought of Argentina as a sort of Wild West, a vast pampa peopled by gauchos and horses. She had no idea of the proprieties of life in a provincial Creole town.

On his part, if Nicolai was drawn to Europe again, it was not because of nostalgia for his hearth and home. "I hope things continue to go well and people continue to interest you," Friederike had answered his first report from Córdoba: "Once you get bored, the situation becomes critical." Nicolai *was* bored. The only event to interrupt the tedium of that first South American winter was a *conferencia* for the benefit, once again, of the starving Russian people, which he and Goldschmidt held not in Córdoba but in Villa Maria, some hundred miles to the south. As early as May he had begun to toy with the idea of a visit to Germany at Christmas. By August the situation had become "critical." His sister Eva voiced her concern: "I have the feeling that you are not exploiting your rich talents. I hear nothing of your work, yet you are capable of doing research as few others today. Ideas just come flying to you. Why are you coming home this winter? I know you; it isn't because of your family."

The pull of Europe was irresistible. He was invited to give a series of lectures in Madrid on the electrocardiogram, on which, in those days of comparatively slow scientific progress, he was still considered an authority. With expenses paid as far as Spain, the chief obstacle to a transatlantic voyage was removed. By Christmas Nicolai was in Madrid. Although he confined himself to scientific topics, the "large and select audience," as *El Heraldo* described it, came to hear the great pacifist. In 1918 the liberal magazine *España* had acquainted the public with his battle against Prussian militarism. Now the leftist writer Luis Araquistain, writing in *La Voz*, hailed him as "a breed which those who do not know him consider non-existent, a German professor who is above all a human being," a man who was treated as a heretic because of the depth of his patriotism, "just as the true Christian is a religious heretic nowadays." Only at a university like Córdoba, he wrote, "freed from the professorial mummies of the past and controlled by a youth whose spirit was kindled by the faraway fires of the Russian Revolution," could such a man have found asylum. In its own way Araquistain's vision of Córdoba was no less romantic than Friederike's.

In France, too, Nicolai was remembered, even though—or rather because—his mission of the previous winter had not borne fruit. In January, when Poincaré seized on a minor pretext to invade the Ruhr, the *Cahiers des Droits de l'Homme*, in a four-page article by Suzanne Colette, called attention to the "Appeal to the Europeans": "One shudders to think that his appeal has lost nothing of its urgency and that five years after the 'Peace' it still sounds like a tocsin." When *Le Temps* called for the shooting of German hostages in retaliation for the assassinations of a French officer and a railway agent, the Socialist *L'Ere Nouvelle* protested: "Shall France adopt Prussian methods? *Le Temps* asks us to imitate Bismarck. For our part, if we must choose our models in Germany, our preference is for Nicolai."

At home, however, Nicolai's visit went unsung. The Germans had other things to think about in that terrible winter of 1923. The country was approaching the nadir of its postwar fortunes. Political murder was more common than ever. The previous June, Walther Rathenau, the Weimar Republic's ablest statesman, was assassinated for the dual crime of being a Jew and of attempting to fulfill the conditions set at Versailles. Chancellor Wirth called for stricter laws to protect the Republic, but—as if to show their contempt for the government—another gang of right-wing hooligans promptly made a brutal attempt on the life of Maximilian Harden. Accommodation with the enemy became a dead issue on 11 January 1923, when French troops invaded the Ruhr. A wave of patriotic indignation swept Germany. Even Nicolai supported the call for passive resistance. Hatred for the invader united all parties, and the country was plunged into the most catastrophic inflation in history.

Nicolai's personal affairs were now in a desperate state. His finances had suffered from his absence from home, as well as from inflation. The lawsuit against the academic senate was still dragging on without hope of success. His medical practice was a shambles. The rent control office had forced Frau Nicolai to sublet most of her apartment. In the cramped space that remained, the presence of Otto, now almost three years old, was a constant reminder of a bitter blow to his father's pride. In December, Elly von Schneider had given birth to Nicolai's child, and although she nobly renounced all claims for child support, the court-appointed guardian insisted on protecting the infant's interests and, in the face of Nicolai's indifference, took the matter to court.

Other legal matters were pending. The return to Argentina had to be planned. Nicolai had been given funds with which to buy instruments for the Physiological Institute of Córdoba, and they had to be selected or specially designed. A group of prospective settlers whom he had at first encouraged to follow him to the New World was at his door day and night, hoping that he would lead them there. He had been considering a divorce so that he could marry Frau Grete M.—, the wife of a Berlin banker and mother of two children, whom he wanted to bring back to Córdoba with him. Only Grete's decision not to desert her family (one of her sons was crippled) saved what was left of Frau Nicolai's marriage. It was agreed that wife and daughter would follow him to Córdoba when Friederike had wound up her husband's tangled affairs but that little Otto would stay behind. Most of what remained of the apartment was to be sublet, leaving the family worse off than before. Nicolai chose the furniture, books, china, silver, paintings, and rugs he wanted for the house he planned to buy in Córdoba. The rest, except for the barest necessities, was to be sold. The die was cast. Life in the Argentine hinterland might be dull, but it was paradise compared to the nightmare that was Berlin. He had no desire to stay a day longer than absolutely necessary.

Fortunately, he had received an invitation to speak in Vienna. The Austrian pacifists were desperate for help. What was left of Austria after the breakup of the Habsburg Empire was a German state whose inhabitants wanted to rejoin the Reich, from which Bismarck had excluded them, and in Germany the desire for the reunion was equally strong, but the Treaty of Versailles had expressly forbidden it. The issue taxed the pacifist position in both countries and supplied ample propaganda fodder for the budding Austrian Nazi movement.

Nicolai's Viennese speech, entitled "German Nation and German Culture," was a rationalization of this state of affairs. Germany, he said, was a unifying cultural idea rather than a political one; therefore Austria could be a part of German culture without a political union (a notion that might appeal to intellectuals but would carry no weight with the masses). He also took the opportunity to ridicule the doctrine of racial purity and "Aryan" blood as "manifest nonsense," scientifically and historically untenable and ideologically inferior to the values of a common culture.

This was too much for the Nazi ruffians who, armed with brass knuckles and rubber truncheons, had come to disrupt the pacifists' meeting. They stormed the podium and would have assaulted—perhaps killed—the speaker had not a starry-eyed young girl named Agathe Woelfler thrown herself in front of him with outstretched arms, demanding that the attackers kill her before they harmed a hair on the great man's head. Startled, they fell back, but in the ensuing battle a member of the audience was seriously hurt.[8]

Apart from the disturbance at the meeting, Nicolai found Vienna most enjoyable, a continuous round of parties, sightseeing, and visits to the theater. Not the least of its attractions was Lotte H.—, Nicolai's guide, a good-looking, intelligent pacifist who devoted her days—and, very shortly, her nights—to the fascinating visitor. He lingered as long as possible, adding a week for an improvised idyll in the Vienna Woods.

En route to Rotterdam for the return voyage, he visited his sister Eva and her family in Karlsruhe. On the spur of the moment it was decided that his nephew Dietrich would follow Uncle Georg to Córdoba, where he could complete his medical education and at the same time make himself useful. Nicolai needed an assistant, and there would be ample room in the new house. No one thought of consulting Frau Nicolai, with whom the boy was to sail and who would have one more person to look after when she came to Córdoba. Her consent was taken for granted.

Having settled this matter to his satisfaction, Nicolai sailed from Rotterdam, this time on a Dutch boat and without incident. Late in April he was in Buenos Aires, where he was again warmly welcomed by the German Republican Club. He reported his European impressions at an improvised reception at the same keller at which he and Goldschmidt had first been welcomed. He returned to Córdoba after an absence of four months. He now had no other place to go.

NOTES

1. Elly soon returned to Germany and in due course bore a son, Arne. Like most of Nicolai's ex-mistresses, she tried to be useful to him even after the affair was over. In 1929 Nicolai sent her the manuscript of his recently completed novel, *Herr der Erde*. After suggesting revisions, she placed the book with Rudolf Kayser, Ilse Einstein's husband, who was an influential writer and editor. Two years later she was Nicolai's companion on his visit to Einstein's retreat at Caputh. In 1932 Nicolai visited her in Geneva and met his son Arne. Mother and son were later interned by the Nazis, but were released and emigrated to France, only to be imprisoned again when the Nazis occupied that country. Arne escaped from prison and joined the French Resistance. In 1944 he took part in General Leclerc's drive to Belfort, where his father once narrowly escaped being shot as a spy. At the end of the war, after attempting to enlist in the regular French Army and being rejected as an alien, he enlisted in the Foreign Legion, was decorated for bravery in the Algerian war, and vanished in the jungles of Vietnam at the time of Dien

Bien Phu. The reaction of Nicolai, the great pacifist, to this irony is not known. As for his mother, after the war she lived out her days in the French fishing village of Gard-sur-Mer. Her correspondence with Nicolai continued until shortly before his death.

2. This account of the events connected with Nicolai's arrival in Buenos Aires is based on contemporary newspaper reports in the Nicolai archive.

3. See his "La Reforma Universitaria y la Facultad de Derecho de Córdoba," in vol. 3 of *La Reforma Universitaria*, ed. Gabriel del Mazo (Lima: Universidad Nacional Mayor de San Marcos, 1968). The account was originally published in 1922. All the quotations that follow are from pp. 11–12, 14.

4. *Ibid.*, vol. 1.

5. For an account of these events, see *ibid.*, vol. 2.

6. Francisco de la Torre, *Recepción a los profesores Nicolai y Goldschmidt*, Cátedra Universitaria 2, no. 6 (Córdoba, 1922).

7. The text is found in *ibid.*

8. Aggie Woelfler's selflessness was rewarded many years later, when Nicolai helped her and her family to find refuge in Chile after the Nazi takeover of Austria. It was she who looked after him in his old age.

22. The Obverse of the Coin

The two public images of Nicolai at this time were as different as night and day. To his German enemies he was a scarcely human creature of fiendish intelligence and resourcefulness whose very memory must be obliterated. To his Latin admirers he was a bringer of light and spiritual freedom, as well as an approachable and attractive human being. People who expected a stern biblical prophet found a man of flesh and blood, a martyr with a sense of humor, a thinker with an interest in here and now, a scientist with charm, a delightful *raconteur* and man of the world. Young and old were seduced by his informality and wit, his forthrightness and fire.

But there was a third side to his personality that did not square with either of these images. The Great European was a petty domestic tyrant; the "free and serene spirit" (Romain Rolland's epithet) was quarrelsome and suspicious; the apostle of reason was a philanderer; and the philanderer was a woman-hater. His humanitarianism stemmed from his rational convictions, not from love of human beings. The notion of a mankind freed from the horrors of war and the inequities of a flawed economic system captured him by its logic but left him free to indulge his selfishness in private life. During and after the war he had been able to identify his personal cause with that of humanity. Now that he had exited from the stage—for to him Europe was the stage of history, in the best Hegelian tradition—he could no longer wrap himself in the mantle of martyrdom. He stood naked before those who knew him well.

Those who did know him well were the women around him, his wife, his sister, his mother, and the many mistresses past and present who had remained under his spell. Friederike, the chief sufferer, was still his most loyal defender. Her letters during the year in which she remained in Berlin trying to disentangle her husband's affairs while he was in Córdoba form an indictment that is all the more devastating because it comes from a loving heart.

While he was on the ship returning from his visit to Europe in the spring of 1923, she wrote to him from Bonn, her childhood home:

> In the midst of so many memories I am beginning to find myself. So many of our mature ideas and reactions rest on our early experiences—yours too, you old scoundrel. Will you ever learn to respect a woman, at least in her own home? Suddenly I find myself saddled with an unmanageable nephew, and Eva—who shares all your tyrannical habits—is giving me detailed instructions on how I am to treat him. Is that nice of you? Not one word to your *mater familias* about plans that create new duties for her. It isn't as if one wouldn't gladly do anything if one were asked nicely, whereas chains forcibly applied hurt and are borne unwillingly. You know how I long for a little freedom. I have only one favor to ask of you: grant me a little relief;

don't let me become a slave to your desire for expansion; don't buy too large a house whose upkeep I shall then have to squeeze out of the household money.

As it happened, the "unmanageable nephew" did not add to Frau Nicolai's burdens. He preceded her to Córdoba by almost a year, aroused his uncle's displeasure and suspicion, and was gone before she arrived there.

The next letter summed up Friederike's unsentimental view of her marriage:

When this reaches you, we will have been married exactly nine years. Not many shared experiences have come of them. Viewed from a purely factual viewpoint, these nine years have brought us only three years together in our home, and then I spent two years camping alone amidst our furniture. For four years we were jointly packing suitcases in strangers' houses.

I am having these thoughts because last week was once again very "Nicolaian" in character. My good husband did not finish anything before he left. The lease and other pressing matters are up in the air. The situation is catastrophic, the architects, the banker, the lawyers, the authorities—everything is in a muddle. The architects demand fifty million marks for the alterations, but that price, needless to say, is valid only for today. I shall have to give up still more rooms. Yes, your stupid little wife does everything wrong; now she interferes even with your freedom of movement. You will probably make her sleep in a hammock in the hall.

Referring to her husband's intention to have his newly imported German secretary, Alice Schultz, live under his roof, Friederike, well aware that this arrangement was not strictly a matter of business, added: "If having your secretary in your home is only a question of economizing, I shall cover the added expense of her living outside. Maria is desperate at the thought of having yet another person to wait on. She says she will work for Herr Professor and Herr Dieter, but another person, no!" Nicolai disregarded the protest, and Alice was duly installed in the sumptuous house on the Paseo Sobremonte which he bought on his return to Córdoba.

Frau Nicolai's troubles were legion. She would have to take a later boat: "You can't expect me to finish in one month what you could not accomplish in three." Fräulein van Kampen was a nervous wreck, "confused by all the work with which you have saddled her." In the few weeks since his departure his twelve million marks had shrunk to four. The twenty thousand pesos he had promised to transfer had turned out to be only sixteen. "I shall have to share a cabin with a stranger. In a word, your alleged riches have evaporated—and I was going to splurge! You believe that, of course, and furrow your brow à la Napoleon. I miss having you around to tease. It is terribly cold here; the house is unheated; we all have colds and walk around in woollens; I even had frostbite." Her daily battles with the various authorities were "at once nerve-wracking and comical." The troubles with the rent control office were coming to a head: "Now they want to confiscate and remodel the apartment. Is it worth fighting for? But yes, as long as you have citizenship rights here, why let them take the roof over our heads? This business has political undertones. Once more they refuse to let the dreaded Professor Nicolai have a place to live." Of twelve rooms she would be allowed to keep only two and the "ballroom," with access through the servants' stairs only.

"The shipment of household goods has gone off," she reported in May.

> I am sad. I have no plates, Irene has no bed, but I wanted you to have everything you might like. Like true Christians, we live in the hope of Paradise in the other world. I cannot quite overcome my sentimental feelings, the longing for a family home once in my lifetime. Irene, too, will never know one, but at least she should learn that she belongs somewhere. She is beginning to understand Otto's limitations and longs for a sister, but not one as dumb as he is. It could have lived—you have to answer for that!

Thus, almost in passing, she touched on the most painful subject of all, an abortion she had undergone at her husband's insistence. He blamed her for Otto's backwardness, and in any case he wanted no more children. "Thus one loses one's self in sad thoughts, partly a matter of being overtired, but there remains much to look forward to for me. I would like to be with you, who are creative."

Nicolai did not answer these letters. For almost a year he wrapped himself in all but total silence, making his wife's rearguard battles even lonelier and more difficult than they might otherwise have been. But she did the best she could, and if despair closed in on her at times, she tried to hide it. Most of the time she was factual, brave, even humorous. Though she could no longer deceive herself about her husband's shortcomings, she believed in his greatness. Neither religious nor unduly optimistic by temperament, she had what upper-class Germans of her day called "*Haltung*," literally, "carriage," a bearing compounded of natural pride and a code that sustained the forms of human intercourse long after the substance was destroyed. She had made a bargain and would keep it, trying to put a good face on it, come what may.

She wrote about the children, not too much, for the subject bored him, but enough to relieve her maternal feelings and stir his conscience, if possible. Irene was bright, a quick reader, drew well, made puppets—as her father and Eva had done at her age—and had a quick mind but was inattentive at school. Friederike bought her a watch, pretending that it was a gift from her father. When a business telegram from him arrived, she told a white lie: "What it really says is that *Vati* is thinking of Irene and sends her many wishes." But the child was not fooled: "As if *Vati* thought about such things! He doesn't even know when my birthday is." In the summer Irene was sent to the seashore as the guest of Grete M.—, the woman for whose sake Nicolai had wanted to divorce Friederike, and her mother went to visit her there. Suppressing her own feelings, she reported that the little girl was happy and in sturdier health. "I hardly dared eat my fill at those prices. Lunch, though far from fancy, cost thirty thousand marks. But it is a wonderful feeling to know that my children have fresh air and good food, and that my big boy is in his marble palace."

The fact that her husband had bought a "marble palace" with two patios and a garden had come to Friederike through Eva, who learned it from her son in Córdoba. "Is your silence deliberate?" the humiliated wife asked in October. "I am too simple and straightforward, dear Georg, I cannot understand it. Your behavior saddens and confuses me. Think of the distance between us. It leaves no room for petty feelings; otherwise I, too, would stop writing. Irene wrote you three or four times. In the beginning she waited anxiously for the replies; now she has given up waiting. It is up to you to restore the ties. In any case we have a right to hear from you."

Much of this correspondence dealt with practical matters. She was doing as well as could be expected in three rooms with the two children, Fräulein van Kampen, and Maria. She had taken a roomer, whose boy friend spent his nights with her. "Life sees to it that I don't become lazy but remain elastic in the face of circumstances." The Court of Appeals had ruled against Nicolai in the matter of the academic senate: "I am not very comfortable in the face of this disaster." The rent control office advised her that she would lose what was left of the apartment if she went to Argentina. How permanent was his position in Córdoba? "The news others are getting from you—Gumbel, for instance—does not sound as if you could stay over there." She reminded her husband that two years of his official leave of absence had now elapsed.

Meanwhile the inflation was galloping on: "Today the dollar stands at 136,000 marks. I shall not be able to take a summer vacation—and I wanted to save money for you, for all of us, for the dream of my heart: a carefree life with the patriarch. While you were here I resigned myself to the fact that others came first, for I lived in the expectation of a permanent reunion. Now that the separation has become permanent I feel all the more keenly how little you belonged to us."

The uncertainty of her own fate and that of her children weighed on her mind. From the Argentine consul she learned of new battles between *reformistas* and traditionalists in Córdoba and was certain that her husband was in the thick of it. "The consul advises against buying more equipment, given the difficult internal situation at the university." The apparatus ordered by Nicolai was nearly ready, and she had taken it upon herself to inspect it at the shop. "The settlers, poor devils, call every three days. They are still without word from you. Irene is a nice little person, in spite of many rough spots. May things work out well for you, and don't take it out on me if circumstances are against you. We imagine ourselves in our house in Córdoba and live with you there in our dreams."

But ultimately Friederike's patience began to wear thin.

So much thought went into the shipment of the things for the house—don't you realize what it means to be cut off? We write at least twice a month. Even Eva is without news from Dieter. The settlers' constant calls see to it that I stay worried, but Buek consoles me by saying "There is nothing about you in *La Nación, ergo* you haven't been assassinated." I accept that. Is it perhaps censorship of the mails? Anything is possible in Germany. Whatever the reason, your silence is paralyzing, Georg. Just now I learned from Fräulein G. [unidentified] that her relatives in Argentina are deeply grateful to you for all you did for them. You see, at heart you are such a nice person that I must remain halfway faithful to you.

There was other news. Wilhelm Herzog—Nicolai's erstwhile coeditor of *Die Republik*—"is going to Argentina and counts on your help. He has

Fig. 37. Friederike at the time of her arrival in Córdoba.

offered to be a pack mule and bring the apparatus. Are you being productive? Your intellectual and scientific progeny will be your true and immortal children." There was gossip to report, about Rose Thesing, Curt's wife and a lover of Nicolai in his Eilenburg days, who had divorced her husband and was marrying the finance minister, Hilferding; about Schwann, Nicolai's associate in the wholesale paper business, who was betrothed. "And we—well, we wait. After five months we still don't know your address. Like true fools we continue to believe in your ties to us. The mark has fallen precipitously again; the dollar is now worth more than a million marks. I am glad, my hothead, that you are over there. Here you would explode at every turn, but of course, we long for you—in a subdued way, that is, for I must avoid becoming too emotional."

But by October, still without word, Friederike was losing control of her emotions. "Our last letter was sent by registered mail eight weeks ago. Your silence makes it impossible for me to go on writing. At first I thought it was due to external circumstances, but lately I feel shaken. Last winter, after mature reflection, we decided not to give up our marriage. Why then this total silence? Is it peevishness? But no, for that we are too old, meaning too wise, too responsible toward the children."

The battle with the rent control office was continuing; there was still time for him to give his advice. The two thousand pesos he had sent were used up. "Perhaps you will give us your ideas concerning money. How do I finance our emigration?" A week later she had to cable for a thousand pesos. Nicolai told her peremptorily to come immediately. "After your long silence your telegram was disturbing," she answered. "Too bad, for everything could have been discussed at leisure instead of being insisted upon dictatorially. You are more hasty than practical. I cannot get tickets right now. Also, Fräulein van Kampen is ill and needs surgery. What is to become of Otto? Last spring I was looking forward to Argentina; now— well, we haven't exactly come closer to each other. I have only a hundred pesos left till December and shall have to sell my fur coat."

The man who at this time was exhorting Argentine youth to build a better world remained obdurate. By November Friederike's situation had become still more desperate. Fräulein van Kampen's condition was serious, and the money was now completely used up. "You *must* finance us," she wrote. "It is hard enough to leave Otto behind, but we cannot leave him without subsistence. My big boy is too smart and my little one not smart enough." Fräulein van Kampen had developed a thrombosis just as she was about to be discharged from the hospital in the care of a sister. "Now I shall have to take her into our home and care for her—for how long? I was just about to book our passage. I become more and more apathetic in the face of obstacles that are all the more paralyzing because no faith sustains me. Save a nice quiet spot in your palace for a quiet, delicate *alma de casa*." Her sense of humor rarely failed her.

Nor did she permit herself to be disloyal. She rejoiced at his every success, even though she was not allowed to share in it. The *Biology of War* had come out in a Spanish translation that would bring in revenues, "also a Japanese edition, did you know?" But good news was scarce and her mood was generally black. An anonymous threat from a Nazi caused her to write: "In my imagination the unlucky star above our heads has taken the shape of a two-legged monster with the brain of an Aryan hero, but then I tell myself that it is silly to take the general shouting so seriously."

Meanwhile, unknown to his wife, Nicolai had made some inquiries to see whether he might seek refuge in Russia, for the situation in Córdoba remained volatile, but in the end he decided to stay where he was. The students had elected him as their representative on the Consejo Superior. With the purchase of the "marble palace" he had made a substantial investment. He had begun to write his magnum opus on the biological basis of relativism, his first venture into the realm of abstract science (Fig. 38). The final defeat at the hands of the academic senate had destroyed any

Fig. 38. Nicolai's drawing of a bi-dimensional continuum for *La Base biológica*.

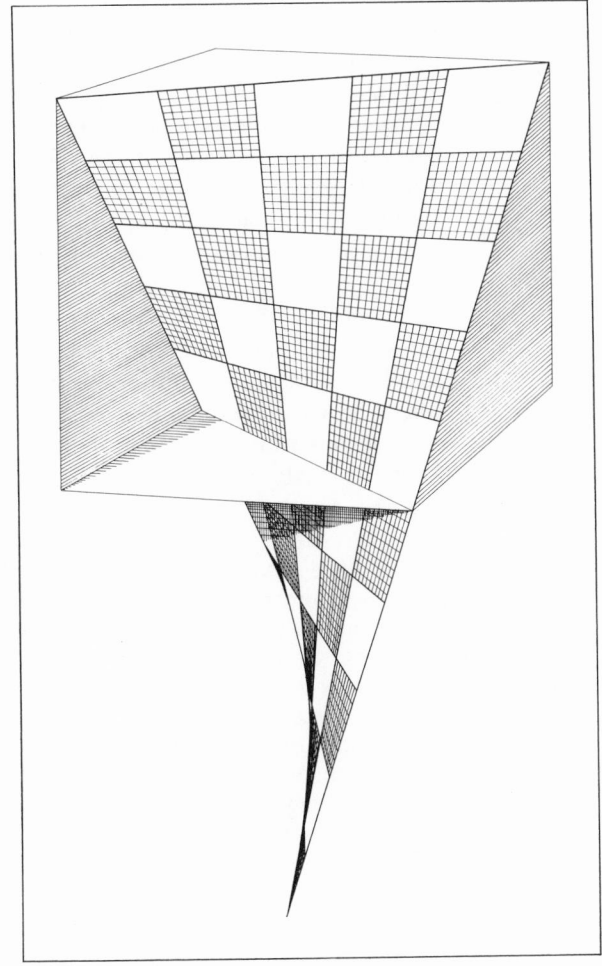

hope of returning to Germany. Now he wanted Friederike to come as soon as possible, not because he longed for an *alma de casa*, but because the household in Berlin had become an unnecessary expense and the marble palace needed her competent hand. It was her duty as a wife to come now.

Unfortunately, she did not share his thinking. "Your wish to have us come immediately and—as I see from Eva's letter—for good requires an entirely new way of thinking from me. I am very reluctant to cut all ties here for the sake of a nomadic existence." She must establish a home for Otto. She had borrowed money, "which I hope will last until you begin to support your family. Christmas will be a very modest affair." Christmas brought a renewed demand from Nicolai for her immediate departure, but no money. She answered that she could not possibly leave before June, as even the best lawyer could not wind up their affairs in less time. "What to do with the fresh little sparrow that is closest to my heart? I would rather bring him with me if only I knew what the climate is like. He would not disturb, only amuse you. Or are there boarding homes, so that he would not be so far from me? I cabled you again yesterday for 1,000 pesos. It is now 1 A.M., the temperature is 8 degrees, and I am shivering with cold and fatigue."

In January Friederike pulled herself together for a birthday letter. "My beloved big boy—your birthday! Remember the fortieth, ten years ago? Then we thought of one another often and happily, though I was not there for the celebration. But that will exhaust the echo of those days. Meanwhile, you have established your reputation, surely quite different from what you had dreamed, years of battles, often petty and wearying but always full of life—as you need it—and yet at times, in the regions of the purest spirit, quite beautiful. I have always enjoyed them and thus felt the drawbacks but little." But now, after sacrificing ten years to his ideals, surely he would resume his vocation: "You will use the next decade to coax secrets from matter and point the way for the younger generation. Matter is stubborn, but at least it doesn't spurt venom and gall."

As for family life,

> I have never considered you as having a talent for marriage and therefore never seriously fought for a matrimonial establishment. Thus it never came into being. For you I don't regret that. It matters little to your personality and it will only delight your biographer when he finds—in the chapter "The Famous Man and His Family"— that you have trod the broad path of respectability only now and then. Of the offspring, only Irene has turned out well, but that isn't much. She is coming along nicely, and it may even turn out to be an advantage that she is under only one parent's influence. She is losing her tantrums and her irritability. In Córdoba, Georg, we must show unity, at least in front of the child, though I hope we will be of one mind in any case.

Later that month things looked momentarily brighter. The consul transmitted some pesos, the apparatus for the laboratory was almost ready, and the wayward husband sent a belated New Year's greeting. But Friederike was far from reconciled to the idea of leaving Germany for good, and the categorical order to sell everything that was not to be shipped brought a cry from the heart:

> You say, sell! I suppose you mean the furniture. Aren't you attached to the dining room set? Ten years ago you made the sketches for it.

For three years we lived with our things, and now I have to sell and destroy everything. *Este es la vida.* My mind does not take these things as tragedies, but my deepest being longs for roots before I can unfold myself. Because of this moving from place to place I always bleed from hidden wounds and feel my strength ebbing away. I go along with everything because it is right and because it has to be done for your sake, but it gnaws at my vitality because my truest self suffers. Since I have no real hopes for over there but only expect to get through the years, I pull myself together with all my might to get ready for the departure. Please leave me Fräulein Maria, even if it is a financial burden on you. I would not ask if I were not afraid of myself, that is, of the faltering of my willpower. These months without news, the undermining of my position by the general knowledge of your fathering [of Arne] in circles that will hold it against you—all that has taken its toll. If I now have to dissolve the household alone with the two little ones, I might collapse.

Apart from her own troubles Friederike was supporting other people's burdens. There were the "settlers," a group of would-be immigrants gathered by Nicolai during his visit the previous winter, who were waiting anxiously for a word from him and naturally turned to his wife when none came. Somehow, after his earlier encouragement, he had become obsessed with the notion that they were right-wing extremists, Nazis and spies, bent on spreading their ideological poison overseas. In reality, they were decent citizens and good democrats, small tradesmen and artisans hoping to escape strife-torn, inflation-ridden Germany to build a new life in a free country under the leadership of the great pacifist. They submitted all kinds of affidavits to dissipate his suspicions, and at Christmas they came once more to Friederike for help: "I would describe their unshakable loyalty in one phrase: 'Your servants await your orders.'" But Nicolai remained adamant, and the settlers stayed at home.

Then there was Georg's mother, now approaching eighty and virtually blind but as alert as ever. Friederike had managed to squeeze enough pesos out of her own allowance for the old woman to make a last visit to her East Prussian relatives, but she had kept the matter secret, for she knew that her husband would disapprove of such sentimental luxuries and that he was not even aware of her desperate attempts to stay within her meager allowance. "Remember your silly little wife, who runs through all the money?" she had written recently. However, Nicolai learned of his mother's trip to Königsberg from the old lady herself. "Of course, you didn't know to what use your pesos were put," she wrote in her unsteady hand. She, too, had grounds for complaint. "You bad boy, you don't let us hear from you. All we know—from Dieter—is the floor plan of the house you bought." She added: "This letter has become longer than I intended, and perhaps you won't even read it, but remember that it is your mother who is writing it and that these may be her last lines. Receive them kindly." As far as we know, these *were* her last lines to her son, although she lived for another five years.

Eva, too, was unhappy, for her son Dietrich had fallen into disfavor with his uncle Georg. The *ménage à deux*—or, rather, *à trois*, for it included Alice Schultz—had begun auspiciously enough. The young medical student, happy to escape from the stifling atmosphere of a German university, delighted to live in a beautiful house in an exotic country, eager to please his famous uncle, had sent glowing reports to his mother. Even Nicolai seemed pleased. "Thank you for your kind words about Dietrich," Eva responded. "He writes that he is very happy about his relationship with you. At heart he is quite sentimental. He is very excited about the lovely house. You must be counting on Friederike's arrival. Now at least I know something about your life, your horseback riding, the student strike, your election, the furniture, and the chickens." Dieter was assisting his uncle with a project that involved measurements of brain weight and intelligence in some two hundred dogs, Nicolai's first and only major piece of original research on a biological subject in Argentina, and received a modest salary for his labors. There was even talk of bringing his parents Eva and Edwin Blos to Córdoba. In a burst of optimism Nicolai talked of founding a clinic in which his brother-in-law would be chief surgeon.

Suddenly the atmosphere darkened. "Your letter came like lightning out of the blue," Eva wrote. "That you don't accept Dietrich is too bad, for I had hoped for a strengthening of our family ties, but that you reject our kind in principle is to condemn Edwin and myself and the upbringing of our children."[1] He himself had suggested Edwin's moving to Argentina "because for once you were interested in making money and needed his practical experience. If you changed your mind, you could have told us in a friendly manner, not so brusquely. Naturally we have abandoned any thought of help from you. We had no objection to Dieter's staying in Argentina, for here the universities are threatened with closure and everything points to another war." It was another episode in the old love-hate relationship between brother and sister, so similar in temperament and so different in outlook.

However, there were still other, more immediate, reasons for the estrangement. Eva had come under the influence of a woman whose mysticism offended her rationalist brother, and Edwin had developed a mystical streak of his own, dressing and acting more like a saintly hermit than a working surgeon, but money was at the root of the quarrel between uncle and nephew. Dietrich had sent his parents a few pesos, thereby triggering both Nicolai's miserliness and his paranoia. He accused the boy of theft, blackmail, and other crimes. When she heard this, Eva wrote to Nicolai indignantly:

> Blackmail, embezzlement! But then I understood the facts from Dietrich's letter. I had hoped, by openly admitting the difficulties in his character, to bring about a reconciliation, for you are the older man and a responsible guide. From his earlier letters I knew that he was working so hard for you that he had no time to study but that he was learning so much and was enjoying himself. Even if you find him so inadequate, that gives you no right to withhold his wages. If he used

the money to pay our debts, it was because he considered it his. There can be no question of embezzlement. I wrote him immediately not to send the money. You treated him harshly, yet with his temperament at twenty-two you could have foreseen how he would react. What you refused him as his uncle he claimed as a stranger.

As so often happened, sister and brother-in-law took the first step toward reconciliation. Edwin wrote a soothing note "in spite of everything," and Eva, with an aching heart, fell into line: "Yes, Georg, you, Edwin, and perhaps all of us are peculiar people, but since each of us has become somebody in his own way, we should not present the spectacle of mutual rejection. And to your expression of interest but a remnant of your former affection and you will feel kindlier toward your sister, whose attitude remains unchanged and whose hand reaches out across the distance." She urged her brother to make up with her son, for "we are a close family and every hurt is felt by each of us. And no matter how much you speak against me, somewhere your brotherly feelings are still alive." But if they were, Georg kept them hidden. Dietrich left the house, worked as a dockhand in Buenos Aires to earn his passage, and sailed back to Germany. The hand Eva had held out across the ocean was not grasped, and the relationship between Nicolai and the Blos family remained strained for many years thereafter.

Friederike was further saddened by the rupture. "I had hoped you could handle Dietrich by means of kindness and sympathy," she wrote. "Youth wants to be won with love. He has many of your personality traits—like Irene!" And she permitted herself one of her rare outbursts: "You are all alike in your arrogance, whether you act in a moral or amoral manner." It was the protest of the outsider in the family—the sensible, practical, middle-of-the-roader—against the superiority of a brilliant clan.

> You as the older man, the *pater familias*, should have shown wisdom. I had been happy to see the beginnings of a mellowing process, an attitude of live and let live, of smiling at the weaknesses of those around you. Georg, one achieves more by being accommodating and kind. Dearest boy, you have as much talent for building up as for tearing down—human souls as well as other things. In old age one quickly becomes lonesome. May your children grow up in warming sunshine. The strongest human beings are those who have been nurtured in joy. Frightened people turn into obnoxious creatures.

But even as she was writing, she succumbed once more to her husband's spell, the spell few women could resist. The letter ended with a surrender: she agreed to leave Otto behind.

Nicolai was unmoved. He had an unlimited fund of self-righteousness and very little human kindness. Whatever his reasons for maintaining his marriage, love and charity were not among them. When he did not ignore his wife's appeals and questions altogether—in desperation she went so far as to send him questionnaires that required only the checking off of "yes" or "no" boxes—his answers were coldly factual, if not peremptory. He never entered into her little jokes or responded to her tenderness. "I would have preferred not to answer your typewritten letter," she protested once; "one should not dictate overseas correspondence in such a mood." He adopted the manifestly absurd fiction of the "silly little wife," a joke devised by her in self-defense, as the actual basis of the marriage. Her sense of humor failed to amuse him, whether she was teasing him or mocking herself. She reached out for the child in him that, according to Nietzsche, is hidden in every man, but in vain. The sexual bond between husband and wife had never been strong and was now completely broken.

But Friederike was useful to Nicolai in many ways, for instance, as a housekeeper and, despite her disclaimers and his scoldings, she was an intelligent and knowledgeable helper in his complicated legal and financial affairs. Then too, her mere presence as his wife shielded him to some extent against scandal. She was presentable in any setting and could be expected to adapt herself well to the role of faculty wife in Córdoba. Her unselfishness, verging on masochism, complemented his ruthless egotism, and in this sense they were well matched. She offered him admiration and admitted his intellectual superiority without being blind to his faults. Her sense of humor enabled her to laugh at all but the worst slights she had to endure, as if he were only acting the part of the tyrant instead of being one. She made no scenes, and if she ever had a jealous impulse she knew how to control it. She left him complete freedom to pursue both his work and his pastimes, including his constant sexual liaisons. She was tolerant but not gullible, practical but not prosaic, resigned but not without spirit.

What made her position so ironic was the fact that she was a wealthy woman in her own right but could not touch her money without her husband's consent, which was not forthcoming. "I have borrowed money and shall wire you for more," she announced at a critical moment. "Why should I, poor miserable creature, pull your chestnuts out of the fire?" Beneath the humble facade there was a proud woman, though she seldom stood up to her husband. "Georg," she wrote on that same occasion, "you want to rebuild our marriage. So do I. I begin with a plea: be so chivalrous as not to demand diplomacy from me. I am too straightforward—and so are you, when all is said and done. You are not a businessman, and neither am I. My undemanding manner is forced, for at heart I have the *grand seigneur* instincts of my Von Lilienthal ancestors."

But it never occurred to her to escape from her bondage. She wanted to protect the children, Otto, "the little idiot," whom she regarded with a mixture of tenderness and horror, and Irene, a bewildered little girl who needed the stability of a home. She had to sacrifice Otto, but Irene would have as normal a family life as it was in her mother's power to provide. At the same time Irene would become the link between her estranged parents. Through her, the gifted daughter, Friederike would redeem herself in the eyes of a husband who blamed his son's defectiveness on her genetic background. (There had been a case of mental illness in her family, and the cause of Mongolism was still unknown, a fact which could excuse Nicolai the physician from connecting the two conditions, though not Nicolai the husband from the cruelty of putting all the blame for Otto on his wife.)

But above all Friederike saw Nicolai not only as her husband but as a great man whom it was unthinkable to desert. For her, as for his other admirers, male and female, he was larger than life, the prophet of a new age and a genius whose path must be kept clear of petty obstacles. He needed her whether he knew it or not, and she would serve him, come what may. For her to think otherwise would have been to admit the utter failure of her life.

In the spring of 1924 she at last could think of leaving Berlin. "Things are very uncomfortable here," she reported. "The lift van has gone off, and Irene and I are without beds. I could travel on the S.S. *Köln*, but I will not. You, with your thick skin, would not understand." In her own way Friederike was as brave as her husband, but after his run-in with the *Köln*'s skipper two years ago she would not expose herself and her child to needless embarrassment. Nor would she go to the expense of traveling first class on another ship. She would wait, bedless and all, until she could get a suitable passage. "But don't worry, Bübele, I always keep my word. You won't find anyone as staunchly and boringly honorable as your lawful wedded wife." In June, having settled her husband's affairs, sold her furniture, and placed her son in an institution for retarded children, Friederike sailed on the S.S. *Crefeld* toward the New World and a future she dreaded.

On the eve of her departure Friederike received a cable from Córdoba that must have buoyed her spirits. The message, wishing her *bon voyage* and a happy reunion, was conventional enough, a gesture a woman traveling thousands of miles to rejoin her husband after a long separation might well take for granted. But Friederike was not accustomed to such thoughtfulness. She could not be blamed for thinking that it signified a new beginning, that Nicolai had indeed mellowed and there might be a hope of rebuilding her all but defunct marriage. The friendly message, however, was actually a well-meant piece of deception (in which, it must be said, her husband had had no part). The sender of the cable was Alice Schultz, the secretary whose unchaperoned presence under Nicolai's roof had so offended Friederike.

Fired from her job and facing expulsion from the house in expectation of the family's arrival, Alice may have been inspired by a kind of sisterly solidarity with the neglected wife, by vicarious embarrassment for her employer-lover, or by sheer pique over her abrupt dismissal. Certainly her departure had been an unhappy occasion. "You told me rudely not to disturb you," she wrote Nicolai from Buenos Aires, in a letter in which she confessed her deed, "yet I was brave and reasonable, for I remembered your saying that you would throw me out when the family came, and I thought it best to leave, at least temporarily." Alice expected to return, like most of Nicolai's lovers, she refused to believe that he could do without her, yet she could not deny that he had given her no grounds for this belief. "You always said that I was free to leave at any time, that you loved no one, and that I was not that much of a treasure." But she pleaded: "Please let me have a word to show me that you love me a little. I have to thank you for those beautiful nights when I slept by the open window; I could hear you rustling your papers or, if you had company, moving chess pieces, or an occasional word, then I would sink back into the arms of Morpheus—or sometimes yours." Written "in the same cheap hotel room, by coincidence, where a year ago I tossed on my bed, unable to sleep because of my longing for you," the letter was Alice's swan song. Nicolai, who had hired her because of her proven willingness to combine business with pleasure, had no further use for her modest talents in either field.

Alice's feelings would have been hurt even more deeply had she known that her name would not even appear on the list of feminine conquests Nicolai compiled not a few years later. He had simply forgotten her, so casually had he possessed her at the end of an evening of chess or study. Yet, with his peculiarly systematic mind—part of which reduced love or any other personal experience to statistics as objectively as if it were a matter of population growth or coal production, while another part examined the existential meaning of all his conscious moments—he had clearly tried to make his Leporello's list as complete as possible. He searched his memory conscientiously and in order to avoid inadvertent omissions arranged the names both in chronological and alphabetical order, making insertions as he went along, adding brief notations to identify the woman or the occasion, and neatly categorizing and tabulating the totals. It was an impressive achievement, if only as a feat of memory, and he might be forgiven if he forgot one or another of the flowers he had gathered along his way.

The list comprised one hundred and six names. He made it while traveling in the Soviet Union in 1931, perhaps on a train or in a hotel room, for it was part of a notebook containing Russian addresses, travel notes, calculations, graphs, and the intricate geometrical doodlings at which he was a master. Later he extended it through 1938. Eighty-nine entries were complete, giving first name and family initial. The rest were designations such as "the violet vendor," "the ranger's wife," "Copenhagen secretary," "English violinist," "woman doctor from New York," and "G. R.'s sister," with the last of these carrying the notation "challenged to duel." It was the girl the young Georg had seduced while he was her brother's locum tenens in the little town of Osthofen. With complete impartiality Nicolai listed the most casual encounters next to the women who had played the most important roles in his life, "Liesel K., the first," "Olga, great love," Johanna, Friederike, and Grete M.—, the objects of his mature passion. His conquests ranged from virgins to widows, from seamstresses to titled ladies, and from A (Ada) to Z (Zulema). Twenty-four were Jewesses, eight were noblewomen, twenty-five were of non-German nationality, seven bore him a child, counting the two legitimate ones. Geographically, the list covered the Far East ("Virginia L.," in Sumatra), Russia, Scandinavia, Austria, Switzerland, France (Emilie), Spain, Argentina, and, of course, Germany. To identify the more fleeting encounters he added notations such as "after lecture," "wore glasses," "in black," "on the train," "sailing," and in two instances "wanted to go home," suggesting that these surrenders had not always been entirely voluntary. There were intellectuals, house-wives, landladies, students, secretaries, poetesses, actresses, feminists, and—in the classical Don Juan tradition—at least one case of mother and daughter.

There is something ludicrous about such a list and about a man who compiles it with quasi-scientific thoroughness. Mozart's (or Da Ponte's) Don leaves the bookkeeping to Leporello, the stock-in-trade comic servant of eighteenth-century comedy who draws the laughter of the audience and, by handling the vulgar details of the business at hand, makes it possible for his master to be all *grand seigneur* and to embody the elemental force of sexual energy in its purest form. Even at that, Don Juan skirts the farcical. It is his blaspheming of the dead and his bold defiance of Hell that makes him, through the medium of Mozart's music, a demonic figure. As the seducer of "one thousand and three" Spanish ladies he belongs in the realm of comedy. The number itself is comical. It has, in Kierkegaard's words, "a lyrical foolhardiness" and suggests that "the list is by no means closed, but that on the contrary Don Juan is in a hurry."

The difference between Don Juan's one thousand and three and Nicolai's one hundred and six (not counting omissions and later additions) is un-important. There is a sameness about an experience so frequently re-peated. For Don Juan, Kierkegaard says, "to see her and to love her is the same thing; it is in the same moment, in the same moment everything is over, and the same thing repeats itself endlessly." In yielding to the sedu-cer's routine the woman is stripped of her individuality: she becomes a mere sexual receptacle. Mozart succeeds in giving individuality to the frigid Donna Anna, the smitten Donna Elvira, the naive Zerlina, but for Don Juan himself they are all the same: "Purché porti la gonnella, voi sapete quel che fa." As long as she wears a skirt, he wants her.

But while there is something Don Juanesque in Nicolai's attitude toward women, what is most comparable is the unfocused sexual energy, the per-petual hunger for the ultimate satisfaction which each new experience seems to promise and never fulfills—the pairing of a strong sex drive with an incapacity for love. Like Don Juan, Nicolai is dashing, suave, virile; he has all the essential characteristics of the seducer, and like Don Juan he becomes insensitive, inconsiderate, rude, even cruel once he has attained his goal. But there the similarity ends. Don Juan and his women, creatures of the eighteenth century, have no relationship to each other other than that of seducer and seduced. He exercises a kind of *jus primae noctis* over every woman and moves on. As for his partners, the experience may re-main merely a piquant memory or may be transformed into love or hatred. The seduction itself is what matters.

Nicolai, on the other hand, belongs to the twentieth century. His person-ality has many dimensions, and he is conscious of all of them. His ana-lytical mind is never idle. He too responds to every female *purché porti la gonnella*, but he gives a meaning to all but the most casual relationships. He takes something individual—other than her virtue—from every woman he possesses, and gives something other than mere sexual gratifi-cation in return. To some extent his Leporello's list is an expression of

369

male vanity—the elderly Casanova savoring his memories—but it is also a record of his personal history, or at least an important part of that history.

He himself was intrigued by the apparent paradox that he needed women, yet at the same time despised them almost without exception. "It was his fault that he needed women at all; it was women's fault that they were not as he needed them," he wrote of "Hans von Doppler," the fictitious hero of his novel *Herr der Erde*, clearly a self-portrait. Hans' social instincts, which he called "the cowardly need to lean on somebody which we descendants of herd animals have inherited," are centered on the woman with whom he happens to be intimate at the moment. "He could do without friends but not without an arm that caressed, a body that yielded to him, the pliable soul of a woman with whom he could let himself go. This dependence was an embarrassing remnant of mortality that annoyed him if he were reminded of it. But above all he regretted that this need always led to conflicts, for conflicts in general, let alone conflicts with women, were unproductive."

Women, then, were creatures of a different order, almost a different species, close enough to the male to arouse his sexual desire, indispensable, alas, for reproductive purposes, and intelligent enough to serve as foils for the masculine genius, "attenuated anthropoids," in the bitter phrase of one of his Argentine mistresses. Women might be less intelligent than men, or at least than "El Dios" Nicolai, the Creole lady conceded, but she failed to see how their intelligence could be of a different order. Did the correlation between intelligence and brain weight which he had observed in dogs (a reference to the research project with his nephew) not hold for females? "Did you by any chance weigh only the brains of male animals?"

The biological explanation was unsatisfactory, and in *Herr der Erde* Nicolai returned several times to the nature of his relationship with the opposite sex. Asking himself why he "toys with women," Hans attempts a psychological explanation: "He saw clearly that it was an animalistic hunger for power to which he, too, was subject. He needed women because only through them did he feel that he possessed power. But why power over women and not over men?" And Hans concludes reluctantly that he takes the path of least resistance: "it is easier to seduce women than to seduce a nation." The passage, written when Nicolai was fifty-four, ends with a quotation from Talleyrand: "Jusqu'à quarante ans l'amour, plus tard le pouvoir."

As a literary device the aphorism was an effective means of ending a passage that was for Nicolai a cul-de-sac. Clearly bothered by the incongruity between his achievements as a thinker and public figure and as a womanizer, between his public and his private morality, he found no answer. The psychoanalytic route was blocked, for he utterly rejected Freud's theories, whose emphasis on sex as the central factor in human psychology he considered an unscientific oversimplification. But was it possible to invert the Freudian concept of the sublimation of the sex drive? For a fleeting moment the hero of *Herr der Erde* toys with the idea: "For me humanitarian impulses do not represent a substitute for sexuality;

rather, I seek humanity through sex." He then rejects this notion as too superficial and takes refuge in a rather trite reflection: "Everything flows from a mysterious, unified, primeval source."

He might have taken comfort from the *vie amoureuse* of Goethe, a thinker whom he admired above all others, a man who had reconciled a life of extraordinary creativity with the enjoyment of many loves. But love is surrender, and Nicolai—except for the youthful affair with Olga in Heidelberg long ago—was incapable of surrendering himself. His gargantuan sexual appetite was born neither of sublimated aggression nor of the subconscious need to prove his virility. Rather it seemed to flow naturally from the fullness of his life. Physician, scientist, teacher, writer, orator, historian, linguist, he was also a world-traveler, connoisseur of food and wine, chess expert, huntsman, and sportsman. He was bound to pursue women as the leopard pursues the gazelle.

As for the women whose path he crossed, it was as though they caught fire from the sparks which—almost against his will and in spite of his low opinion of the sex—his personality emitted. Even when his interest was of the most fleeting kind and purely physical, his intellectual passion transmitted itself to all but the dullest of them. The awakening he caused was often painful to his partners, not only because he left a void afterward but because it had the force of a conversion. In yielding to him as a lover, women had thrust upon them the potent but difficult gospel whose apostle he was. It was, one might say, a permanent seduction of the spirit, as is evident from the letters many of his mistresses wrote him years later. Their tenor was much the same as that of a letter written to him by Lotte H.—, the woman who was his guide and lover during his brief visit to Vienna in 1923, a highly intelligent woman and a public figure in her own right. In 1928 she wrote from London:

> Why do I suddenly write out of a clear blue sky? I am not a rational being and I do not know why, but I do know that despite all the changes in my eventful life I must again and again think of you as one of the true Europeans and a person close to me. You are, moreover, one of those interesting variants of whom one does not know whether they are a whim or a necessary step of nature: a scientist who is not ossified, a physician who can speak of the heart as a poet does, a university professor with vitality, a serious man who can play.

Would Friederike have made the sacrifice of coming to Argentina if she had known that the welcoming cable was a forgery? Probably so. She had long ago resigned herself to her husband's extramarital escapades, as a mother might resign herself to the temper tantrums of a gifted child. Early in her marriage she confided to Eva that she could not expect to have a man of such vitality all to herself. Though by no means unattractive, she knew that she was neither beautiful nor brilliant, nor was she endowed with what would later be called "sex appeal." She also understood that Nicolai would not remain faithful to her—or to any other woman, for that matter—even if she had possessed the attributes of the Queen of Sheba.

But without fully understanding the flight of his ideas she believed in his genius and accepted the notion that he could not be measured by the yard-stick of ordinary morality. She herself was conventional enough, but un-less her dignity was publicly assaulted—as it had been when Elly von Schneider openly proclaimed her purpose in sailing with Nicolai—she re-mained silent or put the best face on the situation. No disappointment, no coldness, harsh words, or flagrant proof of infidelity ever cured her of the illusion that she had a role to play in her husband's life.

The sultry Alice Schultz could never be a threat to the legitimate wife. The full measure of Friederike's martyrdom was heaped on her by a woman with whom she knew her husband to be deeply infatuated, Grete M.—, the banker's wife. A year after Nicolai asked her to marry him and then returned to Córdoba, she came to Friederike, of all people, for help in arranging a visit to Argentina to see him. Friederike complied with this odd request, pleading her rival's cause in a letter which reveals not only her boundless capacity for self-effacement but also the depth of her insight into Nicolai's character. She explained that Grete was now ready to leave her children in order to join Nicolai. She quoted Grete: "If your husband were to invite me (it has to be an invitation, for otherwise I can't afford it, the journey is too expensive), I would come right away, I think. Now I have reached the point where I can even leave the children." It was in his power to call his lover to him "with the help of the riches life had tossed into his lap in a far-away country." Friederike wrote, unable to suppress a touch of bitterness at the thought of the Argentine pesos that were not coming *her* way. The visit would be short, but its glow would enrich his existence and spur his creativity. She ended by giving her blessing to the plan: "Everything is ready, all the portents are auspicious. I am taking care of things at this end. Do your part—if you want to."

Grete was indeed Friederike's only competitor for the dubious privilege of being Nicolai's wife, the only one in a long history of seductions for whose sake he would have gone to the trouble of obtaining a divorce. Grete knew Frau Nicolai and, like Alice Schultz, must have been sorry for her. Whether she was genuinely fond of her or whether the remark in one of her letters to Córdoba—"Your wife is so attractive! You should send her some money"—contained some sarcasm is an open question. The compliments paid wives behind their backs by their husbands' mistresses are seldom sincere.

But Grete could afford to be generous. While Friederike was pleading for news and support in her desperate financial plight, Nicolai had written to *her*, had even sent her, a banker's wife, a sum of Argentine pesos, which she gave to her husband to invest. (The climate in which it was possible for a woman to confide in her lover's wife and to turn her lover's money over to her own husband throws a startling light on the morality of the once straight-laced German middle class in the postwar era.) Grete took an interest in Irene and invited the forlorn little creature to her sum-mer place on the North Sea where she could eat her fill, breathe the salt air, and play with her own children. It was here that Friederike visited her, only a day or two after writing this letter.

What qualities did Grete possess to make Nicolai forget his contempt for women, waken his generosity, spur him to write long letters, compose poems, join her in planting a "lucky clover," offer to marry her, and, in short, behave as devotedly and as foolishly as any lover? Only a pale reflection of the charm she undoubtedly possessed appears in her letters. Nicolai used her as the model for his fictitious mistress in *Herr der Erde*. There he endows her with a serene beauty, a keen but unobtrusive intelligence, and a tranquil but by no means passive temperament. She is the wife of an Alsatian banker, whose name, Josephine—in a play on the Alsatian pronunciation of the letter J—he turns into the pet name "Chose" ("thing"). In the opening chapter the hero has a falling-out with Chose because of her lectures on his failure to put his genius to work in the service of humanity. "You may impress people with your ideas," she says, "but you make them feel that they are nothing more than objects of your whim." Paraphrasing First Corinthians, she tells him that he has no love with which to warm human beings. Unlike a Jesus or a Socrates, he would have no disciples to write his *apologia*. The hero, though recognizing—as did the author himself—the truth of this judgment, is nonetheless annoyed "because the slave presumed to lecture the master," the slave to whom he had remained faithful for all of three years "only because he had had such an easy life with her until now. If that were to change, he would leave her, as he had left others before her." The hero does leave, but returns to her many years later. These passages do not suggest that the hero pined very long, nor did the author.

Grete had what her contemporaries called a delicate constitution. "I live like a nun, as I promised you I would, in spite of temptations," she wrote Nicolai while waiting for his visit to Berlin in the winter of 1922. She had become his mistress willingly enough, but she was a shy lover. "I am not at all suited for a sex object," she excused her reticence, "but I know that at heart you love me nevertheless." Had she known that even at the height of his infatuation her lover was availing himself of other "sex objects," she might not have been as tolerant as Friederike, not because she had a jealous disposition, but because she was more vulnerable. She would brood for months over some trifling incident or casual remark that she took as a sign of his indifference. "Once you hurt me deeply when you said that at bottom you love only children," she wrote long after he had left for Argentina. She might have suspected that his fondness for children was either self-deception or a pose, for she could not have remained unaware of Irene's unrequited attempts at engaging her father's affection. (A revealing incident occurred in 1931, when he visited Elly von Schneider in Geneva and dutifully took his son Arne to the zoo. "I never want to see that man again," the eight-year-old is reported to have said afterward.) People who knew Nicolai late in life did speak of his fondness for children; perhaps he changed in old age.

Whatever the attraction Grete exerted on Nicolai, Friederike's diagnosis was correct and her way of handling the situation was not only genuinely sympathetic but psychologically sound. He did not send Grete the money for the trip to Argentina, nor did he see her when he passed through Berlin in 1931 on his way to Russia. He loved this woman, at least for a time and to the extent that he was capable of loving. Neither the pressures upon him when he met her nor the vagaries of the masculine psyche at the approach of middle age can wholly explain the effect she had on him.

Friederike's marriage, such as it was, was never again in jeopardy. Nicolai had no reason to upset an arrangement that was—for him—on the whole quite satisfactory. Thus, cheered by Alice's cable, Friederike went across the ocean like a lamb to the slaughter. Her case was perhaps unique and certainly extreme, for her husband combined superior intelligence with unbridled conceit, unassailable ideals with the cruelty of a petty tyrant, willingness to sacrifice all for a noble cause with sexual proclivities worthy of an August the Strong or a Casanova. But the tragedy—for hers was indeed a tragedy—was shaped not solely by the interplay of personalities between husband and wife. Precisely because she was not a "silly little wife" but a capable, sensible woman, it is clear that she was playing a role, perhaps not consciously and not from choice but because the script called for it, a badly written script with only a few stereotyped parts for women of her generation.

NOTES

1. By "our kind" Eva means her brother's rejection of the whole philosophy of life of the Blos family. Edwin Blos had become a sort of mystic, wore Hindu garb, had become a vegetarian, and had notions about the sanctity of all life, including flies and worms. Eva, and through her the rest of the family, had fallen under the spell of a semi-religious fanatic, one Frau Lörchen.

23. Another Nicolai Case

The shadows on Nicolai's private character must not obscure our vision of the public figure, the thinker, the teacher, the indefatigable fighter for humaneness, justice, and reason. In his South American exile he became a unique intellectual and moral force, preceptor of several generations of students and scholars and in the end mentor of the entire continent. From an observer's point of view, if not from his own, this second half of his life was in many ways more rewarding than the first, for it was in his maturity that his genius fully unfolded. Controversial to the end, aggressive and defiant at an age when most men mellow or resign themselves to fate, he was nevertheless respected, admired, and even loved by a large circle of friends, audiences, and readers of his writings, among them the finest minds of Latin America.[1]

When he died in Santiago in 1964 at the age of ninety, his body lay in state on a catafalque erected in the Sala de Consejo of the Casa Central of the University of Chile, and the flags flew at half-staff over the buildings of the Faculty of Medicine. The dean of the faculty paid his respects and sent condolences to the German embassy, which was represented at the funeral and bore its costs. A cortège of some forty academic dignitaries escorted the coffin to the cemetery. Members of the faculties of philosophy, education, and medicine spoke at the graveside. "Nicolai's work represents an extraordinary blend of scientific rigor and human passion," his friend and colleague Dr. Hector Orrego Puelma said. His library, "which encompassed all human knowledge, history, philosophy, psychology, biology, clinical medicine, economics, physics, mathematics, and so many other subjects," was the mirror of his intellect, "and yet he was not a dilettante, nor doctrinaire, nor a pontificator." If his opinions had shocked some, Orrego said, they were always well founded.

The press was equally generous with its tributes. "With the demise of Georg Frederico Nicolai," said *El Mercurio*, Chile's leading newspaper, "one of the significant personalities of the century is gone." "He lived rich in ideas, poor in material things," another commentator wrote. He spoke of Nicolai's "exalted rationalism" and acknowledged the debt the nation owed to the great *maestro europeo* for having shared his scientific and philosophical knowledge with the people of Chile. In his last visit to Nicolai the dying man had thanked him for his kindness. "It is we as good Chilenos who should have said thank you for coming to Chile and giving our country world-wide prestige by living among us and publishing some of your writings here." A month after the funeral, an old friend and recent political adversary, the Communist deputy Cesar Godoy Urrutia, rose in parliament to pronounce a eulogy for "the eminent, universally renowned *sabio* Professor Jorge F. Nicolai." It had taken three centuries for the Ecumenical Council to redress the injury and humiliation the Church had inflicted on Galileo. Would Nicolai have to wait as long for his posthumous vindication, he asked.[2]

Allowing for Creole hyperbole, one nevertheless senses the sincerity of these tributes. The path that led to such honors, such admiration and affection, was a thorny one, for the very qualities that made Nicolai the hero of youthful idealists and of the liberal intelligentsia also made him a target for both the conservative forces in Creole society and the orthodox Marxists in the opposite camp. Once again he fought these battles alone, unsupported by any political party or professional organization. His "exalted rationalism" was offensive to the Church, his vast erudition put most of his academic colleagues to shame, and his uncompromising stand on human rights and insistence on absolute intellectual honesty made less dedicated souls uncomfortable. His lack of humility, his all too obvious contempt for mediocrity, and his irrepressible penchant for sarcasm did the rest.

And yet Nicolai and Latin America were made for each other. The Creole intelligentsia of the time, proud and sensitive yet conscious of its backwardness and respectful of European culture, welcomed him as a man who represented the best of that culture without its imperialistic pretensions. He was seen as an ally in the struggle against the colonial past. In contrast to other famous visitors, he had come to stay; he had learned the language and mastered the customs of the country. He seemed to embody the very ideal of the *Reforma*: the teacher who was an outstanding scholar and a moral and intellectual force in the life of the university, a leader and inspirer of youth and a comrade-in-arms to the forward-looking spirits among the faculty. His contract with the University of Córdoba, drawn up by the *reformista* De la Torre, spoke explicitly, almost naively, of Nicolai's "cultural mission," a term no European university would have used in appointing a professor of physiology. His universal outlook was appreciated by audiences eager for guidance in almost every field of learning. His flamboyant personality appealed to the Latin temperament, his informal manner easily overcame the ceremonial stiffness of his hosts, and his conversation both shocked and delighted men and women accustomed to the sterile talk of provincial drawingrooms.

For his part, Nicolai was warmed by the spontaneity and the geniune idealism of the Latins. Here his ideas fell on fertile ground; here the vital link between science and truth, between learning and freedom—the link his enemies in Germany had been unable to see—seemed to be understood almost instinctively. Here life was calmer and sweeter than in the Old World, and contact with others seemed easier, once the barrier of Spanish formality was penetrated. Here he was not an outcast but a figure of authority. He was human enough to enjoy the adulation of the Cordobese students, which was doubly sweet after the humiliation he had endured at the hands of their German counterparts. He served dutifully on faculty committees and, to no one's surprise, was soon elected by the students as their representative on the Consejo Superior, the university governing body. He found a few kindred spirits among the *reformistas* on the faculty,[3] and, with the arrival of wife and daughter, a semblance of normal family and social life was established. The Nicolais settled down comfortably, free from financial worries for the first time in many years, in their "marble palace" (Figs. 39–40)

In his first year Nicolai had not yet become disenchanted with the *Docta y Santa* and spoke with genuine warmth of the "quiet colonial houses and great patios, so conducive to meditation and serene work." The atmo-

Fig. 39. The Nicolais in their "marble palace" in Córdoba, early in 1927.

sphere provided the ideal setting for a project that had long been in his mind, a monumental work that would embody a biologist's ideas on the Relativity Theory. Soon after his return from Europe in the spring of 1923, he began preliminary studies. His film had been his first attempt to convey Einstein's concepts of space and time to non-physicists by a novel educational technique, but it dealt only with their physical aspects, not with their broader philosophical implications. Nicolai recognized these implications at a time when most philosophers dismissed the theory as of interest only to physicists and astronomers. He understood that Einstein's discovery profoundly affected the theory of knowledge. All previous epistemological systems had rested on subjective perceptions shaped by the physiological peculiarities of the human organism. Einstein had liberated the intellect from this "tyranny of the senses." In *La Base biológica del relativismo científico y sus complementos absolutos*[4] Nicolai would

Fig. 40. Irene Nicolai, aged about ten, in Córdoba.

ask, from the physiologist's point of view, why space and time had escaped recognition as relative or subjective perceptions, and what the consequences of the new insight were for other spheres of human thought and behavior.

It was an ambitious undertaking, involving not only a thorough grasp of mathematical and physical theory—as well as an overview of biological evolution as it relates to the development of human intelligence—but a critique of every epistemological system from Protagoras to Kant and of all earlier concepts of space, time, and motion from Ptolemy to Copernicus and Kepler, from Galileo and Newton to Michelson and Lorentz. As a tribute to the University of Córdoba Nicolai wrote the book in Spanish, a language whose subtleties he had not yet fully mastered, although he succeeded—with help from dedicated students—in expressing himself clearly, if not elegantly. The lavish illustrations from his own hand added a unique touch to the text.

The work was rich in original ideas, many of which have stood the test of time and become common property, though not, alas, as the result of Nicolai's labors, for it remained untranslated abroad. In Latin America and in Spain it was greeted as a major achievement. The *Revista de Filosofía*, whose editors were the distinguished Marxist philosophers José Ingenieros and Anibal Ponce, published its concluding chapter as an article before its publication in book form, along with a commentary on it by Gregorio Berman.[5] Anticipating Einstein's impending visit to Argentina, Berman predicted that Nicolai's book would be epoch-making and called it "the finest present the country could offer Einstein."

Gratifying as this tribute was, the prediction proved wrong. Einstein arrived in Córdoba on 11 April 1925, bearing greetings from Ilse and from Elly von Schneider, but it seems that he did not appreciate Nicolai's reverently offered gift. We have no record of the encounter between the two old comrades-in-arms,[6] but we can surmise that it was disappointing. We know that Einstein was overtired and travel-weary.[7] In any case, he was not concerned with the philosophical or biological implications of his work. In a footnote to the article on Nicolai's book in *Revista de Filosofía*, added when the journal went to press several months later, Berman reported: "We had occasion to converse with the great physicist about the themes with which this article has dealt, and we continue to believe, now as then, in the value of this biological contribution to relativism." The defiant "now as then" tells the story. As we know from another source,[8] Einstein was cool to Nicolai's ideas. As a loyal friend and disciple of Nicolai, Berman could not hide his disappointment.

Despite Einstein's lack of enthusiasm, Nicolai's book was not only a labor of love but, in its day, a novel and significant contribution, not to the Relativity Theory but to epistemology. Why had time and space prior to Einstein's discovery successfully masqueraded as absolutes or, as Kant had been forced to call them, as a priori categories of perception? Nicolai's answer was that the subjective perception of time and space is inseparable from the process of living itself—that it is the oldest and most deeply rooted sensation in evolutionary history, a universal experience which, unlike all other sensations, does not depend on the development of specialized sensory organs but is common to all living creatures from amoeba to man. This biological fact explains why man failed to recognize the non-objective or relative character of time and space, as opposed to other sensations, for example, color, whose subjective nature had been understood long ago. In a typical digression into comparative physiology, Nicolai traced the evolution of the color sense from invertebrates and fishes (where it is absent or poorly developed) to amphibians (where it is first encountered) to higher animals (where it is well established but still not of vital importance) to man (in whom it is a useful but not indispensable function).[9] As a relatively recent acquisition, then, the color sense was far less well fixed in the human psyche and therefore more readily recognized as a separate faculty than the sensations of space and time, with which all living organisms had been familiar for some five hundred million years.

The essence of the Relativity Theory resides, Nicolai wrote, in "the demonstration that on the one hand our concepts of space and time are relative, while on the other hand a space and time—or rather a space-time continuum—is given which, unlike our familiar relative space and time, cannot be represented in a natural way but which in truth are absolute in the scientific sense, for they permit us to explain by means of coherent formulas phenomena which until now were simply inexplicable." In this sense Einstein's achievement was "the conquest of subjective relativism and the triumph of objective relativism." As Einstein himself told Nicolai once, "the only thing that is wrong with my theory is its name."

Nicolai was happy to be able to repeat Einstein's remark, not so much because as a former Kantian he found it uncomfortable to be adrift in the shallow waters of relativity but because his very existence was anchored in the conviction that science could provide absolute truth. Science was immune against the fallacies of subjective perceptions, for it dealt not with objects themselves, whose true nature could never be known, but with relations among objects. Science, Nicolai wrote in *Fisica y moral*, his next major work, began when the Pythagorean school recognized numbers as essential attributes of objects, "for a number is nothing but a relation between objects which we assume to exist, an abstraction from any actual property they might possess." Two apples, for example, were objects whose real nature remained unknown. "Certainly no phenomenal reality attaches to the number 'two.' It is nothing more than a relation, the double of the number 'one.' But this relation is *segurísima* ["utterly certain"]. It is another kind of reality than the assumed one of the apples. More than that, if one thinks about it carefully, it is the only unshakable reality. One can argue about apples and about the world, about God and politics, but no one can argue about the number 'two.'"[10]

By confining itself to relations among objects, science could provide answers to every question, even if the question involved sensations, for "sensations are merely a special case of relations among objects, to wit, among objects within and without the organism." In dealing with such relations, science had created a split between two kinds of reality, the scientific and the sensory one, but ultimately it would show that relations, even the most complex ones, are legitimate and therefore real. Seen in this light, "the Relativity Theory is not something foreign to the realm of science; on the contrary, it is the usual process. It is only that Albert Einstein has 'relativized' the most inverterate notions of our senses, those of time and space, which hitherto no one has been bold enough to relativize, at least not on a scientific basis."

Even Einstein could not have objected to this reasoning, which served a useful purpose at a time when his theory was considered by many either as a threat to the certainties of the Newtonian universe or—in the words of some respected German physicists—as "destructive Jewish pseudo-science." But then Nicolai left the solid ground of scientific reasoning and ventured forth into uncharted waters. The epistemological revolution unwittingly set in motion by Einstein must have profound consequences for moral philosophy, hitherto the domain of the absolute, and it was these Nicolai wished to explore, for until now human behavior had been governed by moral rather than scientific principles. Had all moral values—the concepts embodied in the great religions, in Kantian ethics, and Hegelian dialectics—now likewise become relative? Was the social consensus built on these concepts suddenly invalid? Was Ortega y Gasset justified in proclaiming "the equality of all perspectives" in the moral sphere?[11]

Nicolai answered his own question with a resounding "No." Relativist physics had its own immutable and absolute laws, and relativism was valid only in consequence of these laws: "The fact that different measurements apply to two systems moving relative to each other in no way excuses the blunderer who has taken an erroneous measurement." Ortega could hardly mean that the viewpoint of a murderer had the same merit as that of a St. Francis. The Relativity Theory would have to be wrong if the perspective of those who hate (here Nicolai named Rector Meyer and the academic senate of the University of Berlin) could destroy all others, "including the man who, according to Ortega y Gasset, is the discoverer of all perspectives. For it is they who with their chauvinist perspective have tried to drive from their fatherland Einstein and so many others with a different view of Germany's mission." "Neither in physics nor in ethics are all perspectives equally valid." That way lay anarchy and "leveling nihilism." Rather, one must seek to discover whether there was a supreme, all-encompassing moral law comparable to that which the Relativity Theory had now established in the realm of physics, a law to which all perspectives related, "as the different systems of measurement relate to the speed of light."

This, then, was Nicolai's main concern: an objective, absolute morality based on scientific truth rather than on subjective or instinctive attitudes. It was ground that had last been plowed by Spinoza almost three centuries earlier, when he tried to link ethics and science, asserting that man must understand the faculties of the human spirit and the order of nature so as to be able to regulate his conduct and refrain from evil. Since nothing can exist in nature which does not conform to the fixed causal laws that govern the universe, and since man is part of that universe, it follows that man will execute the purposes of the Creator once he fully understands those laws. Nicolai, strangely enough, never mentions Spinoza, though he gave the Spinozist ethic a characteristic biological twist. An objective (absolute) morality must benefit the whole of mankind, he said, and since man's biological destiny is linked to his uniquely human attribute, namely, his intelligence, an absolute morality is that morality which favors the development of ever-higher intelligence in the human race as a whole. Until now humanity had progressed toward this goal instinctively "and often unconsciously and against its own will." As men are now able to recognize their biological destiny, they must henceforth "subordinate morality to reason [*inteligencia*], thus fulfilling the injunction of Socrates, whom the world has justly called the wisest of all philosophers." This central idea, which first appeared in the *Biology of War*, was now fully elaborated into a moral system.

In Córdoba Nicolai had become a scholar concerned with scientific and speculative ideas, seemingly removed from polemics and politics. Pi Suñer, the Spanish physiologist, who reviewed *La Base biologica* for the Madrid newspaper *El Sol*, concluded that his old friend was contented at last. He congratulated America: "Happy the nations where intellectual activity is *amable y amado*.[12] We are learning yet another lesson from them, a lesson that free nations are those which strive for greatness and respect. A free man, persecuted at home, arrives in a free land and writes a work that honors his adopted country as well as the language in which he writes it! The flowering of the spirit is a beautiful thing to behold."

Pi Suñer's tribute was a token of the respect in which Nicolai was still held by European intellectuals, but his words had already been made meaningless by events. Contrary to his romantic notions, intellectual activity in Córdoba was far from *amable y amado*. Rather, it was seen as a threat to the tranquility of the parochial spirit that had already reconquered the *Docta y Santa*. The conflict began at the very time when Nicolai gratefully dedicated *La Base biologica* to the university. The gesture seemed to indicate that he had indeed found a congenial environment in Córdoba. But the following year the conflict broke into the open, and in October of 1927 *La Acción* of Rosario informed its readers that "Dr. Jorge F. Nicolai, in consequence of the incidents in which he has been involved with the University of Córdoba, has abandoned that city and moved to Rosario, where he has established his residence and opened an office as consultant in cardiology." What had happened?

As best one can determine from the record, Nicolai had given no offense other than that of being himself. As a thorn in the flesh of the *Docta y Santa*, a liberal among ultraconservatives, an agnostic among believers, a superior mind among mediocrities, a modern scientist in a scholastic "diploma mill"—above all, as the hero of a volatile youth that was in open rebellion against its elders—he had fallen victim to petty jealousies and backstage maneuvers. He had behaved with dignity and discretion, refusing to be drawn into quarrels and ignoring the overt slights and covert intrigues of his enemies. He had counseled restraint to the hotheads among the students, even submitted a conciliatory proposal for academic reform to the faculty. But in the overheated political atmosphere of the *Reforma*—the students called it "the revolution"—he became a symbol despite himself. To say, as he had in his opening lecture, that he had come "not to teach subjects but to teach you to think" amounted to a declaration of war against the Old Guard. There was constant agitation and excitement; the students organized demonstrations, strikes, and public meetings. Every university election was fiercely contested; every event was magnified by a partisan press to which the famous exile was always good copy, whether it was reformist or traditional, socialist or clerical. "You called me here from Europe," he once candidly told the students, "not because of my work on the electrocardiogram but mainly because I had written a book [*Biology of War*] which, characteristically, not one of you had read."

In 1925 Nicolai resigned his seat on the Consejo Superior in protest against new regulations which effectively barred students from participation in the governance of the university. But when the students resorted to a strike which resulted in violent clashes with the police, he took a statesman-like attitude:

> There is room for improvement, yes, and here perhaps more than elsewhere. But such improvement is not achieved by force but by discussion. You want qualified scientists as professors. You speak of the ideals of youth, but you know better than I that most of you study only to obtain an easy job. I believe in the sacred fire of youthful idealism, but I disapprove of the methods of the struggle. You want great battles and the support of the masses, but neither in a university, nor in a nation, nor in mankind at large are the masses ever strong, intelligent, or idealistic, nor can they be. Men are not made thus. The masses always cry "Betrayal!" when their leaders come to power. The workers of Germany, France, England, and Russia are examples in the political realm; the letters some of you have written to your friends of yesterday, Messrs. De la Torre and Palacios, are examples in the academic realm. Men are not necessarily traitors if, having taken on the responsibilities of power, they find it impossible to achieve everything they had believed possible. It is dangerous to speak of Utopia to the masses.

According to Auguste Comte, every new epoch must build on the legacy of the past, Nicolai wrote, and even a Lenin had had to persuade his followers that the slow way was the practical way. "I had just begun to work in the Consejo Superior in this way, that is, in my own way, on behalf of *your* interests. It is therefore a pity that you are withdrawing your confidence at this very moment. I do not know whether this is the wish of the majority, but my resignation is irrevocable, for I do not think that my pacific intentions and conciliatory sentiments can be helpful at this moment."[13]

Nicolai might be moderate and conciliatory, but clearly he had not been transformed into a diplomat. The examples he chose to illustrate the wisdom of making haste slowly could not have endeared him to a staunchly Catholic faculty which abhorred the Positivism of a Comte almost as much as the Bolshevism of a Lenin. He had been foisted on the most conservative university in Argentina by the victorious *Reforma*, whose champion he made himself on the very night of his arrival with his dramatic speech from the balcony of the Federación. The forces of conservatism had regrouped quickly. De la Torre had long since been eased out of office. The present rector, Leon Morra, was an arch-conservative whose election had been carefully arranged by the enemies of *Reforma*. Recognizing the futility of resisting the momentum of the Reaction, Nicolai had abstained from voting in that election, thus antagonizing both the Old Guard and the rebels.

With Morra in the office of rector and another conservative as dean of medicine, there now began what a reliable observer, Alfredo Castellanos, professor of geology at Rosario and a respected scientist, later described as "a guerrilla war against the *sabio*, using the system employed earlier against Goldschmidt, the system of 'making noise in silence.'" Nicolai's crime, said Castellanos, was that he "tried to maintain moral and intellectual standards against inept and small-minded men."

Goldschmidt lasted barely a year in Córdoba before seeking a more hospitable environment in Mexico. Every attempt on the part of the *reformistas* to import competent scientists from abroad—especially from Germany, where there was a plethora of unemployed scholars—had been thwarted by overt or, if necessary, secret maneuvers on the part of the entrenched forces. The mood at Córdoba was one of outspoken xenophobia, despite the desperate need for an infusion of academic talent from the more advanced countries.

Nicolai was one of the few foreigners who had gained a foothold here. He was also the most formidable and the most objectionable. Ways had to be found to get rid of him, and they were found, the familiar methods by which a bureaucracy can make life unpleasant for a misfit. He was given the silent treatment; his budget was cut without explanation; his requests for badly needed staff members were ignored. The renewal of his contract was delayed again and again. His claim for reimbursement for the laboratory apparatus he had purchased in Europe was challenged on the flimsiest of pretexts, and he was even accused of irregularities in the handling of the funds entrusted to him. A delegation from the Comisión de Enseñanza was dispatched to his house to search for university property which he was alleged to have removed for personal use. Rumors were circulated that he was a speculator in real estate, based on the fact that, by a stroke of luck, he was able to sell his property on Paseo Sobremonte at a profit when the municipality wished to acquire the site for a courthouse.

Nicolai had had much experience with hostile academic authorities. He wrote to the Minister of Public Instruction in Buenos Aires, as he had written to his counterpart Haenisch in Berlin under similar circumstances, and met with similar lack of success. When he protested to the Consejo Superior that the administration had failed to respond to his repeated requests for a new contract, a spokesman for Rector Morra—in a maneuver reminiscent of the tactics of Rector Meyer—lulled his suspicions to rest with suave assurances that the matter would be settled amicably, but nothing happened. In April of 1926, after three of his formal protests had been ignored, his patience gave way. Since he no longer had a valid contract, he informed the rector, he would neither hold classes nor give examinations to doctoral candidates until such time as the Consejo chose to normalize the situation. It was a drastic step, but it did not have the desired effect. The war of nerves dragged on for another year, with charges and countercharges filling the air, until at last it was announced that Professor Nicolai had been relieved of his post for non-performance of his duties. The same day a certain Dr. Barilari, a local talent of no particular distinction, took over the Physiological Institute.

The scandal provoked an outcry from *reformistas* and other enlightened spirits throughout Argentina. It was, Castellanos wrote in *La Acción*, the act of those determined to lead the country into intellectual bankruptcy: "Compare Nicolai's *curriculum vitae* with that of any of the tenured professors of that university, and you will see what distance separates him from them. The men who were brazen enough to expel him and close the portals behind him are incapable of comprehending the worth of his monumental work. They can never appreciate the life of a scholar and a man of science."

In a similar vein, Juan Lazarte, a leading light of the *Reforma*, a graduate of the University of Córdoba and now a prominent physician in Rosario, recalled the arrival of Nicolai and Goldschmidt at his *alma mater*: "The entire youth of the university was on its feet, welcoming them as liberators. We never ceased to feast our eyes on Nicolai." What had happened? "Nothing more than that Dr. De la Torre, the students' choice, was no longer rector, and the hatred of the professors found a new target." *Reforma* had brought a change of form, not of substance. In 1921, the year of De la Torre's election, Lazarte wrote, "everything was ripe for a change. But if it is true that ideas had taken hold of the students, it is no less true that the faculty had not changed by one iota. A few of the old ones left, but the spirit remained the same, as subsequent events have proved. Reformism was only skin-deep."[14]

Nicolai had become the symbol of the struggle of Argentina's intellectuals against the entrenched forces of the Reaction in the universities. He himself was not the man to take the challenge lying down. "The Doctor of the Academic Pincushion will depart and never return," he said in a bitter farewell speech to the students. "Coming from one who has been expelled and whom no one has asked to turn back, such a statement may seem arrogant, but that is how I feel. This city no longer pleases me." He had sought peace at Córdoba, where, as a stranger, he found nothing to distract him from his work. He would always remember "with gratitude and even a bit of nostalgia my old house on the Paseo Sobremonte, where I planted a few trees whose fruit I shall never taste." One of his students had written a satirical poem about the city, he said, "where cultural and artistic life is limited to the cinema, chess, sleeping at siesta time, betting on the elections, and bragging about one's genealogy to the barber," but the past few weeks had proved that the Cordobese were capable of other things, that they could destroy a man's life.

> The methods they have used leave a bitter taste in my mouth. With what can they reproach me? Nothing! Nobody has tried to justify his stand in this affair. An outsider might think I am departing without an enemy. Why, then, have they tried to get rid of me? The sole reason, I think, is the fear of every animal in the face of anything unfamiliar, whether good or bad. We belong to different worlds, I and the people on the other side of the ditch. I did not succumb in an honorable fight, I simply fell into a jelly jar.

To fall into a jelly jar was more ridiculous than painful. He would soon forget "the viscous, soundless jelly of mediocrity" in which he could find no foothold: "One can fight ideas and men, wolves and even octopuses, but not jelly." He was leaving, but the students had to stay, "and that is sad, for the jelly will engulf you in its clammy, shapeless mass." Where were those students who greeted him with shouts of "*viva* Nicolai, *viva* the *maestro*, the *sabio*" five years ago? Today almost all were successful doctors and lawyers with an automobile and a good income. "They are on the other side of the fence, and I fear that you too will be on the other side five years from now": "in another five years or at the most ten you will be like them, contented, satiated, silent." Youth in any case deserved little credit for being idealistic, for that was its natural inclination. Idealism was meaningful only if one made sacrifices for one's ideals, because, he told the students, "one can make a profit on ideals just as easily as on wheat or cattle."

But when he went on to speak of *his* ideals, one can understand why he was idolized by the students. Universities exist to provide useful knowledge,

> but then they have another purpose, that of giving the few who want and need it the idea of universality, of giving every student the sense of a higher life that does not perish in the monotony of everyday existence but looks heavenward to sun and stars with that longing which makes human beings out of brute animals. Thus it comes about, my young friends, that you know neither science nor conscience. There is a profound meaning in the fact that these two words have a common root in almost every language, proof that when they were coined human beings everywhere were aware of the common origin of science and morality. Nowadays this link is generally denied but that is an abnormal attitude, a negation of the deepest feelings on which humanity rests.
>
> Why am I telling you all this in the hour of my departure in brief words you can hardly comprehend? Because I fear for your souls and want to tell you that they are in danger. The fate of the world may some day depend on your generation. We live in an age that resembles in many ways the final days of Greek civilization. The decline of the West is on everyone's lips nowadays. You can save our culture or destroy it and perish with it. The future is in your hands if you remain faithful to the ideals in which you surely believe today. My word and my example may serve a purpose.

All those who followed the path of truth (in an odd juxtaposition, here he named Jesus, Socrates, Prometheus, Spartacus, Liebknecht, and Jaurès) had been killed by their fellow men.

> But hope does not die, and we must continue to hope that some day people will be inspired by justice, morality, and science. And therefore I believe—as a child believes in miracles—that one, two, or perhaps three young minds will retain this childish faith. I call it childish because it separates us from all the honors, riches, and beauties of this world; because we know in advance that it serves no useful purpose and that mankind will continue for a long time to be

the brutish horde it has always been; because our example will only serve to frighten the intelligent and the strong who have seen where the pursuit of the ideal can lead: to misery and wandering from place to place.

But he would not count his five years in Córdoba as lost if even one of his listeners remained faithful to the oaths of his youth, for science and the enthusiasm for truth were passed from hand to hand like the Olympic torch of ancient Greece, and "it is our mission to keep the flame from being extinguished."

Nicolai ended on a bitter note: "I am unwanted by the men who manage the politics of the university with an eye to elections and compromises. From now on they will be able to bestow their jobs and buy their votes. Therefore I must go. Like my predecessors, I have suffered shipwreck at this university. But this great satisfaction remains: I consider this shipwreck as a mark of honor in my existence, and so do all those who know my work and my life."

Once again there was a Nicolai Case, and although his enemies had carefully avoided all issues of principle, no one was in doubt that principles were at the root of his "shipwreck." The liberal press called the affair an insult to the spirit of a free country. Because of Nicolai, Córdoba had risen in the esteem of the world, one commentator wrote. A kindly fate brought him to Córdoba at the right moment, "but the evil genius of the *Docta y Santa* has driven him away," lamented another. The Buenos Aires magazine *La Antorcha* published the farewell speech on 17 June 1927 under the title "La Profesión de fé de Nicolai." It was indeed a profession of faith such as the Cordobese had never heard before.

When his rage had subsided, Nicolai saw that irony was a better weapon than pathos in the battle against "jelly." He wrote a satire, *Homenaje de despedida a la tradición de Córdoba docta y santa*,[15] which delighted his friends and infuriated his enemies. It was a merciless exposure of the backwardness, obscurantism, and ignorance of his former colleagues. Those who complained about the lack of tradition in the New World did not know Córdoba. There the spirit of the glorious past was fully alive; there modern ideas did not threaten the attitudes of those "who are firmly resolved to keep things as they are." Every university honored the memory of its great men, Bologna that of Galvani, Heidelberg that of Bunsen, Königsberg that of Kant, Göttingen that of its great mathematicians, Córdoba that of—Padre Trejo y Sanabria! Even its scientific laboratories, in their "archeological beauty," bespoke this respect for tradition. Like the ancient monastery of Solovets in the icy wastes of the Arctic, which long ago he had visited during his stay in Russia in 1906, the University of Córdoba had retained its medieval splendor, though here it was the sacred spirit of the past rather than geographical isolation that had caused the miracle.

But let no one say that the Cordobese lacked originality; on the contrary, as someone had said, "Would that they were less original!" It was a pity that Europeans knew so little about the "mysterious science of the pampa."

Where else could they find a chemistry professor who had at last rooted out the thousand-year-old error that the sun was a ball of fire, proving instead that it was simply a mirror that reflected the heat of the earth? Where else would a physician have consulted him about the case of a woman with a body temperature of 100 degrees Celsius? Nicolai reported that he had advised his colleague to stick his finger in the patient's mouth: "If it burns, you are right."

As for the lack of scientific discoveries at Córdoba, "it would be absurd to assume that such complete sterility was not intentional. It was, and in this heroic abnegation, which one finds as a rule only in the schools of the Jesuit order, lies the memorable achievement of this university." It had not been easy; "How much hypocrisy, how many lies, were necessary, doubly painful for men who must at all times call themselves the servants of science and truth?" Some day Córdoba would go the way of the Indian with his feather headdress and the gaucho with his braids, lariat, and silver spurs, "but we can have faith that that day is distant. Córdoba the tricentennial remains unconquered."

This little volume earned its author exorbitant compliments from some, enduring hatred from others, and a well-intentioned warning. The Buenos Aires writer Elias Castelnuovo praised Nicolai's "fine irony, more French than German, more Voltaire than Heine." But Dr. Fuld, an old friend, was worried. "I don't know whether it will harm or help you," he wrote from Berlin, "but I fear the former, if only because you attack the Church and, what is worse, the Jesuits. You have played chess long enough to know that one does not attack on all fronts at once without weakening one's position." Fuld's prognosis was correct: Nicolai would soon pay the price for ridiculing the *Docta y Santa*.

NOTES

1. This chapter is based largely on interviews with surviving friends and acquaintances of Nicolai conducted in Argentina and Chile in 1972, six years after his death (see the Bibliography for a list of these sources). This information was supplemented by Nicolai's collection of newspaper clippings and by a folder of correspondence, "Briefe von Freunden," in the Nicolai archive.

2. Godoy Urrutia's eulogy of Nicolai is published in his book *Hombres y pueblos* (Santiago: Editorial Austral, 1966).

3. Among Nicolai's friends in Córdoba, for example, was Deodoro Roca (1896–1942), a professor of jurisprudence and one of the foremost Argentine *reformistas*.

4. [The biological basis of scientific relativism and its absolute complements], rev. ed. (Córdoba: Universidad Nacional de Córdoba, 1925).

5. The article, "Sentido filosófico de la teoría de la relatividad," appeared in *Revista de Filosofía* 11, No. 4 (July 1925):1–26. For Berman's comments, see pp. 27–34.

6. Nicolai's otherwise all-inclusive collection of newspaper clippings of his activities contains only an article in *La Voz del Interior* welcoming Einstein as one of the four signers of the *Appeal to the Europeans* and reminding its readers that "another signer lives in our midst." Yet it is inconceivable that the University of Córdoba would not have staged an *acto academico* in honor of the world's greatest living scientist, or that, if it did, Nicolai should not have been chosen to welcome his compatriot and fellow-pacifist. He was always the one called upon to speak for the faculty on special occasions, such as the great protest demonstration against the banishment of Miguel de Unamuno by the Spanish dictator Primo de Rivera in 1924, or the memorial service for José Ingenieros after the latter's untimely death in 1925, at the age of forty-eight.

7. See Ronald Clark, *Einstein: The Life and Times* (New York: World Publishing Company, 1971), for details.

8. A biographical sketch of a colleague of Nicolai's in Rosario, Simon Neuschlosz, by the Rosarine historian Ricardo Orta Natal ("Los Estudios rosarinos sobre la historia de la filosofia," *Revista de Historia de Rosario* 7, nos. 17–18 [1969]:112–41), refers to the fact that Neuschlosz had reached conclusions concerning the biological implications of the Relativity Theory similar to those of Nicolai. These notions, said Natal, "Einstein as a pure mathematician had roundly rejected during his visit to Córdoba, when his old comrade in the pacifist struggles reverently presented them to him" (p. 126).

9. In discussing the color sense of mammals Nicolai referred to his early Pavlovian experiments (see Chapter 13 above), recalling that his dogs learned to distinguish between a square and a circle but never between blue and red.

10. *El Mundo físico y moral en su concepcíon cientifica, un ensayo biológico-social*, 2d ed. (Santiago: Editorial Engranaje, 1934), pp. 21–22.

11. Nicolai's argument was directed at Ortega's *El Tema de nuestro tiempo*, which appeared first in 1923. The Nicolai archive contains a copy of the twelfth edition, published in Madrid in 1956.

12. This play on words may be roughly translated as "both enjoyable and appreciated."

13. The quotation is from a draft of his remarks in the Nicolai archive. Though undated, the context indicates that he is speaking of the student strike at Córdoba in 1925.

14. "Nicolai y la universidad," *La Acción* (Rosario), 20 June 1927.

15. Georg Fr. Nicolai, *Homenaje de despedida a la tradición de Córdoba, docta y santa* (Buenos Aires: Sociedad de Publicaciones "El Inca," 1927), pp. 24, 28–29, 77.

24. The Ship That Passes

Rosario, derisively called "La Ciudad Fenicia," the Phoenician city, the city of traders, had none of the academic arrogance of Córdoba. Its university was only a branch of the still young Universidad del Litoral, whose administration was at Santa Fé, the provincial capital some hundred miles to the north. This port city on the Paraná River was a navigation and rail center and the site of grain elevators, textile mills, and sugar refineries. Prosperous and progressive, it was open to the world and accustomed to strangers. But it was a commercial city, flat and drab, resolutely utilitarian in its architecture and its spirit. At the university the humanities were represented by a single chair of philosophy, located, significantly enough, in the school of economic sciences. To have to make a fresh start here, without even an academic appointment, was a distinct comedown for Nicolai.

Nicolai took a spacious house on Boulevard Oroño, one of the best residential streets, and announced in the newspapers the opening of his consulting practice. His household goods—the ornate furniture from Berlin, the monogrammed china with which he and Friederike had begun their troubled marriage, and above all his great library were shipped from Córdoba as if he planned to settle down permanently in Rosario. Irene, a gifted, pleasant girl of twelve, was enrolled in a private school; a piano was bought and a music teacher engaged for her (Fig. 41). Señora Nicolai as *alma de casa* did her best to make life tolerable in a strange city.

Nicolai was not completely unknown in Rosario, however. The previous fall he had given a series of lectures at the Biblioteca Argentina, the cultural center of Rosario, a superb library endowed long ago by a wealthy physician. There he had first presented the ideas from which *Fisica y moral*, the most powerful and most concentrated expression of his thought, would soon evolve. His arrival as a permanent resident was eagerly awaited by Rosarine students—who had not yet followed their Cordobese brethren to the "other side of the fence"—and by a small core of intellectuals hungry for spiritual nourishment. These men—scientists, mathematicians, historians, physicians and teachers—formed a loose community of kindred spirits, rather like people washed up on a desert island and glad of one another's company. Nicolai found many friends in this group and made a lasting impression on its members. Shipwrecked though he was, he would be happier here than anywhere else in Argentina. "I would sacrifice five years of my life to live in the same city and be able to work with you," a physics professor, Caplán, wrote Nicolai after he had left the city.

A close friendship developed quickly between the Nicolais and the family of Alfredo Castellanos, a professor of geology and supporter of Nicolai in his Córdoba days. Irene, who was somewhat intimidated by her father, was adopted, as it were, by Señora Castellanos and her kindly husband and spent many weeks at their cottage in the Sierra Cordobese. With Caplán, an immigrant from Russia who spoke better Yiddish than German or Spanish, Nicolai played chess and discussed socialism, science, and the state of the world. Another friend was Simón Neuschlosz, a native of Hungary, whose background as a pacifist and a biologist with

Fig. 41. Irene, aged twelve, and her father in Rosario, 1928.

a wide range of cultural and philosophical interests was remarkably similar to Nicolai's own. As Nicolai's peer, Neuschlosz refused to join in what he called the "incense-burning" of his Creole admirers, but their friendship was stimulating and rewarding for both parties.[1] There were others: Dr. Lelio Zeno, the wealthy owner of the Sanatorio Britanico, a somewhat erratic personality with a deep interest in Soviet medicine; Juan Lazarte, a leading *reformista* and critic of the university and spirit of Córdoba; the young physician and student of the Nicolaian philosophy David Ostrovsky; and Francisco Benedicente, then a student of economics, and his sister Julia, whose admiration for the *maestro* knew no bounds.

Among these friends Nicolai was able to relax, smoke his cigar, drink his beer in the best German style—"without spirits no spirit," he would tell his guests—reminisce about his battles in Germany and in Córdoba, and expound upon his ideas, sure of a sympathetic and intelligent audience. Now in his fifties and graying, he had begun to mellow. However much he thrived on conflict, at heart he was an Epicurean, happy to enjoy life when there was no battle to be fought, rather than a zealot. Rosario might be a backwater, but it was a haven. He seemed reconciled to his fate and indeed was prepared to spend his life there. His consulting practice was flourishing. His teaching urge was satisfied by a course in biology at the university. He wrote two books in Rosario, one in German, the other in Spanish.

The first, *Herr der Erde*, is a tale of a misunderstood genius who, having failed to convince the world of his vision of a peaceful and progressive humanity, in the secrecy of his laboratory invents a miniature atomic-type bomb. With this weapon he forces the rulers of the world to disarm and renounce violence. To this science-fictional/Utopian plot is added a liberal dose of good-natured satire on life in a Creole society. The rest of the story consists of thinly disguised autobiographical reminiscences. With a kind of nostalgic humor he recalls his school years at the Ernestinum and his sentimental education by women (here we can easily recognize Olga, Johanna, and Grete, the three most attractive of his lovers). *Herr der Erde* is the book of a man at peace with himself and, surprisingly, with the world.[2]

He sent the manuscript to Elly von Schneider, who tried unsuccessfully to find a German publisher for it. It was rejected, she reported, because it contained too many speculative ideas and not enough action. This was perhaps unfair. *Herr der Erde* is an extraordinarily imaginative book—we must remember that the atomic bomb was not invented until almost twenty years later—though it is true that Nicolai was a better scientist than a novelist. The manuscript was returned to him and never published.

The second book, *Fisica y moral*, fared better. It was the most important of the books Nicolai wrote in Spanish, and it made a deep impression in Latin America. It was the ultimate profession of his faith in humanity, not as it is but as it is capable of becoming, the credo of the scientist, a profoundly pessimistic book with an unexpectedly optimistic ending. Taking up the problem of the moral basis of human behavior where he had left it at the close of *La Base biológica del relativismo científico*, Nicolai examined the religious and philosophical foundations of morality with the detachment of a visitor from another galaxy and found them, without exception, wanting.

The moral sense, far from representing a rational system of thought, is only an instinct not much different from those of our primitive forebears, a kind of magical faculty. "But the magic seems to me to lie in the fact that man, in spite of being instructed by this interior voice since time immemorial about what is good and what is evil, has not learned its lesson." The moral sense has the peculiarity of being compatible with immoral acts. The bloodiest war in history was fought by nations whose leaders called themselves Christians and who were educated in the ideas of Kant, Descartes, Locke, and Montesquieu. There have been great "subjective" moralists—Jesus, Socrates, the authors of the *Zend Avesta*—but, seeing what mankind has done with its teachers and their teachings, it is inexcusable, even "immoral," to rely on subjective morality. Voltaire exposed the absurdity of the free will with supreme irony in *Candide*. Kant, the great moral philosopher, unwittingly underlined the unreality of an autonomous moral sentiment by calling it "transcendental," a term which in plain language means "incomprehensible" and supposedly can be understood only by "pure reason," which is itself incomprehensible. Having brushed the Kantian cobwebs out of his way, Nicolai made his point: "I propose to show that anything resembling a moral sense does not exist in reality either in a positive or in a negative sense, being only one of the sensory images with which we see the world and ourselves. That which exists, here as in all other spheres, is the relation." The moral law is only a special case of universal relations. To entrust it to the free will of the individual is to remove it from rational examination. It is a fundamental error to consider science and ethics as separate spheres, the former that of immutable laws, the latter that of the free will, as the Argentine thinker Alejandro Korn had proposed.

Once again biology is the key to a philosophical problem. One would expect the moral instinct to be the same in all humans Nicolai said, like the impulse to eat when one is hungry, like the father rushing to the aid of his daughter, like the scream of the virgin when she is attacked. But there is a difference: "Everybody eats when he is hungry, but not every father defends his children, and not every virgin screams." The behavior of animals is much more consistent. Some defend their young, others do not, but within a given species all behave in an identical manner: "The ethicist calls this confusion [of human behavior] moral freedom, but the naturalist speaks with equal justice of poorly fixed instincts."

The acquisition of instincts is a learning process associated with the evolution of the different species. Bees have been building their honeycombs since the Cretaceous, many millions of generations ago, and have observed their "moral laws" for the same length of time. The "morality" of mammals is much more recent and their instincts less well fixed, though conditions since the lower Eocene have been stable enough to allow patterns of behavior to become firmly established. Predators always behave like predators, herbivores like herbivores. From such evidence one could derive an approximate idea of the time needed for instincts to become fixed. But man has not had millions or even thousands of generations in which to fix his moral instinct: "It is clear that he has fixed nothing. He has not resolved the problem of whether to scream or not." In at most fifty generations humans have gone from cave to skyscraper. The progression from primitive tools to modern technology has been so rapid that the few moral instincts man possessed were almost all "residues of primitive barbarism, in conflict with the technical civilization we have achieved." Instruments, once they are invented by human ingenuity, remain available for all time, whereas moral ideas take thousands of years to become established. Technical progress is cumulative, moral progress is not.

Moral crises are thus inevitable. "With the head of Louis XVI the last totem of mankind fell, the last check on instinct was removed. The last century sought in vain to replace it with human rights. With neither king nor God to frighten him, the only thing man fears is restraint on his egotism." Religion which promises in afterlife the rewards it cannot deliver on earth, and nationalism, which as a secular religion excludes the rest of humanity from the rewards of belonging to a particular group, have both proved ineffectual.

> Since laws are nothing but means of controlling egotism, it follows that egotism must reappear where there are no laws, and so it happens: the only ones who live officially outside the law are the sovereign states, and they—or rather, their citizens—boast openly about their egotism. Individuals would not call "just" that which only benefits their own well-being or their purse, but most people approve this attitude as the foundation of the state. They do not call the state immoral, but they call immoral those who oppose the distinction between collective and private egotism and who apply a single yardstick to all acts whether they take place within or without the national borders.

Conventional morality is therefore the enemy of "true, or social" morality. Moral man has never been tolerated, except when deified and thereby rendered harmless—after first being killed. It is hard to find in all of history a fighter for humanity who escaped the hatred of his fellowmen. Of all of them Socrates was the most tragic "because he simply said that virtue is something that can be learned." The old morality—which actually consists of many different and mutually exclusive moralities, all subjective and resting on our sensorial image of the world—must be overcome before a new beginning can be made.

Every morality must serve a common purpose, and that purpose can only be the welfare of humanity as a whole, given the interdependence of modern nations. "Objectively, morality is embodied in the habitual conduct of living individuals." In nature there is great diversity in this respect. Most animals kill their sick, while man, in contrast, "cares for them with growing concern, meanwhile sacrificing the healthy by wars and in other ways." Moral standards often change, and no common denominator exists except that of a common purpose as perceived at a given time by a given community. "So great is the power of the community that people believe in the rule of the civil code, the penal code, the decalogue, or the state— and some in all of these at once, despite the fact that they are contradictory. To call such an accommodation of conscience 'morality' is to negate every definition that has ever been given of the word. But man is in the habit of constructing ideological roofs that are higher, the lower the floor of the underlying reality." How else explain the tendency to speak of the most monstrous cruelties as humane, for example, "humane electrocution," "humane war," "humane treatment" of slaves, prisoners and exiles? This is not mere hypocrisy, however, but rather the expression of a perfectly sound sentiment, "proof that the subconscious mind harbors a natural instinct which says that what is useful for the majority of a collective entity is what is moral."

The "morality" of animals is in perfect harmony with their biological needs, the propagation of the species, and the unfolding of its characteristic properties. Individual animals sacrifice themselves for the good of the group "with a simplicity which the most disciplined hero must envy." Man lost this instinctive morality as his intelligence began to determine his behavior. The ancient legend which identified curiosity as the original sin had a deep meaning, "for intelligence has made of the moral animal the immoral human being." But no return to nature is possible: "we are prisoners of our evolution." Fishes must live with their fins, birds with their wings, man with his highly developed brain.

Linking morality and rationality on a biological foundation had been the goal of *La Base biológica*. Now Nicolai enlarged upon this conception. Man's fate is tied to the evolution of his characteristic organ, the brain. The history of the species is the history of "cerebralization." Man's past must determine his future. He who understands this, "he who understands intellectually what it means to be human, is ipso facto objectively moral."

But there was one more obstacle to be overcome. Given man's deplorable behavior throughout recorded history, how can one expect that in time he will adopt this objective morality? It is an undeniable fact that humanity learned little or nothing from the confused events of forty or fifty centuries: "These struggles often end with the triumph of barbarism or the death of a civilization." Historians try to detect a direction in these events, and each system of history has its merits, but "none gives us the satisfaction we derive from the study of any other zoological species." The reason is the difference in scale between human and natural history: the latter deals with general, the former with individual aspects; human history encompasses a few thousand years; the evolution of a species is measured in geological ages. The historian concerns himself with so many details that "if we knew equally much about horses, or even about simple physical phenomena, we could never discover a general law." Physicists are not interested in the individual molecules of a gas but in the sum of their velocities, that is, in the frequency and probability of events. If one applies the same method to humans, determining the frequency of, say, murders, suicides, births, and deaths, one can see that so many individual events cannot significantly affect humanity as a whole.

The irresistible progress of mankind is not revealed by the ordinary kind of records but becomes apparent only if one looks at the "great outlines of history." In the evolutionary scale that leads from hominids to humans, a century is the equivalent of a few hours, and "we cannot determine the direction of a life in hours, nor in days." The laws of history can be discovered only if one looks at intervals of tens of thousands of years, beginning with paleontological finds. Then a much more satisfactory picture emerges:

> Then we see man in the trees, later descending to the ground, taking shelter in caves, making the first tools, fighting wild animals; then we see him leaving the cave at night, becoming a nomad, following or being followed by semi-domesticated animals; we see him as fisherman, hunter, cattle-raiser, eventually becoming sedentary, building with wood and stone. Meanwhile he perfects language, invents writing, develops technical and scientific skills, while at the same time his social relationships become more complex. First families, then hordes, then nations, then states are formed.

This was the pattern everywhere, modified by climate and geography but remarkably consistent in its basic aspects. "He who fails to see a meaning, a direction, a law in all of this is blind."

One can therefore assume that human development will continue in the same direction, that is, toward a higher, more intelligent, and therefore more socially and objectively moral humanity. It will follow a zig-zag course, just as in the past, but the general direction is certain. This is the basis of Nicolai's "exalted rationalism," his religion, as it were, a religion founded on biological laws as revealed by science. "We cannot escape our destiny," he wrote, "any more than Eohippus could avoid developing into the horse." The human race is destined to develop its brain and its intelligence "until this dizzying development leads to the ultimate human being." If we knew how this human being will behave, we would have "perfect knowledge of the true Platonic idea of mankind or, what amounts to the same thing, objective morality." Nicolai had given Nietzsche's superman a biological *raison d'être*.

In a footnote to this discussion he expressed a reservation: his description of the ultimate man was not to be taken literally. Later generations of humans might possibly go mad or degenerate as the result of inhospitable conditions, but "the principle is an ideal, arrived at by extrapolation."

Half a century later we might criticize Nicolai for not considering the possibility that man's technical creations (in our day nuclear energy, computers, DNA technology, and the like) might acquire an autonomous existence with which man, still in his primitive moral and intellectual state, could not cope. We might point out that he did not allow for a revolt against the rule of reason by the irrational and anti-intellectual forces in the human psyche. In the past the death of a civilization was not fatal to mankind because another civilization could spring up elsewhere. Today the technology available for destroying all life on this planet would make it impossible for the survivors of such a death to start afresh. Within Nicolai's frame of reference the conclusion that human reason can solve all moral and practical problems of mankind is tenable, at least in theory, but it is a dangerous creed. Can man in his present state of imperfection make the decisions that were formerly left to God, or to nature? Nicolai would answer—as, in fact, he later did in *La Eugenesia*, which dealt with the necessity of controlling both the quality and the quantity of the population in a Malthusian universe—that mankind has no other choice.[3] His "great outlines of history" are compelling, as is his radical rejection of the moral illusions of the past. But extrapolation is a dangerous thing. To consider human beings as one does so many gas molecules is to ignore the very quality that makes them human.

Fisica y moral embodies the essence of Nicolai's philosophy. By the time of its publication in 1931, the *Biology of War* had appeared in a Spanish translation, and, of course, Latin American scholars all knew his *Base biológica del relativismo*. With these three books he had become one of the foremost—if not *the* foremost—thinkers of the continent. Sculptors made portrait busts of him, cartoonists drew him in every conceivable pose, newspapers printed his picture and his pronouncements on social, political, and scientific events, crowds flocked to his public appearances, and a society called Amigos de la Ciencia, with branches in Argentina and Chile, Uruguay, Bolivia, and Peru, was later formed to propagate his ideas and, incidentally, to provide financial assistance for the *maestro* when he became impoverished. He was frequently compared to Nietzsche, Spengler, Jung, Freud, and Einstein as one of the great modern iconoclasts.

His admirers were Nicolai's undoing. The students of Rosario soon began to agitate on his behalf. Why was he not given the vacant chair of physiology? "The savant Jorge Nicolai lives in Rosario," the liberal newspaper *América* wrote on 19 March 1928. "Does the town know it? What are we doing to make this great man of science ours? Are physicians aware of what they have in him? Is the university indifferent? We do not demand a public tribute; we simply ak Dr. Gatti, the dean of medicine: 'Don't, you think the scholar Nicolai could well play a role in our scientific life?'" In case the dean was thinking of events in Córdoba, said *América*, "Don't think of Córdoba, think about this: in Rosario Nicolai could find a spirit that is freer and less devoted to the Establishment." *Democracia* chimed in a few weeks later, complaining about the shabby treatment of the great man by the university: no notices of his (volunteer) lectures had appeared in the course bulletin, no information about them was available at the registrar's office, and the anteroom outside his classroom was so noisy that his classes were frequently disrupted. It concluded: "Our doctors cost us many thousands of pesos, mostly undeserved. There are professors who have not met their classes in a long time. It is not too much to ask that the university create at least an adequate environment for a distinguished man of science." *El Bisturi*, the medical students' newsletter, was even more outspoken: "The studious and liberal youth of Rosario salutes the eminent *maestro* and is proud to be at his side to listen to words of inspiration and love of pure science in this . . . house that teems with mercenary souls."

The authorities turned deaf ears to this agitation. Perhaps they *were* thinking of Córdoba, afraid to open their doors to an outspoken champion of *Reforma*. In June Nicolai, the students' choice to speak at the commemoration of the tenth anniversary of the revolution of 1918, once more declared his sympathies with youth and progress. At any rate, Nicolai was passed over, and the chair of physiology was awarded—without the requisite formality of a *concurso*—to a native Argentine.

But the students would not accept defeat. A chair of sociology had just been established in the Faculty of Economic Sciences. Nicolai had recently lectured on population problems, and *The Biology of War* was a work of profound sociological significance, the students argued. *La Capital* could soon report that "a pleasing rumor concerning Nicolai's appointment" was circulating in academic circles. *América* urged him to take part in the obligatory *concurso*, for it would be unfortunate if he were appointed "solely because of the pressure of his overwhelming knowledge in the face of the ignorance that surrounds him."

This time the students won. Nicolai was appointed—without a *concurso*—to the chair of sociology. On 16 October, 1929 he gave his inaugural lecture in the great hall of the university before a large audience which, *Crónica* predicted, would grow even larger because of the importance his incumbency lent to the chair. In his opening remarks he cautiously alluded to the provisional nature of his appointment, warning that he might not be able to finish his course of lectures. But then he plunged into his subject, recommending a list of books[4] and defining the concepts of the individual, the organism, and society. In subsequent lectures he examined society in its animal, primitive barbarian, and civilized phases. At the end he described with enthusiasm the society ruled by culture. Evidently his concept of "sociology" was an all-encompassing one.

Nicolai was in his element and happier than he had been in years. But the honeymoon did not last long. The Faculty of Economics was peaceable enough, but the administration in Santa Fé was not. Nicolai was allowed to lecture but received no support for such departmental essentials as a seminar room, assistants, a library, and secretarial help. Though his teaching duties forced him to neglect his practice, the university would not compensate him for the time he had to take away from it. Soon it stopped paying him altogether. At this point a quarrel between Rosario and Santa Fé was triggered by a strike of the medical students. A mediator was appointed by the government, and the fight now became openly political. There were the usual charges and countercharges, proclamations from the mediator and the Ministry of Public Instruction. President Yrigoyen, a believer in political patronage, thought that a plum such as the Rosario chair should go to a member of his Radical Party, not to a foreigner with potentially dangerous ideas. A candidate appeared, in the person of a Dr. Baldrich, who had the advantage of being not only a native and a Radical but also the son of a high-ranking general. A *concurso* to decide the matter was announced but not held. Acrimonious exchanges followed. Nicolai's partisans called Baldrich an inferior candidate; Baldrich attacked Nicolai as a man who, despite his record as an opponent of German militarism, had clung to the arrogant ways of the Prussian Junkers, an observation that was not wholly unjustified. In the end Dr. Izzo, the mediator, whom Nicolai had already offended by a pun, "Izzo hizo nada" ("Izzo did nothing"), sided with Baldrich. Once again Nicolai was without a teaching position.

This time a wave of indignation swept the entire country (Fig. 42). A Comité de Defensa Cultural was formed for the express purpose of pro-

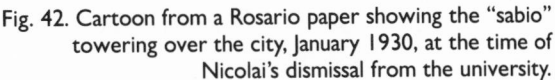

Fig. 42. Cartoon from a Rosario paper showing the "sabio" towering over the city, January 1930, at the time of Nicolai's dismissal from the university.

testing Nicolai's dismissal. Mass meetings were held: men like Anibal Ponce, Alfredo Palacios, Deodoro Roca, Juan Lazarte, and Gregorio Berman signed manifestos denouncing the deed as a danger to the republic and a symptom of the corruption of its educational system. Letters poured into Yrigoyen's and Izzo's offices, inflammatory editorials were written, and the picture of the great man whom Rosario had treated more shabbily than had Córdoba was in every newspaper.

The respect and affection in which Nicolai was held by the Argentine intelligentsia is clearly shown by an offer of hospitality which he received at this moment from a stranger in Buenos Aires, an educator named Luis Reissig. He had read of Nicolai's misfortune, which was no doubt engineered by the Cordobese *doctores*, Reissig wrote. "They will persecute you as far as Rosario and wherever you may go. Everywhere you will find a Cordobese eager to avenge the insult to his 'family.'" He offered Nicolai a place to stay in his house, "as a place for rest and study for as long as you may wish. Understand me well: not as an asylum, but so that you may be free in this world, where so many live in chains." He was welcome to bring his wife or his *compañera*, Reissig added. Nicolai, thanking him for his offer, agreed with his assessment: "You are right about Córdoba. I fear I must rethink my situation. My work in this country has come to an end, and since I cannot live unmolested in Germany, I do not know where I can take root. I have thought about Mexico."

But for the time being he stayed in Rosario, giving up the large house on Boulevard Oroño in favor of more modest quarters in Cafferata and storing much of his furniture with the Bendicentes and other friends. He made a triumphant lecture tour to Tucumán, Santa Fé, Buenos Aires, La Plata, and Montevideo and was surrounded everywhere by tumultuous crowds of students. But no university would offer him a position. His Rosarine friends came to the rescue, organizing a program of adult education or, as they called it, a "free university," which gave him both a forum and a livelihood. Luis Reissig took up the idea in Buenos Aires and, together with Anibal Ponce, created there the Colegio Libre de Estudios Superiores which, until its demise under the Perón regime, survived as a lively force in the intellectual life of the nation and a leaven in its educational dough. It was designed with Nicolai's ideas and personality in mind. It was he who formally opened the Colegio Libre before a huge and enthusiastic crowd. On 1 June 1931 he gave the first of five lectures on a wide range of topics, topics which he might well have addressed in his course at the Universidad del Litoral had his career there not been cut short: "The Influence of the Environment on Cultural and Political Development," "Immigration and Foreign Labor," "Energy Resources," and "The Mission of South America." They were another triumph.

Nicolai was now on his way out of the country, but not to Mexico. His wealthy Rosarine friend Dr. Lelio Zeno, who wanted to study Soviet medicine at first hand, had invited him to accompany him to Russia at his expense. Nicolai spoke Russian, knew the country, and was acquainted with many Russian scientists and clinicians from his former travels there. He accepted with alacrity, for appealing as the Colegio Libre was, it was an uncertain venture that offered no security to a man approaching sixty. The voyage with Zeno would give him an opportunity to explore, without obligation, as it were, the possibility of settling in the Soviet Union. Although he remained firmly opposed to Bolshevism, he was hoping that he might find conditions tolerable in a society that called itself the hope of mankind. Scientists were in short supply in the Workers' Paradise. Raïssa Golant, his lover of many years ago, had written encouraging letters to him from Russia on various occasions. If nothing came of these vague possibilities, he would at least have an interesting journey and perhaps find material for a book. On the way back they planned to visit Spain, the young republic where an independent spirit like Nicolai ought to be welcome. His wife and daughter were to stay in Rosario for the time being.

For Argentine liberals the departure of the *Gran Europeo*—presumably forever—was an emotional shock, coming as it did on the heels of the triumphant opening of the Colegio Libre. *La Vanguardia*, *El Hogar*, *El Pais*, *La Capital*, *Tribuna*, *Critica*—all the newspapers and magazines of the Left that had championed him over the years—expressed their sorrow and their indignation. Creole hyperbole ran rampant. "Maestro, perdón," one commentator ended his lament. From Rosario came a poem entitled "Salutación," in which Nicolai, "the second Jehovah of the solemn realm of science," turned his back in righteous wrath on "this Sodom and Gomorrah where the spirit has been forsaken," or, in another verse, abandoned the "glacial climate of America" to seek new Edens elsewhere. The sincerity of the sentiment made up for the confusion of the imagery.

The final tribute came from Anibal Ponce on 13 June, the day of Nicolai's departure. *Vanguardia* carried the article on its front page. "Without banquets or speeches, with the simplicity characteristic of his exemplary life, Jorge Federico Nicolai leaves Argentina's shores today—forever?" First Córdoba and then Rosario had repudiated him for reasons of pettiness, hypocrisy, and pharisaism. "Nietzsche would have included him in his circle of free men. From *The Biology of War* to *El Mundo físico y moral*, his farewell gift to Argentina, as it were, there is not a line in which he does not rise up against the petty barriers of nationalism to uphold the noble ideal of humanity as a single organism with a single conscience. Only yesterday in his last class he spoke in emotion-charged words of the destiny of our America and the future of mankind." Ideas, Ponce said, were like waves reaching the shore long after the ship that causes them has vanished in the distance: "Nicolai leaves us this afternoon, but in the waters of Argentine life he has been that passing ship."

NOTES

1. An exhaustive study of Simón Marcelo Neuschlosz by Tibero Gombos ("La Tragedia del Dr. Simón Marcelo Neuschlosz. A Tres lustres de su muerte," *Revista de Historia de Rosario* 4, No. 11 [January-June 1966]) reveals striking biographical parallels. Neuschlosz came to Argentina in the 1920s, taught biology and philosophy at Rosario, was deprived of his position by the Perón regime, and died in exile in Santiago. His farewell letter to Nicolai of 10 June 1931, written on Nicolai's departure for Russia and preserved in the Nicolai archive, illuminates the relationship between the two:

A few days ago you made a remark indicating your belief that, while I had not joined the enemy camp, I did not always support your cause with the necessary warmth and determination. I most decidedly reject this suspicion. For temperamental reasons I have not behaved like your Argentine friends, with hymns and incense, but you must know that I recognize your importance as a human being and a scientist, a man who has the courage of the pro-fessor like no other contemporary, who stands up for what he recognizes as the truth without regard for position or personal advantage.

2. This manuscript was written in German in Rosario in 1927–1928. Its four volumes are preserved in the Nicolai archive.

3. *La eugenesia cómo gloriosa culminación de la medicina* (Buenos Aires: Editorial SAC, 1957).

4. The list included Aristotle, Augustine, Machiavelli, Comte, and Kropotkin.

25. Ahasuerus on the Lecture Circuit

Traveling in the company of Lelio Zeno and his brother Artemio, Nicolai disembarked at Hamburg and proceeded to Berlin to await visas for the Soviet Union. It was a strange and uncomfortable homecoming. His enemies were more powerful than ever, in the universities and elsewhere in Germany. He still had loyal friends, but time had taken its toll, and he himself seemed to be a ghost from the past. He was a spectator now, Gulliver among the Lilliputians or perhaps Dante in the Inferno, more familiar with the scene than his Argentine companions but no less a stranger.

The shadows over the Weimar Republic were lengthening rapidly in the summer of 1931. Nowhere had the Great Depression been more devastating and demoralizing than in this country. The psychological wounds of the war had never been allowed to heal, and the brief prosperity of recent years had not sufficed to stabilize the new democratic republic. Hitler was on the march, his legions swelled by the unemployed and the dispossessed, his war chest filled by the largesse of industrialists. Uniformed Nazis formed the second largest delegation in the Reichstag. Although as yet no sane person could imagine the horrors of the Third Reich—the ravings of the Nazi press against the people whose heads would later roll surely were not to be taken literally—there was a sense of doom in the air. Some otherwise intelligent people, including a few of Nicolai's former associates at the Weltbühne, had persuaded themselves that it would be best to let Hitler take power, for he could not possibly last very long. Once he was gone from the political scene, they argued, Germany could regain her political health.

Parliamentary government had already succumbed to the concerted onslaught of Hitler supporters and Communists. Chancellor Brüning, a man of good will and poor judgment, had administered the coup de grâce by dissolving the last Reichstag that might have supported a democratic regime. He was now ruling the country by means of a string of barely legal emergency decrees backed by nothing but the righteousness of his intentions and the confidence of a president, Hindenburg, who was old, unpredictable, and himself at best only a dubious defender of the Republic. Avowed Nazis were in the ascendancy in the faculty councils of the universities, and Nazi students could now terrorize their fellow students at will, silence Jewish or otherwise "undesirable" professors, and even force their removal. In the streets a bloody civil war was being waged nightly between Brown Shirts and Reds, their forced alliance in the Reichstag notwithstanding. The police force was impotent, and the Reichsbanner, the only force dedicated to the defense of the Republic, lacked both the weapons and the will to enter the street fights and contented itself with orderly demonstrations.

On Constitution Day, 11 August, Nicolai, his old friend and erstwhile counselor Schweitzer, and Schweitzer's wife Lotte watched the Reichs-banner's torchlight parade through the Brandenburg Gate. The sight of the black, red and gold banners against the summer sky was impressive. Ni-colai had been away from Berlin too long to judge the situation with his usual acumen, and the Schweitzers, like so many future victims of the Terror, were blind to the threat that was hanging over them.[1] The three friends ended the evening at Die Taverne, reliving their old battles and drinking to a happier future.

Such happy moments were rare, however. The pacifist movement was in complete disarray. Veterans like Quidde, Ossietzky, and Hiller had been prosecuted as traitors for having attempted to expose the illegal rearma-ment efforts of the Reichswehr. Gumbel was the target of Nazi agitation at the University of Heidelberg, under circumstances reminiscent of Nico-lai's own expulsion from Berlin. Wehberg had fled to Geneva, F. W. Förster to Paris. Gerlach had given up the editorship of his once-eloquent pacifist weekly, Kessler, more interested now in art than in politics, was commuting between London, Paris, and the Riviera, and Beerfelde had retired from political life altogether. Nicolai himself was forgotten.

The only pacifist of stature whose voice was still heard—though not in Germany, where he was under attack as a Jew and an internationalist—was Albert Einstein. During this period Nicolai visited him several times at his retreat in the village of Caputh.[2] Einstein was contemplating emi-gration himself: he was one of the rare liberal thinkers in Germany who did not indulge in wishful thinking and had just written a letter to his colleague Max Planck indicating that "in view of the events of recent days" he wished to renounce his German citizenship.[3] He must have lis-tened with profound attention to Nicolai's past experiences and future plans.

As the world's best known and perhaps best beloved scientist, Einstein would be welcome almost anywhere he might want to go, but for Nicolai, who had been "shipwrecked" in South America and who had no ties to the Anglo-Saxon countries, the choices were very limited. In the West only Spain, where the monarchy had been swept away and the June elections had just given the parties of the Left a commanding victory, offered a ray of hope. Spain was doubly promising because Nicolai spoke and wrote the language and was well known to the liberal intellectuals who were now coming to the fore (Einstein himself three years later seriously con-sidered the offer of a chair at the University of Madrid).

The only alternative seemed to be Soviet Russia, not as far-fetched a notion in 1931 as it had been in the violent days of the Bolshevik Revo-lution or as it would become again when the show trials of the Old Bol-sheviks exposed the horrors of Stalinism to the entire world. Here, it ap-peared to many, rational and dedicated men were striving to build a new order of social and economic justice, an effort all the more appealing in view of the seemingly inevitable collapse of the capitalist system and the rise of Fascist dictatorships. In the West a depression of global dimen-sions, with its attendant business failures, mortgage foreclosures, unem-ployment, hunger, and despair, was accompanied by a surge of imperialism, militarism, chauvinism, and anti-Semitism. In Russia one saw a planned economy, industrialization on a gigantic scale, full employment, equitable redistribution of wealth, repudiation of imperialist wars, abolition of national prejudices. The skillful propaganda of the Soviets had thus far succeeded in concealing the oppressive nature of the Workers' Paradise from all but the most critical eyes. If the kulaks had to suffer from the collectiveness of agriculture, so much the worse for a class that stood in the path of history. Trotsky was a special case, a doctrinaire revolutionary whose expulsion was necessary if Socialism in One Country were to be achieved. Middle-class intellectuals were not yet being persecuted as such, for they were needed in technology, education, and science.

Nicolai was willing to accept at least the last of these propositions, for it was borne out by his own sources of information. Raïssa Golant, his one-time lover who had resumed contact with him after the Revolution, had written him in 1923 that her parents had lost their fortune but otherwise had been left in peace. She was now a professor of physiology in Leningrad, happily married, with a school-age son, working hard and satisfied with her life. Should Nicolai come then, she said, he could write his own ticket: he was still remembered as the great pacifist to whom the Soviets had offered citizenship in 1918, and even now, in 1923, he would be able to find a good position. Four years later, E. J. Gumbel, who for a time held an academic post in Moscow, described life in that city to Nicolai as "incredibly intense on the intellectual plane, though extraordinarily modest on the material plane." To Nicolai, who at that moment was turning his back on Córdoba, where intellectual life was anything but intense, this appraisal must have been appealing, all the more because Gumbel added that with hard work and willingness to take on extra jobs a professor of medicine could secure a "tolerable existence" in Russia and, incidentally, could maintain a private practice on the side.

Gumbel was in the Soviet Union at the time when Lenin's New Economic Policy had temporarily alleviated the hardships of strict socialization. With the advent of the First Five Year Plan the economic screws had been tightened again, but Nicolai had no reason to think that scientists and intellectuals were worse off than before. In contrast to most Western sympathizers who had only second-hand knowledge or who visited Russia briefly and saw only what they wanted to see—Henri Barbusse and Romain Rolland in France and Nicolai's erstwhile co-editor of *Die Republik* Wilhelm Herzog in Germany were cases in point—Gumbel was a reliable observer of working conditions under Communism. It was important, he wrote Nicolai, "to emphasize once more the immense intellectual interest that prevails in Russia and the enormous effectiveness and intellectual influence you could attain there, though only if you are willing to go along—at least *pro forma*—with the established fictions, of which that of belonging to the proletariat is the most essential."[4]

However tempting the thought of being able to mold opinion in a country engaged in the most momentous social experiment of modern times, the prospect of having to join the proletariat gave Nicolai pause. As he had said in his farewell address to the Córdobese students, individuals, educated or otherwise, lose that most precious of human attributes, the ability to think, when they become part of a mass. At bottom he did not consider the masses capable of governing themselves. Long ago, in his disenchantment with the reactionary professorial caste of Germany, he had briefly placed his hopes in the cultural mission of the proletariat, but as a political reality the Marxist doctrine of the dictatorship of the least advanced class, or of any class for that matter, was anathema to him. For that matter, the German workers had been well educated in political and cultural matters, whereas he knew the Russian proletariat to be backward in both respects. It was not without reason that he had declined Kamenev's offer of citizenship in 1918.

It seems more than likely that Einstein reinforced these misgivings. In the summer of 1931 he had not yet publicly expressed his opinion of Stalinist Russia, but it could not have been favorable, for less than a year later he refused to sign an anti-war appeal sent to him by his fellow-pacifist Henri Barbusse solely, he said, because it included a "glorification of the Soviet Union." With the realism that was so curiously blended in his nature with cosmic vision, he had seen well in advance of most liberals that Stalin was turning Russia into a police state. "At the top," he wrote to Henri Barbusse in mid-1932, "there appears to be a power struggle in which the foulest weapons are used by power-hungry individuals acting from purely selfish motives. At the bottom there seems to be complete suppression of the individual and of freedom of speech. One wonders what life is worth under these conditions."[5] He could not have reached such conclusions overnight, and he would surely have mentioned them to an old comrade who was about to leave for Russia.

Nicolai was no less concerned with freedom than Einstein, but he reserved judgment. Much of what was happening in the Soviet Union might be attributable not to the Communist regime but to the history of the country and the people, the autocracy of the tsars, the backwardness of the peasantry, the lack of democratic traditions, the physical and intellectual isolation from Europe. He was by no means committed to staying in Russia, but he was determined to see for himself what the truth of the matter was. The birth of a new society was an exciting event, and there might indeed be a role for an apostle of scientific reason in a country struggling to shake off the fetters of the past. At heart he was a Russophile; he had come to admire the vitality of the Russian people during his stay in St. Petersburg a quarter of a century earlier. "You know that I have always been fond of the Russians as human beings who are alive and full of curiosity," he wrote to Raïssa in 1923, at a time when he still considered his position at Córdoba as a temporary arrangement and was exploring other possibilities: "I should like very much to work at a decent Russian university."[6] He revered Pavlov, under whose guidance he had worked for six months, and knew that he was still alive and apparently held in great respect by the Soviets. He knew enough Russian to communicate easily with people in all walks of life. Physiologists were scarce in the Soviet Union. Things could hardly be worse there than in Argentina, where pettiness and indolence had denied him a place in the sun, or in Germany, where he was on the proscribed list. If Paris was worth a mass to Henri IV, the chance of a new beginning might be worth taking on the nominal status of a proletarian.

We know little about his personal experiences during the three months of his stay in Russia. It seems that he was free to travel and talk to the man in the street. As he took pains to declare later, he had no contact with political leaders. (His would-be sponsor Kamenev was already in disgrace, and Nicolai was too shrewd to venture into the jungle of Soviet politics.) Since he was serving as interpreter for the Zenos, whose purpose it was to study Soviet medicine, he must have visited many hospitals and met many physicians. He did see Raïssa, and she opened many doors for him. But he was more interested in social and economic conditions than in medicine, and he kept his eyes and ears open.

His first impressions must have been favorable, or at least more positive than negative, to judge by a surviving letter from Irene, now sixteen, in Rosario. "I did not answer your question," she wrote on 31 December 1931,

> because I did not really know what you meant, for I don't know anything about the proletarian life, after all, and you don't write anything about Russia. Since you are asking again, I think it might be quite good for me, then again, perhaps not. I don't have any clear ideas because I really don't know what it is all about. I imagine that to be happy in Russia the main thing is that one believes in the Soviet and its future and is convinced of its ideals. I will be able to adapt to proletarian life if I recognize the purpose or the necessity and believe in it. I have no picture; for example, I don't know how this life will be different from my previous life, except for the work.

Until a year ago she had thought of her life as desirable, but she had changed. "That is the reason why I said I wanted to go to Germany; later it might be too late. Dear Vati, I never go along with the things other people tell me to think, only those which I think myself, and that is the reason why you are getting such a funny letter in which there is really very little said. We are very sad that you don't write."[7]

The letter gives us an unhappy picture of the relationship between father and daughter and of Irene's desperate quest for an identity—were her roots in Argentina, where she had lived since she was nine years old, in Germany, where she wanted to go before it was "too late," or with her strange and forbidding father in a strange and forbidding land? It also indicates that at some point in his journey Nicolai considered staying in Russia permanently and was sounding out Irene (though not her mother) before making his decision. Allowing for the time it must have taken for mail to go from Moscow to Rosario, the date of this letter suggests that as late as mid-November of 1931 he was still undecided. Her letter reached him in Spain. We do not know when he came to the conclusion that the proletarian life was not for him, though we can easily guess why he did so. Had he stayed, he would have ended in Siberia, if not before a firing squad.

But as a visitor he found Russia utterly fascinating. Even the most skeptical visitor could see that gigantic strides were being made in virtually every field: steel, coal, and oil production; construction and modernization of plants; transportation; electrification. The Turk-Sib railroad was already completed, the great Dneproges was nearing completion, new metallurgical plants were springing up in many places, tractors were replacing manual labor on the farms. Simultaneously the enormous problem of illiteracy was being tackled, and results were impressive. It was certain that the First Five Year Plan would be met ahead of schedule and that further plans would follow. It was the first example of a planned economy in the industrial age. Not only did it constitute a startling advance over conditions in tsarist Russia, familiar to Nicolai from his first visit in 1906, but, despite the ravages and losses the country had suffered in the war and the Revolution, it compared favorably with the economic state of the rest of the world, then in the throes of the Great Depression and still untouched by Keynesian ideas.

In a letter to the Spanish physiologist Gregorio Marañon, Nicolai later summed up his conclusions:

> I believe that Russia's practical economy, whether Communism continues or not, constitutes a better adaptation to machines, that is to say, to the conditions of heavy industry, and that in this respect Europe can—and therefore must—learn from her. I hope that her cultural aspirations, which (with the exception of a few details worth studying) are so utterly narrow and despotic as to be a menace to the European spirit, will never be realized. But I *know* that this hope will be in vain and that the free and rational spirit of Europe cannot survive unless this same Europe learns to defend its economic interests, which it cannot do without adapting itself better to our times.[8]

It was the "adaptation to machines" that most impressed Nicolai. He went so far as to assert that this advance had nothing to do with Communism: "Russia has let herself be guided by realities rather than by programmatic determinants," he declared. But in the perspective of his "grand outlines of history" the adoption of a planned economy by a country of the importance of Russia amounted to nothing less than the next step on the ladder of human evolution, as momentous as the invention of the wheel or the harnessing of steam and electricity. The full benefits of modern technology, which a faulty system of production and distribution had hitherto denied to all but a fortunate few, were now becoming accessible to everybody. Freed from drudgery, poverty, and unemployment, humanity could now rise to new heights of cultural achievement. The fact that the Communists happened to be the first to try the experiment might be deplorable but, as seen from Nicolai's vantage point, did not lessen its importance.[9]

Like Einstein, he was convinced of the pacific intentions of the Soviets. The danger to "Euro-Yanquia," he predicted, would come neither from armed aggression nor from Communist propaganda but from the superiority of a controlled economy over the vagaries of free enterprise. The Soviet Union would—indeed, had to—compete with Western industrial nations in world markets (the capitalist manufacturers were only too eager to sell their Communist rivals the necessary equipment to do so).

But the key to the success of the Soviet economy, in Nicolai's opinion, was the abolition of private property, allowing the government to set prices and wages, control production and distribution, and regulate exports without regard to the profits of stockholders or the demands of labor. To meet this threat, he believed, the capitalist nations would have to adopt some form of "state socialism." At a time when governments had not yet assumed any direct responsibility for the economic well-being of their citizens, this call for "state socialism" was heresy. But the laissez-faire system had collapsed, and within a few months Roosevelt would institute the kind of measures Nicolai had in mind—"Pump-priming," the W.P.A., the Social Security System, unemployment insurance, and all the other innovations of the New Deal.

The likelihood that the Russian experiment would fail, as predicted by the experts, was decreasing with every passing day, Nicolai asserted. As for the hoped-for collapse of the Soviet regime, his observations had convinced him that the Russian people would not rise against rulers who, both by their achievements and by "intelligent propaganda," had given them a sense of dignity and self-confidence: "In teaching the people to believe in themselves, Communism has given them the tools to overcome all obstacles." Not all Russians were Communists, let alone Stalinists, but "this does not keep them from being supporters of the Soviet government, whose greatness [grandeza] they have come to recognize. Perhaps the world will forget the word 'Communist,' but the general effect of the economic feats of the new Russia can never be erased from history."

In Nicolai's view the new Russia was the creation of the political genius of one man, Lenin, the supreme opportunist whose entire doctrine was "pieced together from Machiavelli, Marx, and the Jesuits," as Nicolai put it, Lenin who in 1917 overcame the pacifist scruples of the Mensheviks by declaring that in the hour of decision the man of action could not be hamstrung by principles, Lenin who in 1919 persuaded his colleagues to throw their most cherished Socialist principles overboard by letting the rebellious peasants keep the lands they had seized from the aristocrats— to this day no one knew what he had told the party chiefs in that secret session, Nicolai related. Lenin alone had made the Revolution; Lenin, the "greatest psychologist of all politicians," had given the Russian people a new religion, that of sacrifice for an idea. How else explain their willingness to live under a tyranny without improvement of wages and living conditions? Whatever one might think of Communism, Lenin was one of the giants of history, a leader who had imposed his vision on a great people.

The new dynamism of Russian life, "this psychic phenomenon that drives a world," was reflected not only in industrial production but in a dramatically rising birth rate. "How interesting," Nicolai commented, that while the rest of the world feared an increase in population, a state which had destroyed the family and legalized abortion welcomed it.

Mistakenly he asserted that forced labor did not exist in Soviet Russia.

He had talked to many workers, he reported, and although he was fully aware that the Russians among them might have been afraid of speaking out for fear of being labeled as enemies of the regime and that the foreign workers were ardent Communists whose testimony was suspect, he had satisfied himself that morale was generally high. The people accepted great privations for the sake of a better future, which was more than he could say of the demoralized proletariat of the West. Manual labor had ceased to be looked upon as degrading. The sons of the bourgeoisie were forced to work in factories for three years, which was a hardship indeed, but he himself had seen every member of the Physiological Institute of Moscow, including the director, volunteer to unload coal from a train stalled fifteen kilometers outside the city. The atmosphere in the city was calm, and the streets were so safe that female police officers sufficed to keep order. More people were dying in Germany and Spain in one week as the result of political violence than in an entire year in the Soviet Union.

As an inveterate rationalist, Nicolai was not overly sympathetic to the plight of the church in Russia. "In my opinion it is a good thing that the Soviets allow people to choose between heavenly and earthly paradise," he said. Religion was by its nature opposed to change, for "those who believe themselves in possession of eternal truth have no use for new ideas." Christianity was admirable, but in stressing the afterlife it deflected human beings from that present reality which, after all, was the main concern of the Communists. "We must understand that a creed whose aim it is to create paradise for humans could behave toward religious creeds in only one way: the struggle against the church was unavoidable." To understand this fact was not to condone the persecution the clergy had suffered during the Revolution, though one had to remember that "in the midst of the general famine the servants of the Lord refused to part with their immense riches." Today, however, Christians were well treated, for the government did not wish to create martyrs. They could hold high civic and governmental posts but were not allowed to join the Party: "One thing is clear: one cannot belong to the Communist Party and the church at the same time." But the incessant anti-religious propaganda was effective. The peasant who had trusted in divine powers for his harvest was taught to improve his soil and rotate his crops instead. The five-day week made him forget the biblical division of time. The old faith was dying, but then this was true everywhere in the world today. The only difference, Nicolai thought, was that irreligiosity was "more strident" in Russia.

Unfortunately, he pointed out, instead of building their new society on scientific principles the Soviets had created a theology of their own, a new "Holy Trinity in which Marx is the Father, Engels the Son, and Lenin the Holy Spirit." In Moscow, "a few feet from the huge placard proclaiming that religion is the opiate of the people, there rises the mausoleum in which the earthly remains of Lenin are preserved," Nicolai noted. No saint had ever been worshiped with greater fervor. But the worst was the rigid orthodoxy which had replaced the robust pragmatism of the early years after the Revolution. The pronouncements of Marx and Lenin had been given a "certificate of infallibility." Every word in their writings had become sacrosanct, down to the misprints. A whole exegesis, Nicolai related, had sprung up around the cleearly nonsensical combination "graphico-Asiatic," which had slipped into a text by Marx. Lenin had become the supreme authority even in scientific matters. An acquaintance of Nicolai was ordered to prepare, in ten days, a lecture on "higher algebra in accordance with Lenin's principles." "The poor wretch searched the books like a fool for writings on algebra by Lenin. I don't know how the matter came out."

The Marxist obsession with dialectics, "that deceitful art which I am at a loss to define," had given rise to an "excess of abstract reasoning" which not only violated the spirit of scientific reasoning but led to a tyranny that was utterly incompatible with freedom of thought. "I am not an unconditional defender of freedom," this former disciple of Proudhon and Kropotkin declared. "I believe that the human process leads the individual to a progressive submission to natural laws. But there exists a freedom which we can never renounce: that of using the marvelous instrument which is our reason, that reason whose exercise cannot be suppressed without committing a crime against humanity. This freedom does not exist in Russia." The present rulers might not be able to perpetuate this state of affairs, "but it is dangerous that an entire generation should live without knowing spiritual freedom." Obviously, the state was not withering away, as predicted by Marx. On the contrary, it was infringing on the rights of the individual as never before, claiming jurisdiction over the minutest details of human life.

But while the constitutional freedoms of the democracies were unknown, the rights of women and national minorities were held in greater respect in the Soviet Union than in most Western countries. In this regard at least the Communist notion of freedom could stand comparison with "the travesty of liberty that is enacted daily in the capitalist world." It was a matter of viewpoint, and one might even argue that, whereas "capitalism uses coercion as a means of degrading and deceiving the people, Communism uses it with the intent of perfecting society and improving the quality of life." The Soviet experiment had begun under the worst possible conditions, making dictatorial rule a necessity. Stalin and the men around him were unable to relinquish their power, for "it is easy to enter dictatorship but difficult to exit."

Such were the opinions with which Nicolai returned from Russia, and they decisively affected his future. Such views provoked storms of indignation both on the Right and on the Left. Once again he was disregarding the reminder of his old friend and chess partner Dr. Fuld that it was dangerous to attack on all fronts at once. His socialist heresies infuriated the conservatives; his indifference to the plight of Christianity the Catholics; his blunt indictment of the Stalinist tyranny, his contempt for Marxist dialectics, and his lack of proper reverence for the sacred person of Lenin the Communists. In a world in which all things political were seen either as black or white, he committed the crime of saying that many things in Communist Russia were gray. A regime whose ideology he rejected and whose oppressive character he abhorred nevertheless deserved credit for adopting a rational and practical economy whose virtues the West ignored

411

at its peril; for embracing pacifism; for giving a new dignity to labor; for respecting the rights of ethnic minorities; and for recognizing women as equals. So much objectivity might become the scientist or the historian; a homeless wanderer could ill afford to be so outspoken.

On the whole this appraisal of the realities of contemporary Soviet life seems remarkably sound. Nicolai overestimated the ability of the bureaucratic apparatus to overcome its own inertia and inefficiency, but he recognized the soundness of the concept underlying the Five Year Plan at a time when traditional economists recoiled in horror at the notion of criticizing the sacred cow of private enterprise. Although he could not have foreseen the disruption of the Soviet economy by the next world war, he did perceive the loyalty of the citizens toward the regime and correctly assessed Russian nationalism as a more potent force than Marxist ideology in holding the country together. On the other hand, he was badly mistaken to discount as malicious propaganda the rumors concerning slave labor that were circulating in the West. His judgment of the morale of those workers he met during his visit was probably correct. His comparisons between Russia and the West were colored by his unhappy experience as a double exile. Mussolini was in power in Italy, Hitler was on the rise in Germany, England and France were suffering from a paralysis of the national will, and the United States was helpless in the face of the worldwide economic debacle. In 1932, when Nicolai was lecturing and writing about the Soviets, General Douglas MacArthur was using troops armed with machine guns, tanks, and tear gas against the unemployed veterans of the Bonus Expeditionary Force in Washington, and no less a defender of democracy and free enterprise than Franklin Roosevelt was speaking of "the Four Horsemen, Destruction, Delay, Deceit, Despair." At this moment in history many observers could find little to choose between East and West.

Nicolai's next stop was Spain, the repository of his hopes. Spain was a great European nation awakening to a new dawn. Here a revolution had been accomplished virtually without bloodshed, here intellectuals and workers were joining forces to build a just society. The new constitution called Spain a "democratic republic of workers of all classes" in which all citizens were equal, no state religion was recognized, and war was renounced as an instrument of national policy. To see a republic of workers of all classes instead of a dictatorship of the proletariat, in which pacifism was a national policy, must have been an exciting prospect for Nicolai as he crossed the Spanish frontier in the closing days of 1931.

He was not entering the country as an unknown. His visit to Madrid in 1922 had made a lasting impression, his protest from Córdoba against the banishment of Unamuno in 1924 had won him additional friends, and his books had been read at least by scholars. Now he returned, a legendary figure, with exciting tales to tell about the "Russian Sphinx," as he chose to call the subject of his first lecture. Once again he was *El Gran Europeo*, the illustrious *sabio* and *profesor de gran valia* (distinguished professor). His progress through Spain resembled a triumphal procession.

In Barcelona his old friend and admirer Pi Suñer introduced him at the local Ateneo. Then he went to Valencia to inaugurate the Universidad Popular, a new institution dedicated, like the Colegio Libre de Estudios Superiores in Rosario, to the education of those who lacked the means or the academic background to enter a traditional university. In the words of *El Mercantil*, Nicolai's participation lent a special splendor to the occasion. Introducing him as "an adventurous and romantic spirit," a Professor Puche spoke of the sacrifices he had made for the sake of his integrity and admonished the youth of Valencia to take him as a model of scientific and ethical valor. The auditorium was filled to the last seat. Nicolai expressed his pride in being called upon to inaugurate the new university and his happiness to see so many workers in the audience, for "the highest goal of the university is the ennobling of labor." He then launched into a cultural-anthropological history of manual labor from paleolithic times to the machine age, ending with the prediction that some day people would work for the pleasure of it rather than from necessity. The crowd loved it. But in his elation Nicolai failed to notice that most of the faculty were absent, a fact that should have given him food for thought.

From Valencia he traveled south to Alicante and Murcia, then north to Madrid and the Castiles. "May he be as welcome everywhere in Spain as he has been in this city, whose beauty and climate he praised so warmly," *El Dia* said in wishing him farewell.

In Madrid his reception at the Ateneo, the famous literary-political club, exceeded his fondest hopes. Here, before an audience of Spain's best minds, he was to present his impressions of Soviet Russia and debate political issues with his peers. He was at his best, dazzling his listeners with anecdotes and sketches of people and things he had observed, with paradox and sarcasm, and above all with the force of his reasoning. He gave three talks, to which a fourth evening was added for discussion. Each session lasted well into the night and was reported in detail by every newspaper in the city. Challenged on many points by articulate opponents, he defended himself brilliantly, proving—in the words of Cánovas Cervantes, a respected commentator for the liberal *La Tierra*—that he was "not only a first-rate mind but a great polemicist."

The sharpest attacks, naturally, came from the Communists in the audience, who objected violently to his description of the Stalinist regime as an "atrocious dictatorship," to his "Franciscan doctrine of non-violence," to his assertion that practical necessity rather than Communist theory was the basis of Soviet actions, to his prediction that socialism would triumph in the end with or without the Russian experiment, and most of all to his complete rejection of the dialectical method as unscientific and metaphysical. Dialectics, Nicolai insisted, was invented by Hegel to justify the reactionary Prussian monarchy and could be used to defend any system one might choose. Revolutions could serve a purpose, but only if social conditions were ripe, as shown by a comparison between the French Revolution, which succeeded in sweeping feudalism away, and the German Revolution of 1918, which only strengthened reactionary elements.

Unamuno, Spain's greatest living writer, was among the invited discussants but—to the disappointment of the audience, which had hoped to

413

witness a verbal duel between two masters of the craft—declined to take the floor; in the words of a reporter, he "did not venture to challenge Nicolai or discuss the Russian situation." At one point, when the speaker had made a particularly provocative statement, "all eyes were fixed on Señor Unamuno, but Don Miguel lowered his gaze and smiled."

At the end of the last session Nicolai received a tumultuous ovation. Dr. Bartolomé Más, the president of the Section on Economics, which had sponsored his appearances, made a motion to the effect that the Ateneo petition the government to establish a chair at a Spanish university for this eminent *sabio*, whose services the country could not afford to lose. In response to this unprecedented gesture, the audience rose to its feet and shouted its approval. Nicolai was visibly moved, although we may suspect that he was not surprised. In all probability he had had a hand in Dr. Más's motion. A chair at a Spanish university was the goal of his visit, and he was not one to leave such an important negotiation to chance.

"*El sabio* Nicolai triumphs in Spain," *La Tribuna* of Rosario reported on 22 March 1932. According to a dispatch from Spain the Minister of Public Instruction, Fernando de los Rios, had authorized him "to work as an integral member of Spanish cultural life." It was gratifying news for his loyal Rosarine friends: "Nicolai has found what he did not find in our country: appreciation. There he will be able to unfold his scholarly talents and influence a new generation with his vast knowledge—to be, in other words, a volcano in action. A volcano which in our midst remained almost inactive. In Rosario, as in Córdoba, the atmosphere asphyxiated him." The transatlantic rumor had a basis in fact. His colleague Gregorio Marañon had personally introduced Nicolai to De los Rios and to Prime Minister Azaña, both liberal intellectuals who were aware of his accomplishments and in sympathy with his political views. Their response had been cordial enough to encourage Nicolai to linger in Spain in hopes that an academic appointment would be forthcoming shortly. However, it was not to be.

The first sign that things were not going well was at Salamanca in May. Nicolai was scheduled to speak in the *paraninfo* of Spain's oldest and most famous university under the auspices of the local Comité de Cooperación Intelectual. On the eve of his first lecture, on the theme "the economic force of Russia," the Comité issued a cryptic announcement. It was grateful to the university for having offered a setting worthy of the guest speaker, but "in view of certain attitudes which have changed the meaning of the agreement the Comité will not avail itself of the offer." It was against its principles to enter into a discussion of the problem, "whose resolution rests with the authorities of the university." The printed invitations were hastily changed, and Nicolai spoke at the Teatro Moderno.

Had the ancient University of Salamanca belatedly decided that Nicolai was too radical or that his topic was too controversial? An exchange of letters between Nicolai and Marañon sheds light on the change of atmosphere that had occurred in recent months. He did not wish to trouble his good friend again, Nicolai wrote, "but could you tell me at least whether

I have a chance, before I go back to Argentina? Why is everybody silent after such promising beginnings? I have heard rumors to the effect that I am accused of being a secret Soviet agent, rumors so absurd that I did not want to insult you by crediting them. My talks at the Ateneo are a matter of record. If you had asked, I would have told you: I have no ties whatever, official or otherwise, with any party or government on earth." Marañon's answer confirmed his worst fears. He had followed up on their joint visit to Azaña and De los Rios: "Both are well disposed toward you but cooling. I made inquiries and learned that our officials have received malicious and slanderous accusations against you from the Argentine republic. I did not hear this from the ministers, who gave me only polite evasions, but I can assure you that it is true. The impression is that you are sympathetic to Communism, though nobody has accused you of actually being a Communist. But they will exploit the slightest pretext to attack the government if you are named professor at a Spanish university."[10]

Marañon's diagnosis was correct. The Azaña government was under attack from all quarters, monarchists and Catholics, anarchists and Communists, Catalans and Basques. The appointment of a highly controversial foreigner might well precipitate the government's fall, whether or not the charges were true. It was a cruel irony of fate. If the accusations indeed originated in Argentina (and there is no reason to doubt the reliability of Marañon's sources) they could have come only from Córdoba. Once more Nicolai's enemies were "making noise in silence." As Luis Reissig had warned him in Rosario, the Cordobese would never forgive him for having ridiculed the *Docta y Santa*. Their revenge, the revenge of mediocrity, would pursue him to the ends of the earth.

Nicolai refused to believe that the country which so recently had welcomed him with open arms, the country whose government was closer to him in its political philosophy than any other on earth, was denying him asylum on the flimsiest of grounds. Even after his departure from Spain in June 1932, he did not completely give up hope, but in his heart he knew that the golden moment had passed. In September, Marañon promised to make further inquiries; then the matter was dropped. By then Nicolai was back in Argentina. He had nowhere else to go.

In Buenos Aires he was met by his wife and daughter. It was a brief and joyless reunion. Friederike and Irene were on their way to Germany. They too had nowhere else to go. They had been left to their own devices in Rosario for more than a year, virtually without news of Nicolai. Frau Nicolai still had remnants of her inheritance in Germany, and Irene wanted to return to the country of her birth. Had the two women rebelled against the authority of the absent father? The household in Cafferata had been broken up, the furniture sold or put in storage, the china given away, the precious library shipped to Buenos Aires in the care of friends. For Friederike the experience was all too familiar.

Nicolai was now truly homeless—as well as jobless—but his friends and admirers in Buenos Aires gave him a hero's welcome. Within weeks after his return he was giving a course on *Rusia actual y futura* at the

415

Colegio Libre, displaying his usual bravura, drawing huge crowds, and fanning the fires of controversy with provocative statements. He chose to disregard the lesson of his Spanish trip.

The attacks on him began immediately. On 22 July, *La Libertad* reported that "Señor Carlos Ibarguren, the official theorizer against whom the Colegio Libre has had to defend itself in the past, has now resigned in protest against Nicolai's course." A campaign of defamation (inspired by the Church, according to this violently anti-Catholic source) had gotten under way against the *maestro*. "The reactionaries cannot forgive the Colegio Libre," *La Libertad* wrote, "for putting its impartial tribunal at the disposal of persons who are capable of giving us objective and reliable information about Soviet Russia. They think one can speak impartially about the beauties of Fascist Italy without mentioning castor oil, shootings, and the like, but when it comes to Russia, only defamatory statements are permitted." Nicolai was the man who was always in the middle, but "we who oppose the Third Internationale for the same reason as we oppose the Church, we want to know the objective truth."

Nicolai himself was pleased, for at least the matter was out in the open. He issued a statement to *Crítica*, which was reprinted in *La Prensa*:

> Dr. Carlos Ibarguren has resigned from the faculty [of the Colegio Libre] because the "Communist" professor Nicolai is to speak there and because he repudiates such tendencies. The first of these statements is a lie. I am not a Communist in any sense, nor do I approve the Russian doctrine, nor do I belong to the Party, nor do I have the slightest connection, official or unofficial, with any government in the world. I know not a single politician in Russia, only men of science and letters. On what does Ibarguren base his action? I expect that as an honorable man he will inform himself. The world is divided into pro- and anti-Communist camps: those who belong to neither and try to see the world with open eyes, objectively and impartially, are shunned by both. The scientist has the obligation to study every phenomenon, even cannibalism, without letting his feelings interfere. He who fears the Russians is doubly obliged to understand them.[11]

We do not know how Dr. Ibarguren responded to this forthright declaration. As for the Church, whether or not he was a Communist Nicolai in his own way was more anti-Catholic than the Russians and, in South America, perhaps more dangerous. But the Colegio Libre, which, under the leadership of the formidable Anibal Ponce, had become a force in the cultural life of Buenos Aires, stood firmly behind him. He completed his cycle of ten lectures on Soviet Russia without further incidents and departed for a well-advertised "barnstorming tour" of the provinces that kept him on the road for the rest of the year.

Despite the uncertainties facing him at this moment he was as ebullient as ever on his trip, relishing the publicity generated by his appearances, enjoying reunions with old friends, lecturing in his best style, granting interviews in the manner of visiting royalty. Outwardly at least he was a man at peace with himself. He still wore his forbidding monocle, but he had shaved off the goatee that he had recently affected and allowed himself to be photographed in a poncho, a glass of wine in his hand and the inevitable cigar in his mouth, smiling benignly into the camera. As in former days, the students gave him stormy ovations wherever he went. For them, he was still the "maestro de la juventud."

In his dealings with the press Nicolai presented himself not merely as an expert, a man who had the latest and best information about Russia and Spain, but as a veritable oracle. The outlook for peace was grave, he told reporters. Another great war was coming, a war that would be even worse than World War I because it would be a war mixed with revolutions, a war both international and civil, a catastrophe comparable to the Thirty Years' War that would destroy Europe, a war which would "benefit no one and solve nothing." It might yet be averted, but only if Russia and the United States joined in making the League of Nations an effective force. In his lectures he talked mainly about Russia but also about Spain, about the need for South America to unite and to industrialize, about the past and future of manual labor, and about his favorite topic, intelligence as a function of the human brain. He was optimistic about Spain and, despite his personal disappointment in Azaña, generous in his judgment of his government. Azaña's leadership was providential, he said, for while he was not an innovator like Lenin, he was a skillful politician who had been able to keep the military under control and to reduce the national debt while building an orderly state. In this context, he could not resist telling his audiences the old story in which God grants the Spaniards three wishes—plentiful harvests, the best wines, and the most beautiful women—but refuses them a fourth, good government, for if they also had that, Spain would be competing with Paradise. It is clear that he had been enchanted with the country and the people of Spain.

In August he was back in Rosario, a place he had hoped never to see again. But he was warmly greeted by his former disciples and by his old supporters in the local press, *La Acción* and *La Tribuna* above all. Flanked by the Zeno brothers, who were his hosts at their Sanatorio Britanico, he was photographed for *La Tribuna*. He paid a call to the editorial offices, signed autographs for his admirers, and sat for a portrait bust by a local sculptor. It was an extraordinary performance for a man who had suffered shipwreck here less than three years ago.

His reception in Santa Fé was hardly less cordial. But the climax of the tour was his triumphant return to Córdoba, where he arrived in October. The Federacíon Universitaria had succeeded in extracting an invitation from reluctant authorities for him to give a public lecture. A large crowd led by his friend Gregorio Bermann and the prominent Cordobese attorney Vizcaya greeted him at the station. Before a bigger audience than the hall of the Sociedad Francesa had ever before held, "he spoke as only he can speak," *El Dia* reported. The eminent jurist and *reformista* Deodoro Roca introduced him. It was several minutes before the applause subsided sufficiently to allow him to speak. It was a bittersweet moment. "I feel a deeper emotion than when I left," Nicolai began. "It is a great joy to be able to speak to you once more. I am here not as a physiologist but to talk about more important things."

He spoke briefly about the industrialization of Russia, about the quasi-religious spirit of its people, which he compared to the evangelistic zeal of the early Christians, and about his surprise in finding himself not in a truly proletarian republic but in "the most aristocratic state that has ever existed," a state in which the workers and soldiers have almost nothing to say about public decisions and all the power resides in a small elite. Then he turned to the role of Lenin, the personification of the Russian Revolution, "this fanatic with the soul of an innocent who preached death and terror," clinging to the idea of revolutionizing the masses at a time when most of his comrades had abandoned it, only to become the savior and the god of the nation. Lenin's thought was not as important, said Nicolai, and "in truth it would be a small loss if it remained unknown, for he produced nothing original."

At this point he was interrupted by catcalls from a small group of hecklers in the back of the hall. Adjusting his monocle, he broke off his lecture in mid-sentence. "Look, *señores*," he said, "this is a matter that has nothing to do with socialism, the bourgeoisie, or Communism. It is a description of Lenin as a politician. I am unlucky: the Communists call me a bourgeois and the bourgeois call me a Communist. Both are wrong."[12] But the hecklers, members of the local Communist cell, persisted. The next night they greeted his lecture with a mimeographed handbill: "Workers and Students! Jorge F. Nicolai is a paid agent of the Reaction, a tool of that imperialism which is pouncing on revolutionary China [an allusion to the Japanese invasion of Manchuria], which is provoking a war of rapine in all of Latin America, and which is preparing an assault on the land of socialism. The local of the Communist Party of Córdoba denounces Professor Nicolai as a clever instrument of imperialism. *Viva la Union Sovietica!*" Nicolai was indeed the man in the middle.

As if to underscore the irony of the situation, a city official in the town of Rio Cuarto, where he was to speak next, raised objections to allowing the "Soviet propagandist Nicolai" the use of the Teatro Municipal. Undaunted, Nicolai continued his journey, Ahasuerus on the lecture circuit, traveling slowly north to the remote towns of the interior, Santiago del Estero, Tucumán, Tara Viejo, Salta, and Jujuy. One wonders how his provincial listeners responded to this strange foreigner who talked about unimaginably distant happenings and brought them the gospel of reason with a German accent.

At last there were no more towns to visit in Argentina. Crossing the Andes by train, he came to Antofagasta in northern Chile, where he addressed the national convention of Chilean school teachers on the subject of education in Russia. Here he was once more an honored guest, cordially received by an audience that was aware of his reputation. A teacher from Santiago, Cesar Godoy Urrutia, had arranged the invitation and looked after his needs. Though Nicolai did not know it, Chile, the remotest corner of the Western world, would be his home for the remainder of his life. The time was January 1933, the month in which Hitler came to power in Germany.

NOTES

1. A letter dated 11 August 1932 in the Nicolai archive from Lotte Schweitzer to Nicolai after his return to Argentina illustrates the illusions prevailing among German liberals immediately before Hitler's takeover: "If your path leads you back to Germany in another few years you will, I hope, find conditions better than they are now. By then, God willing, Herr Hitler should have reached the end of his tether."

2. Information kindly supplied by Helene Dukas of Princeton, New Jersey, formerly Einstein's secretary.

3. The letter is dated 17 July 1931. Apparently it was never sent. See Otto Nathan and Heinz Norden, eds., *Einstein on Peace* (New York: Schocken, 1960), p. 155.

4. Letter of 20 April 1927, Nicolai archive.

5. Letter of June 1932, quoted in *Einstein on Peace*, p. 178.

6. Letter of 9 June 1923, Nicolai archive.

7. Letter of 12 December 1931, Nicolai archive.

8. Letter of 8 August 1932, Nicolai archive.

9. This summary of Nicolai's views on Soviet Russia is based on three sources: a summary of his lecture series, "Rusia actual y futura," by Sergio J. Bagú, which appeared in two undated issues of the Socialist magazine *Claridad* about October 1932; Nicolai's own book, *Rusia, actual y futura* (Santiago: Editorial Moderna, 1932); and newspaper clippings from Buenos Aires, Rosario, Córdoba, Santa Fé, Rio Cuarto, San Justo, Tucumán, etc., reporting his views during the period from August to December 1932, in the Nicolai archive.

10. Undated draft letter from Nicolai to Marañon and Marañon's response, dated 9 July 1932, Nicolai archive.

11. *Critica* (Buenos Aires), 23 July 1932.

12. These events were reported in *El Dia* (Córdoba), 4 October 1932.

26. The Calm after the Storm

The beginning of this last journey was no different from so many in the last ten years, in Córdoba and Rosario, Santa Fé and Tucumán, Montevideo, Barcelona, and Madrid—a series of spectacular triumphs that soon turned to ashes. As the famous German expatriate traveled down the length of Chile from Antofagasta in the remote north to Valdivia and Osorno more than a thousand miles to the south, huge crowds flocked to his lectures, students fervidly applauded him, educators, intellectuals, physicians, and public figures declared their support, the liberal press reported his every word, and soon the familiar clamor was heard: keep this man here, create a position worthy of the great *sabio* whose services the nation cannot afford to lose. But the authorities turned a deaf ear, the clamor died down, and Nicolai, now in his sixtieth year, was still forced to live by his wits.

To his supporters it would not have mattered whether he received an appointment in medicine or sociology, in biology or philosophy. In their view he overshadowed the experts in any of these fields: apart from possessing as much technical knowledge as most of them, apart from being unmatched as a teacher and scholar, he seemed to personify the spirit of science as a universal principle that transcends artificial academic boundaries. "He roams the world as a passionate student both of biology and social phenomena, the latter being for him essentially biological facts," a commentator wrote in *La Nación*. He preached the gospel of salvation through rational thought to an irrational world teetering on the brink of disaster.

The authorities, on the other hand, were wary of this foreigner with the reputation of a troublemaker, an iconoclast, and, some said, a Communist. Indeed, the Nazi sympathizers in Chile lost no time in denouncing him, although he was careful not to become embroiled in domestic politics or even to comment publicly on the ghastly events in Germany. He had been incautious enough, however, to begin his scheduled lectures in Antofagasta with a talk on education in Russia, a topic that would interest an audience of schoolteachers but made him suspect of being a Communist sympathizer, despite the fact that—as always—he had criticized the Soviets, praising their efforts to educate a nation of analphabets but condemning the accompanying regimentation. He saw no point in "organizing the spirit." The Chilean authorities for their part saw no point in courting trouble. Another "Nicolai Case" must be avoided if at all possible.

It was not an easy thing to avoid. The pressure of the pro-Nicolai sympathizers was considerable. Thus, inspired by reports that Albert Einstein had turned his back on his country and accepted the offer of a chair at the Sorbonne, the well-known writer and poet Vicente Huidobro urged the University of Chile to "honor itself" by making a similar offer to "a great scholar in our midst, likewise German, likewise ashamed to see his country in the hands of a mediocre rabble-rousing *caudillo*."[1] Nicolai had told Huidobro privately that he wanted to become a Chilean citizen should Hitler come to power. "Some benighted souls among us are saying that he is dangerous because he is not afraid of Russia," said Huidobro. "As if a true scientist were afraid of anything!" The authorities were burying their heads in the sand, and "for the ostriches Doctor Nicolai is a dangerous man," but was he not under attack by the Communists themselves? "For me," Huidobro declared, "he is a man of science who strives to maintain his independence and defends his judgment against both sides. Like a scientific investigator, he observes, and records what he has observed, relying solely on his records because he considers only them to be trustworthy." One might even say that Nicolai was the victim of a "scientific rigor" that made him overlook the existence of "certain factors that escape science." In rejecting Marx as "unscientific," for example, said Huidobro, he forgot that "perhaps the most important things about Marx lie outside the realm of science." But no one could deny that he was a great *maestro* whose presence would benefit the university and the country at large.

The students at Santiago and Concepción were no less emphatic in their clamor for the man whom they, like their brethren in Argentina and Uruguay, considered the *maestro de la juventud*. They staged a great *acto academico* in his honor, escorted him to his residence in a torchlight parade after each lecture, mobilized speakers for pro-Nicolai rallies, and gathered signatures on petitions in his behalf from such academic dignitaries as Don Pedro Godoy, the former rector of the University of Chile.

But the strongest pressure came from the schoolteachers, whose national organization, the Asociación General de Profesores de Chile, had brought Nicolai to the country in the first place and which was sponsoring his appearances at Antofagasta and elsewhere. It was no accident that these teachers were among his most ardent supporters. Primary education was a burning issue in a country that still suffered from a high rate of illiteracy, in which 90 percent of the arable land was in the hands of owners of large estates who were naturally conservative and had little enthusiasm for educating the *campesinos*. To be a schoolteacher was to be idealistic and to believe in the perfectibility of human beings through education. Like Cesar Godoy Urrutia, one of their leaders and Nicolai's first Chilean benefactor, the bulk of the teaching profession was socialist in its political outlook. For these men and women Nicolai, as a life-long champion of popular education, was an inspiring figure. Therefore, the Asociación de Profesores joined with the Federación de Estudiantes and many liberal individuals in strongly supporting the demand of *La Nación* for a chair of "social biology" for the *maestro*.

The right-wing press objected vehemently, and the university vacillated. After several months of waiting, the Asociación went on the offensive. In August 1933 its executive committee issued a remarkable statement:

> In the face of the attacks and diatribes of the fascist movement against the scientific and personal character of the *sabio* Nicolai, and

the unwillingness of the University of Chile to take him to its bosom as professor of sociology, the national secretariat of the Teachers' Association of Chile, in extraordinary session assembled, resolves to declare before the country:

1. That it is prepared to fight with determination until the *sabio* Nicolai has been made a part of the Faculty of the University of Chile.

2. That it will make every effort within its power to see to it that the *sabio* Nicolai—one of the glories of the world culture—does not leave our country.

3. That it will support any initiative designed to give the endangered *sabio* complete satisfaction.[2]

But even this extraordinary gesture on the part of an influential group failed to move the authorities. It would be three years more before the University of Chile took the "*sabio* Nicolai" to its bosom, and then it did so without much enthusiasm. It did not create the hoped-for chair of social biology for him—this novel concept of his, "social biology," did not begin to find acceptance until some forty years later—but gave him a modest appointment as professor of physiology at the School of Veterinary Medicine. Still, it was a tribute to a man who by then was past the age of sixty and just one more refugee in a world crammed with refugees from the Third Reich.

From 1933 to 1936 Nicolai lived from hand to mouth, earning his keep like a wandering scholar of the Middle Ages by going from place to place to lecture. Fortunately, he also received a modest income from the sale of his books, both those he wrote in Chile and those published elsewhere, which Chilean publishers now brought out in new editions. His books had always sold well in Latin America, not only in Chile and Argentina but in Uruguay, Peru, Bolivia, and as far north as Mexico. His *Fundamentos reales de la Sociología*, which found more than two thousand readers immediately after its publication in 1936,[3] was reissued as late as 1962. Even *Biology of War*, long since forgotten in Europe, continued to be read as a classic in these countries ("one of the great books of our time," as one publisher called it), kept appearing in new editions, and attracted a devoted public. In addition, Nicolai was much sought after as a contributor to magazines and newspapers. His income was more than adequate for the spartan style in which he now lived, in a modest boardinghouse on Casilla in the university district of Santiago, where Godoy Urrutia was his neighbor.

It was here, not long after his arrival in Chile, that he received the news that his daughter, who had recently gone back to Germany, had committed suicide by throwing herself out of the window of a Berlin apartment. Was she schizophrenic? Had it been "too late" for her to find out where she belonged? Or had she (she was a Nicolai, after all) found herself overwhelmed by the hatred of the Nazis for the people and the ideals she was brought up to respect?

Her father did not know. In a letter to his old friend Dr. Fuld, who looked after Irene in her last few months, he spoke of her melancholia, which, "when I saw her in Buenos Aires after a year's separation, often seemed alarming." But since her condition had improved before her departure, he had thought that it was a "passing melancholia of puberty, even though her rigidity at times made me think of something like *dementia praecox*." But "whether it was stupidity [*Blödheit*] or a precocious intuitive understanding of the sorrows of a life she did not want to face," he wrote, made little difference. "What use if we knew? It cannot change, it cannot heal anything." Had the autopsy shown any organic disease? he asked Fuld. Apart from that question, he would rather not pry into the secret she had (perhaps intentionally) taken with her: "Call it dread [*Angst*] or sentimentality on my part."

This document is revealing. Was it organic disease, schizophrenia, or encephalitis that had driven Irene to suicide? Though her father, a physician, had let her sail for Germany after observing "an alarming rigidity and depression" during their last brief reunion, the letter to Fuld betrays no guilt. If his daughter's suicide was merely an act of "stupidity," it made him angry. The possibility that she was merely a young, intelligent, serious girl adrift without a compass in a confusing adult world, a human being who needed warmth and love, apparently did not occur to him. "I secretly wish that my friend Georg would value not her intellect but the child-like and spontaneous qualities of his daughter," Friederike once wrote. Irene had been a brilliant student, always at the head of her class. Her father insisted that she skip two school grades and receive special tutoring in preparation for college. "My classmates are so much older, I have no one to play with," she wrote her grandfather Busley when she was eleven. She played chess and read only scientific books, modeling herself on her father in both respects, but her efforts at emulating him gained her nothing.

Nicolai's grief may have been genuine, but it did not lead to introspection. We are told that he was in the lounge of the boardinghouse on Casilla when he received the cable about Irene's death. Putting it in his pocket, he said "Esta idiota de hija mia se suicidió" ("that idiot daughter of mine has committed suicide"), as if she had unexpectedly dropped out of school instead of out of life. But there were tears in his eyes.

Among the letters of condolence was one from Albert Einstein in Pasadena, addressed to both parents:

> With deep sympathy I have heard of the terrible misfortune that has befallen you. I can feel all the more deeply for you because I suffered a similar fate. The more sensitive [*der feinere*] of my sons, whom I felt truly to be one of my own kind, was seized by an incurable mental illness. Thus we can perceive a meaning in our life only if we can liberate ourselves from the shackles of the "I" in our attitude toward the world. The Hindus have taught it and the strong among them accomplished it: living for all things alive, feeling for everything that has feeling, receiving joy from the beauty of that which exists, independent of the wretched "I." In this sense I greet you both; may you find the inner strength fate is demanding of you.[4]

423

Nicolai had little joy from his children. Of the two legitimate ones, the daughter committed suicide, the mentally retarded son was forgotten by his father—though never by his mother—and in his institution narrowly escaped death by gassing as part of the Nazi's "euthanasia" program. As for the illegitimate ones, Arne, the child conceived aboard the S.S. *Köln* by Elly von Schneider in hopes of creating another Nicolai, remained completely outside Nicolai's orbit. He grew up in Geneva, where his father saw him once briefly on his way from Russia to Spain in 1931—and failed to win his affection—spent most of the Second World War in a French internment camp, joined the Foreign Legion after the war, and perished in the jungles of Vietnam at the age of thirty-four. Georg Wolfgang Lenz, the son of the seamstress Else Lenz, never amounted to much. In Santiago he served as a sort of errand boy for Nicolai in the late 1930s and ran a newstand on the side. After ten years in Chile he went to New York and became a waiter at the Waldorf-Astoria Hotel. He too died in his thirties. The fate of Nicolai's other offspring is not known; evidently they played no part in his life. Yet he once told Grete M.— that at bottom he loved only children.

Irene's death did not reunite her parents. Friederike remained in Germany for the time being; Georg, of necessity, stayed in Chile, where he soon carved out a niche for himself in the intellectual and scientific life of Santiago. The publication of a new edition of *Fisica y Moral* by a Chilean firm brought laudatory reviews from the local press. *Psicogenesis*, a summation of Nicolai's views on the genesis of the human psyche, published in Santiago by the university press in 1935,[5] and *Fundamentos reales de la Sociología*, published by Ercilla the following year, compelled the attention of the academic community. In the literary and social salons of the capital, where everybody knew everybody else, Nicolai's pungent wit and depth and range of knowledge became legendary. He debated literature with Huidobro; life with Pablo Neruda; politics with Godoy Urrutia and his socialist friends; medicine with Alejandro Lipschutz, the renowned endocrinologist, a political refugee like himself whom he had met at the international socialist congress in Bern in 1919 and who preceded him to Chile; and psychology with Oscar Fontecilla, professor of psychiatry and editor of the *Revista de Psiquiatría*, which opened its pages to him.

In August of 1936, at the age of sixty-two, Nicolai at last received a professorship at the University of Chile. "For those who know him," *La Nación* commented, "this scientist of exemplary honesty and industry is the personification of scholarship, totally dedicated to the noble tasks of research and analysis." His presence gave a new vigor to the scientific and philosophical life of the capital: "There is in the personality of this modest scientist and possessor of a vast culture a deep sense of humanity and a contagious personal *simpatía* which enable him to move with ease between the intellectual and the scientific circles of our city."

Modest as it was, the salary he now received, added to his other sources of income, allowed him to enjoy the amenities of life, but he continued to live like a pauper, whether from habit after so many lean years or because he was becoming more miserly with advancing age. Friends in Buenos

Aires had to take up a collection to pay for shipping his personal library to Santiago. From the boardinghouse on Casilla he now moved to a large but sadly rundown apartment on Castro, not for his own comfort but to have space for his books and papers. Friederike, who now rejoined her husband, was appalled: the wallpaper was in shreds, and the sparse second-hand furniture consisted mainly of dusty bookcases and tables. "It's no use cleaning," she reported; "the bugs come back through the cracks, gnaw away at the books, and bite me." Georg was hoping for a raise, and "I keep quiet, so as not to arouse his fighting spirit. When I am not cleaning the layers of dirt away, I type the manuscript for his latest book."

There was always a manuscript to be typed, for Nicolai's productivity at this point in his life actually increased. Nor was he at a loss for new themes. But at bottom each of the many books he wrote during the next

Fig. 43. Caricature of Nicolai lecturing, 1937, by an unknown hand.

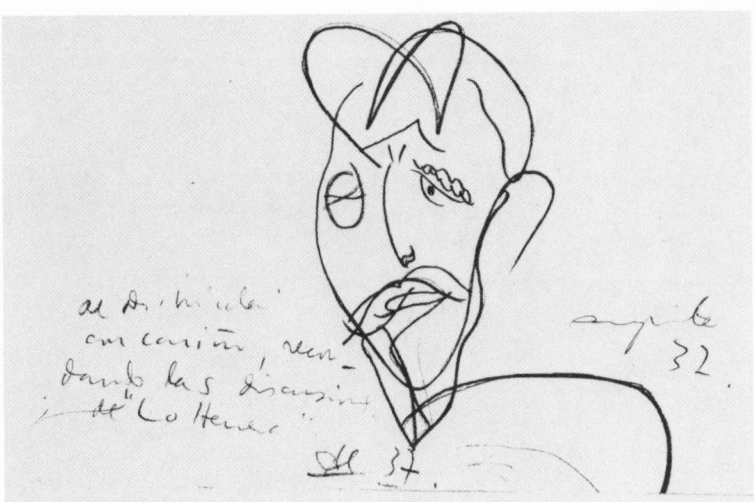

quarter of a century—he was eighty-three when the last of them first appeared—was a variation on the central Nicolaian theme that man's actions as a rational being must conform to his biological destiny. Whether he was dealing with the physiological basis of the human psyche, as in *Psicogenesis*; with the significance of technological progress for human freedom, as in *Liberación del Trabajo*; with population control, as in *Mortalidad infantil y Natalidad* and, twenty years later, in *La Eugenesia*, his last book, which is also a study of the changing role of the physician in the history of mankind; with a critique of the dialectical method as propounded by Hegel and applied by Marx, as in *La miseria de la dialectica*; or with Freud's theory of the unconscious, as in *Analisis de Psicoanalisis* (Fig. 44), each book was consistent in stressing this theme.[6] All represented careful research and contained a vast amount of factual information, much of it not found in standard sources. All were provocative and permeated by a kind of ruthless logic that respected no shibboleths and made no concessions to human frailty or historical circumstances.

Together with *La Seguridad científica*,[7] a series of essays on the method of natural science that occupies a central place in Nicolai's theoretical writings, these books constitute a monumental attempt to show that sci-

Fig. 44. Nicolai's humorous sketch of the Freudian psyche, in which, he explains, the Ego (the monkey) contemplates the Id (the octopus), while the Superego (the bearded figure) mediates.

ence is capable of providing true insights and, ultimately, solutions for humanity's problems in every sphere—social, economic, psychological, and technical. This thesis, already foreshadowed in the *Biology of War* and fully developed as a general principle in *Fisica y Moral*, attributes man's woes to his inability or unwillingness to use the tool evolution has put at his disposal, namely, the reasoning power of the human brain. Instead, he continues to rely on emotion, intuition, tradition, or—as in the case of Hegel and Marx—on metaphysical dogmas disguised as science.

With the exception of a few select spirits like Einstein and Pavlov, no one was exempt from this criticism, least of all those who guided the destinies of nations. Huidobro erred when he faulted Nicolai for overlooking the existence of "certain factors that escape science," for, according to Nicolai, there were no such factors.

Nicolai had never been a zealot and did not become one in later life. In his universe there was room for beauty, nature, art, and poetry. But for him the measure of a poet's or writer's worth was the degree to which his work clarified the relationships of human beings to one another or to nature. Goethe had been such a one. "Whoever strives for perfection we are allowed to save," sings the chorus of angels in *Faust*.[8] The lines "Turn toward clarity, ardent flames! Those who condemn themselves truth shall heal, so that joyous redemption from evil may give them cosmic beatitude"[9] Nicolai translated into Spanish as a tribute to Einstein on the latter's death in 1955 because he believed that in them Goethe foretold Einstein's mission.

Another great clarifier among the writers of the pre-scientific age Nicolai admired was Cervantes, whose liberating irony had helped to dispel the fog of the Middle Ages. In *El "Poema" de Don Quijote*,[10] an excursion into the realm of literature, or rather a *tour de force*, Nicolai paid homage to the "modern" mind of the Spaniard, contrasting him with Dante, whom he condemned for having added to the darkness of false beliefs and superstitions in which medieval man lived.

With his book *Psicogenesis* Nicolai returned to an early love, the study of psychic phenomena by physiological (that is, "scientific") methods along Pavlovian lines. As both pupil and collaborator of Pavlov, he had a unique claim on the attention of the psychologists and psychiatrists of Santiago. On the occasion of Pavlov's death in 1936 the Neurologic-Psychiatric Society invited him to speak about the work of the Russian master,[11] and that talk tells us as much about Nicolai at this stage of his life as it does about Pavlov. He recalled that at the time of his apprenticeship in St. Petersburg three decades earlier Pavlov, already famous but "eternally young," had embarked on a new career, deciding to investigate the psychic effects of reflexes which until then were believed to be purely vegetative. He had approached a hitherto speculative subject, the psyche of animals, through strictly empirical methods, "a novel concept which enchanted the neophyte." The neophyte was still enchanted, he said. Pavlov had introduced a degree of precision into his experiments that made them valid for all time. It was regrettable that the associative psychology which the master had constructed on the foundation of thousands of painstaking experiments had lately fallen into direpute, largely because of the pernicious influence of Bergson, who was a "metaphysicist" rather than a scientist and who, "at the very moment of Pavlov's death," Nicolai commented ironically, "crowned his metaphysical career by entering the Catholic Church." But Pavlov's science was alive today, while Bergson's metaphysics was dead.

Nicolai too wanted to embark on a new career. He was asked to repeat his talk on Pavlov before so many professional societies that he mockingly called himself a "specialist in Pavlovian eulogies," and after it the Neuro-logic-Psychiatric Society had made him an honorary member. "I am now your *Vereinsbruder*" (fellow club member), he wrote happily to his old friend Gregorio Bermann, the professor of psychiatry at Córdoba. But such honors were unimportant; what he wanted was to go back to the bench to resume the experimental studies of psychic mechanisms which he had abandoned in favor of work on the electrocardiogram on his return from Pavlov's laboratory. The times were out of joint, a mass psychosis a thousand times worse than that of 1914 had his native country in its grip, and things were not much better in Fascist Italy, Stalinist Russia, and imperialist Japan, to say nothing of Spain. Nothing could be more impor-tant than the study of psychic mechanisms that might shed light on these suicidal aberrations.

Nicolai envisaged nothing less than an "institute of psychogenesis" (we might call it a laboratory of experimental psychology), which he would direct and for which he hoped to assemble a sizable staff. The program reflected his specific concept of the psyche, which, "as the form in which the organism reacts to the environment," was the only proper subject for empirical research. There was no point in studying the origins of con-sciousness, which Nicolai defined as the ability of the human mind to contemplate and interpret the objective relationship between external stimuli and sensations, for he considered consciousness in this sense as an *Urphänomen*, an irreducible fact, an attribute of human existence just as matter is an attribute of the universe. Nor did the subconscious have a place in his scheme, for he viewed it as a "construction intended to fill the gap between physical and mental processes" rather than as a scientifically verifiable reality. This position, which he later expanded into a formal critique of psychoanalytic theory, naturally aroused the scorn of the Freudian school, which was then at the height of its popularity.

In spite of this and other obstacles, however, he succeeded in establish-ing his institute in 1939. But it was an institute in name only. It lacked adequate funds, and university support was lukewarm. Still the master of persuasion, Nicolai convinced the Ministry of Education to send him on an official mission to the United States to seek advice and, above all, financial support from the American government or the Rockefeller Foun-dation.

The mission was unsuccessful. In 1939 the attention of the world was riveted on Hitler's threats to peace. New York was teeming with refugees whose needs were more urgent than those of this German professor from Chile, with his heavy accent and shabby clothes. For some unknown rea-son none of his books except the now obsolete *Biology of War* had ever been translated into English, no matter how influential in the Spanish-speaking world and no matter how hard he and some of his disciples had tried to interest American or British publishers in them.[12] His ideas were unfamiliar to American scientists and intellectuals and were unacceptable to both Freudian and traditional psychologists. No one in New York or Washington was interested in this uncertain venture into experimental psy-chology by an obscure elderly scientist from Chile.

The trip had its compensations, however. There were reunions with family and friends, among them Eva, who had found shelter in Virginia, and his old friend Dr. Fuld, who had settled in the little town of Weedsport in upstate New York. In that idyllic place the troubles of the world were momentarily forgotten in the glow of friendship. Nicolai and his old friend and chess partner resumed their erudite battle of wits, reminisced about life in Berlin, played chess as in the old days, and walked in the countryside. Nicolai also occupied his time in Weedsport by restoring Fuld's valuable antique chairs, thus repaying his host's hospitality and proving that he had lost none of his old manual dexterity.

But the events of Europe cast a shadow over the rural pleasures of Weedsport. Like their mutual friend Albert Einstein[13] and all their erstwhile comrades-in-arms of the German peace movement, the two veteran pacifists had had to abandon their unconditional opposition to war. Fuld, a pessimist by temperament, had always feared the worst. Nicolai, a more sanguine nature and a man who was incapable of really comprehending irrationality except in psychiatric terms, at first refused to take Hitler seriously. He was convinced that this raving maniac was bound to be repudiated once Germans realized the extent of his madness. From his refuge in Chile Nicolai shocked his old friend, then still in Berlin and, as a Jew, in imminent danger, with the whimsical prediction that the Führer would cure the Germans of their anti-Semitism. "The speed of contrary developments is such that for the rest of my life span the question is academic," Fuld answered wryly. Nicolai had long since been forced to concede that even the most frightful barbarities had failed to rouse the "moral instincts" of a supposedly civilized people.

The outlook was darker than ever in the summer of 1939. The march of the totalitarian powers seemed irresistible. The civil war in Spain came to its tragic end in March, with the victory of Franco and his Nazi and Fascist helpers. Nicolai's Spanish Republican friends were dead, in jail, or scattered over the globe, as were his German and, more recently, his Viennese friends. In the same month Hitler seized what remained of Czechoslovakia after the debacle of Munich. In April Mussolini occupied Albania. Hitler's threats against Poland were daily becoming more vociferous. The European democracies were in all but total eclipse, the Soviet Union had been neutralized, and the United States was locked in a struggle between isolationists and interventionists. Collective security had proved to be a snare and a delusion. For those who had eyes to see, the outbreak of another world war was only a question of time.

For Nicolai, the foremost European pacifist in Latin America, the switch from uncompromising rejection of war to recognition of the need to defend civilization against armed aggression was painful, but not inconsistent with his principles. The developments on the international stage since the First World War had confirmed his warning of 1914 that the conditions of the peace must not become the source of future wars. But the root of the evil went deeper. Even the classical Marxist interpretation of war as a necessary consequence of capitalism was inadequate, he wrote in 1935, for it gave too much weight to economic conditions and ignored the instinctual factors and quasi-religious elements of human behavior.[14] The simultaneous trend toward dictatorship and toward Fascism—which were not the same thing, since dictatorships could equally well be Communist—reflected the persistence of two attributes of primitive man: his fear of the unknown and his herd instinct. The former made him rally behind the god-like leader, as his simian ancestors had rallied behind the "Great Ape," the dominant male. That instinct was the legacy of the horde, the urge to seek safety in numbers and to belong to a group: it was, in a word, nationalism, of which Fascism was but an extreme and degenerate form. The creation of a new economic order, however necessary, would still not lead to permanent peace as long as these residues of animal-like behavior could flourish, in other words, as long as national states were allowed to retain their sovereignty. For this reason socialism by itself could not eradicate war, and indeed armed conflict between socialist countries was conceivable in the future. The remedy, Nicolai said, lay in the abolition of national sovereignties in favor of a world government with the power to enforce its jurisdiction, an international organization, backed by an effective police force, to which the national states would relate as individuals now relate to the state.

Nicolai put forth these views at a gathering honoring the memory of the recently deceased French pacifist Henri Barbusse, which took place while he was visiting his friend Bermann in Córdoba. He must have known that they would displease the audience, for Barbusse had been a Communist, and the hall was filled with Communist sympathizers who interpreted his remarks as a veiled attack on Stalin's "Socialism in One Country." His call for a global government was criticized as a futile attempt to resurrect the all but defunct League of Nations. There was some justice in this criticism, for in 1939 Nicolai was no more able to explain how sovereign states could be made to relinquish their authority than Woodrow Wilson had been in 1919.

But Nicolai challenged his critics to suggest a better solution. That spring, just before his departure for New York, he again stated the argument: the fact that the original League of Nations had failed was deplorable, but the fault lay not in concept but in execution, he told Luis Alberto Sanchez, the future rector of the University of San Marcos of Lima, who interviewed him for the magazine *Hoy*. "What I did not foresee was the possibility that the United States would abandon the idea proposed by her own president, Wilson. This failure, which can only be explained as national egotism, is the principal reason why Europe must again suffer the consequences of the politics of gangsterism." Perhaps Franklin Roosevelt would "correct this mistake," he said. What would be the effect of a rectification of United States policy? Nicolai had the numbers with which to buttress his argument. Together, the United Kingdom, France, the United States, and the Soviet Union controlled 57 percent of the earth's surface. If the European neutrals, South America, and China were added—for at bottom they were part of this combination of powers—they represented over 80 percent of the world's population. The totalitarian nations, Germany, Italy and Japan, controlled only 3.2 percent of the earth's surface and 11.3 percent of its population. Surely order *could* be imposed. "Therefore I maintain that the inevitability of war is only the consequence of the lack of initiative and decisiveness on the part of those who do not want war." "Then you believe there will be war?" Sanchez asked. "There will be!"[15]

The Hitler-Stalin pact of August 1939, which profoundly shocked the many liberals who had rested their hopes in the Soviet Union, upset Nicolai's calculations but did not otherwise disturb him, for he had never shared these illusions. "The Nazi-Soviet pact," he wrote after the two dictators had swallowed up Poland, "eases the task of recognizing that the enemy front is the totalitarian front, the alliance of those who would reduce human individuality to the vegetative submissiveness of unreasoning ants."[16] The countries whose citizens wished to live in freedom must now unite. Thus far, England and France stood alone. "The rest, out of fear, try to remain neutral, but will have to fight under worse conditions later." This attitude was appalling. "Neutrality is criminal and moreover stupid, for the war can end tomorrow and forever, if the whole world joins in the defense of human values."

War, then, could be a moral duty, Nicolai concluded, but not a moral duty in the "patriotic" sense. It was justifiable only if aimed at ending the conditions responsible for wars in the first place. The failure to recognize this principle was the reason for man's failure to end war a thousand years ago. Those who did not understand that even the most benign form of nationalism was incompatible with culture and progress could do nothing to make the future better than the past. The victors of 1918 had had absolute power to do what they wanted, but despite their good intentions they had failed. They did not understand the fundamental causes of war, being nationalists themselves and therefore unknowing propagators of war. Apart from lacking political foresight, the leaders of the world did not see it as their obligation to defend culture. With the burning of the Reichstag the *guerra libertadora*, the war of liberation, had become inevitable. Political leaders, however, had seen it only as an attack on culture and thus as a problem with which they did not have to deal. But culture, human well-being, prosperity, and progress formed an indissoluble entity.

After his return from the United States Nicolai applied for British citizenship. He no longer attached any value to his German nationality, he wrote in very bad English to Sir Charles Orde, the British ambassador in Santiago, for it made him "to a certain degree responsible of all what Nacis [sic] have done, do and will do," and he "can hardly think that the Hitlerian government will renew his passport after what he has written in his books and in South American newspapers about the Nacis and their actual [sic] war." Since he did not expect things in Germany to improve in his lifetime, "even when the principal person will be eliminated," he had decided to change his nationality. He could become a citizen of Chile, but "I believe that a man's nationality is a serious thing, and therefore I would wish to embrace one that corresponds as much as possible to my principles. And in that respect I have been convinced for more than thirty years that of all the peoples on our earth the English resembles the most to my ideal of a nation." He pointed to *The Biology of War*, which had appeared in an English translation in London at a time when it was forbidden in Germany. "You have perhaps seen in the papers of Chile and Argentina that I have always espoused England's cause. Yet, my manner of acting twenty-five years ago seems to me still more convincing, because it indicates that my predilection for England is not only brought about by my antipathy against the Naci government. Considering all that, I would beg your Excellency to tell me if, on the basis of these antecedents of more than twenty-five years, there is any possibility to acquire the English nationality, and what I ought to do in that case."[17] The request was denied on the grounds that Nicolai failed to meet the residency requirements for

Fig. 45. Nicolai's rendition of the view from his couch at the Sazié house.

British citizenship. For reasons that are unclear, he did not choose to become a citizen of Chile at this time, although he remained in that country for the rest of his life.

Friederike had gone to Germany for a visit and was trapped there when the war broke out. Nicolai was annoyed, but he did not miss her. Lately his material circumstances had improved. The wealthy owners of a house on Sazié, then a quiet, pleasant street, had put an entire building at the back of the property at his disposal for a nominal sum. For the first time in many years he had a place he could call his own, modest but spacious and well suited to his needs. On the ground floor there was a dining room, a kitchen, and a large alcove that served as his bedroom. Upstairs there was enough space for his reassembled library of some six thousand volumes (Fig. 45) and a study, described by one reporter as an alchemist's retreat on account of its many strange instruments, retorts, jars, and Bunsen burners. In the sun-drenched patio the old man could plant vines and geraniums and even raise chickens.

A fat, motherly woman named Rosita, who was utterly devoted to her master, looked after Nicolai's creature comforts. Carlos Lovazzano, a medical student, joined the household as a faithful amanuensis and disciple. Life took on a regular rhythm. Nicolai was a creature of the night. He worked in his study until three or four o'clock in the morning, slept until noon, breakfasted in bed, then lit the first cigar of the day and jotted down the ideas that had come to him on awakening. In the afternoon he went for long walks, partly to keep fit, partly to save cab or bus fare. Once a week, rain or shine, he would walk to the house of Doña Amelia Asenjo, at whose *jour* he would find not only the writers, artists, and scientists of Santiago but political figures and members of the diplomatic corps.

In 1940 *La miseria de la dialectica,* the most complete statement of the mature Nicolai's political philosophy and perhaps the most brilliant of his books, was published. One cannot appreciate his genius without at least a glimpse into this quintessential work, which he completed in 1937 but whose appearance was delayed for three years by circumstances beyond his control. The delay proved to be fortunate, for the Hitler-Stalin pact gave special meaning to the uncompromising rejection of Marxism which was the message of the book. But this rejection was based not on the political situation of the moment but on a scientist's searching examination of philosophical and political systems based on the dialectical method.

In a word, in *La miseria* Nicolai rejected the dialectical method *in toto* as unscientific or—worse—pseudo-scientific. He was not doctrinaire: science was not a fetish or an *idée fixe* with him, but the scientific method was, he believed, the only approach to understanding reality. He recognized the profound importance of Marx's achievement. Historical materialism, the recognition that economic and technical realities largely determine human history and morality, was Marx's "permanent contribution," he wrote. But Marx had overlooked the fact that other instincts beside possessiveness also governed human behavior—that while man would prefer to live by economic principles, other "passions" kept him from doing so, passions which natural science and objective sociological and behavioral methods must elucidte. Marx's insight that it is not man's consciousness which determines his conduct but the reverse, that it is adaptation to the methods of production which leads to codes of behavior and systems of ethics, was a great truth. The rest of Marx's work, however, was not, "as he would have us believe, simply a consequence of that concept" but was heavily influenced by political expediency and would thus share the fate of all things political. The ultimate socialist society would bear little resemblance to Marx's projections, but the path opened by the concept of materialism would never be abandoned, though socialism would have to be freed from the evils that beset it if it were to survive. The danger of negating the individual must be removed. Man has a dual mission, to develop his society and to perfect his personality. The former depended upon the latter, but neither the Prussian state idealized by Hegel nor Marx's theory recognized this interrelation. Both Hegel and Marx demanded the complete subordination of the individual, not to the will of the majority but to a tyrannical dogma and an established program.

While Nicolai unmercifully attacked and ridiculed Hegel, he respected Marx, in whose works not dialectic but that which he had accomplished by truly scientific methods was the essential thing. "The fundamental principle of dialectics is the belief that the logical manipulation of notions can procure knowledge of reality," Nicolai scoffed. When Marx deals with concrete facts, he forgets his dialectic, Nicolai wrote, "but the cursed dialectic keeps intruding everywhere and transforms everything." Because of its dialectical trappings, historical materialism in the hands of Marx's political successors had ceased to be a scientific method in any sense and had become a mystical force through which social forms were assumed to evolve without human intervention, a new form of divine providence invoked in the shape of "historical necessity."

The remedy was a return to pragmatic, scientific principles. Unless it is recognized that the brain is part of the physical world and that understanding the manner in which it functions is all-important for the study of human behavior, Nicolai asserted, historical materialism can shed little light on history, nor can it be a useful basis for socialism: "Ideas don't come from nothing; they have their real causes, and if one calls them 'superconstructions,' that does not mean that they can be considered simple epiphenomena. At least in their relation to social problems they must be taken as real and unshakable phenomena."

Here we cannot follow Nicolai through his critique of the absurdities of "proletarian science," a science determined by the political and ideological needs of Stalinist Russia, nor through his reflections on revolutions and on modern history in general. He was accused of placing too much emphasis on the formal aspects of dialectics with his criticism of the Hegelian triad thesis-antithesis-synthesis, which he called an irrational scholastic construction. "Dialectical science" was for him a contradiction in terms. The changes that have occurred in Marxist theory in the four decades since *La miseria de la dialectica* was first published have made some of Nicolai's arguments out of date, though in the context of the times they were original, courageous, and weighty. His criticism of the belief that "logical manipulation of notions can procure knowledge of reality" remains valid, however, not only for the dialectical method but for ideologies and "ism"s in general.

The Second World War ran its course, avidly followed by Nicolai. Once the United States entered it, his apprehensions diminished, for he believed that now, like the previous one, this would be a war of resources. He again pondered the question of what was to be done with the Germans after their defeat. It was imperative that the Nazi mentality be studied if a recurrence of the Hitlerian madness was to be averted. Fascism, he had declared in 1939, was one of the most interesting phenomena of modern times. It represented the resurgence of animal instincts and fetishist, totemistic, and other atavistic attitudes in an industrial society. It was most regrettable that the Fascist states had not allowed scientists to study the beast in its natural habitat. Now, with victory in sight, the opportunity was at hand. The prime object would be Hitler himself, if taken alive. Nicolai wrote a letter to Winston Churchill to suggest Hitler's examination and "re-education" by trained psychologists and other experts "whose political understanding is far better than mine." The Moscow "show trials" of 1936 had shown the effectiveness of such manipulations, he added.

Clearly, what Nicolai had in mind was what would later be called "brain-washing." He considered it justified in the case of so important a prisoner as Hitler, for he saw the phenomenon of Nazism as a collective mental aberration that required a psychological approach, and in any case one had to fight fire with fire.

This principle was also applicable to the use of the atom bomb against the Japanese. When the reporters came rushing to get his views about Hiroshima and Nagasaki, he passed over the moral aspects of the tragedy and expatiated instead on the triumph of science that gave mankind access to unlimited energy for future peaceful uses. Nuclear power would enable man to conquer outer space, change climates, and transform deserts into gardens, he said. It would revolutionize international relationships, for small nations would no longer be dependent on the great powers. "Today the liberated atom has transformed the islands of Japan into desolate craters. Tomorrow it may be possible that men will recover their good judgment and put the atom into the service of humanity."[18] It did not occur to Nicolai that it could be otherwise, man being a rational creature.

Given the preponderance of the United States in resources and technology, Nicolai had great hopes for the United Nations as the instrument of international control which the League of Nations had failed to be. The Second World War had provided a horrible example of the evils of nationalism. Now was the time to curtail national sovereignty. But nationalism was far from dead. At this moment pressures for the creation of a national Jewish state were building up. Nicolai, sympathetic, but still wedded to his concept of One World, rejected the idea. "However worthwhile," he wrote the Chilean committee "Pro Palestina Hebrea," "Zionism does not seem to me to be the proper solution of the Jewish problem. Convinced as I am that the consequences of nationalist sentiment constitute the gravest danger for the unity of the world, I cannot wish the nationalization of the Jews, but rather the de-nationalization of the rest of the world." The Jews had rendered valuable services to humanity.

> precisely because they were not a nation but a group devoted to an idea, which is the only kind of group worthy of rational beings. The Jews over their tragic history of thousands of years have educated themselves to combine economic with cultural internationalism and to foster the concept of hospitality. In their most illustrious representatives they have proved that they have understood their historical mission, and in my opinion it would be a pity if they were deprived of this privilege and turned into just another nation.[19]

Once again Nicolai was allowing the logic of idealism to triumph over emotional and practical realities.

Every position which he took was consistent with his idealist logic, which itself rested on his belief in the linkage between progress and man's biological evolution. On an evolutionary scale the differences between races became negligible. Nicolai had long since shed his instinctive prejudice against non-whites, the prejudice that had shocked Romain Rolland as unworthy of him. The potential of the human brain was so great, he had said as early as 1930, that in seventy years the North American Negro had advanced from slavery to an average level of intelligence comparable to that of Caucasians. "There is no doubt that, if we wanted to, we could raise all races to the same level as the European average in a few generations. In this sense there are no races; humanity is a single family, or at

Fig. 46. On a cultural mission, with dignitaries of the University of San Potosí, Bolivia, 1938.

least could be one." In 1938, when the government of Chile sent him on a cultural mission to Bolivia (Fig. 46), Nicolai returned to the subject. The Indians of Bolivia were backward but not inferior, he told a reporter: "Nobody has tried to educate the backward races, Indians and North American Negroes." In Bolivia the Indians were advancing rapidly because they had good schools, but in the United States the blacks lived in forced inferiority, "which prevents them from free and responsible development, wherein lies the only true education."

Nicolai remained mentally and physically active almost up to his death at ninety. He continued to give courses and to write books and articles on a wide range of subjects—pedagogy, psychology, sociology, the history of religions, and the history of medicine. It is impossible to trace all of his ideas here, but we should mention briefly the last of his books, *La Euge-*

nesia (Eugenics), published in 1957, for here he had to face the consequences of the "objective morality" which he had first expounded in *Fisica
y Moral* thirty years earlier, not as a philosophical concept but as a concrete problem.[20] What were the responsibilities of the physician in a Malthusian universe? Overpopulation was becoming an imminent danger, and
medical science, both as a cause and as a potential means of repairing the
damage, must come to the rescue. Modern medicine had created a dis-
equilibrium by reducing the death rate and increasing life expectancy
while simultaneously increasing the birth rate. Nicolai met the challenge
head on: "He who says 'A' must say 'B,' and he who diminishes deaths
must also diminish births." Otherwise, there would be thirty people living
on each square meter of the earth's surface within a few centuries.

At first blush, Nicolai wrote, the death of the elderly would seem to be
the natural solution to the problem of overpopulation, for they had served
their purpose. But in reality the survival of the species depended on infant
mortality or, rather, on death before the reproductive age was reached.
This was nature's solution, as exemplified in the death of untold millions
of bacteria and immature fishes which made it possible for a relatively
small number of survivors to thrive. Humans had always resorted to killing, but now it was possible to substitute control for killing—better yet,
to choose who should be eliminated, that is, to choose the progeny most
useful for the future of the species, a feat which blind nature had been
unable to achieve. "As incredible as it may seem, the Church and the
traditional moralists reject this obviously humanitarian intervention of intelligence." But it was impossible, prejudicial, and even criminal not to
take the enormous changes in knowledge into account. Jesus had broadened the decalogue from an ethical standpoint; "we must broaden it today
from the biological standpoint, a duty which only creatures wholly devoid
of ethical sentiment and compassion for their fellow humans can shirk."
The Fifth Commandment needed to be broadened to read, "Thou shalt
respect human life as sacred and do nothing that might directly or indirectly endanger it, but do everything that to the best of your knowledge is
necessary so that life in its entirety will grow and progress, with the largest
number of individuals compatible with its well-being." The key term here
is "life in its entirety," meaning the welfare of mankind as a whole. The
physician traditionally considered himself responsible to the individual patient, but today, in Nicolai's view, he was obliged to think of the species
as a whole.

In practice this meant not only birth control but sterilization when and
where indicated. The ethics of eugenics in no way contradicted the decalogue, Nicolai asserted: both served life, and the interest of life required
the elimination of certain individuals, though these were not the same type
of individuals as in biblical times. Let no one think that "the biologist who
dedicates his life to the study of life holds it less sacred than the theologian
and would ever oppose the Fifth Commandment. On the contrary, he
wants only to make it more meaningful by adapting it to new conditions
and new knowledge." Either large numbers of people will die in misery
and hunger as the result of overpopulation or a small number will live

437

happily for a "higher purpose." In the past human beings, lacking the knowledge on which to base a rational choice, had gone blindly to their doom. Rational beings should not follow their example: "Nature has worked blindly for two billion years to produce the miracle of human intelligence, and now this glorious breed [of rational beings] resigns itself to the inevitability of dying of overpopulation as meekly as dumb animals!"

The war between traditional morality and the future had begun with Malthus, but his alarm had sounded prematurely. The greatness of the species was based on quality, not numbers. Darwin and Galton had completed Malthus's work with their studies of evolution and heredity. The knowledge of genetics was still fragmentary, but even in 1957, sterilization of the "most dangerous cases" was justifiable. To oppose eugenics on the grounds that Hitler had misused it was as if one were to deny the blessings of morphine to cancer patients because it was abused by drug addicts. The Hippocratic ethic, formulated in a thinly populated world, had become indefensible and indeed immoral in a crowded one. With his customary optimism Nicolai passed over the practical difficulties arising from deeply ingrained beliefs. He saw clearly that the success of eugenics hinged on its acceptance by an enlightened society, but "if only this once we suceed in avoiding the danger of a new Middle Age," one could hope that the technical and scientific revolution of the past century would be overshadowed by the social and humane revolution of the future. Biological reason would triumph over sentimental idealism in the end. The full title of this last book makes the point: *La Eugenesia como gloriosa culminación de la medicina*, "Eugenics as the Crowning Glory of Medicine."

The rest of our story is quickly told. Nicolai's life was now the quiet one of a scholar and patriarch. He never lacked disciples, friends, and willing female helpers. Friederike never returned to Chile. She had been standing on the dock in Hamburg waiting to board ship for Valparaiso when Hitler's government canceled all exit permits on the eve of the war. All communications between Germany and Chile were interrupted, and Nicolai, with typical suspiciousness, attributed her failure to rejoin him to her preference for the Nazis. In the meantime, a substitute wife had appeared, in the person of Frau Agathe ("Agi") Feldmann, née Woelfler, the same Agi Woelfler who as a young girl in Vienna in 1923 threw herself in front of Nicolai to shield him from the brass knuckles and rubber truncheons of his Nazi attackers. She was now the wife of a Viennese businessman who had been forced to leave Austria, and the family had come to Chile at Nicolai's invitation. Still his devoted admirer, Agi took the solitary bachelor under her wing, helped him with his shopping, kept him company on his walks, nursed him when he was ill, and took him home to play chess with her husband and impart his wisdom to her young son Peter (Fig. 47). After Herr Feldmann's death this idyllic arrangement continued until Nicolai's failing health made living alone on Sazié impossible, at which point Agi and her son Peter took him into their home.

Although utterly forgotten in Europe and never known in the United

States, Nicolai in his later years received many honors in Latin America. In 1938 he was appointed professor of "biological philosophy" at the Pedagogical Institute of Santiago. In the same year the Chilean government sent him on a cultural exchange mission to Bolivia. He continued to receive—and accept—speaking invitations from all over the continent— Argentina, Peru, Brazil, and, of course, within Chile itself. He was elected corresponding member of the prestigious Brazilian Centro Cultural Euclides da Cunha. In 1953 he was named president of the Chilean section of the Congress for Cultural Freedom and attended its international meeting in Hamburg. In 1960, at the age of eighty-six, he was the guest of honor of the International Congress of Sociology in Mexico City.

In Hamburg, at the Congress for Cultural Freedom, he was celebrated

Fig. 47. Chess with Carl Feldmann in Santiago, 1942. Peter Feldmann looks on.

as a martyr. The newspapers of the post-Hitler era told his story, and for the first time, belatedly, Germans learned of his protest against the First World War and of his treatment at the hands of German professors and students. But these admirers were not the people he had known, and the Hamburg rising from the ashes of the war meant nothing to him. He visited both West and East Berlin. The hunger in East Germany, he commented, was "a fact no dialectic can overcome." In Karlsruhe he saw Eva, who had returned to live out her days in the country of her birth, and Friederike, with whom he had made his peace. On the way back to Chile he stopped in London and Paris. Still more francophile than anti-Communist, the old man attended a reunion of the staff of *L'Humanité* in the Bois de Vincennes. He retuned to Santiago exhausted, but still lively enough to angrily accuse the driver of his taxi of having rifled his luggage. His personality had changed remarkably little over eighty-six years.

Nicolai's participation in the Congress for Cultural Freedom aroused vehement attacks from the left-wing press, for the group was inspired and financed by the United States Central Intelligence Agency as a propaganda

Fig. 48. Portrait at eighty-four for a new printing of *La miseria de la dialectica*, 1958.

front against the Soviet Union. Nicolai was completely ignorant of this fact, but even had he known, it is unlikely that such knowledge would have deterred him, for his opposition to Communism was stronger than ever. He broke with his old and devoted friend Godoy Urrutia when the latter moved from socialism to Communism and joined the Chilean parliament as a Communist deputy. Later he would break with Salvador Allende when Allende, though remaining a Socialist, seemed to him to be moving too far to the left.

The finest tribute Nicolai could have wished for was the foundation of the society "Amigos de la Ciencia" ("Friends of Science") by his disciples throughout the Continent, on the occasion of his eightieth birthday. These were the men who, in the words of one of them, "in the decade 1920 to

Fig. 49. Nicolai's copy of the announcement of his course in the history of medicine, May 1948, sponsored by the Sociedad Amigos de la Ciencia. The drawing is his own.

1930 received direct inspiration from the *maestro* and hoped to transmit to the new generation the interest, understanding, and love of science which they owed to him."[21] The *maestro* himself was asked to draft a constitution for the group. It began with an eloquent profession of his unvarying creed: "Science is the most formidable instrument we possess to emancipate ourselves from our own irrationality and from the external forces that dominate our lives. Whenever man has let himself be guided by science, he has significantly improved both his existence in his own time and the ultimate destiny of humanity."[22]

The Sociedad Amigos de la Ciencia had its seat in Lanus, Argentina, with branches and correspondents in many places throughout the continent. It published and distributed Nicolai's later books, most notably *La Eugenesia*. After his retirement from the University of Chile it arranged for his lectures with the object of providing both a forum and financial support for the still vigorous but impecunious old man (Fig. 49). Few teachers and fewer scientists have inspired such devotion.

In his last years Nicolai mellowed somewhat. Although he showed some of the traits of old age—miserliness, suspiciousness, and intolerance for the opinions of others—they were merely magnifications of long-standing character traits and were forgiven by those around him. He busied himself with wood-working tools and invented various gadgets for his own amusement. He still played chess and took up bridge. Through all the years of his exile he carried some mementoes of his early battles, among them the memorable pillow artistically adorned with red blood cells and malaria parasites embroidered by the Misses Rohlfing and Schreiber of Danzig and, of course, his books and papers. He bequeathed his library to the University of Chile.

His last illness was long and tedious. He fought death like a lion, Agi wrote to Friederike. He died on 8 October 1964, aged ninety. Few lives have been richer.

NOTES

1. Huidobro's comments appeared in an article, "El Doctor Nicolai," *La Opinión*, 7 April 1933.

2. Quoted in *Cauce*, 5 August 1933, clipping in the Nicolai archive.

3. *Fundamentos reales de la sociología* (Santiago: Editorial Ercilla, 1936).

4. Letter of 14 February 1933, in the Nicolai archive.

5. *Psicogenesis, o del origen del alma* (Santiago: Prensas de la Universidad de Chile, 1935).

6. *Liberación del Trabajo*, 2d ed. (Buenos Aires: Editorial Americalee, 1941); *Mortalidad infantil y natalidad* (Santiago: Prensas de la Universidad de Chile, 1934); *La eugenesia cómo gloriosa culminación de la medicina* (Buenos Aires: Editorial SAC, 1957); *La miseria de la dialectica, Dialectica y marxismo frente a la ciencia, un ensayo de una critica constructiva* (Santiago: Ediciones Ercilla,

1940); *Analisis del Psicoanalisis a la luz de la psicología fisiológica* (Buenos Aires: Editorial "B," 1953).

7. *La seguridad científica, Cuatro discursos del método de la ciencias natural.* (Santiago: Publicaciones del Department o de Extensión Universitaria, 1948).

8. "Wer immer strebend sich bemüht, den können wir erlösen."

9. "Wendet zur Klarheit Euch, liebende Flammen! Die sich verdammen, heile die Wahrheit, dass sie vom Bösen froh sich erlösen, um in dem Allverein selig zu sein." Both quotations are from Part 2, Act 5 (my translation).

10. *El "Poema" de Don Quijote, ensayo psicológico sobre el fundamento de la poesía* (Santiago: Editorial Nascimento, 1947).

11. "Homenaje a I. P. Pawlow," *Revista de Psiquiatría* 1, no. 3 (July 1936): 1–14.

12. In a letter dated 7 September 1948, Nicolai wrote (in English) to the publisher Appleton-Century: "An author who writes in Spanish that other people hardly ever read, and in South America, . . . , must have the natural wish to be published in a language of world-wide circulation and in a country where the interest for the popularization of science is greater. . . . The object is not to gain dollars but to aid in bringing about a greater diffusion of my conviction that on principle the results of science are trustworthy (what is now so often denied), and with that to increase the regard for science."

13. The Fulds and the Einstein family were on a friendly footing in Berlin. Dr. Fuld came to the United States at an advanced age and practiced medicine in Weedsport for a time. When he became incapacitated, Albert Einstein was instrumental in obtaining a place for him and his wife in a rest home for displaced persons in New York. (This information was supplied by Dr. Fuld's daughter-in-law.)

14. "La Lucha contra las Dictaduras, el Facismo y la Guerra Imperialista," *La Flecha*, 2 November 1935.

15. Luis Alberto Sanchez, "Georg Frederic Nicolai, 'El Gran Europeo,' 'Ciudadano del Mundo,'" *Hoy*, 1 June 1939, pp. 13–18.

16. Jorge F. Nicolai, "La guerra y la soberanía de los estados desde un punto de vista universal," *Timón* 1, no. 1 (November, 1939):27–46.

17. Draft letter to Sir Charles Orde, ca. fall 1940, Nicolai archive.

18. Interview with Nicolai, unsigned, *Ercilla*, 14 August 1945, Nicolai archive.

19. Letter of September, 1944, Nicolai archive.

20. The quotations from *La eugenesia* which follow are from pp. 94, 98, 99, 100, 101, 126, 129, and 130.

21. Brief Biographical Notice, *ibid.*, p. 14.

22. *Ibid.*

Chronology of G. F. Nicolai: Life and Selected Writings

LIFE

1874	Born Georg Lewinstein in Berlin, 6 February.
1885–90	Attends boarding schools.
1890	Expelled from gymnasium at Schwedt for dueling.
1890–94	At Ernestinum in Gotha; boards with Kurd Lasswitz.
1894	Expelled from Ernestinum; graduates at Hagenau.
1894–95	Studies medicine at Königsberg.
1895–96	Studies medicine at Berlin; joins FWV dueling fraternity.
1896–97	Studies in Paris; changes name from Lewinstein to Nicolai.
1897–98	Resumes medical studies in Berlin; resigns from FWV; expelled from university.
1898–1900	Completes medical studies at Heidelberg; becomes drama critic for newspaper.
1900–1901	Studies zoology at Leipzig; completes doctoral dissertation.
1901–2	Travels in Far East.
1903	Instructor at Physiological Institute, Halle.
1903–8	Instructor at Physiological Institute, Berlin.
1906	Visits Russia and works with Pavlov in St. Petersburg.
1908	Research at marine biological institute in Naples.
1908–14	Senior physician at Charité Hospital, Berlin.
1909	Named titular professor by state Ministry of Education.
1910	Publishes *Das Elektrokardiogramm* (with Friedrich Kraus).
1912	Founds sports laboratory and private diagnostic laboratory (with Leonor Michaelis).
1914	Speaks at International Congress for Electrophysiology at Lyons; becomes chief of cardiac service at Tempelhof on outbreak of world war; writes "Appeal to the Europeans"; gives anti-war lectures at University of Berlin.
1915	Transferred to Graudenz; writes *Biology of War*; transferred to Tuchel for expressing "anti-national" views; contracts rheumatic fever and convalesces in Berlin; resumes anti-war lectures.
1916	Transferred to Danzig; drafted into army as medical orderly but refuses oath; galleys of *Biology of War* confiscated.
1917	*Biology of War* published in Zurich; author court-martialed for violating press laws and insulting superiors; transferred to Eilenburg as infantry rifleman.
1918	Publishes *Six Facts*; refuses to carry sidearms; flees to Den-

445

mark; writes *Why I Left Germany*; declines offers of Soviet citizenship; after Armistice returns to Germany.

1919 Active in Bund Neues Vaterland; gives pacifist speeches; at meeting of Second Internationale in Bern as reporter; spokesman for German delegation to Bern conference on League of Nations; visits Romain Rolland and later translates and sponsors Rolland's postwar manifesto.

1920 Resumes medical lectures; courses disrupted by rioting right-wing students; academic senate deprives him of teaching privileges for alleged treason and desertion from the army.

1921 Loses lawsuit against academic senate.

1922 In Paris as delegate of Bund Neues Vaterland; appointed head of department of physiology at University of Córdoba; emigrates to Argentina; visits Madrid, Berlin, and Vienna.

1923 Begins work on *La Base biológica del relativismo científico*.

1924 Friederike and Irene Nicolai arrive in Argentina.

1925 Publishes *La Base biológica*; conflict with university administration begins.

1927 Leaves Córdoba for Rosario.

1928–29 Professor of sociology at Rosario.

1930–31 Colegio Libre de Estudios Superiores founded in Rosario and Buenos Aires in his honor; *El mundo físico y moral* appears.

1931 Travels to the Soviet Union.

1932 In Spain gives lectures on his Soviet visit; attempts to get teaching position unsuccessful; returns to Argentina; lives on fees as traveling lecturer.

1933–36 Tours and teaches in Chile.

1936 Appointed professor at University of Chile; settles family there.

1939 Founds "institute of psychogenesis" in Santiago; visits United States to seek funding for institute.

1940 Publishes *La miseria de la dialectica*.

1954 In Hamburg for Congress for Cultural Freedom.

1964 Dies in Santiago.

SELECTED WRITINGS

Note: the bulk of Nicolai's medical publications before 1914 has been omitted. His writings in Spanish are not completely listed here, but I believe that all his books and most of his published essays and articles are included. I have drawn upon Eugen Relgis's list in *Georg Fr. Nicolai, Un sabio y un hombre del porvenir* and on the lists of Nicolai and others found in the Nicolai archive.

1896 [Georg Lewinstein.] "Zur Kenntnis der verdünnten Luft." *Archiv für die gesamte Physiologie* (Bonn) 65: 278–80.

1901 "Über die Leitungsgeschwindigkeit im Riechnerven des Hechtes." Doctoral dissertation, University of Leipzig. Published in *Archiv für die gesamte Physiologie* 85:65–85 in the same year.

1904   *Anleitung für den praktischen Kursus der Physiologie*. Berlin: Kunstanstalt Albert Frisch.

[with O. von Fürth and A. Kreidl.] "VI. Internationaler Physiologenkongress zu Brüssel." *Zentralblatt für Physiologie* 17, no. 25:816–39.

1905   "Zu Pawlows 60. Geburstag." *Medizinische Klinik*, no. 11: 1–9.

1907   "Die Gestalt einer deformierten Manometermembran, experimentell bestimmt." *Archiv für Anatomie und Physiologie* 3:129–40.

"Noch einmal die Franksche Paraboloidmembran." *Zeitschrift für Biologie* (Munich) 50:456–58.

Die physiologische Methode zur Erforschung der Tierpsyche. Leipzig: Ambrose Barth.

1908   *Die Mechanik des Kreislaufs*. Braunschweig: Friedrich Vieweg and Son. Reprinted from Nagel's *Handbuch der Physiologie des Menschen*.

"Das Lernen der Tiere auf Grund von Versuchen mit Pawlows Speichelfistel." *Zentralblatt für Physiologie* 22, no. 11:1–3.

1910   [with Friedrich Kraus.] *Das Elektrokardiogramm des gesunden und kranken Menschen*. Leipzig: Veit.

1917   *Die Biologie des Krieges, Betrachtungen eines deutschen Naturforschers*. Zurich: Orell Füssli. Reissued as "first original edition," i.e., authorized version, in two volumes in 1919, translated into English (*The Biology of War*, trans. Constance A. Grande and Julian Grande (London: J. M. Dent, 1919), Danish, Swedish, and Spanish; abridged versions in Romanian, Russian, Finnish, and Japanese.

1918   *Sechs Tatsachen als Grundlage der heutigen Machtpolitik*. Edited by O. Nippold. Bern: Freier Verlag (authorized); Copenhagen: Steen Hasselbalch (authorized). Second edition published in Berlin by Verlag Gesellschaft und Erziehung in its Revolutions-Bibliothek series in 1919; included in *Aufruf an die Europäer* (1921).

Warum ich aus Deutschland ging. Copenhagen: Steen Hasselbalch (authorized); Bümplitz-Bern: Benteli A.G. (unauthorized).

1919   *Naturwissenschaft und Pazifismus*. Oldenburg: G. Stalling. Pamphlet.

Romain Rollands Manifest und die deutschen Antworten, mit einem Anhang über den Fall Nicolai. Charlottenburg: Mundus Verlagsanstalt. Nicolai's translation of Rolland's postwar appeal to the intellectuals of the world and his commentary on the response in Germany.

1920   *Professor Nicolai und die deutschen Professoren, eine Selbstverteidigung.* Zurich: Buchdruckerei Genossenschaft Schweizerischer Sonntagsblätter. *Richtigstellung des Urteils des Senats.* Berlin: privately printed. Nicolai's formal rebuttal to the charges of the rector and academic senate of the University of Berlin.

1921   *Aufruf an die Europäer, gesammelte Aufsätze zum Wiederaufbau Europas.* Edited by Hans Wehberg. Leipzig: Verlag der Wiener graphischen Werkstätte. A collection of political essays written between 1914 and 1921.

Preface to E. J. Gumbel, *Zwei Jahre Mord.* Berlin: Berger.

1922   *¿ Qué es la vida?* Córdoba: University of Córdoba. Inaugural lecture at the university, published in the series Cátedra Universitaria, vol. 2, no. 6, pp. 175–80.

1923   "An Appeal for Sanity." *Atlantic Monthly* 316, no. 4104:507–9. Translated from article in *Neue Zürcher Zeitung*, 17 January 1923.

Deutsche Nation und deutsche Kultur. Berlin: Schwetschke. Text of speech given in Vienna in March.

"Las Isopsicas de los animales y la relación entre la inteligencia y el cerebro segun observaciones en 192 perros." *Revista de la Universidad*

Nacional de Córdoba 10, nos. 7–8:1–44.

1924   "La Influencia de la guerra mundial sobre los deportes." *Revista de la Universidad Nacional de Córdoba* 11, nos. 1–3:3–19.

1925   *La Base biológica del relativismo científico y sus complementos absolutos.* Córdoba: Universidad Nacional de Córdoba. Interpretation of the biological implications of the Relativity Theory and their extension to a biological morality.

"Sentido filosófico de la teoría de la relatividad." *Revista de Filosofía* (Buenos Aires) 11, no. 4:1–26.

1926   "In memoriam de José Ingenieros." *Revista de Filosofía* 12, no. 1:83–90.

1927   "La Ciencia y la moral." *Revista de Filosofía* 13, no. 3:301–17. Speech given at Córdoba meeting organized by students protesting Nicolai's dismissal from the university; reprinted in *La Antorcha* (Buenos Aires), 17 June, under the headline "La profession de fé de Nicolai."

Homenaje de despedida a la tradición de Córdoba, docta y santa. Buenos Aires: Sociedad de Publicaciones "El Inca."

1928   *Herr der Erde*. Unpublished manuscript of an autobiographical-science fiction novel.

1929   "La influencia de los estudios puros en la formación de la nueva conciencia." *Universidad Nacional de la Plata, Extensión Universitaria* 7:9–52.

       El sentido de la ciencia. Buenos Aires: Asociacion Trabajadores del Estado.

1931   *El mundo físico y moral en su concepción científica, un ensayo biológico-social*. Buenos Aires: Talleres Gráficos Argentinos. Second edition published in Santiago by Editoral Engranaje in 1934. The major repository of Nicolai's philosophical ideas.

1932   "Cerebro y Intelligencia." *Crónica Medica* (Valencia) 36, no. 780:169–78. Reprinted by Editorial Engranaje, Santiago, in 1933 and by Ediciones Iman, Buenos Aires, in 1935.

       Origen y desarollo del trabajo humano. Buenos Aires: Ediciones Nervio. A 52-page pamphlet; second edition revised and enlarged (185 pages) published by Editorial Americalee, Buenos Aires, in 1941 with an essay by Romain Rolland, "La Biologia de la Guerra de Nicolai."

       Rusia, actual y futura. Libros de Política y Sociología no. 11. Santiago: Editorial Moderna.

1933   "La mujer y la agricultura." *Crisol* (Santiago) 5, no. 9:214–18.

       "Población." *Revista de la Facultad de Ciencias económicas, comerciales y políticas de la Universidad Nacional del Litoral* 2, no. 3. A 48-page pamphlet; reprinted by Imprimería "Nacional" de J. Lajouane & Cia, Buenos Aires, in the same year.

1934   "Instintos sociales." *Acción Social* 4, no. 51:6–9.

       Mortalidad infantil y natalidad. Santiago: Prensas de la Universidad de Chile.

       "La necesidad de una Liga de Naciones." *Acción Social* 4, no. 49:6–9.

       "Significación de la obra de Pawlow para la sociologia." *Acción Social* 4, no. 50:4–8.

       "Tres disgracias modernas." *Acción Social* 4, no. 48:3–5.

1935   *Psicogenesis, o del origen del alma*. Santiago: Prensas de la Universidad de Chile.

1936   "Las divergencias de la izquierda." *Bases* (Valparaiso) 1, no. 1:16–19. Published in the official organ of the Socialist Party of Chile.

       Fundamentos reales de la sociología. Santiago: Editorial Ercilla. Reprinted by Editorial José M. Cajica, Jr., Puebla and Buenos Aires, in 1962.

"Homenaje a I. P. Pawlow." *Revista de Psiquiatría* 1, no. 3:1–14.

[with Oscar Fontecilla.] "El problema de la conciencia." *Revista de Psiquiatría* 1, no. 3:24–29.

1937   "La ciencia y la fé en la convicción personal." *Acción Femenina* (Santiago) no. 11:7–10. Year of publication uncertain.

1939   "La guerra y la soberanía de los estados desde un punto de vista universal." *Timón* 1, no. 1:27–46.

Reflexiones sobre Bolivia. Santiago: Editorial Nascimento. A 38-page pamphlet.

1940   *La miseria de la dialectica, Dialectica y marxismo frente a la ciencia, un ensayo de una crítica constructiva.* Santiago: Ediciones Ercilla. Reprinted by Editorial Jose M. Cajica, Jr., Buenos Aires, in 1958. A critique of Hegelian and Marxist dialectics from the viewpoint of the natural scientist.

"La selección en las prisiones." *Readaptación Social y Reeducación* (Santiago) 1, no. 1:12–18. The official organ of the Chilean Department of Prisons.

1942   "La perfectibilidad del hombre y el problema del progreso." *Acción Social* 12, no. 112:2–7.

1944   *Cómo un biólogo ve la filosofía.* Santiago: Prensas de la Universidad de Chile.

1946   "Créditos comerciales e industriales." *Economía y Finanzas, Revista mensual de circulación panamericana* (Santiago) 10, no. 122:3–6; 11, no. 123:9–12.

"La igualdad y la educación clasificadora." *Revista americana de Educación* (La Plata), no. 2:5–14.

"El mecanismo psiquico explicado por doble inervación a la Base de las Experiencias de I. P. Pavlov." *Revista de Psiquiatría* 11, no. 1:77–88.

1947   *El "Poema" de Don Quijote, ensayo psicológico sobre el fundamento de la poesía (Cervantes comparado con Dante y Shakespeare.)* Santiago: Editorial Nascimento. A rationalist *tour de force* leading to the rejection of Dante as the perpetuator of the Dark Ages and the glorification of Cervantes as a realist.

"Por qué soy anticomunista." *Revista de afirmación chilena* 16:18–19.

"La Sociología (Economía) biologica y el principio de Fermat." *Economía y Finanzas, Revista mensuel de circulacíon panamericana* 10, no. 125:3–8.

1948   "Eugenesia o proletarización, 1) La necesidad de preparar la acción por 'Historias Familiares.'" *Acción Social* 15, nos. 129–31:12–16.

La seguridad científica, Cuatro discursos del método de la ciencias naturales. Santiago: Publicaciones del Departamento de Extensión Universitaria, Universidad de Chile.

1949   "Eugenesia o proletarización, 2) La selección negativa." *Acción Social* 16, nos. 132–33:5–10.

1950   "Ave y Avión." *Revista Universidad Nacional de San Agustin de Arequipa* (Arequipa, Peru) 22, no. 32:135–60.

Goethe cómo educador politico (Revolucionario-Anárquico-Aristócrata). Santiago: Editorial Universitaria.

1953   *Analisis del Psicoanalisis a la luz de la psicología fisiológica*. Buenos Aires: Editorial "B." A radical critique of Freudian psychoanalysis from the viewpoint of experimental psychology.

Ciencia, Libertad y Cultura. Santiago: Publicaciones del Congreso por la Libertad de la Cultura.

1957   *La eugenesia como gloriosa culminación de la medicina*. Buenos Aires: Editorial SAC [Sociedad Amigos de la Ciencia]. Contains brief authorized biographical résumé.

"El invento de la rueda como símbolo del sol." *Occidente* (Santiago) 12, no. 110:3–10.

451

Selected Bibliography

MATERIALS ON G. F. NICOLAI

Bleuel, H. P. *Deutschlands Bekenner, Professoren zwischen Kaiserreich und Diktatur*. Bern: Scherz Verlag, 1968. Contains a brief account of Nicolai's battle against the University of Berlin.

Godoy Urrutia, César. "Jorge Nicolai, Un sabio contradictorio." *Hombres y Pueblos*. Santiago: Editora Austral, 1966.

Guardia Moyarga, C. A. "Georg Fr. Nicolai." *Revista* 32 (1950): 127–34.

Relgis, Eugen. *Georg Fr. Nicolai, un sabio y un hombre del porvenir*. 2d ed. rev. Buenos Aires: Cajica, 1965. Originally published in Buenos Aires by Ediciones Reconstruir in 1949.

Rolland, Romain. "Un Grand Européen: G.-F. Nicolai." *Demain* 2, nos. 18–19 (October-November 1917):337–57, 13–30. Later reprinted in Rolland's *Les Précurseurs* (Paris: Albin Michel, 1923).

Souchy, Augustin. *"Vorsicht, Anarchist! Ein Leben für die Freiheit: Politische Erinnerungen*. Darmstadt and Neuwied: Luchterhand, 1977.

GENERAL SURVEYS

Germany

Andrae Fr., and S. Schönfeldt, eds. *Deutsche Demokratie von Bebel bis Heuss*. Hamburg: Fischer Bücherei, 1968.

Bramstedt, Ernest K. *Aristocracy and the Middle-Classes in Germany: Special Types in German Literature, 1830–1900*. Chicago: University of Chicago Press, 1964.

Eyck, Erich. *Bismark and the German Empire*. New York: W. W. Norton, 1964.

——. *A History of the Weimar Republic*. Science Editions. New York: John Wiley, 1967.

Haffner, Sebastian. *Die verratene Revolution*. Bern: Scherz Verlag, 1969. An unorthodox but well-documented and convincing account of the Revolution of 1918.

Heiber, Hellmut. *Die Republik von Weimar*. Munich: Deutscher Taschenbuch Verlag, 1966. Excellent summary of the political history of the Weimar Republic.

Laqueur, Walter. *Weimar: Die Kultur der Republik*. Frankfurt-am-Main: Ullstein, 1976. Originally published in English by Putnam in 1975 as *Weimar: A Cultural History*. Invaluable source of information on Nicolai's German contemporaries.

Mann, Golo. *Deutsche Geschichte des neunzehnten und zwanzigsten Jahrhunderts*. Büchergilde Gutenberg. Frankfurt-am-Main: S. Fischer Verlag, 1958.

Taylor, A. J. P. *The Struggle for Mastery in Europe, 1848–1918*. 2d ed. London: Oxford University Press, 1974.

Valentin, Veit. *Geschichte der Deutschen Revolution, 1848–1849*. Cologne: Kiepenheuer and Witsch, 1970. First published in 1930; a classic study of the March Revolution.

Latin America

Allende, Salvador. *La via chilena hacia el socialismo*. Santiago: Joan Garcés, 1971.

Arciniegas, Germán. *El Continente del siete colores*. Buenos Aires: Editorial Sudamericana, 1965.

Gil, Federico G. *The Political System of Chile*. Boston: Houghton-Mifflin, 1966.

Liss, Sheldon B., and Peggy Liss, eds. *Man, State and Society in Latin American History*. New York: Praeger, 1972,

Maurer, Gerhard. *Blickpunkt Südamerika, die Revolution der steigenden Erwartungen*. Cologne: Kiepenheuer and Witsch. 1967.

Palacios, Alfredo. *Nuestra América y el Imperialismo*. Buenos Aires: Editorial Palestra, 1961.

Petras, James. *Political and Social Forces in Chilean Development*. Berkeley: University of California Press, 1970.

Ponce, Anibal. *El viento en el mundo*. Santiago: Sociedad Imprimería Horizonte, 1968.

Puiggrós, Rodolfo. *Las Izquierdas y el Problema Nacional*. 2d ed. Colección Los Porqués. Buenos Aires: Carlos Peres, 1971.

Ramos, Jorge Abelardo. *America Latina: Un Páis. Su historia, su economía, su revolución*. Buenos Aires: Editorial Octubre, 1949.

————. *La Bella Epoca*. 4th ed. Buenos Aires: Ediciones Del Mar Dulce, 1970.

————. *El Sexto Dominio*. Buenos Aires: Editorial Plus Ultra, 1972.

Roca, Deodoro. *Prohibido Prohibir*. Buenos Aires: Ediciones La Bastilla, 1972.

Romero, José Luis. *Las Ideas politicas en Argentina*. Mexico-Buenos Aires: Fondo de Cultura Economica, 1969.

Silvert, Kalman H. *Chile Yesterday and Today*. New York: Holt, Rinehart and Winston, 1965.

HISTORIES OF THE FIRST WORLD WAR

Baldwin, Hanson W. *World War I: An Outline History*. New York: Grove Press, 1972.

Fischer, Fritz. *Germany's Aims in the First World War*. New York: W. W. Norton, 1968.

Förster, Wolfgang. *Ludendorff, Deutscher Feldherr, deutsches Unglück*. Wiesbaden: Limes Verlag, 1951.

Kielmannsegg, Peter Graf. *Deutschland und der Erste Weltkrieg*. Frankfurt-am-Main: Athenaion, 1968. An invaluable comprehensive study of military, political, and diplomatic history.

Koszyk, Kurt. *Deutsche Pressepolitik im Ersten Weltkrieg*. Dusseldorf:

Droste Verlag, 1968. An authoritative study of the German press in the period.

Schieder, Wolfgang, ed. *Erster Weltkrieg, Ursachen, Entstehung und Kriegsziele*. Neue Wissenschaftliche Bibliothek. Cologne: Kiepenheuer and Witsch, 1969.

Stern, Fritz. *Bethmann-Hollweg und der Krieg, die Grenzen der Verantwortlichkeit*. Tübingen: J. C. B. Mohr, 1968.

Wernecke, Klaus. *Der Wille zur Weltgeltung*. Düsseldorf: Droste Verlag, 1970.

MEMOIRS BY CONTEMPORARIES

Erzberger, Mathias. *Erlebnisse im Weltkrieg*. Stuttgart Deutsche Verlagsanstalt, 1920. Political memoirs of a key parliamentarian.

Groener, Wilhelm. *Lebenserinnerungen*. Göttingen: Vanderhoeck and Ruprecht, 1957. Memoirs of a moderate military man, Ludendorff's successor and later defense minister.

Herzog, Wilhelm. *Menschen denen ich begegnete*. Bern: Francke Verlag, 1959. This book and the two following are memoirs by German pacifists.

Hiller, Kurt. *Ein Leben gegen die Zeit*. Reinbeck-Hamburg: Rowohlt, 1969.

Kessler, Harry Count. *Tagebücher 1919–1937*. Edited by Wolfgang Pfeiffer-Belli. Frankfurt-am-Main: Büchergilde Gutenberg, 1971.

Ludendorff, Erich. *Kriegsführung und Politik*. 2d ed. Berlin: E. S. Mittler, 1922. Critique of the civilian authorities by the mastermind of the High Command.

Moser, Otto von. *Die obersten Gewalten im Weltkrieg*. Stuttgart: Chr. Belser Verlagsbuchhandlung, 1931. Critical study of the German military and civilian powers in the First World War by a military expert.

Mühsam, Kurt. *Wie wir belogen wurden*. Munich: Langen, 1918. Revelations about German propaganda and censorship by a journalist.

Payer, Friedrich. *Von Bethmann-Hollweg bis Ebert*. Frankfurt-am-Main: Frankfurter Sozietätsdruckerei, 1923. A liberal parliamentarian's view of the prelude to the November Revolution.

Rolland, Romain. *Journal des années de Guerre 1914–1919: Notes et documents pour servir à l'histoire morale de l'Europe de ce temps*. Edited by Marie Romain Rolland. Paris: Albin Michel, 1952. The most comprehensive and authentic source on pacifists and pacifism during the First World War; many references to Nicolai, as well as Einstein, F. W. Förster, Anatole France, Karl Liebknecht, Lenin, Franz Pfemfert, and other interesting contemporaries of Nicolai.

Scheidemann, Philipp. *Der Zusammenbruch*. Berlin: Verlag für Sozialwissenschaft, 1921. A leading Social Democrat exposes the Socialist position in the First World War.

DOCUMENTARY COLLECTIONS

Eckart, Rolf, ed. *Das Zeitalter des Imperialismus, Kaiserreich und Erster Weltkrieg*. Munich: Wilhelm Goldmann, n.d. [ca. 1965].

Hannover, H., and E. Hannover, eds. *Politische Justiz 1918–1933*. Frankfurt-am-Main: Fischer Bücherei, 1966.

Kotowski, Georg, ed. *Historisches Lesebuch 1914–1933*. Frankfurt-am-Main: Fischer Bücherei, 1966.

Mazo, Gabriel del. *Estudiantes y Gobierno Universitario*. Buenos Aires: Libreria El Ateneo, 1955.

Weber, Hermann, ed. *Völker hört die Signale. Der deutsche Kommunismus 1916–1966*. Munich: Deutscher Taschenbuch, 1966.

UNIVERSITIES AND STUDENT MOVEMENTS

Bleuel, H. P. *Deutschlands Bekenner, Professoren zwischen Kaiserreich und Diktatur*. Bern: Scherz Verlag, 1968.

———, and Ernst Klinnert. *Deutsche Studenten auf dem Weg ins Dritte Reich*. Gütersloh: Sigbert Mohn, 1967.

Feuer, Lewis S. *The Conflict of Generations: The Character and Significance of Student Movements*. New York: Basic Books, 1969.

Mazo, Gabriel del. *Estudiantes y Gobierno Universitario*. Buenos Aires: Librería El Ateneo, 1955.

———, ed. *La Reforma Universitaria*. 3 vols. Lima: Universidad Nacional Mayor de San Marcos, 1967–68. A comprehensive collection of documents on all aspects of the *Reforma* by a participant.

Orgaz, Jorge. *Reforma Universitaria y Rebelión Estudiantil*. Buenos Aires: Ediciones Libera, 1970.

LITERARY VIEWS OF POLITICS

Pross, Harry. *Literatur und Politik*. Olten-Freiburg: Walter Verlag, 1963.

Raabe, Paul, ed. *Ich schneide die Zeit aus, Expressionismus und Politik in Franz Pfemferts "Aktion."* Munich: Deutscher Taschenbuch, 1963.

Rothe, Wolfgang, ed. *Der Aktivismus 1915–1920*. Munich: Deutscher Taschenbuch, 1969.

Index

Wolf Zuelzer, M.D., emeritus professor of pediatric research at Wayne State University, was most recently director of the Division of Blood Diseases and Resources, National Heart, Lung and Blood Institute. He studied at the Sorbonne and at the universities of Heidelberg, Berlin, Bonn, and Prague, receiving his medical degree from Prague. His specialties, hematology and human genetics, are the same as those of his subject. Like Nicolai, Zuelzer is a physician, a writer, and a humanist.

The book was designed by Edgar Frank. The typeface for the text is VIP Times Roman, based on a design by Stanley Morison in 1932. The display face is VIP Gill Sans, based on a design by Eric Gill about 1930.

The text is printed on S. D. Warren's 60-lb. "1854" text paper. The book is bound in Holliston Mills' Roxite vellum finish cloth over binder's boards. Manufactured in the United States of America.